TALES OF FOREVER

For comments or questions about this book, visit
our web site: *The LostStories Channel*, at
loststorieschannel.com

Published in the United States by
Lodestar Cinema Creations
West Covina, California
Smith, W. Kent (1959-)

Includes Analyses, Tales,
Selected Biographies, Source Material,
Endnotes, and Cast of Characters

Front Cover and Title Page Painting:
The Creation of Adam, Michelangelo, 1512

Front Cover Inset Poem:
Faith, Ephrem the Syrian, c. 360

Book Exterior and Interior
Designed and Executed
by W. Kent Smith

ISBN 0-9675869-2-5

Manufactured in the U.S.A.
August 2016

Tales of Forever

The Unfolding Drama of
God's Hidden Hand in History

Analyses

and

Dramatization

by

W. Kent Smith

Books by W. Kent Smith

Fish Tales (From the Belly of the Whale): Fifty of the Greatest Misconceptions Ever Blamed on The Bible, Reel One, The Hook #50-34

Fish Tales (From the Belly of the Whale): Fifty of the Greatest Misconceptions Ever Blamed on The Bible, Reel Two, The Line #33-18

Fish Tales (From the Belly of the Whale): Fifty of the Greatest Misconceptions Ever Blamed on The Bible, Reel Three, The Sinker #17-1

Fish Tales (From the Belly of the Whale): Fifty of the Greatest Misconceptions Ever Blamed on The Bible, The Complete Edition, Hook, Line, and Sinker #50-1

Tales of Forever: The Unfolding Drama of God's Hidden Hand in History, Book One: The Analyses – Part One

Tales of Forever: The Unfolding Drama of God's Hidden Hand in History, Book Two: The Tales – Part One

Tales of Forever: The Unfolding Drama of God's Hidden Hand in History, Book Three: The Tales – Part Two

Tales of Forever: The Unfolding Drama of God's Hidden Hand in History, Book Four: The Analyses – Part Two

Tales of Forever: The Unfolding Drama of God's Hidden Hand in History, The Complete Edition

For Ted,

Best Friend and Dad

Contents

THE SUBPLOTS

THE CREDITS

Although the contents of the following work are instructive, their sole purpose is not simply to instruct. Instead, they are offered as a catalyst to fuel one's God-given imagination so that the infinite mind of the Word might shed some small part of Himself upon all who dare to embrace a knowledge of the sublime as a child seeks to embrace the ineffable mystery of a clear blue sky.

W.K.S. 4.10.16

A List of the Five

FIVE THINGS ... five *sacred* things... The Ark of the Covenant, The Spear of Destiny, The Shroud of Turin, The Great Pyramid of Giza, and *The Septuagint Bible*.

Believe it or not, these five things all have one thing in common. And as it turns out, this one thing just happens to provide the key to a startling proof of God's control over every aspect of world history, proof of God's faithfulness to every promise He has ever made to the children of Adam.

Now, just in case there is anyone reading this who does not know what these five things are, let me briefly describe them without bogging down in the endless debate over the authenticity of the various claims made about them:

> One, **The Ark of the Covenant**, also known as The Ark of Testimony, is the wooden chest overlaid in gold, in which the Israelites carried the two stone tablets of the Ten Commandments.
>
> Two, **The Spear of Destiny**, also known as The Holy Lance or The Spear of Longinus, is the Roman centurion's spear that pierced the side of Jesus as He hung on the cross.
>
> Three, **The Shroud of Turin**, also known as The Holy Shroud, is the linen burial cloth that bears the image of the resurrected Christ.
>
> Four, **The Great Pyramid of Giza**, also known as *The Bible* in Stone, is the only remaining structure among the Seven Wonders of the World and is said to contain the prophetic history of Scripture in its geometric dimensions.
>
> And five, ***The Septuagint Bible***, also known as *The Greek Old Testament*, is the vernacular translation of *The Hebrew Bible*, produced around 250 B.C., and is the book most often quoted by the writers of *The New Testament*.

To anyone who doubts that God's control and faithfulness can be proved to be a tangible and verifiable fact of life, these five things hold the key to that proof—proof of God's hidden yet potent hand at work throughout the course of human affairs.

Five things ... five *sacred* things—and the knowledge they convey—though scattered through time and space, have now, within the pages of this unique book, been pieced together to tell the ultimate tale of God's intention toward humanity.

Some Foreword Thinking

Stranger than Fiction

THIS A TALE beyond imagination yet true—a tale stranger than any fiction ever conceived by the mind of mankind, because in order to tell the ultimate tale of God's intention toward humanity, this tale of five *sacred* things and the knowledge they convey, one must weave together all the elements of the greatest tales ever told.

An ancient prophecy, a promise of "days," which precisely foretold the Advent of Christ, given to the primordial parents of our race and recorded in the oldest story contained in the biblical record—a prophecy that bears a striking similarity to the messianic chronology found in *The Septuagint Bible*, the book most often quoted by the writers of *The New Testament*. But, as so often happens, this most ancient of all stories, and a knowledge of the prophecy it contained, eventually fell out of favor in the wake of certain political movements and was swept away, never to be seen again in the West for over a thousand years.

One man, set apart from all others, who was said to have talked with God, face to face, having a conversation that took place not in any earthly realm but at the very pinnacle of Heaven itself—a conversation written in a book for all humanity to read. Yet, because of its startling and enigmatic message, it was considered unsuitable for viewing by the common people, so sometime in the latter half of the fourth century of the Christian Era, it was banned and subsequently thought to much of the world for more than a millennium.

And an array of sacred artifacts, each one a talisman well known to emanate an uncanny power to affect the hearts and minds of those who encountered them. Although every one of these objects appear insignificant at first glance, according to legend, they are all said to be more potent than any man-made weapon—The Ark of the Covenant, The Spear of Destiny, and The Shroud of Turin. The other object amongst this array, however, is not so much an artifact as it is a colossus of a structure—The Great Pyramid of Giza.

All these elements, then—a man and his heavenly conversation, a promise of "days," an ark, a spear, a shroud, a pyramid, and a book, that is to say, everything needed to demonstrate a startling proof of God's control and faithfulness—have for the first time been forged into a single storyline, to tell the *Tales of Forever: The Unfolding Drama of God's Hidden Hand in History*.

From Out of Nowhere

BUT BEFORE I BEGIN, one would do well to keep several important points in mind as we proceed with the telling of this tale of five *sacred* things, of the special connection they hold in common, and the startling proof this connection conveys to an onlooking world—a proof that naturally has its origins in the written record of Scripture. And rest assured, although readers of this work will find themselves on a firm foundation of biblical truth, the process of investigating these origins will undoubtedly challenge their traditional view of *The Bible* as it is known today in the West. This is because a fundamental requirement in penetrating the veil that hides the truth concerning these five things is that one must first be willing to venture into territory familiar only to those who have encountered such works as *The Septuagint Bible*, one of the earliest known vernacular translations of *The Old Testament*—one of several books that, as we will soon be discovering, have all, at various times throughout their history, fallen in and out of favor.

This leads us, then, to important point number one: Throughout the entire course of history, the process of choosing which books were to be considered "acceptable" has been a veritable roller coaster of political correctness. As much as we would like to believe otherwise, the harsh reality is that the primary factor in deeming certain books as either inspired or heretical has been based not so much on matters of personal conscience as it has been on which political system was in power at a particular time and place. Still, this does not mean that these decision makers have always been able to enforce their political will in all places and at all times. More importantly, when it comes to the history of the formation of the Biblical Canon, what we are dealing with is, and always will be, an international struggle of global proportions. Ever since the Great Schism of the eleventh century, the Orthodox Church has occupied the East, while the Catholic and Protestant branches of Christianity have occupied the West. And because of this, the fact that some books are said to have been rejected and excised actually means that they were—contrary to popular opinion—not so much lost as they were marginalized and subsequently forgotten by a specific geographical segment of Christendom.[1] This overriding fact, in turn, has several consequences that are critical to this present-day study, both of which have occurred as a direct result of the point-of-view of this work, which happens to be a Western Protestant one.

Important point number two that emerges from this admittedly Western view is that when we speak—as we often will in this work—about lost books, lost chronologies, and lost truths of *The Bible*, keep in mind that we are not implying that these things have ever been lost in the strictest sense of that word. What we are really saying is that they simply lost their foothold in the West, while remaining part and parcel of the orthodoxy in the East; or in some cases, what fell out of favor in the Protestant West held fast in the Catholic West. This more than anything else accounts for the apparently sensational aspect of the so-called "discovery" of manuscripts, all which had generally been thought to be lost forever.

It is also critical to realize—important point number three—that this sort of thing is not at all unusual in terms of the overall landscape of biblical history. The same idea undergirds our understanding of the so-called Lost Tribes of Israel. Although the northern kingdom of ancient Israel was punished and scattered throughout the nations, they were never truly lost in the sense of their having been totally annihilated; rather, they were driven "underground," so to speak. In fact, the prophet Hosea clearly spoke about this very thing, in that the ten tribes to the north were to be punished for their idolatrous ways but only for a divinely appointed period of time, after which they were to reappear upon the stage of world history, as if from out of nowhere.

This, in turn, brings us to important point number four. I am one who firmly believes that this same phenomenon is at work when we as a Western people, dominated by a Protestant view of the Biblical Canon, are now the recipients of lost books that have all been—according to God's set time—rediscovered and restored to the West after centuries of having been deprived of their contents. And rather than scoff at such a possibility, one might humbly reconsider it in light of the facts that come forth from an in-depth examination of these various manuscripts, many of which will prove to be more than capable of standing side by side with the traditional books of Scripture, as we will shortly demonstrate.

And finally, for important point number five. Unlike those who profess to believe in God's ability to protect His written revelation but reject the great antiquity alleged by the authors of that record, this writer believes that when *The Bible* declares that men like Enoch, the scribe—that is, *the writer*—received a message from God, which Enoch conveyed in books, that declaration should be accepted. Furthermore, if the biblical record states that these books were written prior to the Great Flood, then I, for one, have no problem believing that other books were also written many centuries before typical scholarship has been willing to admit. After all, is it not written: In the beginning was the Word, and through the same Word, the entire Universe was created?[2] How absurd, then, to relinquish the inevitable conclusion that if the Word of God communicated His truth to not only Enoch but also Adam before him and Abraham after him that the end result of those communications would not have produced some form of written record. Therefore, it is with all the preceding ideas in mind that I now carry on with this tale of five *sacred* things, with the unfolding drama of God's hidden hand in history, that is to say, with *The Tales* that are … forever.

The Unfolding Drama

IN 1650, ARCHBISHOP James Ussher published one of the most influential biblical chronologies ever set forth as the unassailable word of God. By using texts in *The Book of Genesis*, together with other passages from Scripture, Ussher calculated that the world was created on the 23rd day of October, in the year 4,004 B.C. To this day, most Christians would never think to dispute such a finding, and if ever challenged would undoubtedly defend this "fact" to the death, not knowing why, other than that it had been included in so many copies of their *Bible*. But sadly, as well-intentioned as these defenders of the faith are, they may, upon further review of all things scriptural, actually be defending a proverbial Trojan horse.

Nearly lost to history is the knowledge that long before Archbishop Ussher offered his chronology as the "gospel truth," there was already another chronological system that had been universally accepted for the first fifteen centuries of Christendom. This chronology, derived from *The Septuagint Bible*, adhered to a five thousand, five hundred year period from the Fall of Adam to the Advent of Christ. And though it had withstood the test of time for so many centuries, it ultimately fell victim to one of the most ironic twists in history and was replaced by a more politically correct translation, which influenced all subsequent versions of *The English Bible* as we know it today. So, with *The Septuagint* having been officially relegated to the dustbin of apocryphal literature, the way was unwittingly paved for Ussher's "new and improved" chronology—one that most biblical scholars will admit is at odds with every known historical account, both Jewish and Christian.

Of course *The Septuagint* was not the first book to have suffered the wrath of ecclesiastical scorn. Included in the halls of the similarly excised were such legendary texts as those ascribed to Enoch, the man who famously walked and talked with God. And though one can assume that the truths conveyed in that conversation might be of great interest, this natural human curiosity was summarily short-circuited when religious authorities, declaring these books unsuitable for common folk, banned them. Such are the perpetual tug of wars—theologically-speaking—that have plagued the entire history of *The Bible* so that what was once perfectly acceptable is almost overnight deemed an object of holy revulsion. As a result, many of the world's most revered manuscripts, rejected and suppressed, have sadly been lost to history forever ... or so it would seem.

It is to the tumultuous story of these lost books, lost chronologies, and lost truths, then, that this work will turn in an effort to shed new light on what I believe to be the ultimate tale of God's intention toward humanity. To do so, this book—unlike any other that deals with such subjects as scriptural interpretation, biblical chronology, and religious artifacts—will not only offer evidence from history but also from the very books that have, down through the ages, generated so much derision and controversy. By analyzing the historical and theological validity of texts like those penned by the likes of Enoch, the scribe, as well as inviting the reader to peruse several of them in their entirety, *Tales of Forever* will provide a unique window into our biblical past. And in the process, even the layperson will be able to judge for themselves what has, for so very long, been the exclusive domain of the elite and the scholar, the esoteric and the clandestine.

Consequently, readers will find themselves on an unprecedented journey in which the traditional notions concerning the so-called *Lost Books of The Bible* are turned completely upside down. What appears to be one of the great failures of history will, within the pages of this book, be portrayed not as having occurred in spite of God's best efforts to reveal His truth but as a direct result of His desire to hide it. No doubt Solomon had this in mind when he uttered his proverb: "God in His greatness has concealed many things, while kings have the honor of discovering them."[3] Simply put, in order to fully apprehend the manifold truths of Scripture—particularly as they pertain to the five *sacred* things and the proof of God's control and faithfulness that they convey—one must come to grips with a peculiar paradox: In the course of the unfolding drama of history, God has made it abundantly clear that He is far less concerned with how obvious He has made the truth than with how artfully He has hidden it in plain sight.

A Spoiler Alert

HIDDEN IN PLAIN SIGHT: This is a concept you will hear a lot about in this book. What is more, you will not only be told what it means—that is, in the context of this particular work—but you will also be challenged to test your own skills of discernment in the process. The reason for this is because this book just happens to be one that was written to both expound and conceal the truth at the same time. Naturally, you may wonder why I would do something that seems so blatantly contradictory, but before you judge me too harshly, please understand one more very important point. I am not doing this out of some twisted desire on my part. In my own defense, I am doing this because what I am writing about is, itself, a thing that is hidden in plain sight. In fact, it is nothing less than the unveiling of a heretofore hidden drama of the ages, the true nature of which we, like an audience sitting in a darkened theater, are scarcely aware of, even as we are watching it on the screen. To be sure, we are all participants of this living drama, yet the vast majority of us who are playing our part are doing so without ever appreciating the extent to which it is being orchestrated by none other than God Himself, the Ultimate Director of human history. And just as the story of the Lord's redemptive drama is one that is artfully hidden in plain sight, this work endeavors to mirror this same quality.

Therefore, the real story contained in this book—that is, the unveiling of God's control and faithfulness conveyed in the five *sacred* things—has been written as a story-within-a-story concerning the lost truths, lost chronologies, and lost books of our collective biblical past. And because of my acute awareness of this paradoxical nature of the divine drama, I, too, have sought to maintain a similarly delicate balance between the two equal but opposite forces that seek to expound as well as conceal its essential meaning. As such, I have attempted to design this book in such a way that it might adequately communicate the truth for the sake of a genuinely open-minded audience, while at the same time not trying too hard to convey it to an admittedly cynical one.

That said, I wish to introduce this book with the following explanation. The book you are reading is not one book but two. Ordinarily, a book is classified as being either a work of nonfiction or fiction, with the first kind of book reading like a documentary, and the second, like a movie. In this way, every book is written specifically for one segment of the population as opposed to another. However, this one was not. To my knowledge, no book has ever been written that contains elements of nonfiction and fiction in equal balance; that is, until this one, which was written to meet the twin demands of the readers of scholarly and dramatic narratives alike. Therefore, let the reader of this work be advised: There is more than one way to read it. What does that mean? It means that, because this book was written with both skeptics and believers in mind, the kind of person you are will determine your approach to the material in it. If you are the critical type who has to know all the behind-the-scene facts of a given scenario, then by all means you should read this book from start to finish. If, however, you are the carefree sort who prefers to avoid sweating the details, then feel free to skip *The Prelude* and *The Analyses*. In your case, you will only need to read the two sections entitled *The Translation* and *The Interlude* before moving on to *The Tales.*

But keep in mind, it does not mean that one approach to reading this book is any better than another. It just means that it was written to anticipate more than a single mindset. Put another way, some people are only inclined to crack open a history book about, say, the American World War II general George Patton after seeing a movie about him, while others would only think to read a novel about him after watching a documentary on the subject. The main thing—as far as I am concerned—is to, once and for all, introduce this all-too-often taboo subject to a much broader audience after having been confined to such a narrow one for so long. If this happens, then at least I will have accomplished the one thing any writer hopes for when attempting to interest an audience in historical events or characters: People from every walk of life will finally look for themselves upon a subject that has generally been confined to the darkened rooms of the cloistered and cryptic.

It is also important to note that when I say this book supplies the reader with a dramatic narrative in addition to a scholarly one, it should not be assumed that this narrative is entirely fictional in nature. Far from presenting mere fiction, what this book does, in fact, is to expand the original narratives found in the ancient documents we will examine in terms of everything that a full-blown dramatization has to offer. This, of course, I have done in accord with what I previously alluded to. Whereas all other books on extra-biblical texts seek to dissect their subject matter in such a way that the reader never has a chance to experience their contents in the same context that was intended by the original authors, this book will provide that opportunity by presenting the stories as complete narratives.

However, just in case there is anyone out there who insists that this is a most unscholarly approach to such a scholastically demanding subject, I have also included what I believe to be a thoroughly systematic analysis as well, specifically presented for the sake of the more investigative segment of the audience. This systematic documentation is what has been provided in *The Prelude* and *The Analyses* sections before and after *The Tales* themselves. The only drawback to this more penetrating approach is that it does come with a spoiler alert. That is to say, in order to convey the historical and theological significance of the manuscripts presented in this book, it was necessary to discuss the narratives in their entirety, and because of this, certain plot points in the stories have unavoidably been "given away" in the process.

So, to review one's approach to reading this book: Are you the kind of person who needs some convincing before you are comfortable taking a leap of faith? Do you prefer more of a documentary approach to your subject matter? If so, you should read *The Prelude* and *The Analyses* before *The Tales*, even though you will be subjected to the occasional plot spoiler. Or, are you someone who enjoys solving a good puzzle on your own? Would you rather let the movie "do its own talking," as it were? If so, you only need to read *The Translation* and *The Interlude* before moving on to *The Tales*. Then, after you have been sufficiently tantalized by first reading the narratives, take the time to peruse *The Prelude* and *The Analyses* before and after *The Tales*. I guarantee you will not regret it, particularly if you are one who hopes to solve the mystery of what connects the five *sacred* things. Still, either way you go, realize this: Whether you embark on this journey as a confirmed skeptic or as a true believer, every aspect of this multifaceted work will provide something special for your unique literary palette.

The Disclaimer

I WOULD ALSO LIKE to insert a disclaimer before I begin, which I feel is necessary because of the sensitive areas of knowledge into which a work like this delves. In order to present the material in its proper light, one must go into detail concerning the history of such controversial subjects as scriptural interpretation, biblical chronology, and religious artifacts, subjects that are still fraught by impassioned debates to this very day. As a result of this historical presentation, one inevitably runs the risk of stepping on numerous theological "toes," as it were.

Without a doubt, the following story involves just as many villains as it does heroes, and consequently, like all great stories, its villainous elements are often more intriguing—and therefore more interesting—than its heroic ones. Due to this ironic nature of storytelling, it is all too tempting to swing the sword of blame and accusation, especially when it comes to a story like this one that involves so many negative forces and characters. In order to tell the whole truth about the age-old controversy of why certain biblical books, chronologies, or truths were either sanctioned or banned, the story could never be written without having to insist that someone was "at fault" for having made a decision that was deemed unwarranted by some political or religious entity. As contemplative, questioning creatures, we simply cannot avoid this very real dilemma. For every controversial issue in life, one can only confront the pros and cons of a given subject, and therefore, it is only natural to land on one side of the fence or the other.

My real concern, however, with this completely normal response, is the lengths to which some people will go to prove their point. By that I mean, if history teaches us anything about the debates that mankind is inevitably drawn into—especially when it comes to theological issues encountered in books like this—the quest for truth sometimes becomes so important that the participants lose sight of their original goals. In such a case, truth is no longer important, and the humble realization that we are all mere humans, reaching to know the unknowable, is swept aside. What began as a holy cause soon escalates into a holy war. Winning the argument, then, becomes the only goal, because it is often easier to appear the winner of the debate, while at the same time never coming one iota closer to the truth, which was the actual purpose for engaging in the quest in the first place.

As a matter of fact, this seems to me to be at the heart of every war that is waged in the name of "religion," or "truth," or "God," or whatever one chooses to call it, and it is this kind of thing that, above all else, I am committed to renouncing with every ounce of my being. Therefore, the contents of this book should never be construed as an effort on my part to deride any particular doctrine of faith, which I believe—as I am sure every true American believes—is a matter of strictest conscience, and as such is off-limits to criticism by anyone.

This, then, is the essence of my disclaimer. To anyone who reads the present volume of *Analyses* and *Tales*, please keep in mind that I bear no ill will toward any person or group of persons, even while trying my best to present what I believe to be the unbiased facts that are central to this story. Just because certain individuals made decisions—as a result of their heartfelt convictions—that certain books should be excised from the Canon of Scripture and therefore suppressed from public circulation, does not mean that I hold those people to be evil or deluded. No one but God, I believe, is qualified to make such a judgment. Similarly, I feel no animosity or hatred toward any religion or denomination just because I point out from history that those who excised certain books belonged to a specific religious group.

And the reason I feel this is never an option is because of my own view on the nature of truth as I perceive it to be revealed in *The Bible* and by the One Who is the final arbitrator of the truth contained in it. To the best of my knowledge, I have never known the Jesus that I see in Scripture to have ever condemned an individual *per se*. What I do see Him condemning are the attitudes and beliefs of certain ones that have their origin in what can best be described as institutionally-oriented, or, to put it another way, system-oriented mindsets. In other words, Jesus seems less concerned with condemning individual sinners and more interested in attacking the root source of what keeps those people spiritually, emotionally, and intellectually imprisoned by the state of sin into which all humans are naturally born. Simply put, Jesus does not condemn people; He condemns institutions, or systems.

Now, before you insist that what I have just proposed is too absurd to believe, and you do so based on the idea that only people and not institutions or systems can go to Heaven or Hell, please keep the following in mind. There is an old adage, attributed to one Lord Acton, which states: Power corrupts, and absolute power corrupts absolutely. Of this very thing Abraham Lincoln spoke when he wisely observed: "Nearly all men can stand adversity, but if you want to test a man's character give him power." If there is any truth to such statements, then what follows is also likely to be true: No individual in the history of mankind, that I know of, has ever been corrupted by power while living alone on a desert island. It is therefore axiomatic that the power that both Acton and Lincoln were referring to is power that can only be exerted by an individual who exists within the matrix of an institution or system, whether it is political, economic, or religious in nature.

Now, mind you, I am not trying to say that individual humans are sinless just because they withdraw from the world and live on a desert island; that, sadly, is the fallacy of living the life of a hermit. What I am saying, though, is what any social psychologist will tell you. The typical individual left to his or her own devices is benign, but when you thrust that same individual into a decidedly hostile group, even if the sentiments and proclivities of that group are very different from that of the individual, a person will eventually succumb to the herd mentality and align themselves with the attitudes and beliefs of that group. Therein lies the logic of Jesus not condemning people so much as the system or institution that indoctrinates people with the attitudes or beliefs that He does condemn.

To see how all of this applies to the teachings of Scripture one need only turn to the words and actions of Jesus Himself. When the Pharisees came to Him demanding a sign to prove that He was the Messiah, Jesus flatly informed them: "An evil and adulterous generation insists on seeking signs, but none will be given to it except the sign of Jonah."[4] First, notice how Jesus did not point an accusing finger at any of those individuals who were standing right in front of Him. Was it because He was too timid to accuse any single individual from within the group? Was He unsure of exactly who were the guilty ones among the demanding crowd? I hardly think so. What we have is simply a clear-cut example of what I am trying to point out. Jesus was less concerned about condemning individuals and more concerned with warning them about the kinds of attitudes and beliefs that they should avoid—attitudes and beliefs that only come as a result of associating with the institutions and systems that are united by like-minded individuals.

This becomes all the more evident when one takes the time to notice that Jesus did not say that a sign would be withheld from "them," that is, those "individuals" who made up the group that was addressing Him. What He did say was that a sign would be withheld from "it," that is, the "generation" that was demanding a sign from Him, which constitutes the world system, or present order. The same idea is expressed when Jesus spoke concerning those who believed in Him. "If you were of the world, the world would love you, but because you're not, the world hates you."[5] The Greek word being used here for "world" is *kosmos*, the word we transliterate directly into English as *cosmos*, a word that literally means "something ordered," as in an "ordered system." So what we see here is Jesus choosing to condemn a world system that is alien to His way of thinking, as opposed to targeting the individuals who had fallen victim to that system by virtue of their simply being born into it.

Next, we see that when Jesus came to the Temple at Jerusalem, He famously drove out those who were buying and selling there, even going so far as to overturn the tables of the moneychangers. "It is written," He bellowed, "My house will be called a house of prayer, but you've turned it into a den of thieves!"[6] What does this mean in the context of what I am trying to articulate by way of this disclaimer? Was Jesus condemning the people for the way they were presenting their offerings to God? Was He angry at the act of their buying and selling, as if one could actually buy or sell the favor of God with mere money? If so, then who did Jesus hold to be of greater guilt? Those who bought? Or those who sold? But, as usual, such a surface-oriented interpretation would miss the point entirely. Certainly, it was no more in the nature of Jesus to be angry with those buying *or* selling, any more than a doctor is angry with a patient for being sick. Undoubtedly, what disgusted Him was the fact that what had begun as a God-given impulse, that is, the desire to offer sacrifice to the Lord, had over time succumbed to the humanly-inspired forces that had crept in and undermined the original divinely-instituted purpose of giving the burnt offering. In other words, He was angry because what had begun as a sublime expression of a single heart offered to God had devolved as a result of the machinations of an institutionally-inspired system.

This same process can be seen repeatedly down through the corridors of history, like "*déjà vu* all over again," as it were. The Lord of the Harvest calls individual men and women of faith, who, in turn, teach their children the ways of God. In time, however, and always over the span of several generations, the ways of God are slowly but surely subverted, and in their place a mere shell of their original intention is all that remains. In the end, the faith of "the one" has become the dogma of "the institution," which then creates a situation where God, as He does in every age, seeks the next individual who will heed the call in order to initiate the process all over again.

Therefore, when I attempt to convey the history of who decided which books should be excised from the Canon of Scripture, and in doing so, I quote certain ones who claim that "this person" belonging to "that religious group" made those decisions, remember I prefer to take to higher ground. And remember I, too, am less concerned by the actions of individuals and more interested in the process of institutionalization, which is constantly at work to undermine the original greatness of said person or group. In this, everyone is equally guilty or innocent, however the case may be, whether they are called Sethites, Semites, Hebrews, Israelites, Jews,

Pharisees, Christians, Catholics, Protestants, Lutherans, Episcopalians, Methodists, Baptists, Presbyterians, Fundamentalists, *et al.*

In short, all these designations, in my view, are just like everything else in this God-ordained Universe of ours, which is to say, they are merely representative of both sides of the same coin. They are good when they willingly cooperate with the good as proscribed by the dictates of the One Who inspired their creation, and they are bad when they willingly succumb to the forces that forever seek to subvert the dictates of that same One. And because of this ironic nature of the human dilemma, I, for one, choose not to assign guilt or condemnation in regard to any of their particular actions; I only seek to report, impartially and with malice toward none.

Roll Call of the Intrepid

THE LAST THING I have to do before beginning is to express my gratitude to the intrepid pioneers who provided the core narratives for this work. Just in case anyone thinks that I have concocted the following storyline entirely on my own, I would like to offer this list of discoverers, translators, and scholars whose monumental contributions have provided the biblical texts that form its backbone. For a more in-depth look at their lives and accomplishments, please refer to the *Selected Biographies* section in *The Credits*.

Among the discoverers who have restored to the world such an unexpected array of lost manuscripts, there are: Johann Grynaeus (1540-1617), a Swiss Protestant divine, professor of *The New Testament*, and collector of biblical manuscripts; Giuseppe Assemani (1687-1768), a Lebanese Orientalist and Vatican librarian; James Bruce (1730-1794), a Scottish explorer and travel writer; and E.A. Wallis Budge (1857-1934), a British Egyptologist, Orientalist, philologist, and author.

Among the translators who have turned many of these manuscripts into works that could be understood by an English-speaking world, there are: William Wake (1657-1737), a British clergyman, dean at Exeter, bishop at Lincoln, and archbishop of Canterbury; Richard Laurence (1760-1838), a British Hebraist, Anglican churchman, and regius professor of Hebrew at Oxford; Moses Samuel (1795-1860), a British author and translator of Hebrew works; S.C. Malan (1812-1894), a British biblical scholar and linguist of Oriental languages; William Wright (1830-1889), a British Orientalist and professor of Arabic at Cambridge; B. Harris Cowper (1822-1904), a British archeologist, historian, and translator; W.R. Morfill (1834-1909), a British professor of Slavonic languages at Oxford; and R.H. Charles (1855-1931), an Irish biblical scholar and theologian.

Among the scholars who invested their considerable skill and effort into making the various manuscripts accessible to the general population, there are: Theophilus of Antioch (c. 120-181), a Syrian theologian, apologist, author, and chronologist; Julius Africanus (c. 160-240), a Libyan historian, traveler, and chronologist; Hippolytus of Rome (c. 170-235), a Greek theologian, apologist, and chronologist; Ephrem the Syrian (c. 306-373), a theologian, deacon, and hymn writer; Giambattista Vico (1668-1744), an Italian historian, political philosopher, and apologist of classical antiquity; George Smith (1800-1868), a British historian, theologian, and author; Joseph A. Seiss (1823-1904), an American theologian, Lutheran minister, and author; E.W. Bullinger (1837-1913), a British clergyman and theologian; Louis Ginzberg (1873-1953), a Lithuanian professor of Judaism and Talmudist; Edgar J. Goodspeed (1871-1962), an American theologian and scholar of Greek and *The New Testament*; and Cyrus H. Gordon (1908-2001), an American biblical scholar and professor of ancient Near East culture and languages.

Thanks to the visionary efforts of "so great a cloud of witnesses," then, I hereby present the following work; I now present *Tales of Forever: The Unfolding Drama of God's Hidden Hand in History*.

ACT ONE

The great fragments of antiquity, previously useless to science because they lay neglected, broken, and scattered, shed great light when cleaned, pieced together, and set into place.

Giambattista Vico, *New Science*

THE PRELUDE

The important fact is ... that for 700 years after the commencement of the Christian Era ... the average estimation of the period from Adam to Christ was some 5,500 years.

Nathan Rouse, *A Dissertation on Sacred Chronology*

The Hidden Books

This Journey of Discovery

IN A WORLD WHERE evil so often triumphs over good, several burning questions linger in the face of such tragedy and despair. Is the God of *The Bible* really in control of human history as the Scriptures declare? And if He is, does He actually keep His promises to mankind? Fortunately for us, these first two questions are inexorably bound together, and they are bound in the following manner. God's control over history is clearly confirmed in direct proportion to His faithfulness to the promises He has made to humanity. In other words, in order to verify that God is in control, all one need do is confirm that He is faithful to the promises He makes. This leads us, then, to the next question, which is: Where does one look to confirm God's faithfulness to His word of promise? Naturally, the obvious solution to a problem framed this way would be: I guess one finds the answer in *The Bible*, right? Needless to say, though, as both believers and skeptics have discovered, such a straightforward solution is much more elusive than that. To begin with, one must first ask: To which promise of God should we look to confirm this faithfulness? And having decided upon which promise, how do we go about establishing a clear-cut way to determine whether or not God has kept that promise?

To that end, it would be useful to focus our quest. By that I mean that, out of the countless promises that fill the pages of Holy Writ, it would help if we could narrow down our choice. Fortunately, we do have the Apostle Paul to assist us in this matter. Speaking of Jesus, in his letter to the Corinthians, Paul said, "For all the promises of God find their 'yes' in Him."[7] Or as Weymouth's *New Testament* puts it: "All the promises of God, whatever their number, have their confirmation in Him."[8] In other words, if one were to gather together every promise that God has ever made to His people, they could all be confirmed by the fact that His Son came into this world to live and die and resurrect just as had been predicted. Therefore, if this Advent of Christ can be adequately confirmed, then—based on this verse in *Corinthians*—every other promise in the book can be counted on as well.

That said, it should be the mission of every student of Scripture to determine the extent to which the promises of God have been fulfilled in the Incarnation of Christ. Admittedly, this is not the easiest thing to do, considering all the roadblocks that stand in the way of one's quest for historical certainty. However, just because it is a difficult task does not mean that it is an impossible one. After all, although there are many pitfalls along the way, the God of *The Bible* does not hesitate to beckon us onward in this journey of discovery. Therefore, if one can appreciate that it is God Himself Who is guiding our quest, then it should come as no surprise that He is also the One Who has provided sufficient signposts to help us along the way.

With this in mind, one simply turns to the various ways in which *The Bible* portrays the manifestation of Christ in history, right? To which I must confess that—for me, at least—this is where things get a little tricky. Let me take a moment to explain what I mean by that.

A Body of Wisdom

NATURALLY, SPEAKING as I am from an admittedly Christian frame of reference, I do look to *The Bible* as one of several sources for such evidence—that is, the traditional *Bible*. But notice how I said the traditional *Bible*. The reason I say this is because after more than forty years of research, I have become convinced that there is another source of God-inspired wisdom that is just as capable of confirming the truth of the divine promise concerning the Advent of Christ. Make no mistake, though, I am not referring to any literary source that has not, at one point or another, been considered part of Holy Scripture. On the contrary, what I am referring to are books that were once considered inspired by God but which have, over the course of time, been excised from the canon of so-called "accepted texts," generally for reasons that seem more motivated by the whims of politics than by the dictates of conscience.

I am referring to a body of ancient wisdom literature that has come to be known in modern parlance as the *pseudepigraphical* books of *The Bible*. *Pseudepigrapha*—chances are if you are neither a biblical scholar nor an archeology professor you may not even know what this word means or what it implies. According to the dictionary, the word is derived from two Greek words, *pseudo*, which means "false," and *epigraphein*, which means to "inscribe," thus, "to write falsely." By that definition, any book considered *pseudepigraphical* is one that is believed to be a "falsely attributed work," that is to say, a work that erroneously purports to be written by some noteworthy biblical personage. As such, any book labeled as *pseudepigrapha* is to be discounted as being outside of the canon of books that have been deemed truly inspired by God. In addition to labeling these books as *pseudepigrapha*, they are often designated as "apocryphal" literature because a number of these titles remain in a separate section of *The Catholic Bible* and *The Greek Orthodox Bible* called *The Apocrypha*. Among these books are *The Wisdom of Solomon*, *The Epistle of Jeremiah*, *The Prayer of Manasseh*, *The Book of Judith*, and *The Second Book of Esdras*.

It is one of the great tragedies, in fact, in the history of *The Bible* that there is so much ignorance in regard to the peculiar assumption that we as a Western Protestant people received our Canon of Scripture like some hermetically-sealed document handed down from On-High. Fortunately, though, for the sake of those with the courage to examine this critical aspect of history, the work of intrepid scholars has greatly aided in dispelling such myopic thinking. Among them are Cyrus H. Gordon, professor of ancient Near East studies at Brandeis University, whose work shed much-needed new light on this age-old controversy. Said Gordon:

> *The Bible* is of a complex composition, varying in scope according to the different ecclesiastical bodies. The Samaritans include only the Five Books of Moses in their *Bible*, and it is evident from *The Dead Sea Scrolls* that before the start of the Christian Era *The Pentateuch* was the most stabilized part of the Hebrew Scripture. Normative Judaism embraces the conventional *Pentateuch*, *Prophets*, and *Hagiographa* of the familiar *Old Testament*. *The Septuagint*, however, is far more inclusive, containing as it does, *Apocrypha* and *Pseudepigrapha*. Qumranite and other sectarian Jews possessed still other sacred writings. *Protestant Bibles* usually contain the normative *Jewish Old Testament* plus *The New Testament*; *Catholic Bibles* have, in addition, *The Apocryphal Books*. Various Eastern Orthodox Churches include different *Pseudepigrapha*. Accordingly, there is no one biblical corpus; and the component books of either *Testament* are in many cases extremely heterogeneous individually.[9]

Concerning the variegated process of the formation of our *Protestant Bible*, Edgar J. Goodspeed, described as "America's greatest *New Testament* scholar,"[10] pointed out:

> *The Apocrypha* formed an integral part of the *King James* Version of 1611, as had all the preceding English versions from their beginning in 1382. But they are seldom printed as part of it any longer, still more seldom as part of the *English Revised* Version, and were not included in the American revision.
>
> This is partly because the Puritans disapproved of them; they had already begun to drop them from printings of their *Geneva Bible* by 1600, and began to demand copies of the *King James* Version omitting them as early as 1629… We moderns discredit them because they were not part of *The Hebrew Bible*, and most of them have never been found in any Hebrew forms at all.
>
> But they were part of *The Bible* of the early Church, for it used the *Greek* Version of *The Jewish Bible*, which we call *The Septuagint*, and these books were all in that version. They passed from it into Latin and the great Latin *Bible* edited by St. Jerome about 400 A.D., *The Vulgate*, which became the authorized *Bible* of Western Europe and England, and remained so for a thousand years. But Jerome

found that they were not in *The Hebrew Bible,* and so he called them *Apocrypha,* the hidden, or secret, books.[11]

The Apocrypha, however, does not contain all of the books included in the pantheon of apocryphal literature. Most notable among the other titles are *The First Book of Adam and Eve, The First Book of Enoch, The Secrets of Enoch, The Book of Jasher, The Book of Jubilees, The Testaments of the Twelve Patriarchs, The Letters of Herod and Pilate,* and *The Gospel of Nicodemus.*

Grounds for Exclusion

OVER THE YEARS many reasons have been offered to justify the rejection of any book that is no longer found in many of our modern versions of *The Bible.* Chief among them are: One, they were written under assumed names; two, they contain historical errors; three, they were not quoted by Jesus; and four, they contain no prophetic elements. Yet ironically, these same objections, which seem to confirm the correctness of rejecting the apocryphal books, have also been leveled against the very books that reside in the accepted Canon of Scripture.

For example, regarding *The Pentateuch,* or the first five books of *The Old Testament,* critics have often doubted the Mosaic authorship of *The Book of Genesis.* As their argument goes: While the last four books could have been written by Moses by virtue of the fact that he lived during the years described by the text, he certainly could not have been around to witness the events depicted in the first book. Yet according to most biblical scholars: "Long before the first century A.D., Moses was declared the author of *Genesis,* and Josephus, the first-century Jewish historian, in keeping with this tradition, accepted Mosaic authorship."[12]

Still other books in *The Old Testament* have had their authorship called into question, such as *Isaiah, Ezekiel,* and *Daniel.* Because they so precisely predict future events, these books, critics insist, must have been published after the fact and therefore must have been written under assumed names. Similarly, certain books in *The New Testament* have in recent times come under fire concerning their genuine authorship. Most notably are those attributed to the Apostles Peter and Paul. According to much modern-day scholarship, both epistles of Peter and several letters of Paul were allegedly written as amalgamations by authors other than the ones to which Scripture has subscribed. Yet the simple fact is, though the identities of many of the best-known biblical authors remain subject to such doubt and speculation, the books that bear their names are still regarded as integral to *The Holy Bible.*

As far as rejecting certain books because they contain historical errors, again I should point out that this same argument applies to texts well within the accepted limits of scriptural sanctity. And again one need only turn to the first book in Scripture to prove my point, because as many biblical scholars are well aware it has been a longstanding bone of contention that the account of Noah's gathering of the animals into the Ark contains two contradictory versions. In one rendition, the animals enter in pairs,[13] while in another, they enter in groups of seven.[14]

The same thing occurs in *The New Testament* regarding Judas Iscariot, whose infamous demise is reported in two separate yet contradictory accounts. In *Matthew,* it is said that a grief-stricken Judas hung himself after betraying Jesus,[15] while *Acts* has him falling headlong into a field and being disemboweled in the process.[16] Naturally, scholars are quick to point out the various ways in which such contradictions can be logically reconciled, and justifiably so. Yet this still does not change the fact that there are obvious contradictions to be found in the received texts, which if they were found in books that critics were seeking to excise would be considered clear grounds for exclusion.

Its True Spiritual Child

AS FOR THE CLAIM that Jesus never quoted from any of the apocryphal books, one need only consider *The Testaments of the Twelve Patriarchs* to undermine such an objection. R.H. Charles, in his scholarly work on pseudepigraphical literature, said this about *The Testaments:*

> Its ethical teaching has achieved a real immortality by influencing the thought and diction of the writers of *The New Testament,* and even those of our Lord. This ethical teaching, which is very much higher and purer than that of *The Old Testament,* is yet its true spiritual child, and helps to bridge the chasm that divides *The Old Testament* and *The New Testament.*
>
> The instances of the influence of these writings on *The New Testament* are notable in the Sermon on the Mount, which reflects the spirit and even uses phrases from these *Testaments.* Saint Paul appears to have borrowed so freely that it seems as though he must have carried a copy of *The Testaments* with him on his travels. Thus, the reader has before him in these pages what is at once striking for its blunt primitive style and valuable as some of the actual source books of *The Bible.*[17]

A perfect example of the way in which the apocryphal literature has made its indelible mark on the world of *The New Testament* can be seen in relation to *The First Book of Enoch.* Consider for a moment, if you will, the evidence of all four Gospels, in which Jesus refers to Himself as the Son of Man some eighty-one times. This is certainly a peculiar title when one considers the fact that most people assume Jesus was condemned for calling Himself the Son of God, not the Son of Man. The Jewish leaders repeatedly demanded to know if He claimed the title of the Son of God for Himself, but never once did any of the gospel writers record that Jesus did so. To a man, what they did reveal was, in response to this question, His reply was purely rhetorical. Said Jesus:

> "From now on, the Son of Man will be seated at the right hand of the power of God."
>
> And they all said, "Are you the Son of God, then?"
>
> And He replied, "You say that I am."
>
> Then they said, "What further need do we have of testimony? We heard it ourselves from his own mouth."[18]

But notice that Jesus never claimed here to be the Son of God; yet His enemies insisted He did. Was this simply a case of their having heard what they expected to hear, even though He never said what they claimed? Unfortunately, such an oversimplification is itself a product of wishful thinking by anyone who insists that Jesus never quoted from the apocryphal books, because all one must consider is that even though He never verbalized that He was the Son of God, His critics acted as if He did. But how?

In fact, they "heard" Jesus "say" so by way of His more than eighty references to Himself as the Son of Man. To the average listener, the title Son of Man carries no divine significance whatsoever, but to the Jewish religious community of that day, the Son of Man was an even more potent title than that of the Son of God. And much to the chagrin of the apocryphal naysayers, this disjointed string of logic in the minds of Jesus' enemies proves it, because the title Son of Man finds its origins in none other than *First Enoch,* as is demonstrated by the following excerpt:

> There I saw the Ancient of Days, Whose head was like wool, and with Him stood another, Whose countenance resembled that of a Man. His face was full of grace, like that of the holy angels. Then I asked one of the angels who had been showing me all of these secret things…
>
> And he answered me, saying, "This is the Son of Man to Whom righteousness belongs … and Who will reveal all the treasures that are concealed, because the Lord of Spirits has chosen Him, and His portion surpasses everyone else in everlasting uprightness. This Son of Man Whom you see … will break the teeth of sinners. He'll hurl kings from their thrones and

their dominions because they won't exalt or praise Him, nor humble themselves before Him, by Whom their kingdoms were granted to them."[19]

Hopefully, excerpts like this will put to rest any question as to whether or not Jesus quoted from the apocryphal literature. It should also help to explain the level of implacable hatred that the Jewish religious leaders displayed toward Jesus when this apparently ordinary man insisted on equating Himself with the loftiest and mightiest figure in their Hebrew pantheon.[20]

A Thread of Prophecy

FINALLY, WE TURN TO the insistence that the apocryphal literature must be rejected because, unlike its legitimate counterpart of canonical Scripture, it contains no prophetic elements. This is perhaps the most spurious claim of all, because even a cursory examination of the many texts in this group will yield, on this point alone, a bounty far beyond the scope of this book.

In *The First Book of Enoch*, one finds innumerable descriptions of the future events concerning the long-awaited coming of the Son of Man and His subsequent judgment of mankind. Certainly, the most famous example of this is the quote by Jude in his *New Testament* letter: "Enoch, the seventh from Adam, prophesied, 'See, the Lord is coming with ten thousand of His saints to judge everyone, and to convict them for their ungodliness and all the defiant words they've spoken against Him.'"[21]

Again, there is *The Testaments of the Twelve Patriarchs*, which, while ostensibly a series of exhortations to Jacob's grandchildren, also provides a prophetic window into the future of Israel, one which speaks not only of the resurrection of Christ but also of the saints who were to rise in His wake. As Benjamin, the youngest son of Jacob, lay on his deathbed, he admonished his children with these words—both chilling and hopeful in their implications:

> The Lord will send His salvation in the form of an Only-Begotten Prophet. He'll enter into the Temple and there be treated with outrage. He'll be lifted up on a tree, the veil of the Temple will be torn, and the Spirit of God will pass on to the Gentiles as a flame pours forth, and He'll ascend from Hades and pass from Earth to Heaven...
>
> And then you'll see Noah, Shem, Abraham, Isaac, and Jacob, rising on the right hand in gladness. Then we'll rise, too, each of us at the head of our tribe, worshiping the King of Heaven, Who appeared on the Earth in the form of a Man with all humility.[22]

In *The Second Book of Esdras*, the visions of Ezra reveal the signs of the approaching messianic kingdom, the general resurrection of the dead, the final judgment, the New Jerusalem, and the coming of Messiah. In it, one finds the following prediction, written more than four centuries before the Advent of Christ:

> The time will come when the signs I've told you about will take place... Whoever is delivered from the evils I've predicted will see My wonders. For My Son, the Christ, will be revealed to those who are with Him, and those who are left will rejoice in Him, that is, in four hundred years, and it will be after those years that My Son Christ will die.[23]

Clearly, anyone who insists that the apocryphal books lack the prophetic elements that are in the canonical texts is blind by choice or by nature, but either way, they are blind to what even a rank amateur can detect, if only they are willing to honestly examine the evidence for themselves.

In our particular case, however, the extent to which we will be investigating this literature will be limited to a lone prophetic thread, though it is one that has everything to do with the all-important issue of the Advent of Christ. Unlike anything else in these ancient texts, this thread of prophecy is of paramount significance due to the fact that it weaves its way through no less than three of these books. Known as the prophecy of The Great Five and a Half Days, this messianic promise originates in *The First Book of Adam and Eve*, is then alluded to in *The Secrets of Enoch*, and finally culminates in *The Gospel of Nicodemus*. It is this prophecy, then, of The Great Five and a Half Days—which, as we will see, refers to a five thousand, five hundred year period from Adam to Christ—that will provide the framework we require to unravel the two mysteries this book has set out to solve. By verifying the historical reality of this *five and a half* "day" timeline, it is our intention to establish the criterion we are seeking in order to, one, demonstrate the Lord's control by way of His faithfulness to His promises, which is to say, "all the promises of God" that are "confirmed" in the Incarnation of Christ, and, two, demonstrate how this prophecy provides the key to revealing the hidden connection between the five *sacred* things.

Meanwhile, at this moment, I can imagine the reaction of everyone who has ever studied biblical chronology and who are all asking the same question: "But what about Archbishop Ussher's seventeenth-century timeline of *four* thousand years from Adam to Christ? I thought *it* was the accepted version derived from *The Bible*." And to such a question, my response is: For many years I thought the same thing, too. I did, that is, until I encountered an alternate timeline—and, mind you, a timeline that offers a vastly superior method for verifying God's faithfulness to His promises. As it turns out, my original view changed in light of the evidence found not only in the apocryphal record but in the historical record as well—evidence that is still, to this day, being overlooked by the general public.

Just consider this potent statement offered by Nathan Rouse, who wrote in his 1856 book entitled *A Dissertation on Sacred Chronology*: "The important fact is ... that for 700 years after the commencement of the Christian Era ... the average estimation of the period from Adam to Christ was some 5,500 years."[24] Imagine that: For the first seven hundred years of Christianity, no one ever once considered the possibility of a *four* thousand year period from Adam to Christ. Why? The reason for this was because, as historians like Rouse were right to point out, all the Church Fathers subscribed to a biblical chronology that was found in the earlier Greek Version of *The Old Testament* called *The Septuagint*—one that differed drastically from the later *Hebrew* Version, or *Masoretic* Text. Concerning this ecclesiastical controversy between the *Septuagint* and *Masoretic* Versions of *The Old Testament*, Rouse went on to say:

> Bishop Michael Russell, in his observation on this subject, states that, "The *Septuagint* chronology was used before the Advent of Christ, was followed by the Church Fathers, and appears not to have been called into question until, in the eighth century, a disposition to exchange it for the rabbinical method of reckoning was first manifested by the Venerable Bede.
>
> "But his innovations were ill-received by his contemporaries. He was denounced as a heretic for taking it upon himself to assert ... that the Redeemer of our race was not born in the sixth millennium of the world. Notwithstanding this attempt, however, and the high reputation which Bede possessed, his system was generally rejected and the *Septuagint* chronology prevailed. This will be evident from the following facts, for which we are chiefly indebted to Dr. William Hales.
>
> "In the year 691 A.D., a general council was held at Constantinople, and in its recorded acts it is stated that the members of this council assembled in the Imperial City in the year of the world 6,199, which places the Creation 5,508 years before Christ. This council, it is true, was held in the nineteenth year of the life of Bede, and therefore prior to his attempt to introduce the Hebrew numbers.

> However, the date here assigned to the Creation was the act of a general council, and as such it furnishes the most decisive evidence that down to the close of the seventh century, the Christian Church continued to use the *Septuagint* chronology."[25]

Not only was this particular chronology in place until then, but if one takes the time to review the historical evidence, it will reveal that the lengthier time frame of five thousand, five hundred years from Adam to Christ was maintained by Orthodox Christianity for another eight centuries after that. It was actually not until the Reformation—and then only as an unforeseen consequence of one of the more ironic twists in history, to be discussed later in this book—that the *Septuagint* numbers were finally replaced by those in the *Masoretic* Text.[26] Concerning this fateful switch, Rouse wrote some three hundred years after the fact:

> A sufficiency of evidence shows that, notwithstanding the attempt of Venerable Bede, the *Septuagint* chronology prevailed down to the time of the Reformation... In this grand chronological blunder, however, the reformers stood alone, and have continued to stand alone, to this day. It does not appear that any other church has followed them in this path. They have the merit and glory of it entirely to themselves. The Greek Church, as is well known, still adopts, as she has always done, the *Septuagint* chronology. The Roman Church, too, and ... the Egyptian Copts, the Abyssinians, the Armenians, the Ethiopians and the Georgians. So that, although the followers of Luther ... adopted the Hebrew numbers, all other churches have continued to reject them to this day.[27]

It is to such evidence that the present work will turn in an effort to shed new light on this critical lost chapter of biblical history. What is more, this book will present, as far as I know, the first attempt to connect the five thousand, five hundred year timeline of *The Septuagint Bible* with The Great Five and a Half Day prophecy so prevalent in apocryphal literature. And if this can be adequately accomplished, then it is my hope that they will never again stand apart; but in their being brought together in a sublime continuum, they will finally be seen in the context that the God of *The Bible* had originally intended for them.

Rest assured, however, this effort will not constitute some new revelation of my own conjuring. On the contrary, the storyline contained in this book will stand as the inevitable ancestor of previous generations who have paved the way with their courage and tenacity. Moreover, in turning to these gems of forgotten wisdom—like *The First Book of Adam and Eve*, *The Secrets of Enoch*, and *The Gospel of Nicodemus*, which provide us with the most comprehensive scriptural view of this prophecy of The Great Five and a Half Days—it will be just as it was intended by those intrepid scholars who gave mankind the first modern translations of these books. According to their mission statement:

> All of these apocryphal volumes are presented without argument or comment. The reader's own judgment and common sense are appealed to. It makes no difference whether he is Catholic or Protestant or Hebrew. The facts are plainly laid before him. These facts, for a long time, have been the peculiar esoteric property of the learned. They were available only in the original Greek and Latin and so forth. Now, they have been translated into plain English before the eye of every reader.
>
> The ordinary man has, therefore, the privilege of seeing upon what grounds the commonly accepted Scriptures rest. He can examine the pile of evidence, and do his own sifting... In other words, the ordinary man is invited to take his place in that council chamber which accepts or rejects the various writings of Scripture. It is safe to say the conclusions desired can be left to his common sense.[28]

To that end, this work is divided into three acts. Act One offers several chapters concerning the validity of those books that are intended to lay a firm foundation for demonstrating God's control and faithfulness—a foundation that just happens to involve examining books that have so often been presumptuously dismissed as "apocryphal" literature. Act Two will present a collection of *The Tales* themselves, in their entirety, with Enoch, the scribe, acting as both narrator and custodian of God's intention toward humanity. And Act Three will provide several follow-up chapters that will tie all the loose ends together in finally revealing the way in which the aforementioned five *sacred* things prove that God really is in the business of keeping His promises to mankind.

That said, I would like to present the reader with the following proviso. In trying to prove that these so-called "apocryphal volumes" are valid sources of divinely-inspired wisdom, and therefore worthy of their role in establishing the foundation I am seeking to build, my methods will not be—I repeat, *not be*—presented in the traditional manner found in most biblical treatises. Instead of offering a purely "scholastic" approach to authenticating the various manuscripts in question, the methodology presented in this book will be derived more in terms of the "story," as it were, that comes from directly investigating the narratives on their own terms. Whereas language loses something in the process of translation and mistranslation, and science reduces all reality down to what can only be measured and quantified, the approach in this book will be one that transcends the foibles of mere language and the limitations of brute science, which most analytics typically focus on. What does that mean? It means that the debate over the legitimacy of these ancient documents will not revolve around such things as linguistic comparisons and manuscript carbon dating. Instead, it will focus entirely on the story elements found in the narratives themselves, and the way in which these elements correlate with the more familiar ones found in the canonical books of Scripture—particularly as they pertain to the biblical doctrine of typology, which we will explain in the next section.

And to echo the words of those provided by another publisher—as it perfectly expresses my own wish in producing this volume of *Tales* retold—I offer this earnest sentiment in the hopes that:

> The publication of this book will do good because it takes away the veil of secrecy that has hidden, for many years, the act of the Church in accepting certain Scriptures and rejecting others. All of the grounds are rendered intelligible to the common man.[29]

A Word to the Wise

HIDDEN BOOKS, hidden in plain sight, God's hidden hand in history: To anyone reading this, it must certainly appear as if there is a very strong element of hide-and-seek to this story, and in describing it this way, I admit that one is not so far from the real truth after all. In my own defense, however, I would like to point out that I am not the first person to characterize the God of *The Bible* along these lines. Moreover, as a result of more than forty years of biblical research and exegetical training, I would like to think that I have even learned a thing or two from the Master of the game, that is, the One Whom the prophet Isaiah described as the God Who hides Himself.[30]

Keeping this mind, then, I would next like to offer the following word to the wise, en route to diving into the rest of this work. This word just happens to involve some key points already touched upon and to which I will briefly turn in order to better equip anyone who is truly interested in discovering the way that the five *sacred* things demonstrate tangible proof of God's control and faithfulness. The key points are these, that of the divinely-inspired principle of concealing and revealing truth, and that of the humanly-inspired endeavor of discerning and mining truth that has its origins in the Divine. To those of you determined to make this journey of discovery with me, know this as you embark on the trip: I respectfully submit to you, here and now, that if you think that I will simply be blurting out the special connection conveyed in the five *sacred* things in Act One, you will be sorely disappointed. In fact, the true significance of what connects these five things will not be entirely apparent after reading Act Two, either. Furthermore, you will find yourself halfway through Act Three, and still you will probably be wondering what it is that connects them all.

Of course, considering such a dilemma as this, I suppose that the overwhelming temptation would be to bypass all the preliminary business just mentioned and skip ahead to the last half of Act Three, right? But unfortunately, I can assure you, this will not, and cannot, produce the desired results, if, in fact, you are one who earnestly wishes to know the startling proof of God's control and faithfulness of which I have spoken. If this really is what you desire, then you will resist such a foolhardy enterprise, and take to heart the folly of all those who dare to tread the path of the sacred without first attaining the prerequisites to prepare oneself for such a journey. Remember well: To those who rush ahead recklessly, only misfortune awaits, just as it did for those misguided ones who brazenly sought to behold the mysteries contained inside The Ark of the Covenant and lifted its lid with such devastating results.[31] Needless to say, in this case, I do not expect such spectacular results as all that, but what I am suggesting is that such a preemptive approach to penetrating the mystery of the five *sacred* things will only short-circuit one's ability to grasp the true significance of the hidden link that can only be properly understood after taking the appropriate steps.

But why, you may ask, must this always be the case? If what you propose is true, then why not just tell us what connects the five things and proceed with your concluding arguments? What point could there be in dragging it out? And the answer to each of these questions is, I believe, the same answer that one might hear in response to the age-old question: Why is it not possible to open *The Bible*, point to a specific chapter and verse, and discover—just that simply—the meaning of life, or faith, or God's will? The truth is: Wisdom, as prescribed by the God of Scripture, is always such that it is intended to be dispensed incrementally, "bit by bit, action by action, and level by level." That is to say, what is required in the first year of one's journey of faith is no longer viable in the second; and what holds true in year two does not remain so in year three, and so on and so forth. A primary example of this can be seen in the history of God's people. When the Israelites originally faced the Red Sea, under Moses, the only thing that the people were required to do was look upon Moses and his raised staff, and God parted the waters, enabling them to pass through.[32] But forty years later, when they came to the Jordan River, under Joshua, God raised the stakes on them. This time, before the Lord would invoke His miraculous power to part the waters, He commanded that the priests who were responsible for transporting The Ark of the Covenant were to wade into the waters, at which point the river stopped flowing and piled up on itself, allowing the people to cross over into Palestine.[33]

Thus, like the peculiar phenomenon that someone experiences in seeing a mirage in the desert that ultimately evaporates from view upon arriving at its source, which then forces them to seek yet another one just over the next horizon, the journey that *The Bible* describes is not one that promises the attainment of its goal quickly, easily, or effortlessly. Instead, it is a journey that is, and always will be, one that is "*from* faith *to* faith."[34] As such, it requires a willingness and a determination to carry on from quest to quest, from the discernment of hidden truth to the mining of that truth, seeking a God Who reveals Himself one day, while concealing Himself the next. In short, the answer to the mystery of the five *sacred* things is that, first and foremost, it is a mystery instituted by a God Who habitually hides His most precious truths, and Who only reveals them to whom He chooses, where He chooses, and when He chooses. And from an understanding of all this comes the realization that this mystery of the five things is, likewise, one that requires a process that is similar to anything indigenous to the endeavor of faith as it is revealed in Scripture.

In other words, the same incremental process that is required to penetrate the truth of *The Bible* itself will be the same one required to grasp a complete understanding of what connects the five *sacred* things. It will require an extended journey of discovery that necessarily leads a person from one foundational truth to the next, followed by the one after that, and the one after that, and all of it eventually building toward a crystallizing moment of insight that can only come from the hindsight that one gains after completing the whole journey. And to the ones who do make the whole journey, through to the end, I can at least promise you that the process will grant you the gift that once attained will forever endure in your hearts and minds, just as the treasure of God's word, once mined from the depths of obscurity, can never be diminished from any human soul.

THE ANALYSES

We speak a message of wisdom, but not the wisdom of this age or of the rulers of this age who are coming to nothing. We speak of God's secret *wisdom, a wisdom that God has* hidden *and destined for our glory before time began.*

The Apostle Paul, *Letter to the Corinthians*

Arguments for Authenticity

The Seed of Truth

WHAT IS TRUTH? asked Pontius Pilate of his supplicant prisoner; and in doing so, he was essentially asking this question on behalf of all humanity. But according to the canonical record, Jesus offered no reply to Pilate. So why did He not answer him? If God is no respecter of persons, as the Scriptures assure us, then the One Who was to give His life as a ransom for mankind would certainly have answered such an important question. After all, Jesus stated that this was the very reason He came into the world: "To testify to the truth."[35] Yet based on the Apostle John's account, Jesus was inexplicably silent as to the exact nature of this truth.

Fortunately, for us, though, John was not the only person who recorded the events surrounding this pivotal moment in history. As it turns out, there is another take on this same conversation, which can be found in the apocryphal record known as *The Gospel of Nicodemus*, formerly called *The Acts of Pontius Pilate*. According to this version of the story, Jesus did answer the question.

> So Pilate asked, "What is truth?"
>
> And Jesus replied, "Truth is from Heaven."
>
> To which the somewhat disappointed Pilate followed up with another question. "Then truth is not of this Earth, is it?"
>
> But Jesus looked the governor squarely in the eye and replied, "Don't be too sure, my friend, because truth does exist on this Earth, but it does so among those who, having the power of judgment, are governed by the truth and who form proper judgment because of that truth."[36]

Confronted by such an alternate version, one must then ask the obvious question. Which version of this story should be accepted as the truth? To which I would reply: Maybe they are both true. After all, as we already noted concerning the divergent accounts of Noah's animals and Judas' demise, history is not made up of only one version of the life of any historical character. So why should we expect there to be only one version of this event in the life of Jesus? It seems to me that one should look to their own conscience in such matters, because in the final analysis this is all any of us can do in our all-too-human pursuit of historical truth. In other words, one must honestly ask themselves: Do the words of Jesus in this particular story sound like those that would have been spoken by the One Who is the very embodiment of truth? Or do they contradict what one might expect Jesus to have said? The words ring true in both versions, do they not? If so, then why not simply accept the fact that what we are dealing with are two complimentary versions of the same event.

This, in turn, brings us face to face with the central issue encountered by anyone who reads a book like *Tales of Forever*, because it is a book that incorporates, at its core, stories that have all been stitched together from the so-called "apocryphal" record—in particular, *The First Book of Adam and Eve*, *The Secrets of Enoch*, *The Book of Jasher*, *The Letters of Herod and Pilate*, and *The Gospel of Nicodemus*. Naturally, in my own defense, only those stories that could be corroborated by the canonical record were drawn from, while any that contradicted it were summarily rejected, but far from expecting anyone to accept it all at face value, I am attempting, by way of these opening remarks, to provide a framework to make one's own judgment as to whether the apocryphal record can be trusted as a valid source of truth. Notwithstanding the centuries-old debate surrounding this literature, there are ways that one can approach the issue, and, as previously stated, the process I am offering will assuredly originate from the teachings and principles that are firmly grounded in the Biblical Canon.

What is truth, then? If one is a staunch believer in the traditional view of only the so-called "received texts," then I would quickly remind them that even Jesus taught that truth was not the same thing to each and every person. According to Him, the whole world can be divided into four distinct groups. Each group, when confronted by "truth," will interpret this information based on their own personal frame of reference, and by virtue of these four different perspectives, what constitutes truth will inevitably end up producing four different results. Truth, then, no matter how obvious it seems can never be received in the same way by all people. Consequently, when Jesus spoke of the dispensing and receiving of truth, He compared it to a farmer who went about scattering seeds in a field, and as can be expected, He predicted four very different outcomes. Some seeds were gobbled up by the birds before they even got planted into the ground. Some seeds fell on rocky ground and sprouted, but, because they lacked depth of soil, withered in the heat of the Sun. Some seeds fell among thorns so that when the plants grew up they choked and died before too long. And finally, there were some seeds that fell among good soil; these proved to be the only ones that were able to produce a healthy crop.[37]

By the Middles Ages, this idea of the four-fold nature of assimilating the seed of truth became the impetus of a tradition of biblical interpretation that had its origins in the commentaries of the early Christian Era. Said Stephen A. Barney, professor emeritus of English at the University of California, Irvine, the four levels of interpretation involved: One, a "literal" interpretation of the events of the biblical story for historical purposes, with no underlying meaning. Two, a "typological" interpretation that connected the events of *The Old Testament* with *The New Testament*, particularly in the way that events of Christ's life related to the lives of earlier messianic figures who preceded Him. Three, a "moral" interpretation, which involved how one should act in the present, that is to say, a meaning derived from the "moral of the story." And four, an "analogical" interpretation, which had to do with an understanding of prophetic, or future, events of Christian history, that is to say, Heaven, Hell, and Judgment Day. In this way, the four types of interpretation correspond to all three modes of existence—past, present, and future; literal, with our past; typological, connecting the past with our present; moral, with our present; and analogical, with our future.[38]

To illustrate how this four-fold approach applies to Scripture, Dante, called "one of the greatest literary icons of the Western world,"[39] offered this example:

> To clarify this method of treatment, consider this verse: "When Israel went out of Egypt, the House of Jacob from a barbarous people, Judah was made His sanctuary, and Israel His dominion." (*Psalm* 113:1-2) Now, if we examine the letters alone (literally), the Exodus of the Children of Israel in the time of Moses is signified; in the allegory (typologically), our redemption accomplished through Christ; in the moral sense, the conversion of the soul from the struggle and misery of sin to the status of grace; in the analogical sense, the exodus of the human soul from the slavery of this corruption to the freedom of eternal glory.[40]

Furthermore, this same idea of the four-fold nature of truth was no stranger to either Jewish or Islamic theology. In Judaism it is known as *Pardes*, which refers to four different approaches to interpreting the biblical text. *Peshat* pertains to the "surface," or literal, meaning; *remez*, the "deep," or symbolic, meaning; *derash*, the "comparative," or similar, meaning; and *sod*, the "secret," or mystical, meaning.[41] And in Islam this idea was expressed by Jafar al-Sadiq, the Muslim scholar and Imam, who stated that *The Koran* has four similar levels of interpretation: "*The Book of God* has four things—literal expression (*ibara*), allusion (*ishara*), subtleties (*lataif*), and the deepest realities (*haqaiq*). The literal expression is for the common folk, the allusion is for the elite, the subtleties are for the friends of God, and the deepest realities are for the prophets."[42]

No wonder that when Jesus spoke about understanding the things of God, He referred to this four-fold principle of awareness. Therefore, it is with this four-fold aspect of knowledge in mind that I would now like to address why I have become convinced of the authenticity of the books that all but the ancient world—while in the case of *The Gospel of Nicodemus*, the pre-

Reformation world—have deemed apocryphal. The reasons for this conviction stem from the following: First, in an etymological meaning revealed in the very word *apocryphal*; second, in the prophetic nature of the biblical record itself; third, in the internal logic of the books which comprise the apocryphal record; and fourth, in the striking relation with which those books correspond with the Canon of Scripture. For some, only one aspect of this explanation will prove sufficient in lending credence to this work, while others will require more convincing, more evidence, more time. Yet, alas, some will never open their minds to the truth presented here, no matter how hard one tries, and for that, the Lord of the Harvest reminds the best intentioned among us, they have no one to blame but themselves.

The End of Secrecy

TO BEGIN WITH—IN A truly ironic twist—there is the simple fact that this word *apocryphal* contains an obvious clue as to the mystery of why these books were deemed unacceptable and lost to humanity for so many centuries, because, over time, the word has come to signify something very different from its original etymological meaning. To the modern mind, something deemed apocryphal is anything that is considered "doubtful," "spurious," or "untrustworthy." In actuality, its true meaning, based on its root word, is something that is "secret" or "hidden," as in, anything considered apocryphal is merely a hidden thing to outsiders. In other words, the secret only remains a mystery to those who do not possess the tools of interpretation, but to those "on the inside," as it were, the otherwise hidden meaning of the thing is fully comprehensible.

When understood in this fashion, the nature of the message contained in books like *Adam and Eve*, *Enoch*, *Jasher*, and *Nicodemus* have been exactly that—a body of divinely-inspired wisdom literature, which has precisely fulfilled this desired intention. In this, it is just as the Scripture declares: "No eye has seen, no ear has heard, no mind has conceived, all the things that the Lord has prepared for those who love Him."[43] Continuing in this same vein, Paul then said, "The man without the Spirit does not accept the things that come from the Spirit of God, for they are foolishness to him and he cannot understand them because they are spiritually discerned."[44]

Truth seen from this view, then, is never something that is as straightforward as one would hope for. From a biblical perspective, truth is always something that is veiled, hidden, obscure—the very essence of which is perfectly conveyed via the word *apocryphal*. Consider Matthew's words when he said, "Jesus spoke all these things to the crowd in parables. He did not say anything to them without using one. In this way, what was spoken through the prophet was fulfilled: 'I'll open My mouth in parables; I'll utter *secret* things which have been *hidden* since the creation of the world.'"[45]

The word being used here for "secret" is the Greek word *krupto*, which means, "to conceal (that it may not become known)." Notice that this word *krupto*, from which we get our English word *cryptic*, is the central component for the word *apocryphal*. According to *Webster's Dictionary*, the word *apocryphal* comes to us from the Greek word *apokryphos*. What Webster does not mention, however, is that the prefix *apo* denotes the cessation, or reversal, of the word that it precedes; as in, if the root word means "secret" or "hidden," then when it is preceded by the prefix *apo*, the meaning of the word changes to that of "the end of secrecy" or "the reversal of being hidden." Clearly, this means that the real definition of the word *apocryphal* is the "unveiling" of a secret that was previously hidden from view.

Imagine that: The very people who were trying to discredit this so-called "forbidden wisdom" inadvertently chose a word that actually conveyed a latent truth about its destiny. No matter how many centuries of doubt and skepticism obscured its true meaning, the knowledge in these books would one day become "uncovered truth," and finally be seen for what it truly was—the wisdom of God that had been hidden away until it was time to be revealed. In this, it is exactly as predicted in one of the most ancient texts known to mankind—*First Enoch*:

> The word of the blessing of Enoch, how he blessed the elect and the righteous who would exist in the time of trouble, rejecting all the wicked and ungodly. Enoch, a righteous man, who was with God, answered and spoke while his eyes were open and while he saw a holy vision in the Heavens. This the angels showed me. From them I heard all things and understood what I saw; that which will not take place in this generation but in a generation which is to succeed at a distant period, on account of the elect.[46]

Search for Hidden Treasure

APART FROM THE CLUES that the etymological root meaning of the word provide, the prophetic nature of Scripture also supports the idea of the existence of a body of wisdom which—even though it proceeded directly from God—would be lost for an intended duration. Then, at some preordained "set time," this hidden wisdom would, for the sake of a future generation, be hurled back into the light of day, as if from out of nowhere. This is precisely what Jesus was saying when He announced: "The time is fulfilled and the Kingdom of God is at hand!"[47] Though the world had experienced various degrees of awareness of God's existence until Jesus arrived on the stage of history, the world remained in a perpetual state of spiritual dysfunction. But upon being baptized by John—an event that was punctuated by a voice from Heaven—the earthly ministry of Jesus was inaugurated and with it a new era of enlightenment and awareness.

Again and again, the biblical authors spoke of God's deliberate pattern of hiding and revealing His most important truths. In every age—from the time of Adam, right up to the present hour—the world has ridden a veritable roller coaster of ignorance and awareness concerning the ebb and flow of God's manifestation. Yet even in those most harrowing of days, when God had withdrawn His presence because of mankind's utter disregard for Him, there still remained a modicum of God-inspired revelation. In other words, there is, and always will be, more than one level of truth that the Lord is in the business of revealing. First, there is a general revelation of truth that all humanity is capable of perceiving as described by Paul. "Since the creation of the world, God's invisible qualities—His eternal power and divine nature—have been clearly seen, being understood from what has been made, so that mankind is without excuse."[48]

In addition to this universal awareness of the Divine, there is another aspect of understanding the reality of God, which is not something that can be grasped by the general population. The reason for this is clearly spelled out in *The Bible* so that there can be little doubt as to God's intention. Once again, Paul, as the great interpreter of Scripture, said it best: "We speak a message of wisdom, but not the wisdom of this age or of the rulers of this age who are coming to nothing. We speak of God's *secret* wisdom, a wisdom that God has *hidden* and destined for our glory before time began."[49]

When one begins to see the revelation of God's word in these terms, which could be described as a cosmic bank vault with a time-specific point of unlocking, it is much easier to understand that the role the apocryphal literature has played throughout history is no aberration in the plan of God.

The knowledge of God, then, is not something that one is simply born with or inherits from one's parents. It must be sought after with tremendous effort and determination. Certainly, Solomon, renowned as the wisest man in history, must have had this in mind when he declared: "God in His greatness has concealed many things, while kings have the honor of discovering them."[50] The knowledge that *The Bible* speaks of is never merely surface-oriented; it must be dug for much in the same way that precious metals must be unearthed. "If you cry out for insight and understanding, and search for it like you'd search for *hidden* treasure, then you'll begin to understand and find the knowledge of God."[51]

Ironically, however, not only must mankind search for wisdom, but the true Wisdom of God, Whom Solomon personified as a living force, also has the ability to search for us. "Wisdom calls out in the street. She shouts in the public squares; from the top of the walls and the gateways of the city, she cries out."[52] In this way, Solomon made it clear that the Wisdom of God is a thoughtful entity, capable of both pursuing and being pursued. As a result of this unique attribute of knowledge as an active, living force, God and mankind are in a veritable wrestling match when it comes to appropriating it. As so often happens, mankind foolishly spurns the advances of the very wisdom that reaches out to it:

> If you had responded to My rebuke, I would've poured out My heart and soul to you. But you rejected Me when I called, paid no attention when I reached out. You ignored all My advice and refused to listen to Me. So, I, in turn, will laugh when disaster overwhelms you. As you mocked Me, I will mock you when calamity overtakes you.[53]

In this, Isaiah further elaborated:

> I know how stubborn you are, with necks as unbending as iron. You're as hardheaded as bronze. That's why I told you ahead of time what I was going to do. That way you could never say, "My idols did it. My wooden image and metal god commanded it to happen!" You've heard My predictions and seen them fulfilled, but you refused to admit it. Now I'll tell you new things that I've never mentioned before, *secrets* that you've not yet heard.[54]

With all this in mind, it should come as no surprise that the average citizen of planet Earth thinks that God is either dead or not paying attention. Neither should one be surprised when the typical Christian doubts the possibility that the word of God could actually encompass more than the traditionally accepted sixty-six books. As one can detect from a brief scan of Scripture, truth as God defines it is simply not something that is easily or casually appropriated. For the most part, truth is a *hidden* thing—a *secret* that resides deep in the heart of God, Who apparently shares it only with those of His choosing.

So the next time some super-spiritual know-it-all starts pontificating about how the apocryphal books were not included in the Canon of Scripture because God declared them unholy or uninspired, just remind them that the Lord is always confounding the self-proclaimed geniuses of this world. "I thank You, Father, Lord of Heaven and Earth," Jesus said, "for *hiding* the truth from those who think themselves so clever and wise, and for revealing it to the child-like."[55] And be bold in your conviction, as you fearlessly remind them of the words of our Lord: "The Kingdom of Heaven is like a treasure that a man discovered *hidden* in a field. In his excitement, he *hid* it again and sold everything he owned to get enough money to buy the field—and to get the treasure, too!"[56]

Imagine that: How many people would even notice what is being said here? Admittedly, it is a subtle point, but for the purposes of our discussion it looms as an important subtlety, because contained in this parable is a clue for the existence of a body of *hidden* wisdom that someone discovered and then, after having gone to a great deal of trouble to find it, *hid* it again! If I am not mistaken this sounds exactly like the scenario surrounding the apocryphal literature with so much of its inherent mystery and intrigue. What else can this mean but that someone attained, by way of intense search, an understanding of God's long-lost kingdom and, having acquired this treasured awareness, then *hid* their discovery again in the hopes of recovering it at some future point in time? Like echoes reverberating down through the corridors of time, this same idea resounds throughout the ages; from the days of Enoch, the scribe, down to that of Asaph, the psalmist:

> Oh, my people, hear my teaching; listen to my words. I'll open my mouth in parables, I'll utter *hidden* things from days of old—what we've heard and known, what our Fathers have told us. We'll reveal them to our children; we'll tell the next generation about His power, about the wondrous things that He's

> performed on our behalf. He decreed statutes for Jacob and established the Law in Israel, which He commanded our forefathers to teach their children so the next generation would know them, even the children who were yet to be born, and they, in turn, would tell their children. Then they'd put their trust in God and would not forget His deeds but would keep His commands.[57]

Then, from the mouth of Asaph, the words were reiterated by the Incarnate Word, Jesus, Who, contrary to popular belief, spoke in parables to veil the truth so they would remain ignorant of the *hidden* wisdom that the Lord chose to reveal to His elect ones. And just in case none of you believes that God is in the business of unveiling apocryphal wisdom, then simply revisit the words of Jesus as recorded by Matthew, Mark, and Luke:

> The disciples came to Him and asked, "Why do You speak to the people in parables?" And He replied, "The knowledge of the *secrets* of the Kingdom of Heaven has been given to you but not to them. Whoever has will be given more and he will have an abundance. Whoever does not have, even what he has will be taken from him.
>
> "This is why I speak to them in parables: Though seeing, they do not perceive; though hearing, they do not understand. In them is fulfilled the prophecy of Isaiah: You'll be forever hearing but never understanding. You'll be forever seeing but never perceiving. For this people's heart has become calloused. They hardly hear with their ears, and have closed their eyes. Otherwise they might see and hear, and understand with their hearts and turn, and I would heal them."[58]

An Improbable Connectivity

IN ADDITION TO considering etymological meanings and prophetic aspects, one must also be struck by another clue as to the authenticity of the apocryphal texts—that is to say, what one could call the internal logic found in the books when examined in their totality. Mind you, what we are talking about here is nothing new when it comes to analyzing the degree of scriptural integrity. It is actually the same methodology used to demonstrate the veracity of the canonical books. One of the most pervasive misconceptions that mankind has ever entertained about *The Bible* is that because it was written by so many different authors there is no point in believing in its so-called "divine authorship." Skeptics and critics alike are unanimous in their appraisal that if the Scriptures are merely a compendium of scattered, indiscriminate writings there could be no way that it constitutes an infallible document "from God's mouth to our ears," as it were. It is therefore assumed to be a fraudulent book, which only an idiot or a fool would treat as an object of trust. On the face of it, this assumption might seem to hold true; yet, ironically, this thread of logic unravels in an instant when one considers the following alternative. Of course, *The Bible* is comprised of numerous perspectives, provided by way of many different authors, but this does not negate the possibility of its divine origins, in and of itself. In fact, this very diversity provides us with the clue that it could not possibly be the crude by-product of human imagination.

What makes *The Bible* such an amazing document actually arises from the fact that even though it is a book written across the entire span of human history it still bears the unmistakable stamp of a singular point of view. In other words, although so many hands have stirred the pot, although so many perspectives have added to its mix, the integrity of the scriptural record still bears a remarkable similarity through in and throughout. From age to age, what begins as a germ of thought in *The Old Testament* unfolds with astonishing continuity in *The New Testament*. From author to author, every book contained in *The Bible* echoes from cover to cover, clearly testifying that this cannot be the product of mere coincidence; it is undoubtedly the greatest proof as to its divine authorship.

Taking this into consideration, then, let us examine the internal logic of the apocryphal literature, that is to say, the way that scattered references throughout these documents demonstrate a remarkably high degree of confluence, or textual continuity, from book to book. One of the greatest examples of this internal logic is something that has come to be known as the prophecy of The Great Five and a Half Days—a prophecy introduced in *The First Book of Adam and Eve*, then alluded to in *The Secrets of Enoch* and finally brought full circle in *The Gospel of Nicodemus*.

Part one of three: When Adam and Eve were expelled from the Garden of Eden, God promised them that they would someday be allowed to return to the place they had forfeited through their disobedience. This return, however, would not take place, explained God—though in typically veiled terms—for another *five and a half* "days." Confused, Adam and Eve thought that God was telling them they would only have to wait *five and a half* days in human terms.[59] But much to their chagrin, they discovered that God was really saying they would have to wait *five thousand, five hundred years* before they could expect to return to the garden, at which time: "One would come to save them and their descendants."[60] Now anyone familiar with *The Bible* is already well aware that, from God's perspective, time is very different from our own. Typically, it is accepted, as per our understanding of Scripture, that one of God's "days" is equal to a thousand years from our human frame of reference.[61] In this way, the apocryphal and canonical records are in agreement. Okay, so far, so good.

On to part two of three: With the death and resurrection of Jesus of Nazareth, events came to a head in the confrontation between Pontius Pilate and the Jewish religious authorities who instigated the crucifixion of Christ. In a final showdown, as depicted in the pages of *The Gospel of Nicodemus*, Pilate demanded that Annas and Caiaphas come clean concerning their crime against Jesus. Then it happened. Smitten by guilt, compounded by the astonishment over numerous reports of the resurrected Christ, Annas, the chief priest at Jerusalem, made a startling confession. In checking the record of their own Scripture—described by Annas as *The Seventy Books*—they encountered a prophecy concerning the coming of the Messiah, a prophecy stating that, counting from the time of Adam, "After *five thousand, five hundred years*, Christ, the most beloved Son of God, was to come to Earth."[62] What is more, Annas even went so far as to make a fascinating connection between this prophecy and the dimensions of The Ark of the Covenant. As he described it:

> We further considered that perhaps He (speaking of this Messiah) was the very God of Israel Who spoke to Moses instructing him to build The Ark of the Covenant with dimensions of *five and a half* cubits. From this we surmised that the Christ would likewise come in an ark, or tabernacle, of a body after *five thousand, five hundred years*.[63]

In this correspondence of the dimensions of The Ark of the Covenant, it appears that there is again an uncanny agreement between the apocryphal and canonical records.

Now for part three of three: Before Adam and Eve were told about the promise of "days" and before Annas and Caiaphas learned about it, an event seems to have triggered God's choice for this numerical figure of *five and a half* in connection with the coming of the Messiah, an event recorded by none other than Enoch. Ironically, it exists as a mere sidebar—a "footnote," if you will—in *The Secrets of Enoch*. In it, Enoch describes Adam's creation on the sixth day, his subsequent fall, and the Lord's response to that first act of disobedience. "Finally, the seventh day arrived and God said, 'Because of what they'd done, I only allowed Adam and Eve to remain in Paradise for *five and a half* hours before I forced them to leave.'"[64]

The significance of this numerical value will no doubt escape those who are unfamiliar with what *The Bible* has to say about divine judgment but will not go unnoticed by those who are. The reason is this: Already firmly established in Scripture is that when it comes to God's decrees involving His chosen ones there is always a direct correlation between the nature of their crime and the severity of their punishment. In other words, when the people willingly rebel against God's commands, the Lord makes an extremely conscious decision to punish them in direct proportion—no more and no less—to the exact extent of their disobedience. So, according to this divine law of crime and punishment, *The Book of Jubilees* states that when Cain died it was as a result of his house collapsing on top of him.

> And he was killed by its stones because he had killed his brother Abel with a stone, so in this way his death by stone was considered an act of righteous judgment. This is why it was ordained on the tablets of Heaven: With whatever instrument a man kills his neighbor, he will be killed with a similar object, and in whatever manner he wounds another, his punishment will be meted out in the same way.[65]

Louis Ginzberg, a Lithuanian professor of Judaism, provides us with some useful scenarios to illustrate this point in his book *The Legends of the Jews*. Of particular interest are the trials and tribulations of Joseph, the beloved son of Jacob. When his jealous brothers sold Joseph to Ishmaelites on their way to Egypt, they received twenty shekels of silver in exchange for him; therefore, according to this law of crime and punishment, God commanded that every firstborn son of Israel be redeemed with the same amount. Also, every Israelite must annually pay the sanctuary this amount that each of Joseph's brothers received as their share for his sale.[66] According to Zebulun, the sixth son of Jacob and Leah:

> When the brothers sold Joseph as a slave, eight of them, including Simeon and Gad, bought sandals with the money. Having acknowledged that it was blood money, they refused to buy food with it. But because Joseph had prophesied that he'd eventually be their king, they wanted to see what would become of his dreams. Therefore, it is written in the Law of Moses that whoever refuses to raise up a descendant on behalf of his brother, his sandals will be removed and they should spit upon him.
>
> So because the brothers of Joseph wanted him dead, the Lord made sure that they'd have to remove the sandals they wore in their conflict with Joseph. That's why, when they went to Egypt, the servants of Joseph forced them to remove their shoes and bow down to Joseph as the viceroy of Egypt. Not only that, but all the brothers were spit upon, having been put to shame before the Egyptians, just as the Lord had decreed.[67]

Taking this into account, let us look at the most eloquent example of God's chastening of His people to be found in Scripture. I am referring to what is known as the Seventy Weeks of Daniel. Almost everyone who is familiar with biblical prophecy has heard of it. In this case, though, I want to focus on an aspect of the story that is often overlooked when discussing the implications of Daniel's prophecy, but first, let us set up our scene.

The prophet Daniel discovered while reading *The Book of Jeremiah* that God intended to extricate His people who had been in Babylonian captivity for seventy years.[68] He went on to say this seventy year bondage had been a microcosm of a greatly extended period of punishment—that is, seventy "weeks" of years—that the people of God were to endure, which would ultimately conclude with the advent of a glorious millennial age ushered in by none other than the Messiah Himself.[69] Until that day, however, God would be teaching His people to trust Him via incremental stages, which would gradually lead them from one phase of salvation history to the next.

Now, to the significance of all this for the purpose of our present study. Long before God decreed seventy years of Babylonian captivity, which prefigured the extended period of punishment, was the fact that when the people of Israel dwelled securely in Palestine there was an unusual law they were told to keep. Unfortunately, though, it was a law that was regularly neglected.

> For six years, you are to sow your fields, and harvest the crops, but during the seventh year let the land lie dormant, unplowed and unused. This way the poor and the stranger among your people may get food from it, and the wild animals may eat what they leave behind. Do the same with your vineyards and your olive groves.[70]

The reason for this prohibition was that, as every seventh day was a Sabbath day, every seventh year was likewise a Sabbath year. In doing this, God intended to not only nurture the Israelites' attitude toward the poor, the stranger, and the animals but also to nurture their trust in His divine provision during every seventh year of their existence in that land. But sadly, history records that they did not abide by this prohibition, and because they continued to farm their fields during those Sabbath years, God punished them with the Babylonian captivity, thereby ensuring that the land would remain untouched.

> So the Israelites were carried into captivity and became servants to the king of Babylon, and during the entire time of its desolation, the land finally enjoyed its Sabbath rests, until the seventy years were completed in fulfillment of the word of the Lord as it was spoken by Jeremiah.[71]

So, returning to our story of the first couple's exile from Paradise: Just as the Israelites were expelled from Palestine in direct proportion to the amount of time that they were in it, Adam and Eve were exiled from the garden according to a similar scale of divine judgment. But could these parallels of time-specific lengths of judgment really be a simple case of coincidence? Or is it possible that the God of Set Times actually built into the scriptural record these kinds of clues to His control over human history? And if so, what can one surmise from it? If Enoch wrote his texts long before such patterns of God's judgment were established, then it was certainly no mere whim that compelled him to mention seemingly trivial information like Adam and Eve living in Eden for *five and a half* hours prior to their God-ordained exile of *five and a half* "days." Naturally, from a strictly humanistic point of view, it might seem like an impossible leap of logic to assume such a thing, but, if one possesses a biblical view, it is not absurd at all.

One thing, however, is certain. We do have in our possession three separate manuscripts—*The First Book of Adam and Eve*, *The Secrets of Enoch*, and *The Gospel of Nicodemus*—all which were written long ago when the preservation of such ancient works demanded an improbable mixture of luck and determination. Yet they have somehow managed to survive to the present day. Even more astonishing to the modern mind, these manuscripts, which have all been scattered throughout time and geography, bear a similarly improbable connectivity, revealing a pattern that was generally believed to be confined to the Biblical Canon. Therefore, far from giving us the impression that they are the by-product of primitive human thought, they instead present a finely wrought synergy that no mere mortal, or group of mortals, could have ever conceived, separated by so many centuries, so many miles, so many improbabilities.

A Peculiar Puzzle

NEXT, WE WILL examine the external logic that is found in apocryphal literature; that is to say, we will consider the degree to which these texts coincide with the more familiar accounts in the canonical record. In actuality, the examples are so abundant that if every correspondence between the two were presented, this present study would likely double, if not triple, in size. Suffice it to say, then, we will be limiting our investigation of this particular point to a single—though pervasive—through-line story.

It has long been accepted that Moses, the famed lawgiver of Israel, was the original author of *The Pentateuch*, or the first five books of *The Old Testament*, which include *Genesis*, *Exodus*, *Leviticus*, *Numbers*, and *Deuteronomy*. Naturally, because it is common knowledge that Moses was around during the events of the last four books, most biblical historians have had little problem accepting that he could have written those books. But it has never been sufficiently answered as to how he could have written *Genesis*, considering it depicts events that he could not possibly have witnessed firsthand. The standard answer, of course, has always been some variation of: "Well, he was a prophet, wasn't he? Naturally, he must have been inspired by God, right?" However, the more logical answer would lead us directly to the apocryphal record. Specifically, we are brought face to face with a book referred to by two well-known figures of *The Old Testament*; both Joshua and Samuel refer to it in their texts. The work I am referring to is *The Book of Jasher*. According to biblical scholar Cyrus H. Gordon, such ancient writings as *Jasher*—among them also, *The Book of the History of Man* (*Genesis* 5:1) and *The Book of the Wars of Yahweh* (*Numbers* 21:14)—undoubtedly provided literary fodder for *The Old Testament*, as he explained in no uncertain terms:[72]

> It is clear that some of the early sources were comprehensive writings excerpted more than once by the biblical author. For example, *The Book of Jasher* is excerpted twice: First, in *Joshua* 10:13; then, in *2 Samuel* 1:18. But the incorporation of such earlier sources does not mean that *The Pentateuch* or *Former Prophets* is the work of an editor who pasted together various documents. Once we view the work as a whole, we see that it is a fresh creation, though not a *creation ex nihilo*.[73]

It is this text of *Jasher*, then, that, upon careful review, will prove to be the actual source material that supplied Moses with the knowledge of the events of mankind's history prior to his own life. When Joshua was leading the army of Israel into battle against the Amorites, he prayed in the midst of the clash:

> 'Oh, Sun, stand still over Gibeon, oh, Moon, over the Valley of Aijalon.' So the Sun stood still and the Moon stopped, till the nation avenged itself on its enemies, as it is written in *The Book of Jasher*. The Sun stopped in the middle of the sky and delayed going down a full day. There has never been a day like it before or since, a day when the Lord listened to a man. Surely the Lord was fighting for Israel![74]

Samuel referred to it when David was told that King Saul and his son Jonathan had been killed. Even though Saul had jealously sought his life in revenge for his having been chosen to replace him as the new king of Israel, David still mourned Saul's death as one who had once been the anointed of God.

> And David took up this lament concerning Saul and his son Jonathan, and ordered that the men of Judah be taught this lament of the bow, as it is written in *The Book of Jasher*: Oh, Israel, your glory lies slain on your heights. How the mighty have fallen![75]

The connections between *Jasher* and *The Old Testament*, however, do not end with these two events. A thorough examination will reveal endless parallels between them. The importance of this is that *Jasher* helps provide missing pieces to a puzzle that often leaves the reader to question whether texts like *Genesis* can tell us anything reliable about events that clearly took place in remotest antiquity. But seen together, the two records converge in an unexpected way, and occurrences that at first seemed too strange to believe are thrown into an entirely new light. Take, for example, an apparently disjointed array of facts as they are found in the traditional narrative of *Genesis*. First, upon eating from the Tree of Knowledge, the eyes of Adam and Eve were opened, triggering the rude awakening that they were naked, which then caused them to use fig leaves to cover their nudity.[76] God, however, had a different plan for them, and provided garments made from skins to cover their nakedness.[77] But as to the kind of skins they were and why fig leaves were insufficient, while these unspecified skins were adequate in God's view, the *Genesis* narrative does not reveal.

Later we are told that when God announced to Noah that He would be sending the Great Flood upon the Earth, the patriarch was somehow able to persuade thousands of animals into the haven of the Ark.[78] But as to how he did this is never explained or even suggested. We are simply expected to assume that he waved some sort of magic wand, and every species of animal—both herbivore and carnivore—came waltzing in, happily cohabitating inside the Ark for forty tumultuous days and nights.

Then in one of the more puzzling scenarios described in *Genesis*, it is recorded that Noah, upon vacating the Ark, took to growing a vineyard, became drunk from the wine it produced, and passed out naked in his tent. Afterward, Ham, the father of Canaan, saw his father's nakedness and told his two brothers outside, but Shem and Japheth took a garment and, walking in backwards, covered their father's nakedness. Upon waking from his drunken stupor, Noah realized what his sons had done and, for reasons that are never made clear, pronounced a horrific curse on the descendants of his grandson, Canaan.[79] And because this dreadful curse was so incommensurate with the apparent actions of Ham, who merely looked upon his father's naked body and gossiped about it to his brothers, numerous biblical scholars have resorted to all manner of bizarre speculation as to the true nature of Ham's crime. Some have even gone so far as to conjecture—in their convoluted efforts to justify the punishment with the crime—that Ham must have resorted to some form of incestuous, homosexual activity. Unfortunately, however, the canonical record never provides a shred of evidence as to why a momentary peepshow and the subsequent gossip thereof would have warranted the invocation of such a sweeping curse as that of the enslavement of an entire people.

Next, there strode onto the biblical landscape the first great figure after the Flood, one Nimrod by name—a man who grew to have so much power over the animal kingdom that he became world renowned as "the mighty hunter before the Lord."[80] Soon, his ability to subdue the wild animals throughout the land caused such a sensation among the people that they eventually made him lord and master over all the sons of Noah. But as to how he developed such remarkable skill as a powerful hunter and charismatic king, once again, the *Genesis* record completely neglects to inform us.

Later still, we read the strange story of Abraham's twin grandsons, Jacob and Esau. Jacob it is said was a modest, quiet fellow—a "homebody," if you will—while Esau, who took to the open fields, grew to become a skillful hunter.[81] What is more, because Esau preceded his brother Jacob at the time of their birth, he stood to gain all of the birthright privileges as the firstborn son of their father, Isaac. Not only that, but Isaac was very fond of meat, which Esau, the hunter, was so adept at providing him. As a result, *The Bible* states, in no uncertain terms, that Isaac grew to love Esau more than the less flamboyant Jacob.

This leads us, then, to the final piece of our peculiar puzzle. From our earliest days as Christians, we have all been weaned on one of the more perplexing chapters in Scripture. In it, we are told the story of an exhausted and hungry Esau, who has returned home after a fruitless day of hunting. There, he encounters his brother Jacob, who offers him a mere bowl of lentil stew in exchange for his birthright blessing, which, quite inexplicably, Esau accepts to feed his empty belly.[82] But why would Esau have so foolishly sold away his birthright inheritance when he was such an obvious shoe-in to receive it from his father? What could have possibly led him to such a tragic blunder? He certainly was not stupid. Described as a cunning man, capable of tracking and hunting down an elusive prey, he does not exactly fit the picture of someone who would forfeit such an obvious opportunity for wealth and power. A man like that would never despise such an offer; not in the real world, at least. Yet the *Genesis* record never even attempts to address such a glaring conundrum. We are simply led to believe by every typical account that Esau was less spiritual than Jacob and, therefore, unworthy of all that the birthright offered. And they believe this, mind you, even though they know full well that Jacob—whose name means *usurper*—deliberately tricked his blind father, with the help of his duplicitous mother, into transferring this birthright from Esau to himself. How odd that most people never seem puzzled by such blatant incongruities. They simply accept whatever trite interpretation is offered them by way of the traditional view of the *Genesis* narrative.

Yet all of these scattered mysteries—the truth about Adam's adequate covering, Noah's power over the animals and his cursing of Canaan, Nimrod's domination as a hunter of both man and beast, and Esau's hunting prowess and lack thereof in procuring Abraham's birthright—can be explained when one simply takes the time to examine the apocryphal record. In this case, one need only turn to a passage in *The Book of Jasher* and another in *The First Book of Adam and Eve*. And make no mistake, these are mysteries that lie at the heart of a crossroad that leads to two entirely different modes of disbelief—one of doubt and the other, delusion. One road leads the skeptic to further dismiss *The Bible* into the realm of absurdity and foolishness, considering the endless list of *non sequiturs* offered in response; the other leads the believer to dull their own sensibilities when it comes to questioning the obvious, lest they even hint at a betrayal of their beloved, childhood interpretations.

So how can one hope to find an antidote in the face of such a cloud of confusion? First, we must ask ourselves: What are the incongruous pieces of this jumbled puzzle as we have presented them so far, and how can one possibly fit them all into a harmonious whole? Let us take a moment to count them down again, one by one. Adam and his wife receive mysterious animal skins that God gives them to wear instead of the fig leaves they had originally chosen. Then Noah, through some kind of unspecified animal magnetism, persuades all the animals to enter the Ark and for forty days manages to restrain the carnivores from devouring the herbivores. Then upon leaving the Ark, Noah gets drunk and naked, and pronounces a horrific curse on Ham's descendants because his son not only witnessed the debacle but also gossiped about it to his two brothers. Then Nimrod acquires such power over the wild animals that his fame causes the people to make him supreme leader over all the land. And finally, Esau, renowned hunter and favorite son of wealthy patriarch Isaac, inexplicably sells his family inheritance in exchange for a bowl of lentil stew. Got all that so far? Good. Then, as alluded to before, let us look to the passages in both *Jasher* and *First Adam and Eve* in order to untangle this odd mess of undifferentiated madness! Says *Jasher*, it all began in the days just after the Great Flood when:

> Cush, the son of Ham, the grandson of Noah, took a wife in his old age and she bore him a son, which they named Nimrod, saying, "At that time mankind began again to rebel against God." And the child grew up, and because he was the son of his old age, his father loved him very much.
>
> And the garment of skin which God made for Adam, when he went out of the garden, was given to Cush. For after the death of Adam, his garment was given to Enoch, the son of Jared, and when Enoch was taken up to God, he gave it to Methuselah, his son.
>
> After the death of Methuselah, Noah took it and brought it into the Ark, and it was with him until he left the Ark. Then, Ham stole the garment from Noah, his father, and he concealed it from his brothers. And when Ham had his firstborn, Cush, he secretly gave him the garment, and it was with Cush for a long time. Cush even went so far as to hide it from his sons and brothers; but when Nimrod was born, he decided to give him the garment because he loved him so much. So when Nimrod turned twenty, Cush gave him the garment of skins.
>
> And Nimrod became strong when he put on the garment because God gave him his tremendous strength, and as a result he became a mighty hunter in the Earth. Throughout the land, Nimrod hunted the wild animals and soon he began to build altars where he offered up the animals as burnt offerings to the Lord.

> Nimrod strengthened himself, and over time he rose up through the ranks of his brothers because he was so effective in fighting battles on behalf of his family, defeating all of their enemies in the process. It happened this way because it was the Lord Himself Who was delivering their enemies into the hand of Nimrod. And God prospered him in all his battles, and because of this he began to reign as a king upon the Earth.
>
> Therefore, it became a common occurrence in those days that after a man who'd been trained for battle was ushered off to war, the people would say to him, "As God has done for Nimrod, the mighty hunter who succeeded in all his battles and rescued his family from their enemies, so may God do the same for you."[83]

So there we have it. The first missing piece to our puzzle, as revealed in *Jasher*, is the garment of animal skins that God had provided for Adam after his expulsion from the garden. But what could possibly be so special about a simple loincloth made from animal skins? Once again, the apocryphal literature provides us with an all-important clue.

In *First Adam and Eve*, we discover that God instructed the first couple where they could find something to cover their nakedness. The Lord told them: "There you will find skins of sheep that were left after lions ate the carcasses. Take them and make garments for yourselves, and clothe yourselves with them."[84] But Satan overheard God telling Adam about the sheepskins, and—consumed by his hatred of these humans—raced ahead of the couple, hoping to destroy the garments before they could use them as they had been instructed. Fortunately, as the story goes, the Word of God—or rather the pre-incarnate Jesus—bound the devil in chains before he could carry out his plan so that when Adam and Eve arrived they got their first real look at the hideous creature they had only previously encountered in the guise of the elegant serpent.[85]

Gazing upon the sheepskins that lay at his feet, Adam was the first person in history to experience an insight into the true meaning of what theologians would many centuries later come to label as "vicarious substitute," a term that referred to the death of Christ as an atonement for the sins of the people of God. According to *First Adam and Eve*:

> Standing over the sheepskins, Adam stood and stared blankly down at them for several moments.
>
> "What's wrong now, Adam?" asked Eve.
>
> "I'm sad thinking about how we got these skins, that's all."
>
> "Sad, why?"
>
> "I'm sad because these skins have come from owners who have died, and when we put them on, we'll be wearing emblems of their death."
>
> "And someday," continued Eve, beginning to realize what he was saying, "we'll die just like they did, won't we?"[86]

The significance of these garments made of sheepskin lies in the fact that God was conveying a truth not only to them but to every one of the descendants of that first couple as well—to all of us, in fact. These sheepskins, which were the result of an attack by a lion, represented the first "type" in history that was to foreshadow the sacrificial death of the Lamb of God, Jesus, Who was slain before the foundation of the world.[87] And as God allowed evil men, compelled by the devil, to shed the blood of His Son,[88] it was a roaring lion, as a type of Satan, which killed the sheep that provided the first adequate covering of its kind for fallen humanity—sheepskins, which came as a result of the shed blood of their owners.

This same idea of Satan as a roaring lion is perfectly illustrated by E.W. Bullinger in his groundbreaking study entitled *The Witness of the Stars*, where he pointed to the significance of the constellation of Orion as typifying the conquering Hero of Heaven. As is well known to any biblical scholar, this constellation is mentioned three times in Scripture—twice by Job and once by Amos.[89] Both men, in no uncertain terms, proclaim that Orion was created by God, and, according to Bullinger, the purpose revealed in such a creative act was to corroborate the truth as it is portrayed in God's written word. In this case, Orion—the brightest constellation to be found in the night sky—is a mighty warrior who holds in his left hand the head of his vanquished prey, a lion's head.

Just who is this conquering hero, one might ask? The names of the stars that comprise this impressive constellation, said Bullinger, provide us with the necessary clues. In the raised foot of this figure is the star *Rigel*, which means "the foot that crushes." One of the stars in Orion's belt—the most famous among this trio of lights—is called *Al Nitak*, which means "the wounded One." Another star in his right leg is called *Saiph*, which means "bruised," the same Hebrew word found in the primordial prophecy of the Redeemer described in the first book of *The Bible*.[90] "And the Lord said to the serpent: 'Because you've done this thing, I'll create hostility between you and the woman, between your children and her children; he will crush your head, and you will *bruise* his heel.'"[91] Here we have a perfect illustration of none other than Jesus Christ, in a dual role as both the Suffering Servant and Conquering Hero. Having crushed His enemy, while in the act of being bruised Himself, He triumphantly holds aloft the head of his ancient foe, that is, Satan, who is forever seeking his next victim—in this case, the sheep killed by a lion that provided Adam's garment.

No wonder that Adam's sheepskin garment, as it was handed down from generation to generation, became such a remarkable source of divine power. It provided the initial step in the reconciliation between God and Adam after the tragic expulsion and alienation of that first couple. It enabled Noah to tame the animals so that they not only cooperated in their entering the Ark but also were temporarily freed from their adversarial nature while confined in it. Next, it was stolen from Noah by his son Ham, who undoubtedly took advantage of the fact that his father was passed out, dead drunk, in his tent. This, in turn, would explain why Noah pronounced such a harsh punishment on Ham; not because he merely peeped and tattled on him but because he stole such a prized artifact—one that Noah knew would never again be used for the God-ordained purpose for which it had been originally provided. And finally, once in Ham's possession, the garment was handed down to his grandson Nimrod, who found in it a virtually limitless source of power prior to his inward turn to self that ultimately weakened its efficacy, even though he wore it on his person until the day of his death.

All this brings us to the next series of questions that again only the apocryphal record is able to answer; and the questions are these: What happened to Adam's garment after Nimrod had it? Did he pass it on to one of his sons like his father before him? How was it that Esau, apparently following in the tradition of Nimrod, became such a powerful hunter? And finally: Why did Esau so carelessly forfeit the birthright blessing of Abraham when it would have bestowed untold wealth and power on him? One need only continue reading further in *Jasher* to find the answers. With these answers, one comes face to face with some very important clues en route to our attempt to solving the ancient mysteries that we are presently investigating. According to *Jasher*:

> At that time, Esau, after the death of Abraham, often went out hunting in the fields. Around the same time, Nimrod, king of Babel, who was also known as Amraphel,[92] was in the habit of hunting during the coolest part of the day, accompanied by his most powerful warriors. As he did, Nimrod would see that Esau was also hunting in the same fields, and, over the course of time, the king of Babel grew jealous of the grandson of Abraham.
>
> One day while Esau was hunting, he spotted Nimrod wandering through the wilderness with two of his bodyguards. At the time, Esau could see that the rest of Nimrod's warriors were yet a great distance from the king, all heading in different directions, each in search of their own prey. So concealing himself there in the bushes, Esau began to stalk Nimrod as though he were hunting a wild animal, and because Nimrod and his men had no idea they were

> being stalked, they eventually wandered right into the place where Esau was hiding.
>
> Without warning, Esau lunged from behind the bush, sword drawn, and ran toward Nimrod intent on engaging him in hand-to-hand combat. Furiously, Esau slashed at Nimrod and his two bodyguards, and in mere moments he beheaded the king of Babel and hacked the bodyguards to death. And when the rest of Nimrod's warriors heard their cries from a distance, they came running to find out what had happened.
>
> From a distance, Esau could see Nimrod's men running toward him, so he grabbed the valuable garment of Nimrod, which had enabled him to subdue an entire kingdom and, as quickly as he could, ran home with the garment securely in his grasp.
>
> Arriving home, exhausted and still shaken from the thrill of battle, he found his brother Jacob cooking a delicious meal and hungrily sat down next to him.[93]

It is at this crucial stage that the canonical record states that the famished Esau sold his birthright at the cunning behest of his brother. What tradition does not point out, though, is why he made such a reckless, foolhardy decision. We are simply expected to accept the age-old tripe that because Esau was such a profane person he simply had no respect for such spiritual matters. However, considering the additional testimony of the apocryphal record, this view is forever altered. Far from seeing Esau as one who was incapable of appreciating the value of the family blessing, the picture that *Jasher* presents to us is definitely one of a very ambitious man.

In fact, Esau is portrayed as someone who was so rabidly ambitious that he was willing to take on the might of the most powerful man of the age. Once he had managed to kill Nimrod and rob him of the talisman that had enabled him to subjugate the entire world, he simply had no further need of the birthright of men like Abraham and Isaac. Certainly, these were not men who Esau aspired to emulate. These men were not known as world conquerors but as lovers of the kind of world that a benevolent God was attempting to establish, a God Who, above all, called men to offer their goods and services as a means of blessing humanity. In other words, however much the patriarchal blessing offered a man like Esau in terms of wealth and power it was still one that was implicitly meant to be shared and thus, in his view, squandered upon a pathetic, needy world. In contrast, the promise that Adam's garment held out to Esau was one of unmitigated fame and fortune. No wonder that Esau was suddenly so willing to trade away something that had previously been seen as a thing of value but in light of his newfound situation was only useful for filling his empty belly. In this, the canonical record is quite correct in describing Esau as a profane and foolish man with no depth of spiritual understanding. It simply misses the mark when it comes to revealing the specific underlying motive for such a rash decision on Esau's part.

Still, I can hear the grumblings of the casual reader of this who might be asking, "But if you say that Moses used *Jasher* as his source material for writing *Genesis*, then he must have had a good reason for leaving that part out, right?" To which I would reply: "But I have already offered a plausible explanation as to why he might have left it out." Based on the divine intention of teaching in parables, God causes some of His deepest truths to be hidden away until some future date when mankind is finally ready to hear them again, like the man in the parable of buried treasure who, after having discovered the truth, then decides to rebury it.[94]

Was it an unconscious decision, then, on the part of Moses to delete this all-important connection? Or was it an inspired decision willed upon him by the Holy Spirit? No one, I believe, will ever know for sure. Suffice it to say, that considering God's cosmic game of hide-and-seek it is a truth that deserves the attention of anyone fortunate enough to be confronted by it once it has resurfaced. The real tragedy is when people receive such enlightening forms of truth but fail to appreciate them, just as when old wineskins are filled with new wine but are incapable of containing it. Sadly, like those proverbial old wineskins, instead of embracing the newness of fresh truth from God's word, their minds figuratively burst because of their rigidity of thought.[95]

Still, I can hear others say, "Maybe Moses didn't record the part about Adam's garment because God wanted to suppress the knowledge of such things so people would no longer expect divine power in mere objects but in Him alone. After all, since Jesus came along, stuff like that just doesn't happen anymore, right?" To which I would reply in typical style: "You think?"

Famous throughout the history of Christendom are numerous legends that would suggest otherwise. One example of this is found in a collection of letters exchanged between Herod Antipas and Pontius Pilate, in a document entitled *The Death of Pilate, who Condemned Jesus*. In it, there is an interesting story that refers to a famous object that has over time permutated into a variety of forms, all of them, however, involving a single element—that of an image of Christ. As the story goes: A woman named Veronica—or Berenice, depending on your language frame—encountered Jesus during His travels throughout Judea. Then at some point during their conversation, Veronica acquired a picture of the face of Christ on canvas, or as depicted in other versions, either a handkerchief or a cloth.[96]

Later in this same account, Veronica was met by an emissary of Tiberius Caesar sent to Jerusalem seeking the assistance of a man who had allegedly been healing the sick by merely speaking to them, namely Jesus. The reason this emissary had been sent there was because Caesar had fallen gravely ill, and because the emperor was unable to find a cure from his Roman physicians, he had been driven by desperation to seek help through any means possible. When Veronica told the emissary that she possessed a painting of Jesus, he suggested that they travel to Rome, whereupon presenting the image to Caesar he was miraculously healed from his disease. Pretty far-fetched, right? I mean, really, how can anybody believe something as ridiculous as that? This story is nowhere in the Biblical Canon, so naturally it must be treated with grave suspicion.

But wait. What if there were similar examples to be found in the received text of the Church? Would that suffice to deter one's skepticism? Then consider this: Such an incident can be found; and not just one but at least two. One of them has to do with ordinary articles of clothing that merely came into contact with the skin of the Apostle Paul, and from that point onward they supposedly took on healing properties. "Now God worked unusual miracles by the hand of Paul so that even handkerchiefs or aprons were brought from his body to the sick, and the diseases left them and the evil spirits went out of them."[97]

So, as in the case of Adam's sheepskin garment—which clearly conveyed spiritual power over the forces of nature—Veronica's painting and Paul's handkerchief were said to have contained similar properties.

Then, there is an even more important example of this in *The Bible*, one that involves none other than Jesus Himself. Certainly, you are aware of the story of Jesus' seamless robe, are you not? No? Well, let me tell you about it then. See how it compares with the stories of Adam's garment, Veronica's painting, and Paul's handkerchief, and when you have heard it, you decide if such things are still sanctioned by the God of canonical Scripture. Said John:

> When the soldiers crucified Jesus, they took his clothes, dividing them into four shares, one for each of them, with the undergarment remaining. This garment was seamless, woven in one piece from top to bottom. "Let's not tear it," they said to one another. "Let's decide by lot who will get it."
>
> It happened this way so that the Scripture might be fulfilled, which said, "They divided my garments among them, and cast lots for my clothing." So this is what the soldiers did.[98]

Now, in telling the story of Jesus' seamless robe, I would like to add a sidebar. Just in case the reader thinks that we are dabbling in nonessential matters here, let me assure them of one simple fact. Although the discussion of such things as garments, paintings, and robes may not seem like legitimate subjects for the serious *Bible* student, they are subjects of tremendous importance to the writers of Holy Writ, no matter how much the darkened mind of humanity tries to trivialize them. Case in point is a passage in *The Gospel of John* regarding the crucifixion of Jesus. In fact, it contains a reference to one of the most profoundly mournful psalms ever penned by King David, called a man after God's own heart. Later, it intrudes into John's Gospel as a brief insertion, but its implications far outweigh its brevity, as anyone who loves the Scriptures will attest. It does this by virtue of the uncanny way in which words that were spoken in *The Old Testament* are spoken again by One Who inhabits the world of *The New Testament*. As it turns out, by speaking these words afresh, the old words are imbued with new meaning, creating startling, unexpected connections between past and present. The twenty-second psalm of David's, then, which has Jesus breathing new life into his words, is so marvelous that the discerning reader will be astonished by its sheer poignancy. And I mention it here to lend credence to the overall importance to the words being quoted, because, in point of fact, so much of this remarkable psalm could have been spoken by Jesus, yet all but two verses are lifted out of it.

As Jesus hung on the cross, poised between Heaven and Hell, the haunting words of David flowed through Him like a rippling wave in time. Before Jesus quoted the words, no one in history could have ever anticipated them being spoken that way, because no one at the time understood the extent to which the lowly Nazarene really was the word of God made flesh. Only then would it be revealed how inseparable were the past and the present, as the words of messianic figures like Enoch, Moses, and David found their ultimate expression in the mouth of Jesus, and never more poignantly than in the final moments before His death on the cross. A thousand years before Jesus would echo his words, King David lamented:

> My God, my God. Why have You forsaken me? Why do You remain so distant? Why do You ignore my cries for help? My enemies surround me like a herd of bulls; fierce bulls of Bashan have hemmed me in. Like roaring lions attacking their prey, they come at me with open mouths. My life is poured out like water; all my bones are out of joint. My heart is like wax, melting within me. My strength has dried up like baked clay. My tongue sticks to the roof of my mouth. You have laid me in the dust and left me for dead. My enemies surround me like a pack of dogs; an evil gang closes in on me. They've pierced my hands and feet. I can count every bone in my body. My enemies stare at me and gloat. They divide my clothes amongst themselves and throw dice for my garments.[99]

Only later, in the tumultuous events of the crucifixion, would the poetry of the psalmist take on the flesh and blood of actual history. As David mourned his plight as the hunted king of Israel prior to his eventual rise to the throne, Jesus would fulfill His own destiny in a similar manner, though in His case through death and resurrection. But en route to His ultimate exaltation, Jesus famously sighed, "My God, My God, why have You forsaken Me?"[100] And during His humiliation on the cross, the Roman soldiers gambled to see who would win His seamless robe.

But whatever became of this seamless robe of Jesus? Was it lost to history after those fateful days following the crucifixion? If the canonical record were our only source for such inquiries, then, yes, it would appear that it did. But how could something so important in the minds of the biblical authors simply vanish without a trace? Fortunately, for the sake of those who love the truth when they hear it, there is another source to be had concerning the history of Jesus' robe. In *The Death of Pilate*, the story is told how, in the days following Caesar's healing by way of the painting of Christ, Pontius Pilate was brought to Rome to be interrogated about his role in the crucifixion of Jesus. Continuing in the apocryphal record, we read:

> So Pilate was apprehended by order of Tiberius Caesar, and brought to Rome. When Caesar heard he had arrived in the city, he was so overwhelmed by an unquenchable fury that he demanded that the governor be brought before him right away.

> Now Pilate brought the seamless robe of Jesus with him, and he wore it when he appeared before the emperor. And as soon as Tiberius saw Pilate, all his anger subsided, and he rose to warmly greet him. He was unable to speak harshly to him about anything. Before Pilate's arrival, Caesar had been furious, but in his presence, he acted gently.
>
> Dismissing Pilate from the room, Caesar became enraged again, chastising himself for not expressing his anger. So he ordered to have him brought back in, swearing that Pilate was nothing but a child of death, unfit to live, but when he saw him again, he instantly greeted him with kindness, laying aside all his fury. Everyone there was quite astonished, as was Tiberius.
>
> Eventually though—either by divine suggestion or persuasion by some Christian—Caesar had Pilate stripped of his robe and quickly the original fury of his mind returned. As the emperor pondered what was happening, someone explained to him that Pilate had been wearing the seamless robe of the Lord Jesus.[101]

What can one surmise from all of the aforementioned examples? First, we have Adam's garment, which not only procured divine favor for him and his wife but subsequently bestowed awesome powers upon Noah, Nimrod, and Esau after them. Then there is Veronica's painting of Jesus that brought healing power even to Tiberius Caesar, followed by Paul's handkerchief that brought healing to those who came into contact with it. And finally, there is Jesus' seamless robe and with it the uncanny power that was imparted to Pilate, who wore it with such dramatic results in the presence of the Roman emperor. Seen separately, as they have been for so many centuries, these various accounts lay about—like scattered jewels—without a proper context, without rhyme or reason, but seen together, in relation to the canonical texts, they coalesce to solidify and substantiate one's overall faith in *The Bible* as a whole. Seen as points on a continuum, the garment, the painting, the handkerchief, and the robe present a string of unlikely but powerful connections, which, to the discerning, clearly reveal God's hidden hand in history.

Of course, anyone familiar with *The Bible* knows full well that, from cover to cover, it is, and always has been, a book of miracles. The ultimate question we are trying to ascertain here, however, is not whether or not miracles are possible. Even much of today's scientific way of thinking lends credence to the possibility of the miraculous, the fantastic, the magical, led by such luminaries as English physicist and science fiction writer Arthur C. Clarke, who famously stated, "Any sufficiently advanced technology is indistinguishable from magic."[102] According to this worldview, the only thing that distinguishes the natural from the supernatural is one of perspective, not in anything that is inherent to nature itself. Therefore, it is best to keep in mind that anyone who urges the spiritually-oriented person to abandon their faith in biblical utterances on the grounds that no one was there to prove any of it really happened would do just as well to urge the scientifically-oriented person to abandon their faith in Big Bang utterances on the same grounds. On the other hand, it is important to realize that someone does not need to shake hands with Abraham Lincoln or George Washington any more than they would Jesus of Nazareth or John the Baptist to prove that they existed. Historical certainty—which is what we are after here—is not comprised so much of scientific empiricism as it is of consistent patterns of eyewitness testimony, much in the same way that the legal proceedings of any court of law rest upon the overwhelming evidence of eyewitness testimony as much as it does on the evidence of DNA testing.

So what does any of this have to do with the preceding assortment of talismans of power? The importance of it lies in the all-important question: What do all these objects have in common? The most obvious answer appears to be *"power."* But this association, in and of itself, seems to reveal nothing to genuine students of *The Bible*. No, what we are looking for here is more at: What is the nature of this power that all these items seem to possess? Or more specifically: What is the common principle that connects the power that emanates from these objects? Let us take a look, one by one.

First, we have Adam's garment, which as we have seen came from sheep that were killed by a lion. From this fact one can surmise that God intended to convey a message to Adam and his descendants, that is to say, only through the shed blood of another is there adequate appeasement of sin—the root cause of spiritual alienation—in the divine view. The garment, then, clearly typifies the sacrifice of Jesus as the Lamb of God. The same can also be said of the painting of Christ that Veronica presented to Caesar. This event took place after the crucifixion, and as such the healing powers it bestowed upon the Roman emperor can be seen as a function of the efficacy of the shed blood of the Savior. Likewise, Paul was a minister of the risen Jesus, Whom He chose as "one born out of due time," endowing him with an extraordinary gift of healing as witnessed by the unique virtues of a handkerchief that had simply come into contact with his skin.

And finally, we see the same thing happening in regard to the seamless robe of Jesus, which was worn by Pilate with such powerful results in the presence of Caesar. Just like Adam, Noah, and Nimrod before him, Pilate possessed a talisman that provided its wearer with a power that nullified the potency of his adversary, in the same way that the wrath of God is quenched by the sacrifice of His Son. For one brief moment, Pilate stood before the furious emperor of Rome as a type of all mankind who stand guilty before the righteously indignant Emperor of the Universe, but because he had been wearing Jesus' seamless robe he was "covered by the skins," as it were, of the Lamb of God. As such, the wrath of the emperor was momentarily appeased. As long as Pilate wore it, Caesar was gripped not by unquenchable fury but by boundless compassion for this pitiful man who had been manipulated by forces—both human and divine—beyond his wildest imagination. But as soon as he was stripped of the robe, the emperor's anger was unleashed once again.

So the underlying principle that binds all these talismans of power together is the sacrifice of Christ, the Lamb of God Who gave His life as a propitiation for sin and thus as a vicarious substitute for the sake of mankind. In this way, the very thing that Jesus predicted is revealed in all its splendor. Then some of the scribes and Pharisees answered, saying, "Teacher, we want to see a sign from You." So He said to them, "An evil and adulterous generation seeks a sign, but no sign will be given to it except the sign of the prophet Jonah. For as Jonah was in the belly of the whale for three full days, so the Son of Man will be in the heart of the Earth."[103]

Upon first reading this passage, one might surmise that Jesus is saying that no matter how much you ask for a sign from Heaven, you are never going to get one. But far from refusing their request, what He was saying was that whenever God reveals Himself, as He so often does, the sign that He is performing has the sole purpose of typifying the death and resurrection of Jesus, of which Jonah in the belly of the whale is the primary example. According to this view, each and every one of the talismans of power we have examined so far conform to this paramount function, just as Cinderella's foot perfectly fits into the proverbial glass slipper.

Hidden in Plain Sight

THIS IS WHY, FROM beginning to end—in establishing a foundation to demonstrate God's control and faithfulness via the five *sacred* things—the present exercise has been one in which we have sought to establish an argument for the authenticity of the apocryphal record on the basis of a holistic approach. In this case, we have sought to examine the question via a four-fold approach—in the etymological meaning of the word itself, in the prophetic nature of Scripture, in the internal logic that exists within the corpus of apocryphal texts themselves, and in the external logic that exists between the apocryphal and canonical records.

In a nutshell, we found that the very word *apocryphal* contains a meaningful clue as to its function and purpose in God's unfolding plan of the ages. Accordingly, true wisdom is always something that the Lord deliberately hides in the secret place of His heart, and which is brought forth only for the sake of truth seekers worthy of the task. This truth, though, is one that was predestined to have been lost amidst the sands of time until a future generation would both rediscover it and bear witness to its reemergence. And not only would this truth one day resurface, but it would do so in such a way that it would remain on the threshold of human awareness.

In this context, truth exists in the world as a bittersweet paradox. Perceived by some, as though they had a key to unlocking the divine vault, it would, however, *not* be understood by others who upon hearing the same "truth" would remain ignorant of its genuine significance. In this, Paul, as usual, expressed it best:

> Of which I became a minister according to the stewardship that God gave me for your benefit in order to fulfill the word of God, which is the *mystery* that has been *hidden* from past ages and generations but is now *revealed* to His saints. To them God willed to make known what are the riches of the glory of this *mystery* among the Gentiles, which is Christ in you, the hope of glory.[104]

Then, while examining the internal harmony that exists within the numerous apocryphal texts themselves, we discovered an amazing synergy in God's decrees of judgment upon His chosen ones. In the case of the Children of Israel, who dwelled safely in Palestine, and Adam and Eve, who lived happily in the Garden of Eden, the length of the divine judgment that God decreed on them was found to be directly correlated to their time spent in obedience to His commands. Seen together, these two timelines display a remarkable confluence that the human imagination could have never devised, especially when considering that all the pieces of this extended puzzle exist in ancient documents scattered throughout the globe.

In the case of Israel and their descendants, we found that, after having defiled seventy years of Sabbath rest while in the Promised Land, they were to be banned from the territory for seventy weeks of "years," until the time when a glorious millennial age was to be ushered in by none other than the Messiah Himself.[105] As a result of this awareness, it became apparent that a similar scale of judgment had been meted out to Adam and his descendants. In their case, after having been in the garden for *five and a half* hours, they were to remain outside of God's direct presence for *five and a half* "days," or five thousand, five hundred years,[106] at which time, "One would come to save him and his faithful children."[107]

And for the final aspect of our inquiry, as it pertains to an external logic that exists between the apocryphal and canonical records, we discovered an uncanny relationship between them that helped to shed new light on many of the more perplexing passages in the received texts. In this way, the strange experiences of Adam, Noah, Ham, Nimrod, and Esau came together in a way that the Biblical Canon, with its threadbare narrative, has never been able to achieve. In the process of our study, we saw how the scattered accounts of Adam's garment, Veronica's painting, Paul's handkerchief, and Jesus' seamless robe, all were brought into sharp focus, forming a unique convergence that ultimately confirmed the words of Christ Himself Who revealed the truth about divine power. To all those who seek a heavenly sign, Jesus said, "The only sign that God is willing to perform is the sign of Jonah, who like the Son of Man would also be in the heart of the Earth for three full days."[108]

In all of this, we have pursued our four-fold approach, utilizing interconnected lines of inquiry. Hopefully, in doing so, it has become clear that these apocryphal accounts, contrary to popular opinion, exist in perfect harmony with the canonical record, and as such are able to illuminate what the traditional texts have only dealt with in a superficial manner. If this has become sufficiently obvious, then it is self-evident that both the canonical and non-canonical records should stand together as a unified body of divinely-inspired wisdom. And set free from its struggle, mankind might finally see this once upon a time forbidden wisdom not as some offshoot of heretical literature but as the ultimate key to unleashing latent truths, which are even now lying about like so many scattered jewels, hidden in plain sight.

Shadow and Substance

Things to Come

AS HAS BEEN SHOWN in our previous discussion, one of the greatest proofs of the authenticity of the apocryphal literature is its ability to reveal a coherence within the very fabric of its textual presentation. There is an internal logic in the information found throughout the corpus of books deemed non-canonical; and there is an external logic in the consistency between the apocryphal and canonical texts. In other words, just as the accepted texts of Scripture convey a harmonious relationship, both internally and externally, the stories found in the apocryphal record bear a strikingly similar set of relationships.

An internal harmony is revealed in the case of the prophecy of the Great Five and a Half Days, begun in *The First Book of Adam and Eve,* alluded to in *The Secrets of Enoch,* and fulfilled in *The Gospel of Nicodemus.* As detached prophetic wisps, they float about as disjointed blips on the divine radar screen, but stitched together they coalesce into a genuine pattern, obvious to even the most obtuse observer of biblical timelines.

Similarly, an external harmony can be seen in the case of the divine attributes displayed by various individuals mentioned throughout the received texts—some of them heroic figures, like Enoch and Noah, and some villainous, like Nimrod and Esau. Until now, all these lives had been traditionally viewed as discordant pieces of a scattered tapestry. Upon further review, though, we found there really is a common thread that makes sense of their apparently disarrayed experiences. This thread, which can only be found in the apocryphal record, involves the strange story of the most ancient talisman known to mankind, that is, the garments of sheepskin that God made for Adam and Eve after they were expelled from the Garden of Eden.

Having established this kind of logical structure, which binds the apocryphal and canonical record into a cohesive whole, I would now like to proceed further in light of this newfound awareness. Next, we will examine the extent to which the apocryphal record lends itself to deepening our understanding of the biblical doctrine known as *typology.* In theological terms, typology is the doctrine that expounds the idea that certain events, persons, or statements in *The Old Testament* are "types" that represent "shadows" that pre-figure specific attributes relating to the Advent of Christ, which, as you will recall, constitutes our primary focus in demonstrating God's control and faithfulness. Paul articulated this idea best when he said, "Don't let anyone judge you about food, or drink, or festivals, or new moons, or Sabbaths, which are all but *shadows of things to come,* but the substance is Christ."[109] This very thing, as we have already seen in the last chapter, is what happened when Annas confessed to Pilate that because they had discovered that Moses had been instructed to build The Ark of the Covenant with the dimensions of *five and a half* cubits, they deduced from this seemingly random bit of information that the Messiah was to arrive on the stage of world history five thousand, five hundred years after Adam. In this, both Paul and Annas were doing exactly what Jesus had done when He compared the experience of Jonah in the belly of the whale with the death and resurrection of the Son of Man.[110]

That said, my purpose in analyzing the role of typology in apocryphal literature—en route to laying a foundation for revealing the hidden connection between the five *sacred* things—is to provide answers to questions that have, down through the ages, plagued anyone attempting to either believe or dismiss the truths found in *The Bible.* For those who wish to believe them, I would like to offer fresh hope in their quest to ground their faith in the promises of God; and for those who wish to dismiss them, I would like to offer an alternative to their outmoded conclusions based on short-sighted interpretations.

These questions pertain to so-called "truths" offered up by various preachers that, on the surface, may sound correct, but due to stale repetitions of shallow traditional views, they instead constitute so much useless pabulum. According to Paul, God has given "gifts" to His Church in the form of apostles, prophets, evangelists, pastors, and teachers, whose job it is to administer His word, which when done faithfully accomplishes God's stated purpose.

> His people are to be equipped to do His work in order to build up the Church, the Body of Christ. That way we'll all come to such unity in our faith and knowledge of God's Son that we become mature in the Lord, measuring up to the full stature of Christ. Then we'll no longer act like children, forever changing our minds just because someone's told us something different or because they deceived us by making a lie sound like the truth.[111]

All too often, however, humans want the purpose of God's Church to revolve around them and their needs, that is, to heal them, bless them, prosper them. But Paul insisted that the true purpose of these gift ministers is to bring the scattered individuals who comprise the Church into a "unity of faith," which can only come from a "knowledge of God's Son." Therefore, it behooves those who are attempting to become part of this Body of Christ to find someone who can adequately inform them about what the Scriptures say about faith in Jesus Christ. Sadly, though, much of today's *Bible* teaching focuses on catering to the human needs of its parishioners as opposed to God's specified desire to build a body of believers who truly understand Who Jesus is.

Part of the problem, as I see it, rests squarely on the shoulders of those individuals who—while claiming to be gift ministers of God's word—willfully insist on feeding their unsuspecting congregations the same old stories, regurgitated from their pet *Bible* commentaries. Never mind that intelligent people with the courage to ask difficult questions prefer meaningful answers rather than trite homilies. Never mind that these so-called "gift ministers" seem to be so oblivious to the inconsistencies in their own teaching of God's word, in spite of the glaring contradictions that their worn out clichés attempt to gloss over. We are simply expected to marvel at their well-intentioned genius while we politely resist the urge to ask any question that might make our fellow saints think we have lost faith in the traditional interpretation of the brethren.

For example, as long as I can remember, I have been taught that when God asked Abraham to offer his son Isaac as a burnt offering on Mount Moriah, it was supposedly a "type" of God offering up His Son Jesus as a sin offering on Calvary. In this comparison between Abraham and God, and between Isaac and Jesus, I could clearly see a direct correlation in theological terms. What is more, because I already had an appreciation for such cinematic concepts as "foreshadow" and "payoff," this interpretation of biblical history seemed quite plausible, as though God, the Cosmic Director of the Universe, had planned it so that we could not fail to recognize a connection between the two events. In fact, never once in all my years have I ever felt that such "parallels in time," so to speak, were not consistent with God's attempts to convey the truth of His plan of redemption throughout the ages.

To this very point, Cyrus H. Gordon spoke most eloquently:

> Scripture makes it quite clear that … Isaac was conceived through divine agency. Like the Mycenaean Greek heroes, Isaac could claim paternity at two levels; the human and the divine. His human father, through whom he obtained his specific position in his people's history, was Abraham; but his superhuman quality was derived from the deity that visited Sarah. This is of a piece with the dual paternity of Homeric heroes, who hold the office of their human fathers, but are supernatural because of their divine fathers… It is in every way conceivable that some of the original Isaac Cycle survived to re-echo in Christianity. Jesus derives His human office of Messianic King from Joseph, but His divine quality from His Divine Father. Moreover, the Church tradition that connects the sacrifice of Isaac with the sacrifice of Christ apparently rests on sound exegesis, for the sacrifice of Isaac would have meant not only the sacrifice of Abraham's son but of God's.[112]

Understood in this context, then, it has always made perfect sense to me that if Abraham were the father of faith, one could easily accept the view that Isaac was the son of faith. What I did find confusing, though, was the seemingly incomplete picture that the canonical record seemed to offer in the actions of Isaac in relation to those of Jesus. Let me explain what I mean.

To begin with, if Isaac is supposed to be a "type" of Christ in this scenario, then why does *The Book of Genesis* depict him as an ignorant, little boy who has no idea what his father is planning for him? In my view, this could never adequately fulfill the typology of Christ, Whom the Scriptures tell us, repeatedly, was a willing participant in drinking from the cup of suffering prepared by God. "I'm the Good Shepherd," Jesus said. "The Good Shepherd lays down His life for the sheep. The reason My Father loves Me is because I lay down My life—only to take it up again. No one takes My life, but I willingly offer it on My own."[113] So if I am to believe in the unerring word of God, how can the traditional picture of an ignorant son of Abraham qualify as the devoted Son of God? To me, this has always presented a lingering contradiction, even as I have tried to reconcile this blatant gap in terms of what *The Bible* is supposedly offering as God's control over every stream of history. No wonder intelligent people continue to question the teaching of preachers who sanctimoniously offer up the Lord as the Omnipotent Master of the Universe, yet He Himself, it seems, is just as determined as they are to sidestep such nagging inconsistencies in His word.

So imagine my reaction when I came upon the story of Abraham and Isaac in the apocryphal literature. In *The Book of Jasher*, I had finally come upon a rendering that satisfied my desire to prove that God actually knew what He was doing with Isaac when He set out to prepare humanity to recognize what He would someday accomplish with Jesus at Calvary. In *Jasher*, we are presented with a picture that adequately fleshes out the idea that not only did Jesus fulfill His destiny as the obedient Son of God, but Isaac also fulfilled his role as a genuine type of Christ when he made that fateful journey to Mount Moriah with his father.

But before we look at the scenario presented in *Jasher*, let us take a moment to examine what would be required of Isaac to ensure that he might truly be called a type of Christ. First of all, unlike the canonical record implies, Isaac could not have been a mere child who was not yet old enough to act on his own accord. If Isaac had been a child, then he still would have been under the jurisdiction of Abraham, and any action performed by Isaac, the boy, could not rightly be compared to those being performed by Jesus, the adult. Furthermore, Isaac would have to know why he was going to Mount Moriah with his father. He would have to fully appreciate the fact that he was going to be killed and presented as a burnt offering to the Lord. And above all, he would have to willingly consent to the wishes of Abraham in what was being done to him. Without any one of these necessary components, the idea that Isaac represents a type of Christ is simply not consistent with any form of logic that I am aware of; and anyone who says otherwise is either stubbornly ignorant, or worse still, downright hypocritical. But fear not, God is quite capable of making sure that all the streams of history conform to His will, because as the story is revealed in *Jasher*, all these criteria have been adequately met. Let us see for ourselves, then, how all these elements come together in *Jasher's* depiction of the drama of Isaac as it pertains to Abraham's most important mission to Moriah.

> When Isaac was thirty-seven years old, Ishmael was visiting him in his tent.
>
> "I was thirteen," said Ishmael to Isaac, "when the Lord told Father to circumcise us. I gave my life to Him, and since then I've never disobeyed."
>
> "Why brag to me about something like that?" asked Isaac. "You cut off a piece of your skin because the Lord told you to. As the God of Abraham lives, if He told Father to cut me into pieces and burn me as an offering, I wouldn't hesitate. I'd gladly consent."
>
> And when the Lord heard what Isaac said to Ishmael, He decided that it would be exactly how He would test Abraham.[114]

The first thing that one cannot help but notice in this account is that according to *Jasher*, Isaac was not a mere child as the canonical record implies. He was actually thirty-seven years old. So why would *Genesis* describe Isaac as a lad? The word *lad* denotes a child, not a thirty-seven year old man. Why the discrepancy, then? Did Moses make a mental error when he penned *Genesis*? The discrepancy lies, I believe, in the simple fact that when Moses wrote his version of the story, he knew full well that human beings lived much longer in those days. Based on the apocryphal record, when Abraham was eighty-seven years old, his great-great-grandfather Reu, the son of Peleg, died at the age of two hundred and thirty-nine.[115] And when Isaac was one hundred and ten years old, Shem, the son of Noah, died at the ripe old age of six hundred.[116] These numbers are also borne out by the canonical record, so by no means was Moses making a mental error when he described Isaac as a mere lad; he was simply describing the situation based on his understanding of the life spans of that era.

In retrospect, the discrepancy lies not in the numbers given to us by Moses but in the fact that we all judge things in relation to our own particular frame of reference. And when this reality, which was simply taken for granted by the biblical authors, is accounted for, it seems quite natural that Moses would call Isaac a lad, even though we moderns would never describe a thirty-seven-year-old man in that way. With this in mind, then, one can easily see that Isaac was, in reality, an adult, and as such can now be considered responsible for any of his own decisions, just as any normal adult might be.

The next thing one will notice is that, far from being ignorant of his father's intention in offering him up as a sacrifice to God, Isaac was actually the one who first thought of the idea. Of course, at the time, he could have never anticipated the possibility that God might actually take him up on his brash offer. Meanwhile, I can almost hear some people ask the inevitable question: Why would God make Isaac go through such a harrowing ordeal simply because he was the one who suggested it first? Is He some kind of cosmic sadist? If by that do you mean to ask: Is God in the habit of helping people perform any and all foolish acts because He enjoys watching people suffer? Then, no, He most assuredly is not a sadist.

Instead, what we have here, when one cares to examine *The Bible* as a whole, is simply another situation where God finds someone who has chosen to do something that He can use to communicate His purpose to an onlooking world. The same could be said when Enoch agreed to go along with the angels in his ascension to Heaven. Before God found that He could use Isaac to communicate what it means to be a type of Christ, He found Enoch. Though fearful of losing his life in the process, Enoch willingly accepted the inherent risk in ascending into the very presence of Almighty God. Thus, he became a heavenly mediator of His word, just as Jesus ascended to His Father where He continues to act as the eternal mediator between God and humanity.[117]

Subsequent to Enoch and Isaac, there was Moses, who also functioned as a type of Christ. In turning his back on the riches of Egypt in order to fulfill his calling as the deliverer of the Hebrews, Moses foreshadowed what one day Jesus would do, in emptying Himself of His divine power in the Incarnation and dying a cruel death on a Roman cross in order to provide a ransom for the people of God.[118]

In the case of Abraham and Isaac, then, God saw the same potential to lay down a shadow of things to come concerning the death and resurrection of His own Son, Jesus, when Isaac volunteered himself as a sacrificial offering. And though Isaac's desire to demonstrate his love and devotion to his father was a noble one, he certainly must have regretted it while having to follow through with his pledge by actually going to Mount Moriah with Abraham. Naturally, from a strictly humanistic point of view, Isaac could never have imagined that God would eventually provide a substitute in the form of a ram, who having appeared out of nowhere was sacrificed by his father instead of him. In this, the canonical record is again misleading. According to *Genesis*, Isaac, in being led up the mountain, appeared completely ignorant as to his father's intention.

As the two of them went on together, Isaac spoke up and said to Abraham, "Father?"

"Yes, my son?"

"The fire and wood are here," said Isaac, "but where is the lamb for the burnt offering?"

And Abraham answered, "God Himself will provide the lamb for the burnt offering, my son."

And the two of them continued on together.[119]

In *Jasher*, however, Isaac is portrayed in a much different way. To be sure, he is afraid of the situation into which he has gotten himself. He does undeniably waver, quite naturally. Who among us would not have done so if we were thrust into that same situation? He was, after all, only human, and in this it was to be the same with the human side of Jesus. Though the Son of God, the Incarnate One in human flesh, yet He likewise prayed in His darkest hour that the cup of God's wrath might pass from before Him. Still, as the obedient Son that He was, He willingly accepted the role that had been foreordained for Him before the foundations of the world had been laid. And as Jesus revealed His own humanity in a moment of overwhelming dread, so, too, did Isaac momentarily buckle under the pressure. Says *Jasher*:

And Isaac carried the wood for the burnt offering while Abraham held the torch and the knife. After walking along in silence for quite a while, Isaac stopped and turned to Abraham. "Father, I see the fire, and I see the wood, but where's the lamb to burn on the altar?"

"Oh, Isaac, you already know that the Lord has chosen you to be the burnt offering, not a lamb."

Isaac tried his best to smile. "Yes, Father, I know. Then, I'll happily do everything the Lord told you."

"You don't think what we're doing is wrong, do you?" asked Abraham. "Tell me now, son. Please, don't try to hide anything from me."

"As the Lord lives, Father, nothing is going to keep us from doing what God wants. I'm completely resolved. In fact, I thank the Lord for choosing me to be a burnt offering for Him."

Relieved, Abraham hugged his son, and they resumed their journey.

Soon, they arrived at the place that the Lord had described, and Abraham began to build an altar on that mountain. He cried as Isaac went around gathering stones and mortar to help him complete it. Then, placing the wood on the altar, he began tying up Isaac.

"Make sure the rope is good and tight, Father. That way I can't roll around. I don't want to ruin the offering by breaking loose when your knife cuts me."

So Abraham tied him securely with cords and carefully placed him atop the pile of wood.

"And Father, please, promise me you'll take some of my ashes to Mother. Tell her: This is the sweet-smelling savor of Isaac. But make sure you don't tell her if she's sitting near a well or anywhere high up. I don't want her throwing herself off trying to come after me."

Abraham cried even more. His tears spilled onto Isaac, who started crying, too. "Hurry, Father, do with me as God has instructed."

Strangely enough, though, their hearts rejoiced in with what the Lord had told them to do. Outwardly they wept, while inwardly they celebrated. Then, Isaac stretched his neck out for his father, and Abraham raised the knife, preparing to cut his son's throat.[120]

From all this added detail, found only in the apocryphal record, one can clearly see that Isaac was not at all ignorant of what his father had in store for him. Though Abraham's son was human and Jesus was both human and divine, the two were yet one in spirit. Both were adults of sound mind and body, both willingly offered themselves to their father's will as supreme proof of their love and devotion, and both completed their journeys to the bitter end. Away forever, then, with the idea that just because the canonical version unnecessarily waters down a genuine parallel between these two heroes of *The Bible*, never let it be said that Isaac, the faithful son of Abraham, was not in every respect a worthy type of Christ, the obedient Son of God, after all.

Mining the Depths

HAVING DEMONSTRATED the awesome potential of the apocryphal record to elicit a deeper appreciation of the role of typology in Scripture, I would next like to elaborate on its ability in this regard. What I am about to undertake will, as far as I know, constitute a new thing never before discussed within the confines of theology. Yet, hopefully, it will be received with due consideration. My endeavor in this is two-fold: First, I hope to cement the validity of any remarks that I have already made concerning the authenticity of the apocryphal record. Second, I hope to place such a firm capstone on its authenticity that anyone who has been reading this presentation will become so convinced they will continue the journey throughout the rest of this work.

The capstone I am speaking of involves another familiar chapter in the Biblical Canon, though as we have seen in the previous illustration, a version that is distinctly watered-down. It is the moment in *The Old Testament* when Joseph, the beloved son of Jacob, after being elevated as the viceroy of Egypt, is trying to decide if he should reveal his identity to the brothers who had many years earlier sold him into slavery. And just as the story of Abraham and Isaac has been told and retold to countless generations, so the story of Joseph and his brothers has also been the subject of many a church sermon or Sunday school lesson.

The generally accepted significance of this scene, like nearly every other phase of Joseph's life, is that it represents yet another type of Christ, just as Enoch and Isaac before him and as Moses, David, and Jonah after him. In fact, so many comparisons can be made between the lives of Joseph and Jesus that biblical scholars have surmised there are no less than seventy ways in which Joseph can be considered a type of Christ.

To name just a handful of parallels, consider this: Both Joseph and Jesus were quite outspoken about their glorious futures in which they were fated to rule as kings, and as a result they engendered skepticism, animosity, and hatred from their family members.[121] Subsequently, both men—though destined for greatness—were imprisoned at the instigation of their own brothers.[122] Both were punished in the company of two other men, of which one was to be spared and the other condemned—Joseph, in prison, encountered Pharaoh's butler and baker, while Jesus, on the cross, hung alongside one thief to His right and another to His left.[123] Similarly, the evils that were perpetrated upon Joseph and Jesus were providentially "turned inside out," so to speak. Rather than destroying the two men, the very circumstances that should have obliterated them led to their eventual exaltation. In the process, both men endured the pangs of death, yet both were ultimately rescued and glorified by a miracle of God.[124] And after being supernaturally elevated to the royal position that was prophetically anticipated for them, neither of them was immediately recognized by the very brothers who had been instrumental in their degradation and near demise.[125] In these and many more ways, Joseph can be regarded as the most fully developed type of Christ to be found in all *The Bible*.

However—notwithstanding all of these remarkable similarities—my focus here in light of our study of typology will be somewhat different in its approach from most other biblical treatises on the subject of Joseph as a type of Christ. The reason for this is my desire to demonstrate the authenticity of the apocryphal literature, which has waited far too long to be appreciated for its true potential in mining the depths of God's revelation. And considering that the apocryphal record goes into so much more detail in terms of character development and storyline than do the canonical texts, it would not surprise me that once they are fully appreciated for their genuine value, they might one day enjoy the same respectability they originally knew before they were unjustly stigmatized.

Having said all that, I would like to proceed with a completely new insight into the life of Joseph, especially as it pertains to his momentous decision to reveal himself to brothers who were acting as hostile outsiders in their quest to obtain food for their starving families still living in famine-stricken Canaan. According to *Genesis*, when the ten sons of Jacob were forced to beg Joseph for food, they initially had no idea who they were dealing with.[126] Then, because Jacob had refused to allow his youngest son, Benjamin—Joseph's only brother by Rachel—Joseph stooped to subterfuge in order to get them to bring him to Egypt.[127]

Eventually, all eleven of Joseph's brothers stood before him, though they were still ignorant of his true identity.[128] It was then that Joseph resorted to one last bit of chicanery. Before he allowed his brothers to return to Palestine with the food they had bought, he instructed his Egyptian servants to hide his silver chalice in Benjamin's bag and to follow the brothers on their way back home. But before they could cross the border, Joseph's servants were to stop them and declare that their master's silver cup had been stolen. Then upon searching through the brother's baggage, they were to reveal that the chalice was in Benjamin's possession. At that point, the group was returned to Joseph with Benjamin as their prisoner, accused of stealing the royal cup from the viceroy.[129]

Naturally, the ten brothers were mortified, vehemently declaring their innocence before Joseph and resorting to every form of histrionics in the process.[130] Eventually, Joseph could stand it no longer. Ordering all his Egyptian attendants out of the room, he finally broke down and, in a tear-filled moment, revealed that he was their long-lost brother. At first, according to the canonical record, none of the brothers believed him, more terrified than skeptical, considering that this powerful man might have another trick up his sleeve.[131] What apparently turned the tide in his efforts was the way in which Joseph, who perceived the foresight of God in his ordeal, was able to convince them that he had been divinely guided to his present position in order to provide a way of escape to Jacob and his descendants.[132] So, as the story goes, after much insistence, the brothers finally came to the realization that this grown man really was the same boy they had so callously imprisoned in a bitter act of jealousy.[133]

But notice how I said: As the story goes. The reason for this is because in our previous example, when using only the canonical record as our source, the notion of Abraham and Isaac representing a type of God and Christ was found to be inadequate. Only when we turned to the apocryphal literature did we find the necessary elements required to call the drama of Abraham and Isaac a true type in theological terms. In the same way, the idea that Joseph revealing himself to his brothers represents another type of Christ seems, on the surface, a legitimate claim. Upon further review, however, certain elements of the traditional account simply fail to add up. Let me take some time to explain what I mean.

As you will recall, in order for someone to fulfill the role of a true type, they must, by necessity, correspond in kind to the substance, which is Christ. In other words, what history records as having occurred in the life of Jesus should correspond in the previous personage who is said to be a shadow of Him Who was to come—in this instance, Joseph. So what should one expect to find in this supposed correspondence? According to most theologians, the reason that Joseph is pointed to as a type of Christ is because, even though he sat before them as the viceroy of Egypt, his brothers did not recognize him until he revealed his true identity as their long-lost brother. This, say the experts, corresponds to the fact that even though Jesus was the Omnipotent Son of the Most High, his fellow man did not recognize Him as such until He revealed Himself after the resurrection.

The only problem with this comparison, while sounding perfectly plausible, actually breaks down when one simply takes the time to ask a few difficult—and by difficult I mean uncomfortable—questions. For example, to test whether or not this scenario bears itself out as a genuine type, one must review the scene as *Genesis* plays it for us. In it, we find that none of Joseph's brothers ever recognized him as the viceroy of Egypt; therefore, to be a true type of

Christ, one would expect to find that no one among the Children of Israel ever recognized the true identity of Jesus until after His glorification via the resurrection.

But clearly this interpretation does not correspond with the actual facts of biblical history, because obviously the twelve disciples of Christ were among those who, even before the resurrection, recognized the kingship of Jesus of Nazareth.

> When Jesus came to the region of Caesarea Philippi, He asked His disciples, "Who do people say the Son of Man is?"
>
> They replied, "Some say John the Baptist; others say Elijah; and still others, Jeremiah or one of the prophets."
>
> "But what about you?" He asked. "Who do you say I am?"
>
> Simon Peter answered, "You are the Christ, the Son of the Living God."
>
> Jesus replied, "Blessed are you, Simon, son of Jonah, for this was not revealed to you by man but by my Father in Heaven."[134]

So if the disciples recognized Jesus as the long-awaited Son of God prior to His exaltation, how, then, can one view the life of Joseph as a true type of Christ? One of the necessary elements of correspondence is missing, even if it appears at first glance to be a minor one.

In addition to this inconsistency, there is also the mystery of why Joseph went to such lengths to incriminate his younger brother, Benjamin. What could have possibly been the point of such a charade? Clearly, Joseph had succeeded in humiliating his brothers, if that was his true intention in repeatedly deceiving them, but as to the actual motive of such a complicated game of intrigue the canonical record does not provide the slightest clue. Fortunately, though, there is another view of this same scenario to be found in the apocryphal record. And just as before, it is in *The Book of Jasher*, where not only the answers to these perplexing questions can be found but also all the necessary elements that are required to view the life of Joseph as a true type of Christ.

Let us take a moment to outline some of the things one should expect to find if Joseph were a type of Christ before we turn to the record in *Jasher*. First, if the disciples of Jesus recognized His kingship before the rest of the Children of Israel, then one would expect to find some correspondence in the case of Joseph and his brothers. Moreover, when one considers the strange trial that Benjamin was forced to endure at the hands of the viceroy of Egypt, one would expect to find some kind of similar correspondence in the life of the Shepherd-King of Nazareth. Certainly, I can already hear some asking: Is not this a rather tall order? How can one ever hope to find such a correspondence? Besides, so what if there is a correlation between these events in the apocryphal literature? What could it possibly add to our understanding of *The Bible*? And how could it possibly help solidify a correct adjustment in our view of Joseph as a true type of Christ? The answer, I believe, might astound even the most ardent skeptic; and it goes as follows.

In *Jasher*, we find that Joseph arranged for a great feast where he gathered his eleven brothers, and under the pretext of using his silver chalice of divination, he told them that he was able to discern their birth orders. As a result, he sat them at the dinner table accordingly, and declaring that because Benjamin was the youngest son among them and was, like himself, without a brother, he wished to have him seated next him on his throne.[135]

> Then, Joseph ordered his servants to bring him his map of the stars of Heaven whereby Joseph knew all the times, and Joseph said to Benjamin, "I've heard that the Hebrews are acquainted with all wisdom. Are you aware of anything like this?"
>
> "Yes, I am," replied Benjamin. "I learned all about it from my father."
>
> And Joseph said to him, "Good, then look at this instrument and tell me if you're able to discover the present location of your brother Joseph, who you said went down to Egypt."
>
> So Benjamin looked at the map of the stars and concentrated very hard,

hoping to perceive within its contents the whereabouts of Joseph. To do this, Benjamin divided the land of Egypt into four sections and eventually came to discern that the one who was sitting upon the throne before him was his brother. Astonished at this revelation, Benjamin looked up at Joseph with ever-widening eyes.

Seeing the odd look on Benjamin's face, Joseph asked, "What is it? What have you seen? Why do you look so amazed?"

And Benjamin replied, "I can see by this instrument that Joseph, my brother, sits before me, here on this very throne."

Then, with a wry smile, Joseph said to him, "Very good, Benjamin. Yes, it's true; I am your brother Joseph. But I don't want you to reveal this to your brothers."

Confused, Benjamin asked, "But why?"

"Because I plan on testing them, that's why. Because I need to find out, once and for all, what is yet in the hearts of the men who threw me into that miserable pit so long ago. Don't be afraid, Benjamin, but I'm planning on taking you away from them. And if they're willing to risk their lives and fight for your sake, I'll know they've repented of what they did to me, and I'll reveal myself to them. But if they forsake you when I've taken you from them, then you'll remain with me. I'll contest their right to you as a brother and send them away empty-handed, and in the end, I'll never let them know who I really am."[136]

How, then, does the apocryphal record differ from the canonical version? First, it reveals that not all of Joseph's brothers were ignorant of his identity prior to his revealing who he was to the entire group. In this, we are a step closer to a more accurate comparison to that of Jesus, Who also was recognized by His disciples prior to Him revealing His true nature after His resurrection. Now, of course, I can already anticipate some people questioning such a need for this alteration in the events of Christ's revealing of Himself. Some might insist that, even though Jesus revealed Himself after the resurrection to His disciples, the whole world will not be privy to this revelation until He returns in His Second Coming in clouds of glory, where He reveals Himself to all humanity. But I insist that this has never been the context of Joseph's revealing his true identity. The crux of this scenario is Joseph and his brothers, not Joseph and the Egyptians, which in such a case would represent the world in general. It is unquestionably a story of Joseph as a type of Christ in which he is revealing himself to brothers who were all recipients of the promises of Abraham, yet who had abused that high calling when they jealously sought to eliminate him. In this context the fact that, unlike in *Genesis*, one of his brothers—that is, Benjamin—recognized who he was, we finally have a new reason to better appreciate Joseph as a true type of Christ.

What is more, the fact that Benjamin is the first among his brothers to recognize Joseph is no mere accident in the providence of God. In this, we have a direct correspondence between the events of Joseph in Egypt and those of Jesus in Palestine, because it is well known among biblical historians that after their release from the Babylonian captivity the descendants of none other than Benjamin came to inhabit the territory in Judea that is identified with Galilee. What does this mean in terms of our examination of Joseph as a type of Christ? It means that when Jesus was recognized for Who He was in Galilee, He was first being recognized by men who just happened to be descendants of Benjamin. Of this connection between Galilee and the ministry of Jesus, biblical scholars are quick to point out the verse in Matthew's Gospel:

And when Jesus had heard that John the Baptist had been put in prison, He returned to Galilee. Leaving Nazareth, He went and lived in Capernaum, which was by the lake in the area of Zebulun and Naphtali, in order to fulfill what was said through the prophet Isaiah: "The land of Zebulun and Naphtali, the way to the sea, along the Jordan—Galilee of the Nations—the people living in darkness

> have seen a great light. On those living in the land of the shadow of death, a light has dawned."[137]

In these Galileans, then, what we see are men of the tribe of Benjamin, who were the first to accept the teaching of Jesus, that is, those who were the first to perceive the "great light" of Messiah. In doing so, they constitute nothing less than the fulfillment of the original type of Benjamin himself, who was the first among the sons of Jacob to recognize Joseph for who he really was.

Furthermore, there is a remarkable twist that clinches the notion of Benjamin being a type of the first "seer" of Christ. As it turns out, when Judas Iscariot—the only man among the original twelve disciples who was not a Benjamite—hung himself, the disciple whom God chose to replace him, Paul of Tarsus, was, in fact, born of the tribe of Benjamin.[138]

Then consider another unique aspect to biblical history. In one of the most peculiar stories in *The Old Testament*, the tribe of Benjamin was nearly wiped from the face of the Earth when they refused to cooperate in bringing to justice a group of criminals within their midst. In a chapter reminiscent of a modern-day horror story, a man's concubine was brutally raped by thugs during their travels through the territory of Benjamin. After his concubine died as a result of her ordeal, the man was so outraged by the wanton nature of the crime against her, he did the unthinkable. In an act of unmitigated fury, he cut her body into twelve pieces and sent the separate parts into all the tribes in blatant protest.

Horrified delegates from eleven of the tribes demanded that the rapists who had caused the death of this woman be handed over to answer for their crime. But for some unknown reason, the Benjamites refused to comply with their request. At that point, a civil war ensued in which the eleven tribes aligned themselves against the single tribe of Benjamin. Initially, the Benjamites unleashed tremendous casualties against their opponents, but eventually they succumbed to the sheer numbers of the combined forces of the other tribes. In the end, the overmatched Benjamites suffered catastrophic losses.

Then, to make matters even worse, in retribution for their actions, the rest of the tribes established a law amongst themselves to never again allow any of their women to marry a Benjamite. These two factors combined with devastating effect, nearly annihilating this tribe with such an important role in the salvation of mankind. Eventually, however, the rest of the tribes regretted what they had done and made special arrangements to give a large sum of their women to them so they could replenish their diminished population, thereby averting their extinction.[139]

Later, God, though just as angry as the rest of the tribes for what the Benjamites had done, understood all too well the importance of their future role. When the Lord was ordering the division of the Kingdom of Israel—to the north and to the south—God declared:

> However, I will not tear away the whole kingdom. I will give one tribe (speaking of the Benjamites) to your son (speaking of Rehoboam, the son of Solomon, the king of Judah) for the sake of My servant David and for Jerusalem, which I have chosen. And to his son (Rehoboam) I will give one tribe (the Benjamites) that My servant David may always have a light before Me in Jerusalem, the city which I have chosen for Myself, to put My name there.[140]

In this single promise, we see both the tragedy and the hope of the descendants of Benjamin, the light-bearer son of Jacob. In it, we see the light of awareness in the eyes of the first one to recognize the man who had been miraculously transformed from the irritating boy with dreams of glory. In it, we see the same awareness in the eyes of the first men who though "living in the land of the shadow of death" recognized that the One speaking to them was the Light of the World. And in it, we see the unspeakable fury of the enemy of God's people (speaking of Satan) who would do anything he could to inspire the obliteration of this special tribe in order to avert the possibility of such a momentous promise of God from ever coming to fruition.

Yet, thankfully, God is in charge, and ultimately the descendants of Benjamin were able to fulfill their destiny in a most remarkable fashion. After the Babylonian captivity, they journeyed back to Palestine, occupying the land that just happened to include the future territory of Galilee, where Jesus would one day venture, there to be recognized first by the men who could all trace their heritage to the one whom God had ordained as a perpetual light in Israel.

And on a more poignant note, there is further prophetic significance concerning Benjamin's ultimate destiny, in this case in the unique capacity of a dual role, as both a seer of the light and as a light-bearer himself, because not only is Galilee located in his territory but the famed city of Bethlehem resides there as well. To better understand the relationship between the birthplace of Jesus and its links to Benjamin, one must read a brief but potent section in *Matthew*, and by way of its contents, an astonishing connection will be revealed.

In the second chapter of his Gospel, Matthew tells of Herod's response to his visit from the three Magi who were seeking the Christ Child. From the Jewish priests and teachers, Herod received disturbing news when he asked them where this Christ was supposed to come from. They replied: "In Bethlehem of Judea, for this is what the prophet has written: 'But you, Bethlehem, in the land of Judah, though you are among the least of the tribes, out of you will come a Ruler Who will be the Shepherd of My people, Israel.'"[141]

Upon learning that the Magi had deceived him concerning the whereabouts of the Child, Herod the Great ordered the slaughter of all the male babies in and around Bethlehem. Then, continued Matthew, what was spoken through the prophet Jeremiah was fulfilled: "A voice is heard in Ramah, a tremendous mourning, Rachel weeping for her children and refusing to be comforted because they are no more."[142] Rachel, beloved wife of Jacob, and mother to both Joseph and Benjamin; Rachel, who died an untimely death giving birth to Benjamin, whose descendants upon returning to Palestine resided in the very territory in which the Christ was destined to be born.

Tell me, please, am I the only one who is amazed by all this connectivity? Am I the only one to appreciate that not only is Joseph a type of Christ in this scenario but that Benjamin—who received the promise that his descendants would be perpetual light-bearers among the Tribes of Israel—can himself be seen in a dual role as a type of both Christ and His disciples? I certainly hope I am not.

Echoes in Time

FINALLY, WE TURN TO the matter of the ordeal that Joseph put Benjamin through when he tricked his brothers into believing he had stolen his royal chalice. And in reviewing this act of Joseph testing his brothers, we will again have a chance to marvel at the precision with which the apocryphal literature portrays Joseph as a type of Christ, and Benjamin as a type of the twelve disciples of Christ, who having first recognized Jesus as the Messiah were all destined to pay the ultimate price.

As we have seen in our previous examination of the sequence of events, the *Genesis* account has Joseph insisting that the ten sons of Jacob bring their youngest brother Benjamin to Egypt if they were to expect to buy any more food for their families in Palestine.[143] Therefore, in order that his children avoid starvation, Jacob reluctantly consented to allow Benjamin to journey with his brothers to Egypt where Joseph treated all his brothers to a great feast.[144] Then, unlike the *Jasher* account that has Benjamin recognizing Joseph before any of his other brothers, the *Genesis* record immediately skips ahead to the part where Joseph instructed his servants to hide his silver chalice in Benjamin's bag. Then when the brothers left for home, the Egyptians, in staging their mock surprise search, placed Benjamin under arrest, whereupon all the brothers, disheartened and dismayed, marched back to confront Joseph.

Again, biblical historians who fail to acknowledge the apocryphal account of *Jasher* can only speculate as to the exact nature of Joseph's action, causing some to correctly infer that Joseph was testing his brothers. However, as to the precise motives that led Joseph to force this test upon his brothers, based on the disparity of opinion, is apparently anybody's guess. Whether he was motivated by revenge, anger, or simply a petty desire to humiliate his brothers for what they had done to him, none can, with only *Genesis* as their guide, say for sure. Only *Jasher* takes the time to provide the parenthetical explanation to reveal the specific motive of Joseph, who said to Benjamin:

> Because I need to find out, once and for all, what is yet in the hearts of the men who threw me into that miserable pit so long ago. Don't be afraid, Benjamin, but I'm planning on taking you away from them. And if they're willing to risk their lives and fight for your sake, I'll know they've repented of what they did to me, and I'll reveal myself to them. But if they forsake you when I've taken you from them, then you'll remain with me. I'll contest their right to you as a brother and send them away empty-handed, and in the end, I'll never let them know who I really am.[145]

Fortunately, for all involved, the brothers—spearheaded by Judah—did fight to rescue Benjamin from the clutches of the viceroy of Egypt. After much discussion, heated and impassioned, Joseph finally chose to reveal himself to the entire group.

> I'm your brother Joseph, the one you sold into Egypt! But don't be distressed or angry with yourselves for selling me to this place, because it was really God Who did all this, sending me ahead of you in order to save lives. He sent me ahead so He could preserve our family on this Earth by means of a great deliverance. So it wasn't really you who sent me here but God.[146]

In this, of course, both the canonical and apocryphal accounts agree. The only thing that differs in the two versions is the critical role of Benjamin found only in *Jasher*. It is this role of the youngest son of Jacob that we will be taking a closer look at in our examination of Benjamin as a type of the disciples of Christ, together with Joseph as a type of Christ Himself. Until now, we have focused on Joseph and Jesus as the main characters of our investigation, while whatever roles that Benjamin or the disciples have played, they have done so in a merely supportive capacity. But in the final portion of this chapter, we will be elevating the bit players to that of "primary cast members," as it were, so as we turn our attention to Benjamin as a type of the disciples of Christ, we will portray them as the main characters of the following drama.

And just as a more thorough study of Abraham's offering of his son, and Joseph's revealing himself to his brothers has provided a fresh appreciation of the theme of shadow and substance, our examination of Joseph's testing of his brothers in regard to Benjamin will also provide a deeper awareness of this continuing theme. The reason for this is because, as it turns out, the testing of Joseph's brothers revealed a critically important truth to both Joseph and a world that still looks back upon this chapter in the history of God's people. And as so often happens in the process of historical hindsight, this backward look speaks not only of the character of the sons of Jacob in the life of Joseph, the viceroy of Egypt, but also of the people of Israel in the life of Jesus, the Prince of Peace.

But as usual, in order to attain this fresh awareness, one must step away from the canonical version, which has left out so many necessary elements, and return again to the apocryphal record. According to *Jasher*, after Joseph confided in Benjamin concerning the test that he had in mind for his other brothers, the viceroy instructed his servants to hide his royal cup of divination in the bag of his younger brother. Then, when his servants stopped the caravan that was headed back to Palestine, the Egyptians were to conduct their search of all the men's bags. Naturally, because they were so convinced that none of them had stolen Joseph's cup, they were quite indignant with such a baseless accusation. Boldly, they declared that if their master's chalice were found among them then the one who had stolen it would die by their own hand, and they would become slaves to the Egyptians.[147] And when Joseph's servants opened Benjamin's bag, they took out the silver cup, much to the dismay of the entire group. Horrified, the brothers all tore their clothes.

According to Louis Ginzberg, this constituted another example of divine judgment—as described in a previous chapter—whereby God repays anyone committing a sin, "coin for coin," so to speak. So, said Ginzberg, as the brothers had caused their grieving father to tear his clothes when they lied to him about Joseph being killed by a wild beast, they were now, providentially, being led in their despair to tear their own clothes as a form of divinely-inspired justice.[148]

Next came the unexpected aspect of Joseph's trial regarding his brothers. Certainly, his stated intention was to find out if they would fight for Benjamin once he had been returned to Egypt. In Joseph's view, this act of fighting for their youngest brother would provide proof enough that they had, as he put it, repented of the evil they had done to him. However, I am quite sure, despite Joseph's confirmed powers of divination, he did not anticipate the dire consequences that his act of trickery would bring down upon Benjamin. On their return journey to answer the charge of theft, however baseless it may have been, the sheer frustration of their ordeal caused an emotional implosion among the brothers, who were all convinced that this would surely bring an end to their aged father's happiness, if not his very life. Not only had they recklessly committed themselves to Egyptian servitude, but, just as Jacob had inadvertently cursed his own wife, Rachel, under similar circumstances,[149] they had also committed Benjamin into the hands of the executioner. This tragic realization, together with their fear of the potential consequences of their complicity in Joseph's disappearance, would inevitably catalyze into an all-consuming force in the brothers as they headed back to Egypt. And that was to exorcise their guilt on the one person who, in their view, represented the emotional foci of all their wrongdoing to that point: Benjamin.

In this case, their overwhelming grief, as so often happens with people under intense duress, came out in a most unexpected way. According to *Jasher*, as they were returning to face their accusers, the sons of Jacob repeatedly struck Benjamin along the way.[150] Not only did they physically assault him, but they afflicted him psychologically as well, referring to the time when his mother Rachel stole her father's religious icons.[151] Jeered one of the brothers: "You miserable thief and the son of a thief, no less. Just look at how you've shamed us, just like your mother brought shame upon our father."[152]

But through it all, Benjamin silently bore the pain of his brothers' physical and verbal abuse, and, Ginzberg added, for humbly submitting to the blows upon his back, God rewarded him.[153] In the blessing given by Moses, Benjamin was called "the beloved of the Lord," and it was appointed that the Holy Spirit would "dwell safely and securely between his shoulders."[154] That is to say, the Temple of God would reside in Jerusalem, a city famously flanked by the two most dominant of the Twelve Tribes of Israel. Above it lies the territory of Joseph, chief of the ten tribes to the north, and below it, the territory of Judah, chief of the two tribes to the south.

Yet even as the brothers outwardly unleashed their rage upon their innocent brother, inwardly they were ashamed of themselves, because in their dire predicament they could clearly see the providential hand of judgment. As the brothers stood contritely before the viceroy of Egypt, Judah uttered this veiled confession:

> How do we plead to the charge that we stole your royal cup? We know all too well we are innocent. Yet we admit we do not stand completely innocent in our present situation, because God has obviously ensnared us in this, like a creditor Who goes about seeking to collect an outstanding debt that is owed to Him.[155]

That said, let us return to our present investigation of Benjamin as a type of the disciples of Christ. In the previous scenario, notice that Benjamin not only recognized Joseph before any of his siblings, just as the disciples of Benjamite ancestry first recognized Jesus for Who He was, but there is also the added dimension of Benjamin having physically suffered at the hands of his brothers. In other words, the smiting of Benjamin by his own brothers clearly constitutes a precursor to the persecution of the disciples by the people comprising the kingdoms of both Judah and Israel. Having rejected the lordship of the humble Nazarene and eliminating Him—in their minds, at least—they next proceeded to unleash their fury upon His apparently defenseless followers.

As a matter of fact, the importance of the events surrounding the scattering and subsequent martyrdom of the disciples of Jesus goes far beyond the immediate circumstances of their collective deaths. What is most important about their otherwise tragic ends is that they were able to bequeath to humanity in death something far beyond what they could have ever given in life. To be sure, one might expect the world to be a better place as a result of the message of grace and peace that the disciples received from Jesus and then carried into every corner of the world after persecution forced them to flee Palestine. This, in and of itself, certainly could have constituted a singularly significant contribution to the enlightenment of world consciousness. Their message of love in the face of hatred, of tolerance in the face of persecution, of forgiveness in the face of condemnation, all of these revolutionary ideas might have been seen as tremendous contributions to the social development of humanity, had it not been for one overriding element to their lives that completely overshadowed everything else. Not only did these men penetrate a darkened world with the message they had received from their Teacher, but they also suffered martyrdom—all except for John, who miraculously survived every attempt on his life. That is unquestionably the ultimate legacy they have bestowed upon mankind. Had they merely wandered through life spouting their pleasantries of love, tolerance, and forgiveness to a typically disinterested population, in all probability they might have departed this life quite unharmed, yet never having made so much as a dent in the chink of the mighty armor of this God-forsaken world.

This might have remained their tepid and thoroughly forgettable legacy were it not for the fact that this bunch of heretofore-timid disciples insisted on repeating the same ludicrous story wherever they went. They all claimed, to a man, that this unassuming minister of grace and peace, Jesus of Nazareth, rose from the dead after three days and some forty days later bodily ascended to the right hand of God. So, for their persistent, unwavering position in this regard, they were forced to suffer the same agonizing death of which their Master had partaken.

In this degradation of the disciples of Jesus, one can see another type to be revealed in Scripture—this time in the humble submission of Benjamin, who as a type of the disciples of Christ similarly bore the self-loathing hatred of his kinsmen. Just as everyone is a part of the same human family, born by Noah and his sons after the Flood, then overspread into every part of the globe, this greater family of mankind turned their anger upon that band of twelve and remorselessly sought to slay them in the hopes of banishing them from their collective memory.

At this stage, one would do well to remember the words of Joseph to his younger brother regarding the conditions of his trial:

> Don't be afraid, Benjamin, but I'm planning on taking you away from them. And if they're willing to risk their lives and fight for your sake, I'll know that they've repented of what they did to me, and I'll reveal myself to them. But if they forsake you when I've taken you from them, then you'll remain with me. I'll contest their right to you as a brother and send them away empty-handed, and in the end, I'll never let them know who I really am.[156]

My point, regarding our present understanding of typology, is that not only does Joseph represent Christ, and Benjamin represent His disciples, but the other ten sons of Jacob can also be seen to have their own counterparts in this unfolding drama of the ages. In this context, they constitute types of the larger population comprising the rest of the people of Israel, that is to say, the southern kingdom of Judah, which was residing in Palestine at the time of the crucifixion of Christ, as well as the northern kingdom of Israel, which had been many centuries earlier scattered throughout Western Europe.

Understand this, then, as one considers the implications of what Joseph expressed as the terms of his trial: Not only was he was speaking about how he would presently judge his brothers, but he was also speaking prophetically as to how his future counterpart, Jesus, would judge His human family. In this instance, the words of Joseph could just as easily be uttered by Jesus Himself so that the dialog might be seen accordingly: "If they fight for your sake, Benjamin (that is, if they fight for your sake, My disciples), then I, Joseph (that is, I, Jesus), will reveal Myself to them. But if they forsake you, I'll send them away empty-handed, and in the end, they'll never know who I really am."

Considering the facts of history, can anyone seriously argue that this is not what transpired? To those who received the teaching of the disciples of Jesus—to those who fed, sheltered, and protected them—the risen Lord revealed Himself, but to those who rejected, reviled, and hunted the disciples of Jesus wherever they traveled after having been driven from Palestine, the risen Lord deprived them of His revelation. What a remarkable fulfillment, then, of the drama of Joseph, Benjamin, and the rest of his brothers.

Like echoes in time, one drama foreshadows the next, and together they convey the awesome power of a God who knows all too well that His doubting creatures will require such reassurance in the face of so many generations of withering persecution. When one considers Satan's every attempt to abort the promises of God to Abraham, Isaac, and Jacob, it is one of the great mysteries of history that the whole enterprise has not collapsed in the face of such inhuman onslaughts. No wonder that the faithful would need an even firmer bulwark against the unthinkable when, after all the obvious enemies of God had been vanquished, an enemy even more insidious than Nimrod, Pharaoh, or Goliath would raise its ugly head. Now the most ominous threat that the faithful would have to endure would be those of their own household, that is, one's own brother, sister, father, mother. No longer would the enemies of faith be so obvious, as those who were counted among the heathen, as Cain or Esau, but as among the chosen sons of Jacob, the twelve pillars of the House of Israel—as Judah from whom the scepter would arise, and Levi from whom the Law of the Lord would be born.

> And when Joseph went looking for his brothers, they saw him coming from a distance, but before he reached them, they conspired to slay him. "Look, here comes the dreamer," they said to one another. "Why don't we kill him and throw him down a pit? Then we'll see what happens to all his dreams."[157]

Who could have ever believed that something like this could be within the scope of God's plan? Certainly, it must be an aberration. Certainly, God never foresaw that something like this would happen. God forbid; He saw it all. But before it ever happened, He made sure to prepare His chosen ones for its tragic eventuality. Since time immemorial, He prepared their hearts in order that they might endure it, just as the Master Himself was to endure the same fate at the hands of His own brothers, His own creation. Before Jesus endured it, God led Joseph through it, and before the disciples of Christ, He led Benjamin. In this way, each generation of the faithful is sufficiently prepared in order that we all might resist the urge to doubt that He is yet in the midst of circumstances that so often seem devoid of God's presence. And instead of losing our grip in the heat of battle, we can hold on even tighter in the knowledge that before He led us into our own mess called "the stuff of life," many others have already trodden the same path.

Patterns of History

IT IS THIS AGE-OLD drama, then, that has laid the groundwork for anyone who has ever submitted to martyrdom for the sake of Christ—whether that involves the actual death of the physical body or merely the psychological death of our earthly hopes and dreams. As Jesus said, "I tell you truthfully that whoever seeks to saves his life will lose it, and whoever loses his life for My sake will live forever."[158] Therefore, whether actual or psychological, the death and rebirth of the self is the drama to which the call of Christ beckons His saints—one that brings us full circle in our study of biblical typology.

In doing so, we are driven to the inevitable question: What, exactly, is the point of all this so-called "typological" evidence? Simply put, because God understands how stubborn and skeptical we humans are as a species, He has deigned to communicate the vastness of His truth by way of the patterns of history, which, by their very nature, are hidden in plain sight. In other words, these patterns through time are uniquely designed to be recognized by some but not by others. In this way, the truth of God conveyed by these patterns exists like so much gold lying about in a treasure chest, but which is only open to the virtuous who will use this wisdom to find their way home, while remaining inaccessible to the unscrupulous who would squander such riches on their own selfish purposes.

Therefore, in terms of our present study on shadow and substance, we are hopefully better able to appreciate the "predicament of God," if you will, so that in this instance of Joseph and Benjamin, we can see the persecution the disciples of Jesus endured was not an unfortunate aberration in the plan of God, as it has so often been portrayed. It was, in fact, a necessary cog in the wheel of the ultimate—dare I say—evolution of the redemption of mankind.

Notice, though, I did *not* say the evolution of *mankind*. In using the word *evolution*, I am not referring to a biological process but to a historical one, which we—limited as we are by our human frame of reference—have only come to grips with as the centuries roll on and our understanding of the divine roadmap matures. What I am speaking of here is the evolution of the *redemption* of mankind, in that the salvation of the world was never something that was going to take place overnight, would never happen without the requisite sacrifices that such a miraculous redemption demanded. By necessity, it has been nothing short of an agonizingly slow procedure, much akin to that of the alleged process of biological evolution.

Mind you, however, I am not talking about the godless sort of evolution that seeks to eliminate the role of divine intervention from human history. What I am talking about is a God-ordained process of historical evolution—one that, as we have seen, necessitates the role of numerous messianic figures who lead each generation of the faithful to the next level of awareness of God's plan for humanity, which ticks away like some great celestial clock, with its persistent, methodical unfolding of time.

To reiterate: When God revealed to Adam that He would rescue him and his righteous descendants, He said it would take place in *five and a half* "days." Naturally, Adam did not understand until it was explained to him that it would not occur after just five and a half days as they were perceived in human terms. These *five and a half* "days" represented days from God's perspective, in which a day for Him constituted a thousand years from humanity's view. That is to say, the redemption that God spoke of would occur upon the completion of a period that encompassed five thousand, five hundred years. And not only did Adam misunderstand the actual time frame that was involved in this salvation, but he was also just as ignorant about its progressive nature. From God's point of view, this process of rescuing us from the clutches of death, Hell, and the grave has taken just a few days to fulfill, but from our perspective, it has required many long and excruciating centuries for this rescue effort to unfold.

So for us, this protracted process—where we are literally spoon-fed a gradual knowledge of God's redemptive plan—requires our understanding of the types of Christ in each succeeding generation. Moreover, because of the incremental nature of this awareness, it is entirely incumbent upon us to have a new revelation for each and every wave of mankind, much in the same way a traveler requires a series of milestones along the roadside so that he may complete his journey without getting lost. In other words, without a clear understanding of who—and what—God is calling us to pay attention to in our journey of discovery, which is leading us back to Paradise, we are like sheep without a shepherd, in need of the sort of guidance that only the Lord of the Sheep can provide.

This is why, when Jesus asked His disciples Who they thought He was, they were actually expressing an awareness—however limited—of this age-old dilemma concerning the gradual dispensation of God's revelation. In the disciples' responses were telling clues to anyone who has taken the time to understand that their various answers were not merely random guesses along the way to solving some sort of cosmic whodunit. So Jesus asked His disciples:

"Who do people say the Son of Man is?" And they replied: "Some say John the Baptist. Others say Elijah. And still others, Jeremiah or one of the prophets."[159]

In light of our present study, which demonstrates the extent to which both the apocryphal and canonical records converge in this exegetical tool of shadow and substance, one can better understand the disciples' view of this guiding principle. To a man, the disciples had all been born and bred into Hebraic messianic theology, and as such, they were trained to expect not just anyone who came along talking about God. They were seeking Someone Who conformed to a timeless tradition of prophetic utterances – a specific Man Whose birth and appearance among men had been precisely predicted.

Above all, they were seeking a Man Who fit a particular mold in terms of the heroes of faith who had all foreshadowed the coming of this Promised One, that is, the Son of Man spoken of so prominently in the books penned by Enoch. So when Jesus continually referred to Himself as the Son of Man, He was unreservedly confirming this tradition of messianic figures who in succeeding generations had prefigured one another until His very day, and this was the hidden meaning behind the disciples' apparently random answers, which to the untrained reader might seem like so many guesses. But to those in the know, their answers actually revealed the extent to which this messianic view of world history had been digested by the people of Israel in that day and age. And when the disciples replied that the people thought Jesus was John the Baptist risen from the dead, or instead a reincarnation of Elijah, Jeremiah, or some other messianic figure in their pantheon of heroes, they were actually testifying to something that only makes sense in light of our study of typology.

This is especially evident when Jesus Himself attested to this phenomenon to which His disciples obviously subscribed. Matthew described the scene where Jesus was speaking about John the Baptist. He asked the crowd what they had expected to see and hear when they came out to the desert to find John. "A prophet?" asked the Lord. "Yes, of course, and more than a prophet, I tell you. In fact, this is the one of whom it was written: I'll send My messenger ahead of You, who will prepare the way before You. And if you're willing to accept it, he is Elijah who was to come."[160]

Once again, Jesus in His own unique way was demonstrating the validity of typology as it is portrayed throughout *The Bible*. According to Him, God has always been in the business of foreshadowing the events of His salvation throughout the ages. So when Jesus spoke of John the Baptist as being the one of whom it was written, He was actually quoting from *The Book of Malachi*, the last book of *The Old Testament*. In it, Malachi was expressing the lament of God at the perpetual infidelity of His chosen people. Eventually growing weary of their unjustified complaints, the Lord had no choice except to turn away from them; but, in a moment of divine inspiration, Malachi prophesied a different fate for God's people:

> "See, I'll send My messenger who will prepare the way before Me. Then suddenly the Lord you're seeking will come to His Temple; the Messenger of the Covenant, Whom you desire, will come," says the Lord Almighty.
>
> But who can endure the day of His coming? Who can stand when He appears? For He'll be like a refiner's fire or a launderer's soap. He'll sit as a refiner of silver. He'll purify the Levites like gold and silver. Then the Lord will have men who will bring righteous offerings to Him, and the offerings of Judah and Jerusalem will be acceptable to the Lord, as in days gone by, as in former years.[161]

So what can one make of all this in light of our new understanding of typology? The first thing to notice is how Jesus locks into the portion of Scripture that pertains to His coming to the Temple as the Messiah Who has the way prepared for him by Elijah, whom He clearly saw as typifying John the Baptist. The next thing one cannot help but notice is that Jesus did not continue beyond the point that represented His First Coming. "Then suddenly the Lord you're seeking will come to His Temple; the Messenger of the Covenant, Whom you desire, will come," says the Lord Almighty.[162] Beyond that point of the mission of Messiah, He did not relate, because hidden in the plan of God—the mystery so difficult for the disciples to grasp—was that there were two distinct phases that comprised the coming of the Deliverer and not just one, as had always been believed by the people of Israel.

The same thing happened when Jesus read aloud from *The Book of Isaiah* in the Temple concerning the acceptable year of the Lord—a time that involved the healing, deliverance, and liberty of God's people. Closing the book, He stopped midsentence at the very point that segued to the day of God's vengeance.[163] Similarly, Jesus at that moment in history spoke only of "the Messenger of the Covenant, the One Whom you desire, Who will come." But He did not continue with the next part of the text in *Malachi* that spoke of the future phase of His coming in which His life would no longer function as a ransom for sin but as the refiner's fire.

Therefore, in both the quoting of the portion of Scripture that pertained to His present situation and the omitting of the part He chose to avoid, there was a clear and telling message, which in the context of shadow and substance reveals a great deal about the mind of Jesus. The most obvious thing is that, in light of the challenges facing Him in communicating God's unfolding plan, Jesus focused on the portions of Scripture that illuminated the most misunderstood aspect of salvation, that is, the nature of His First Coming as the Kinsman Redeemer Who would give His life as a ransom. In order to do this, Jesus made it a point to echo what He found in *The Old Testament* that spoke of this phase of His work, while avoiding what did not.

This is why Jesus sought to highlight the fact that in the person of John the Baptist, they were witnessing the very messenger of God who had been prophesied to prepare the way for the Christ Who was to come. By referring to *Malachi*, Jesus was impressing upon them the lengths to which God had undergone to first raise up Elijah so that they could more readily accept the genuineness of John's role in the redemptive scheme of things. In doing this, God was revealing an enduring truth not only to them but also to an onlooking world. The Lord of the Harvest has forever been in the business of confirming His word by means of this process of shadow and substance—a fact which, as we have seen thus far, is clearly borne out in both the canonical and apocryphal records.[164]

In light of this truth, an understanding of the history of mankind can ultimately be divided into two camps. One view states that history is a series of random actions that results in an endless array of open-ended and meaningless outcomes. The other view states that, however random the actions of humanity appear, there is an underlying principle that is unifying the events of historical time, particularly as they pertain to the so-called "people of God." According to this latter view, specific events in the past foreshadow future events in such a way that the past, the present, and the future are all intertwined so that one day they will ultimately confirm the controlling influence of the God of the Universe.

As a result, certain historical facts can, and should be, re-evaluated in terms of this unique principle of shadow and substance. When we might be tempted to view the disciples of Jesus as the most miserable of men because they were savagely persecuted and martyred for their testimony concerning the risen Christ, we might instead marvel at God's mastery over every stream of time and space. Rather than seeing the martyrdom of the Galilean disciples as a jagged edge in an otherwise perfect plan, one might look at these events in the context of God's foreshadowing them by way of Benjamin's ordeal at the hands of his jealous brothers and thereby gain a new appreciation. If one is able to grasp this connection, which clearly reveals God's hidden hand down through the corridors of history, then it might finally impart to us in today's world that there is nothing He does not anticipate in the lives of those who recognize Jesus as their long-lost brother. And though we may be called to endure our own bewildering trials and tribulations because of this same recognition, we can rest assured that—like Benjamin and his "twelve sons" before us—the Lord of Resurrection, the Lord of Life, will always be there to see us through, just as He did for them, to the very end ... and beyond.

The Stage is Set

Anchor of Faith

BEFORE WE PROCEED to *The Tales* presented in this volume, I would like to take one last opportunity to review the scenario that we have established so far. When comparing the so-called "apocryphal" texts with those of the canonical books of *The Bible,* it is abundantly clear that they are deserving of our attention and admiration. First and foremost, they are "worth their weight in gold," as it were, because of the way in which they consistently elucidate the more enigmatic portions of the Canon. Some of the greatest mysteries that have haunted humanity throughout the ages are thrown into an entirely new light when one simply takes the time to consider the implications of the apocryphal record. How did Noah get all those animals into the Ark? Why did he pronounce such a devastating curse on his grandson, Canaan, just because Ham, his father, found him lying in his tent, naked and passed out? And why would Esau, who was described as a cunning, greedy man, so casually sell away a birthright that by all accounts would have brought him untold riches and power? The answer, if the apocryphal record is to be believed, lies in the mystical power of the sheepskin garment that God provided for Adam, which was unmistakably a type of the covering that would one day be provided by none other than the Lamb of God, Jesus, Who was slain before the foundations of the world were laid.

The apocryphal literature also demonstrated its supreme importance when it revealed its ability to provide a clearer picture in terms of God's salvation of Adam by way of Abraham, Isaac, and Jacob. When God promised to rescue Adam and his descendants after The Great Five and a Half Days of prophetic time, He laid the groundwork for this rescue effort by utilizing Abraham and his son. Not only was Isaac a willing participant in volunteering himself as a burnt offering to the Lord, but as a type of God's Son in every dimension he—quite unlike *The Book of Genesis* portrays him—was a grown man, completely aware of what his father was doing when he was led to Mount Moriah. Most importantly, as a result of their audacious act of obedience, Abraham and Isaac uniquely foreshadowed the way in which the ultimate salvation of mankind would someday be carried out on Calvary.

Finally, in verifying how a study of God's usage of typology provides an anchor of faith, it was again demonstrated that the apocryphal record can be counted on. When biblical historians seek to exemplify God's preponderance for using types in *The Old Testament* to foreshadow the life of Jesus, they consistently turn to Joseph—the dreamer so despised by his brothers. In the life of Joseph, it is said, one can find, more than anyone else in Scripture, a type of Christ Who was to come. The only problem is: There are so many elements in the life of Jesus that are missing from the canonical record of Joseph's life that this prophetic correspondence between the two becomes very difficult—if not impossible—to accept. However, many of the important elements that are missing from the received texts can be found in the apocryphal literature when one simply takes the time to examine it.

For example, according to *Genesis,* there was no distinction in the sons of Jacob's hatred of Joseph. All his brothers, it states, conspired to slay him in order to nullify the fulfillment of his dreams.[165] Therefore, in order for the life of Joseph to represent a genuine type of Christ—as biblical scholars purport—then all the Children of Israel, as they came to occupy Palestine in the time of Jesus, would also be expected to hate and reject the Nazarene as well. But this is not what history has recorded, because a remnant of Israelites certainly did believe, receive, and love Him. Why is that important? It is important because it just so happens that the Galileans at the time of Christ were actually descendants of none other than Benjamin, and when *Jasher* reveals that Benjamin never resented Joseph and that he recognized him before any of the other brothers, one comes face to face with exactly the kind on correlation one might expect to find in the way of typology. In this prophetic correspondence between Benjamin and the Galilean disciples, we have yet another example of the apocryphal literature's ability to undergird this remarkable aspect of the divinely-appointed dramas involving typology.

A Universal Language

IN ALL THESE REMARKABLE ways, the apocryphal literature was found to be a valuable ally in the war against skepticism and doubt. This eventually leads one, then, to ask the next series of inevitable questions: Why, exactly, is the God of *The Bible* so interested in typology, in shadow and substance? What is the point of all this melodramatic subterfuge, anyway? Is there no easier way to get His message across? The answer, I am convinced, is quite an obvious one. But just as important as it is to answer questions like these, it is even more important to provide an answer that lends itself to solving the greater mystery of how we are to confirm God's control and faithfulness in the context of the five *sacred* things. As you will recall, we have thus far established a connection between two of the five things, that is, between The Ark of the Covenant and *The Septuagint Bible,* in that The Ark's dimensions correspond to the *Septuagint's* chronology, and together with the prophecy of The Great Five and a Half Days, we see a clear-cur connection that binds them together. But en route to connecting the other three of the five things in question, we must first understand the underlying issue that adequately explains why God is so involved in communicating His message of salvation by way of all this so-called "melodramatic subterfuge." And in providing such an answer, it is my earnest hope to provide the hidden connection between the five *sacred* things in such a way that there can be no other way to "see" them ever again. However, before I simply blurt this answer out, let me first take a moment to outline what must surely precede this answer. That is to say, before one can entertain a possible answer to such questions, one must first understand the underlying problem that the answer is intended to address.

To begin with, the initial hurdle one is confronted with has everything to do with the nature of communication. By that I mean that it is a problem that rests squarely on the shoulders of the fact that we are neither God-like, nor are we capable of communicating in a God-like manner. As a result, we, as a species, are devoid of the necessary tools to communicate with a God-like being. To which one might reasonably respond: Of course, that is a given; so what is your point? My point is this. If we lack the ability to communicate with God, as we normally communicate with one another, then how might God choose to communicate with us? He is, after all, the One Who first conceived of this thing we understand as language, is He not? Certainly He does not lack the ability to communicate. Therefore, if anyone has a problem with this process of communication between God and humanity, I would have to assume that the problem lies with us.

From an awareness of this ironic nature of communication, which affects not only mankind's relationship with God but also with itself, one is confronted with the oldest complaint ever introduced into a conversation that ponders whether or not *The Bible* can be trusted as a valid source of truth. Naturally, of course, this complaint is argued all the more passionately by those who proudly embrace their skepticism in the face of anything that even remotely postulates the communicative power of a higher being such as God. Their arguments generally run as follows: How can anyone believe in the divine origin of a book that was written by so many different people, living in different times and places, and speaking different languages? Everyone is familiar with the infamous parlor game where a line of people attempt to convey a message introduced at one end of the line and then passed on from person to person until eventually it comes out completely different on the other end. Is not this exactly what has happened with the countless regurgitations of *The Bible*?

To which I would respond: Yes, madam, or, yes, sir. I completely understand your dilemma. I would never think to argue with you on such a point. On this one thing we can all agree. This is certainly the true nature of the problem we are facing when it comes to depending on a compendium of books that have clearly been translated via a plenitude of language frames. Only a fool would try to dismiss such a valid criticism; a fool, or worse still, a simpleton—neither of which I am sure God needs to affirm His ability to communicate with His own creation. Therefore, any attempt to unravel such a mystery without addressing such an obvious objection would constitute a complete failure on the part of anyone who was endeavoring to validate the truth of *The Bible*.

How sad, then, that so many sincere people, wrestling with these same issues, have been forced to endure the same old stale clichés, like "You just gotta believe, brother!" Not to mention, "There are just some things in life that require blind faith!" And worst of all, "Blessed are those who believe without seeing." What a tragedy that such bold pronouncements constitute the kind of faith that we are typically being told the Scriptures are calling the true believer to embrace, yet, ironically, nowhere in *The Bible* does God demand that someone believe simply for the sake of believing. And before anyone tries to write me off as being anti-biblical, let me first explain what I mean by that.

The initial thing that should be addressed is that neither of the first two statements even appear in *The Bible*, although over the course of time they have insinuated themselves by way of the traditions of mankind, just as the phrase "God helps those who help themselves" has somehow passed from being something that was quoted by Benjamin Franklin to it having been uttered by the Lord Himself. But trust me when I tell you: Nowhere are these words to be found in Scripture. However, a variation of the last of these admonitions, "Blessed are those who believe without seeing," can be found there; the problem is, though, it is almost always quoted out of context and consequently becomes the basis for all sorts of mischief that might otherwise be avoided if only one is willing to examine the actual text as it is written in *The Bible*.

There is a critically important maxim in regard to interpreting such statements of truth, not only those contained in Scripture but all truth in general, and that is: "Text without context is error." In other words, even genuine truth, when it is lifted out of its proper context, no longer conveys the original truth it once contained but is now, in point of fact, a clear distortion of said truth and is, instead, error. Such a maxim would apply in the following manner. When anyone contemplating the question of God's faithfulness is challenged by the preceding admonitions calling for "blind faith," the first thing they should do is ask: What is the specific setting in which such a statement was made? And in doing so, one might finally penetrate the veil of disinformation that centuries of misapplication have engendered. Take for example, then, this classic misconception of *The Bible*: "Blessed are those who believe without seeing." As it stands, all by itself, it constitutes nothing less than an outright indictment upon anyone who would dare question the veracity of Scripture as it is presented from any number of pulpits; and as such, it stands as a nearly impenetrable shield against any objection offered in opposition to some pet theory of biblical analysis that is being espoused in the name of almighty truth, no matter how spurious that theory might sound to thinking, rational human beings. So it has been; so it ever shall be, amen. But, wait, not so fast.

Fortunately, for the sake of all those with the courage to investigate such matters, there is a sure-fire method for bringing down such a perennial house of cards; and it proceeds as follows. When trying to decipher the genuine truth of any given biblical pronouncement, ask yourself three simple yet revealing questions: Who said it? To whom was it said? And in what situation was it said? In this particular case, Jesus said it, the person He said it to was His disciple, Thomas, and the situation in which He said it was that time right after Christ's resurrection when He was revealing Himself to His disciples, each in their own turn, with Thomas, according to *The Gospel of John*, being the last. It was in this context, then—after Thomas had infamously refused to believe that Christ had risen from the dead until he could touch where the nails had been, and put his hands into His side—that Jesus said to him: "Because you have seen Me, you have believed; blessed are those who have not seen Me and yet have believed."[166]

So, now that we have properly set the stage, as it were, ask yourself again: How is the admonition that "you just gotta believe without seeing" altered by drawing out its context in this way? Seen against the backdrop of this full-orbed scene, several questions instantly spring to mind. Is Jesus saying this to someone who did not have the benefit of being one of His twelve disciples? Are we to dismiss the fact that Thomas had walked and talked with Jesus for three and a half years? And finally, are we to assume that Thomas witnessed none of the miracles that He had performed in all that time? Of course not. So, far from admonishing someone to believe in Him without having had a personal awareness of His faithfulness, what we are presented with, instead, is a scene in which Jesus is addressing someone whose belief was entirely predicated on this direct connection with Him in terms of everything that Thomas *had seen* up to that point in time. In other words, the admonition to believe without seeing, which is generally aimed at the so-called "unbeliever," when examined in its proper context, it is actually an admonition to all the doubting Thomases of this world to never forget "in the dark" what you previously saw "in the light." It is not so much an admonition to believe without seeing, then, as it is a call to embrace all the more what you already know to be true, even in the darkest of times when one's confidence in the truth inevitably wanes, just as it had in those dark days immediately following Christ's death.

And as if to make this point perfectly clear, the last verse of John's Gospel provides us with one last piece of this contextual puzzle, when it states, "Jesus performed many other signs that were not recorded in this book, but these have been written so that you may believe that Jesus is the Messiah, the Son of God, and that by believing you may have life in His Name."[167] So, if Jesus is only impressed by those individuals who "believe without seeing," to the apparent exclusion of all others, then why would John even bother to make such a statement? And if God expects people to "believe" without the benefit of their first being made aware of His faithfulness, then what is the point of providing mankind with a written record of that faithfulness—you know, that thing we all know and love called *The Bible*? How odd that such a classic misconception as the necessity of "blind faith," which is itself blindly held forth as the supreme example of God's call, falls apart so easily when one simply takes the time to investigate its original context.

One's belief in the Lord, then, as it is found throughout Scripture, is always predicated upon a person's awareness of His control and faithfulness, which, through the sheer weight of it being adequately communicated, engenders a faith in the God of *The Bible*. Faith, as it is biblically defined, comes from a Greek word, *pisteuo*, which being translated means "to trust," as in, to trust someone or something in a tangible way, as one trusts a staff or cane by leaning on it. No one blindly leans on a non-existent staff or cane. Understood this way, one is better able to see that "blind faith" in God is an absurd myth never once found in *The Bible*. Moreover, I defy anyone to prove me wrong—assuming, of course, that they are willing to provide the context for such a claim. As just demonstrated, without slicing and dicing Scripture into random bits, one simply cannot accomplish such a feat.

When *The Book of Hebrews* speaks of Abraham believing in God as One Who is invisible, advocates of "blind faith" are quick to point to this verse as proof of their absurd notion. The only problem with this logic is it completely avoids the fact that Abraham repeatedly experienced God's ability to rescue him. When Nimrod threw him into his fiery furnace, he walked around inside it for three days, much to everyone's amazement, without even being singed.[168] But wait. One might argue: That story is nowhere in the canonical record. How do you expect anyone to believe in something like that? Well, it just so happens that an event just like it is recorded in the third chapter of *The Book of Daniel*, when Shadrach, Meshach, and Abednego miraculously survived their own harrowing ordeal of being thrown into Nebuchadnezzar's fiery furnace after they had refused to bow down to his image of gold. If I am not mistaken, these two events stand together as yet another example of the kind of connectivity of which I am attempting to convey. In fact, this kind of parallelism, which is found throughout Scripture—both canonical and apocryphal—will comprise a portion of the argument that I will be attempting to formulate here. More will be said about that later.

In the meantime, I mention this here in the context of refuting the idiotic notion of "blind faith" as opposed to the kind exhibited by the heroes of faith who, like Abraham, were led through a series of increasingly difficult challenges, each of which elicited "real faith" in a God

Who demonstrated His faithfulness by repeatedly rescuing them. Just as we love the Lord because He first loved us;[169] likewise, we have faith in Him because He first was faithful to us. That is to say, the only kind of faith that *The Bible* is describing is one that occurs as a reaction to God's faithfulness to His promises, whereas anything else merely perverts the truth of a biblically-oriented faith—a perversion that leads someone to either reject the necessity of faith in God, or, worse still, embrace the fallacy of blind faith, both of which lead to a needlessly tragic end.

Having defined the true nature of faith, parenthetically, let us return to where we left off. Moments ago, we were contemplating the yawning chasm between the infinite mind of the Creator and the finite mind of mankind, and with it the question of how we, in the twenty-first century, are to validate the truth of Scripture if the only evidence left to us consists of books written long ago and communicated down to the present day via an array of translations. Admittedly, when one addresses the dilemma in these terms, our problem certainly does appear hopeless, does it not? Yet this is exactly the series of obstacles that the biblical record as a whole is claiming to surmount. But how? Could it be that there is actually a key to unlocking the mysteries of *The Bible* as so many throughout the ages have suggested? And if there really is a key of interpretation, then why has mankind been unable so far to establish some kind of consensus with this process?

Strangely enough, I believe, the answer to such a conundrum is really quite simple, if by the word simple one inserts the word *non-mystical*, because, contrary to popular opinion, finding the answer does not involve delving into the murky realm of *Bible* codes but rather into the all-too-human domain of the cinema. For in the cinema, one is presented with a very specific language—a language not comprised of words but a dialectic of visual imagery, that is to say, a series of images made more meaningful via their sequential arrangement. In the more than one hundred years of its existence, this international art form has managed to accomplish what was best described by American film director D.W. Griffith. "We've gone beyond Babel, beyond words. We've found a universal language."[170] As a result, this language of the cinema—composed entirely of images, of symbols, of meanings—is uniquely capable of imparting a message that transcends any known language barrier. Moreover, it is this simple usage of symbolism to convey meaning—as opposed to a more arcane approach—that most closely resembles the way in which *The Bible* manages to articulate its deepest truths.

Consider this: Prior to the industrial revolution of the late eighteenth century, the world remained compartmentalized—geographically, culturally, ideologically. As a result of industrialization, there came an explosion in mass transportation technology in the form of steam locomotion, which within a few short decades laid the foundation for everything that followed. With electrification came the telegraph, the telephone, the phonograph, the automobile, the cinema, the radio, and the airplane, which physically connected the world in a manner previously unimaginable. But, while all these inventions abolished the barriers between physical spaces, none of them could provide the much-needed means to eliminate the psychological barriers that remained. Consequently, a world without geographic barriers has only managed to create an environment where previously disparate regions of the globe began to commingle in unanticipated ways. Rather than unite the world, the abolition of borders has done far more harm than good, as evidenced by two world wars, followed by decades of regional war ever after.

Amidst all this technologically-induced strife, only one invention has succeeded in rising above the mayhem of clashing titans, of south rising against north, of east rising against west. Only the cinema has provided humanity with the potential to bridge the psychological gap that was laid bare in the wake of the tearing asunder of physical barriers, and only masters of the cinema have learned over the course of time to perfect an art form that has managed to transcend all cultural and ideological boundaries, proving once and for all that the peoples of the world are not so different after all. North, south, east, west: When seen through the eyes of the universal language of the cinema, these so-called "pockets of ideology" bear a striking, if not haunting, similarity to one another.

It is this unique language of imagery, symbolism, and meaning, then, that, I am convinced, is the key to understanding God's message in *The Bible*; not the vague, surreptitious sort that only a computer genius can hope to decipher, but one that is laid bare for all to see on pages of black and white. This is why, when pioneers of the cinema sought to distance their product from their childish reputation as mere nickelodeons, they did so by cleverly embedding the universal message inspired by Holy Writ. By virtue of this infusion, the world's first patently modern art form soon took on an unprecedented maturity. Inspired by the timeless tapestry of biblical history, prescient producers breathed new life into their creations: Heroes and heroines alike strove against overwhelming odds, brother pitted jealous will against brother, merciless overlords sought to enslave the free, and amidst it all, the Divine One dipped His benevolent hand into the well of human misery. In theaters around the globe, themes of tragedy and hope, of crime and punishment, of ruin and rebirth, resonated deeply, from city to city, state to state, and country to country.

Furthermore, in a truly ironic fashion that I am sure no one has yet to fully appreciate in terms of its prophetic significance, for its first thirty years of existence the cinema was forged into being without uttering a single, spoken word. The silver screen was above all a silent one. To be sure, the written word was periodically inserted, but primarily it was an art form that conveyed its story entirely by way of a series of visual images. Concluded British film critic David Robinson: "This was the most truly international era in which was created a new art of great subtlety and sophistication."[171] Through all manner of metaphor, allegory, and simile, the cinema perfectly conveyed its poetic vision in a way that could be understood in every corner of the globe without an ounce of its intended message ever being lost to mistranslation.

This to me is what God—in His preponderance for using types and shadows—had in mind when He set out to communicate His truth to mankind. He speaks through dramas that transcend interpretation, that is to say, through universally recognizable symbols of dramatic significance that supersede the brute limitations of the intellect and speak directly to the heart and soul of humanity. This is why *The Bible* repeatedly focuses on the enduring elements that constitute the human condition in all its ignominious glory—of courage and cowardice, of sacrifice and greed, of faith and doubt, of honesty and deceit, of revenge and mercy, of loyalty and betrayal, of love and hate. This is why the truths of Scripture are so often couched in double and triple parallels of events that span many generations, as when the likes of Isaac, Joseph, Moses, and Jonah all foreshadow the life of Jesus.

In this way, the Lord demonstrates His acute awareness that we, as members of a fallen race, require this process of foreshadow and payoff to apprehend the true nature of the Divine, much like an audience sitting in a darkened theater requires the necessary clues to penetrate the mystery that is being played out on the screen before it. And though we can only gaze in rapt anticipation upon these iconic dramas, as those who "look through a glass, darkly," we are still able to grasp the truth conveyed in these scattered moments through time, and perceive in them a remarkable synergy that no mere mortal could have ever contrived.

Milestones of the Millennia

TO ILLUSTRATE THIS point, we will now take some time to examine one of the most controversial—and therefore most important—concepts to be found in *The Bible*, and due to the sweeping implications of this particular subject, it is also the one that most people have the greatest difficulty with, that of the resurrection of the dead. For example, just try to point out that of all the so-called "good and wise" men who have ever lived and died throughout the ages—men like Jesus, Buddha, Confucius, and Mohammed—only one among them ever predicted that three days after His death He would rise from the grave.

As a matter of course, everyone is perfectly willing to admit that Jesus was a good and wise man, considering all the wonderful things He said and did, but that He actually rose from the dead, that is where they draw the line. Never mind that if Jesus did not rise from the grave,

He could not be called good and wise, because anybody who claimed that he would rise from the dead was either a liar, in that he expected people to believe something he knew he was incapable of doing, or crazy, in that he actually believed the impossible about himself. Either way, such a man could never be deemed good and wise, and would therefore have to be removed from this pantheon of good and wise men.

How, then, does one go about determining the possibility of such an event? Well, one might argue, posterity has received the testimony of the Galilean disciples, not to mention upwards of five hundred additional eyewitnesses who also testified to the resurrection of Jesus.[172] But many would insist that such antiquated reports, dating back more than two thousand years, constitute evidence far too tenuous from which to deliver such an important verdict. And if such claims of Jesus' resurrection were actually admitted as testimony, one could still never rule out the possibility that once things had failed to pan out as predicted these so-called "eyewitnesses" simply lied in an attempt to save face. Certainly even the most ardent believer must consider such likelihoods, if they are willing to be honest with themselves. So how can the sincere investigator of such mysteries ever hope to penetrate so many layers of historical uncertainty?

Fortunately for us, our investigation does have the one thing that we have presently been learning about, insofar as the Lord of Time has established His own unique way of undergirding our pathetically human approach to such dilemmas. There are, in essence, still the dramas that transcend interpretation. What does that mean in terms of whether or not Jesus might have risen from the grave? It means that when I see someone literally gag on the sheer improbability that a man might actually have raised from the dead, I am perfectly happy to begin addressing the problem with the same systematic approach that I believe God has provided throughout the entire *Bible*. First and foremost, I will focus on the way in which the theme of the resurrection of the dead permeates Scripture from beginning to end. In other words, in the resurrection of Jesus of Nazareth, we are by no means being confronted with an isolated incident, an event that illogically appears from out of nowhere, an apparent aberration that has no historical antecedent. Let me demonstrate what I mean by that.

It has been said that *The Bible* is above all a book of miracles, and certainly there is no greater miracle depicted within its pages than that of the resurrection of the dead. In *The Old Testament*, Elijah raised the son of a widow.[173] After him, Elisha was involved in two resurrections: The first time occurred when he raised the Shunemite's son;[174] the second time, when a corpse was placed in Elisha's sepulcher and came back to life after just touching the bones of Elisha.[175] In *The New Testament*, Jesus famously raised Lazarus, among others;[176] God raised Jesus;[177] and Peter raised Tabitha.[178]

Yet oddly enough, though all these passages record the resurrection of various individuals, their occurrence throughout Scripture still seems so random somehow. That is to say, this person resurrected over here, and that one resurrected over there, and then, oh, yeah, Jesus resurrected, too. But never before—in my experience, at least—have any of the "lesser resurrections," if you will, ever been examined in the context of the greater resurrection of Jesus. Never before have I been told that the proof of Christ's resurrection could be bolstered by virtue of the knowledge that before He rose from the grave, others rose as a God-ordained "shadow of things to come." That is until now; because it is my earnest hope that with the next cataloging of risen ones, it might finally provide this added dimension in determining whether or not the resurrection of Christ should be seen as merely an isolated, illogical, aberrational event.

To properly do this, we will again find ourselves turning to the apocryphal record, because, as has already been demonstrated, when looking only to the narratives found in the Biblical Canon, one is left with the aforementioned haphazard view of the resurrection of the dead. But when one takes the time to balance our view of Scripture, which involves including information from the apocryphal record, one is suddenly provided with a much more complete picture of what the God of *The Bible* clearly intends as His overall intention for humanity.

Case in point is mankind's first experience with the concept of the resurrection of the dead, which for some strange reason was completely skipped over in *Genesis*. Nevertheless, while this critical detail was omitted from the canonical book, this omission does not occur in the apocryphal record. In fact, it seems as if it is the most important theme of *The First Book of Adam and Eve*. Of course, this does not seem so hard to believe when one simply puts "flesh and blood," as it were, on that first couple who alone knew what it meant to fall from grace. What else would Adam and Eve be more obsessed with than the restoration of the life-force they had been deprived of the moment they ate from the Tree of Knowledge? This is never more evident than immediately after they found themselves exiled from the Garden of Eden. They were so heartbroken, their behavior bordered on the suicidal. Like desperate, confused children, Adam and Eve tried to entice God to let them back into the garden, again and again, but far from achieving their earnest desire, they instead suffered the dire consequences of their misguided recklessness, which led to their deaths on numerous occasions. Only through the direct intervention of the pre-incarnate Christ was the couple spared each and every time. Appearing to Adam and Eve by the same name that John, the gospel writer, would later describe Him,[179] the Word of God raised them from death, repeatedly explaining to them that He was restoring their lives so they could fulfill the years God had decreed for them.[180]

The second example of the resurrection of the dead, and the first to be found in the received texts, is one that is expressed in allegorical terms. "And Enoch walked with God, and he was no more because God took him."[181] But because the description in *Genesis* is so sparse, one is again forced to turn to the apocryphal record to better understand how this event typifies resurrection. In *The Secrets of Enoch*, we find that when Enoch was taken up to Heaven, his family had no idea where he was. In their view, Enoch was the ancient equivalent of the modern-day "missing person," having vanished without a trace.[182] Enoch's family—assuming the worst—thought perhaps that a wild beast had carried him away. Then as suddenly as he had disappeared, Enoch was back among them once again, alive and well. So from their view, Enoch's family received him back into their lives as one returning from the great beyond, as though he had been raised from the dead.

Yet another type of the resurrection of the dead occurred in *Jasher*, where we read that Abraham as a young man survived for three days in the fiery furnace into which Nimrod threw him for brashly insulting him to his face.[183] Although this story does not appear in the canonical record, a similar ordeal by fire does appear there. In *The Book of Daniel*, three Hebrew men, Shadrach, Meshach, and Abednego, survived a parallel event at the hands of Nebuchadnezzar.[184] In both cases, we can see a striking similarity in symbolism, as together they form a powerful allusion of the three days in Hades that Christ was to endure between the point of His death and subsequent resurrection.

Next, we come to, by far, the most familiar type of the resurrection of the dead to be found in *The Old Testament*, which involves the story of Abraham and Isaac. For all intents and purposes, both men went to Mount Moriah with the firm assumption that there would be a death involved. As it turned out, they were right. To be sure, Isaac was bound and laid upon an altar. To be sure, Abraham was poised, knife at the ready, to slay his beloved son, but instead of Isaac dying, it was a ram that was, in the end, sacrificed in his place—the one that God provided as a type of the Lamb of God slain before the foundations of the world were laid.[185] In this way, Isaac experienced a kind of psychological death and resurrection in a foreshadowing event that would prepare the hearts and minds of humanity for the sacrificial death that Christ would one day undergo in reality and not merely symbolically.

The next well-known type of the resurrection of the dead took place when the brothers of Joseph threw him in a pit, sold him into Egyptian bondage, and told their father Jacob that a wild beast had killed him.[186] Unbeknownst to his brothers, however, Joseph's life took on a new dimension in the land of his servitude. Through a miraculous turn of events, he threw off his chains and ascended to a position of great power as the viceroy of Egypt.[187] Then according to the providence of God, Joseph's family was forced to travel to Egypt because of the terrible famine raging in Canaan.[188] And like Enoch being restored to his family, alive and well, Joseph revealing himself to his brothers bears a striking similarity to the moment when the risen Christ would miraculously return from the dead and be received by His astonished disciples.[189] In this way, Joseph's trip from the pit to the throne perfectly parallels the same journey that Jesus was destined to make in which He was cast into the pit of Hades, yet ultimately rose again and ascended to the right hand of the Father.[190]

In regards to this theme of the journey of Christ—one which took Him from the lowest realms of the underworld to the highest point of creation—we come to another example of this recurring drama. This time we have but a slice of a man's life; still it is a very potent slice in terms of its prophetic meaning. The man I am speaking of is Moses. In this case, however, we are not interested in the full-blown deliverer of Israel who boldly raised his staff and parted the Red Sea, or the great lawgiver who strode down from Mount Sinai to defy those who were worshiping the Golden Calf. No, what we will be focusing on this time is the story of Moses as a babe wrapped in the blanket of a Hebrew slave.

The scene is a familiar one. Yet ironically, the reason that this aspect of Moses' life is so familiar is not as one might expect because of what we read in the canonical version of *The Bible*. In fact, anyone who relies on *The Book of Exodus* for this part of the story might otherwise miss out on the fact that this portion of Moses' life bears a striking resemblance to the birth of Jesus of Nazareth. In this, I have to admit, I would have been just as wrong, because when I set out to draw from this well of typological truth concerning the lives of messianic figures of *The Old Testament*, I simply assumed that my memory of it had been derived from *Exodus*. But much to my considerable shock it was not. Before too long, however, I did locate the flaw in my thinking. Eventually, it occurred to me that the actual source for the connection I had in mind between the lives of Moses and Jesus—as it pertains to the slaughter of the Innocents in the reigns of Pharaoh and Herod—came not by way of a book written by Moses but a film produced by Hollywood.

The movie I am referring to is the 1956 classic *The Ten Commandments*, starring Charlton Heston and Yul Brynner. Every year, at the same time, this movie is replayed. For Christians, it is Easter; for Jews, it is Passover. For everyone else, the fact that both of these holidays occur at the same time is merely a coincidence. From my point of view, however, one that is constantly seeking out the patterns in history, events like these are never coincidental. To me, they represent milestones of the millennia—sacred signposts of a God Who is continually providing humanity with a clearly marked path in the unfolding drama of the ages. What we are dealing with, then, in both Easter and Passover, is yet another example of parallel events, which together form one of the major linchpins in proving that Jesus of Nazareth is none other than the Lamb of God sacrificed as a propitiation for the sins of the world.

Clearly, it was God's intention to foreshadow this prophetic connection when He instructed Moses to institute the feast of Passover on the eve of the Exodus of Israel from Egypt. There was the nation Israel; there was the Passover lamb; and there was Egypt. In this timeless drama, Israel was a type of all those who would put their trust in God, who "ate the bread of haste, with staff in hand and sandals on their feet," ready to move, though still apparently enslaved to Egypt.[191] The sacrificial lamb was a type of Christ, Who would one day shed His blood, just as Isaac had offered to do on Mount Moriah. Finally, Egypt was a type of sin—that is, the world, the flesh, and the devil—which holds all mankind in its seemingly perpetual vice-like grip. These three elements came together, then, in the Passover feast that Moses instituted, which was nothing less than the nationalization of Abraham's actions on Mount Moriah, when he sacrificed a ram instead of his son, Isaac. Ever after, the priests of Israel continued this tradition throughout the life of the nation, right up until the time that Christ strode upon the stage of world history.

Of all this Jesus was clearly mindful when He chose to go to Jerusalem. Prior to this decision, which He knew would trigger events that would lead to His crucifixion, He had refused to make the trip, because, as He put it: "It's not My time to go yet."[192] More to the point, when Jesus finally did decide to go, He did it specifically at Passover time.[193] Even the Jewish authorities who opposed Him understood that it would not be in their best interests to have Him crucified as the Paschal lambs were being slain in the Temple because they were justifiably worried it might lend credence to His claim to be the Lamb of God.[194] Yet crucify Him they did, right on schedule, according to the "set times" of the Lord.

In this, we see another prime example of parallelism in biblical typology. Not only have the many messianic figures represented types of Christ throughout history, but all the blood sacrifices that have ever been carried out down through the ages have also been part of God's plan in foreshadowing the ultimate sacrifice, which is Jesus, the Lamb of God. This prophetic timeline—often referred to by theologians as the scarlet thread of redemption—began when the lion killed those first sheep that provided adequate coverings for Adam and Eve. It continued when Abraham sacrificed the ram on Mount Moriah, through the days of the first Passover feast on the eve of the Exodus, right up to that fateful day when Jesus shed His blood at Calvary.

With all this mind, let us return to the movie *The Ten Commandments*. Prior to this, we have pointed out how events in the life of Moses and Jesus were connected in ways that are similar to Enoch, Abraham, Isaac, Joseph, David, and Jonah. Now we come to another instance of parallel lives. In this case, though, it is not one that pertains to types of Christ but to types of Anti-Christ. It is well known to biblical historians that both Pharaoh and Herod the Great instigated a slaughter of the Innocents in each of their days. In this diabolical connection, we have another clear example of typological truth—although a decidedly negative version. Before Herod sought to eliminate the birth of the Christ Child, Pharaoh similarly sought to eliminate the child Moses, who was himself a type of Christ. Strangely enough, though, I had always assumed that these two events were linked in the received text, but I soon realized how mistaken I had been. Come to find out: The story as I remembered it was only hinted at in *Exodus*; and I do mean hinted. Like so many of the canonical versions, the text is so deficient of detail that in retrospect I am shocked at the extent to which my own memory had embellished what is hardly there in the traditional narrative. Let me demonstrate what I mean.

In the gospel record, we do find an explicit version of the attack on the male babies of Israel—one of the last acts to be instigated by Herod the Great. As the story goes, Herod received news from the Wise Men of the star that purportedly heralded the birth of the long-awaited Christ. In response to this news, the king ordered that all the male Israelite children under two years of age should be killed in order to prevent this legendary Child from ever growing up to replace him.[195] In this regard, the canonical version of *The New Testament* is as explicit as any movie that Hollywood has ever produced on the subject, such as *King of Kings* or *The Greatest Story Ever Told*. However, what I found so surprising was that I thought *The Old Testament* was just as explicit when it came to the events surrounding the birth of Moses.

The story—as I had remembered it—went as follows. Fearful of a prophecy of a Hebrew deliverer who was destined to free his prized slaves, the king of Egypt unleashed a terrible pronouncement: All the male babies born to the Hebrew slaves were to be drowned in the Nile River. By doing this, Pharaoh was convinced he would rid his kingdom of the threat of a potential slave revolt that might be led by this so-called "Hebrew Messiah." In my mind, then, I could clearly see a link between the prophecies of the births of both Moses and Jesus. To me, all this made perfect sense in light of everything I had learned so far about typological consistency. In other words, if Christ really did represent the fulfillment of all prophecy, then one might naturally expect to find examples of births of messianic figures involving prophetic utterances that would foreshadow His eventual birth. Most notably among these, in *The Old Testament*, is Samson, of whom it was said that "he will be a Nazarite from his mother's womb, and will begin to deliver Israel out of the hand of the Philistines."[196] And, in *The New Testament*, there is John the Baptist, whose birth clearly foreshadowed that of his cousin, Jesus, because it was said of John that "he will be great in the sight of the God, and will be filled with the Spirit of the Lord, even from his mother's womb."[197] The surprising thing, however, was when I examined *Exodus* to confirm this correspondence concerning the birth of Moses, I found that this aspect of the story simply was not there. According to it, the Egyptians were only concerned with their inability to control the Hebrew population in their midst, which then led to their plan to rid themselves of the threat by drowning all the male infants.[198] In short, there was not a single word in the received text about the prophecy of a deliverer destined to lead the Hebrews to freedom.

So where had I come upon this idea that the events of Moses' birth were a mirror image of Jesus' birth? If it was not in *Exodus*, then where had it come from? That was when I finally realized that I had gotten the idea not from Scripture but from Hollywood. In reality, the idea had been planted in my mind by the 1956 film *The Ten Commandments*. Thoroughly disappointed, I felt I had no choice but to abandon this train of thought and move on to something else, when suddenly it dawned on me. Maybe I should check the account of Moses' birth in *Jasher*. That was when I discovered that, once again, the apocryphal record had provided me with the necessary cog in the wheel that made my "typological machine" run. There it was in the sixty-seventh chapter: The Pharaoh at the time, just like his father before him in the days of Joseph, had had a nightmare. In his dream, the king saw an old man with weighing scales in his hands. Onto one side of the scales, the man placed all the noblest men of Egypt, while, onto the other side, he placed a kid goat. And much to the amazement of Pharaoh, this single, insignificant goat outweighed all of his best men. When he woke up, the king immediately gathered all of his wise men so that they might interpret such a confusing dream. Then Balaam, the son Beor, stepped forward—of whom it would later be famously recorded that he had a conversation with his donkey. According to Balaam:

> This could only mean one thing, My Pharaoh. Something terrible is going to happen to Egypt someday; and all because a son is going to be born to Israel who will destroy Egypt and everyone who lives there. And afterward, he'll lead the Israelites out of Egypt with a mighty hand. So, if I were you, I'd make sure you do everything you can right now to destroy the hopes and expectations of these people before they ever have a chance to rise up and crush the land of Egypt.[199]

So there it was: The connection I had been seeking. Until now, I had always thought that the parallel between the births of Moses and Jesus had been derived from the received text, but not anymore. To my amazement, I realized it had actually come from one of my favorite movies. Even more amazing, it now seemed more obvious than ever that filmmakers had not only borrowed from the canonical texts in their attempts to make their movies more meaningful, but they had turned to apocryphal literature as well.[200]

Parenthetically, it should be noted that this is not the first time that artists have been known to draw from apocryphal literature to enrich their art. According to Philip Jenkins, professor of history at Baylor University, the same thing happened repeatedly in the case of *The Gospel of Nicodemus*, in which the narrative of Christ's descent into the underworld after His death—referred to as the Harrowing of Hell—provided "rich opportunities for dialog and dramatic interaction."[201] As Jenkins observed:

> The Nicodemus story spread across Christendom. In the visual arts, the Harrowing story was portrayed in thousands of paintings and carvings, windows and wall-paintings, which reached a climax between 1380 and 1520, the years leading up to the Reformation. Major Renaissance artists who treated the theme included Andrea Montegna, about 1470, and the German Albrecht Dürer, about 1510. In the Eastern Church, the common *ikon* theme of the *Anastasis*, or Resurrection, depicts the Harrowing and the liberation of the righteous dead…
>
> The Harrowing was a central theme of the vernacular literatures that emerged across Europe from the twelfth century onward. It featured in every major language, in plays, sagas, chronicles, pious poems, and bloody epics…

> Each country developed its own Harrowing mythology. The story was sung in French verse, and it drew the attention of Europe's greatest medieval poet, Dante Alighieri.[202]

Apart from Dante's *Inferno*, which clearly draws a parallel between the poet's main character, in his own descent into Hell, and that of Nicodemus' Christ character, the story, said Jenkins, "even has a claim to rank as the origin of European drama ... given the theatrical character of the *Descensus* itself, with its extensive dialogs in scenes that cry out for dramatization."[203]

So, now that we have demonstrated the extent to which the apocryphal literature exerted its influence upon other works of drama, and having established that, in his birth, Moses was another type of Christ, we can now tie up the loose ends of all the ideas that I introduced several paragraphs ago. I began this train of thought when, in discussing the theme of the journey from death to life, I had compared the plight of Joseph with that of Jesus'. In both of their lives there ran a consistently familiar chord. Both were cast into a pit of apparent hopelessness. By the hand of their own brothers, Joseph had been consigned to a snake-filled pit and Jesus to the pit of Hades itself. Yet because of their absolute faith in God, both were raised from the degradation to which they had been subjected. What is more, the instrument with which their oppressors had intended to destroy them instead became the very tool by which the God of Resurrection and Life brought about their exaltation.

And so it was that a similar destiny was in store for Moses—in his case regarding the events surrounding his birth—because no matter how hard Pharaoh tried to nullify the prophecy of the birth of the Hebrews' deliverer, it was his own edict to drown all the male babies that ended up backfiring on him. In a form of poetic justice that no Hollywood writer could have conceived, the Nile River—the same body of water that was used to drown the Hebrew infants—became the vehicle that floated the baby Moses into the court of Pharaoh's daughter. In other words, the Nile became, for the Hebrews, the most improbable vehicle, which, against all odds, ensured that their hopes and dreams would be resurrected from the very crucible of death with which the Egyptians had intended to destroy them.

Fortunately, the apocryphal literature and Hollywood are not the only places that one finds these typological truths concerning this recurring theme of the resurrection of the dead. In fact, I am pleased to report that another of the most familiar of these types is found in *The New Testament*. Moreover, the expositor of our final lesson concerning this much-misunderstood aspect of biblical typology is none other than Jesus of Nazareth. As it so happens, it concerns the tale of Jonah and the whale. In it, we come face to face with one of the most improbable stories to be found in Scripture—yet paradoxically—one of the most enduring. So, why is it that such a whopper of a fish tale should attach itself so vigorously to the human imagination?

Undoubtedly, it is because Jesus Himself insisted on endorsing the story. Without such a validation, the drama of Jonah, residing in the belly of the whale for three full days before being spit out on the shores of Nineveh, might certainly have been relegated to a lesser status in the annals of fanciful tales. But endorse the story He did. In the Gospels of both Matthew and Luke there is corroborative evidence that Jesus did so without reservation.

> Then some of the Pharisees and teachers of the Law said to him, "Teacher, we want to see a miraculous sign from you."
>
> And Jesus answered, "A wicked, adulterous generation asks for a miraculous sign! But none will be given to it except for the sign of the prophet Jonah. For as Jonah spent three days and nights in the belly of the whale, so the Son of Man will be three days and nights in the heart of the Earth. The men of Nineveh will stand up at the judgment against this generation and condemn it because they repented at the preaching of Jonah, and now someone even greater than Jonah is among you."[204]

In addition, as if to establish a clear precedence for the story, Matthew has Jesus refer to it again when He is reprimanding the Pharisees and Sadducees for their unrelenting demands for celestial signs. "You know how to interpret the appearance of the sky," Jesus said to them, "but you can't interpret the signs of the times. A wicked, adulterous generation looks for a miraculous sign, but none will be given to it except for the sign of Jonah."[205]

From this, it is quite evident that, in the mind of Jesus, the story of Jonah was no mere sidebar. Every time the religious authorities of His day demanded a sign to prove His deity, He unflinchingly referred to it. No wonder that this granddaddy of all fish tales has continued to endure to the present day, in spite of the story's apparent implausibility. In short, it seems obvious by the way Jesus compared His hellish descent with Jonah's perilous journey that we are left with but one conclusion. Before one dismisses the outrageous claim that the crucified Jesus had risen from the grave, one would do well to remember the story of one of Christ's greatest forerunners, whose own story of peril and redemption stands as a shining beacon in the face of mankind's most dreaded enemy—typified by the belly of the whale—death. Moreover, as Jesus undoubtedly took courage from the fact that He could seek deliverance from the same God Who had rescued Jonah, we, too, would do well to remember the same thing. As it is written in *The Book of Hebrews*:

> Now faith is the substance of what we hope for, the certainty of what we do not yet see. This is what the ancients were commended for... By faith, Enoch was taken from this life so that he did not experience death; he could not be found because God had taken him away, in that before he was taken, he was commended as one who pleased God...
>
> By faith, Abraham, when God tested him, offered Isaac as a sacrifice. He who had received the promises was about to sacrifice his one and only son, even though God had said to him, "It is through Isaac that your offspring will be reckoned." Abraham reasoned that God could raise the dead and, figuratively speaking, he did receive Isaac back from death...
>
> By faith, Joseph, when his end was near, spoke of the Exodus of the Israelites from Egypt, and gave instructions concerning the burial of his bones... By faith, Moses, when he had grown up, refused to be known as the son of Pharaoh's daughter. He chose to be mistreated along with the people of God, regarding disgrace for the sake of Christ as of greater value than the treasures of Egypt...
>
> Not only that, but women received back their dead, raised to life again, while others, who were tortured, refused to be released so that they might gain a better resurrection... All of these, then, were commended for their faith.[206]

Therefore, based on all of these shining examples, it seems fairly certain that this concept of the resurrection of the dead is no mere afterthought in *The Bible*. If anything, it is its most resounding theme—one which found its ultimate expression in the life of Jesus, the Risen One. From it, we have evidence for the assurance of resurrection by way of the lives of Adam, whom God repeatedly raised in order to fulfill his ordained time on Earth; of Enoch, who was miraculously restored to his family after they had given him up for dead; of Abraham, who, like Shadrach, Meshach, and Abednego, survived for three anxious days in a fiery furnace; of Isaac, who survived the harrowing ordeal of offering himself as a burnt offering; of Joseph, who rose from the pit of despair to the heights of divinely-ordained power in order to save his family from starvation; of Moses, who, abandoned as a baby to an unknown fate, was floated by the very instrument intended to destroy him into the shelter of a mother's nurturing arms; and of Jonah, who, though hopelessly imprisoned in the belly of the whale, was three days later, according to the "set times" of the Lord, cast forth into the light of a new day.

The Author of the Universe

IN REVIEW, WHAT CAN one surmise from all of this? If it can be summed up concisely, I guess our storyline would run as follows. If God has apparently gone to such great lengths to speak to mankind by way of types and shadows, then He must have done so because He understands that, more than anything else, we are creatures with brains that are uniquely tuned to these tried-and-true storytelling elements. In an attempt to prove such a point, we not only have the biblical texts to offer up as evidence, but we also have a continuing record of many millennia in which humans, as a species, have spent endless amounts of energy in the business of telling stories.

As for the precise origin of storytelling, there is much debate as to how far back one must look to discover history's first example, particularly in respect to its conveyance in written form. This is due primarily to the fact that the modern view simply cannot accept the idea that the ancients were—as *The Bible* clearly implies—recipients of a "written tradition" prior to the so-called "oral tradition." In this way, a strictly humanistic interpretation of world history has won the day in its ability to rewrite an unabashedly biblical one. According to this humanistic view, primitive mankind simply lacked the necessary cognitive skills which were required for such things as writing—a skill that would only later supersede the more "primitive" phase of human development indicated by a "simpler" oral transmission of cultural wisdom.

Unfortunately, because this present analysis on the function of storytelling is a limited one, we have neither the time nor space to delve into the arguments for or against such a view. Suffice it to say, this work embraces a biblical frame of reference in opposition to a humanistic one that assumes that storytelling began with caveman drawings. As such, we view its true origins as having occurred with the production of written works like those attributed to Enoch, the first narrator of *The Bible*. And should anyone ask why there is no evidence for this written tradition prior to the oral tradition—apart from the straightforward testimony of Enoch's texts themselves—one may simply point out that this "missing chapter" of history was entirely in accordance with the plan of God, in that these earliest examples of storytelling were meant to be lost for a time. Only later, following a period similar to that of the Dark Ages of medieval Europe, would writing give birth to the more traditionally accepted version of storytelling as it has come to be known today.

Needless to say, however, the importance of telling stories as a cultural phenomenon, both past and present, can hardly be overstated. In fact, many historians and anthropologists believe storytelling to be one of the most widely influential factors in the development of civilization, the common denominator that binds our collective humanity. Since time immemorial, stories that define the human race have been handed down from generation to generation. Many are viewed as merely myths, legends, fables, or fairy tales; others are deemed epics, adventures, or morality plays. But in every case, at the heart of the tale that stands the test of time, is a story of what it means to be human—or more specifically—what it means to become "more" human. In other words, at the center of all the stories that have carved out this universal tradition of storytelling is an element of *transformation*.

As the old adage goes: The only constant in the Universe is change; and just as it is with the Universe, so it is with every great story. Transformation, metamorphosis, transcendence, call it what you will. Whether literally or figuratively, characters that speak to the human heart are ones who are striving to become something more than what they started out to be. And in this process of "becoming"—as when a caterpillar morphs into a butterfly, thereby becoming something altogether different—mankind is face to face with God's age-old work of recession and renewal, of extinction and rebirth, of death and resurrection. Old things are passed away; behold, all things have become new.[207] Death is swallowed up in victory,[208] and resurrection—again whether literally or figuratively—has provided a brand-new start.

This, then, is the essence of drama and the reason, I believe, that God Himself is to be considered the Author of the Universe. After all, did not John, in the opening chapter of his Gospel, specifically state that the Word of God created all things?[209] According to this view, the Godhead literally spoke the Universe into existence by way of the articulated word. "And God '*said*' let there be light."[210] From this, one might gain some insight into the biblical passages that refer to Jesus as the Author of the Universe. The Apostle Peter called Jesus the "Author of Life."[211] Additionally, Paul referred to Jesus in much the same vein, twice calling Him the "Author of Salvation," and once, the "Author of Faith."[212]

No wonder that all the processes in the known Universe, both natural and supernatural, are undergirded by this same articulated word, which speaks of the irresistible cycle of life and death. According to both biological and spiritual precepts—each according to its own frame of reference—the death of an organism is but a gateway to another form a life, however mystifying that new life form appears from our limited view. In scientific terms, matter is never lost; it is regenerated into a different form. Similarly, in theological terms, spirit is never lost; it, too, is retranslated into a new dimension.

The Wondrous Circle

SO WHAT IS THE point of all the foregoing analytics? The point is: If God is the Author of the Universe, then it should no longer come as a surprise that He determined every aspect of creation would embrace the message of redemption that He uttered to Adam and Eve. In fact, given this understanding of God as Author, it makes perfect sense that He would choose a messianic figure like Enoch to proclaim the first prophecies of the Son of Man Who would one day carry out this mission of saving Adam and his descendants. It would similarly follow that—as critical as the articulation of such a message was—this message of Enoch, and others like him, would have been rejected and subsequently lost for many long ages. And finally, when the time had finally come to initiate a new era of spiritual awakening, it seems only natural that this Author God would do so via this same articulated word, specifically uttered for the sake of the chosen people of His calling.

More to the point, this is why I am convinced that God has chosen to convey His message not in terms that stifle the faith of His people, that is to say, in the minutiae of laws, regulations, and restrictions, which invoke such a burden of guilt and shame that it does nothing but quench the Spirit of Truth. Instead, God, as the Author of the Universe, has chosen to manifest His redemption via the power of the dramas of life and death, of war and peace, of doom and deliverance, as they are portrayed throughout the history of His chosen ones. As it was written by the hand of the Apostle Paul: "Faith comes through the hearing of God's word."[213] And again he wrote: "So I ask you, does God give you His Spirit and work miracles among you by the works of the Law or by your believing what you have heard?"[214]

In other words, God's plan has always been to rescue mankind by way of its response to the message He has entrusted to His light-bearers who have woven their artful tales of the rising and falling of the human spirit, of the rebellion and rebirth of the human heart, of the death and resurrection of the human body. In this way, these inspired tales of wonder and awe have fulfilled their divine purpose in their simply being spread abroad and received by those individuals who have had but eyes to see and ears to hear.

Such are the *Tales of Forever*, tales like those first penned by Enoch, which were handed down to inspire subsequent generations of prophetic genius, producing such works as *Jasher*, *Genesis*, *Isaiah*, and *Daniel*. All this until finally the One Who had set His redemptive plan of *five and a half* "days" into motion strode upon the stage of world history to give His life as a ransom to fulfill that promise made to Adam and Eve.

In turn, we would one day partake of the drama of their lives in such a way that—though dead and buried long ago—they would impart meaning to us, not in a didactic way that leads to disenfranchisement and despair but one that conveys truth that resonates from age to age, from life to life. In examining the meaning of these lives, we would in some special way detect in them a way of interpreting the meaning of our own lives, and as a result of this peculiar connection, which stretched to us in our own time, we, too, though destined to die like Adam, would be able reach for the impossible and thus be imbued with the same force that transformed Jesus' mortal coil from death to life.

In this way, the wondrous circle of life as God has intended it is made complete. In the beginning was the Word; from age to age, it is the Word that sustains the Universe; and through to the very end, it will be the power of this Word that communicates His eternal purpose to all the world. And one day a generation will arise—perhaps this generation—that Enoch spoke of so long ago when he recorded his conversation with the Lord, Who said:

> I'll describe two mysteries for you, Enoch. First, many rebels will violate the word of truth. They'll speak incredible things and pronounce many lies. Tremendous civilizations will be created, and many books will be composed in their own words.
>
> But My people will begin to write all My words properly in their own languages without altering or diminishing their meaning. They'll perform the task correctly, and then they'll possess everything I've said about them from the beginning.
>
> The other mystery to tell you about concerns the faithful and wise, who will be given books of joy, integrity, and remarkable wisdom. And having received the gift of those books, they'll believe in what they have to say. They'll rejoice in them, and all the faithful ones will acquire the knowledge of every righteous path through them and be rewarded.
>
> And someday, they'll call out to the people of Earth and make them listen to their wisdom.[215]

Time to Move On

SO ENDS PHASE ONE of *The Analyses* into the potential validity of *The Tales*, with Phase Two at the end of this book, beginning in Act Three. So far, in Phase One, we introduced a four-fold investigative approach that hopefully helped to eliminate the stigma that has for too long tainted these neglected gems of biblical wisdom. In the process of doing this, one can now better see the extent to which these narratives correlate with the more familiar texts of the Canon, as well as the way that they clarify some of its most perplexing mysteries. Not only that, but they also help to explain why the God of *The Bible*, as the Ultimate Director of human history, has so persistently couched His message to mankind in what can best be understood as "the dramas of the ages."

Having set the stage this way, we will next turn to examining the process by which a disparate set of ancient manuscripts, depicting long-forgotten worlds, was updated and adapted so that a modern audience could relate to them. This will be followed by a brief history of the restoration of these manuscripts that were once thought to be lost forever.

Finally, after previewing *The Tales*, you will be ready to digest the actual narratives in all their dramatic glory, the contents of which include Enoch and his heavenly conversation, and the all-important promise of "days" given to that first couple after their having been exiled from the Garden of Eden—the length of which just happens to bear an uncanny relationship to the five thousand, five hundred year chronology found in *The Septuagint Bible*, and the dimensions of *five and a half* cubits built into The Ark of the Covenant.

This will be followed by the tale of Abraham and his journey toward faith, a story that chronicles the peculiar role that Adam's garment of sheepskin played in the lives of both Nimrod, the mighty hunter and rebel before God, as well as Esau, Abraham's grandson, so infamous for his ambition and greed.

From there, we will next turn to the tale of Pontius Pilate, who, after a lifetime of political scheming, had his life turned upside down when he came face to face with his most perplexing circumstance yet, in a story that involves Veronica's mysterious painting of Christ, and the equally mystifying seamless robe of Jesus.

More importantly, it should be noted here, that in the digesting of *The Tales*, readers will not only be partaking of the sublime wisdom contained in the narratives themselves, but they will also be assimilating all the ingredients needed to properly apprehend the forthcoming proof—so artfully hidden in the five *sacred* things—of God's control and faithfulness that this entire work is building toward.

So, without further delay, it is time now to move on to *The Translation*.

THE TRANSLATION

The test of a translation, like the test of a book ... is not a line here and there but coherence, movement, action; not how easily we may pull it to pieces and what interesting pieces it makes but how it first interests us, then absorbs us, and finally sweeps us along.

James I. Cook, *Edgar J. Goodspeed: Articulate Scholar*

A Matter of Style

The Latent Message

ONE OF THE MOST difficult aspects in bringing these stories to life for the sake of a modern audience was the all-important decision concerning the style of translation employed in their retelling. Crucial to this process were certain considerations, the first being the original style of writing in which the stories had been presented in their various incarnations up to the present day. As previously stated, *Tales of Forever* is a book that has been synthesized from manuscripts some of which date from the remotest periods of antiquity, such as *The First Book of Adam and Eve, The Secrets of Enoch, The Book of Jasher, The Letters of Herod and Pilate,* and *The Gospel of Nicodemus.*

When I learned of the existence of these stories more than three decades ago, they only existed in collections that had been published in the 1920s, while these in turn were reproductions from even earlier versions of the original manuscripts. Upon my initial reading of them, I felt much like someone who encounters the unfiltered works of William Shakespeare for the first time. These were definitely not stories that one could simply breeze through. Poetic yet mystifying, inspiring yet exasperating, they were written in a style that was clearly as archaic and outdated as anything penned by the Bard of Avon. Nearly incomprehensible at first glance, the sublime meaning of the texts seemed to arise only after a great deal of reading and re-reading, which required many hours of study and contemplation. Over the course of time, however, I not only became enthralled with the stories in these books, but I also became convinced that they were literary treasures in their own right. Unfortunately, because of the convoluted style in which they were written, I could also see why most modern minds would remain unimpressed and untouched by the latent message embedded in them.

After several years of sharing these stories with friends and colleagues—with admittedly mixed results—I noticed that something unusual began to happen as I attempted to engage others with their contents. Gradually, as I continued to read the narratives aloud to those around me, I ceased to simply recite them verbatim as they were found in the books. I found myself "translating them on the fly" in order to better convey the meaning that I felt was trapped in their pages. Only then did people begin to become engaged, with the end result that they started offering remarks like: "These are some very interesting texts. They shed new light on questions I've always had about certain aspects of *The Bible*." And: "This is fascinating stuff. I wonder why we've never heard anything about these stories in church."

Finally, after countless readings of the stories, I came to the conclusion that they represented a startling, behind-the-scenes version of *The Bible*—an extended storyline that constituted an intriguing counterpart to the familiar versions of Scripture. Not only that, but at some point in my journey through this collection of *Tales*, I began to see them as more than a collage of random texts. Slowly but surely, there emerged a distinct pattern of connectivity, which transformed this scattered compendium into a single, continuous timeline—one that literally pivots upon the little-known prophecy of The Great Five and a Half Days—with Enoch as the narrator of a series of stories, beginning with Adam and Eve, then Abraham and Nimrod, and finally Jesus and Pilate.

Unfortunately, there was still one seemingly insurmountable problem with my grandiose plan. Apart from biblical scholars and literary aficionados, I wondered, who in this modern, skeptical world would ever take the time to decipher the content of these stories when they were trapped in a language frame that only hardcore Shakespeare fans could appreciate, let alone understand?

So, like every other author before me, the question remained the same: How could I go about creating believable dialog for characters who existed in some of the remotest chapters of human history? Would I simply resort to parroting the style of the *King James Bible* translators when attempting to depict the biblical past? For me, this would constitute the ultimate failure of nerve, because, quite frankly, I have never been satisfied with biblical movies that took this route. I mean, really, who in their right mind would ever believe that anyone in *The Bible* actually talked like people who inhabited the world of Elizabethan England? Does anybody think, for one second, that Jesus, Abraham, or Adam spoke in iambic pentameter? Of course not. So why should audiences continue to endure such artistic nonsense? To me, it has always been nothing less than a gross oversimplification that just because a story involves historical characters who inhabit worlds unlike our own they must be portrayed as speaking with dialects and accents in order to convey their unique time and place.

A Clarity of Language

WITH THIS AGE-OLD dilemma, one comes face to face with the next critical consideration in trying to present the most ancient of tales to a modern audience. Throughout the history of storytelling, authors have made a concerted effort to flesh out their narratives by means of presenting three crucial elements—the *time* when a story occurred, the *place* where it occurred, and the *characters* who existed when and where that story occurred. Primarily, the way in which the first two aspects of storytelling are portrayed, that is, the "time" and "place" of any given story, have been done in a fairly straightforward manner. Whether the author's presentation of such matters can be characterized as either profoundly poetic or merely functional in style, the conveyance of time and place is generally more an indication of the author's personal writing style rather than anything intrinsic to the story itself.

On the other hand, the one aspect of a story that exists apart from the author's style is the way in which the "characters" of a story are presented, which is done not so much by way of what they *do* but how they *speak*. In other words, regardless of the background and origins of an author, the characters of a given narrative—either fictional or nonfictional—should always speak in a way that is true to that character's unique background and origins. Whereas an author may depict the time and place of a story in a multitude of ways without altering it, the way that characters speak will inevitably alter the reception of that story. More than any other aspect of the story, how characters speak must ring true to the time and place that they inhabit, or else the audience might interpret everything they do as false or contrived. The depiction of the dialog of a story's characters, then, is the paramount hurdle with which an author must contend, and never more so than with a narrative like *Tales of Forever*, which attempts to portray characters that clearly have a specific historical setting.

A prime example of dialog that uniquely conveys the setting of a story can be found in the literary works of Mark Twain. Through his clever use of dialect, Twain not only conveys a character's personality but, with little or no back story at all, he also conveys their education level and position in society. On the positive side, Twain's use of dialect provides insight into his characters through a dialog that, by way of texture and sound, reveals a great deal about the setting of the story—one which conveys a truth far beyond the author's mere description of the time and place in which the characters exist. On the negative side, however, trying to read dialog that is steeped in a peculiar dialect is sometimes very difficult to decipher. Often narratives that resort to foreign dialects to convey the background of certain characters work on one level, but because the dialog is so stultified, the actual message of the work is literally lost in translation. As a result, books or movies with dialect-laden dialog might be applauded by one segment of the audience, such as critics or other artists, while the average patron winds up on the losing end because of the difficulties that arise from trying to decipher the dialog. Unable to follow the plot, the reader or viewer disengages from the narrative before they even have an opportunity to get involved with the story.

To avoid such a potential death knell to box-office success, many filmmakers have pursued an alternate route in attempting to convey the settings of their stories. Rather than employ characters that resort to hard-to-understand dialects, they use those who speak in the language of the people they portray while providing subtitles for the sake of the audience. Such is the case in films like *The Longest Day*, *Dances With Wolves*, and *The Passion of the Christ*. In *The*

Longest Day, unlike most war films of that time, all the German and French characters speak in their own language, accompanied by English subtitles. *Dances With Wolves* has much of its dialog spoken in Lakota with English subtitles. And not to be outdone, *The Passion of the Christ* does not contain a single word in English. The entire film is comprised of characters who speak Aramaic, Latin, and Hebrew. Yet ironically, in order to convey its ancient message to a modern audience, the filmmakers chose to subtitle the film in what can only be described as "vernacular English."[216]

Therefore, when it came time to establish the style of dialog in this modern adaption of ancient tales, all of these potential pitfalls and possibilities loomed large in my mind. As a result, I decided to make every effort to avoid any of the aforementioned clichés. What kind of historian would I be, I asked myself, if I sought to make Enoch and his counterparts speak like characters who had just stepped out of one of Shakespeare's plays simply because audiences expected biblical characters to speak that way? Above all, I sought to achieve a clarity of language with this newly forged rendition. I was not content to simply convey the meaning of these stories in the same way that a literary scholar might do. More than anything else, I wanted these timeless tales to be expressed in a language that could be understood by every strata of society, from the scholarly critic to the ordinary individual.

As it turns out, I am not alone in such an effort. As a matter of fact, the same thing has been happening for many years in respect to updating the Elizabethan English of the *King James* Version of *The Bible*. Not until 1885, with the creation of the *Revised* Version, had any significant changes been made to it since its inception in 1611. Then, in the wake of the growing popularity of modern-day revisions, the twentieth century saw more and more similar endeavors, spearheaded by leading theological minds like Edgar J. Goodspeed, who, in 1939, published *The Bible: An American Translation*. Although these kinds of translations have always been met with a mixture of praise and criticism, Goodspeed insisted that such efforts constituted a necessary evolution in the language of *The Bible*. Said James I. Cook, in his biography of the man:

> Nothing horrified Goodspeed more than the popular notion that the modern *Bible* translator merely tinkers with the *King James* Version, replacing its archaic words with their modern equivalents. For him, the case for a new translation rested ... upon the papyrus discoveries of the late nineteenth and early twentieth centuries. He was convinced that these rendered intolerable, not simply the individual words but the entire linguistic style of the *King James* Version and its revisions. The papyri solved the problem of what kind of Greek was in *The New Testament*. It was not the classical or literary Greek of its own day... The papyri showed that *The New Testament* was written in the vernacular Greek of its time, the language of everyday life.[217]

This is why Goodspeed was so determined that despite all the well-intentioned protestations: "*The New Testament* must be retranslated if it is to reach the modern reader with anything like the force it had in antiquity."[218] And for Goodspeed that meant: "The only appropriate vehicle for such retranslation is the common vernacular English of everyday life."[219] Therefore, just as Goodspeed sought to make the canonical *Bible* more accessible by updating its language, I have sought to do a similar thing with the apocryphal books. Rather than assigning so many lines of ill-conceived dialog to the people in these stories, I chose to allow them to speak in a language entirely devoid of inappropriate dialects, which, in my view, contradicts an accurate depiction of reality. Let me explain what I mean by that.

Of Accents and Idioms

IMAGINE A CLASSIC film like *Gone With the Wind*, a drama set entirely in the Confederate South during the American Civil War. Because everyone in the story is a southerner living in the 1860s, the characters should all speak with a nineteenth-century southern drawl while invoking every known southern expression of that era. Right? But wait. Before you answer too quickly, take a moment to ask yourself one question, assuming that everyone reading this is also from a variety of ethnic backgrounds: When you converse with someone who possesses a mutual ethnicity as yourself, do you ever notice yourselves speaking with peculiar accents or idioms? I sincerely doubt it.

The only time that someone would ever detect such peculiarities is when there are people or, in this case, characters, who are interacting with individuals of *other* nationalities. In other words, only when a story depicts characters from different language frames should an author employ the use of unique accents and idioms. Unless the dialog is intended to reveal the cultural difference between their characters, as might occur in a war movie where an American soldier is talking to a German one, or in a Western that has a cowboy conversing with an Indian, there is simply no logical—let alone artistic—reason to invoke the use of accents or idioms. Yet invoke them they do.

Such is clearly the case in a "period piece" like the aforementioned *Gone With the Wind.* Do most of its characters speak in that southern drawl so indicative of the late nineteenth century in order to convey a sense of time and place? Not surprisingly, the answer is yes. On one hand, most of them invoke classic southern accents, like Vivien Leigh, with her perky exclamations of "fiddle-dee-dee" and "great balls of fire." On the other hand, Clark Gable, whose character stems from Charleston, South Carolina, exhibits barely a hint of an accent, as evidenced by his famous tag line: "Frankly, my dear, I don't give a damn!" Either way, it appears that screenwriters are just as guilty as most *Bible* translators in their clichéd attempts to telegraph the "who," "where," and "when" of their plots. Fortunately, though, this has not always been so—in the case of both Hollywood and Holy Writ.

The employment of *non*-archaic dialog in a "period piece" is never more evident than in the critically acclaimed film *Butch Cassidy and the Sundance Kid*. Though set at the turn of the nineteenth century, the movie does everything it can to avoid the sort of "countrified" dialog that is typically heard in most Westerns. As the story goes, this was a conscious, creative choice made by both the film's writer and director, William Goldman and George Roy Hill, respectively. Said Internet movie critic Eric D. Snider: "The dialog ... is casual and nonchalant in a strikingly modern way, and their attitudes are not what you expect of people from the late 1800s... This is all by design. It's part of the reason the film was so popular with audiences at the time, and why it's still so well regarded today."[220]

Case in point: When Butch and Sundance are being pursued by a posse and are desperate to formulate an escape plan, Cassidy proposes that they go to Bolivia, but the Kid is far from enthusiastic about the idea. "You just keep on thinking of stuff, Butch," he replies with a mocking tone. "That's what you're good at." Frustrated, Cassidy grumbles back, "I got vision, and the whole world wears bifocals."

As it turns out, this is precisely the kind of thing that Edgar J. Goodspeed had in mind as he approached his updating of the Elizabethan English of the *King James* Version of *The Bible*, in his 1939 translation of *The New Testament*. His biographer, James I. Cook, described it this way: "Goodspeed's aim was to avoid translation English, which he regarded as almost no English at all, to exclude all echoes of the familiar '*Bible* English' of the older versions, and, in their place, to use American idiom."[221]

Another way of looking at this same problem might be to imagine two Eskimos having a conversation. If we, as English-speaking individuals, were listening in on this conversation, we would naturally detect accents and idioms that were very different from our own. However, from the point of view of the Eskimos who were speaking to one another, they would not notice anything unusual at all. To them, they would just be having a normal conversation. So, based on this assumption, if an author were to translate this conversation for their readers, then why, for Heaven's sake, would they resort to such illogical and unnatural gimmicks like foreign accents or peculiar idioms simply to convey the fact that they were Eskimos?

With all this in mind, then, I set out to depict the characters in *Tales of Forever* as individuals who are indigenous to the same world, whether it is Adam conversing with Eve or Abraham talking to Nimrod or Jesus speaking with Pilate. And, therefore, like southerners speaking with other southerners, or cowboys with other cowboys, or Eskimos with other Eskimos, the characters in this book have been deliberately stripped of dialect-laden speech so that the concise meaning of what they have to say can finally resound from their ancient origins and penetrate our own world of modern sensibilities.

Foreshadow and Payoff

IN ADDITION TO updating the language of *The Tales*, they have also been thoroughly "fleshed out" in admittedly "cinematic" terms. This was done for several reasons, the first of which is because, as we previously noted, there is such a clear parallel between the dramatic narratives found in *The Bible* and those in the theater, literature, and cinema. The second reason was because, considering the significance of the first reason, the fact that it had not been done yet seemed so incongruous. That is to say, it was done because, in the opinion of this writer, it was long overdue in terms of the development of the dramatic narrative as a cultural phenomenon. What does that mean? Consider this, if you will. Historically speaking, in both the sacred and the secular realms, the earliest examples of storytelling were confined to a much simpler and condensed format. Only since the birth of modern literature and its ancestor, the cinema, has a more expanded mode of expression evolved with the subsequent maturation of the secular narrative—one which was only hinted at in the theatrical productions of ancient Greece and medieval Europe. Conversely, the sacred narrative has traditionally lagged behind in terms of this natural progression, and they have undoubtedly done so because of the built-in resistance to what is generally perceived as "tampering" with the original narratives themselves. Such resistance is certainly the very thing that intrepid pioneers like Goodspeed experienced regularly, even as he correctly envisioned the potential boon to humanity as a result of his updating of not just the archaic language but also the outmoded narrative style of existing translations of *The Bible*.

The next reason for adding this new dimension to the original stories was because, even in their unembellished state, they were stories that were predominantly told through the actions and dialog of their characters as opposed to a litany of religious precepts or ideology. In other words, *The Tales* inhabiting the world of apocryphal literature were already steeped in dramatic elements so that one only needed to ask a few questions when deciding how to make them truly "cinematic." One example of this latent cinematic element appears throughout the original stories in that, much akin to earlier forms of the narrative, the "dialog" in them was usually expressed through extended "monologs." Such a mode of expression might have seemed perfectly natural in the past, but, typically, modern audiences find them tedious and artificial. Therefore, in order to bring these portions of antiquated storytelling into the present day, one simply needed to "translate" these *mono*logs into a scenario in which two characters are expressing the original content of the story in the form of *dia*logs. Mind you, though, the primary content of the original stories was never changed in this process of retelling them. Their inherent potential was merely "fleshed out." Altering their content—that is, the explicit intent of the original authors—was never an option. Instead, what we are talking about here is not a matter of changing their "content" so much as changing the conveyance of said content.

Another way in which these stories were updated harkens back to our earlier discussion on the concept of parallel elements in both sacred and secular storytelling. By that I mean, because of the inherent similarity between the dramatic narratives found in Scripture and those in the theater, literature, and cinema, the potential for elaborating *The Tales* was always an obvious one. Though these two modes of communication have generally been viewed as being alien to one another, they are not so different after all. Consequently, in sacred terms, the dramas of *The Bible* unfold according to a principle known as "shadow and substance," while in secular terms, the dramas of the theater, literature, and cinema are conveyed by means of what has come to be known as "foreshadow and payoff."

What, exactly, does "foreshadow and payoff" mean? In filmic terms, foreshadow and payoff means that, in regard to both plot and character, the main body of a motion picture is in balance with its climax. In other words, through a filmmaker's clever use of plot details and character elements, a film's beginning and middle will naturally flow toward its inevitable end, and thus, from the audience's perspective, the finale will not seem to come "from out of nowhere." Otherwise, it does not matter how dramatic the ending of a movie is, without this proper balancing act of foreshadow and payoff, the audience will detect such foul play and quite rightly feel cheated by a finale that has clearly been tacked on simply for effect. Only when the "big ending" of a picture grows "organically," as it were, from all that has preceded its climax is that movie favorably received. This idea is never more evident than when one takes the time to see how this narrative device has been used in the proper way, in just the right doses, in some of the most successful films of all time. Generally, foreshadow and payoff are executed filmically in one of two ways—either through plot devices or thematic devices. Two films that have famously used plot devices to achieve this effect are *Jaws* and *Goldfinger*.

In *Jaws*, the finale comes when Chief Brody shoots and detonates the compressed air tank lodged in the shark's mouth, blowing it to kingdom come. But long before this occurs, it is cleverly foreshadowed in the main body of the film. During the early stages of the men's hunt for the man-eater, one of the oxygen tanks aboard their ship accidentally breaks loose and is quickly grabbed and secured. "Damn it, Martin!" exclaims the oceanographer Matt Hooper. "This is compressed air. You screw around with these tanks and they're gonna blow up!" With typical cynicism, Quint, the hard-bitten shark hunter, retorts, "Yeah, real fine gear you brought out here, Mister Hooper. But I don't know what that bastard shark's gonna do with it. Might eat it, I suppose. Seen one eat a rocking chair one time." At first, when this tension-filled dialog takes place, the audience experiences it as but a random flow of events that contribute to the mounting drama. In reality, however, it is all that and more; it also serves as an artfully planted clue that prepares the audience for one of the great climaxes in cinematic history, when Brody kills the shark by taking advantage of information that previously seemed incidental. Thus, the big ending does not materialize out of thin air but is a direct payoff of a foreshadowing event woven into the story entirely for the sake of the audience.

In *Goldfinger*, there are actually two instances of the foreshadowing of the demise of the villain—in this case, the sinister mute servant, Oddjob, as well as his boss, the namesake of the picture, Goldfinger himself. First, James Bond takes care of Oddjob by acting swiftly in connecting a loose electrical wire and electrocuting Oddjob as he is dislodging his deadly flying steel-brimmed hat from an iron cage. But prior to this, it was perfectly mirrored in the opening scene of the film when Bond outwits an assassin whom James shoves into a water-filled bathtub, then tosses a "live" appliance into the tub, also electrocuting him. In this way, the filmmakers not only demonstrate the inimitable Agent 007's resourcefulness in eliminating one of his enemies, but they also foreshadow the way he will eventually bring down one of his most famous opponents. As for the demise of Goldfinger: In another example of foreshadow and payoff, Bond is finally able to rid himself of this criminal mastermind when a stray bullet blows out the airplane's window and sucks the villain out, thus ending Goldfinger's tyranny. But before this happens, it, too, is adeptly foreshadowed. Having been captured, Bond is being transported by plane to Goldfinger's headquarters by his personal pilot, Pussy Galore, who holds him at gunpoint, saying, "Do you want to play it easy or the hard way?" Bond, however, cool as ever, replies, "Now, Pussy, you know a lot more about planes than guns. That's a Smith and Wesson .45, and if you fire at this close range, the bullet will pass through me and the fuselage like a blowtorch through butter. The cabin will depressurize, and we'll both be sucked into outer space together." So again, what initially appears to be just a passing remark actually serves to provide the necessary information to the audience when, in the final scene, the very thing that Bond had warned about occurs.

Apart from using plot devices, such as a particular action or piece of dialog to foreshadow a film's finale, another form of this principle of foreshadow and payoff involves the use of thematic devices. As such, films that utilize this format are much broader in their technique. Instead of interjecting a single foreshadowing event that results in an eventual payoff, these films rely on a whole series of subtle but potent moments throughout the picture, which, together, help build toward its climax. Famous examples of this type include such classics as *Shane*, *The Searchers*, and *The Godfather*.

In *Shane*, a mysterious drifter rides in from out of the desert and befriends a family of desperate homesteaders, caught in the throes of a range war, sometime after the American Civil War. No sooner does Shane arrive on the scene, however, than he reveals that he is a man with a haunted past. At the slightest provocation—the young son's cocking of his toy rifle, the crunching steps of a stray deer outside the cabin window—and instantly, like a coiled rattlesnake, Shane is ready to draw his six-shooter on his imagined foe. Embarrassed by his own abruptness, Shane proceeds to exchange his buckskins and pistol for a pair of jeans and a pickaxe; in short, Shane the gunman becomes Shane the sodbuster. And although he quickly takes sides with this family, in opposition to Rufus Ryker, the heartless cattle baron who is hell-bent on running roughshod over every family in the valley, Shane seems just as determined to do it without resorting to gunplay ever again. Emboldened by Shane's apparent weakness, Ryker brings an even more menacing threat into the situation in the form of a hired gun by the name of Jack Wilson, who soon taunts one of the homesteaders into an obvious mismatch and ruthlessly guns him down in a mud-filled street. For the already-anxious homesteaders, this is the last straw, as more and more of them decide to pull up their stakes and leave. Still, Shane seems strangely unmoved. Only one man is willing to oppose Ryker, and that is the father of the family, Joe Starrett. In vain, his wife pleads with Shane to stop her husband from such a foolhardy enterprise, but the quiet stranger declines, much to the chagrin of the man's family. Only when Shane is informed that Ryker is drawing Joe into an ambush does he finally relent; only then does Shane put away his jeans and axe, and once again dons his buckskins and pistol, confronting Ryker and his hired gun in a final showdown. As Ryker looks on, Shane coolly stares down the malevolent Wilson—a man who is clearly unimpressed with the reticent drifter standing before him. Then it happens: The man haunted by his past, the man so reluctant to take up arms ever again, finally unleashes all his pent-up anger, and like the coiled rattlesnake that he is, explodes in a fury of gunfire, killing Wilson and then Ryker before they barely have time to pull their weapons. And just like that, every finely crafted moment in this classic film comes to a resounding crescendo—an absolutely perfect example of cinematic symmetry, if ever there was one.

In *The Searchers*, Comanche raiders kidnap Debbie Edwards, the young niece of Civil War veteran Ethan Edwards, initiating an intense and extended search for her by Ethan and her adopted brother, Martin Pawley. But what ostensibly begins as a rescue effort by Ethan and Martin changes over time. As the years roll on and they still have not been able to locate Debbie, Ethan's fierce hatred of all things Indian begins to blind him to his niece's humanity. Because Debbie has lived among the Comanches for so long, Martin comes to realize that Ethan feels she is no longer worth rescuing, and he must now do everything he can to rescue her before his uncle can do her any harm. When they finally find Debbie, Martin must physically shield her from Ethan, who menacingly aims his pistol, demanding that he step aside. But before Ethan can make good on his intentions, he is shot in the shoulder by a Comanche arrow, thus reprieving Debbie for the time being. Only later do the men track her down again in the camp of her kidnapper, fully realizing that if they do attack the Indian's camp, it means that Debbie will probably be killed by her captors rather than their relinquishing her. "That's what I'm counting on," rages Ethan, to which Martin protests vehemently, "She's alive, and she's gonna stay alive." Ethan then roars back: "Living with Comanches ain't being alive!" Only in the final sequence of this nightmarish search does Ethan catch up with Debbie, who, seeing the blistering anger in her uncle's eyes, recoils in terror. And then it happens: Upon seeing his niece face to face after all these years, Ethan is smitten and, disarmed of all his fury, his compassion overcomes his quest for vengeance. With quiet resolve, he tells her at last, "Let's go home, Debbie."

In *The Godfather*, Vito Corleone is the Sicilian head of a crime syndicate who rules with an odd blend of honor, justice, and vendetta. Known as the Don by his enemies who fear him and the Godfather by his family who respect him, he is a ruthlessly shrewd man who nonetheless displays great love and compassion for his three grown sons, each one with their own unique personality. Two are clearly destined for a life of crime—Sonny, the hotheaded firebrand, and Fredo, the ne'er-do-well oldest son, who cannot hold a candle to his younger brothers. Then there is Michael, the war hero who returns home on the day of his younger sister's wedding. Dismayed by his family's reputation and openly critical of their activities, Michael insists to his fiancé that he has absolutely no intention of following in his father's footsteps. However, when Don Corleone is nearly killed in a failed assassination attempt, Michael inadvertently becomes ensnared by the very world that he had so adamantly refused to be a part of. At first, he is merely acting true to his nature by bravely guarding his father from further harm as the Don recuperates from his wounds, but then in a bold and impulsive move, he volunteers to strike back at the men responsible for his father's attack. Upon gunning down a rival crime boss and a corrupt police captain, Michael embarks upon a completely new path, and as the years go by, he plunges deeper and deeper into the life that neither he nor his ailing father had intended for him. In the end, upon Vito's passing from the scene, Michael masterfully orchestrates the deaths of all his rival crime bosses, and as his incredulous wife looks on, the door slowly closes between her and the Godfather.

Now that this principle of foreshadow and payoff has been illustrated by way of a variety of films, one might naturally ask the question: How can any of this pertain to a discussion of adapting *Tales of Forever*? First and foremost, it should be noted that all five of the previously mentioned films were adapted from novels, which means that the source material, as such, contained more plotlines and characters than a movie is capable of sustaining. Consequently, the screenwriters who were adapting these novels into movie scripts were all faced with the same challenges that I faced in adapting *The Tales* from what they once were to what they are now. In other words, the primary task on both our parts was to sift through an array of events and personalities, and to forge them into a single, cohesive through-line story. To do this, the first order of business was to decide which aspects of each story, from among this plethora of information, were best suited for this framework we have just described, that is to say, a narrative that conforms to this filmic principle of foreshadow and payoff. Fortunately, this was not nearly as difficult as one might imagine, because as I previously stated, these ancient narratives, even in their most primitive form, already possessed this innate potential. Like so many diamonds in the rough, these essential elements were just lying about, ready to be mined, cut, and polished in the hands of the master jeweler. And as it so happened, the key to unleashing this potential was to develop and adapt them in accordance to the aforementioned principle of foreshadow and payoff.

Still, in view of such elaborate alterations, one may ask the next series of inevitable questions: Do you not feel guilty "meddling" with what might otherwise be deemed sacred territory? After all, are you not in the process of trying to convince us that these apocryphal stories should be held on par with the canonical books? Why not simply stick to updating the stories from their archaic language into a more modern form while remaining faithful to the original stories, word for word, and be done with it? Why insert all this added business of foreshadow and payoff? Well, to answer such questions, I return to the thinking of Goodspeed, who was adamantly against this very thing when he said, "The most serious translation errors made in updating the language of *The Bible*, from Tyndale to the *Revised* Versions, was their adoption of a word-for-word method, with never a glance at the line of thought."[222] On this subject of updating the narratives of Scripture into those that were more suitable for a modern audience, James I. Cook had this to say about Goodspeed's thinking:

> A translation which was faithful in its individual parts but unfaithful in its total impression would be wrong in principle. That had been the greatest weakness of

> earlier translators. They had been more concerned with words than with phrases, with clauses than with sentences, with verses than with paragraphs. The test of a translation, like the test of a book, said Goodspeed, "is not a line here and there but coherence, movement, action; not how easily we may pull it to pieces and what interesting pieces it makes but how it first interests us, then absorbs us, and finally sweeps us along."[223]

Never has this advice been taken more to heart than in one of the finest examples of adapting a story from *The Bible* to the big screen, in a film that we have already examined in a previous chapter of this book. However, we will now be doing so after having come to understand this narrative principle of foreshadow and payoff. That film is *The Ten Commandments*. And just in case you think it sacrilegious to "add" to *The Bible*—a prohibition directed only to *The Book of Revelation*, by the way—imagine how this epic tale would have played out if those who had adapted it had not been audacious enough to "meddle" with its original storyline? Does this mean that those who did the "adding" were being disrespectful of Scripture when they chose to interject events and characters that were not already there? Fortunately, the end result and the test of time have answered both of these questions in resounding fashion. Clearly, they were more than respectful in their audacity; they were downright reverential. More to the point, they expressed this reverence by way of an overriding sense of foreshadow and payoff. Let us take a moment to revisit the movie in light of what we have just learned, and you will see exactly what I mean.

In *The Ten Commandments*, the film opens with Pharaoh's soothsayers warning the Egyptian king about an ominous prophecy concerning a Hebrew deliverer who will one day lead a slave revolt, declaring, "A star has proclaimed his birth." In starting the picture this way, with a scene that is nowhere to be found in *The Book of Exodus*, anyone familiar with the original story in *The Bible* is immediately struck by the fact that this rendition of Moses as Messiah is no longer simply an *Old Testament* story; it is also one that is deeply rooted in *The New Testament*. In other words, the film's payoff as Moses, the deliverer of Israel, is derived entirely from the way in which *The Bible* itself depicts the meaning of Moses' life as it is seen through the prism of Jesus, the Deliverer of humanity. As it is written: "By faith, Moses, when he was come to years, refused to be called the son of Pharaoh's daughter; choosing rather to suffer affliction with the people of God than to enjoy the pleasures of sin for a season, esteeming the reproach of Christ greater riches than the treasures of Egypt."[224]

And so, as the first scene of the movie goes in regard to Moses as Messiah, so goes the rest of the picture, and—I repeat—all made clear by way of the ingenious usage of this principle of foreshadow and payoff. For example, before Moses ever delivers the nation of Israel as a whole, he first rescues a pair of Hebrew slaves. One is a woman who just happens to be his aged mother, Yochabel, although Moses, as a prince of Egypt, raised in secrecy by Pharaoh's daughter, is still unaware of this fact; the other is Joshua, whom Moses sets free from a death sentence for striking an Egyptian while attempting to save Yochabel from being crushed by a quarry stone.

Later, when Pharaoh asks his son Rameses if he has learned the identity of the would-be Hebrew deliverer, Rameses insists that they do not need a deliverer because they already have Moses, who, even before God had ordained the people their Sabbath day of rest, had instituted a day of rest for the Hebrew slaves, much to the chagrin of Rameses. Then, when Bithiah, Moses' Egyptian adoptive mother, tries to persuade Yochabel to leave the country before Moses learns the truth of his Hebrew heritage, Yochabel resists her plea. When Bithiah challenges her priority as Moses' mother, Yochabel poignantly confesses that though she had yearned to reach out to her son, she resisted the urge, lamenting that she "dared not even touch the hem of his garment," a phrase that is clearly an allusion to Moses as a Christ figure.

When Moses finally does learn the truth about his Hebrew heritage, he is confronted by the two Egyptian women in his life whom he loves most, and in doing so, he must endure words of temptation as tearing as any offered by Satan to Jesus in the wilderness. First, Bithiah begs him to hide the truth that will only lead to certain servitude and hardship, asking plaintively, "Cannot justice and truth be served better upon a throne, where all men may benefit from your goodness and strength?" Then, his first love, the Egyptian princess Nefritiri chides Moses after retrieving him from the mud pits: "First Friend of the Pharaoh, Keeper of the Royal Seal, Prince of Thebes, and Beloved of the Nile God… A man of mud!" But when Moses takes it all in strides, Nefritiri scoffs, "Is this what you really want? To be a slave? If you want to help your people, come back to the palace. Oh, Moses, the gods have fashioned you for greatness … and when you are Pharaoh, you can free your people." But just as *The Book of Hebrews* would later record, Moses summarily spurns their offers of instant gratification and chooses the more difficult path that God has personally laid out for him, forever turning his back on the throne of Egypt.

And again, to reinforce the Christ allusion, when Yochabel sees that Moses is willing to give up his Egyptian royalty in favor of pursuing his daring role as their destined deliverer, her words clearly echo those of another mother who would also come to realize the messianic role that was to be played by her son. That mother's name is Mary. Says Yochabel, "Blessed am I of all mothers in the land, for my eyes have beheld Your deliverer."

Still, before Moses ever takes on the mantle of deliverer, he first suffers in the mud pits alongside his fellow Hebrew slaves, where he is personally confronted with the brutality of their Egyptian taskmasters. When an old man is attacked for his dignified protest, the mortally wounded fellow reveals his lifelong wish to Moses, that of one day seeing the promised deliverer with his own eyes. With bitter irony, Moses asks under his breath, "What deliverer could break the power of Pharaoh?" "You!" barks the taskmaster to the others standing there. "Clay carriers. Throw this carrion to the vultures." Then the taskmaster snaps at Moses, "You. Take his place." And just as Jesus willingly took our place as the recipient of God's wrath for the consequence of the sins of all mankind, Moses, too, willingly and without a single word of protest steps down into the muck and mire of that muddy pit to stand side by side with his kinsmen slaves.

Finally, after receiving God's call from the burning bush, Moses explains to Joshua that he is to lead the Hebrews out of Egyptian bondage, and Joshua, like the Apostle Peter in his day, brashly looks to the sword for deliverance. But once again reminiscent of Christ, Moses declares, "It is not by the sword that the Lord will deliver His people but by the staff of a shepherd." In the end, it is this very staff that Moses stretches out toward the Red Sea, which temporarily bars the escape of the Israelites as Pharaoh's fierce charioteers move in on them. Then in one of the most memorable climaxes in cinema history, Moses, with staff in hand, confidently utters a mighty word of faith, as he and the people with him watch in awe as the waters part in a spectacular display of God's power, thus enabling the people to cross over through the midst of the sea as if it were dry land.

In foreshadow after foreshadow, then, this artful movie lays down its marvelous tapestry of clues that all eventually reveal the true depth of their meaning in the story's final payoff, as Moses slowly but surely rises to embrace his grand destiny. And just as God, the Ultimate Director of human history, must have surely directed the steps of the real-life Moses, Cecil B. DeMille, the director of *The Ten Commandments,* in audacious stroke after stroke, masterfully directs the heroic life of his cinematic counterpart. More importantly, far from diminishing the message of faith and hope contained in Scripture, as some might argue, this classic film actually makes these biblically-inspired realities even more accessible, all through the unparalleled power of the dramatic narrative.

Thus, it was with all the foregoing ideas in mind that *The Tales* were reworked, that is to say, not just in the updating of their language but in the extent to which they could be infused with the same vital elements that are found in a modern-day narrative. And all with the utmost intention that this new adaption of *The Tales* should "first interest us, then absorb us, and finally sweep us along." In the final analysis, it will be this radically modern, dramatic approach to the reworking of these *Tales* that sets this work apart from any other in dealing with the subject of whether or not the so-called *Lost Books of The Bible* should be restored to their former status in the hierarchy of God's wisdom.

THE INTERLUDE

Men take it for granted today that in order to understand anything human ... they should search out its history... So pervasive has historicism become that we tend to forget it is itself a historical phenomenon.

Tom F. Driver, *Romantic Quest and Modern Query*

The Curtain Rises

Impossible Wonders

IN 1768, AN ANCIENT manuscript known as *The First Book of Enoch* was located in the mountains of Ethiopia. At the same time, Britain and America and, in effect, most of Europe were hopelessly embroiled in what was actually the first world war of ideas. Then, just when it seemed that our troubled world needed them most, more and more of these literary treasures from antiquity began to be rediscovered.

Ironically, though, after managing to recover these impossible wonders from the depths of oblivion, no one bothered to translate them. Rather than being seen as potential gems of spiritual wisdom, these priceless documents were relegated to the status of rare artifacts. So, for more than half a century, they sat unopened and unread on various museum shelves, simply gathering dust. But once the arduous task of decipherment had been completed, manuscripts like *First Enoch* began providing the West with a vivid, haunting glimpse into humanity's spiritual origins and destiny. Almost overnight, an entirely new way of understanding ourselves had been unveiled, as old as time itself.

Centuries of Suppression

STILL, AS MUCH AS these manuscripts have managed to illuminate the human condition, they have also sparked an inordinate amount of derision and controversy. Having survived for twenty centuries or more, these priceless documents depict events that reach far beyond normally accepted limits of prehistoric time. Most notable among these – besides *First Enoch* – are *The First Book of Adam and Eve*, *The Secrets of Enoch*, *The Book of Jasher*, *The Letters of Herod and Pilate*, and *The Gospel of Nicodemus*. Sadly, however, they have all generally been ignored, dismissed, or suppressed, presumably because of their provocative rendering of historical events and persons.

A typical example of this is *First Enoch*, which had been read and respected by Jews and Christians alike, and which had stood side by side with *The Book of Revelation* during the first four centuries of the Christian Era. While many of the Church Fathers, such as Clement, Ambrose, and Tertullian, endorsed it, others did not hold to this favorable view, and because of the efforts of influential opponents of the book, like Augustine and Jerome, who were critical of Enoch's description of those peculiar angels, or Watchers as they were called, the book was eventually deemed heretical. Along with other Enochic writings, it was banned from the mainstream of Scripture. Shredded and burned, the book was lost to the West for over a thousand years. Yet with remarkable persistence, many of these ancient gems have, slowly but surely, made their way back into circulation. Today, thanks to the efforts of a handful of men who were uniquely capable of seeing beyond the veil of skepticism and doubt, nearly everyone has heard something about these remarkable books.

Still, this never seems to answer the inevitable question: What relevance could a bunch of ancient manuscripts provide for an increasingly cynical world? The standard answer has always been that these books were designed so that a chosen few could understand them, but as to how this special remnant is supposed to assist in ushering in this awareness of God's truth, the canonical record does not reveal; which brings us back to the subject of extra-biblical texts. With the unexpected occurrence of the Qumran findings of *The Dead Sea Scrolls*, the notion of recovering "hidden" wisdom literature has become more and more widespread. Consequently, it no longer seems so far-fetched that there might be other sources of biblical truth not found amongst the traditional sixty-six books of *The Bible*. What is more, these sources of truth are able to provide critical missing pieces to the biblical record. In this way, these remarkable texts are helping to answer questions that have puzzled scholars for hundreds, if not thousands, of years.

This is why, even before a place like Qumran could ever have been imagined, when mere rumors of a surviving Enochic text began to surface, the Scottish explorer James Bruce was eager to get his hands on a copy, no matter the cost to him personally. So in 1773, Bruce endured an extremely hazardous journey to Ethiopia, where he was able to secure three copies of the rare book. Then in 1821, Dr. Richard Laurence, regius professor of Hebrew at Oxford, translated the work into English, providing the West with its first glimpse into Enoch's "forbidden mysteries." No longer would we remain a victim of centuries of suppression. No longer could the traditions of men keep us in ignorance concerning the role of spiritual pioneers like Enoch, the scribe.[225]

As a result, we can study these so-called "apocryphal" texts for ourselves. Now we are free to digest the contents of these remarkable books on our own. We can meditate on their mystical sayings and relive the fantastic journey of Enoch as easily as any described by the likes of Jules Verne or H.G. Wells. We can now witness firsthand how God is still using Enoch as a type of Christ, even after his supposed "death," from his being taken up to Heaven, where he served as a divine mediator, right up to his reappearance as one of the Two Witnesses described in *The Book of Revelation*.

Thanks to the courage and dedication of men like Bruce and Laurence, who succeeded in restoring these ancient texts to our Western world, almost everyone who has ever studied biblical history has come to learn about Enoch and the strange angelic beings called the Watchers. Their fabled story provides the building blocks for countless mythological motifs, particularly concerning their respective roles in the construction of The Great Pyramid of Giza. Since time immemorial, one civilization after another has told and retold its own version of a miraculously exalted hero, poised to usher in an age of enlightenment for the faithful. But what does tradition have to say about the rest of Enoch's life? Unfortunately, except for the brief passages in Scripture, tradition has very little to say. What really happened to Enoch during his ascension to Heaven? Did God simply spirit him away without leaving humanity a single word of explanation afterward? And why does there seem to be so little written about Enoch's role in the creation of *The Bible*?

Furthermore, how did Enoch react when an angel told him he was being recruited as a conveyor of the mysteries of God? What was the reaction of Enoch's family after he told them the news? What did his family do with the books he wrote? And could the accounts produced so long ago by Enoch and others like him finally be starting to prove their relevance, not simply to a few appointed people but to an entire world, ready and waiting for their lost message?

These are just some of the questions that this book, *Tales of Forever*, will attempt to grapple with, but it will do so in a way unlike any other that you have ever encountered. It will not seek to approach the issue in a strictly formal manner, and although many decades of scholarship have contributed to its creation, it will not attempt to do so in a purely scholastic way, either. Rather, the stories in this book will attempt to reveal a radical new approach to the key personalities and events of biblical history.

Admittedly, however, the unique approach to the historical events and persons contained in this book was not entirely my own creation. It came instead as an outgrowth of the development of mankind's evolving understanding of the nature of historicism itself and the subsequent pursuit of historical certainty. About this evolution of historical thought, Tom F. Driver, professor emeritus of theology and culture at Union Theological Seminary, said:

> Men take it for granted today that in order to understand anything human (often to understand natural phenomena as well) they should search out its history—its genesis and the processes by which it has come to its present state. For modern man, historical investigation is not only a method, it is very nearly *the* method, an approach to reality that conditions all modern thought. So pervasive has historicism become that we tend to forget it is itself a historical phenomenon. As a matter of fact, it revolutionized human thought only in the nineteenth century and then only in those places where European culture was dominant.[226]

According to Driver, the most important pioneer in this revolution in historical thinking was the eighteenth-century Italian scholar Giambattista Vico. More than anything else, it has been Vico's philosophy of history, which Driver called "a theory of historical cognition,"[227] that ultimately provided the impetus for the present narratives found in *Tales of Forever*. Concerning this theory, Driver articulated Vico's belief that:

> Since man is native to history ... man is capable of re-evoking the past in the depth of his own consciousness. Given a certain amount of historical data to begin with, man is able, through his imagination, to overcome the gap that separates the past from the present.[228]

This, in essence, is what this book sets out to do; it aims to provide the reader with all the necessary historical data that these ancient manuscripts have been offering all along. This data, however, is not reconstructed according to the dictates of intellectual inquiry alone. Instead, the persons and events depicted in them have been presented as a full-blown dramatic narrative, and it is this narrative that provides the ultimate foundation for the re-examination of said persons and events. In doing so, readers are invited to utilize their own God-given imagination to psychologically and emotionally bridge the seemingly insurmountable gulf between past and present. In other words, instead of the typical piece-meal approach so common to most historical treatises, *Tales of Forever* will provide a completely unique insight into many of the watershed moments of our collective history through the imaginative power of the dramatic narrative.

The Stuff of Legends

IN OUR FIRST installment, we witness firsthand Adam and Eve's expulsion from the Garden of Eden and God's reaction to their child-like response as they desperately try, again and again, to get back into His good graces. We see the establishment of the very first promises from God as He explains His plan to save them from a tragic fate.

For this wondrous tale, two men must be acknowledged for their selfless pursuit of biblical knowledge, men whose reputation in the Western world of theological studies was unimpeachable in their day. They are S.C. Malan, a British biblical scholar and linguist of Oriental languages, and W.R. Morfill, a British professor of Slavonic languages at Oxford. In 1882, Malan produced the first English translation of *The First Book of Adam and Eve*; and in 1896, Morfill gave us his translation of *The Secrets of Enoch*. Thanks to the efforts of this intrepid pair, humanity is able to once again partake of the long-forgotten world of the most famous couple of all time.

The story of Adam and Eve is literally the stuff of legends, from their prior glory in Eden to their disgraceful expulsion from the garden. Every culture the world over has incorporated some version of the Forbidden Fruit being offered up by some shape-shifting monster, poised to bring about the downfall of the first family of the clan. But what does tradition have to say about Adam and Eve after they were kicked out of Eden? Unfortunately, except for the brief passages in *The Book of Genesis*, it has little to say. What really happened to them during their exile experience? Did God simply abandon them to a life of hopeless despair? And why was nothing else written about the rest of their lives?

In *Tales of Forever*, we discover for ourselves how God continued to nurture Adam and Eve during every phase of their lives, from providing them with sheepskins for clothing, right up to His teaching them how to make their first offerings to Him. How did Adam and Eve learn to survive on their own after being deprived of direct access to God? What did Satan do in his attempt to thwart God's every effort in restoring them to their former state of grace and peace? How did Adam and Eve react when confronted with the idea of marriage? How many children did they have? What were their names? And could the woman that Cain was destined to marry actually have been his brother Abel's twin sister?[229]

In our next installment, we begin in the palace of Nimrod, the first great rebel against

God after the Flood. There, young Abraham is born to Nimrod's chief prince, Terah, as an awesome celestial event heralds his birth, thereby inaugurating the next phase of God's remarkable deliverance of Adam and his descendants.

For this adventurous tale, we Westerners are greatly indebted to one man: Moses Samuel, the British author and translator of Hebrew works, who, in 1838, gave us the first English translation of *The Book of Jasher*. Thanks to Samuel, we can now understand, like never before, what really inspired the one person, who, in the face of such opposition and peril, survived to spawn the mightiest lineage the world has ever known.

Nearly everyone has heard the story of the man whom God told to sacrifice his son. Their tale is an epic one, retold in countless ways, with nearly every culture ever since incorporating some form of sacrificial offering in order to ensure the clan's ultimate survival. But what does tradition have to say about why Abraham seemed so willing to do something like that in the first place? Unfortunately, except for the brief passages in *Genesis*, tradition does not have much to say. Did Abraham always have such unswerving faith? If so, then why was he so devoted to God? And if not, what enabled this one man, apart from all other men, to become the father of faith?

In *Tales of Forever*, we discover for ourselves how God guided Abraham throughout every stage of his life, from rescuing him as a young man from the furnace of Nimrod, right up to the time when He asked him to sacrifice Isaac on Mount Moriah. What role did Noah and Shem play in the development of Abraham during his formative years? What lengths did Nimrod take to kill Abraham before he could fulfill his world-changing destiny? How did Satan react to Abraham's attempts to sacrifice his son to God? Was Isaac really unaware of his father's intentions as he was being led up that mountain? And when Abraham told Pharaoh that Sarah was his sister was his story really so far from the truth, considering that she was his brother's daughter?[230]

Finally, in our third installment, we come face to face with the most amazing chapter in God's rescue effort yet, the very hour when the ransom for that deliverance was to be paid in full. In it, we confront many of the lesser-known facts behind the trial and execution of Jesus of Nazareth, as well as the startling events that took place afterward, despite every attempt to erase them from the pages of history.

For this most pivotal tale of all, the Protestant West owes much to a trio of men. They are William Wake, a British clergyman who went on to become the archbishop of Canterbury; William Wright, a British Orientalist and professor of Arabic at Cambridge; and B. Harris Cowper, a British archeologist, historian, and translator. In 1693, Wake gave us the first English translation of *The Gospel of Nicodemus*, while in 1865, Wright gave us *The Letters of Herod and Pilate*, and Cowper, *The Epistles of Pilate to Caesar*, *The Trial and Condemnation of Pilate*, and *The Death of Pilate, who Condemned Jesus*. Woven together into a continuous dramatic narrative, these texts combine to reveal an unparalleled glimpse into the hearts and minds of the players who took part in the most notorious trial ever recorded.

There is hardly a person alive who is not familiar with the scene of Pontius Pilate washing his hands before the angry mob that is demanding the death of Jesus. The story is renowned throughout the annals of world history, with every culture around the globe incorporating some version of the dying-and-rising hero providing his life for the sake of the group's continued existence. But what does tradition have to say about why Pilate really sentenced Jesus to die? Unfortunately, except for the brief passages in *The Gospels*, tradition has little to say. Did Pilate condemn Jesus because he was trying to avoid another bloody riot on his watch? Or was he really acting on orders from Rome, which required the pitiless end to all threats to the Empire? And when his wife tried to warn him about the innocence of the Man he was about to have crucified, did Pilate really believe her after all?

In *Tales of Forever*, we discover for ourselves why Pontius Pilate acted the way he did during his encounters with Jesus, from his early career as a ruthless politician, right up to his reaction to the machinations of the entrenched religious leaders in Judea at that time. Were the disciples of Jesus the only people who believed in Him or supported His cause? How did Satan react to Jesus' attempts to sacrifice His own life? What was Jesus really doing during the three days and nights prior to His resurrection? Was Jesus the only person Who was reported to have risen from the dead? And after everything was said and done, what was Pilate's real motive in turning Jesus over to a Roman crucifixion, even after he had openly declared Him innocent of every charge?[231]

Beyond the Veil

TALES OF FOREVER, then, is no ordinary rewriting of the same old stories. In this telling, for example, we find that, contrary to popular opinion, Enoch not only walked and talked with God, but he also left behind a written record of the history of all mankind's activities—past, present, and future. Adam and Eve were never totally abandoned by God just because He expelled them from the Garden of Eden. Isaac was very much aware of what his father Abraham was doing when the two of them made their way to the top of Mount Moriah. And Tiberius Caesar actually put Pontius Pilate on trial for allowing Jesus to be railroaded by religious leaders under his jurisdiction.

These are just some of the amazing things you will discover for yourself in *Tales of Forever: The Unfolding Drama of God's Hidden Hand in History*, where you will finally find answers to questions you have wondered about your whole life, not to mention a few that you never even thought to ask. Like marvelous links in a chain of time, these *Tales* provide an unprecedented view into our historic past, unlike anything you have ever experienced before. So prepare yourself for a starkly original journey beyond the veil of time and space; because instead of analyzing the past in a merely abstract manner, the reader of this book will experience firsthand the events of antiquity through the very lives of those who have inhabited our biblical past. As nearly as possible, these stories are authentic representations of a timeless wisdom that has been handed down from generation to generation. They are, in fact, stories from a land where all legends and lore collide. They are *Tales of Forever.*

The time has come, then. The players are assembled, the lines have been rehearsed, the stage has been set. All that remains is for you to begin the journey, one page, one chapter, one book at a time. And now, the curtain rises.

ACT TWO

Truth is sifted from falsehood in everything that has been preserved for us through long centuries by those crude traditions which, since they have been preserved for so long and by entire peoples, must have had a public ground of truth.

Giambattista Vico, *New Science*

THE TALES

Oh, my children, listen to what I have to say, because I've been allowed to come to you today so that I may make an announcement, not from my lips but from those of the Lord's Himself—all that is, and was, and will be, until the Day of Judgment.

Enoch the Scribe, *The Secrets of Enoch*

The Man from Forever

Adapted from

The Secrets of Enoch,
also called
The Slavonic Enoch
or *The Second Book of Enoch*

God took Enoch, Gerard Hoet, 1728

The Man from Forever

A Hole in Space and Time

THIS IS THE STORY of a man who soared through a hole in space and time, where space was without limit, and time stood still. There was only the man and his journey, and this journey took him to a land where all legends and lore collide, where the man found himself standing before the Face of God, the Lord of Eternity Who holds space and time in the palm of His hand.

When this man asked the Face why he was there, he was told simply that he should tell the *Tales of Forever*. Then he was given a pen of quick-writing and told to write them down as fast as he could. So for what seemed like but a moment, the man beyond time wrote down everything he heard. He wrote stories of everyone's lives, of those who *have* lived, of those who *were* living, and of those who *were yet to* live.

And after he was done writing, he awoke on his couch, wondering what he should do next. Until finally, he realized that he had no choice in the matter, because unless he did what he was supposed to do, no one else would ever know the *Tales of Forever*, because no one but him had witnessed the things that he had. So he looked in the mirror and understood what he alone had to do, because he recognized the face staring back at him, and it was the face of the man from forever.

Sparks and Secrets

IN THE SEVENTH generation from Adam, one of his sons became famous, not only for his skill as a master craftsman but also for his remarkable wisdom. His name was Enoch. Living before the Great Flood, in the days when people often lived more than nine hundred years, Enoch was still a young man at the age of three hundred and sixty-five.

One afternoon, he was at home, relaxing on his couch, when he fell fast asleep. As he slept, a horrible depression overwhelmed him, and he began to weep. Without warning, two angels materialized at the end of his couch. Their faces glowed like the Sun, their eyes flashed like beacons, and they had brilliant wings of gold.

"Wake up, Enoch," said one of them.

Confused and groggy, Enoch opened his eyes. Jumping to his feet, he stared oddly at the two luminous beings standing before him. "Hello, uh, how are you?" he stammered.

"Fine, thank you," replied the second one politely. "My name is Sariel, and this is my associate, Raguel."

Enoch nodded nervously. "Nice to meet you both." Rubbing his eyes, he blinked widely.

"We're very sorry for intruding unannounced like this," said Raguel. "Did we startle you?"

"Oh, no, of course not." Enoch did his best to stay calm in the presence of this disturbing pair of visitors. "How can I help you two?"

"Relax, Enoch," said Raguel. "There's no need to be afraid. The Eternal God has sent us to tell you something."

"What is it?" asked Enoch, gulping in anticipation.

"Today," replied Sariel, "you'll be going up to Heaven with us."

"But how is that possible?" wondered Enoch, bewildered at the very idea.

Sariel extended his arm toward Enoch. "Take hold of my cloak and find out."

His eyes wide with anticipation, Enoch reached out his trembling hand and placed it on Sariel's luminous sleeve. Then the two angels abruptly extended their tremendous white wings, and up they went with Enoch in tow.

TO HIS AMAZEMENT, Enoch was instantly lifted through Earth's atmosphere, and rising upward to the first level of Heaven, he saw a vast crystal sea, even greater than that of the Earth's ocean.

Soaring onward to the third Heaven, with the aid of his winged escorts, Enoch caught sight of a beautiful garden with an amazing tree growing at its heart. Around the tree flew a swarm of bright, white angels, flitting about, limb to limb, manicuring the exquisite leaves and robust fruit, which resembled delicate grapes. From the lips of these angels came beautiful singing, more incredible than any human voice could have ever sung.

Enoch turned to his angelic guides. "Is that really what I think it is?"

The angels both nodded.

"Yes, it is," said Sariel. "The Tree of Life."

"And those are the three hundred angels," added Raguel, "who tend to the tree, day and night, without end."

The singing of those angels sent out such a hypnotic effect that Enoch became transfixed by it. "Remarkable," he murmured.

Onward, the two angels carried the awestruck Enoch, upward still, as yet another astonishing sight rolled past his eyes. Vast columns of warrior angels, armed with jewel-encrusted shields and swords, glided past the trio. They, too, sang a remarkably haunting song as they went by.

"This can't really be happening, can it?" Enoch asked incredulously. "I must still be asleep on my couch. I'm dreaming all this, right?"

"No, of course not, Enoch," replied Sariel.

"You are *seeing*." Raguel smiled back knowingly.

"And who are these troops I'm seeing, then?"

"These are the legions of the Almighty," said Raguel. "They all march under the banner of a single Ruler, the Omnipotent Lord, the King of Heaven."

Astonished, Enoch shook his head. "Simply amazing."

Still, the trio continued to soar upward, until they reached the seventh Heaven. Fiery archangels flew about everywhere, darting every which way. Wherever Enoch turned, he saw the same thing, row after row of dazzling thrones. Upon each of them sat a ghostly apparition staring down at him with smoldering eyes.

"What is all this?" asked a wide-eyed Enoch.

"These are the dominions of the Lord," Sariel said, quite casually. "From them proceed the order and government of God."

Enoch was dumbfounded as he watched cherubim, seraphim and other strange angelic beings, with numerous eyes wrapped around their heads, flying all around him. Turning to his two traveling companions, he asked, "Are you sure we're in Heaven?"

Sariel smiled reassuringly. "Don't worry, Enoch. We're getting very close to God's throne, that's all. This is no place for ordinary humans. Look!" The angel pointed up, and Enoch craned his neck to see.

Above them and still at a great distance, a brilliant purple light beckoned them onward.

"It's so beautiful," Enoch said quietly. "Is that God's throne?"

Together, the angels nodded reverently.

"It is," Raguel stated, quite matter-of-factly.

"Is that where you're taking me?" wondered Enoch.

"That is where *you* will be going, yes," Sariel replied with a benevolent smile.

"But I don't understand."

"Not everyone is as lucky as you are, Enoch," said Raguel.

"What do you mean? I thought you were taking me to see the Lord."

"Yes, Enoch, we have been taking you there," Sariel assured him. "But we've only been allowed to bring you this far, and no further."

"Beyond this point, we're not permitted to venture at this time," Raguel explained.

"But why?" asked Enoch nervously. "I don't understand."

A tremendous gust of wind suddenly blew the two angels off into the distance.

"No, wait!" shouted Enoch. "Don't leave me!" Looking about, he realized that he was very much on his own, while still, all about him in the air, the frenzy of angelic flight carried on.

"What is that strange smell?" grumbled a cherubim as it buzzed past Enoch.

A seraphim then flew by. "I think it's this human."

"A *human*!" groaned the cherubim. "Who let *him* in here?"

"Don't ask me," the seraphim snorted. "How should I know?"

Terrified, Enoch began to panic. "Now what am I supposed to do? Why is this happening to me? Please, Lord, help me."

The fiery cherubim flew right up to Enoch, sniffing at him disapprovingly. "You're not supposed to be here! Who let you in?"

"I was brought here by angelic escorts," replied Enoch.

The seraphim buzzed back. "You're an intruder, I tell you!"

"Human flesh is not allowed here," growled the cherubim. "Get out of here right now, or we're going to kill you."

"No, you can't do that!" exclaimed Enoch with a shudder. "I told you, I was brought here by two of God's angels. Honestly."

The cherubim eyed him suspiciously. "You're lying."

"No. I was invited here; really I was."

"*You*?" scoffed the seraphim. "Why you?"

"But I'm not sure why. They didn't say, exactly. They just told me the Eternal God had sent them to bring me here."

"Enough of your lies, human!" barked the seraphim.

The cherubim drew out a fiery dagger. "I say we kill him, and be done with it!" He hovered closer to Enoch and raised his blade, poising it to strike. And then a hand grabbed hold of the cherubim's wrist.

"No," said an angelic voice. "You'll do no such thing. Nothing will keep this chosen vessel of God from fulfilling his destiny."

Enoch turned and looked up into the eyes of a handsome archangel.

"Gabriel!" howled the seraphim.

"What are you doing here?" the cherubim exclaimed, releasing his dagger.

"Mind your own business!" snapped Gabriel. "Now all of you get out of here this instant, or else I'll kill you instead." Gabriel shoved the startled cherubim several feet away. "You hear me?"

"Yes, Gabriel, of course," replied the cherubim, blinking wildly. "Anything you say."

The whole group of bewildered angels instantly darted off, and Gabriel turned to Enoch, who was still obviously traumatized from his close call. "It's all right, Enoch. They won't bother you anymore."

"Thank you so much. Gabriel? Is that what the others called you?"

"Yes, that's right. I'm Gabriel. I was sent to help you in the rest of your journey to see the Lord."

"Oh, thank God you got here when you did. I was so worried. First, these two angels brought me here, and then, suddenly, they were gone. I didn't know what I was going to do next."

"Yes, well, you can relax now. I'm here. Are you ready to see the Lord, then?"

Enoch thought about it for several tense moments. Taking a deep breath, he carefully replied, "Yes, I think so; I do believe I am."

"Good, because it's time," said Gabriel, who then took hold of Enoch by the arm and gently carried him upward. Like two leaves caught in a breeze, the pair soared up through two more levels of Heaven before they finally reached their destination.

"Well, Enoch, here we are," continued Gabriel as he set Enoch down, "the tenth level of

Heaven."

"Thank you, Gabriel, for all your help."

"You're welcome." The archangel smiled radiantly. "Goodbye for now." There was another gust of wind, and just as suddenly Gabriel was whisked away, leaving Enoch all by himself again.

Looking around, Enoch finally saw what he had come for; right before his very eyes was the dazzling throne of the Eternal One. Awestruck, Enoch gazed up at the Face of God, like molten iron, emitting sparks as it glowed, a Face as awesome as it was beautiful.

"Welcome, Enoch," said the Lord with a crackle of thunder.

Trembling, Enoch fell to his knees and bowed to the ground. "Lord, I am most honored to be here."

"Don't be afraid, Enoch. Stand and talk with Me."

Suddenly another archangel appeared, carrying a luminous robe and a jar of light.

"Here; Michael will provide you with some things to protect you while you're in My presence. He'll dress you in a special suit of My divinity and anoint you with the oil of My Spirit."

Reverently, Enoch rose to his feet and the archangel wrapped him with a robe, as dazzling as God's throne itself. Then Michael reached out his fingertip, glowing with a brilliant purple light, and touched Enoch's forehead, leaving a dab of glowing ointment, which quickly absorbed into his skin. Then with an eerie flash of white light, Michael vanished as quickly as he had appeared.

Inhaling deeply and exhaling with a sigh, Enoch cautiously looked up into the glowing Face. "Thank You for that, Lord; and thank You for inviting me here. What can I do for You?"

"I want you to listen to Me very carefully, Enoch, because I'm about to tell you things I've never even told the angels."

"Yes, Lord, I'm listening."

"Good, because I've never told the angels about their origins or described My endless realm to them. They understand nothing about My creation; but I have decided to tell you about it."

"Me? Why me?"

"I'm telling you because I require someone who will be faithful in all I ask him to do. Will you be that man?"

"I will, Lord. Just tell me what You want me to do."

"Your mission is a very straightforward one. I want you to write down everything I tell you. That way you'll be able to hand down this wisdom to your descendants."

"But how will I ever remember everything You tell me?"

With a blur, another angel streaked into view and stood next to Enoch. Bowing gracefully, he said, "Hello, Enoch."

"This is Pravuel," said the Lord. "As you can see, the swiftness of his intelligence excels beyond all my other archangels. His lightning hand will assist you in preparing the books I want you to write."

Enoch bowed to the archangel. "Glad to meet you, Pravuel. Thank you. It will be an honor to work with you."

"Now," crackled the voice of the Lord, "bring Enoch the pen of quick-writing."

A seraphim fluttered over to Enoch, and handed him an odd-looking writing utensil. Fascinated, Enoch examined the pen thoroughly. He was particularly intrigued by the tip of the device, which emitted a faint, purple glow. Then, a cherubim floated over with an endless stack of paper and set it in front of Enoch, who looked up expectantly into the smoldering Face of God.

"Are you ready, Enoch?" asked the Lord.

"Yes, sir, I am."

"Good. Then listen very carefully and use the pen I've given you to write down everything I'm about to describe."

As the Lord began to speak, the archangel Pravuel reached over and placed his hand on Enoch's hand while He dictated. As swiftly as his hand could move, Enoch began to write, page after page, chapter after chapter, book after book, mesmerized by everything he was hearing. His eyes were glued on those scalding lips, emitting so many sparks and secrets as yet unimaginable to any mere mortal.

WITH NO REAL WAY OF knowing how long the Lord had spoken, Enoch watched as the scalding lips uttered their final word, and then Pravuel lifted his hand from Enoch's. As if awakened from a powerful daydream, Enoch refocused his eyes. He shook himself and looked back up into the awesome eyes of molten divinity. "Now what, Lord?"

"Well, to begin with: I want you to apply your mind, Enoch, and realize Who is speaking to you so you'll always treasure the books I've had you write."

"Of course, Lord, thank you. I'm truly honored. I'll always treasure them far above all things."

"Good. Now I want you to go with Sariel and Raguel. Take your books with you to Earth, and when you get back, I want you to tell your children all about what I've told you and all that you've seen, from the lowest level of Heaven to the pinnacle of My throne room."

"Of course, Lord, but pardon me for asking: What if I tell them everything You've told me, and they think I've lost my mind? Maybe they say I'm making it all up. Then what?"

"Just give them the books you've written, Enoch. When they read them, they'll know Me for the Creator, and they'll realize, once and for all, I am the God of the Universe."

Enoch's eyes lit up. "Of course. Why didn't I think of that?"

"Then," continued the Lord, "I want you to distribute your books from person to person, from nation to nation, and from generation to generation."

Enoch was awestruck. "Lord, how will I ever carry out such a grand plan as that?"

"Don't worry. I'll give you an assistant: Michael the archangel. He'll help you preserve all the books you've just written."

Bowing reverently, Enoch smiled sheepishly. "Thank you, Lord. You are way ahead of me, as usual."

"And just think, Enoch, someday there will come a unique generation that will descend from your ancestors, faithful workers of My pleasure, who do not acknowledge My Name in vain. And from among that generation, there will be One Who will finally explain the meaning of the books you've written. What's more, those whom He'll teach will be instructed in the guardianship of the world."

Enoch nodded knowingly. "Yes, Lord, it will be such a wonderful day. I can't wait."

"In turn, they will then communicate those truths to a future generation, and when those people have had a chance to discover them, they'll be blessed even more than those who had read them in the beginning."

"Thank You, Lord, for Your words of truth." Again Enoch felt compelled to bow.

"Now, Enoch, I'll give you a period of thirty days to spend at home with your family. Tell everyone in your household they can all hear about what I've told you. That way they'll be able to understand I'm the only God Who exists. Then maybe they'll keep My commandments and begin to read the books you've written."

"Whatever You want, Lord. Just say the word."

"And after thirty days, I'll send My angels for you again. They'll take you from Earth and from your children, and bring you back to Me. Are you ready?"

Enoch nodded. "Yes, Lord, I am."

"Good, then the time has come for you to leave."

Another angel appeared at his side, more terrifying than any that Enoch had seen up to that point. As this menacing creature stood next to him, Enoch took a good long look. Astonishingly, this fearsome angel was covered in frost and snow. The angel slowly reached out an icy finger and touched Enoch's face, instantly freezing it.

"Don't be alarmed, Enoch," said the Lord. "If your face isn't frozen like this, no one will be able to look at you when you return to Earth, because no mortal man can endure the terror of the Lord, just as it isn't possible to endure a stove's fire or the Sun's heat." Then Enoch turned to see that Sariel and Raguel were at his side once again.

"Now, you two," continued the Lord, "take Enoch back to Earth so he can prepare for the determined day."

The two angels immediately took hold of Enoch and headed back down to Earth. By then, Enoch was so exhausted from his ordeal that he lost consciousness as Sariel and Raguel cradled him in their arms.

ARRIVING BACK AT Enoch's home, the angels gently returned their human cargo to his couch, and there he slept soundly for quite a while, until quite abruptly, Enoch's son Methuselah came bursting into the room where his father was still fast asleep.

"Father, you're back! Finally!"

Groggily, Enoch sat up on the couch. "Good God, Methuselah; what is it now?"

"Thank the Lord above. Pop, you're home!"

Blearily eyeing his surroundings, Enoch muttered, "Well, I'll be. So I am." Then he turned to Methuselah. "Son, have I got something to tell you. In fact, I want you to get the whole family together. I have something to tell everyone."

"I'll say. We thought we'd never see you again. You had us worried sick."

"Worried? Why? What are you talking about?"

"You were gone so long. Everyone thought you'd been killed by wild beasts or taken captive. Who knew what had happened to you?"

"But I was only gone a short time, a couple of hours, maybe. The most amazing hours a man could ever hope to experience, and everybody has to complain because I go missing for a little while. What's the problem?"

"A couple of hours?" blurted Methuselah, staring back at his father, quite incredulously. "Are you kidding me? Are you feeling all right?"

"Of course. I feel fine. There's nothing wrong with me. What are you going on about?"

"Father, you weren't gone for a couple of hours. You were gone for two months."

Enoch squinted oddly at the thought.

"Are you sure you're feeling all right?" Methuselah asked.

"What did you say?" murmured Enoch.

"I asked if you were feeling all right."

"No, no, no. Before that."

"I said, you've been gone for two months!"

"But how is that possible?" A peculiar smile slowly crept across Enoch's face. "Remarkable."

"And Pop?"

"Yes, son."

"Why is your face covered in frost?"

Enoch touched his cheek and examined the tip of his finger, which he could see was lightly covered in snow. "Simply remarkable," was all he said.

THE NEXT DAY, ENOCH was surrounded by a large crowd of people, including Jared, his father, Methuselah, his son, and Lamech, his grandson, along with their wives and children. Cradled in Enoch's lap was a large book.

"My beloved family, I've asked you all here today to tell you about something very important." Enoch caressed the book lovingly in his hands. "So, I'm hoping you'll at least consider what I'm about to tell you, inasmuch as it is in accordance with the Lord's will."

"Of course, Father, we'll listen," said Methuselah, as if speaking for the entire group, who were all nodding, eager to hear what the patriarch had to say.

"Wonderful. Well, you see: These things I have to tell you about," said Enoch, hesitating nervously, his fingers playing lightly across the binding of the book in his lap. "What I'm going to tell you is simply what I've heard from the Lord's own mouth during my absence. To you, it seemed as though I was gone for two whole months, but from my perspective, it felt like just a few hours. You all remember, don't you?"

"Of course, son," said Jared. "How could we ever forget? We were worried out of our heads. We didn't know where you'd gone."

"Well, now I'm here to tell you, Father. But I'm afraid you'll never believe me when I do." Enoch paused thoughtfully again as he carefully scanned the group that was looking at him with such trusting faces. "Does anybody here think I would ever lie about something that concerns the Lord and His inscrutable will?"

"Certainly not, Pop," replied Methuselah. "What on Earth would make you think that?"

Embarrassed, Enoch shook his head. "Because I still find it so hard to believe myself. One moment, I'm sure it happened, then the next moment, I'm sure I dreamt the whole thing. It's all so confusing."

"Don't worry about us, Grandpa," insisted Lamech. "Who are we to judge what did or didn't happen to you?"

"Thank you, Lamech," said Enoch with a sigh of relief. "What a wonderful thing to say. I can't tell you how glad I am to hear that."

"So tell us, Father," prodded Methuselah. "Where did you go that whole time? Please, don't keep us in suspense any longer."

"Certainly, son. I went to Heaven."

"Y—*you* what?" sputtered Methuselah. "Did you say you went to *Heaven*?"

Enoch smiled radiantly, suddenly captured in his recollection of the place. "Yes, Methuselah, that's exactly what I said."

"But how, Grandfather?" asked Lamech.

"With the help of God's angels, that's how. Certainly you don't think I got there under my own power, do you?"

Methuselah and Lamech exchanged a peculiar look, as did everyone else there, including their two wives, who leaned in toward one another.

In hushed tones, Lamech's wife asked, "He didn't say he went to Heaven, did he?"

"No, of course not," Methuselah's wife replied quietly. "He said he *dreamt* he went to Heaven, that's all."

"Oh, okay," said Lamech's wife with a sheepish grin. "For a second, I thought he said he actually went there."

And together the two women laughingly shrugged it off.

"But Grandfather," blurted Lamech, who then hesitated when he saw that his father Methuselah was holding up his hand to caution him.

"Never mind, son, just never mind," Methuselah said calmly. "Just let it go. Can't you see your grandfather has been through enough already?"

Lamech nodded obediently, and Enoch, still flush with excitement, never even noticed that everyone there was quite oblivious to the true significance of what he was trying to tell them.

"So you see, my children," continued Enoch, "it's just that what I'm about to tell you is not something I made up from my own imagination. It comes straight from the Lord Himself. Do you understand what I'm trying to say?"

Methuselah nodded tacitly. "Yes, Father, we understand. Go ahead, please."

"Good. Then today I'll be reading to you from one of the books I wrote while I was in the Lord's presence. Would you like that?"

The group chimed in unison. "Yes, please."

"Yes, Grandpa, please read to us from your book, won't you?" added Lamech.

Enoch smiled like a doting father. "And so I will, just as the Lord has requested."

Opening the book, he carefully slid his hand over the surface of its pages. "In fact, what I'm going to tell you is all about the past, it's about the present, and it's even about the future, right up until Judgment Day."

A hush fell over the entire group. All eyes were fixed on Enoch; and slowly, confidently, he began to read aloud from the book, just as he had been told by God's own mouth.

Dawn of Time

Adapted from

The Secrets of Enoch,
also called
The Slavonic Enoch
or *The Second Book of Enoch*

and

The First Book of Adam and Eve,
also called
The Conflict of Adam and Eve with Satan

Adam and Eve in Paradise, Jan Gossaert, 1527

Dawn of Time

Of Light and Darkness

IN THE BEGINNING the void of darkness was everywhere, and in that darkness there was only silence, all except, that is, for the still, small voice of God, which said, "Before anything visible ever existed, only We, the Godhead, used to traverse the domain of the invisible."

THEN CAME THE DAY when God decided to create the Universe, so He said, "Let the very darkest regions produce a division between the visible and the invisible." Suddenly a tremendous light burst forth, and a great age began.

After that, God decided to produce something from this interplay of light and darkness, so He spoke again: "Let the waters congeal into a dense core of molten glass." And as He saw the light separate further and further from the darkness, God said, "Let an atmosphere encircle this fledgling planet I will call Earth. Out of the ocean waves, let volcanic rock emerge, and from the hardened rock, let the dry land pile up, and the depths of this Earth, I will call the Abyss, or the Bottomless Pit."

ON THE SECOND DAY God took a tremendous lightning bolt, composed of both fire and ice, which neither can extinguish, and He carved out a chunk of molten rock. Then God said, "Having received its remarkable nature from the gleam of My eye, let this firestorm produce the ten invisible orders of angelic troops, with weapons and clothing forged in flames, and let every one of them remain under their own commanders, even as I have decreed."

But among the hierarchy of angelic warriors there was one who grew restless with the existing order, so he turned to one of his companions and asked, "Why should god be the only one who has a throne? If I wanted to, I could place my own throne far above the clouds. Then, I, Lucifer, the Morning Star, could achieve equality with the lord, and nothing would be impossible for me. And if you join me, I promise we'll all have the kind of fame and glory that god thinks is his alone to possess."

So a great war broke out in the heavenly realms between Lucifer's minions and God's angelic warriors, with Lucifer lassoing one third of the angelic troops with his tail and dragging them into his diabolical service. The war raged on for some time as both sides pushed back and forth with the ebb and flow of battle, but before long, God personally intervened, ejecting Lucifer and his legions from Heaven. Like a tremendous cascade of lightning bolts, they all fell, crashing down onto the surface of the Earth, sending shockwaves to its very core as they landed. All across the globe, every mountain and every valley melted away as the planet shuddered violently.

"And there you will remain," declared God, "to fly continuously above the Abyss until Judgment Day. "But no longer will you be seen in the shimmering beauty of your original form as Lucifer, the Morning Star. From now on, you'll be transformed into the epitome of ugliness and filth, to be forever known as Satan, the adversary, and your angels will no longer continue in their prior state of elegance and grace, doomed as they are to become as grotesque and horrid as their despicable master."

ON THE THIRD DAY God turned to renewing and reshaping the devastated Earth, which had nearly been obliterated as a result of the Fall of Satan and his crashing minions, so He said, "Let the mountains and valleys be restored, and upon them let the seeds in the ground produce their plant life with incredibly lush grass and fruitful trees. And let there be a beautiful Paradise in the East, near the border of this world." Instantly, a colossal hedge grew around Paradise, completely enclosing it, except for an ornate gateway that served as an entrance. Then, darting through the air, a fiery angel streaked to the gate of Paradise and took up position at the entrance, where he raised a flaming sword, standing at attention with a menacing look stamped on his face.

THEN THE FOURTH DAY arrived. "Let the Sun appear for illumination of the day," said God, and a great fireball congealed above the blue sphere of the Earth. "And let the Moon appear in the celestial vault to shine at night, along with a vast array of stars." So the day gave way to night, and a cool white orb appeared out of the midst of the inky blackness, followed by countless stars, glimmering all around it.

WHEN THE FIFTH DAY came, God said, "Let the oceans bring forth fish, the sky, vast numbers of birds, and the land, animals of every species." And as they appeared, they all began to spread out in every direction, through the sea, across the sky, and over the landscape.

ON DAY SIX GOD SAID, "Now it's time for Me to create mankind. I'll make Adam by forming him with seven consistencies: One, his flesh will be made from the ground." Immediately, in the dirt, the shape of a human being began to form, first the torso, then the arms and legs, and finally a head. As God described His intentions, the form of this human gradually became whatever He said. "Two, his blood will be made of the dew." Moisture congealed from the air about this nascent creature and flowed into its form. "Three, his eyes will be made from the Sun." A tremendous beam of light flashed into the space that was slowly forming into a face. "Four, his bones will be made from stone." Rock jutted up out of the ground and into his members. "Five, his intelligence will be from the speed of the angels and the clouds." What seemed like part angelic presence and part cloudy substance swirled into the human's skull. "Six, his veins and hair will be made from the grass of the Earth." Blades of grass grew up into this developing body to form the human's circulatory system and the hair on his head and skin. "And seven, his spirit will be made from My breath and the wind." Just then, an ethereal human face appeared above the figure that was still embedded in the ground and hovered there, face to face with the human's prostrate form lying below it. A blast of energy flowed like a gust of wind from the mouth of the hovering face, and the now-living human sucked in a deep breath from this energy-flow. Opening his eyes, he slowly sat up and rubbed his eyes as though he had just awakened from an ancient slumber. The human—Adam—looked around, surveying everything around him. Awestruck, he marveled at all the animals as they made their way about the primordial landscape.

"And I gave Adam seven natures," continued God. "His flesh is for hearing." Adam tilted his head as he heard the call of the animals around him for the very first time. "His eyes are for seeing." He squinted oddly at their unexpected forms. "For the spirit, there is the sense of smell." Inhaling deeply, Adam felt the air flowing through his nostrils and deep into his chest. "There are veins for touching, and blood for tasting." Adam touched his own face, then put his fingers in his mouth, like an infant acclimating itself to its newborn existence. "He has bones for endurance." Adam stood to his feet and took his first, feeble step, testing the solid ground beneath him. "And finally, with his intelligence, there comes enjoyment." Feeling the dirt between his toes, Adam realized that there was a difference between it and himself. He smiled proudly as he made his way about this new world, inspecting each and every thing he encountered, from the tiniest insects to the largest mammals.

"So in the creation of this human, I'd conceived a cunning thing," continued God, "having formed him with both visible and invisible natures, and now his very being reflected that fact, too. He understood speech like a created being, and was fragile in his greatness, yet mighty in his frailty. I placed him on Earth to be a kind of 'second angel,' if you will. Regal and supreme, I appointed him to be king over this planet and to possess My wisdom. In fact, there was nothing like him among any of My creatures that I'd created to that point."

Looking skyward, Adam was amazed at the sight of so many stars, still faintly flickering in the early morning hours, stretching as far as the eye could see. "And because the name of this first human was derived from the four cardinal points of the Earth, I appointed four special stars for him." Then, four points of light, more brilliant than all the rest, streaked across the sky. A mesmerized Adam watched as each star took its new position, one soaring to the east, one to the west, one to the south and one the north.

"Then I showed Adam two ways of life, one of light and one of darkness, and I explained to him what was good and what was evil so that I would be able to find out whether or not he really loved Me. I also wanted to find out who among his descendants would love Me or hate Me, because I understand all too well their true nature, even though they never have. Even worse, because they're so ignorant of their genuine selves, they'll sin even more, and in the end, what is left for them after they've sinned, except death?"

AFTER A BUSY MORNING of investigating his new surroundings, Adam sat down awhile, enjoying the afternoon breeze as it gently blew through his hair. Suddenly he grew so tired that he had to lie down.

"What's wrong with me?" wondered Adam. "I feel so strange."

Slowly closing his eyes, he fell into a deep sleep. As he lay there, a hand suddenly appeared next to his right side, which reached out with its forefinger and caused an incision to appear between Adam's fifth and sixth rib. Then from out of the incision came one of his ribs, which the hand set onto the ground next to the dozing man. Gradually, this rib absorbed into the ground and it, too, eventually expanded into the shape of a human being, filling in, bit by bit, in the same fashion as God had done with Adam.

"And finally I created a woman to abide with Adam," said God. "That way death would overtake him through her, and taking the last word he spoke before he fell asleep, I named her Eve, which is to say, *mother*."

ADAM SLOWLY OPENED his eyes, and to his amazement, he realized that there was someone lying next to him. The woman opened her eyes, too, and sat up. As soon as she saw Adam, she smiled. Adam stood to his feet, and taking the woman by her hand, he helped her up. For the longest time that first couple gazed at one another; and then Adam spoke his first words to her. "Why do I know your name?" he asked with a perplexed smile. "Even though I've never heard it before, I feel like I know who you are. Isn't that odd?"

Smiling back at him, she nodded. Noticing the scar on his right side, she reached out and gently touched it.

"Yes, that's right," said Adam, as if recalling a dream of how this woman had miraculously appeared next to him. In his mind's eye, he glimpsed how God's finger had opened his side and sealed it back up with merely a gesture. "You're bone of my bone, and flesh of my flesh. You are Eve."

Again she nodded with a smile. "Yes, I believe you're right. How strange. I am Eve. And even though I've never seen you before, I, too, feel as though I know your name." Her lips slowly formed a single word as it came lilting from her delicate mouth. "Adam."

"Yes, Eve, yes; I am Adam," he said, as he reached out to embrace her.

TOGETHER, THE COUPLE strolled, hand in hand, through the lush landscape of their garden home without a care in the world. As they did, they marveled at every sight that came into view, like children seeing the world for the very first time. One by one, Adam pointed to each living creature that they encountered. "Before you came into my life, Eve, God inspired me to name every one of them. Look, there's Horse, over there is Sparrow, and here is Butterfly."

LATER, AS ADAM AND EVE sat down to relax on that very first evening of their being together, they looked up at the starry sky.

"I opened the Heavens so Adam and Eve could see the angels singing," said God. "Radiant light never stopped shining for them."

A tremendous array of beautiful angels suddenly appeared above them. Flying down to greet the couple, the angels seemed genuinely intrigued by these two humans, who likewise felt the same way about meeting them.

"BUT BEFORE LONG," continued God, "Satan, who had been doomed to hover the Abyss, began to take notice of this new couple, who now inhabited the world that had, until then, been his, and his alone, to command."

Turning to his lieutenant, the devil grumbled, "God must be trying to create a new world, because this Adam now appears to be king of the Earth. Now he's controlling everything that's happening here instead of me."

"What should we do, Master?" asked the lieutenant.

"Well, I may be a fugitive from Heaven, and god may have altered me so I'm no longer like the rest of his darling angels, but the nature of my understanding is still the same! I still understand all too well that we've been condemned for our crime."

"But, Lord, what does that mean?"

"It means god is never going to forgive us, you fool! It means that unless we do something about this Adam, even this miserable excuse for a planet is no longer ours anymore."

"You mean god will never restore us to our previous condition? And this Adam is going to be our king from now on?"

"That's exactly what I mean, yes! God's completely abandoned us, and now it seems he's starting over with these *humans*!"

"But isn't there anything we can do to stop it?"

Satan's hideous face instantly lit up with a sinister smirk. "Maybe there is one thing we can do?"

"What? Will you enlist the aid of this Adam like you did with the angels before him? Make a pact with him to wage war with god again?"

Satan shook his head. "No, I'm afraid that's no longer a viable option. Openly confronting god again might turn out as badly as it did the last time we tried that. Then god would certainly banish us to a place even worse than this one."

"Worse than the Abyss?" blanched the stunned lieutenant.

"Much worse, yes," growled Satan, still mulling over the new plan in his twisted mind. "No, I think what we need this time is a much more subtle approach."

"What?"

"I propose an invasion."

"An invasion? But if Adam and Eve aren't willing to cooperate, won't they simply enlist god's help in the face of an invasion?"

Then turning to his lieutenant, Satan flashed a malignant grin. "Not the kind of invasion I have in mind, no."

SO, DISGUISED IN the shell of a beautiful serpent, Satan's first act was to seduce Eve, without directly confronting Adam, or even God, for that matter. And offering up the Forbidden Fruit for Eve to eat, she unwittingly took a bite, and as soon as she had, she persuaded Adam to eat as well.

"And even though I warned them never to eat the Fruit from the Tree of Knowledge, they ate it anyway," God said with a tremendous mourning in His voice. "And when they did, their eyes were truly opened. At that very moment, they began to die. So what choice did I have but to curse ignorance? I refused to curse what I had already blessed, so I didn't curse Adam or the Earth or the other creatures, but I did curse Adam's evil deeds and their result. 'You're made of the ground,' I told him, 'so you'll return to it when you die. I won't be destroying you but simply returning you to where I took you from. Then when I return, I can restore everything that you've lost.'"

A Promise of Days

FINALLY, THE SEVENTH day arrived, and God said, "But because of what they'd done, I only allowed Adam and Eve to remain in Paradise for five and a half hours before I forced them to leave."

As Adam and Eve were leaving the Garden of Eden, they came to its gate and stood there, frozen with fear. To their utter dismay, all they saw was an alien expanse spread out before them. Slowly, the despondent couple made their way forward, step by cautious step. Every direction they looked the ground was covered with stones, large and small. Dirt was everywhere.

"Oh, Eve, what have we done?" groaned Adam. "Until now, all we've ever known is our garden home. But just look at this strange place. I've never seen anything like it before."

"It's horrible, Adam," whimpered Eve. "I don't think I can go through with this. My heart is breaking."

Seized by a terrible dread, they both fell flat on their faces and died. But the eyes of God were watching them as they lay prostrate at the garden's gate, and in an instant, a handsome Man appeared at their side. Gazing down at the couple, His eyes beamed with a love and compassion that seemed to transcend time and space. He bent down, took Adam and Eve by the hand, and lovingly helped them to their feet. Still disoriented from their experience, they stood up and gazed into the face of this marvelous Man standing before them.

"Who are You?" asked Adam, obviously sensing this Man was someone special.

"Actually, I have many names," He replied with a quiet reassurance, "as the time and circumstance dictates. In your case, you will know Me as the Word of God."

"What just happened to us?" asked Eve as she oddly examined her hands, then touched her face as if to confirm that she was really alive.

"I'm afraid you died," replied the Word, quite nonchalantly.

"Died?" wondered Adam. "But why? And if we died, how come we're talking to You right now?"

Amused, the Word smiled warmly. "Unfortunately, those are difficult questions to answer, but I'll try to explain all this in a way you might understand. First of all, you died because that's what God decreed for you and your children as soon as you ate from the Tree of Knowledge, and the reason you're talking to Me now is because I raised you from your state of death so you can fulfill the days God has decreed for you on this Earth."

Adam and Eve exchanged a peculiar look.

"So we actually died, but you restored our life again," said Adam, trying to work out this mystery in his confused mind. "Is that what You're saying?"

"It is, yes."

"Then does that mean You'll be restoring us to our garden home now, too?"

With deeply sad eyes, the Word gazed back at these two for several moments. "No, Adam, I'm sorry. Just because I raised you doesn't mean I'll be returning you to the garden right now."

"No?" Heartbroken, Adam nearly fainted. "But why not, Lord? You don't want us to die again out here in this wilderness, do You?"

"Oh, Adam, don't despair," replied the Word. "Rest assured; I haven't completely abandoned the two of you. I promise, someday I'll rescue you both from all of this, and then you can return to the garden home you love so much."

"Really?" said Adam with a tremendous sigh of relief. "Oh, thank You, Lord. Did you hear that, Eve? We're going to be rescued after all."

"Yes, Adam, I heard," replied Eve, sounding somewhat skeptical. "But when?"

"Someday, Eve," said Adam, shrugging his shoulders. "How should I know? Someday soon, I imagine."

"Until then," continued the Word, "I've appointed this Earth to have hours and days and years transpire upon it. And you and your descendants will live here until the determined time is completed. Then, I'll return to rescue you and all your faithful children."

"When, Lord?" wondered Adam. "When will that be?"

"After five and a half days, Adam."

Adam looked as confused as ever. "But, Lord, I don't understand what You mean by five and a half days. You mean we're going to be rescued after just five and a half days. Is that what You're telling us?"

"Not exactly, Adam, no," said the Word. "The days I'm speaking of represent days from My point of view. You and your descendants will experience these five and a half days from your perspective as five thousand, five hundred years. Then I'll come to rescue you and your righteous descendants. But I already told you all about this before, Adam, just as you two were leaving the garden. Don't you remember?"

Adam searched his mind, trying to recall what the Word was describing. "Not really, no." But mental images began to flash into view. "Wait, I do remember something."

In his mind, Adam could see himself, walking side by side with Eve as they were making their way toward the garden gate. As they walked slowly past the Tree of Knowledge, he remembered how it looked, recalling in vivid detail just how much it had changed. Now, it was withered and dry. Adam trembled as he approached the tree and fell at its foot, but suddenly the Word of God was there to gently pick him up.

"Yes, Lord, I remember now," exclaimed Adam. "I remember how You first told me about Your promise to rescue us after five and a half days." Then turning to Eve, he asked, "Don't you remember, Eve?"

"No, Adam, I don't."

"But you must. You were there, too."

But Eve despondently shook her head. "I'm sorry, but I don't remember."

Adam then turned to speak with the Word but found that He had vanished. "He's gone, Eve. Now what should we do?"

"How should I know, Adam? I'm just as confused as you are."

Quite reluctantly, the couple turned from the gate of their old home and started out into the forbidding landscape of their new home.

THE FIRST THING Adam and Eve noticed, having ventured eastward from the garden, was a vast ocean that stretched as far as the eye could see. Stepping up to the shore, they found the water was so clear that they could see into the very depths of the Earth.

"In fact," said God, "the water in this ocean was still so pure, one could even drink it, and if someone was completely stained, washing in it would make them as clean and pure as it was."

As the couple gazed out across the vastness of the sea, their eyes peered further and further into the distant horizon, where it appeared that this ocean was reaching upward to the edge of the sky, and from there it appeared to envelop the entire world in a tremendous canopy of water.

"For My own pleasure," continued God, "I created this sea because I knew that Adam and Eve would fall from grace, and after their banishment from Paradise, others would be born, and faithful ones from among them would die. But on the last day, I would reunite their souls with their flesh, and let them bathe in that ocean so they could all be cleansed from their sins."

Just then, an angel appeared and pointed for Adam and Eve to walk in the opposite direction. "I'm sorry to inform you, but God doesn't want you to stay here."

"But why?" asked Adam, shrugging his shoulders. "This seems like a perfectly good place to live."

"He's worried if you live here in the East, then you might try to wash yourselves in this ocean before the appointed time, and you'll be cleansed from your sins, forget the crime you've committed, and no longer contemplate your punishment."

Saddened by this, the couple turned and started walking the other direction.

AS THEY DREW NEARER to the garden, Adam and Eve could see two more angels, one standing at its northern edge and another to the south. Both were obviously poised as guards, and both were pointing the couple in a westerly direction.

"As for the northern or southern sides of the garden," said God, "I didn't want Adam and Eve to live there, either, because whenever the winds blew in their direction, it would have brought them the sweet smell of the trees in the garden, and smelling their lovely fragrance might cause them to forget about their disobedience, in which case they might never be cleansed from their crime."

Without a word of protest this time, Adam and Eve continued past the garden, traveling along the southern edge so they could at least catch a glimpse of the entranceway, and silently they continued onward to the western frontier of this new territory.

"FINALLY," CONTINUED God, "because I govern everything in a way that only I understand, I made Adam and Eve live on the western border of the garden, where the land was broad, in a cave, hewn out of solid rock."

Having arrived at this cave, Adam and Eve met another angel standing at the entranceway, but instead of barring their way, this angel was beckoning them to enter. "Welcome, you two. This is where God wants you to live. Come inside and make yourselves comfortable."

The couple cautiously stepped up to the mouth of the cave and hesitated as if frozen with indecision.

"Oh, Adam, I'm not so sure about this," moaned Eve. "Do we really have to live in there?"

"You heard the angel. This is where God wants us to live. So I guess that's all there is to it."

"But do we have go in right now? Can't we look around a little while before we go inside?"

Adam shrugged. "I don't see why not. Let's go, then. Maybe we'll feel better about going in when we come back later."

Relieved, Eve nodded, and then the two of them turned and walked away.

ADAM AND EVE WANDERED aimlessly until, much to their surprise, they found themselves very close to the garden gate, where an angry looking cherub buzzed about with his flaming sword. The cherub glared fiercely at them with his sword raised, ready to strike.

"Hey!" shrieked the angel. "You two aren't allowed to be here! Leave this place before I kill you where you stand!"

Paralyzed by fear, the couple fainted, falling flat on their faces, but the cherub felt sorry for them, so he lowered his sword and flew up toward Heaven.

"LORD, I FOUND ADAM and Eve snooping around the entrance to the garden," said the cherub to the molten Face of God. "And when I ordered them to leave, they collapsed, dead away. Did I do the right thing?"

"You've done well, My faithful servant," replied the Face.

"What should I do now?"

"Return to your post, and I'll send My Word to resolve the situation."

SO THE CHERUB returned to the entrance of the garden, and suddenly the Word of God appeared where Adam and Eve lay prostrate. Sadly looking down at their motionless bodies, the Word shook His head. "What am I going to do with you two?" Then He reached down, restored their lives, and helped them to their feet.

"Lord, thank you so much for coming to our rescue," Adam said as he wiped himself off. "We were just wandering around, and before we knew it, we'd gotten too close to the garden gate. We're so sorry if we made You angry. Please forgive us."

"Never mind that now. Just promise Me you won't let this happen again."

"Yes, Lord, we promise," insisted Adam. "It's just that we're so miserable here in this new world. We miss our old home so much."

"I understand. But didn't I already tell you two I was going to save you after five and a half days?"

The couple nodded timidly.

"So relax," continued the Word, "and live in the cave like I asked you. Can you do that for Me?"

They nodded again and replied as one: "Yes, Lord."

"Good. Before you know it, everything you both desire will be restored to you again, and all the misery and sadness you're enduring now will just be a distant memory." And with that, the Word of God vanished.

Adam and Eve looked at each other and smiled reluctantly. "Did you hear that, Eve? I'm beginning to think God really is serious about rescuing us someday."

"Yes, Adam, I heard. The only problem is we don't know how long that *someday* is going to be, do we?"

Adam nodded meekly. "No, but still, something tells me it's going to happen. Our old life isn't so far away after all."

Enemy Within and Without

MEANWHILE, SATAN and his cadre of demons sat watching Adam and Eve from a distant hillside. "Can you believe those two?" groaned the devil. "What spoiled brats they turned out to be. I just don't get it. What does god see in them, anyway?"

"I think he just likes to make things that remind him of himself," replied his lieutenant, quite matter-of-factly. "You know, little versions in his own image that he can boss around and make do stuff."

Amused, Satan smirked. "Well, well, my infernal lieutenant. How clever you turned out to be."

Proud of himself, the lieutenant turned to one of his fellow demons and elbowed him in the side. "See, I told you I was smart."

"Tell me, then, if you're so clever," continued the devil. "What do you propose we do to rid ourselves of these despicable, little vermin before they infest every square inch of what's left of our Universe? Can you tell me that?"

For several tense moments, the lieutenant mulled the question over in his ugly mind. "Well, let's see, now that god has kicked them out of his presence, I say they're easy pickings. I say we go down there right now, rip their hearts out, and eat them while they watch."

Relishing the thought, the other demons howled with grisly delight. Satan, however, was clearly unimpressed. "And you think god will just sit back and let it happen, do you?"

"It's worth a try, isn't it? He is still angry with them, isn't he?"

"Of course he is. But if you've noticed, even after I went to all the trouble to get them kicked out of the garden, he's still helping them. What makes you think he won't just give them new hearts once you've eaten the old ones?"

"Hmmm, I never thought of that," mumbled the lieutenant.

"And if god did that for them," interjected another demon, "just imagine how grateful they'd be to him."

"You see?" blurted Satan. "Now that's exactly what I'm talking about! Open warfare is futile! How many times do I have to tell you that?"

"Well, if we can't overwhelm them with blatant violence," muttered the lieutenant, thoroughly vexed, "then what can we do?"

"We do the only thing we *can* do," the devil replied slowly, thoughtfully. "We go underground."

BACK TO THE ENTRANCE to their cave, Adam and Eve were still quite frustrated as they stood there, staring bleakly at its cavernous mouth, trying desperately to work up the nerve to go inside.

"Adam?"

"Yes, Eve. What is it?"

"Why do I get the feeling it wants to eat us alive?"

"What a strange thing to say." Adam turned to Eve with a peculiar look on his face. "What made you think of something like that?"

Eve shrugged. "I don't know. I just looked at it, and the thought struck me, that's all. Why?"

"Because for a moment, I felt the same way; as if it wanted to tear into our flesh and devour us."

"And now?"

"Now ... it's passed. Now, there's just the sense of a mindless void ... dark and lonely ... waiting for us inside this cave."

"Oh, Adam. I'm not sure which is worse, being eaten alive or swallowed by the dark loneliness."

"Well, there's one way to find out," murmured Adam, and then he cautiously ventured forward through the craggy mouth of the cave, followed timidly by Eve.

Once inside, Adam was clearly dismayed by what he saw. "Just look at this place, Eve! It's so small! This place pales in comparison to the expanse of our garden."

"This isn't a home," Eve whimpered. "It's a prison."

"We used to have the Lord's mercy overshadowing us, but now all we have to shelter us is this slab of stone."

"And it's so dark in here. What's happened to our eyes? We used to be able to see angels singing in Heaven; but not anymore."

"Now our eyes are merely flesh, Eve. Now there's nothing but this gloomy cave to look at."

"Adam, do we really have to live in this cave for the rest of our lives? I feel like I'm going to suffocate."

"But we have to. God's ordered us to live here. And if we don't, we'll be in danger of being rebels all over again."

"Please, can't you at least ask God to let us live somewhere else while we wait for Him to rescue us?"

So Adam looked up at that rocky ceiling. "Oh, God, please release us from having to live in this cave. We don't want to stay under this overhanging rock anymore. We can't see the sky or any of Your creatures inside this place." Agonized, he began to beat his chest with such force that he abruptly dropped dead.

A devastated Eve began to weep. "Oh, God, it's true. We've gone from light to darkness all because of what I did, but please don't hold it against me forever. Just look at how Your servant Adam has fallen. Please restore his life, won't You? Don't leave me in this dungeon all alone. But if You decide not to raise him, will You at least take my life so I can be like him?"

She wept so miserably that soon she fell onto Adam's motionless body and died, too.

Then the Word of God appeared and, with merely a touch of His hand, revived Adam and Eve. Slowly, the couple got to their feet and wiped themselves off.

"Thank you, Lord, for coming to help us," Adam said with a sigh of relief.

"Have you come to take us somewhere else to live besides this cave?" asked Eve.

"I'm sorry, Eve, but that's not why I came."

Adam and Eve exchanged a distressed look.

"But why not?" moaned Eve.

"Stop it, Eve," said the Word. "What makes you think I'm not as upset as you are about all this? You think I'm happy you both chose to disobey Me? You think I wanted you to leave the garden?"

"No, I guess not," muttered Eve, sadly hanging her head.

"Of course not," He continued. "And now you'll simply have to get used to it. I didn't choose this destiny for you; you did. You defied Me because you wanted divinity and greatness, but I took away your luminous nature and made you come here. If only you hadn't eaten that fruit in the first place. I told you not to go near that tree, didn't I?"

Dolefully, the couple nodded.

"There were so many other trees in the garden!" lamented the Word. "But that damned Satan; he just had to make *that one* seem so much more appetizing, until finally you gave in and ate from it."

"But, Lord," groaned Adam, "how could eating something so small cause such a huge calamity?"

"Because when you ate, you were actually cooperating with Satan, a diabolical creature who, though originally created for an awesome purpose, chose instead to scorn Me and reject My first plan for him."

"You mean like us," mumbled Adam. "Don't You?"

"Yes, Adam, I'm afraid so. And because you listened to him, I've allowed the same suffering I unleashed on him to come upon you as well."

"So You do intend to wipe us out after all," replied Adam, thoroughly disheartened.

"Of course not, Adam; I'm the Creator. I would never create living beings simply for the sake of destroying them. But if they manage to make Me angry enough with their persistent rebellion, I will reprimand them with terrible plagues; that is, until they really want to change their ways."

"B—*but*, Lord, we *do* want to change our ways," stammered Adam. "We *have* changed. We realize how badly we've behaved and promise to never doubt what You tell us, ever again."

"Yes, Lord, Adam is right. We're so sorry we didn't trust You before. We really want to prove to You we can do better next time. Will You please give us another chance?"

"Of course, you two, you know I will," continued the Word. "Now remember: I've confirmed My promise with you, and I'll never forget it. But by the same token I can't let you back into the garden until after My contract of five and a half days is completed. So please, for your own sakes, stop trying to persuade Me to do something you know I won't do. Is that clear?"

Together, Adam and Eve replied, "Yes, Lord."

"And Lord," continued Adam. "Before we got kicked out of the garden, remember how all the animals were under my control?"

"Of course I do, Adam. Why do you ask?"

"It's just that ever since we disobeyed You I keep having the strangest feelings. It's like Eve and I are being watched or, worse, hunted. I'm worried one of these days an animal is going to try to eat us. Does that make sense?"

"Of course, Adam, I understand. And you're right. The world you're living in now is quite different from the one you used to know. Since your fall, the creation has suffered along with your rebellion. Even the animals have changed. But don't worry; I'll make sure they realize they're not to harm you or any of your righteous descendants."

TWO BY TWO, MALE AND female, the animals began to approach Adam and Eve, respectfully bowing before them. Among the more ferocious species came lions, bears, crocodiles, jackals, and wolves.

"Greetings, Adam," growled the lion. "God has instructed us to appear before you today."

"He wants us to give you our solemn assurance," grunted the bear. "So we will."

"As long as we're never attacked by you and your kind," snapped the crocodile, "you need never fear us."

"If you promise not to hunt us," yelped the jackal, "we promise never to harm you."

"If this is agreeable to you," snarled the wolf, "then we'll go in peace today with an understanding between us all."

In response, Adam and Eve bowed to the animals.

"We, too," said Adam, "pledge to never attack your kind without provocation, and we'll strive to co-exist in harmony as long as we remain together on this Earth."

"Agreed," the animals said with one voice. Then, they all left the couple in peace.

From a distance, however, the serpent was watching everything with utter disdain. "Just look at the way those pathetic creatures have all prostrated themselves before these humans. What a complete waste of time. What are they thinking? Who is Adam that we should bow down to him? Even God has abandoned him. He's nothing but a miserable animal like us now, just waiting for the day he becomes food; food for me, perhaps. What I wouldn't do to exact my revenge for what's happened to me."

"Revenge, you say?" asked a disembodied voice.

"Who said that?" snapped the startled serpent, his head darting about in an effort to locate the source of the voice. "Where are you? Show yourself this instant!"

Slowly, the hideous, black eyes of the devil materialized before the serpent. "Here I am, Serpent. Remember me?"

"You?" sputtered the serpent. "Why should I remember *you*?"

Then, as if to prepare the serpent for what he was about to see, Satan gradually materialized the rest of his body, bit by dreadful bit. Soon there stood before the dumbfounded serpent a monster of ghastly proportions. As though he were a twisted conglomeration of every ravenous animal rolled into one, the devil's skin was coarse like a crocodile's, his fingernails sharp like a hawk's, face ragged like a wolf's, eyes steely like a leopard's, teeth jagged like a boar's, horns crooked like a dragon's, and wings leathery like a bat's.

"Now do you remember me, Serpent?" sneered the devil.

Momentarily taken aback, the serpent gulped ever so slightly. "Good grief, no, I do not. I've never laid eyes on you before; and believe me when I say, by the looks of you, I'd certainly remember if I had. What manner of species are you, anyway?"

With a cavalier wave of his paw, Satan scoffed, "Ah, that's not important. The important thing is how you *feel* right now. Do tell, Serpent. What will you do with that unquenchable rage welling up in your belly, every day, every hour, every minute?"

"My belly? What do you know of my belly? Or my rage, for that matter? What makes you such an expert of me?"

"Because I know all about you, Serpent, that's why. I know very well how you were once the most respected animal in all of god's creation; that is, until he changed you, made you different, *cursed* you. I remember when you were one of the most beautiful animals in the world, so lovely all the others were awestruck in your presence."

The serpent's head tilted, his eyes thinned, his forked tongue flicked at the air. "Yes, as I still do, each and every moment I breathe."

"But now, I'm afraid, you're the ugliest animal of all," continued Satan, honing every word as sharp as a dagger. "Slippery, cold-blooded, forced to crawl around on your belly like a lowly, miserable worm. Instead of eating the best foods and living in the nicest places like you used to, now you eat in the dirt, live in the dirt, breathe the dirt."

"How I loathe the dirt," hissed the serpent through clenched fangs.

"Your home, once a place where every animal would gather, has now been abandoned, scorned. Before, everyone used to come and drink wherever the serpent drank, but ever since god's curse made you venomous, they all flee as they see the meanest creature alive approaching the drinking hole."

The serpent's eyes grew wide with rage. "Now none of them will drink with me. Now everyone hates me! But why? What did I ever do to them? Nothing!"

LATER, ADAM AND EVE were just sitting in their cave, staring blankly at the walls.

"Oh, Eve, when we lived in the garden our hearts soared. We saw angels singing in Heaven. But now just look at us, staring at the walls, with God's entire creation hidden from view! What's wrong with us?"

Then the Word materialized there in the cave with them. "You're no longer under My control, Adam; that's what's wrong with you. As long as you were, you had a luminous nature inside you. That's why you could see so many amazing things."

"And now that we've been banished," muttered Eve, "we'll never see things the same way again, *ever*."

"But why, Lord?" asked Adam.

"Because your luminous nature has been removed. Now, you're mere flesh and blood. So from now on, you'll only be able to see things close to you." Then the Word vanished once again.

"Did you hear that, Adam?" Eve moaned as she began to pace nervously about. "We've been reduced to mere flesh ... *flesh*. Here we thought we'd become like gods, and what has become of us? Flesh."

"Eve, please, we've got to learn to relax. We can't keep worrying so much about things we can't control anymore."

Halting in her tracks, she turned to him. "What is that supposed to mean?"

"It means we've got to accept what's happened to us. If we're going to survive this mess we're in, then we're going to have to make the best of it."

"I suppose so," Eve replied with a heavy sigh. "What should we do now?"

"I say we go for a walk. See what we can see; I don't know. Anything is better than hanging around this miserable cave."

SO THE COUPLE wandered about aimlessly and again, without their even realizing what they had done, they ended up back at the garden gate. Approaching very close, they gazed longingly at its enclosed walls, comprised of dense, thorn-covered shrubs.

Eve abruptly burst into tears. "Oh, Adam, I thought we told God we wouldn't keep trying to get back into the garden."

"We did," Adam replied sheepishly. "And we're—*we're* not."

"Then why are we here again?"

"But we're not trying to get back in, Eve. We're just looking around, that's all. We're out for a walk."

They slowly stepped away from the gate and walked up a hill near the eastern edge of the garden. From there, they could see a river that flowed right past a huge tree at the heart of the garden and branched out into four rivers, which all made their way in every direction, north, east, south and west. As it so happened, one of those rivers flowed under the garden wall and right past the couple on its way to the ocean in the East.

"Look, Eve, it's the Tree of Life," blurted Adam as he eagerly pointed. "You see it?"

"Of course I see it, Adam. What about it?"

"There's water flowing from its roots. See?"

Confused, Eve shrugged her shoulders. "Okay, so there's water coming from the tree. So what?"

"Well, if water is flowing from the Tree of Life and it connects with this river that goes past us here, then maybe this water will restore us to life."

But as they looked closer, they could see that the water flowing from the roots of the Tree of Life was not moving in their direction; it was moving away from them, turning back toward the garden's interior.

"I'm afraid not, Adam. It doesn't connect with this river. It's going the other direction."

Deflated, Adam hung his head. "It's no use, then."

"But why? Water is water, isn't it? There's plenty of water flowing right past us. It comes straight from the garden. What's wrong with *it*?"

Adam then stepped closer to the water's edge in order to get a better look. "Nothing, I guess." As he stood there gazing at the river, Adam became hypnotized by its crystal-clear current flowing past him, swishing and gurgling, as if speaking some sort of secret language. "I think maybe you're right, Eve. Maybe this water really is special. Do you hear it? Do you hear what the water is saying?"

Stepping forward, Eve craned her neck. "Of course I hear the water, Adam, but I don't understand what it's saying."

Suddenly a thought struck Adam, and he began striking his chest with his fist. "Oh, Eve, why? Why did you have to bring such disaster on us? Why'd you it?"

"Now what's wrong, Adam?"

"There *is* something special about this water, even if it's not the water from the Tree of Life. It was with us in the garden. It used to water every tree there, and now it's flowing right past us."

"So? What about it?"

"We never even noticed it back then, did we? But now, I can't stop thinking about what it means to us, means to our bodies."

"Adam, please," groaned Eve, who was becoming agitated. "What are you saying?"

"This water, Eve. This water is our life now. Without it, we'll die. Now, somehow, we're going to have to use it to help our bodies live."

Adam longingly stared down into the translucent waters where he could see fish swimming around. He leaned forward to get a closer look. "You see, Trout is smart enough to know he needs water to live." Then Adam jumped into the river and began flailing about.

"Adam, no!"

"Jump in, Eve. We need this water. Trust me."

So, Eve jumped in, too, and as soon as she did, she started flailing about as well. "Now what do we do, Adam?" she gurgled.

"How should I know? I just know we need this water to live."

Gasping for air, the couple began to sink, but fortunately for them the eyes of God were upon them as they slowly drowned. Soon an angel materialized at the river's edge, and pulling the couple out, he carefully laid their motionless bodies on the shore. The angel turned to see the Word of God appear next to him and said, "Lord, I'm afraid Your creatures have breathed their last breath."

Then the Word kneeled down next to Adam and Eve and, with a touch of His hand, revived them again.

Slowly, Adam stood up. "Lord, thank you so much for rescuing us."

"Adam, what were you doing in the water like that? You don't know how to swim, do you?"

"Not really, no. I just knew I needed this water somehow. I guess I didn't think it through."

"No, I guess not."

"It's just that while we were still in the garden we didn't even care about water. How come?"

"Because while you were under My control, you were like the angels, so you never *needed* to know anything about water. But now that you've disobeyed My order, you're never going to be able to live without it."

Adam turned to Eve with a knowing look. "See, Eve, I told you, didn't I?"

"If we need water so much," blurted Eve, "then what just happened to us? Water didn't seem to help us live at all."

Mulling this over, Adam turned to the Word. "She does have a point, Lord. How are we supposed to use this water, anyway?"

"You use it for drinking and washing. Drinking it will quench your thirst and help your bodies grow, and washing with it will cool you off and clean your skin. But now, because your bodies are just like the animals, you can't live in the water; only fish can survive in water without drowning."

"Like Trout, you mean?"

"Yes, like Trout." Then, the Word vanished.

Adam and Eve just stared at one another for quite a while.

"Oh, Adam, my mouth is so dry; my insides, too. What should we do? Should we at least try to drink some of this water?"

"I don't know, Eve," said Adam, skeptically shaking his head. "After what we just went through I don't think we should drink any of it."

"I guess you're right. Whether we throw ourselves in or whether we try to drink it, one way or the other we'll probably regret it in the end."

Nodding in agreement, Adam just walked away from the river without drinking, and Eve followed him without saying another word.

Fall of Night

LATER THAT DAY the serpent was slithering across the landscape, rooting about in the dirt. "I am so hungry. If only I had hands and feet like I used to, I could catch myself a decent meal." Frustrated, the serpent reared up on its tail and glared in every direction. "I've had it up to here with all this dirt. I'm so angry at those two humans, I could *spit!*"

"Then why not do something about it?" asked the disembodied voice.

"What's that?" The serpent's eyes darted in every direction. "Who's there?"

Once more the eyes of the devil slowly materialized before the serpent. "Just me again, Serpent."

"Good grief. Do you always have to make such a spectacle of yourself?"

With that, Satan faded completely into view, smirking with satisfaction. "So sorry; force of habit, I guess. But frankly, considering your own flare for the dramatic, I thought you, of all god's creatures, could appreciate it."

"What on Earth does that mean?"

"What with you being so special and all, so sophisticated; I thought you could appreciate my style."

"Style, yes, I see. Well, I suppose so. Tell me, then, what is the nature of your business? I'm very busy. I don't have all day to chit-chat, you know."

"Too busy groveling about in the dirt, you mean; too busy eking out a meager existence, subsisting on rats and sparrows."

"Enough already. I get your point. I still fail to see why you keep talking to me about all this. Why do you even care about my predicament?"

"I care because we have so much in common, because our fates are intertwined."

"Intertwined? Don't be ridiculous. I keep telling you. I don't even know who you are."

"Of course you do. We've been intimate, you and I."

"Intimate? Now you're getting downright revolting. Explain yourself before I bite your face off."

"Dear Serpent, you're hurting my feelings. I thought for sure you'd eventually remember me, but I guess I'll have to refresh your memory. I'm the one who made a pact with you to deceive the humans into eating the Fruit of the Tree of Knowledge. You were so jealous that Adam and Eve were getting all of god's attention you were more than willing to cooperate with me. Don't you remember?"

"You?" The serpent's eyes grew large and his tongued flitted frantically. "That was you? But you looked so different then. What happened? You were such a handsome fellow."

"Yes, well, sadly god and I have had our own falling out, much the same as you."

"And besides that, you lied to me!" the serpent snapped, suddenly furious. "You told me when Eve persuaded Adam to eat the Fruit that God would reject them! You said I'd be elevated in their place as a result. But look at me! Your plan was an utter failure. Now I'll never be the same again, *never!*"

"Well there's no use quibbling about it now, is there?"

"Then what *do you* propose I do in the way of restoring my old life, you impertinent fellow? Is there nothing you can offer me in the way of consolation?"

"As for restoring you to your old life, I'm afraid my hands are completely tied. But there is one other alternative I was hoping you might find appealing in lieu of that fact."

"And what pray tell might that be?"

"Revenge, dear Serpent, revenge."

MEANWHILE, AS THE couple sat in their cave, darkness slowly began to descend all around them. "Adam, what's happening to the light?"

"I have no idea," whispered Adam. "It seems to be fading away."

"But where is it fading *to*?"

"I wish I knew, Eve."

Before long, the couple could no longer see each other.

"Where are you, Eve?" Standing up, Adam groped around in the inky blackness.

"I'm here," she breathlessly replied as she got to her feet. "I'm standing right here. Where are *you*?"

"Oh, Eve, this is terrible."

"What do we do now?"

"Hold out your hand."

"Okay, I'm holding it out. Now what?"

"Now I grab hold of it. There. Now we sit down together and ask God to tell us what's happening."

"All right," continued Eve, through pursed lips. "Now we're sitting. God, are You there? Can you please tell us what is going on?"

But as the couple sat there in hushed anticipation, the darkness showed no sign of dissipating.

"Oh, Eve, remember how radiant we were while we lived in the garden? We never knew anything about this darkness. And remember the Tree of Life? The water flowing from it shimmered across the landscape. Can't you still see its awesome splendor?"

"Of course I can, Adam. But no sooner do we come to this strange place than this *darkness* overwhelms us."

"I wonder why this is happening."

"I don't know, Adam, but I'm scared. Tell me: What good is living a life in a world with no light, no happiness, no hope?"

"I wish I could tell you, Eve. We can only try to ask God to do something and to do it soon."

"I don't think He's going to do anything for us this time. Maybe He's too busy to worry about us anymore. Did you ever think about that?"

"Eve, don't say that. Don't even think it. If that's true, then we're doomed."

Thoroughly frustrated, Adam stood up and started groping around in the dark again, when suddenly he bumped into the cave wall.

"What was that?" exclaimed Eve.

"I just ran into the wall! I can't take this anymore, Eve!" And as he began to strike his chest, Adam threw himself to the ground and died. Hearing him fall, Eve felt around in the dark and eventually found his corpse. Horrified, she tried to scream, but her throat was so dry that nothing came out. Unable to make another sound, she simply clung to his side, weeping over his body.

EVENTUALLY, THE Word of God arrived, filling the cave with His luminescence, and again He revived Adam while at the same time opening Eve's mouth.

"Oh, Lord," moaned Eve as the couple got to their feet. "What happened to the light?"

"And where was that *darkness* before it attacked us?" asked Adam.

"Relax, you two," said the Word, touched by their lament. "As long as Lucifer was obedient to Me, he knew nothing about the darkness, either. He was covered with a bright light just like you, but when he violated My orders, I deprived him of that brilliance and threw him down to Earth. It was that darkness which first overcame him, and now the same thing has happened to both of you."

"I don't understand, Lord," said Eve. "Why was it so dark?"

"As long as you were living obediently to Me, My radiance covered you both, but when I heard about your crime, I took it away."

"Does the darkness come from us, then?" asked Adam. "Is that why it comes?"

"Oh, Lord, have we *become* darkness?" Eve wondered.

"No, no, of course not. I didn't turn you into this darkness. Turning you into darkness would have been like killing you, but in My mercy, I created you as you are, as human beings with bodies that experience heat and cold, light and darkness."

"And when we fell from grace," Adam continued somberly, "You drove us here to live in this cave."

"That's right," replied the Word. "And it was then that the darkness overcame you, just as it did to the one who first violated My order. So you see: This night has actually deceived you. It's not really going to last forever, as you believed. It will only continue for twelve hours. Then, when it's over, daylight will return as usual."

"You don't plan on tormenting us with the darkness from now on, do You?" asked Adam.

"Stop worrying so much, Adam," replied the Word. "The darkness doesn't last forever. And quit thinking I'm trying to torment you with it. The darkness isn't a punishment. I did create the daylight for you, though."

"What do you mean, Lord?" asked Adam. "What did You create for us?"

"Because I knew you'd be sent to this place after your disobedience, I created the Sun and put it in place so you'd have light to live and work by. I never wanted your fall to cause your doom. Just because you had to leave the eternal light and enter this place of darkness, doesn't mean you have to start being afraid of *Me*. I'm not shutting you out completely just because you're here instead of the garden. I made you of the light, and I planned for Eve to give birth to children of light, just like the both of you."

Adam and Eve looked at each other in amazement.

"Oh, Adam, what have we done?" groaned Eve.

"Now, as I've already said," continued the Word. "I've made the day for you and your children to work, and the night for you to sleep. Nighttime will also be when animals come out to search for their food. But now very little of this night remains, Adam. Daylight will soon be reappearing."

"But, Lord," sighed Adam, "won't You please take us somewhere else? Don't let us live in a horrible place like this anymore!"

"Yes, Lord, please, we're begging You," cried Eve. "Take us anywhere there's no darkness!"

"Trust Me, you two. This darkness will pass, and it will do the same thing every day I've determined for you until My contract is made complete. Then I promise, I'll rescue you and bring you back into the garden again, into the place of light you desire so much, where there's never any darkness. In the meantime, none of this misery you've been burdened with is going to help you escape the clutches of Satan. But *I* will save you."

"But what does that mean, Lord?" queried Adam. "How will You save us?"

"By becoming one of your offspring, that's how. I, Who am without years, will be subjected to the reckoning of time. I'll be received as an ordinary human being in order to rescue you, and while in the flesh I'll suffer the same pain and anguish you're now experiencing, and the same darkness that overcame you in this cave will overcome Me in the grave." Then the Word disappeared, plunging the couple back into complete darkness.

Eve began crying. "Oh, Adam, we really won't be returning to the garden until the decreed days are fulfilled."

"No, Eve, I'm afraid not. But what's even worse is, in order to rescue us, the Lord Himself is going to have to suffer, too."

FINALLY, THAT FIRST morning began to dawn. Seeing the light was returning, their fears began to melt away as the darkness loosened its grip around them. Cautiously, Adam and Eve walked to the entrance of the cave and looked eastward. As the Sun gradually peaked up over the horizon with its brilliant, glowing rays, the couple began to feel its heat course over their bodies.

"Adam, look! I've never seen anything like it before. Have you?"

"No. What do you think it is?"

"I think it might be God!"

"I think you're right, Eve. God is a ball of fire!"

"Now that He's agreed to stop tormenting us with the darkness, I guess He's decided to send this fireball to scorch us instead."

Terrified, Adam and Eve fell on their faces.

"Lord," exclaimed Adam, "please don't torture us like this anymore!"

The Word of God returned. "Oh, Adam, this isn't God. It's just the Sun. And how many times do I have to keep telling you? I haven't sent any of these things to punish you. I created the Sun to provide light and heat for you and Eve. That's why I told you earlier that the dawn would be breaking soon and, with it, the light." And again the Word vanished.

Blood and Smoke

LATER THAT AFTERNOON, Adam and Eve left the cave, heading straight for the garden again. As they approached its southern border, they saw the serpent crawling in their direction. Moving toward the gate, it slithered along, despondently licking the dust. Then, when the serpent noticed Adam and Eve coming toward him, it rose up on its tail and swelled its tremendous head, preparing to strike. "I'm going to make you two pay for what you did, if it's the last thing I do!" With blood-red eyes and gaping fangs, the serpent went straight for Eve as she ran away, screaming.

"Help, Adam; it's after me!"

Momentarily, Adam just stood there, panic-stricken. "What do I do? Lord, help us!" Then, with a heart burning for Eve, he ran after the creature and dove for its tail. The serpent dragged Adam for several feet as he held on for dear life. Abruptly it stopped and turned toward him with dripping fangs. Terrified, Adam sprang to his feet.

"It's all your fault, Adam!" the serpent hissed. "Now, because of you and this woman, I have to crawl around on my stomach all the time!"

The serpent lunged at Adam and wrestled him to the ground. Wrapping its gigantic coils around his body, it poised to crush him. "I'll kill you for what you've done to me!"

But suddenly an angel appeared, and throwing the snarling creature away, he helped Adam to his feet.

"Thank you so much," Adam gasped, breathlessly wiping the dust off. "You got here just in the nick of time."

The indignant serpent glared at the angel. "What is the meaning of this outrage? Do you realize the misery these two have caused me?"

Then the Word of God materialized in their midst. "Of course he does, Serpent, but that doesn't give you the right to attack them, you miserable coward."

"How dare you speak to me like that," hissed the serpent. "This is an outrage! An outrage! Do you have any idea who I am, my good man?"

"Do *I* know you?" replied the Word with a hearty laugh. "Of course I do."

"Well, I doubt it. Because if you did, you'd treat me with some respect. After all, I am the wisest of all God's creatures."

"That may be true, but I'm the One Who created you with such wisdom in the first place."

"*You* created *me*?"

"I did, yes."

"Well then, if you're my creator, I have to assume it was you who changed me, forced me to crawl around on my belly; and for what?"

"Well, I may have forced you to crawl around on your belly, but still I never deprived you of everything. But from now on, you and all your kind will never be able to speak another word."

"Don't be ridiculous, you arrogant fellow. Why on Earth would you do something like that? What have I ever done to you?"

"It was *you* who first helped bring disaster to God's children, and now here you are trying to kill them, even though they've never wished you any harm, even after they were condemned because of what you did."

Enraged, the serpent's eyes thinned and his head swelled again. "Well, never in—"

But with a wave of His hand, the Word shoved the serpent's next word back down his throat, and following another gesture, a tremendous wind picked up the speechless creature and hurled him far away.

"See, Lord, I told You this would happen!" Adam exclaimed. "I told You the animals would attack us and try to eat us! Didn't I, Eve?"

Eve nodded, still trembling.

"Relax, Adam," said the Word. "The serpent was only angry at you because I cursed him for helping Satan deceive you and Eve, but none of the other animals have ever tried to harm you. Remember when I had them all visit you before? Remember how you all made an agreement to live in harmony?"

Reluctantly, Adam nodded. "Yes, I remember."

"I didn't invite the serpent, did I? Or else it would have attacked you then. I knew how vindictive it had become. That's why I never even let it get near you. So relax. Quit worrying so much. I'll still be with you until the end of the days I've determined for you."

"But, Lord, please," groaned Adam, "can't You take us somewhere else? Someplace the serpent can never reach us? Or else someday it might find Your servant Eve and attack her again. Its eyes were so horrible, so full of evil."

"From now on, you'll never have to worry about it. I've driven it far from this place, so it won't ever be coming near you again. In fact, none of the animals around here will ever attack you like that again."

"Thank You, Lord. If You hadn't come when You did, that thing would've killed us for sure. Where did You send it, anyway?"

"Right about now, I imagine it's slithering around, quite perplexed and angry, on some seashore far, far away, in a place called India." Then the Word disappeared.

The couple scanned the area with nervous eyes, and finally satisfied that the creature was nowhere to be seen, they returned to their investigation of the garden.

EVENTUALLY, THEY made their way up along a steep ridge facing the garden's western edge, but soon they began perspiring terribly. Exhausted, they stopped near a cliff and looked down at the garden from there. Eve suddenly broke into tears.

"What is it now, Eve?" asked Adam, vexed by her abrupt outburst.

"Oh, Adam, it's no use. Who are we kidding? We keep promising God we won't try to get back into the garden anymore, but just look at us. We're right back where we started."

"You're right, Eve. We'll never get our old life back if God doesn't see we can be honest with Him. Why would He want to save us? All we ever do is disappoint Him again and again with our lies."

Without warning, Adam flung himself from the top of the ridge.

"Adam, no!"

Careening down the mountainside, Adam's face was torn and his flesh ripped. Blood splattered everywhere. Crumpling at the bottom, he died in a heap. Eve stood at the edge of the cliff, screaming through her tears as she looked down at his shattered body.

"Oh, God, not again. I can't go on like this anymore. Adam's only doing this to himself because of me." Then she threw herself off, too. Lacerated and bruised, she tumbled to the bottom of the hill and died alongside Adam.

The Word of God returned again and raised them, sealing up all their bloody wounds in the process. "Oh, you two; punishing yourselves like this won't do a thing to eliminate My decree. It's not going to change the contract of five and a half days in the slightest."

"But, God, we're so sick of this place!" groaned Adam. "We're withering in this heat."

"I think I'm going to faint from all this walking around," Eve sighed. "And who knows how long it's going to be until You let us leave this place."

"Well, it can't be right now," said the Word. "But when the time does come, rest assured, I will bring you out of this dismal land. I promise."

"But, Lord," Adam moaned, "what good is a promise if we don't live long enough to see it fulfilled?"

"Having to live like this is unbearable!" cried Eve. "Ever since we came here, it's been nothing but one disaster after another."

"It's true, Lord, we admit it," said Adam. "We did freely disobey You. When we wanted to become gods like You, Satan was right there to deceive us. But please don't plague us anymore for one little sin. It's just not fair."

"Stop it, Adam. Now I've already told you that whatever you're going through I'll also be enduring for your sakes. Because you've endured fear and suffering and death in this world, I'll be experiencing the same things when I come to rescue you. So if I, Who have done no wrong, am willing to go through what you're going through, then I'm sure you'll survive just fine."

"God have mercy on us," said Adam. "Whatever You're willing to do, I want to do also."

Abruptly the Word vanished, leaving the couple alone once again. Captured in what seemed like an endless silence, Adam and Eve exchanged an agonized look.

"What was that all about?" wondered Adam.

Just as confused, Eve shook her head and shrugged. "How should I know?"

"Come on, Eve; I have an idea." As Adam began walking around gathering stones, Eve stood and watched. Finally, he turned to her and impatiently said, "Don't just stand there. Help me."

"Well, what do you expect me to do?"

"What else, silly? Help me gather more stones."

So Eve started to pick up rocks with him, and when they had gathered a couple of dozen decent-sized stones, Adam began to arrange them into a crude, circular shape.

"Adam?"

"Yes, Eve."

"What are we doing?"

"We're building an altar."

"An altar? What's an altar?"

"Just wait; you'll see."

Then Adam started to pick up some of the leaves from the trees near the garden wall and began wiping up the blood that they had spilled on the rocks beneath the cliff.

"Now what are you doing?" asked Eve, still perplexed.

"Now I'm preparing an offering."

"A what?"

"Eve, I need you to stop asking me questions you know I don't have answers to. All I know is, it just seems like the right thing to do, that's all. Now will you please just help me?"

Together, they stacked up the blood-soaked leaves on the altar. Then Adam started banging two small, flinty rocks near the stack of leaves.

Puzzled, Eve asked, "What are you doing now?"

A perturbed Adam stopped momentarily and shot her a look of disdain.

"Never mind," was all she said as she stepped away, thoroughly confused.

Several minutes went by as Adam continued striking the two rocks together, until several cinders shot out and landed on the stack of leaves. Adam blew gently on the smoldering leaves and before long the whole pile of leaves was ablaze.

Mesmerized by what she was seeing, Eve wandered back to the burning altar. "Oh, Adam, how did you do that?"

But Adam shook his head. "I'm not exactly sure, Eve. I'm just doing what I see in my head."

"Oh, my. What are you going to do next?"

For several moments, Adam thought very hard and finally replied, "Now I think I'll pray to the Lord."

Eve smiled ever so slightly and nodded. "I think that would be wonderful, Adam."

So the two of them turned toward the glowing altar and lifted their eyes skyward.

"Please, Lord," began Adam, "forgive us for our disobedience. While we were still in the garden, our praises went up to You endlessly, like the smoke of this offering, but ever since we came to this strange place we've lost our powers of praise. Without our luminous natures, our perfect understanding is a thing of the past. So help us, Lord. Please look at our blood on these leaves and accept it, like the praise we used to offer You in the garden."

A fireball fell suddenly from the sky and consumed their gift. Adam and Eve stepped back cautiously.

"Adam, wh—*what* just happened?"

Wide-eyed, Adam shook his head. "I'm not sure."

"I hope God isn't mad at us again."

Then the Word of God returned. "No, you two, God isn't mad at you. Actually, quite the opposite is true. He's very impressed with your offering. He's amazed you did this thing without any specific orders from Him. Smelling the sweet savor of your offering, He sent this fireball as an expression of His mercy toward you."

Adam and Eve exchanged a look of tremendous joy.

"See, I told you I knew what I was doing," Adam said with an impish grin.

"And Adam," continued the Word, "just as you've bled, I will shed My blood someday, too. In fact, when I'm born as one of your descendants, I'll even die like you did. You offered your blood on an altar; I'll offer My blood on one, too. And as you asked for forgiveness on the basis of your blood, My shed blood will wipe away every transgression that's ever been committed."

"So what do we do until that day arrives, Lord?" asked Adam.

"In the meantime, whenever despair overwhelms you, make Me an offering, and I'll be kind to you."

Adam stared back, mulling the words over in his mind.

Then the Word continued, "But you have to promise me something, Adam."

"Yes?"

"I don't ever want you to kill yourself like that again. Is that clear?"

"But I *was* going to kill myself, Lord, at once!" blurted Adam. "Without Your radiance surrounding me, there's no point in living."

"Promise Me, Adam; I want to hear you say it."

"Oh, all right, I promise."

Then, the Word disappeared.

"What should we do now, Adam?" wondered Eve.

"Well, you heard Him, didn't you? God was happy with our offering. So from now on, we're going to make it a custom of ours to do the same thing every week."

"And you promise to stop killing yourself, right?"

"Of course, of course," he replied nonchalantly.

Unconvinced, Eve glared back. "Adam? You have to promise me, too. Say it."

"Oh, all right, Eve, I promise you, too."

Angel of Light

ADAM AND EVE HEADED back for their cave, but when they got close enough to see it from a distance, they got very depressed. The Sun was beginning to set beyond the western horizon.

"I hate to tell you this, Eve, but it looks like the Sun is starting to disappear again. The darkness will be returning soon, and we won't be seeing each other for quite a while."

"No, Adam, no," whimpered Eve. "Please ask God to help us."

So they spread their hands toward God.

"Lord, please, hold back the Sun," begged Adam, "and let it keep shining for us. We don't want the darkness to ever return."

"Yes, Lord," Eve lamented, "we'd rather die than endure such darkness again."

Then the Word of God returned. "Oh, Adam, I wish I could accommodate you, really I do, but if I did hold back the Sun, then the agreement I made with you could never be fulfilled."

"But why, Lord?" asked Adam.

"Because without the Sun, there would be no more hours or days or years. Then, I'm afraid, you'd remain banished from the garden. You and everyone you loved would be plagued by endless disaster, and no salvation would reach any of you, *ever*."

Adam and Eve exchanged a concerned look.

"So just try to relax and endure the nights until that time has arrived. Can you do that for Me?"

Eve began to weep. "Oh, Adam, what if something happens to us before the time comes?"

"I wish I could tell you, Eve; really I do," Adam replied sadly.

"You know, you two," continued the Word, "when I think of all the wonderful things you used to have, and why you had to leave them, I'm still more than willing to continue being good to you. But unfortunately, I can't alter the contract I've told you about, or else I would've already returned you to the garden."

Adam perked up. "Did you hear that, Eve?"

Eve nodded meekly as she wiped the tears from her cheek. "Yes, Adam, I heard."

"Until then," said the Word, "be patient and endure living in this cave, because the darkness you're so afraid of will only last twelve hours. Then the light will return, just as I've promised." And again the Word vanished.

UPON ENTERING THE cave, the couple held hands in dire anticipation.

"Oh, Adam, I'm terrified of the dark," groaned Eve. "Just the *thought* of it terrifies me. I'd rather die than endure another night of it."

"I know how you feel, Eve."

Slowly, almost agonizingly, the darkness descended around them.

"Please, Lord," Adam whispered, "be merciful to us throughout this night."

"We need Your help so much," added Eve.

Before long, the couple found themselves enveloped in utter blackness.

"Lord, we're begging You," Eve whimpered. "Please send the light."

THOROUGHLY DISGUSTED, Satan was watching their cave from a distance, even in the blackest of night. One by one, his demons gathered around him, as a murder of crows gathers about its leader.

"Just look at the little vermin, with their simpering prayers," grumbled the devil. "Won't they ever shut up? *God help us. Oh, please, please, please.* You'd think he'd eventually get fed up and blot them out. Why does he keep comforting them? I hate the very sight of them!"

"What will you do, Master?" asked his lieutenant.

"Well, if god insists on tickling their fancy with His shimmering light, then I can't wait to see the look on their faces when I hit them with my little lightshow."

AS ADAM AND EVE huddled together in the darkness, a peculiar singing began to filter in through the mouth of the cave, and trickling in with it was a beam of white light. When Adam and Eve saw it, they became transfixed. "Look at that light, Eve. I wonder what it could be."

"And that singing," added Eve. "It's so beautiful."

"I wonder where it came from. Do you think God is doing it?"

"Don't ask me, Adam; ask Him."

"Good idea. Lord, are there any other gods besides You Who can create a light as bright as this one?"

Suddenly an angel appeared before Adam and Eve, lighting up the cave with his own luminescence. "Don't be deceived, Adam. God isn't the author of the spectacle occurring outside your cave."

"Who is, then?" asked Adam as the couple got to their feet.

"This is the doing of the same one who hid in the serpent, the one who got you and Eve kicked out of the garden, but this time he's tried approaching you as an angel of light."

"But why?" Eve wondered.

"He was hoping you'd worship him. He wanted to mesmerize you, make you believe you were actually in God's presence. And if God hadn't sent me here, he may very well have succeeded."

Then, Adam and Eve followed the angel as he walked over to the mouth of the cave, where they found a group of angels singing their hauntingly beautiful melody. But as soon as this group saw that the couple was accompanied by one of God's angel, they ceased their singing. After a simple gesture from the angel, the group outside the cave was abruptly unmasked, revealing a cadre of hideous demons with their grotesque chief standing at their head. Adam and Eve gasped, as did the demons, who all painfully recoiled at the brightness of God's angel. Abruptly they scattered, leaving Satan standing there, frozen stiff, apparently unable to move.

"Who is this?" muttered Adam, squinting at the hideous creature standing before them.

"*What* is this?" Eve added, just as bewildered.

"This is Satan, your adversary," the angel replied. "Once, he was the most beautiful angel whom God had ever created; but not anymore."

Horrified and confused, Adam and Eve examined him from head to toe. They were repulsed by the very sight of him, with his reptilian skin, wolfen face and bat-like wings, his jagged teeth, claws and horns. As the couple gaped at him, the devil hissed lamentably, trying in vain to spit at them.

"What a despicable monster," said Adam.

"Why is he so ugly?" wondered Eve, almost in awe.

"He looks like this because God cursed him for rebelling against His divine rule. This is how he's appeared ever since he was kicked out of Heaven. Naturally, he knew you wouldn't invite him into your cave looking this way, so he transformed himself into a dazzling angel."

Then God's angel grabbed Satan by the scruff of the neck and hurled him out of sight. "But God wants you to know," the angel continued, "you don't have to be afraid of him, because He Who created you will be your strength." And just as quickly as he had appeared, the angel vanished, plunging the couple back into darkness.

AS MORNING BEGAN to break inside the cave, the couple got up and stretched their weary muscles. "Lord, what should we do now?" asked Adam.

"I don't know about you, Adam," began Eve, "but I'd like to take a trip to the garden. I hope you don't think I'm being silly. It's just my heart yearns to go back. I know I shouldn't keep dwelling on it, but there it is; I said it."

"I don't think you're being silly, Eve. I feel the same way. We'll always be connected to it somehow. Just because we had to leave doesn't mean we have to stop thinking about it, right?"

Eve smiled at the thought. "Right."

AS THEY WERE WALKING along, Adam and Eve looked up and saw a dazzling array of angels flying toward them, soaring through the air like some kind of swirling, white cloud.

"Adam, do you see what I see?"

"I do, Eve. Angels of God. At least they look like angels."

"You don't think it's that monster in disguise again, do you? What was his name?"

"You mean Satan?"

"Yes, him. You don't think it could be him and his angels again, do you?"

Adam shrugged his shoulders as the cloud came closer and closer. "I don't know. He'd have to be pretty stupid to try something like that again. Let's find out what they want, though, before we jump to any conclusions."

"If you say so," Eve said suspiciously. "I just hope you know what you're doing."

Swooping down in front of the couple, the cloud of angels lit upon the ground and graciously bowed. "Greetings, you two," cooed one of the angels, who stepped forward to the head of the group.

"Hello," replied Adam. "Who are you?"

"I'm none other than an angel of the great and glorious God. Simyasa is my name, and these are His holy angels."

"Really?" said Eve. "Hello, Simyasa. What brings you here?"

"Why, God has sent us to help you, of course, in your quest to get back into the garden. Would you like that?"

"Would we ever," exclaimed Adam. "But how?"

"Well, naturally God can't allow you back inside the garden in your present condition, so he's asked us to help you prepare yourselves. Are you ready?"

"Of course," blurted Eve, suddenly eager and hopeful. "Tell him, Adam. Tell him we're ready."

"Good, then follow us," said Simyasa. "We're all going to go to the ocean, where you and Eve will be able to bathe. There, your bodies will be purified so you'll be able to return to the garden. How does that sound?"

His words sank deep into their hearts.

"That sounds wonderful," Adam replied.

Ecstatic at the thought, Eve touched Adam's arm as they exchanged a look of mournful longing. "Can it really be true, Adam?"

"It's time now," said Simyasa. "Let's get going."

BUT AS ADAM AND EVE followed the angels in their journey, they cautiously walked behind them, keeping their distance. They had walked only a short while before Eve leaned into Adam and whispered, "Are you sure we're going in the right direction? This isn't the way you go to get to the ocean."

EVENTUALLY, THEY CAME to the steep hill along the garden's northern perimeter, and there Adam and Eve stopped. Turning back toward them, Simyasa looked almost as perplexed as they did. "What's wrong?" he asked. "Why have you stopped?"

"We thought you said we were going to the ocean in the East," said Adam, who exchanged a nervous look with Eve.

"Yeah," added Eve. "Why are we going this direction?"

Simyasa took several steps toward the couple and held his arms out wide. "Oh, my dear ones, don't be alarmed. I'm merely taking you there by way of a short-cut. After all, you're not accustomed to all this walking about, now are you?"

Again the couple looked at one another, unsure how to respond.

"No," Adam said finally. "As a matter of fact, we *hate* walking. This place is nothing but dirt and rocks."

"You see, then," continued Simyasa. "What better way to get there than by way of a short-cut?"

"Yes, a short-cut," echoed Adam, however reluctantly, and turned to Eve. "What do you say, Eve? Wouldn't you rather take a *short-cut*?"

Eve shrugged again and said, "I guess so, sure."

TRUDGING THEIR way up to the peak of the hill, Adam and Eve were on the brink of exhaustion, when finally they were forced to stop in order to catch their breaths.

"Some short-cut this turned out to be," Adam muttered, huffing and puffing.

Simyasa and the rest of his group stopped and turned toward the couple.

"Don't stop now, you two," said Simyasa with a reassuring smile. "The hard part of our journey is nearly over. It's all downhill from here."

Simyasa waved them on, and the couple walked up to him where he stood very close to the edge of the cliff. Gazing out over the sprawling landscape, he turned to Adam and Eve. "How's this for a view?" he asked with a sweeping gesture of his hand. "Isn't God's creation a marvel to behold?"

Intrigued, the couple moved up to the cliff's edge and looked down. "Look how high we are, Eve," said Adam as the couple inched ever forward.

Still winded from their journey, Adam and Eve stared down, precariously close to the edge of the cliff, and as they did Simyasa surreptitiously stepped up behind them. "Undeniably, my friends, undeniably." He slowly stretched out his hands, preparing to push them.

But suddenly the disembodied voice of God roared from the void. "Satan, you scourge of the Universe! How dare you try to destroy My children!"

Terrified, Simyasa froze and, grunting in frustration, transformed into his true form as the devil. "Damn you, god, *not again!*"

Startled, the couple turned around to see Satan and his leathery claws stretched out toward them.

"What the—" Adam blurted.

To their amazement, the couple watched as the angels that were huddled about the devil were also unmasked, revealing their true demonic forms. Then, a tremendous gust of wind swept them all away, along with their hideous master, who hurled a steady stream of unspeakable insults as they went.

Confused and alone, Adam and Eve stood there looking around.

"Oh, Adam, we did it again."

"And this time God just let it happen."

"Well, what do you expect? We never bothered to ask Him if it was Satan or not, even after we knew better. Now what do we do?"

"What else can we do?" replied Adam, who raised his voice to the Heavens. "Lord, please forgive us for following Satan and his angels. Help us, won't You?"

Then the Word of God appeared. "Aren't you two ever going to learn? What were you doing up here, anyway?"

"We were looking for something to relieve our sadness," murmured Eve, "something to remind us of the life we used to have in the garden."

"Up here?"

Hanging their heads, the bewildered couple just shrugged their shoulders.

"Very well," continued the Word. "Maybe I can help with you that."

An angel appeared suddenly in their midst, and Adam and Eve looked up.

"Who is this?" asked Adam.

"This is the archangel Michael. I'm going to send him to where the ocean reaches India, to get some gold for you and Eve."

Then another angel appeared. "This is the archangel Gabriel," said the Word. "I'll be sending him to the garden, where he'll get you some frankincense."

Finally, one more angel materialized. "And this is the archangel Raphael. He'll be going to the garden to fetch you some myrrh."

The trio of archangels bowed humbly before the Word of God.

"Now go, you three, and be quick about it."

With the speed of the wind, the archangels darted out of view, leaving a vapor trail in their wake.

AS EACH OF THE archangels streaked to their divinely-appointed destinations, they encountered a barrage of demonic opposition. Each one had to slash his way through with the use of their flaming swords, slicing a pathway to their respective quarries. Eventually, Michael got through to the gold near the Indian Ocean, Gabriel made his way to the eastern border of the garden, where he retrieved the frankincense, and Raphael fought his way to the western edge of the garden, where he found the myrrh.

THE THREE ARCHANGELS then returned to where Adam, Eve and the Word of God were still waiting for them.

"Now, I want each of you to dip what you have in the Water of Life," said the Word with a gesture of His hand, and instantly the trio of archangels vanished again.

THE ARCHANGELS ALL found themselves at the Tree of Life in the garden, where they each kneeled down to dip their items in the crystal-clear water flowing from its roots.

THEN AS ABRUPTLY AS they had disappeared, they were back again where the couple still stood in anticipation.

"Now give what you have to Adam and Eve," said the Word of God.

Dutifully, the archangels stepped forward and, one by one, presented the awestruck couple with their gifts.

"So, you two," the Word continued, "you said you were looking for something to remind you of the garden, in the hopes that it might comfort you. Here you are, then. I'm giving you these three tokens to reassure you of My promise of the five and a half days."

And when Adam and Eve saw the gold, the frankincense and the myrrh, they became very happy.

"I'm doing this so you'll realize you can trust Me to keep My promise, because I really will come and rescue you someday."

The couple smiled at one another.

"When I arrive in the flesh, kings will also present Me with gold, frankincense and myrrh."

Adam's demeanor grew somber again, and he remarked, "Gold reminds me so much of the beautiful home we had to leave."

"That's because gold is a symbol of My kingdom," said the Word.

Adam continued, "This frankincense makes me think of the bright light that was taken from us."

"Because frankincense typifies My divinity."

"And this myrrh," observed Adam, "reminds me of all the despair we've been feeling since the day we had to leave."

"Because myrrh is reminiscent of My suffering and death."

Again the couple exchanged a concerned look.

"So Adam," added the Word, "I want you to keep these things with you in the cave. The gold will shed light by night, the frankincense will provide you with its sweet aroma, and the myrrh will help soothe you in your sadness."

"Thank you so much, Lord," Adam said, "we'll never forget Your kindness to us today."

"Yes, Lord," added Eve, "You've been most gracious. We can't thank You enough."

ADAM AND EVE SUDDENLY found themselves back inside their cave again. Looking around in amazement, the couple sucked in a deep breath and reached out to one another to steady themselves.

"Adam, what just happened?"

"I'm not sure; but I think we're back in our cave somehow."

"Yes, you two, God transported you to your cave," said a voice.

And when they turned to see who was speaking, they found Michael the archangel, standing there with everything that the angels had retrieved at his feet. Bowing humbly, Adam and Eve began placing their new things in an appropriate spot. At the south end of their cave, they placed the gold, on the east side, the frankincense, and to the west, the myrrh.

"I hope this will help you both in your time on this Earth," said Michael. "May God richly bless you with His peace which surpasses all understanding." Nodding, he streaked out of view with a puff of smoke.

"You know, Eve, now that we have such nice things from God here in our cave, we should give this place a name to go along with this occasion. What do you think?"

"A name? What kind of name?"

"I don't know; like the Cave of Gold, the Cave of Treasures, something like that."

"Hmmm. I like that, Adam. Yes, the Cave of Treasures. That sounds nice. From now on, we'll call our home the Cave of Treasures."

"God knows if we do have to endure our new life within the confines of a cave, we should try to make the best of it."

AS ADAM AND EVE were acclimating themselves to their new surroundings, the molten Face of God looked down from His dazzling throne. "Did You hear that, Son? Adam and Eve have decided to name their residence the Cave of Treasures in memoriam of the gifts We've bestowed on them."

Then the Word of God turned to the Face. "Yes, Father, I heard. I think it's quite fitting, considering the fact that this is the third day since Adam and Eve have been expelled from their garden home."

"Yes," continued the Face. "And just as You will remain in the heart of the Earth for three days, they now have these three things as a pledge toward that someday."

Hollow

THEN CAME THE DAWN of the eighth day since they had departed from the garden, and for the first time, when Adam and Eve came out of their cave, they seemed happy.

"Oh, Eve, what a beautiful morning," said Adam with a tremendous yawn. "I had such a wonderful sleep last night. How about you?"

"I slept quite well, believe it or not," Eve replied, stretching her muscles. "These last few days I can actually say I haven't been so miserable."

"I think it's because of the sacred tokens the Lord gave us. Now our cave isn't so dark and dreary at night. It's starting to feel like a home instead of a prison."

"I wouldn't go that far, Adam. It's still a cave, you know. All the gold, frankincense and myrrh in the world won't erase that fact."

"No, I guess not."

"Can you believe it's been more than a week since we left the garden? My stomach feels funny."

"What do you mean, funny?"

"It's beginning to feel," said Eve, searching for just the right word. "I don't know." Then she turned to Adam with a mournful frown. "*Hollow*."

"Hollow, hmmm. Yeah, now that you mention it, I'm beginning to feel hollow, too."

"I wonder what that's all about."

The couple exchanged a curious look and shrugged it off.

"What should we do today?" Eve asked.

"You know, Eve, I was thinking. We asked God to give us something from the garden, and He gave us those mementos."

"Okay. So what did you have in mind this time?"

"I don't know. Maybe God isn't so mad at us as after all. Maybe He'd reconsider taking us back into the garden."

Eve nodded thoughtfully. "Maybe. And if He doesn't let us back in yet, then at least He could provide us with a nicer place to live than this one."

"Good, then let's go."

"Go? Go where?"

"Let's go to the ocean."

"Why the ocean?"

"I don't know. It seemed like there was something special about that place. Maybe if we went there to pray, God would see how serious we are about getting back into the garden."

SO THE COUPLE WENT to the ocean and stood by the shore, gazing out across the water.

"Now what do we do?" asked Eve.

"I want you to go down into the water, and I want you to start praying harder than you've ever prayed before in your life."

"For how long?"

"I want you to pray like that for forty days."

"Forty days? Isn't that an awfully long time?"

"Not at all, Eve; not if we really want to show God how serious we are about this. Pray with your sweetest voice. Pray that He please forgive us."

"Well, what about you? What are you going to do?"

"I'm going to walk further up the coast and do the same thing there. Then, after the forty days are up, I'll come back and get you."

"All right," said Eve with a skeptical nod, and slowly she waded into the water. "I sure hope you know what you're doing."

ADAM WALKED UP THE shoreline for quite a while before he, too, waded in and began praying. "Lord, please hear our prayer. We're so sorry for our crime against You and were hoping You might change Your mind about waiting so long to let us back into the garden."

SATAN AND HIS HENCHMEN, in the meantime, came buzzing about the Cave of Treasures.

"I wonder what Adam and Eve are doing today," grumbled the devil. "Begging god to do something else for them, I imagine."

"They're not here, Master," his lieutenant reported.

"I can see that for myself, you idiot!"

"But where can they be?"

"How should I know? You're supposed to be my lieutenant. You find them! If they're up to no good, I want to know about it!"

Splitting off in every direction, Satan and his despicable crew began searching.

WHEN THE DEVIL GOT to the ocean, he absolutely hated what he found there. "Here they are! But what are they doing just standing in the sea? Could it be? Why, yes. They're still begging god to let them back into the garden! What fools!"

Several demons streaked up to Satan's side and looked down at Adam and Eve as they stood praying in the ocean. "What are they doing now, Lord?" asked one of the demons.

"The pathetic, little replicas are begging god to be released from my control. What else?"

"Still? Don't they ever learn? What should we do to them? Just say the word, and I'll go down there right now and rip their hearts out!"

"Well, well, aren't we original? You're as bad as Adam and Eve when it comes to thinking of something new."

Then, when he felt a second demon next to him nudge him with an elbow, the first demon turned with an irritated scowl. "What is it now?"

Surreptitiously, the second demon put his finger to his pursed lips, as if to warn the first not to say anything more.

"What did I say that was so wrong?" mumbled the first demon.

AS EVE CONTINUED to pray knee deep in the ocean, she suddenly found herself with a visitor. A beautiful, little angel was flitting about her, as pleasant as a butterfly, smiling so radiantly. "Well, hello, my dear," beamed the tiny angel with a voice as tiny as itself. "I'm so glad I found you."

Intrigued, Eve smiled back. "Hello there. Well, look at you. I've never seen an angel so small. What's your name, little one?"

"My name is Suriyel. God has sent me to tell you He's heard your prayer, and He's forgiven you."

Eve gazed at him, suddenly perplexed. "He has?"

"Why, yes. First, He sent me to Adam, and I brought him the good news about your return to the garden. He was so excited about it he wanted me to come tell you right away."

"Is that so?" replied Eve with just a hint of skepticism in her voice. "So where's Adam now? Why didn't he come to tell me himself?"

"He wanted to; really he did. But he's already back at your cave, where he's worshiping God as we speak. That's why I was sent to tell you to come with me. So you can both be crowned with the same light you had before your fall."

But far from being overjoyed at the news, Eve still seemed puzzled. "I don't know. Are you sure it's all right?"

"Oh, dear, I can just imagine how you feel right now. Adam said you might react this way. So he told me that if you decided not to come with me to remind you about what you saw on the mountaintop. Do you remember how God transported you to your cave? How you laid the gold to the south, the frankincense to the east, and the myrrh to the west?"

Eve thought for a moment and nodded reluctantly. "Yes, I suppose so."

"Well, then, there you are. You see? There's nothing to fear. Certainly I'm nothing you should be afraid of. Now, come with me, dear Eve, won't you?"

Finally, Eve got very happy, so she came up out of the water and started to follow the tiny, fluttering angel.

THE ANGEL CONTINUED to lead her to the point where they were approaching Adam. As soon as she saw him still praying in the water, Eve frowned and said, "But you told me Adam was already back at our—" And turning to the angel, she found him gone. "Hey, where'd you go?" she exclaimed. Looking in every direction, Eve found that he was nowhere to be seen. Hesitantly, she cautiously waded into the water and stood next to Adam.

"And Lord," he intoned, still unaware that Eve was standing next him, "I can't thank You enough for all the wonderful mementos You provided us." Then, turning toward her, Adam was horrified. "Oh, Eve, no." Striking his chest, he slowly sank into the water.

Just then, the Word of God appeared and dragged Adam to the shore. "Good, Lord," sputtered Adam as he blearily opened his eyes. "Oh, God, have pity on us, won't You?"

"Never mind that now, Adam," said the Word with the sternness of an older brother. "I want you to stand up like a man and explain to Eve what just happened. She's confused and needs to be able to look to you. She needs your sympathy right now. She doesn't need to be condemned. Do you understand Me?"

"Yes, Lord, I think so."

"Then go to her."

So Adam stood to his feet and walked over to Eve as she quietly wept. "Darling Eve, don't cry. Everything will be fine."

"No, Adam, it won't. I've ruined everything again, just when things were starting to get better for us."

Momentarily speechless, Adam turned to the Word, Who just nodded back as if to encourage him onward. "Don't say that, Eve," continued Adam. "It's all right. I promise: We're going to get through this. You'll see."

"Really?" murmured Eve, as Adam wiped the tears from her cheek. "You think so?"

"Of course."

"But I don't understand. Everything was going so well. We were so happy praying to the Lord, and then this little angel, this tiny wisp of an angel, looking as harmless as a butterfly, had to come along and spoil everything. Why would he do that?"

"An angel? What angel? What did this angel do?"

"A tiny angel came to me while I was praying in the water and said that God had heard our prayers, that He'd forgiven us, that we were finally going back to the garden. He said you were back at our cave, thanking God for His forgiveness, but he lied! He lied, Adam. He lied! Why would an angel of the Lord do something like that?"

"Oh, Eve, a true angel of God wouldn't lie."

"Well, that's what I thought, too."

"Eve, I'm afraid that wasn't one of God's angels. I think it was that damned Satan again. He probably saw us praying to God and decided he'd better stop us before the Lord had time to answer our prayers."

Like a bolt of lightning, his words sank into Eve's heart. "Oh, Adam, you're right. I can't believe I was so stupid. What was I thinking? Of course; that has to be it."

Then, Adam reached out and took hold of her hand. "Don't be so hard on yourself, dear. We're all bound to make mistakes with that despicable creature still lurking about."

AS THE SUN BEGAN to peek up over the eastern horizon, Adam and Eve stumbled out of their cave, looking weak and frail.

"It's been forty-three days, Eve, since we left the garden. Can you believe it?"

"Adam, my mouth is so dry. What's wrong with me?"

"Mine, too, Eve. And I'm so *hollow*."

WITH A FEEBLE SIGH, the couple sat down on the hilltop, just to the west of the garden, and there they looked out across the expansive landscape.

"My Lord and my God," said Adam, through parched lips. "You created me out of the ground and brought me into the garden on a Friday. Then You told me all about that tree, the one I was to avoid eating or even approaching. You told me, then and there, 'If you eat from this tree, you'll die.'"

"And when we did die on that very first day," Eve began, "just outside the garden gate, You could've left us like that, and You would've been perfectly justified. But no, in Your wondrous mercy, You chose to raise us so we could experience firsthand what a loving Creator You really are." Her words trailed off in tears.

"So, Lord," continued Adam, "could You help us again today? We're so empty. Our bodies are shriveling up. Our strength is withering away. What's wrong with us?"

Then the Word of God appeared. "Don't worry, you two. You'll be fine. You just need some nourishment, that's all."

Adam turned and meekly asked, "Nourishment? What's that?"

"Food for your stomach, liquid for your mouth; so you won't feel so *hollow* anymore."

"You mean we're not dying?"

"No, of course not. You're just hungry and thirsty."

"But why, Lord?" wondered Adam.

"It's because you don't live in the garden anymore. As long as you were there, you never knew a thing about hunger or thirst. How could you? You never experienced change or even had to sleep, but now you'll need to eat and drink to survive."

"Did you hear that, Eve? We just need to eat and drink, and we'll be fine."

"But we don't dare gather any of the fruit here," remarked Eve. "After all, look what happened to us when we tried that the first time."

"Relax, Eve," said the Word. "There are plenty of things to eat in this world besides the Fruit from the Tree of Knowledge. Feel free to have any of it to satisfy your needs." Then the Word vanished.

The couple exchanged a nervous look.

"But how will we know which is which?" asked Eve.

Adam just shrugged his shoulders.

Just then, the cherub responsible for guarding the entrance to Paradise flew over to Adam and Eve, and motioned for them to approach a fig tree. "Here, you two, God has instructed me to show you what is acceptable for you to eat. Now this is a fig tree, and these are figs."

The couple reluctantly plucked two figs from the tree, but in their weakened condition, they struggled even to hold them in their hands, considering the fact that these figs were, after all, much larger in those days, averaging the size of watermelons. Examining them closely, something struck them both at the same moment.

"Just look at these figs, Eve," groaned Adam, "and these *leaves*. Don't they look familiar?"

"Yes, Adam, they do look familiar; too familiar, I'm afraid."

"This is exactly the kind of fruit tree we tried hiding amongst when we realized we were naked for the first time."

And as if they were scalding hot, the couple dropped the figs and took a step back.

"We have no idea what kind of pain we'll feel if we eat these," sighed Eve.

Adam shuddered. "I don't even want to touch them anymore. Let's ask God if we can have some fruit from the Tree of Life instead."

So Adam and Eve walked away from the figs, and without knowing what else he could do, the cherub threw his hands up and flew back to his post at the garden's gate.

AS THE LATE AFTERNOON Sun began to inch its way toward the western horizon, Adam stood alone, just outside their cave. "Oh, God," he whispered, "it was the sixth hour of the sixth day when we defied Your direct orders. For just an instant, we disobeyed You, and this bitter struggle has been the result. But, Lord, don't be too harsh on us. Please, could You give us some of the Fruit from the Tree of Life to eat? We want to live again. We don't want to suffer like this anymore. After all, God, if anybody can fix a problem like this, it's You. Can't You please make these forty-three days of suffering equivalent to that one violation?"

Then the Word of God arrived. "I'm sorry, Adam, but I can't give you what you're asking for. I can't just give you the Fruit from the Tree of Life. At least not until the five thousand, five hundred years are completed."

Eve came out of the cave and stood next to Adam. "You can't give it to us?" she grumbled pathetically. "Or You won't?"

"Stop it, Eve," said the Word. "You know I would if I could, but there are just some things in this world that cannot be changed, no matter how much you wish them to be different. You're simply going to have to face up to that fact."

"Never mind, Eve, it's no use," insisted Adam. "We're just going to have to deal with it as is. And someday, we'll finally get what we're looking for."

"Someday," ranted Eve, "it's always *someday*. I'm sorry, Lord, but I feel like I'm losing my mind."

"I understand, Eve, really I do," said the Word. "But *someday* is still better than never."

"He does have a point, Eve," added Adam.

"And on that day, you and your righteous descendants will eat the Fruit from the Tree of Life and live forever. I promise."

Adam and Eve looked so disappointed.

"In the meantime, you two, I've already given you something to eat. You have your figs. So go ahead and eat them before you both die of hunger." And again the Word vanished.

So Adam turned to Eve and said, "Come on. I guess we should go back and get our figs."

Reluctantly, Eve nodded and started off with Adam on their journey.

The Fire that Burns

AROUND SUNSET, THE couple was back inside their cave, where they laid their figs down on the ground. Sitting down next to them, they stared at the figs for quite a while.

"Please, God," said Adam, "can't You satisfy our hunger without having us eat these things? I mean, what good will it do, really?"

"Just the thought of eating something again terrifies me," lamented Eve.

Then the Word of God arrived. "You know, you two, you never used to fast and pray like this before. How come? Why didn't you have this kind of apprehension before you violated My orders?"

The couple looked at each other, hoping that the other might offer some kind of reply.

"I'm afraid you're just going to have to get used to the fact that from now on your animal bodies can't survive without earthly food." And that quickly, the Word disappeared.

Slowly, then, Adam took his fig and placed it on the stack of gold. Eve put hers on the frankincense, and together they stood, praying silently well into the night.

AS THE SUN WAS RISING, Adam sat up and turned to Eve. "Come on, Eve, let's get going."

"Where are we going now?"

"I want to visit the spot where we could see the Tree of life, where the river splits in four directions. God may not be able to give us any of the Fruit from the Tree of Life, but maybe He'll let us drink some of the water flowing from its roots."

STEPPING TO THE river's edge, the couple turned their eyes skyward.

"Lord," began Adam, "while we were still in the garden we remember seeing the water that flowed from beneath the Tree of Life, but we never felt any need for it then. Now, here we are outside of Your mercy, and we see this water flowing right past us."

"We're dead, Lord; our flesh is so dry," added Eve. "We need the other water now more than ever. So, please, could You give us some of the Water of Life so we can live again?"

Then the Word of God appeared. "Why do you two keep asking Me for things You know

I can't give you yet. The water from that tree is no different than its fruit. I can't give you either one. It simply isn't allowed until the day I descend into Hades to break the gates of brass and smash the kingdom of iron!"

"But when will that be, Lord?" blurted Adam.

"When the end of the world arrives, Adam; on the day I shed My blood on your head at Golgotha. Then, and only then, will that blood be the Water of Life for you. And not for you alone but for every one of your descendants who trusts in Me."

"But, Lord," groaned Eve, "I don't think we can wait that long."

"Relax, both of you. Now, I've provided you with food, but you refuse to eat. Fine. I won't force you to eat. And just because I can't give you the Water of Life, doesn't mean I'm not allowing you to drink from the water that's flowing past you. So, just as I've instructed you to eat when you're ready to eat, when you're ready to drink, feel free to drink, but I suggest you do it quickly." Then the Word vanished.

Adam and Eve stared longingly into the crystal-clear water for quite a while, but eventually, they left the river, still without drinking any of it, and headed back home.

AROUND NOONTIME, the couple approached their cave. As they did, they noticed a pillar of smoke rising near it. Startled, they stopped and stared, wide-eyed.

"Eve, why is there smoke coming from our cave? We didn't do anything to cause a fire like that, did we?"

"Of course not, Adam."

So the couple sprinted the rest of the way back to their cave, and when they got there, they were horrified to find a huge fire at its entrance.

"How could a fire like this have started, Eve?"

"I'm not sure we should even call it *fire*," she gasped. "I've never seen anything quite like it, except for when God sent that cherub with lightning in his hand. Remember?"

"That's right; this *must* be that same fire from the cherub's sword. He's trying to keep us out of our cave. God must be mad at us because we keep refusing to eat or drink!"

"Oh, Adam, it's true."

"But where will we live now?"

Eve clutched desperately at his arm. "And Adam, what if the darkness there is even worse than it is here?"

"Or worse still, what if He never wants to see us again? What then? All because we keep disobeying Him."

"Because we keep asking Him for so many things, that's why! And after we finally started to find some happiness here."

"Oh, Eve, if we travel even further away from God and the garden, how will we ever find Him again?"

"How will He ever be able to comfort us with His presence?"

"And if we can't find Him anymore, what's going to happen to the promise He made to us about the five and a half days?"

Helpless to do a thing, they just stood and stared as the blaze grew more intense with each passing moment.

UNBEKNOWNST TO ADAM and Eve, however, was the fact that Satan and his demons were at the heart of the matter.

"Quickly, my minions," snarled the devil, "bring me more material for our glorious fire!"

One by one, his demons threw tree branches and dry grass into the rear of the fire, fueling it with a tremendous crackle.

"Oh, my word," cooed Satan, utterly gleeful. "I can just see their pathetic faces as they watch their precious 'home away from home' burning to the ground, and there's not a damn thing they can do about it! Just the thought gives me goose bumps all over."

A sadistic laughter rang out among his legions.

"But, Master," interjected his lieutenant, apparently confused about something. "How come the blaze isn't destroying their cave? It seems to burn right up to its very edge but then no further. Is there some sort of shield protecting it from our fire? Or are my eyes merely deceiving me?"

"What?" blurted Satan, who turned to see what he was describing. "What are you babbling about now?"

Sure enough, as the devil hovered over to get a closer look, he could see for himself that the fire was burning right up to an inch or so from the cave. Reaching through the flames, Satan touched the wall of the cave with his hideous paw. "It can't be; but it is! Even though our fire burns as hot as the Sun, their filthy cave remains cool to the touch. What is the meaning of this outrage? Is there no justice to be had in this god-forsaken Universe?"

From within the thin barrier between the cave and the fire, a peculiar set of eyes suddenly materialized in plain sight.

"What is this, then?" growled the devil.

Then, along with the eyes, a face began to take shape, a cherub's face. "Don't be alarmed, Satan," said the cherub with a satisfied smirk. "It's only me."

Baffled, the devil inched forward, as did several of his confused demons alongside him. "M -- *Me*?" stammered Satan. "Who the Hell is *me*?"

"I'm the cherub who guards the gate to Paradise. That's who."

"That scrawny, little puke I've seen buzzing about with his flaming sword? You mean that one?"

The face proudly nodded. "Undeniably, you foul creature. So glad to meet you, too."

"How dare you spoil my plans this way!" Enraged, the devil thrust his leathery fist in the direction of the cherub's satisfied grin, but because it instantly vanished, he only punched the wall of the cave. The devil let loose an angry, painful howl. "Ahhh!"

AS THE FLAMES continued to blaze out of control, Adam and Eve could only stand and watch the raging inferno, helpless and dumbfounded.

"Adam, are you sure we can't do anything? Can't we at least ask God for help?"

Adam shook his head. "I don't see why God would want to help us if He's already mad at us."

"Oh, that's right; I forgot. Then it's useless. We're doomed."

"There is one thing we could do, though."

"What?"

"If God won't help us put the fire out, maybe He'll at least tell us why the fire got started in the first place."

Eve nodded. "He might. So ask Him."

SATAN KEPT MOTIONING for his minions to continue bringing more tree branches and dry grass to throw into the fire. "I don't care how much that lousy excuse for a cherub tries to thwart me. I'm going to destroy this cave and everything in it, if it's the last thing I do!"

As his lieutenant proceeded to fuel the fire, he mumbled, "But are you sure it will do any good? The cherub said -- "

"I don't give a damn what that little puke said! Bring me more branches, more grass! You hear me?"

"Yes, Master."

Buzzing into action, more demons followed suit and continued to stoke the fire, until the flames engulfed the entire cave. Still, the keen eyes of the cherub peered out from the invisible firewall as he intently watched Satan's futile attempt to breach his protective shield.

Finally, the Word of God appeared. "Enough already, Devil! Can't you see you're wasting your time?"

"This is an outrage, I tell you!" Satan screeched, sheepishly clutching a tree branch in his miserable paw, like a child caught with his hand in the cookie jar. "Why do you keep helping these two? What have they ever done to deserve your favor?"

"I'm sorry you don't understand, Satan, but I'm afraid you wouldn't believe Me even if I told you. Sadly, that is the curse of the liar. The liar doesn't know how to believe the truth, even when it's told to him."

Frustrated, the devil threw down the branch and stomped on it. "I am so sick of your double-talk! Why can't you ever say something I can understand?"

Slowly but surely, Satan's embarrassed minions began to retreat from view, one by one.

"You really are pathetic," insisted the Word. "You manage to deceive My servants and get them kicked out of Paradise, but that's not good enough for you. Now you won't stop until you destroy every last shred of their happiness, even if it means killing them."

"Well, what do you expect? Everything that used to belong to me is Adam's now! You know, if you're such a merciful god as you purport to be, you'd see your way to being kind to *me* once in awhile, too. Don't you think?"

"But I have been merciful to you. If I hadn't, I'd have already destroyed you and all your wretched minions. Instead, I've been patient with you, and will be until the end of the world. Now away with you, before I change My mind."

Satan fled angrily, and just as abruptly the Word vanished.

As soon as the devil and his crew withdrew, the fire began to subside. When Adam and Eve saw the blaze beginning to die down, they began to cautiously approach the cave. Without warning, the fire shifted and began moving toward them with its lashing flames. Horrified, the couple watched as it slowly encircled them.

"I guess God really is mad at us," remarked Eve. "Maybe that's why he doesn't tell us how the fire got started. He assumes we already know."

"I think you're right, Eve. Just look at these flames! Remember when we had the same thing inside us?"

"I do. But that seems like so long ago now. It used to yield to us; but not anymore, not since we've transgressed the limits of our creation."

"But this fire hasn't been affected at all!" shouted Adam, as the flames crept closer and closer. "Now it has complete power over us!"

As the couple moved to evade the fire, it moved to cut off their path of retreat.

"Oh, God," cried Eve, "just look at this inferno! It has a mind of its own. Wherever we turn, it's right there trying to scorch us."

"Lord, please, help us. This wall of flames won't let us get back into the cave that you ordered us to live in. Please tell us what to do!"

Then the Word of God appeared right next to them.

"Thank you, Lord, we're so glad to see You," cried Adam. "We thought You'd abandoned us for good this time."

Gazing into the flames, even the Word seemed mesmerized by the fire as it threw its sparks in every direction. "Just look at this fire, Adam! Do you see how different it is from everything else in the Garden of Delights?"

"Yes, Lord, I do. But why has it changed so much?"

"As long as you obeyed My command, it yielded to you, but as a result of your downfall, it's now able to attack you. So do you see how Satan has exalted you after all? Did you really think he loved you when he said he'd raise you On-High?"

"Then why did he do it?"

Turning from the flames, the Word looked Adam straight in the eye. "Why do you think? He wanted you to leave the light and stumble into darkness, to drag you down into slavery, to see your happiness turn into misery, and your peace become struggle."

"Oh, Eve," murmured Adam, unable to bear the searing eyes of the Word, turning back toward the flames, which were infinitely more bearable than the Lord's penetrating gaze. "Just look at this fire."

"That's right, Adam," continued the Word. "Take a good look at it, and see how it surrounds you. Then realize it will do the same thing to you and your descendants whenever you do things his way. He'll torment you with fire, and after you die, you'll go down to Hades. Then you'll see what it really means to burn in his fire."

Adam and Eve exchanged a terrified look.

"There, you and your descendants will stay until the time of My coming. So just as you're unable to enter your cave because of this inferno, you'll be imprisoned until I make a way of escape for you."

Then the Word raised His right hand toward the flames. "Listen to Me, fire. I want you to make a pathway for My servants to walk through."

The fire began to slowly part in the middle. It continued to spread until a pathway opened up in its midst, and the couple cautiously started through the corridor. Then the Word vanished. As Adam and Eve passed through the gap in the fire, Satan's ugly face materialized and blew into the flames like a whirlwind, causing some of the flames to lash out and scorch their skin.

"Lord, save us!" cried Adam. "Please don't let us be swallowed by this fire!"

Again the Word returned, His arms spread wide, and extinguished the flames once and for all. This time, however, the wounds remained on their bodies.

"What happened, Lord?" asked Adam, grimacing from his burns. "We were so close to making it through unharmed."

"It was that damned Satan again. He couldn't resist one last opportunity to hurt you. So you see: The one who promised to give you divinity, instead burns you with fire. How fitting is that? Do you still believe Satan loves you?"

The couple solemnly shook their heads. "No, sir," they said in unison.

"But look, I'm the One Who created you. Do you realize how many times now I've rescued you from his attack?"

This time they both nodded with a sad smile.

"And Eve," continued the Word, "what did Satan promise you in the garden?"

She meekly replied, "He told us that when we ate from that tree our eyes would be opened, and we'd become like gods, knowing good and evil."

"Well, how is that for sweet irony?" asked the Word with an uncharacteristic smirk. "He's made you see fire's power over you; how it burns. And now you're seeing every evil that Satan has planned for you and your descendants! So, in fact, your eyes have been opened, haven't they?"

Then the Word vanished while Adam and Eve just looked at one another, utterly dismayed.

Rock of Ages

INSIDE THEIR CAVE, Adam and Eve were still trembling from their experience with the fire, still agonizing over the searing burns on their bodies.

"Oh, Eve, if fire burns our skin like this now, just imagine what it's going to be like when we're dead and Satan punishes our souls."

"And right now our rescue seems so far away. If only God in His mercy would come to fulfill His promise sooner."

Even as the daylight was fading the embers from the fire were still smoldering. Just then, a breeze fanned a tiny flame alive, and slowly it began creeping toward Adam and Eve. The couple exchanged a troubled look and cautiously backed away.

LATER THAT NIGHT, the couple walked up to the summit of the hill that overlooked the western border of the Garden of Eden. There they sat bathed in the light of a full Moon, just staring down at the garden, as the cherub buzzed about its perimeter, darting about, here and there, searching for possible intruders. Exhausted, the weary couple then laid back and fell asleep, quite peacefully, under that shimmering, moonlit sky.

BUT SATAN EVEN despised the sight of them sleeping. Like a persistent gnat that will not go away, the devil and several of his grotesque henchman hovered above the dozing couple. "I still don't get it," grumbled Satan. "Why does god keep promising salvation for Adam and Eve, but not me? He's never promised *me* a thing!"

"God isn't so good, after all, is he?" grunted his lieutenant. "If he were, then he'd save us, too. Where's our contract?"

"The goodness of god is meaningless, I tell you," Satan continued, his hollow, black eyes growing wider. "We're doomed to live in a Universe without hope! There's nothing left for us but an unquenchable demand for revenge."

"Then revenge is what you'll have, Master," growled his lieutenant. "What do you suggest?"

"Let me see," muttered the devil, mulling over his options. "Subterfuge has failed again and again. Even my old friend fire has failed me. So what else is left? There must be something we can do to get rid of these miserable humans."

"I say we just kill them and be done with it," replied the lieutenant. "Then the Earth will finally be rid of the pestilence of Adam and Eve."

"Of course," continued Satan, relishing the idea. "And once they're dead and gone, there won't *be* any descendants to inherit our old kingdom. It will be my exclusive domain once again! *Then* god will have to take me back."

With a puzzled look on his ugly face, one demon there turned to the fellow next to him. "I don't get it. Isn't that what I've been saying all along?"

The other demon glared back at him. "Fool, who are you to question the master's wisdom?"

"I'm not," grunted the first demon. "I'm just saying, that's all."

"Well, if I were you, I'd keep my filthy trap shut; unless you want to end up becoming food yourself."

"Forget I even mentioned it," he muttered. Then, returning his attention front and center, he burst out with a blood-curdling scream. "Death to Adam and Eve! Let's rip their hearts out and eat them!"

Inspired by his sadistic sentiment, the whole group resounded with a single, guttural howl. "Death to Adam and Eve!"

"Absolutely, my precious legions," growled the devil. Intoxicated by such a rousing display of bloodlust, he motioned to his minions. "Now, gather round."

As though drawn in by an invisible net, they all moved in closely.

"Our most malcontent Lord," scowled one of them, "what would you have us do?"

"I propose, hmmm, let me see," he began, scratching his furry chin, his malicious eyes scanning the eager faces before him. "Yes, I propose we find a huge rock and smash them into oblivion! That way there'll be nothing left of them for god to restore!"

The whole assembly let out a boisterous roar and eagerly swooped down to where Adam and Eve were still fast asleep. Turning to his lieutenant, Satan snarled, "And make sure the rock you choose has no craters or holes of any kind, or else they might escape being crushed. Is that understood?"

"Certainly, Master," replied the lieutenant. "Consider it done."

THE DEMONS SOON found a gigantic stone, wide and smooth. The group hovered about this stone, meticulously searching for any imperfections.

"This one is perfect, Master," said his lieutenant.

"Good," the devil replied. "Then pick it up and drop it on them! And be quick about it.

The last thing we need is to have that misanthropic god of theirs showing up to foil our plans again."

Then, as if according to a single mind, the legion moved into action and together they hoisted the huge rock from its resting place.

"And I want you to make sure it doesn't roll off of them after it lands!" scowled Satan.

"Yes, Lord," grunted the lieutenant. "Your wish is our command."

So they took the colossal stone and maneuvered it directly over the sleeping couple. Then, they simply let go. The rock headed straight for them and landed with a tremendous thud.

"Good shot, you infernal bastards!" howled Satan. "I don't believe it! We did it! We've killed Adam and Eve. Be still my heart. We're free at last!"

A wave of horrid joy shot through the ranks of his legion. "We did it!" snorted one of them, turning to the fellow next to him. "Did you see that? We dropped that baby right on them, and there wasn't a damn thing they could do about it! Smash, boom, dead! Did you see it?"

Wide-eyed, fangs glistening, the other demon slapped him on the back with a hearty blow. "You better believe I saw it! And it was beautiful! What I wouldn't give to see the look on god's face right now!"

"Or Adam and Eve's faces, for that matter," replied the first. "If they still had faces!"

Their raucous laughter echoed for several moments while Satan continued to look down at the scene with such happiness. "I don't think I've ever seen a more beautiful rock in my entire, miserable life. I think I'm actually going to shed a tear." A sliver of a teardrop dribbled down his cheek, and he wiped it away in an instant. "Oh, there it was. My word, I haven't had a good cry like that in I don't know how long." But as the devil watched his demons frolicking about in such ecstasy, the look of joy suddenly washed away from his despicable face to be replaced by his familiar scowl. "Enough already. The deed is done. Party time is over. We'd better vacate the premises before the meddler god shows up to check on his little darlings. We certainly don't want to be around for that." With a wave of his leathery paw, he shouted, "Now all of you, back to work!"

And just like that, the entire lot of demonic hosts jumped to attention and catapulted out of sight as if they had all been shot from a cannon.

FROM OUT OF NOWHERE, two angels appeared and flew down to the boulder. "Did you see what I just saw?" murmured the first angel.

"I'm afraid so, yes," replied the second with a painful grimace.

"Oh, dear, I can't believe those despicable monsters actually got away with it."

Inspecting the surface of the giant stone, the second angel noticed something. "Look, there's a crack in the rock."

"A crack?" asked the first. "How odd. A rock this size shouldn't have a crack in it after landing on a grassy knoll."

"It's not merely a crack, though. It's actually a small crevice punched straight through the slab."

"That *is* odd. Should we have a look?"

The second angel nodded eagerly.

"Very well, then."

And together the two angels shrank down to the size of two insects. Then they walked straight through the crevice in the stone as if it were a very sizable doorway. Inside, they could hardly believe their eyes.

"Can it be?" gasped the first angel.

"Have you ever seen anything like this in all your days?" the second one said, quietly in awe.

"Absolutely not."

"But we both saw it with our own eyes, didn't we? The devil and his legions dropped a giant boulder on Adam and Eve while they lay sleeping, yes?"

"Yes, that's right; I saw it, too," insisted the first angel. "But it doesn't appear to be a boulder anymore at all, does it? It's..."

Mystified, the two tiny angels gaped upward at their strange surroundings.

"It—*It's* a canopy," stammered the second.

Sure enough, the angels gazed up, not at solid rock, as they had expected to see, but at a hollowed-out cavern, hewn out of the stone's core, and by the moonlight that peeked in through the crevice in the rock, they could also see two figures lying at the center of this, from their miniature perspectives, rocky cathedral.

"And those two figures on the ground there—"

"Are none other than Adam and Eve."

The couple woke up suddenly, and, sitting up, looked at one another, confused and groggy.

"Thank the Lord above," the first angel whispered.

"They're still alive after all," added the second.

And like two flying insects, the pair flitted back out through the crevice in the rock and disappeared.

"Eve?" mumbled Adam as he looked around, completely disoriented. "What is going on? Where are we?"

"You're asking me?" replied Eve, trying to shake the cobwebs from her mind. "How should I know?"

With eyes still weary, the couple peered through the dusty interior, lit only by the streak of moonlight filtering in through the crevice in the slab face.

Confused, Adam struggled to his feet and walked over to the stone wall. "Are we in some kind of cave?" Reaching out and touching the wall, he instantly drew his hand back as though he had been burned. His jaw dropped and he turned to Eve.

"Well," snapped Eve, "don't just stand there, Adam. Tell me. What's going on? Where are we?"

"We *are* in a cave, Eve, but it doesn't look like our cave. It seems more like we're inside a gigantic rock."

"Good Lord, Adam," exclaimed Eve, springing to her feet in a panic and moving to the wall to touch it for herself. "Last night we fell asleep under the stars; and now you're telling me we're inside a rock? How is that even possible?"

"I don't know, Eve. We've seen a lot of strange things since we left the garden, but this is definitely the strangest of them all."

"What did we do to cause a rock to bend itself over us like this? And what's next? Does the ground open up and swallow us?"

"Maybe God is mad at us because we left the cave without His permission. You know we only came here last night because we wanted to."

"We came here," insisted Eve, "because that fire wouldn't stop coming after us. You don't think God would be angry with us just because we tried to escape the fire, do you?"

"I don't know. Maybe God will tell us Himself."

"Then ask Him, Adam; ask Him now, please."

So Adam lifted his eyes toward the ceiling of that rocky cathedral. "Dear Lord, could You please tell us what has happened that we've now found ourselves under this rock? Are You mad at us for leaving the cave?"

Immediately, the Word of God appeared.

"Lord, thank you for answering our prayers," said Adam. "I can't tell—"

But before he could continue with another word, the Word put up His hand to stop him. "Never mind that now, Adam. I have an important question to ask you."

"Certainly, Lord. What is it?"

"Tell me, who told you to leave the cave and come to the hilltop overlooking the garden?"

The couple exchanged a worried look.

"See, Eve, I told you He was mad at us for leaving the cave."

"Don't talk to her, Adam, talk to Me. Now, who told you to leave?"

"No one, Lord," he meekly replied. "We only came here because of the heat from the fire. It wouldn't stop coming after us; not even in our cave."

"Really," said the Word, "you came here because a little flame chased you?"

"I'm sorry, Lord," interjected Eve, "but we're not sure if You're teasing us or what, because if You are, I don't think You're being fair. Adam and I were badly burned in that fire. Just the sight of it coming after us was very traumatic. And here you are chiding us for running away. What should we have done? Laid down next to it and gone to sleep?"

"Of course not, Eve, but seriously, if you're that disturbed by one night with the heat, how are you ever going to endure it while you're in Hades? Not to mention the fact that, by leaving your cave, you risked a fate far worse than the burning of your skin. Did you ever consider that for even a moment? Why didn't you just ask Adam to put it out, anyway? It wasn't that big of a fire, was it?"

"So that's why You covered us with this miserable rock?" wondered Adam. "A rock this heavy could've crushed us. Wasn't there any other way You could've taught us a lesson?"

"What makes you so sure I put this rock on you, Adam? I'm not the one who's trying to kill you, you know. This was Satan's doing. He's convinced himself that if he can kill you two, then I'll have no choice but to restore him to his old life."

"Satan?" exclaimed Adam."But how?"

"His minions dropped a huge boulder on you, but in My kindness, just as the rock was falling, I told it to form this canopy over you."

Eve pointed down at their feet. "Look, Adam, He even lowered the ground beneath us."

"So You're not really mad at us?" asked Adam, embarrassed with himself.

"No, I'm not mad at you, but I am disappointed you didn't stand up for yourself in the cave. I'm disappointed you left without a fight. When are you two ever going to learn? With Me on your side, you can face anything, any storm, any attack, no matter how unsettling it may appear on the surface."

As His words sank into their hearts, they appeared deeply moved.

"Oh, Lord," muttered Eve, "I am so sorry for doubting You."

"Yes, Lord, we're both sorry for doubting You, and especially for not asking You to help us extinguish that flame."

"And thank you for turning this rock into a cave for us," added Eve.

"Of course, you two," said the Word. "I accept your apology."

"And, boy, were we scared when we woke up under this thing, Lord," Adam continued with a sheepish grin, trying to lighten up the somber mood. "You should have seen the look on Eve's face. But I guess You never have anything like this happen to You, what with You being the Lord and all."

"Don't be too sure of yourself, Adam. In fact, this very thing *will* happen to Me when I'm born on this Earth someday. Satan will stir up certain leaders among the Jews and drive them to put Me to death. Then they'll lay Me inside a cave, just like this one, where I'll stay for three days and nights, but on the third day, I'll rise again and provide salvation for you and your descendants."

Adam and Eve exchanged a puzzled look. They had no idea how to respond.

"Now, Adam, because you left the cave and came here without permission, I won't be letting you out from under this rock for three days. But don't despair; after the appointed time, I will set you free. Is that understood?"

Solemnly, the couple nodded.

"Yes, Lord," replied Adam. "We understand."

Then the Word vanished.

THREE DAYS LATER, an earthquake split the rock open, from top to bottom, and Adam and Eve slowly crawled out from underneath it. By then, their skin was extremely withered. Squinting at the Sun, the couple wandered around in a daze for quite a while.

"Thank God we finally got out of there," Adam said, stumbling slightly before righting himself. "I don't think I could've taken it much longer."

"I thought I was going to suffocate at any moment," added Eve, who sat down awkwardly, still trying to catch her breath.

LATER THAT AFTERNOON, the couple was back inside the Cave of Treasures, where the first thing they did was to go around making sure that all their mementos were still intact.

"Well," said Adam, "it looks as though everything is still here. Gold, frankincense, myrrh, all just the way we left it. You know, Eve, I hate to say it, but I've never been so glad to see this old cave as I am today."

"I hate to say it, too," said Eve with an embarrassed smile. "But after that fire nearly destroyed it and after three days under that rock, I feel the same way."

"Funny how something like that could happen, huh?" Adam said as he reached out and hugged Eve.

"Yeah, funny," was all she said.

Emblems of Hope

THEN CAME THE DAWN of the fifty-first day of their having been exiled from the garden, and when Adam got up early that morning, he said, "Come on, Eve, let's go and do some work. It'll be good for us."

"Work? What kind of work?"

"I don't know. I'm sure we'll think of something."

"I'll tell you what I'd like to do."

"What?"

"I'd like to find something to wear besides fig leaves. Do you think we can do that?"

"I don't see why not, if we try hard enough. Let's go."

SO THE COUPLE WALKED along the northern perimeter of the garden without really knowing exactly what they were searching for; they were just searching. Suddenly, Eve stopped and wiped her sweaty brow. Then, looking down at her dirty hands, she tried to wipe them off on her fig-leaf skirt. Finding her hands were no cleaner than they were before, she let out an exasperated sigh.

Watching her intently, Adam asked, "What's wrong, dear?"

"Oh, Adam, just look at us. We've spent so much time walking around in this heat, lying around in musty caves, rolling around in the dirt, we're filthy."

Adam shrugged. "Maybe God can help us figure out what to do about it."

Then the Word of God appeared. "Adam, take Eve with you and go to the seashore where you fasted before. There you'll find the skins of sheep that have been eaten by a lion. Now, just the skins remain. Take them and use them to make clothing for yourselves."

"Did you hear that, Eve? The Lord has clothing for us instead of these useless fig leaves?"

Eve nodded with a grateful smile. "That's nice, Adam. Thank You, Lord."

"And Lord?"

"Yes, Adam."

"What is *clothing*, anyway?"

"It's what you wrap around your body to keep it dry and clean, something you wear to protect it from the cold, the wind and the rain."

"That sounds like just what we're looking for. Thank You, Lord."

"NO, NO, NO, YOU'RE lying!" shrieked Satan. "I don't believe a word of it! You're a filthy liar!"

"But it's true, Master," insisted his lieutenant. "I've seen them with my own two eyes. There's not a scratch on them."

"But how? I watched them get smashed into oblivion! Certainly it must be some sort of illusion. God is playing a trick on me because he knows I've killed his little darlings."

"I don't think so, Lord. We just overheard god instructing Adam and Eve to go to the ocean, where they'd be receiving sheepskins they could turn into clothing, whatever that is."

"What am I going to do now? I thought for sure I'd gotten rid of them." For the longest time, the devil fumed vehemently. Finally he turned ever so slowly to his lieutenant. "When you picked out that boulder, I specifically told you to find one with no holes in it, didn't I?"

"We did, Lord, and the rock was flawless. Trust me. I would never lie to you, *never*."

"Flawless, my eye. And as for your not lying to me, let's not even go there."

"But, Lord—"

"Enough! Off to the Abyss with you!" Satan simply waved his paw, and the howling lieutenant was instantly sucked away into oblivion. Craning his wolfen head, the devil looked around with a vicious scowl. "Now, who's next in line?"

CURSING INCOHERENTLY under his breath, Satan was striding along the seashore, heading straight for the sheepskins lying on the beach. "As usual, when you want something done right, you have to do it yourself. What was I thinking, anyway, asking a bunch of worthless rejects to do something as basic as crushing a couple of humans with a boulder?" Stepping up to the skins, his eyes thinned as he looked them over. "Now, as for these sheepskins, I still haven't decided. Should I throw them into the sea, or should I burn them? Personally, I am so inclined toward burning."

But just as he was reaching down to grab them, the Word of God appeared. "Not so fast, Devil!"

"What the—" Satan sputtered, and before he even had a chance to put up a fight, he found himself tightly wrapped in a brass chain. "Not you again," he muttered, thoroughly deflated as he fell prostrate into the sand.

"Your new outfit suits you," said the Word with a wry smile. "I hope you enjoy it." And then He disappeared, leaving the devil lying there next to the sheepskins.

"Come back here, you coward!" grunted Satan.

EVENTUALLY, ADAM and Eve came walking along the seashore, quite casually, when suddenly something caught Adam's attention. "Look, Eve, there are the sheepskins God told us about."

But as they walked closer, they were confused by the added spectacle of what they had never expected to see. "Adam, is someone lying next to them?" wondered Eve. "What's he doing there?"

"It looks like he's chained up."

"I wonder who it is."

"Who," wondered Adam, "or *what*, you mean."

Then the Word of God returned. "Don't you two recognize your archenemy?"

The couple stared blankly at the prostrate figure awhile, before they shook their heads.

"Not really, no," said Adam.

"Of course, you know who this is," the Word insisted. "The one who tricked you by hiding in the serpent? Who fooled you by disguising himself as an angel? You remember, don't you?"

Adam turned to Eve. "Do you recognize this creature, Eve?"

"Of course you do," pressed the Word. "The one who promised you divinity?"

Eve shook her head in exasperation. "I'm confused, Lord. You say we should know him, but at the same time You say he's different things at different times. First he's a serpent, then he's an angel, now here he is looking like this hideous monster. What is he really? And how are we supposed to recognize him if he keeps changing his appearance?"

The couple expectantly stared back at the Word.

"She does make a good point, Lord," replied Adam.

"She makes a very good point, yes; but therein lies the rub. A creature that can appear as any one of these things *better* be recognized, and recognized quickly."

Then Adam turned to Eve. "Now He makes a good point." Thoroughly confused, Adam hung his head. "This is all very hard to take in, Lord. Could You please start over from the beginning? Who is this monster that we should know him?"

"This is the horror among the angels," continued the Word, "the source of all pride, the father of lies, the one who was responsible for your fall from grace. This is Satan."

Suddenly Adam and Eve's eyes grew wide with rage. "*Him!*" they said as one.

"You mean *he's* the one who tricked us into eating from the Tree of Knowledge?" sputtered Adam.

"*He's* the one who got us kicked out of our garden home?" screeched Eve.

"He's the one all right," added the Word, "lying here in all his miserable splendor. So much for his hollow promises now."

"But why don't You banish him, Lord?" Adam wondered, "like You banished the serpent, like you banished *us*?"

"I did banish him, but his banishment is of a different nature than that of the serpent's or yours, because Satan's nature is altogether different than any fleshly creature."

"Well if you banished him, how'd he get here?" asked Eve.

"He's here because in My providence I lured him here. He thought he could destroy the sheepskins I provided for you, but it was My intention to chain him until you arrived so you could see, once and for all, just how weak and powerless he really is. That is his true banishment, a banishment infinitely harsher than either you or the serpent will ever have to endure."

With just a wave of the Word's hand, the shackles fell away from Satan, and instantly he flew away, spewing his venomous curses as he went. For several awkward moments, Adam and Eve just stood there, and turning to the Word, they found Him gone again.

"Adam, why does He just disappear like that? Couldn't He at least say goodbye, or something?"

"Never mind that now, Eve. Let's just get our sheepskins and go back to our cave, before we get into any more trouble."

"Fine, but before we do, I'd like to wash up. If we're going to start wearing clothes, we should probably be clean before we put them on."

"Whatever you say, Eve. Let's hurry, though, and be done with it."

SO THE TWO OF THEM hastily washed up in the ocean, and before long they came out of the water cleaner than they had been in a long time. To the sheepskins, Adam stood and stared blankly at them for several moments.

"What's wrong now, Adam?"

"I'm sad thinking about how we got these skins, that's all."

"Sad, why?"

"I'm sad because these skins have come from owners who have died, and when we put them on, we'll be wearing emblems of their death."

"And someday," continued Eve, beginning to realize what he was saying, "we'll die just like they did, won't we?"

BACK INSIDE THEIR cave, Adam and Eve laid the sheepskins down, and again they dolefully stared at them for quite a while.

"Lord, now that we have these skins," said Adam, "could You please tell us what to do with them? How are we supposed to *make* clothes with them? We have no idea how to do something like that."

An angel suddenly appeared there in the cave. "Very well, then. God has instructed me to show you how to make clothes. Go get some palm thorns."

RETURNING WITH A handful of thorns, Adam handed them to the angel, who began to diligently work with the skins. First, the angel took a thorn and attached a long, thin string to it. Then, right in front of them, so they could both get a good look at what he was doing, he pierced the skins with the thorn and pulled the string through. So adept was this angel with his thorn that he wove his thread into those skins in such a way that the stitch was virtually invisible and that the entire thing was sown together with a single strand. Then he repeated the same process so that when he was finished he had created two complete outfits, one for Adam and one for Eve. Both were given loincloths for their waists, while Eve received a slender top to cover her breasts. The couple eagerly put them on.

"How does it look Adam?" asked Eve, twirling about the cave in her new outfit.

"It looks great, Eve."

"I love the way it fits. Thank you so much. You really are an angel sent from above."

"You're welcome," he replied. "It's been a pleasure to serve you. Goodbye now."

"Goodbye," said Eve.

Then, the angel streaked out of view.

"See, Adam, the angel says goodbye when he leaves. Why doesn't the Lord?"

"Maybe because when the Lord leaves our presence, He's not really gone. He's still right here in our midst."

Intrigued, Eve nodded. "You know, Adam, I think you might be right. What a comforting thought." Walking over to him, she planted a kiss on his cheek. "I never thought of it that way before. Thank you for that."

Obviously proud of himself, Adam smiled.

As a Roaring Lion

THE NEXT MORNING, the couple got up and surveyed the world from the mouth of the cave.

"Lord, bless us today," said Adam, "and help us to know what we should do so You'll always be proud of us."

"Very good, Adam. What would you like to do today?"

"I don't know," he replied with an innocent shrug. "I was just thinking, since we still have no idea what's off in the West, it might be nice to see what's out there."

HEADING INTO THE West, the pair had not gone very far, when Satan spotted them from a distance. "What have we here? Two wandering doves, I see, helpless as can be." And landing behind a bush, the devil transformed himself into a lion. "My word, this body of mine is absolutely ravenous. I feel as though I haven't eaten a thing for three days. I wonder what's on the menu."

Appearing on the horizon, the unsuspecting Adam and Eve began to approach Satan's position. "Ah, if it isn't the main course," growled the devil, "headed right this way."

With barely a sound, the lion darted out from his hiding place and started to charge Adam and Eve. Instantly, the couple saw him coming. Eve let out a blood-curdling scream, and Adam instinctively stepped in front of her, acting as a shield. "Lord, save us!" he cried.

Still, the lion galloped closer and closer, until finally, just a few feet away, the Word of God materialized in his direct path toward the couple. Too close to stop, the lion tried to swerve around the Word, but with just a touch from His hand, the lion was catapulted into the surrounding brush, where he became thoroughly entangled. Terrified, Eve fell into Adam's arms.

"It's okay, Eve. The danger's passed. The Lord's prevailed again."

"Thank God," murmured Eve, "I thought for sure we were dead."

"Thank You, Lord," said Adam. "What would we ever do without You?"

Still trembling, Eve gaped at the prostrate lion as it struggled to extricate itself, to no avail. "But why, Lord, why did this lion attack us? Didn't they pledge to not attack us as long as we never tried to harm them?"

The Word nodded. "They did, yes, but this is no ordinary lion." And with a wave of His hand, He caused the lion to transform back into its true appearance.

The horrified couple took a step back.

"Satan," was all Adam said.

"That's right, Satan," echoed the Word, "lurking about as a roaring lion, seeking whom he may devour."

"No wonder it attacked us, Eve," said Adam, as Eve still clung firmly to him. "But see, just like I told you, the Lord never left us for a moment."

"Now away with you, Devil!" shouted the Word, and after another wave of His hand, Satan's entanglement loosened and fell from his body. Without a sound, he flew away in a whirlwind of dust.

Then the Word turned to the couple and smiled reassuringly. "I'll bet that's the first time you ever saw the devil completely speechless."

Forcing a smile, they both nodded.

"So tell me, Adam," the Word continued. "What are you doing out here in the West? Isn't your home east of this place?"

"Yes, Lord. Eve and I were just out here exploring. We were curious to see what lay in this direction, that's all."

"I see. You almost paid a very dear price for the sake of curiosity, didn't you?"

Timidly, Adam nodded. "We did, yes."

"You've got to be more careful, Adam. I warned you before, to never go wandering off like this. But still, you don't seem to realize how precarious your situation is. As long as you reside where I've designated, you know you're safe. But when you choose to go wherever you please, then this is the result. Is that what you really want for you and Eve?"

Adam shrugged his shoulders. "Of course not, Lord."

"Then go back to your home and stay close. I don't want you to allow any more opportunities for Satan to attack you."

Then the Word vanished, leaving the couple still trembling from their experience. Once again, without a word, they slowly headed toward home.

BY THE TIME THE couple got back to the Cave of Treasures, their strength was clearly failing.

"Eve, I am so sorry. If it wasn't for me, we'd never have found ourselves in that predicament."

"Don't blame yourself, Adam. It was the devil who attacked us, not you."

"But you heard the Lord. *I* was the one who put us in harm's way. I could never forgive myself if I lost you like that. Damn this insatiable curiosity of mine. I'm sick of this world. What good is it, anyway, if we always have to worry about being attacked by that renegade?"

"But what can we do about it? We keep asking God to let us back into the garden, but all He ever does is tell us to wait."

"I know, Eve, but we can't wait. We have to think of another way."

"Like what?"

"I don't know, but I'll think of something."

THE NEXT MORNING, Eve woke up, and turning to see Adam, she found that he was gone. "Adam, where are you?"

"I'm here, Eve."

Springing to her feet, she met him at the mouth of their cave. "Don't scare me like that. For a second there I thought something had happened to you. Where were you?"

"Out wandering."

Relieved, Eve hugged him tightly, when suddenly she noticed something. "Adam, you're bleeding. What happened?"

Looking down, Adam saw it, too. A trickle of blood was dribbling down his wrist. "Oh, that? It's nothing. I slipped and fell climbing a rock, is all." He bent over, and grabbing a handful of grass, he then wiped the blood away with it. "See, all gone," he said with an innocent smile. "Now, what do you say, Eve; are you ready to go for a walk with me?"

TOGETHER, THE COUPLE was strolling along the southern border of the garden.

"Where are we going, Adam?"

"I told you; for a walk."

"I know that, but where to?"

"You'll see."

Eve started to open her mouth but thought better of it and simply followed Adam.

SOON, THEY CAUGHT A glimpse of the gateway to the garden.

"Adam, look, the cherub's gone. The entrance is clear. Where could he be?"

"Doing his job, I hope," replied Adam with a peculiar look in his eye. Single-minded in his intensity, he stared straight ahead at the empty gateway leading back into the garden.

"I don't get it," murmured Eve. "You *want* the cherub to do his job? Why?"

Still staring at the vacated entranceway, Adam put his finger to his mouth and started toward the garden gate. "Don't say a word, Eve. Just follow me."

MEANWHILE, THE CHERUB responsible for guarding the gate was flying along the northern perimeter of the garden, inspecting the thorny hedge that surrounded it. Suddenly he noticed something. "What have we here?" Streaking down to take a closer look, he was disturbed by what he saw. "If I didn't know better, I'd say someone has been tampering with this hedge." Sure enough, the cherub then found a section where a huge hole had been partially torn into the thorny exterior. "Oh, thank Heaven, it doesn't go all the way through. At least no one has penetrated the wall here." And looking closer still, the cherub was shocked at what he saw on one of the branches. "Blood?"

BACK AT THE GATEWAY, Adam and Eve were drawing near to the entrance, stepping very cautiously so as to not make a sound. Just a few feet away, they were closer to getting back in than they had ever been before, when suddenly the cherub swooped down in front of them, wielding his sword of fire.

"How dare you!" screeched the cherub. "You know you're not allowed back in! Are you two trying to get me in trouble, sneaking around behind my back like this? It's not right, I tell you!"

Rushing forward, the cherub raised his fiery sword to strike them, but before he could, the terrified couple collapsed. Then the cherub's flaming sword flickered and dimmed. "What's this?" muttered the cherub. Inspecting his sword, he found that it was no longer emitting flames, not even a spark. "What's happened to my sword?"

Suddenly an earthquake rumbled through the landscape, shaking the garden walls in its wake, then, just as quickly as it had commenced, it was over. In a flash, a cherubim flew down to the garden gate to see what was happening. Noticing the confused cherub hovering over the two motionless bodies, he flew over to him. "What's all this, then?" asked the cherubim.

"I'm not sure," replied the cherub. "I was making my rounds about the garden's perimeter, when I discovered a potential breach in the wall, and when I returned to my post, I found Adam and Eve trying to sneak back inside."

"So you killed them?"

Bewildered, the cherub shook his head. "That's just it; I never got the chance. When I raised my sword to block their way, they collapsed, and just like that, my sword fizzled out."

"Fizzled out? What do you mean, fizzled out?"

"I don't know. It just went out, as if I'd dipped it in a cold stream. One moment it was a flaming sword, then *whoosh*, it fizzled out."

"I wonder how something like that could have happened. Do you think God might have decided to be merciful to Adam and Eve, even though they nearly outsmarted you?"

"Outsmarted me? What's that supposed to mean?"

"Maybe instead of allowing you to kill them, He chose to spare them, considering it was your fault for nearly allowing them to get back inside."

The cherub earnestly considered his words. "Oh, dear, I never thought about it that way. What should we do now?"

"We? There is no *we*, my dear fellow. This is your responsibility, not mine."

"Then what do you suggest *I* do? Certainly you could offer me some sort of council in this matter. I can't just fly back to Heaven and ask God. He might still be angry with me for nearly letting them back in."

"Yes, that is a distinct possibility. You've certainly gotten yourself in quite a predicament, haven't you?"

Then a group of angels came down to where Adam and Eve were lying, and where they discovered the cherub and the cherubim staring at one another, quite perplexed.

"What is going on here?" asked one of them.

"That's just it," replied the cherubim. "We're not exactly sure. This fellow was supposed to guard the garden gate so Adam and Eve couldn't regain entrance. And just now he found them trying to sneak back in."

"No!" cried the angel, gaping at the prostrate couple.

"Yes!" blurted the cherub.

"So you killed them?" exclaimed another of the angels.

"No. I never had the chance!" insisted the cherub, holding his cold sword out for them to see. "Look, my sword doesn't even work anymore. I couldn't harm a flea with this thing."

"It's true," interjected the cherubim. "When he tried to stop Adam and Eve with it, his sword, *whoosh*, mysteriously extinguished."

"*Whoosh*?" echoed the first angel.

"Whoosh," said the cherubim with a knowing nod.

The angels all exchanged a curious look amongst themselves.

"Well, that's wonderful news," exclaimed yet another of the angels. "God must have changed His mind about letting Adam and Eve back into the garden. Or else why would he have prevented the cherub from striking them down?"

But the first angel remained unconvinced as he stared down at the couple's motionless bodies. "I don't know. They don't look so good to me. There's no way their death in this place could've been an accident. If you ask me, I think God killed them for trying to get back in without His permission."

Then the Word of God appeared in their midst, to the amazement of all the angels. "Don't worry, everyone. I'll handle this."

And with that, the whole group scattered; all except for the cherub, that is. Embarrassed, he just hung his head, rolling his dim sword about in his hands, as if unsure of what to do with it.

"Relax, Cherub. This wasn't your fault. You've done your job well."

The cherub's head popped up with a grateful smile. "Oh, thank You, Lord. I'm so relieved to hear it."

Then, with a wave of His hand, the Word reignited the cherub's sword. "There you are; now, feel free to resume your duties."

"My sword!" exclaimed the cherub, who then cheerfully buzzed out of sight.

Turning to Adam and Eve, the Word reached down and revived them once again. The couple slowly opened their eyes and realized who was standing over them. Reluctantly, they stood up and wiped themselves off, exchanging a serious look as they did.

"So," began the Word, "you two want to get back into the garden that badly?"

Adam innocently shrugged his shoulders. "Who us? No, of course not, Lord."

"No?" blurted Eve, glaring back at him. "What are you saying, Adam?" She grabbed his arm in desperation. "Tell Him the truth. Tell Him: We *do* want back in. Tell Him we're tired of being attacked by falling rocks and hungry lions and flaming swords."

"But I thought we already covered all that," said the Word.

"Yes, Lord, we have," replied Adam, "more times than I can count, I'm afraid."

"Be reasonable, you two. You know you never have to worry about being attacked when you stay within your designated domain. The only time you ever have a problem is when you choose to stray. Isn't that right, Eve?"

Considering His words for a moment, Eve finally nodded. "Yes, Lord, I guess so; when You put it that way."

"Good, now please try to stick with the plan, will you? I really hate to see all this needless suffering you're putting yourselves through. This world is tough enough without your having to add to your own misery." And again the Word vanished.

Just then a strange fluttering sound began to emanate several feet from Adam and Eve.

"Eve, do you hear what I hear?"

"I do. What do you think it is?"

"It sounds like the beating of angels' wings."

"What could it mean?"

"I don't know," Adam replied as he took several steps in the direction of the sound, "but there's one way to find out."

"Be careful, Adam. And for Heaven's sake, don't get mixed up with the devil again, please."

As the fluttering sound continued, it slowly began to spread, until it reverberated in the air all around them.

"Oh, angels who wait upon the Lord, have pity on us," Adam said, flinging his hands about in an effort to grab hold of something tangible. "We used to sing praises just like you, but now, even though we know you're there, we *still* can't see you. You angels of God, you could help us, though, couldn't you?"

"But what could we possibly do for you?" asked an odd, little voice.

Turning toward the voice, Adam and Eve were stunned by what they saw. "Look, Eve, a pair of eyes staring back at us."

Sure enough, a pair of disembodied eyes blinked back at them both.

"Are you really an angel of the Lord?" wondered Eve as she cautiously took several steps toward the eyes.

"I am."

"Then why don't you show yourself?" asked Adam, moving forward to Eve's side.

"I don't wish to be seen, that's why."

"By whom?" asked Eve.

"By Satan, of course. He watches you constantly, seeking any opening, any weakness, never sleeping, never ceasing."

"If you're really an angel of the Lord," said Adam, "then you're committed to serving God's purposes. Isn't that so?"

"Just what are you getting at?" the voice murmured suspiciously.

"If you serve God, then you should want to help Eve and I."

The eyes blinked repeatedly, as if thoughtfully considering his words. "If I were you I wouldn't be so eager to twist me toward your selfish purposes. We've already had that game played on us before, thank you."

"What game is that?" asked Adam, suddenly growing impatient.

"The devil's game, of course," replied the voice, "a subtle game, whereby you propose that your aims are undoubtedly the aims of God. We've seen it all before, I assure you."

"Tell us, angel, what have you seen, and when?" insisted Adam.

"Before you ever got kicked out of the garden, Satan was kicked out of Heaven after he tried to convince all of God's angels it was in our best interest to help him, too. Sound familiar?"

The couple exchanged a frustrated look.

"Go on, angel," said Adam.

"First, Satan promised us all kinds of incredible things, like invincibility, divinity, immortality. Some were foolish enough to think he was telling the truth, so they bowed to him and renounced the majesty of God."

"But you didn't believe his promises?" wondered Eve.

"Of course not. I knew they were all lies."

"Didn't you at least consider his offer for a moment?" asked Adam.

"Absolutely not!" snapped the voice. "I flatly refused him."

"What happened next?" pressed Eve.

"What do you think happened? Satan unleashed his troops on us! If it weren't for God's intervention, we'd never have been able to drive him out of Heaven. And when he fell from among us there was incredible happiness, because had he been allowed to stay not a single one of us would have survived. So you see: When you try to persuade me to believe your ends are God's ends, you merely dredge up old wounds, unforgivable wounds, and you very nearly make me regret why I ever felt sorry for you in the first place."

Adam and Eve looked at one another, extremely disturbed by this.

"Forgive us, angel," said Adam. "We're sorry for our selfish behavior. You were right to doubt our motives after all. Truly you are an angel of the Lord."

"I understand," replied the angel, his eyes slowly fading from view. "Peace be with you, Adam and Eve. I promise we will do everything in our power to help you in your time on this Earth."

The angel's voice then began to ring out in a hauntingly beautiful song. "Dear Lord, our most merciful Creator, we, Your faithful servants, humbly beg You to protect Adam and Eve as the devil seeks to destroy them. Never let the jealousy of the Evil One come between them and Your kindness, and please bear with them until the ultimate fulfillment of Your promise. So be it until the end of time."

Then the Word of God returned. "What a beautiful song that was," He said.

"Yes, Lord, it was," added Adam with a melancholy nod.

"And just think, if only you two had obeyed Me, You'd still be with the angels right now, singing right along with them. But no, you had to cooperate with Satan, and now you're living among his angels, demons more evil than you can imagine."

Adam and Eve exchanged a troubled look.

"Lord, please," Adam groaned. "Why are you torturing us like this?"

"Adam, how can you say that?" asked the Word. "I've done nothing but rescue you, time and time again. But if you think I'm being too harsh, maybe you can ask the devil to help you instead. Ask him to give you the divine nature he promised. Do you think he can make you a garden like I did?"

"I don't know, Lord, can he?" asked Eve.

"Of course not, Eve," replied the Word. "He's incapable of keeping a single promise he's ever made to you. I, on the other hand, am capable of fulfilling every one of My promises. Now hurry, get away from here, or else the cherub will come back and try to kill you again."

Vigilance

SATAN CASUALLY WALKED up to the Cave of Treasures, where he stood at the entrance and called out contritely. "Adam, please come outside. I'd like to have a word with you."

"Adam," said Eve, "do you hear that? Someone is calling you."

"Calling me? Who's calling me?"

"How should I know? Someone is outside our cave calling for you. Why not find out for yourself."

Curious, Adam jumped to his feet and headed for the mouth of the cave. "Maybe it's an angel bringing us a word from the Lord," he muttered, half to himself.

But when he got outside and saw the hideous figure standing there, he took a cautious step back. "Oh, it's you," he said with obvious disdain. "What do you want?"

"I just wanted to talk to you, that's all."

"Since when do you just talk?"

"Since now."

"All right," replied Adam cautiously. "Start talking. In fact, I'd like to know something while you're at it. You told Eve if we ate from the Tree of Knowledge, we'd have our eyes opened and that we'd know what God knew. Isn't that what you told us?"

Satan tilted his head. "I vaguely remember saying something like that, yes."

"And you told her we'd receive a divine nature. Isn't that what you said?"

"I suppose so."

"Well, what happened to all that? When are we going to get what you promised us?"

Satan grinned sheepishly. "I'm so sorry. Did you *actually* think I was going to do something for you just because I promised I would?"

"I'll bet you can't even make us a garden like God did, can you?"

"Me? Certainly not, you pathetic mongrel."

"So tell me. Have we gotten a single thing you ever promised us?"

Then the devil's smirk turned to a scowl. "Of course not. And you never will. So how do you like it?"

"I think it stinks!"

"Good," grunted Satan as he extended his grotesque paw in a mock gesture. "Then let me officially welcome you to the club, because I'm never going to get what I'm asking god for, either!"

"Then why'd you do it? Why'd you lie to us? Why'd you have to go and ruin *our* lives?"

"I did it because god ruined my life and replaced me with you!"

Adam shook his head in disbelief. "Well, that doesn't make any sense. We didn't do anything to you. Why not punish God? Why do you have to take it out on us?"

"That's a damn good question; but sadly it's a question I don't plan on answering."

"Well, why not?"

"Because god is much too uncooperative to reason with, but you, on the other hand," spewed the devil, his eyes black with hatred, "*you* are infinitely more manageable. And now that you're under my control, *I'm* going to be your king from now on! So the fact is: I don't have to answer any more of your silly questions, no matter how clever you think you are."

"And this is what you came here to talk to me about?"

"As a matter of fact, yes; it is."

"Eve, did you hear? This miserable liar isn't going to keep *any* of the promises he made to us in the garden."

Cautiously, Eve stepped to Adam's side, shuddering at what she saw. "Not you again."

"Did you hear that, Eve? He says *he's* our king now. Can you believe it?"

"I don't know what to believe anymore, Adam. God only knows. He created us; maybe He can tell us if it's true or not."

"God?" scowled the devil. "God doesn't give a damn about you. If he did, he'd never have allowed you to fall into my clutches in the first place. And while you mull that bombshell over in your pathetic, little minds, consider this: If you think you're going to inherit *my* kingdom, you've got another thing coming, because I'll *never* cease my quest to destroy you! Not for a day, not for an hour, not for a minute! I'll see you both dead, if it's the last thing I do! How do you like that?"

Then, Adam and Eve joined hands and lifted their eyes skyward.

"Lord, please help us," exclaimed Adam. "Save us from the Evil One. Don't let him destroy us before You've had time to fulfill Your word. Please, drive him far away, won't You?"

Suddenly an angel appeared. "Satan, the Lord rebuke you. Leave this place immediately before God destroys *you* instead."

And like a bolt of lightning, the devil streaked out of sight, leaving a cloud of dust in his wake. Turning to the angel, the couple found that he was gone, too.

Adam then turned to Eve. "Well, now we've heard everything. First, God tells us we're safe as long as we stay put, then the devil shows up on our doorstep, telling us about his plans to murder us; and in broad daylight, no less. It doesn't make any sense. Why would God let him do something like that?"

"I don't know, Adam. Nothing about this upside-down world makes any sense to me. Everything keeps changing, shifting from one day to the next. How will we ever know the difference between the truth and the lies?"

"The only time we really know we're listening to the truth is when the Lord is right in front of us. Then all the lies disappear."

"Yeah, but you know as well as I do," countered Eve, "He never sticks around long enough to keep it that way."

"Maybe if we asked God to help us learn the difference for ourselves, maybe He'd show us the way."

"What makes you think He'll do that?"

"I don't know," Adam groaned in frustration, "but it's certainly worth a try. Otherwise we'll never feel safe in this world."

"What did you have in mind?"

"I say we set up a vigil in our cave. We sit right down and pray like we've never prayed before, and this time we do it for the full forty days."

"But you know we already tried that at the ocean."

"I know, but this time we won't make the mistake of splitting up. This time we stick together till the bitter end, even it kills us in the process. Agreed?"

Eve nodded. "Anything, Adam, anything. As long as it keeps that miserable devil from ruining the rest of our lives."

So Adam and Eve walked back into their cave and sat down.

"Dear Lord," began Adam, "we thank you for sending your angel just now and rescuing us from the wrath of the devil, but frankly we're a little concerned that his attacks are becoming bolder by the day. Is there any way You could help us learn how to prevent these random acts of his violence before they occur?"

MEANWHILE, SATAN and his minions sat watching the Cave of Treasures from a distance, and for the longest time the devil just sat there, staring, without a shred of emotion displayed on his sullen face.

One of his demons leaned over and whispered into his neighbor's ear. "He's been sitting like that for days. Whatever could he be thinking?"

"I imagine he's planning something. Great minds like his are always planning things."

"Oh, of course. How right you are. Something absolutely diabolical, I imagine."

"Simply diabolical."

"I wish he'd tell us what he's thinking, though. I hate the suspense. We don't dare go wandering off. You know as soon as we do, he'll decide to rally us to his cause, or some such thing."

"So shut up, why don't you? And let the great one think."

Satan slowly turned his wolfen head toward them and growled, "Yes, do shut up and let me think, you infernal chatterboxes. How do expect me to come up with something worthy of my diabolical genius, if you're both constantly flapping your ridiculous jaws?"

Startled, the demons looked down contritely.

"Forgive me, Master," mumbled the first demon. "So sorry to disturb you."

"Yes, Master," added the second, "a thousand pardons."

"Oh, don't mention it," replied the devil. "It won't happen again." And with a wave of his paw, Satan sent the pair of hapless demons careening off into oblivion. Turning to his lieutenant, he asked, "What is the weather like in the Abyss this time of the year, anyway?"

The petrified lieutenant just shrugged his shoulders, unable, or unwilling, to utter a single syllable.

"AND THANK YOU, LORD," intoned Adam, "for always hearing our prayers and gracing us with Your presence. Amen." Then he looked over at Eve. "Would you like to say something, dear?"

But Eve vacantly shook her head. "No, you're doing just fine." Then she grimaced ever so slightly as the faint sound of gurgling came from her stomach.

"What's wrong?" asked Adam. "Are you getting bored with all this praying?"

"It's just hard to concentrate, what with all that's going on in my stomach."

"Why, what's wrong with your stomach?"

"You know very well what's wrong with my stomach. It's *empty*. And I'm sure by now yours is just as empty as mine."

"Yes, but now is no time to think about something like that. This is too important."

"Naturally," replied Eve, obviously unimpressed.

"Besides, I thought we both agreed to stay put until the forty days were finished. It's the Lord's will that we remain wherever he's told us is safe. Remember?"

"Sure, but didn't the Lord also tell us that we should eat and drink something before we died of starvation and thirst? Why can't we do both?"

"I thought you were afraid to eat anything."

"I am, but that doesn't mean that eventually I might have changed my mind. Did you ever consider that? This world isn't the only thing that changes around here, you know."

"But what made you change your mind?"

"The emptiness in my stomach, Adam. What did the Lord call it? Hunger? Thirst? It's becoming unbearable. Don't you feel it, too?"

"Of course I feel it, but I'm trying my best to ignore it. I just don't want anything to spoil our plans this time. Now, maybe if you lead us in our next prayer, the emptiness will go away."

STILL, SATAN WATCHED and waited from his perch, like a buzzard sitting on a tree branch waiting for its dying victim to succumb. "Those two have been in that damned cave of theirs for three straight weeks now, and not once have they even bothered to poke their miserable heads out! I don't like it one bit. What are they up to this time?"

"Last time we checked, Master," replied his lieutenant, "they were praying."

"Praying? Praying for what? What could possibly take this long to pray for?"

"From what we've been able to gather, they've committed themselves to a forty day vigil, hoping to convince god to reveal more about our strategy. They realize we want nothing more than to see them dead, and they're begging him to expose our tactics."

"What?" Taken aback, Satan grabbed his lieutenant by the throat. "A prayer vigil, you say?"

The lieutenant nodded timidly.

"For forty days?" croaked the devil.

His lieutenant could only nod again with a hand wrapped around his throat.

"Then why wasn't I informed about this sooner?"

Struggling to speak, the lieutenant gurgled in response.

"What are you saying, you damned fool?"

The lieutenant frantically pointed at the hand clenched around his throat.

"Oh, very well," snapped Satan as he relinquished his chokehold. "If you insist."

"But, Master," sputtered the lieutenant, "we've only just ascertained this bit of intelligence and were waiting for the appropriate time to convey it to you. Naturally, we didn't want to disturb your ... *thinking time*."

"Naturally," grumbled the devil. "So the pathetic, little replicas want to learn more about our tactics, eh? So they think that will do them any good. Well, we'll see about that. Maybe it's time we put them and their god to the ultimate test!"

"But, Lord, what can we do? Until now they've been impervious to our attack in the cave. And now they seem quite determined to stay there until god reveals our secrets to them. What if he actually consents to their request? What if he arms them with a defense we'll never be able to breach? Then what?"

"Enough with your revolting fears! I will never succumb to such pessimism! That is the human's weakness, not ours. Ours is to seek the vulnerable, exploit the opening. And believe me, there is always an opening which is vulnerable to our kind. Now find it and find it quickly, before I find someone else who can. Is that clear?"

"Of course, Lord. I understand all too well."

AS ADAM AND EVE continued their prayer vigil in the cave, it was apparent that they were growing weaker by the moment. "Lord, please, Eve and I are running out of strength. We don't know how much longer we can continue like this. We know you've instructed us concerning our need to eat and drink, but with the devil ever vigilant, we were desperately hoping You could equip us with some way to detect his presence, some way to discern his plan of attack. Otherwise, how will we ever know when we're in danger or, for that matter, when it's safe to eat or drink? For all we know, we might end up eating the wrong thing all over again, and then we'd be right back where we started."

From out of nowhere, the sound of swarming, angry insects began to reverberate in the distance.

"Adam, what's that sound?"

Startled, Adam struggled to his feet. "I'm not sure, but it sounds like it's heading right for us."

"I'm scared, Adam. What should we do?"

"Brace yourself, my dear, brace yourself."

The swarm then streaked into the cave and covered the screaming couple like a dense, dark cloud.

"Hornets!" shouted Adam. "Thousands of angry hornets!"

"And their stingers are all over me!" cried Eve.

In actuality, these fierce, little creatures were no ordinary hornets. Upon closer inspection, they were none other than tiny demons, as miniscule as buzzing insects. With their razor sharp swords, like thousands of painful stingers, they all stabbed at Adam and Eve, until finally the couple collapsed in a heap. Then, just as quickly as they appeared, the malicious horde darted off into the night, leaving the pair for dead.

WHEN THE WORD OF GOD arrived, He not only raised Adam and Eve, but with a wave of His hand, He also healed all their wounds. Stunned, the couple examined their flesh, hardly believing their eyes.

"Lord, what was that all about?" Adam muttered. "And what happened to our wounds. We were just stung to death by the angriest swarm of hornets I've ever seen."

"I'm sorry, you two, but those weren't hornets that just attacked you."

"They weren't?" gasped Eve. "Then what were they?"

"They were thousands of demons, the size of flying insects."

"But how, Lord?" groaned Adam. "How could they attack us in our cave? I thought you told us as long as we remained where You told us to, we'd be safe from the devil's assault."

"I did say that, Adam, yes, but unfortunately that doesn't just apply to your physical location. In and of itself, this cave is no different than any other cave in the world. What I've been telling you all along is that when you're in obedience to My word, wherever and whenever you go, *then* you can be sure that you and Eve will be safe from Satan's attack. Does that make any sense?"

Both Adam and Eve struggled to grasp the meaning of His words.

"Not really, no, Lord," Adam replied. "Apart from just being attacked by a thousand demonic hornets, Eve and I are so weak from hunger and thirst, it's making things much more difficult to understand."

"And that's exactly the point I'm trying to make. That's how Satan was able to penetrate your shield. Even he was shocked when he realized he could overcome you in your cave. Even he thought you were impervious here. And it was true, as long as you obeyed My command. But when you kept refusing to eat and drink the things I've already designated as good and safe for you, that's when you, once again, fell from My grace. That's when you afforded the devil an opening to strike."

Shaking her head in disgust, Eve glared at Adam. "You see, this time I was right, and you were wrong. I knew it was finally time to eat and drink. Why wouldn't you listen to me, Adam, for once?"

"Oh, Eve, this is no time to blame each other," insisted the Word. "Defying My order for you to eat or drink wasn't the only thing that left you two vulnerable."

"It wasn't?" asked Eve, suddenly embarrassed.

"No, just as great a sin as it was to refuse to eat or drink was the moment when you and Adam came to a disagreement between yourselves. Like a wedge that drove you from Me and My power, your division drove a wedge between you and Adam's power."

"You mean I have power, too, Lord?" blurted Adam.

"Of course, Adam. As water has power to cut its course into a riverbed, the spirit I've given you has a similar residual power, and as the riverbed supports and controls that course of strength, so does your individual will direct your power as well."

"Did you hear that, Eve? I have power, too."

"But never forget, Adam. It's still only a power too easily limited by your own hopes and fears and choices, ones that occur during every moment of your existence."

"Eve, darling Eve, let's agree to never quarrel with the will of the Lord again, all right?"

"I agree, Adam, and I'm sorry for arguing with you, too."

"Just think, you two, if only you had have acted this way before you fell from grace, you wouldn't be going through any of these difficulties right now. So, now that we have this understanding between us, how would you like to do something for Me?"

"Anything, Lord," exclaimed Adam. "Anything at all."

"I'd like you and Eve to finish your prayer vigil in the cave, and as soon as you're done, I want you to eat and drink the things I've designated for you. Can you do that for Me?"

Together, the couple nodded wholeheartedly.

"We can, and we will," replied Adam.

Brother of Mine

NINE DAYS LATER, Adam and Eve had very little strength left as they nervously paced back and forth in their cave.

Eve stared dejectedly down at her palms. "My hands, Adam; they're so shriveled. They look awful." Then she turned to Adam, disturbed by what she saw. "Just look at us. We're nothing but skin and bones."

"Oh, Eve, I'm not sure what I want to do more, eat or drink. How about you?"

"I know how you feel."

Overcome by exhaustion, they both collapsed in the cave.

"How much more of this do you think we can take, Eve?"

"Not much, I'm afraid."

"But we're so close."

"How long has it been now?"

"We've been praying for thirty-nine days, as far as I can tell."

"Thirty-nine days? I can't believe it. You mean we only have one more day to go."

"As far as I can tell."

Just then, a middle-aged gentleman, immaculately dressed in dapper sheepskin clothing, complete with staff in hand, wandered up to the entrance of their cave. "Oh, dear me, is the place? Hello, is there anyone in there? Hello, anyone?"

Venturing several steps into the cave, the man peered in and caught a glimpse of Adam and Eve, lying there quite still.

"Adam, is that really you?" wondered the man. "And Eve, could it be you, too?"

The couple exchanged a perplexed look, almost too exhausted to respond.

"Yes, we're Adam and Eve," replied Adam. "Who are you?"

"Oh, dear, I'm not exactly sure how to put this," said the man, thoughtfully considering his words. "My name is Dakar, and I'm your older brother, Adam."

"What?" blurted Adam and Eve with one voice, and as if they had just been invigorated with some new source of strength, they scrambled to their feet and quickly walked over to the man.

"Y—*you can't* be serious?" stammered Eve. "You're Adam's older brother? But that's impossible."

"But look," insisted Dakar, holding out his hand for their inspection. "I'm made of flesh and bones just like you. See?"

Bewildered, Adam shook his head. "This is the craziest thing I've ever heard. If you're my older brother, then how come I've never seen you before?"

"That's because after God created me, He placed me in a garden of my own, located far to the north, at the very top of the world."

"But that still doesn't explain how Adam came to be your younger brother," insisted Eve.

"That, I'm afraid," said Dakar, "is where things get a little *tricky*."

"Tricky?" Adam echoed. "What do you mean, *tricky*?"

"Well, you see," continued Dakar, a bit awkwardly, "one day, a long, long time ago, God put me into a very deep sleep and brought you, Adam, out of my side."

"Adam?" blanched Eve.

"Yes, Eve?"

"Did you hear what he just said?"

"I did, yes."

"I wonder if he's telling the truth," she muttered.

"Of course, I'm telling the truth," Dakar said as he pulled away his sheepskin, offering them a look at his side. "Look for yourself. I have a scar on my side just like Adam's."

The couple leaned forward in bittersweet anticipation and, sure enough, saw the scar on Dakar's right side, directly between the fifth and sixth rib.

"Oh, my God, it's true, Adam," whispered Eve. "He does have a scar like yours."

The couple reached out together to touch it.

Confused, Eve turned to Adam and said, "I thought you said God made you out of the ground."

"That's what I thought, too," he replied, thoroughly bewildered. "So, if I came out of your side Dakar, then how come God never told me about you?"

Dakar smiled so benevolently. "You know, that's what I wanted to know, too, but, unfortunately, He refused to tell me. For some strange reason, He just wouldn't let you stay with me. He took you away from me and placed you in a garden all your own."

"Well, what did you do after that?" asked Eve.

"After that, I got very depressed. I missed you so much, Adam."

"Then what did God tell you to do?" pressed Adam. "You prayed to Him about it, didn't you?"

"Oh, yes, of course. But you know how God is. He just told me to quit worrying and to not interfere with what He was doing with you because He'd already brought a companion out of your side as well. He insisted you were perfectly happy on your own. So what else could I do?"

"That's terrible," grumbled Eve. "Why would God let something like that happen?"

"So if I'm your brother," Adam continued, "then how come you never came back to find me?"

"I never came looking for you because until God just told me, I had no idea where you were living. I certainly had no idea you were enduring such misery and pain; all because you disobeyed God and cooperated with Satan. And now just look at you two, suffering this way."

"So why did God send you to us now?" asked Adam.

"Well, as you know," replied Dakar, "it's been a very long time since you left the garden, and now, God has instructed me to come here to take you home with me. He wants me to keep Satan away from you from now on."

"God did that for us?" wondered Adam.

"Oh, yes. He doesn't want you to be attacked anymore."

"He actually said that?" pressed Eve.

Dakar smiled back. "Of course He did. I mean, just look at the two of you, barely clinging to dear life."

"Did God tell you anything else?" asked Adam.

"Oh, yes. That's the best part. God has ordered me to personally give you fruit and water from the Tree of Life."

"Really?" Adam's eyes opened wide.

"Is that all?" asked Eve.

"As a matter of fact, no," replied Dakar calmly, calculatingly, "then He told me I was to restore you to your original state of grace and to restore all the powers you used to have prior to your unfortunate fall."

Adam and Eve smiled at one another, and reaching out, they held hands.

"Eve, did you hear that?"

"I can hardly believe my ears, Adam."

"Oh, Adam," continued Dakar with such melancholy in his voice. "It's so good to see you again and to finally meet Eve. I've missed you so much. I just couldn't stand the thought of what you two were going through."

"So when you came here to rescue us," asked Eve, "did Satan try to attack you, too?"

"Oh, my word, of course he did. He is such a nasty fellow, isn't he?"

Adam and Eve nodded back in agreement.

"What did you do?" queried Adam.

"Did you ever think about giving up on us?" asked Eve.

"Certainly not," insisted Dakar, putting his hand to his breast as though he were swearing allegiance. "I'd never do something like that, not when it concerned my own dear brother."

"Come on, you can tell us," chided Eve. "You were scared to fight the devil, weren't you?"

"Well, all right, I admit it," replied Dakar, rather sheepishly, "I did at first tremble upon hearing the name of Satan. I thought: Maybe I shouldn't venture out by myself. What if he traps me like he did the two of you? So I prayed: 'Oh, God, Satan's going to meet me on my way to rescue Adam and Eve. He'll challenge me just like he did them.'"

"What did God say?" pressed Adam.

"He told me: 'Don't be frightened. Take this staff for protection, and when Satan confronts you, strike him with it. But whatever you do, don't be afraid of him, because he can't really hurt you. After all, you've been around a lot longer than he has.'"

"Then what happened?" asked Eve.

"I said, 'Lord, I don't think I can go. Please, send Your angels to bring them here instead of me.' But God replied: 'Certainly they won't agree to come with angels. They're not the same as Adam and Eve. They'll never trust them. But I've chosen you because you're Adam's older brother. You're just like him, so he'll listen to what you have to say.'"

"Interesting," said Adam.

"Positively," replied Dakar, smoothly confident. "Then do you know what God said to me?"

Adam and Eve looked at each other, hoping that the other might respond, but neither of them could think of a response, so they turned back to Dakar and shrugged their shoulders.

"No, what?" replied Adam

Dakar beamed back his benevolent smile. "Then He told me: 'But if you don't have enough strength to walk there, my son, I'll send a cloud to carry you. It will drop you off at the entrance to their cave, and if they agree to come with you, I'll send the cloud back to return you all safely to your garden home.'"

"No," said Adam.

"Yes," insisted Dakar. "I'd never lie to you. God actually commanded a cloud, which picked me up and brought me straight here to you."

"That's amazing," said Eve.

"So, my brother, my sister," continued Dakar, "I've traveled so far to get here, and now the time has finally come. We're all going to a wonderful place of peace and tranquility. What a marvelous time we'll all have, finally, together at last." Then, Dakar began to weep so much that tears poured down his face like water. "Oh, dear, I told myself I wasn't going to do this."

Touched by his emotional outburst, Adam and Eve stepped closer to get a better look at him.

"Look at him, Adam; he really does look just like you, doesn't he?"

"Of course he looks like me." Adam nodded proudly. "We're brothers."

Wiping his tears away, Dakar smiled at them and held his hands out. Slowly, Adam and Eve each took hold of one, and then Dakar began to lead them away from their cave.

THEY HEADED STRAIGHT for the hill that overlooked the western edge of the garden, where the couple was so fond of going.

As they walked along, Eve leaned into Adam and quietly said, "Adam, what about the cloud Dakar told us about? I thought *it* was supposed to take us where we were going."

"Oh, that's right, I forgot," replied Adam, who then turned to enquire, "Please, Dakar, we'd like to know: Where's the cloud you told us about? Eve and I are tired of walking. I don't think we can take another step."

"Certainly, my brother, I understand," he replied. "Don't worry. It's just around the bend. You'll see."

MAKING THEIR WAY up the hilltop, the couple continued to follow Dakar, until finally they saw it, extending out from the edge of the cliff, a shimmering cloud, spreading out like an iridescent flying carpet.

"Look, Eve, there it is," said Adam. "There's your cloud, just the way Dakar described it."

"See, you two?" said Dakar confidently. "What did I tell you?"

"It's beautiful," murmured Eve. "But it looks so delicate. Are you sure it'll hold us?"

"Certainly," insisted Dakar. "Just climb abroad, and before you know it we'll be off to your new garden home. Soon, all this misery and suffering will simply be a thing of the past."

The couple inched their way, closer and closer, toward the edge of the cliff, where the dazzling cloud awaited them.

"That's it," said Dakar. "You're almost there. Just step out onto the cloud, and we'll all get going."

To the very edge of the cliff, Adam and Eve looked down at the luminous cloud and then at one another. They were filled with an exhilarating sense of both anticipation and dread.

"Oh, Adam, I'm so nervous. Are you sure we can do this?"

"Sure we can, Eve, if it means a new life far away from this miserable place. Don't you want to go?"

"Of course she does, Adam," said Dakar. "Here, let me help you. All you two really need is a bit of encouragement." And stepping past the couple, Dakar walked right onto the shimmering cloud and turned back toward them with his hands held out. "See how sturdy it is? There's nothing to fear. Now, come, it's your turn to join me, won't you?"

The couple inched nervously forward and reached out to take hold of Dakar's outstretched hands, but instead of walking onto the cloud, they fell straight through it.

"Oops," sputtered Dakar, who then transformed into the devil and burst out laughing. The screaming couple fell helplessly through space, headed straight for the bottom of the ravine, but just before they landed, Adam and Eve abruptly stopped short of the ground. Confused, they looked around as they dangled just a few feet above the ravine floor.

"What the—" muttered Adam.

Looking down from his vantage point, Satan was completely baffled by the sight of Adam and Eve suspended in mid-air. "What is it this time?" he snapped, and swooping down to investigate, he was incensed by what he saw. To his utter amazement, he found that the couple was being held up by two glittering clouds of their own. But of course these were no ordinary clouds. As the devil moved in closer still, he found that these clouds were actually comprised of thousands of miniature angels. Gently, they began to lower Adam and Eve down to the ground, where they were finally able to stand on their own. Then, like a billowy swarm of shimmering butterflies, they fluttered past the devil.

"Are you kidding me?" Satan growled. "What do I have to do to get rid of these two pests?"

Then the Word of God appeared.

"Well, well," snarled the devil, "if it isn't the meddling god, right on time as usual. I see that two can play at this game, can't they? How fitting you've rescued your little replicas by the same means with which I nearly destroyed them; and how *infuriating!*"

Looking Satan dead in the eye, the Word pointed toward the horizon. "Just go, you miserable excuse for an adversary. Go tell your minions how well you did here today. I'm sure they're just waiting to congratulate you on your latest achievement."

"Yes, yes. No need to rub it in, my good man. I already know the drill." And with a cloud of dust in his wake, Satan streaked out of view.

The Word then turned to the couple, who stood there, both relieved and embarrassed. "Oh, Adam," He said, obviously disappointed, "what happened this time? You were so close. Why did you leave your cave this time?"

"But, Lord, excuse me for saying this," sputtered Adam, "but seriously, You are not going to believe what just happened to us."

"Really? Tell Me, then. I'd be very interested to hear it."

"Well, You see, we were in our cave praying like You told us, when quite unexpectedly this strange man came to visit us."

"See, I warned you, didn't I?"

"But this was no angel of light, Lord. This was a man, a real man; but not just any man.

This was a man with a scar in his side, a scar just like mine. And this man told us a story about how You'd taken me from his side, just like Eve had been taken from mine. He said he was my brother, my older brother, in fact."

"And you believed him?"

"But he showed us the scar in his side, Lord," interjected Eve. "We touched it with our own hands. It was real. It was all *so* real."

"But was it real after all?"

Adam hung his head in shame. "Everything but the cloud, I'm afraid."

"So now you realize who you were dealing with, right?"

"Don't tell me it was Satan again?" asked Eve.

"Of course it was Satan, Eve."

"But he looked just like us, Lord," grumbled Adam, as if he were genuinely disappointed. "How could it have been the devil?"

"Didn't I tell you he was the father of evil arts? He's tried everything else, so this time he thought he could accomplish his goal by appearing to look like you. And he was right, wasn't he?"

"But he was so convincing, especially that scar of his," insisted Adam. "And just the way he told us his whole story about being my brother. He even said he was going to take us to his garden home where we could find some peace and quiet for once in our lives."

"Of course he'd say that, Adam. He's going to tell you exactly what you want to hear. That's how he got you kicked out of the garden in the first place. Now he's doing everything he can to eliminate you, because he thinks if he succeeds I'll have no choice but to take him back."

"Where's Satan now, Lord?" asked Adam.

Nervously, the couple looked around to see if he might have returned without them noticing.

"Relax, you two. He's long gone for the time being."

"Thank you, Lord," said Adam with a sigh of relief.

"Now, Adam, take Eve back to your cave and stay there until tomorrow. Then, after your forty day vigil is completed, I want you both to go to the eastern edge of the garden, where I'll give you further instructions."

THE FOLLOWING MORNING, Adam and Eve were waiting patiently at the eastern border of the garden.

"Lord, please give us new strength," said Adam, almost breathless. "We're famished."

"Could we please have something to satisfy our terrible hunger?" asked Eve, ever so frailly.

Exhausted, they fell down, unable to lift a finger.

Again the Word of God arrived. "Adam, Eve, get up. Go home, get the two figs I put in your cave and come back here as soon as you can."

The couple exchanged a serious look. Slowly, they got to their feet and headed back toward their cave.

AS USUAL, SATAN AND his cadre of henchman were watching everything from a distance.

"I am getting so sick of watching god help that miserable pair," grunted the devil. "I still don't get it. Why does he do it?"

"Is there anything I can do to help, Lord?" asked his lieutenant.

"*You*? I certainly doubt it. But go ahead; try me."

"Well, let's see, we tried deceiving them. Oh, that was beautiful how you got them kicked out of their garden, Master."

"Yes, yes, flattery will get you nowhere. A lot of good that did me."

"All right, I was just saying. Okay, so we tried deception. Then we tried blatant violence."

"Keep going, keep going. Tell me something I don't know."

"Begging your pardon, Lord," said the lieutenant as he furled his malicious brow, trying desperately to come up with a decent idea. "Just give me a second; I'll think of something. Have we ruled out blatant violence yet?"

"Yes, we have, you infernal dolt! What we need is a different method to rid ourselves of these two, and preferably one where god doesn't get more credit if he rescues them again."

"All right, then. So what's left? Adam and Eve just spent forty days fasting and praying, and now they're on the brink of starvation. Why? Because they keep refusing to eat or drink anything."

Just then, a twinkle appeared in the devil's beady, black eyes. "Wait a second; wait a second. What did you just say?"

"I asked if we'd ruled out blatant violence."

"No, no! After that, you idiot!"

"I said Adam and Eve were on the brink of starvation."

"Yes, that's it! If we simply oblige them in their persistent refusal to eat or drink, then maybe they'll die of their own accord. Certainly god won't force them to eat or drink anything. He apparently values freedom far too much for that, the sentimental fool."

"What a perfectly diabolical idea, Master. I think you might be onto something." Then turning to Satan, his lieutenant found him missing. "Master? Master? Where did the master go?"

LIKE A STREAK OF lightning, the devil was already hurling through space; and the place he was going to was the Cave of Treasures. Arriving before Adam and Eve had time to get there, he went inside and found the two figs that the couple had left for safe keeping. "Well, well, what do we have here? Morsels, just ripe for the picking."

Stepping outside with the two figs securely in his grasp, the devil searched the horizon. "Now, tell me, where are my insolent minions? You mean to say that no one is with me today."

"We're with you, Lord," rattled a guttural voice. "We await your command."

Turning his wolfen head, Satan was happy to see that a swarm of his demons had followed him on his journey. "Good, very good. Now quickly, bury these damned things, and bury them so deep that Adam and Eve can never find them again."

IN NO TIME, HIS CADRE of demons had dug a huge trench in the ground, and dumping the figs into the hole, they filled it in, taking turns to stomp the ground into a solid mass.

As he watched with tremendous satisfaction, the devil let out a raucous laugh. "Wonderful! I can't wait to see the miserable look on their faces when those two realize their precious figs are gone forever!"

But no sooner had the figs been planted in the ground than they rapidly grew up into a pair of fig trees, complete with dozens of fledging figs hanging from their branches. Horrified, the devil and his henchmen stared at the trees in utter disbelief.

"How did that happen?" grumbled the lieutenant.

"Well, don't just stand there gawking," Satan snapped, "hack the miserable things down, you pathetic worms!"

But as his minions slashed away at the tree, they found that their fiery swords were useless. Each time a demon hacked at a branch, the blade merely bounced away.

"Now what's wrong?" demanded the devil.

"I have no idea, Lord," blanched the lieutenant. "These trees are impervious to our blades, no matter how hard we swing them!"

"No, no, no!" howled Satan. "How could this be happening again? I'd have been better off leaving those damned figs where they were!"

"God is mocking us, Master! What should we do now?"

"God hasn't merely mocked us, my legions, he's turned our brilliant plan inside out! Now I have no idea how to get rid of this revolting *food* of theirs!"

Food for a Change

STROLLING UP TO their cave, Adam and Eve noticed the two large fig trees for the first time. The puzzled couple examined the fruit on them. They also noticed how the trees were now providing such nice shade for their cave.

Confused, Adam shook his head. "I think we're lost, Eve. These two trees weren't here before, were they? We must have gotten off course somehow. What do you think?"

Eve just shrugged her shoulders.

"I say we check inside to see if the figs are in there," continued Adam. "If this *is* our cave, then they should still be there. If not, then we'll know it can't be our cave."

So they went inside and looked all around. Every square inch of the cave was inspected, but still they found no sign of the two figs. They did, however, find the gold, frankincense and myrrh. Stepping outside again, the couple sat down, exhausted from their desperate search.

Adam turned to Eve with a puzzled look on his face. "I give up. Everything else is still in our cave; so where'd our figs go?"

"I wish I could tell you, Adam, but I just don't know what to think anymore. I'm so hollow and dry inside, I can't think straight."

Adam struggled to his feet. "God, You ordered us to come here to get our two figs, but we can't find them anywhere. Did You take them?"

"We're so confused, Lord," whimpered Eve. "Where'd they go?"

"Please explain this mystery, Lord," said Adam. "Where did these trees come from?"

Then the Word of God returned. "Well, you two: As you can imagine, Satan is up to his old tricks again."

"What?" blurted Adam. "What did he do this time?"

"When I sent you to get your figs, Satan went ahead of you. He got here first and buried the figs outside your cave."

"But why?" asked Eve, almost painfully.

"He thought burying them would destroy them, and that by destroying them you'd die of starvation, but I caused them to grow into the two fig trees you see here."

"You're kidding," said Adam. "You mean our two figs are now these two trees? Satan must've really gotten mad when he saw that."

"Is that why you made the trees grow, Lord, to anger the devil?" wondered Eve.

"Of course not, Eve," replied the Word.

"They why *did* You do it?" queried Adam.

"I did it because in My mercy I wanted them to grow for your sakes. That way you'd be able to have their fruit close by, not to mention having the shade from their branches and leaves."

"You did that just for us?" asked Eve.

"Certainly," insisted the Word. "I wanted you to see an example of My power, and I *especially* wanted to show you how cruel and vengeful Satan is. You know, he hasn't stopped trying to hurt you since the day you came out of the garden. Not for a single moment!"

Adam and Eve exchanged a knowing look.

"But remember," continued the Word, "I still haven't given him complete power over you. So from now on, the two of you can enjoy the fruit from these trees whenever you get hungry, and rest under them whenever you get tired or hot. Now each of you may have a fig."

"Now?" asked Eve.

"Yes, now," replied the Word, "before you die of starvation." Then He vanished.

Timidly, the couple each picked a fig from its branches. They went inside their cave, and sat down with the figs.

"What should we do now, Eve?"

"I guess we're supposed to eat them."

"But how do we do that?"

"How should I know? I've never eaten figs before. Just the thought of eating something terrifies me."

"Me, too. What if they make us sick?"

"What if we actually *like* this food. What then?"

So they just sat there, staring at the figs for the longest time, when suddenly an angel appeared before them. Smiling, he sat down in front of Adam and Eve.

"God has sent me here," began the angel, "because He wants you to know you can't go on living without eating something. Now take the figs and peel some of the skin off to get to the pulp inside. Scoop some out, put it in your mouths, and chew. Then, when you've chewed sufficiently, you swallow. Understand?"

Cautiously, Adam and Eve each picked up a fig. They slowly proceeded, just as the angel had instructed them, and began to eat.

"Mmm," said Eve, "this is good. How's yours?"

"Not bad, not bad." Nodding, Adam chewed some more. "I think I like this, eating."

Eve noticed some of the juices running down his chin. "Drooling. Uh, Adam, you're drooling."

Adam wiped his chin with a sheepish grin. "You're one to talk. Look at you."

Smiling playfully, Eve wiped her chin, too. "Sorry."

THAT EVENING, THE couple sang hymns of praise to God, and when they were done, they slept quite soundly because of all the food they had eaten.

THE NEXT MORNING, however, when they got up and left their cave, they felt sick to their stomachs. Pacing frantically in front of the mouth of their cave, they were both terribly distressed.

Adam bent over, trying to catch his breath. "Oh, Eve, I wonder what's happening to us. Why are we in so much pain?"

"We've really done it this time, Adam," gasped Eve as she stumbled to the ground, stabbed by a stomach cramp. "Oh, God. We'd have been better off dying of hunger than to have eaten those figs!"

"At least we'd have kept our bodies from being contaminated with food."

"We never experienced anything like this when we were in the garden."

Dropping to his knees, Adam put one hand to the ground to prop himself up. "My insides feel like they're about to explode!"

On her side, Eve curled into a ball and whimpered, "Lord, no. I don't want to die like this, please, not when I finally started to believe You'd actually fulfill Your promise to us."

"Lord, please help us," groaned Adam. "I realize You may not be ready to keep Your promise just yet, but please don't abandon us now."

At once, something happened to Adam and Eve, something that relieved them of all their pain. As quickly as it had struck them, the stabbing in their gut was no longer there. Equally puzzled and relieved, the couple stood to their feet, cautiously touching their stomachs, as if to check where the pain had gone.

"Eve, what happened? The pain. It's gone. Thank the Lord above."

"You're right, Adam. I feel normal again. God must have answered our prayers."

"Of course He did." Adam nodded with a tremendous sigh. "What other explanation is there?"

AS THE SUN SLOWLY SET, the couple sat at the cave's entrance, trying to relax, when Adam noticed a troubled look on Eve's face as she dolefully held her hand to her stomach.

"What's wrong, Eve?" he asked. "Are you feeling sick again?"

"No, I'm fine."

"But you don't look fine. Something has you upset. What is it?"

Eve stared straight ahead, obviously caught up in some sort of inner turmoil. "Well, as it turns out, ever since the pain left my stomach, it seems as if it's decided to take up residence somewhere else. And though what I felt in here hurt me terribly…" Pausing thoughtfully, she removed her hand from her belly and placed it to her breast, "it's nothing compared to the unbearable ache I now feel in my heart."

Adam nodded with a look of understanding. "I know exactly what you mean, Eve. Our bodies won't ever be the same now that we've eaten *food*. God would never want us back in His garden now, not with earthly bodies with such peculiar functions as ours."

Pitifully, Eve nodded and began to cry. "Which means all our hopes and dreams of getting back into the garden are completely gone now!"

"We just don't belong there anymore," Adam added lamentably.

"From now on, we're nothing but dirt, just like every other creature living in this miserable world."

Adam gazed longingly out across the landscape. He saw the animals roaming about in the murky twilight, and looking up he saw the stars and the Moon. "You know, Eve, for as long as I can remember, I've always felt like a genuine part of God's creation, as if I were actually one with everything in it, you know?"

"I do, yes." Eve nodded sadly and dried her tears. "But now?"

"But now, with every day that passes, I feel more and more like a stranger on this Earth. Do you realize it's been ninety-four days since we left the garden?"

"Ninety-four days," murmured Eve. "Ninety-four days, and what has it gotten us? We've become nothing but strangers … *strangers* in a world we call home."

Bread from Heaven

THE COUPLE WOKE UP the next morning and looked at each other expectantly.

"What should we do now, Adam?"

"Well, we asked God for something to eat and He gave us those figs, so now let's ask Him for a drink of water."

STANDING AT THE riverbank where they had previously thrown themselves in, the couple stared longingly down at the water as it flowed past them.

"Please, God," began Adam, "could You send us Your Word to tell us if we can drink some of this water?"

Then the Word of God arrived. "It's all right, Adam. Now that your body is merely flesh, it requires water. So go ahead, both of you, drink and give thanks."

So the couple stepped closer to the river, and dropping to their hands and knees they began to drink from it.

"Oh, this is so good, Eve."

"You're right, Adam. I can't believe we waited so long to do this."

IN THE MORNING, Adam and Eve went to where they had stored their leftovers, and to their absolute amazement, they found that the figs had been restored to their original size and condition, just as perfectly shaped and plump as they had been the day before.

"Can you believe it, Eve? It's as though we never even ate any of it."

"Maybe these figs have miraculous qualities, Adam. Maybe that's how our bodies were transformed."

"I think you're right. I say we put them in a safe place and find something else to eat."

Eagerly, Eve nodded her approval. So the couple took the two figs, along with the leaves, and hung them up on the wall of their cave.

"This way we'll always have these as a memorial of God's blessing," said Adam, "and someday our children will be able to look at them and remember all the wonderful things God has done for us."

For several moments, the couple proudly inspected the new memorial that graced their cavern wall.

Then Eve turned to Adam with a peculiar look on her face. "Adam?"

"Yes, Eve."

"You said someday our *children* would look at this memorial."

"Uh, yeah, I did, didn't I?"

"What are *children*?"

Tilting his head and squinting his eyes, Adam thoughtfully considered her question and finally shrugged his shoulders. "How should I know?"

OUTSIDE THE CAVE, the couple wandered here and there, searching the landscape.

"Lord," Adam said, "please show us where we can find something else to eat."

Then the Word of God returned. "Adam, I want you to travel west from here, until you reach a land of dark soil. There, you'll find more food."

JOURNEYING WESTWARD, the couple eventually came to a land where the ground was covered in a dark, rich soil. They found wheat growing there, full-eared, ripe and ready to harvest. They even found more figs, too, which they ate right away, so happy with their discoveries.

Again the Word of God appeared. "Take this wheat, Adam, and make bread with it. Eating this bread will also help nourish your body."

THE COUPLE EAGERLY began uprooting the wheat with their bare hands until there was enough to form several large piles. Then Adam began to grind the grain with a flat stone, adding a little water to the mix until it turned to dough. This dough, in turn, he then cooked over a fire, and when it was cooked, the first loaf of bread was broken up by the happy couple and eaten until both of them were full.

"Oh, Adam, I couldn't eat another bite. That was delicious. How did you learn to make—what did the Lord call it again?"

"Bread."

"Right, bread. How'd you ever learn to make bread like that?"

"I'm not sure, Eve. It just came into my mind, that's all."

"It must have been God Who inspired you to make something that good," she replied with a heavy yawn. "Oh, wow. I am so sleepy after all that work. I need to lie down awhile. How about you?"

Adam nodded with a weary, contented smile, and together they found a shady tree and plopped down under it, where a cool breeze quickly fanned them into a deep sleep.

SATAN AND HIS MINIONS, meanwhile, were watching the dozing couple from a distance.

"Damn those two!" snapped the devil. "I had such high hopes the little replicas were going to starve themselves to death. Now look at them, so fat and content with their *food!*"

"Don't despair, Lord," said his lieutenant, "all is not lost yet. There must be something we can do to end their reign of peace."

"First, god provided them with figs to eat," Satan grumbled, "then he caused fig trees to grow up, then he gave them water to drink. Now he's gone and given them wheat, too! Damn their miserable hides!"

"Wheat? What's *wheat*, Master?"

"Wheat! You know, wheat! Humans make bread with it."

"But what's *bread*?" wondered the lieutenant, turning to the other demons, who all in turn just shrugged.

"Apparently, it's what humans use to make a new kind of food, you idiot. Now stop asking me such ridiculous questions! They still have a huge pile of this wheat left over from their efforts!"

"What should we do, Lord?"

"I want you to destroy it, of course," the devil growled impatiently. "And I want it done before they try to eat any more of it. If we're ever going to starve these two into extinction, we must cut off their food supply! Is that understood?"

"Naturally, Master, your wish is our command. It does appear they're still fast asleep from all their hard work. We could attack them right now."

"Good, then hurry before that miserable pair wakes up. Go and burn their grain, *now!*"

"Yes, Lord; we'll burn it all this instant!"

"And can you believe it?" chimed in another demon. "Now Adam and Eve have a bucket to carry water, too."

"A bucket?" spewed Satan. "Where did that come from?"

All eyes turned toward this demon, who started to reply, but much to his dismay the words stuck in his throat. Both frustrated and horrified, he tried to shrug it off with a pathetic, toothy grin.

"Well," snapped the lieutenant, "you heard the master. Where'd they get it?"

"I—I—*I*," croaked the demon, suddenly jolted back to speech. "*I'm* afraid I have no idea, sir."

Turning to his lieutenant, Satan shrieked, "Enough already! Never mind how they got it! Do something, damn you!"

Pointing to another demon, the lieutenant snapped, "You there!"

"Who, *me*?" replied the unsuspecting one.

"Yes, you," barked the lieutenant. "Get down there right now, and take care of that bucket."

"Yes, sir. Consider it done."

"Good," replied the lieutenant. "Now get going!"

"Yes, that should do the trick," cooed Satan. "Then maybe we can kill them with thirst!"

"And if we're lucky," howled the lieutenant, "maybe they'll curse god, and he'll destroy them for us! Then we'll finally be rid of Adam and Eve, once and for all!"

SO THE DEVIL AND HIS horde bellowed with revolting glee as they began to hurl fireballs down onto the remaining piles of wheat, which in turn rapidly engulfed the entire field in flames. Startled, the dozing couple woke up and saw the fire all around them.

"Oh, Lord, not again!" shouted Adam, who reached for the bucket of water next to him but found it tipped over and empty. The terrified couple retreated from the blaze and stood at some distance, helplessly watching their beloved field go up in flames.

"No, Adam. There goes our beautiful field. Now what are we going to do?"

"I guess we have no choice but to go back to our cave."

SMUDGED WITH SOOT from head to toe, the traumatized couple had traveled several miles before finally, too exhausted to continue, they slumped down into the dirt.

Then the Word of God appeared. "Are you two all right?"

"I guess so, Lord," muttered Adam, rubbing his soot-covered forehead. "But all our wheat is gone. Even our bucket of water got dumped out."

The Word calmly replied, "It seems that Satan and his henchmen have been up to no good as usual."

"But how could this happen?" queried Eve. "Did we do something wrong again?"

"Oh, my poor Eve," continued the Word. "That's not an easy question to answer. Sometimes, no matter what you do, the rain is going to fall on the just and the unjust alike."

"What does that even mean, Lord?" asked Adam. "Pardon me for asking: But did we or did we not do something to deserve this?"

"In this case, no. Actually, you could say that the only thing you did *wrong* was follow

My instructions."

"I am so confused," Adam said, shaking his head. "Now what are You telling us? Bad things can happen to us even when we do the *right* thing?"

"I'm afraid so, yes."

"But why?" blurted Eve. "That doesn't make any sense."

"Unfortunately, it makes perfect sense when you consider that you've already willingly handed your kingdom over to the devil by following his advice to eat from the Tree of Knowledge. He is, after all, the king of this world."

Adam and Eve just looked at each, thoroughly frustrated.

"Now do you understand what I'm saying?" asked the Word.

"Yes, Lord, I think so," replied Adam with a heavy sigh. "What You're telling us is: Satan is just as angry, if not more so, when we do follow Your instructions."

"Now you've got it, Adam."

"So if bad things are just as likely to happen to us if we do the right thing," interjected Eve, "then why should we even bother to do it?"

"Because when you do what is evil, I'm against you, but if you do what is right, then only the devil is against you. And never forget, when he attacks you, I'm still more than willing to protect you, but if I'm against you, there's no one in the Universe who can save you from My wrath."

WITH HEAVY HEARTS and still covered in soot, Adam and Eve were silently on the move again. They walked like that for quite a while before Eve finally turned to Adam. "So what's the point of going back to that field if all the wheat has been burned to the ground?"

"The point is," Adam blurted impatiently, "God told us to go back, so we're going; end of story."

"All right, all right. Are you mad at me now?"

"I'm sorry, Eve; I don't mean to be angry with you. It's just that every time we turn around we have something completely unexpected thrown in our faces. I'm losing my mind, I think."

With a knowing look, Eve nodded. Then she stopped and pointed as a peculiar expression swept across her face. "Adam, look, our field!"

"Can it be real, Eve? Or is it just another of the devil's illusions?"

Having arrived back to the wheat field, they were amazed to discover that it had been completely restored to its original condition. Together, they ran, with outstretched hands, through row after row of full-grown stalks of wheat.

"But it can't be an illusion, my love," shouted Eve. "I feel every grain of wheat flowing right through my fingertips."

"You're right, Eve. And look, here's our bucket, full of water again."

They even found a stout, full-blossomed bush with a fluffy, white substance sprouting from every branch.

"That's strange, Eve. I don't remember seeing this bush before."

Eve shook her head, dumbfounded. "Me neither."

Intrigued, the couple stood and stared at it.

"What kind of fruit is this, Adam?"

"How should I know? I've never seen anything like it before in my life."

"It's manna," came a sweet, clear voice.

Turning to see who was speaking, Adam and Eve found an angel standing next to them.

"Manna?" replied Adam. "What's manna?"

"It's bread from Heaven," the angel said with a serene smile.

"You mean like the bread that Adam made for us?"

"Better."

"Better?" blurted Eve. "Impossible."

"If you don't believe me, then go ahead and try it yourself."

The couple cautiously reached out, plucked a handful, and touched it to their lips.

"Mmm, it's sweet," said Eve, who put it in her mouth and chewed. "Oh, Adam, he's right, it *is* better than your bread, and you didn't even have to bake it."

So Adam took a bite, too, and happily nodded in agreement.

SATAN AND HIS MINIONS, as usual, were watching the couple and the angel from a distance.

"This is so infuriating," grumbled the devil. "Every time we come up with a way to strike misery and fear into the hearts of those two, it completely backfires on us. What can we possibly do to counteract something like that?" Silently brooding for several moments, Satan finally turned to his lieutenant. "Well, what do you have to say for yourself this time?"

Stunned, the devil could not believe his black, cold-hearted eyes, because instead of looking into the face of the lieutenant, he was staring into the face of the Word of God, which sat curiously atop the shoulders of his faithful lackey, a totem of astonishing dimensions.

"Wh—*what kind of trickery* is this?" stammered the devil as he rubbed his eyes with his leathery paws.

"What's wrong now, Satan?" replied the Word, sporting a sardonic grin. "How does it feel to doubt what your eyes tell you?"

"Please, state your purpose, if you don't mind. The sooner you tell me why you're here, the better."

"As you wish, Devil. I'm here to warn you."

"Warn me? Warn me about what?"

"I trust you love your minions."

"Love my minions? What's that supposed to mean?"

"Your minions. Do you love them?"

"Love is such a strong word. I hardly think it's a word that even exists in my vocabulary."

"Then you enjoy their company. You love what they can do for you."

"Oh, I see what you're getting at. Of course, I do, yes. Why do you ask?"

"From now on, for every stalk of wheat you destroy, I will banish one of your minions to the depths of the Abyss. Is that clear?"

Satan's eyes thinned as he considered this proposition, and then, without a word, he nodded with a nearly imperceptible groan.

"Very good," said the Word, and just like that His handsome face faded from view, giving way to the lieutenant's grotesque visage.

As if waking from a deep sleep, the lieutenant's eyes rolled back into their sockets and focused on Satan's angry gaze. "What?" mumbled the lieutenant, barely coherent. "Why are you looking at me like that?"

The Perfect Sacrifice

AS THE SUN SLOWLY set behind the mountain where Adam and Eve had brought their first offering of blood, the couple was preparing some grain as an offering. Placing the oblation on the same altar, they burned it. As they stood nearby, they watched as an incandescent pillar of smoke began to rise from the fire.

"When we were in the garden, Lord," began Adam, "our praises rose like the smoke of this offering, and our innocence ascended to You just like incense. So, God, please accept this offering from us, and don't turn us away without Your mercy."

Then the Word of God appeared. When Adam and Eve spotted Him, they walked over and joined Him. "Lord," said Adam, "we're so honored You could be here with us."

"You've done well, Adam. I'm proud of you."

The couple smiled at each other.

"Hear that, Eve? We did something right for a change," he remarked, looking in every direction. "And see, the devil is nowhere in sight."

The Word smiled knowingly. "That's right, Adam, because he can't stand the sight of what you've done here today."

"Why, Lord?" wondered Eve.

"Because you've offered this thing of your own free will. To the devil, it's repugnant, but in the sight of God, it is most precious; so precious, in fact, He's decided to make it My body when I'm born on this Earth to save you. And I'll cause it to be offered continually upon an altar to provide forgiveness and mercy for everyone who partakes of it properly."

Suddenly a fireball hurled down upon their offering, engulfing the whole scene with a tremendously bright light. The astonished couple stepped back.

"What's happening, Lord?" queried Adam. "What's that light?"

"God has accepted your offering and has sent this light to illuminate your hearts with grace and peace."

Then, from out of the flames of their offering, a strange figure began to rise from the altar. It was the figure of a dove slowly ascending into the evening sky.

"What's that, Lord?" Eve asked quietly. "It's so beautiful."

"You two are most honored, because today God has sent the Holy Spirit to visit you and your offering."

In awe, the couple looked at one another in the flickering moonlight.

"Oh, Eve, can you feel it? It's as though the love of God is coursing through every fiber of my being. What an amazing thing. I've never known anything like it in all my days."

"I do feel it, my darling. And you're right, the only way I can describe it is it's as though God's love, His peace, His warmth, is flooding my innermost being. I feel so alive."

Completely transfixed, Adam and Eve stood there, basking in the iridescent glow of that special moment.

"Oh, Lord," sighed Adam, "if only this moment could last forever. Eve and I could be happy even in this darkened world. Please tell us You can make it so."

As the couple watched with such yearning, the dove of the Spirit continued to ascend with majestic wings of light. Gliding upward, further and further, it eventually became a mere speck of light in the celestial vault and then vanished.

"It's gone, Eve," murmured Adam, "gone, all too soon." Then turning to Eve, he saw tears streaming down her face. "Oh, Eve, don't cry, it'll be all right."

"But I'm not crying because I'm sad, silly. These are tears of joy, tears of longing, tears of hope."

Overwhelmed, they embraced and as they did Adam peered over her shoulder to the Word looking on with such happiness. "Thank You, Lord, for this moment. You really have blessed us beyond measure today."

The Word nodded. "You're welcome, Adam."

"If only this sort of thing could happen again and again," said Eve with a contented sigh.

"But what makes you think it can't?" asked the Word.

Amazed at this, the couple turned to the Word. "What are You saying, Lord?" asked Adam. "You mean this could happen again? But how?"

"Whenever you make a free will offering to Me, you're turning from yourselves and the misery of this fallen world. In that moment, when you offer yourselves in this way, it provides a delicate yet powerful conduit into the Divine, a kind of 'new beginning,' if you will, whereby God has the ability to renew your dead selves."

"You mean it's as if, in that brief moment, our old life," mused Adam, "the life we used to have in the garden, is restored."

"Yes, that's exactly what I'm saying."

"Did you hear that, Eve? All we have to do is make an offering whenever we're overwhelmed by pain or depression, and God will fill us with His—what did you call it, Lord?"

"The Holy Spirit."

"Right, the Holy Spirit."

ADAM WAS STILL SO excited the next morning he could hardly contain himself. Vaulting out of their cave, he was a man possessed with a new mission in life. "Eve, Eve, my darling Eve. What a beautiful day this is."

Eve smiled, too, as though she did not have a care in the world. "You're right, Adam, it is a beautiful day. I don't know when I've ever felt better. God knows, this place is no Garden of Delights, but somehow that doesn't seem so important anymore. Somehow the thing I wanted so badly doesn't seem so far away after all. Isn't that odd?"

"Then it's settled. We're going to make a free will offering, just like we did yesterday, three times a week. We'll do it every Wednesday, Friday and Sunday, and we'll keep on doing it that way for the rest of our lives."

Suddenly the Word of God arrived. "Hello, you two. I've come to tell you God is very pleased about your commitment to bring your offerings on a weekly basis."

"That's great news, Lord," replied Adam.

"And because of your resolve to do this thing, you've now determined your fate for both you and your descendants."

Adam and Eve exchanged a curious look.

"Is that a good thing?" wondered Adam.

"Of course it is. It simply means that when I come as a human being and suffer for your sakes, it will happen in such a way as to fulfill the meaning of all your sacrifices offered from this point onward."

"But I don't understand, Lord," Adam said, shaking his head. "I'm afraid I don't follow Your meaning."

"Don't worry about that now, Adam. Someday you'll understand. All I'm saying is that when I come to give My life as a ransom for many, it will also take place on a Wednesday and proceed through the preparation day of Friday. And then, just as I created everything in the beginning and raised the Heavens high above the Earth, so once again, My rising again on Sunday will create joy for everyone Who trusts in Me. So, you two, just remember to continue bringing these offerings to Me for the rest of your lives, and everything else will take care of itself."

ADAM AND EVE APPROACHED their altar again, where they piled their meal offering in a large heap and set it ablaze. As they stepped back, the fire crackled intensely, sending a shower of sparks skyward, shimmering upward in the shape of a dove. "Look, Eve, there's the Holy Spirit. God has accepted our offering again. Can you feel His love flowing through our veins?"

Eve nodded contentedly.

"Can you believe it? We've been bringing our offerings to God for seven whole weeks now, and it seems like we're growing closer and closer to Him every day."

Again, with her sweet smile, Eve just nodded. Then abruptly she withdrew a flinty dagger from beneath her sheepskin loincloth and began slashing into Adam with her blade of stone, piercing him squarely in his right side, causing him to shudder with each blow.

"Eve, no."

Ripping into his side with stab after stab, Eve then threw the bloody knife at his feet as she watched blood and water gush out of his wounds.

"Oh, Eve, what've you done?" gasped Adam. "How could you?"

Slumping at the foot of the altar, Adam died. Eve just stared it his lifeless body, oozing its strange mixture of fluids. Then, slowly lifting his corpse, she placed it up on the altar, extinguishing its flames. With a peculiar look in her eye, she moved her face very near to Adam's and gently pressed her lips against his. Slowly, Eve's countenance transformed into that of the devil's, and his grotesque lips finally withdrew from Adam's mouth.

"So, Adam," sneered Satan, "how does it feel to offer yourself up as a living sacrifice to your beloved god? Not all it's cracked up to be, is it?"

BEHIND THE CAVE OF Treasures, Eve lay prostrate on the ground, her mouth wrapped securely with a sheepskin muzzle. She desperately struggled to break free from the cords that bound her hands and feet. Just then, a pair of hands untied the muzzle.

"What is going on?" gasped Eve as she turned to see that an angel was untying her hands and then her feet.

"There is no time for a lengthy explanation, my dear," he said. "Suffice it to say that Satan and his angels abducted you in an effort to stop Adam from bringing any more offerings to the Lord."

"Adam! Is he all right? Where is he?"

"He's at your altar, Eve, and he needs you more than ever."

Jumping to her feet, Eve bolted away.

"Go quickly, young lady," exclaimed the angel. "Run like the wind!"

ARRIVING AT THE altar, Eve found Adam lying dead on it.

"Oh, Adam, I'm too late." Trembling and crying, she pulled his corpse from off the altar. As she did, blood oozed out over the embers of the smoldering sacrifice. Setting his body on the ground, Eve kneeled down next him, just as the Word of God appeared a few feet away.

Tears streaming down her face, Eve turned and asked, "What happened, Lord?"

"The devil, dear Eve, disguised himself as you and stabbed him."

"As *me*? But why?"

"Why does Satan ever do anything to you two? He's jealous of the peace and tranquility your offerings have brought you. He can't stand the thought of you and Adam growing closer to the heart of God, while nothing he does prevents it from happening."

Turning back to Adam, she fell onto his corpse, weeping uncontrollably. "Poor Adam, how you must have suffered. Please, Lord, please bring him back to me, won't You?"

The Lord reached out His hand toward Adam, and slowly all of his stab wounds sealed back up.

Sucking in a deep breath, Adam sat up, wild-eyed. "Eve, why!"

Dismayed, Eve jumped to her feet, looking to the Word for moral support.

"Relax, Adam, don't be alarmed. Eve didn't attack you. It was the devil again. He transformed himself to look like Eve so you'd never suspect how close your attacker was."

"Oh, thank You, Lord," gasped Adam. "For a second there—"

Obviously offended, Eve protested. "Adam! What are you saying? Did you seriously think for one second I could've done something this despicable?"

"Never mind, Eve," insisted the Word in a reassuring tone. "Appearances can be deceiving. Don't be so hard on him. He was, after all, just killed by a woman. That in itself will always try a man's soul."

"He makes a good point, Eve. You can hardly blame a guy for jumping to conclusions."

"Very funny, you two," smirked Eve.

"Now, go ahead, Adam," continued the Word, "I want you to finish up here with your offering. Just realize how precious this is to God. In fact, the same thing is going to happen to Me while I'm on Earth."

"What, Lord?" asked a confused Adam. "What's going to happen to You?"

"I, too, will be pierced in My side, and blood and water will also flow from My wound, and that blood that is spilled will be the true offering, one that will be laid upon an altar as a perfect sacrifice."

A Message from God

THE COUPLE WALKED westward from their cave early the next morning. They went to the field of wheat and rested under the shade of a large tree. No sooner had they sat down than a pack of wolves appeared from the bushes and moved in toward the relaxing couple. Growling maliciously, fangs extended, the animals crept forward, preparing to rush at them. The startled couple sprang to their feet, and Eve instinctively hid behind Adam.

"What's the meaning of this, wolves?" asked Adam as he boldly stepped forward.

Stepping ahead of the rest of the pack, the lead wolf snarled, "We're hungry, and lately our hunting has been scarce. Provide us with food, and we'll leave you in peace."

"I wish we could help you, Wolf, really I do."

"What, then, should we tell our hungry families when we return to them empty-handed again?" asked the wolf while the pack slowly crept forward several more feet.

Adam put up his hand in protest. "Wait! Certainly you remember the oath we all took to never harm one another. Why would you do something like this?"

For a moment, the wolves hesitated and looked at one another.

"Are you aware of making such a pact with these humans?" asked the lead wolf of his companions.

"I am not," replied one of them.

Turning back to address Adam, the lead wolf shrugged his furry shoulders. "It seems my brothers and I took no such oath. Now, provide us with something to eat, or else."

"But we have no food for your kind," replied Adam.

"Then prepare to *become* food, humans!" growled the wolf, and lunging ahead the pack rushed forward along with him.

"Adam, do something!" screamed Eve.

"Into the tree, Eve, quickly!" Adam nimbly hoisted Eve into the branches of the tree and scrambled up after her, just as the furious pack, fangs extended, swept past them with their snapping jaws. Circling back around, the pack gathered at the base of the tree and began scratching at it, frantically trying to jump up after the couple.

"Now what do we do, Adam?"

"We go higher, Eve, higher."

So climb they did, moving upward from branch to branch. Finally, one of the wolves managed to claw his way up into the lowest branch of the tree. Eve was desperately trying to reach the branch above her when the one she was on suddenly broke. Managing to grab her wrist as she fell past him, Adam held on tightly. But as her feet dangled, the wolf in the tree was very close to reaching her with his vicious fangs.

"Get the female!" snarled the lead wolf as he tried to climb into the tree with his companion. "Get her!"

Eve struggled mightily to hoist herself upward while the branch supporting Adam creaked loudly. Unable to hold their combined weight, the branch finally snapped, sending the pair down onto the wolf in the branch just below them. "Adam, no!" Eve screamed.

Together, all three came spiraling down out of the tree, scattering the pack below. Landing in a heap, Adam and Eve looked at each other and then at the wolf they had landed on. Fortunately for them, the wolf just laid there, quite unconscious. Struggling to their feet, the couple looked frantically about, only to find that the pack, which had temporarily backed away, was now returning to stalk their prey.

"Step aside everyone," said the lead wolf. "Allow me to show you how this is done."

Obligingly, the pack parted to let him forward, and before Adam and Eve had time to react, the wolf was sprinting toward them. Frozen with fear, the couple just stood there.

"Lord, help us, please," whispered Adam.

Just as the wolf began his leap, an angel appeared in front of the trembling couple, and having simply been touched by this angel, the wolf floated past Adam and Eve and fell harmlessly to the ground with a thud. Grumbling angrily, the wolf laid there, huffing and puffing, but obviously incapable of any real movement. Just as abruptly, two more angels appeared and stood before the pack of wolves. They, too, simply motioned to them, and without a whimper the pack scattered and disappeared into the landscape, leaving their immobilized leader to fend for himself.

"Thank you so much, angel," said Adam, still trying to catch his breath. "And not a moment too soon."

As furious as she was terrified, Eve moved forward to examine the prostrate wolf, still lying helplessly on the ground. "Why would you do something like this, Wolf?" she snapped. "We made a pact with you and your kind. How could you?"

"He did it, Eve," began the first angel, "because he is no wolf at all."

Confused, the couple stared at the trio of angels.

"Not a wolf?" blurted Adam. "Then..." A strained look of realization swept across his face. "Oh, no. Don't tell me it's him, *again*?"

And after a simple gesture from the first angel, the startled look on the couple's faces revealed that the answer had become all too apparent.

"Satan," said Eve, blanching at the hideous creature on the ground, no longer looking like the wolf that had just attacked them.

"Yes, Satan," replied the angel, quite calmly. "Doing what he does best, deceiving you with his myriad disguises. And if it were not for the fact that God is so concerned about your safety, he might have succeeded with his clever ruse."

"No wonder, Eve," said Adam. "Of course, the animals would never have attacked us this way. I should have known all along. How stupid of me."

The other two angels stepped over to them, looking down at the monster with equal parts disgust and dismay.

"Don't be too hard on yourself, Adam," said the second angel, "anyone could have made a mistake like that. A creature like this, with the ability to take on any form he chooses, is simply impossible to anticipate."

"Now, be gone, Devil!" snapped the third angel, "and count yourself lucky that God doesn't destroy you for trying to destroy his beloved children!"

And with a cloud of dust, Satan streaked out of view.

Sighing heavily, Adam turned to the trio of angels. "You three certainly look familiar. Have we met before?"

"Of course, Adam," replied the first angel. "We're the archangels who brought you gold, frankincense and myrrh."

"Oh, right," said Adam. "I remember now. What were your names again?"

"I'm Michael. I was the one who brought you the gold."

"I'm Gabriel, and I brought you frankincense."

"And I'm Raphael. I brought you myrrh."

"That's right," said Adam as he turned to Eve with a smile. "Remember, Eve?"

"Of course, I remember, Adam. We're so grateful to the three of you; then and now."

"It is our pleasure to serve you, my dear," said Michael with a perfunctory nod.

"The Lord bless you and keep you always," added Gabriel.

"So tell us," continued Raphael, "have you enjoyed the gifts we brought you in the Name of the Most High?"

"More than words can say," replied Adam. "We'll cherish them forever."

"So glad to hear it," said Michael.

"You bringing us those tokens," interjected Eve, "was the first nice thing that had ever happened to us in this miserable place."

"Tell us, then, angels," continued Adam, "is there any chance you might have something more for us from the Lord?"

"You mean apart from rescuing you both from Satan's attack just now?" asked Gabriel, smiling playfully.

"Oh, Adam," said Eve, clearly embarrassed. "Haven't they done enough for us yet?"

Adam sheepishly hung his head.

"Don't worry, Adam," added Raphael, "the Lord always has more for those who trust Him without reservation. Do you trust Him?"

Looking up with a tremendous smile, Adam replied, "Of course I do, with every ounce of my being."

"Good," said Michael, "because today is a special day, you two. Not only has the Lord rescued you from the jaws of death, but He has also asked us to bring you a very important message."

"Really," mused Eve. "What could it be?"

"Oh, it's nothing really," quipped Michael. "Still it is a message from God. Are you willing to listen and perform it?"

Adam nodded. "Tell us so we can receive it."

"Then you have to promise you'll do it. You have to swear."

"But I don't know how to swear," replied Adam.

"Then I'll show you," said Michael, holding out his hand. "It's easy. Give me your hand."

Adam then placed his hand in Michael's.

"Now, say this," continued Michael. "As God lives and speaks and is rational, Who raised the Heavens in space, established the Earth on the waters, and created me out of the ground, I, Adam, will never break my promise, nor renounce my word."

Adam repeated the oath.

"Very well, then," said Michael with an earnest nod. "You know it's been a long time since you came out of the garden, and in all that time you've never done anything wrong. Now, God wants you to take Eve, who came out of your side, and marry her."

"Marry her?"

Adam and Eve exchanged a curious look.

"But what does that mean?" asked Adam.

"It's when two humans are joined together as one," said Michael, quite matter-of-factly.

"Really," muttered Adam, mulling the idea over in his confused mind. "Do I really have to marry my own flesh and blood now? Wouldn't that mean I'd be committing adultery against myself? God would really want to destroy me then."

Michael blanched. "Adultery? Who said anything about adultery?" Turning to the two angels with him, he asked, "Did either of you hear me say anything about adultery?"

Both of them shrugged and together said, "No."

All eyes returned to Adam, who still looked very confused.

"There, you see?" said Michael with a reassuring smile. "Marriage just means that you and Eve will be able to bear children to comfort you in your sadness. Doesn't that sound like something that would appeal to you?"

"Adam?" interjected Eve.

"Yes, dear?"

"Ask him to tell us what *children* are."

Adam, however, put up his hand in protest. "Hold on, Eve, hold on. We'll get to that in a minute. First things first. What I want to know is: If God exiled us and deprived us of our luminous natures because we ate fruit from a tree, what do you think He'd do to us if we consented to this thing you called—what was it again?"

"Marriage," said Michael.

"Yeah, marriage. I bet He'd wipe us out if we do something like that!"

"But I'm telling you," insisted Michael, quite adamantly, "there is nothing wrong with what God is proposing."

"Wait a second!" blurted Adam, suddenly suspicious. "God never told us anything about what you're saying. Maybe you're not one of God's angels after all. You're really the devil and his henchmen in disguise again, aren't you?"

With that, Michael opened his mouth to reply, but strangely enough, although his lips were moving, no sound came out. Puzzled, the trio of angels turned to one another and tried to converse amongst themselves, but still, though they were all mouthing their words, nothing could be heard from any of them. Nervously, they looked back at Adam and Eve, and then took several cautious steps backward.

"Damn you, Satan," exclaimed Adam, "get away from us right now, in the Name of the Lord!"

Suddenly the three angels transformed into their true appearances as Satan and two of his hideous demons.

"But—*but how*, Adam?" stammered Eve. "Didn't we just see Satan as the wolf? And now here he is again. What is going on?"

Adam and Eve stepped back, but the devil did not advance toward them. Instead, he made a hasty retreat, spewing obscenities, with his demons following close behind.

THE DEPRESSED COUPLE sat in their cave, late into the evening, just staring at each other.

"Oh, Eve, did you see that?" groaned Adam. "I just swore by God's Name and shook hands with the devil."

"I know, Adam, but you have to stop beating yourself up like this. It's not your fault. Those disguises of his are impossible to figure out."

"Please, whatever you do, don't ever tell anyone about this. All right?"

So Eve remained silent while Adam spread his hands toward God. "Oh, Lord, please forgive me for what I've done. I never meant to cooperate with the devil again."

ADAM CONTINUED TO stand and pray like that, day after miserable day. Disheartened at the sight of what Adam was putting himself through, Eve approached him and held out a slice of bread.

"No thank you, dear," said Adam. "I'm busy right now."

"But, Adam, I'm worried. You haven't eaten for over a week now. You need your strength. Please eat something. I made you some bread, just the way you like it."

"I'm sorry, Eve, but I just don't feel like eating right now."

"Please, for me? You know, it's one thing to pray for God's forgiveness, but it's another thing altogether to starve yourself in the process."

"I'm sorry, Eve, really I am; but I need to keep praying until the Lord responds."

"But you know that takes forever sometimes."

"If He never responds, then so be it. I'll die of starvation. Then, without me to take care of you, the Lord will have to let you back into the garden."

"But I don't care about the garden anymore, Adam."

With a look of utter disbelief, Adam turned to Eve. "What did you say?"

"I said, I don't care if I ever get back into that silly, old garden."

"Oh, Eve, don't say that, not even in jest. Don't you want our old life back?"

"Not if it means losing you, no. I don't even know what I was thinking before. What do I need with a garden, anyway, when we have each other, when we have God, the Word and the Holy Spirit? What more do I need beyond that?"

"Wow, I'm not quite sure how to respond to that. Now, would you please just let me get back to my prayers?"

"Fine," she said, and then sadly turned and walked away.

STILL REFUSING TO eat or drink after several more days of determined prayer, Adam, overcome by exhaustion, finally slumped to the ground, very near death.

Lamentably, Eve looked down at his motionless body. "Lord, please, help us. I'm afraid Adam doesn't look so good."

Then the Word of God appeared and revived Adam again, helping him to his feet. "Oh, Adam, what am I going to do with you?"

"I don't know, Lord," replied Adam, hanging his head in dismay. "I feel just terrible about all this."

"You swore an oath by My Name."

"I know, Lord. How could I have done something so stupid?"

"And you made another agreement with Satan."

"I know, Lord. What was I thinking?"

"But, for the very first time in your life, you saw through his deception, rebuked him, and caused him to flee without any help from Me at all."

"I know, Lord. I feel so ashamed. Wait—*what*?" Confused, Adam looked up at the Word. "What did You say?"

"I said, you saw through his deception and caused him to flee without the slightest bit of help from Me. I'm very proud of you, Adam. You're finally beginning to grow into a genuine knowledge of God."

Adam and Eve exchanged a relieved look and a smile.

"Did you hear that, Eve? The Lord is proud of me."

Eve happily nodded.

"Oh, Lord," exclaimed Adam. "I can still hardly believe what happened. There were ravenous wolves. And there were these angels who looked just like the ones who brought us the gold, frankincense and myrrh. And then there I was shaking hands with the devil!"

"But you sent them all packing in the end, didn't you?"

"I did, didn't I?" replied Adam, getting more and more excited.

Quite pleased, the Word nodded and put up His hand as if to calm an excitable boy. "But never forget, Adam. You still have to be very careful with Satan around. Now more than ever actually, since he'll be seeking to exact his revenge for your having outsmarted him for the first time. Will you do that for Me?"

With this sobering thought in mind, Adam quickly calmed down and solemnly nodded. "Of course I will, Lord."

Then the Word disappeared.

Relieved, Adam turned to Eve. "I am so hungry, Eve. Is there anything to eat?"

Beauty and the Beast

ADAM WOKE UP THE next morning and, rolling over, he watched Eve with an intense longing as she lay sleeping.

Slowly opening her eyes, Eve became startled by his scrutinizing gaze. "Adam, why are you looking at me like that?"

"No reason. I'm just looking. Have I ever told you how beautiful you are?"

Bewildered, she shook her head. "No, you haven't."

"Well, then, I'm telling you now. You are very beautiful, my darling; your eyes, your hair, your face, all lovelier than the most beautiful sunset I've ever seen."

Taken aback, Eve stared at him with a peculiar look on her face. "Why, thank you, Adam. What has gotten into you?"

WALKING ALONG THE river on the eastern border of the garden, Adam and Eve got to its bank and sat down. Enjoying a pleasant breeze, they gazed out over its peaceful, flowing waters.

"Tell me, Eve: Do think God would be angry with me if I wanted to marry you?"

Thoughtfully, she considered the question for a moment, then turned to him with her most charming smile. "I don't know. Have you ever thought about asking Him?"

"Frankly, it's all I *can* think about."

SATAN AND HIS MINIONS, of course, were watching the couple from a distance as they were often in the habit of doing. The devil scratched his furrowed brow, staring, brooding, plotting. "What to do, what to do? Those disgusting, little replicas are really starting to drive me crazy. Now they're even beginning to see through my most elaborate schemes."

Seated at the devil's right hand, his lieutenant's face suddenly lit up and his eyes opened wide. He eagerly raised his bony finger and his lips slowly parted, as if he were about to say something significant.

Noticing him, Satan turned his ugly face and sneered, "What is it now, you insufferable dolt?"

Deflated, his lieutenant closed his mouth, lowered his finger, and frowned.

"Just as I thought," grumbled the devil. "Can't anyone offer me anything in the way of a workable plan to convince god to destroy these two troublemakers?"

Then, as if his lieutenant had something else occur to him, he raised his crooked finger again.

"Yes, yes," mumbled Satan. "Out with it already."

"Well, Lord, I was thinking."

"Do tell."

"Well, as I see it, even though Adam has been repeatedly protected from our attacks, there would be no one to protect him if he incurred the wrath of god."

"Naturally, you idiot, that's a given. But how do we accomplish such an aim?"

"But you've already figured it out yourself, Master."

"I have?" muttered Satan, trying to figure out what it was. "Oh, yes, of course I have." Turning to his lieutenant, the devil leaned toward him in anticipation. "What was my idea again?"

"When you persuaded Adam to shake your hand, it revealed his innermost desire to have relations with the female. It revealed his vulnerability to something their god has never given them permission to do."

Mulling over his words, Satan's eyes thinned. "Yes, I see what you're saying. If I can just trick Adam into marrying Eve without receiving permission from god, then he'll kill them for us."

"Precisely, Master! That's exactly what I'm saying."

"Oh, my word. I am diabolically clever, aren't I?"

With an oppressive howl, the whole group of demons shrieked their approval.

Then, as the din slowly simmered down, Satan turned to his lieutenant and quietly asked, "Now, remind me again how I plan to carry out this grand scheme of mine?"

TRYING UNSUCCESSFULLY to relax, Adam sat with Eve on the riverbank, but obviously he was growing more and more agitated about something.

"So what do you think, Eve? How do you feel about marrying me?"

"Marrying you? Why do you want to marry me?"

"Because I love you; isn't that reason enough? Don't you love me?"

"Of course I do, sweetheart. You know that."

"Well, then, marry me. What do you say, Eve, you want to marry me?"

"I don't know," she replied with a sheepish grin, obviously embarrassed by his impetuousness. "What does this marriage involve, anyway?"

Leaning over to her, Adam kissed Eve amorously on her neck. "It involves being in love; you know, being together."

"No, I don't know," she said, pulling away, suddenly uncomfortable. "And what makes you such an expert on marriage? Has God told you something I don't know about?"

"Not in so many words."

"What's that supposed to mean? Has He advised you about marrying me, or not?"

Frustrated, Adam turned away. "No."

And for quite a while, the couple just sat there without a word, unsure of what to do next. Then something caught their eye from the shoreline.

"Adam, what's that in the water?"

Rising from the depths of the river, ten women, exotic, naked and sensuous, came up slowly, not more than fifty yards in front of them.

"I don't know, Eve," said Adam, his eyes widening, much to the chagrin of Eve. "But I think they're women, *beautiful* women."

The entire group of ladies effortlessly made their way through the rivers current. Reaching the shoreline, they stepped out of the water and up to the couple.

"Hello there," said the tallest of the women. "What's your name?"

Adam and Eve exchanged a stunned look, and then returned their wide-eyed gaze back to this group of exquisite visitors.

"My, uh, my name is Adam. And this is Eve. Who are you?"

"Hello, Adam, Eve. My name is Lurana, and these are my sisters."

"Does this mean there's another world beneath our own?" asked Adam. "And is everyone living there as beautiful as you?"

"Why, yes, of course," Lurana replied, her dark, seductive eyes fixed squarely on Adam. "We are an abundant race."

"But how do you multiply?" asked Eve.

"How else does anyone multiply?" replied Lurana, quite nonchalantly. "We all have husbands who have married us, of course. Aren't you and Adam married?"

Eve shook her head, thoroughly confused. "No."

"You mean to tell me you have no children?" asked Lurana.

"Children?" echoed Adam as he shot a furtive glance at Eve. "What are children?"

Clearly taken aback by the question, Lurana replied tersely. "You know, progeny, offspring, *children*."

"But where, exactly, do these children come from?" asked Eve.

"By way of birth, of course," replied Lurana with an awkwardly charming smile. "All my sisters and I have given birth to many children, who then grew up and in turn got married and had children of their own. Of course, if you don't believe us, we can always prove it to you."

So the whole group of women turned toward the river. "Husbands, children, come to us now!" Lurana shouted. "Come and greet your neighbors of the dry land!"

Quite to their surprise, Adam and Eve watched while ten men and twenty children ascended out of the river. Every one of them walked straight to one of those lovely, young ladies and stood next to her.

"You see?" continued Lurana. "Here are our husbands, our sons and our daughters. Say hello, everyone. This is Adam and Eve, our neighbors."

"Hello," said the group as one.

"Hello," echoed Adam and Eve together.

"Just think, Adam," continued Lurana, "you and Eve could get married just like we did, and you could have children of your own." Then, she fell silent. Allowing some time for her words to sink in, Lurana fixed her sensual gaze firmly back on Adam.

Considering her advice, Adam grew even more agitated. "Eve, darling, didn't I tell you? Just think what it would be like to be married, to have children of our own. Wouldn't that be something?"

"But, Adam, what would God say?" Eve said slowly, half to herself, half to him. "Are you sure He wouldn't be angry with us if we got married without His permission?"

"All right, Eve, all right," grumbled Adam, thoroughly frustrated. "Have it your way." So he stood and turned his eyes skyward. "Lord..."

Lurana tilted her head oddly. "But why do you need God's permission to do something so natural?"

Adam adamantly shook his head. "Because if we don't get His permission, He may be angry with us for doing something like this."

"Nonsense. We never required permission to marry, and look at us. God didn't kill us, did He?"

"I'm sorry, but we have to ask God for His advice. Now, please, stop interrupting me." Again Adam lifted his eyes skyward. "Lord, Eve and I would like to get married, but we don't want to make You so angry with us that You'd wish to kill us. Could You please tell us what You think about all this?"

With that, the entire group of exotic visitors exchanged a peculiar look and cautiously stepped back.

"Wait," exclaimed Adam. "Where're you going? You have to stay until the Word of God comes to tell us His decision."

But Lurana resolutely shook her head, and without another word, the entire group walked back to the river, where they slowly descended, one by one, into its depths and disappeared from view.

BACK IN THEIR CAVE around evening time, Adam and Eve were trying to go about their business as if nothing unusual had just happened, but because Adam continued to pace incessantly about, Eve got annoyed. "Adam, would you please sit down and relax? You're not helping this situation with all your pacing."

"But why won't God answer us? Why won't He let us know what to do? I've never been more confused about anything in my life. I can't stop thinking about marrying you. So many thoughts are surging through my mind, my body. I can't take it anymore."

"I'm sorry, but I'm exhausted. I'm going to sleep. You deal with it on your own. I'll see you in the morning. Good night."

But even after Eve had long since fallen asleep Adam was still pacing back and forth.

AT THE BREAK OF DAWN, Adam woke Eve up. "Come on, Eve, hurry. It's time to get up."

Sitting up, bleary-eyed, Eve gaped at Adam. "Did you even go to sleep last night?"

"Sleep? How do you expect me to sleep with so many questions gnawing at me? Now get up; we've got to go."

"Go? Go where?"

"We're going to the hilltop where we received the gold, frankincense and myrrh. I need to ask the Lord about this thing."

Still half asleep, Eve laid back down. "But I'm tired, Adam. I'm not ready to go anywhere right now. Just leave me alone."

"Are you kidding? I need the Lord to explain what it means to marry you! I'm telling you, Eve, those people at the river have set my heart on fire! I can't stop thinking about what they told us! Thoughts of their sensual lives keep racing through my mind! But I refuse to just take you without God's permission, or else He might destroy us for sure!"

"But why do we have to go to the hilltop?" asked Eve, struggling to sit up, yawning and stretching her tired muscles. "Why not just pray to God here in our cave? He'll tell us if marriage is a good idea or not."

Adam then turned his eyes toward Heaven. "Oh, Lord, would You please tell us about this thing called marriage? If it's okay with You, then let us know, but if it isn't, then order us to resist our desires, because if You don't give us permission soon, we'll be overpowered for sure! We'll be following Satan's advice again, and You'll have no choice but to reduce us to nothing!"

Then the Word of God appeared. "Just think you two. Do you realize that if you had been this cautious in the beginning, you'd have never been forced to leave the garden in the first place? You've certainly come a long way since then."

Smiling, Eve stood up and took hold of Adam's hand. Suddenly the three archangels who had brought them the gold, frankincense and myrrh appeared next to the Word.

"So that you won't think this is a mere illusion, I've asked Michael, Gabriel and Raphael to join Me before you now. Above all, I want you to be absolutely sure that I am blessing your union together, and in order to explain everything that you'll need to know about your impending marriage, I'll leave you two in their capable hands."

Adam smiled proudly at Eve. "Did you hear that, sweetheart? The Lord has blessed our marriage."

Smiling back, she nodded.

Then the Word vanished, leaving the archangels standing before the happy couple.

"Now, Adam," began Michael, "take some of the gold you were given and present it to Eve as a wedding gift."

So Adam took a sliver of gold and placed it on Eve's sheepskin blouse, just over her heart. "This I give you, Eve, as a pledge of my undying love."

"Then," added Gabriel, "pledge yourself to her by giving her some of the frankincense I brought you."

As Adam handed Eve some of the frankincense, he said, "This I give as an assurance that I will always be there for you, Eve, to protect you, to shelter you, to care for you all the days of my life."

"And when you present her with the myrrh," said Raphael, "you'll be engaged."

Finally, Adam presented her with some myrrh. "And this I offer you, Eve, so you may know that when we two become one, it will not merely be a oneness in flesh alone, but it will be in spirit and in truth as well."

"Well done, Adam," said Michael. "You two are now officially engaged."

"Now, God wants you both to fast and pray for the next seven days," continued Gabriel, "and after that, Adam, you may go in to Eve, your wife, because then it will be a pure union, a sacred union."

"Then, you are to have children," added Raphael, "who will multiply and replenish the entire planet."

Adam and Eve happily nodded to the archangels.

"We'll do everything just as you've told us," said Adam, "as though it were straight from the mouth of the Lord Himself."

THE COUPLE REMAINED in their cave for several days, fasting and praying, when suddenly four visitors appeared at the mouth of their cave. It was Lurana, with her husband, son and daughter. But much to their chagrin, Adam and Eve refused to even speak to them. The couple simply pointed them in the opposite direction. Reluctantly, the dejected visitors from the river turned and walked away. Kissing Adam on his cheek, Eve proudly smiled and watched as he resolutely strolled back into the cave.

AS THE SUN ROSE THE following morning, Adam rolled over and gently shook Eve awake. "Dear Eve, wake up. It's time."

Opening her eyes, Eve gazed longingly up at him. "Don't tell me, my love. Is it really the morning of the eighth day?"

Happily, Adam nodded, stood up, and helped Eve to her feet.

FROM THEIR VANTAGE point, Satan and his minions watched from a distance, miserable and helpless, as Adam and Eve, flanked by Michael, Gabriel and Raphael, stood reverently before the Word of God. Then, Michael handed a ring of gold to Adam, who gently placed it on Eve's finger.

"I now pronounce you man and wife," said the Word. "Adam, you may kiss your lovely bride."

And as Adam took Eve in his arms and kissed her, the Word and the archangels slowly dissolved from view, just leaving the married couple quite alone and quite in love.

"What a touching sight," said the devil as a lone tear trickled down his furry cheek.

Noticing the desperate look on Satan's face, his lieutenant leaned in toward him and whispered, "Are you all right, Master?"

"I'm afraid," mumbled the devil with a pathetic sniffle, "weddings make me cry."

"Really?" wondered the confused lieutenant. "But, Lord, when have you ever seen a wedding before?"

Irritated, Satan glared back at him. "You idiot! This is all your fault!"

"Me? Why me?"

"It's been two hundred and forty days since I managed to get Adam and Eve kicked out of that horrid garden of theirs, and what've you accomplished in all that time? *Nothing!*"

"B—*but, Master*, please. I'm not the only one who's failed. You're not being fair."

"Fair! Who said anything about fair? This was a war, you insolent worm! A war for our very existence! A war with an entire kingdom on the line, and you want fair? Fair has nothing to do with it!"

"But all is not lost."

"You fool, *it is lost*, I tell you! Our direct war with Adam is over! We have no more tricks, no more deceptions, no more tactics. *It's over!*"

"But, Lord, you said yourself, we must never give in to doubt and pessimism, never give in to merely human weaknesses. Remember?"

"I said that?"

Meekly, the lieutenant gurgled, "Y—*yes*, M—*Master*, y—*you did.*"

"Damn your pathetic hide," screeched Satan with a wave of his wretched paw. "How dare you contradict me!"

Then, with an eerie rush of wind and a whimpering howl, the terrified lieutenant was swept away into oblivion. Still fuming, the devil turned to his trembling cadre of demons and eyed them with the blackest eyes they had ever seen. "So tell me, did any of *you* hear me say something like that?"

A Change of Heart

FOR A WHILE AT LEAST that very first couple lived peacefully on the Earth. Then one day as Eve was bathing in the river, she stopped and tilted her head curiously. Holding her hand to her bulging stomach, she turned with a strange look on her face. "Adam?"

"Yes, dear, what is it?"

"Come here, please," she said quietly.

"Right now?"

"Yes, Adam. Your pregnant wife would like to see you *right now.* Hurry, please."

"Are you all right?" he asked, stepping into the river with her, looking rather concerned. "Is something wrong?"

"Not at all."

"Then what is it?"

"Here, give me your hand," she replied as she took his hand and placed it on her stomach. Confused, Adam went along with her but suddenly jerked his hand away.

"Wh—*what* was that?"

"That was your child kicking inside me."

"No."

"Yes."

"If I didn't know better, I'd say there was a wrestling match going on inside there."

"There is, Adam. And do you know what else?"

"What?"

"It was exactly one year ago today that we were married."

"Is that so?"

"It is, yes."

"A year ago already, wow. How time flies."

"And you're still happy that we got married?"

"Of course Eve, it was the best decision I've ever made. The best decision I will ever make. Right after trusting the Lord, that is," he said with a wry smile. "And you?"

"What about me?"

"Are you still happy we got married? No regrets, I mean? No more imagining what it would be like to have things the way they used to be? To be back in the garden again?"

For just a moment, Eve hesitated and then said, "No, not really."

"Not really." Then with just a hint of skepticism in his voice, he asked, "You mean to tell me that you're still not pining for your old life back? I find that very hard to believe. Tell me, then: If God decided to change His mind tomorrow and offered to let us back into the garden? Wouldn't you want to go, just a little?"

"Of course, silly, but..." Eve paused again, as if unsure of her next words.

"But what?" pressed Adam.

"But if He's doesn't, I'm okay with that, too. I won't be upset. Not anymore. I already told you: What do I need with a garden, when I have everything that was *in* the garden, right here, right now?"

"You make a good point, as usual."

"But what about you?" she asked. "Are you really okay with all this, too?"

"Well, I admit, there are still moments when I miss our old life, sure. The time we spent in the garden was like a dream, a sweet, beautiful dream, filled with cool breezes and the smell of nectar, but..." Pausing, Adam's gaze drifted from Eve and wandered far into the distant horizon.

This time Eve pressed the issue. "But now?"

"But now," said Adam, slowly mulling the words over in his mind, "after all the time we've spent here together, building a new life by the sweat of our brow, the labor of our hands, I'm beginning to feel like this is more real than all that other stuff ever was. And if life in this place means learning to cope with the hardships we face, with your help and the help of the Lord and His angels, then I'm with you, Eve, all the way. Besides, what good is thinking about the past, when it keeps you from living in the present?"

"Good, I'm so glad. I needed to hear you say it for yourself. Now, please, can you get me some more of that delicious manna? I'm really craving something sweet right now."

AS THE COUPLE TRIED to sleep in their cave, Eve tossed and turned so much that finally Adam sat up. "Eve, dear, are you all right?"

"No, Adam, I'm not."

"What's wrong? Is the baby kicking again?"

"No."

"What is it, then?"

So Eve sat up, too. "It's our cave."

"Our cave? What about our cave?"

"It's just that I'm going to have a baby soon, and this cave, well, it's a sacred cave. I mean, because of all the miraculous things that have happened here. You know?"

"Sure, Eve, I understand. What about it?"

"Well, I just don't think it would be proper for me to give birth here, that's all."

"Where should we go, then? Where else *can* we go?"

"Maybe we should go to the rock Satan dropped on us. God did turn it into a perfectly good awning over us, remember?"

Adam nodded. "Of course, it formed a natural cave, didn't it?"

"It did, yes. So, how about we go there? You could fix it up in no time; make it a kind of 'home away from home.' Please?"

ADAM AND EVE THEN went to stay in that sheltering rock until the time of her delivery approached, and when that day arrived, Eve cried out in agony. Adam felt so badly because of what she was going through that he prayed like he had never prayed before.

"Oh, Lord, have mercy. Please, stop torturing Eve this way."

Then the Word of God appeared.

"Lord, I think Eve is dying."

"No, Adam, she's not dying."

"What's wrong with her, then? Have we angered You in some way again?"

"Don't be alarmed. It's true, Eve is experiencing tremendous pain at this moment, but it's not because of anything you've done recently."

"Then why is she going through this?"

"It goes back to the beginning, I'm afraid, when you first disobeyed the command of God, and the Lord cursed your evil deed. She's going through this so God's word to her will be fulfilled: 'In pain and suffering, you'll bear your children.'"

Eve let out a lamentable scream. "Oh, Adam, the pain; it's unbearable!"

"Do something, Lord," begged Adam. "Don't let her suffer like this anymore."

"Don't worry, Adam. Soon, the agony of childbirth will subside, and when the twins are finally born, it will all be a distant memory."

"*Twins*?" Bewildered, Adam turned to the Word. "Good God, what are twins?"

EVE'S CRIES OF AGONY eventually gave way to the crying of her newborn son, and along with him came a daughter, too.

Holding the children in her arms, Eve was feeling much better.

"Oh, Eve, there are two of them, two of them. I can't believe it. No wonder there was such a wrestling in your belly."

"Say hello to your new son and daughter, Adam," whispered Eve, tired but happy. "How does it feel?"

Adam beamed a proud smile. "Wonderful."

FORTY DAYS LATER, Adam brought a meal offering to the same stone altar that they had built with their own hands, and watching from a distance, Eve held her two infants while Adam set fire to the offering.

"Lord," began Adam, "we come here today to consecrate the birth of our two children, Cain and Luluwa, and to ask that You watch over them, protect them, guide them, just as You've done with Eve and I."

A beam of light suddenly came streaming down from Heaven, which shone down on the altar. Amazed, Adam motioned to Eve, and slowly she walked to him with the children. Then with Cain in Adam's arms and Luluwa in Eve's, the couple stood before the altar, basking in the glow of the divine light beam and the warmth of the fire.

"Do you feel the love of God, Eve?" asked Adam with a serene sigh.

"I do, my darling, yes."

"And you're happy?"

"Happier than at any time in my life."

MEANWHILE, AS USUAL, Satan and his minions were watching what that first family were doing, and they looked thoroughly disheartened. With equal parts disgust and dismay, the devil moaned, "And I have never been *less* happy than at any time in my hateful existence." Turning to his new lieutenant, the devil asked with a grim scowl, "Tell me, then, my latest recruit, what miserable news might you have that could cheer me up today? In light of this tragic turn of events, that is."

After thinking very hard for several moments, the lieutenant raised his scrawny finger and emphatically declared, "You are still king of this world, Master, and we are all your obedient and willing slaves."

"Good grief. Tell me something I don't know."

Then a new idea ignited a spark in the lieutenant's sinister eye. "The children, Lord."

"The children? What news concerning those crying brats could cheer me up?"

"Their names, Lord."

"Names? What about them, you babbling idiot?"

"It seems that Adam, as he so often does, has discerned something unique about his future, in this case, his newborns. Before it's come to fruition, I mean; something that you might find very interesting."

"Really?" Satan leaned in, his eyes thinning and nostrils sniffing. "In what way?"

"Well, you see, he named the female Luluwa, which means *beautiful*, because apparently Adam believes she will be even lovelier than her mother."

"Ahhh," grunted the devil. "How in Hell is that supposed to cheer me up?"

"Wait, wait, Master, there's more. He named the male Cain."

"Yes, of course, Cain." Mulling this over in his malicious mind, the devil shrugged his leathery shoulders, shook his wolfen head, and hissed through clenched teeth. "*So*?"

"But, Master, he named him Cain, don't you see?" The lieutenant's beady eyes opened wide. "Cain means *hater*, because he hated his own sister, even while he was still in his mother's womb."

Then, as if a bolt of lightning had hit him, Satan swooned, and donning his most malicious grin yet, he growled, "Oh, that is delicious. Now I see what you're saying. Yes, I do believe I can do something with that one. Good work, Lieutenant, very good work."

EVENTUALLY, EVE GAVE birth to another set of twins, again a boy and a girl, and as she held the babes to her breast, she looked up at Adam with a serene smile.

"Say hello to your new children, Papa."

"Hello, my dear son; hello, my darling daughter."

"And have you decided on names for them yet?" asked Eve.

"I have, yes. Our son is called Abel, and our daughter is Aklia."

ADAM MADE AN OFFERING for Abel and Aklia forty days later, and as a beam of light cascaded down upon the couple and their four children, they huddled together around the offering that burned so brightly against the night sky. And for that first family, yet another year had transpired, which meant they were at least that much closer to the time when God would finally rescue them and bring them back into the garden home they had longed for so very much.

Day of a Thousand Years

ENOCH CLOSED his book and looked out over this gathering of his family. By then, there were more than three times as many people listening to him since he had begun telling the story. He smiled graciously at the blossoming crowd. "Well, well, everyone. What did you think? Did you all enjoy the story of the Lord's creation and our very first parents?"

"Very much, Papa Enoch," chirped a child, around ten years old, in the front row.

"Good, Eli. That's very good. Did anyone learn anything from their example?"

Then Lamech stood up. "Of course, Grandfather. I learned that the Lord is faithful to all His promises, whether for good or for bad."

Enoch smiled proudly. "Excellent, Lamech."

"I must admit, Father," said Methuselah, "I also found your story to be most intriguing. If I didn't know better I'd swear you were telling the story as though you'd been there yourself."

"But that's what I've been trying to tell you. I was taken up to Heaven where I stood before the Face of God. Like molten iron, it glowed like the Sun. I've seen it with my own eyes. I've heard His voice with my own ears. Now everything He told me is in the books I've written for you."

Again everyone exchanged a look of consternation. Only Lamech's wife seemed sure of herself as she leaned in to Methuselah's wife, who looked just as perplexed as everyone else. "See, I told you he said he went to Heaven," Lamech's wife said quietly, much to the chagrin of her aunt.

Enoch grew suddenly melancholy. "But now He's only given me thirty days to tell you about it in person. It just doesn't seem fair somehow."

Baffled, Methuselah shook his head. "Please, Father, try and relax. You've obviously been through a very trying ordeal. You need your rest. You're delirious."

"Nonsense. I'm fine. It's just that what I'm trying to tell you is so important, and I don't have much more time to tell you." Enoch sprang to his feet, setting the book down in the seat behind him. "If only I could somehow get you to see what I've seen, hear what I've heard. Doesn't anyone here understand what I've been through in the slightest?"

Methuselah hung his head. "I wish I did, Father, really I do; but I'm afraid I don't."

"Well, then, try to imagine something for me, if you can. You've all seen me using my compass, haven't you?"

Methuselah looked up and, with the rest of the family, nodded. "Of course, Father, more times than I can count. You're a master craftsman."

"Yes, well, then try to imagine seeing the world from God's point-of-view: A Universe stretched out using the Lord's perfect compass. With it, I analyzed the Sun's orbit and counted off the hours it marks with its arc. I investigated everything concerning the Earth, every plant, every flower, every blade of grass. I discovered where the clouds live and how they create raindrops. I even saw the way of thunder and lightning, and how angelic guardians protect the Earth by restraining their power so their violent nature, harnessed in the thunderheads, won't destroy everything on the planet."

"Please, Pop, we understand," said Methuselah. "Now, have a seat, will you? You look tired."

"Tired? But I keep telling you: I'm fine! I've never felt better in my whole life!"

"What else did you see, Papa Enoch?" asked little Eli.

"Well, I saw the treasure houses of wind and ice, where I discovered the secrets of the wind, how they're brilliantly balanced throughout the globe to prevent earthquakes. I observed the key to the changing seasons, and I measured all the mountains, hills and rivers, all the fields and trees, right down to the very last stone."

"That's amazing, Grandfather," sighed Lamech. "And you say there are more books where we can read about these things?"

"That's exactly what I'm saying, Lamech, yes. If I saw it, I wrote about it, from the exalted Heavens, down to the depths of Hades and the place of judgment, where I saw tortured prisoners who all understood the nature of their judgment. I made a record of everyone being sentenced by the Eternal Judge, everything the accused have done, as well as all the verdicts. And that's when I saw *them* for the first time."

"Them?" blanched Methuselah.

"Yes, my son. *Them.*"

"What did you see, Grandpa?" asked Lamech in hushed tones.

"I saw the gatekeepers of Hades, huge serpents that had faces like extinguished lamps, with eyes of fire and teeth sharp as razors."

"Awesome," whispered Eli.

Aghast, Eli's mother stepped forward. "All right, Grandfather, enough with your spooky stories, really. The children will be having nightmares for weeks."

Taken aback, Enoch stared at her. "Nightmares? Why? From hearing the truth about God's creation? Nonsense, I tell you. It's good for them."

"So scaring children is a good thing now, is that it?" quipped Eli's mother.

"If having the privilege of understanding the Lord's actions is a scary thing," Enoch replied with a defiant nod, "then yes, I guess it is."

"It's all right, Grandfather," Lamech chimed in. "We're not scared. We appreciate what you're doing. You're a great man. The Lord has blessed you above all others by choosing you to be His mouthpiece."

"Oh, my dear boy," sighed Enoch. "God bless you for that. But now just look at me. What do you see? You see the Lord's eyes shining through me, like the Sun's rays, filling every one of you with awe." He then turned to the youngest member of the family. "I'm not frightening you, am I, Eli?"

"No, Papa Enoch," said Eli with an impish grin. "Not really."

"Of course not. God is wonderful. In fact, I saw how His actions are always good, unlike that of mankind, who sometimes does good and other times bad, and through this work of God, the heart of every evil person will be revealed for what it truly is."

"Then how come God didn't let Adam and Eve back into the Garden of Eden after five and a half days like He said He would?" The voice came from yet another young man, around the same age as Lamech, who stepped forward from out of the crowd.

"What's that, my boy?" Enoch squinted at the young man. "I'm sorry, my son, but I seem to have forgotten your name."

"My name is Jubal," said the young man.

Eli's mother nodded. "He's Lamech's cousin, twice removed."

"Oh, of course, yes," said Enoch apologetically. "The resemblance is most striking. You two could pass for brothers, twins almost. What was your question again, Jubal?"

Jubal calmly looked Enoch straight in the eye. "Didn't you tell us God promised to rescue Adam and Eve after five and a half days had transpired? So God never really did keep His promise to them, after all, did He?"

"Excuse me, Jubal, but I distinctly recall saying God promised to rescue Adam and Eve after five and a half of *His days*, not the kind of days you're thinking of."

Jubal shrugged his shoulders. "I still don't follow your meaning."

Not getting the response he was looking for, Enoch paced about for several moments. "Hmmm, let me see, maybe if I put it another way. I want you to stop and think about something for me, all right?"

Everyone except for Jubal respectfully nodded, but Enoch never even noticed him, having become so absorbed in his attempt to explain what was on his mind. "Good. Now, everyone remembers how God told Adam that he'd die the day he ate from the Tree of Knowledge, don't they?"

Again everyone but Jubal nodded in agreement.

"But he didn't die the same day, now did he? No. In fact, Adam actually went on to live to the ripe old age of nine hundred and thirty years before he finally died. Can anyone tell me why?"

Dumbfounded, the group stared back as they silently tried to figure out the answer.

"Come now, everyone?" urged Enoch. "How long do God's days last?"

"A thousand years?" said Lamech timidly.

"That's right. Now you're getting it. So, if God's days last a thousand of our years on Earth, then what?"

His eyes growing suddenly wide, Lamech raised his hand like an eager student.

"Yes, Lamech," said Enoch, nodding in approval. "Have you figured it out?"

Lamech smiled proudly and said, "Then, when Adam died at the age of nine hundred and thirty, it means that he still died on the first day of creation from God's perspective."

"Very good, Lamech. And?"

"And that means that when God told Adam that He'd rescue him after five and a half days, He was actually saying that He'd rescue him after five thousand, five hundred years had transpired."

"Exactly, Lamech, that's right! Very good, my boy. You're most observant. What's more, the Lord even went so far as to confirm this same promise to Adam and Eve's third son, Seth. When he was old enough to understand the truth, God also told him that He'd rescue Adam and his faithful descendants after five thousand, five hundred years. But that's not all, everyone. Do you know who else God personally told about His promise of five and a half days, besides Adam and Seth, I mean?"

Everyone there sat quite still, thinking the question over in their minds. Some of them looked to the person next to them to see if they knew, while others shrugged their shoulders or shook their heads, revealing that they had no idea.

"I know the answer, son," said Jared, quite matter-of-factly, as all eyes then turned to him.

"You, Grandfather?" wondered Methuselah. "How come you know who God told about His promise of days?"

"I know, my boy, because it was me. After God told Seth … many, many years later, God told me about it."

A subdued hush rippled through the crowd.

"Wow," sighed little Eli. "That is so amazing. But Papa Jared?"

"Yes, Eli."

"How come *you* never told us about the five and a half days?"

"But I did. I told you all about it. Don't you remember?"

"You did?" Looking rather puzzled, Eli squinted curiously. "You told me?"

"Of course, I did; certainly."

"But when did you tell me?"

"Just now. I told you about it just now."

"No you didn't," said Eli with an amused, little grin. "That was Papa Enoch who told us about it."

"Well, who do you think told him about it, my boy?"

Then turning to his mother, Eli smiled precociously at her. "Papa Jared is being silly, isn't he, Mama?

"He is, my love," she replied with a smile of her own. "That he is."

"So what do you think of that, everyone?" asked Enoch. "Now, all of you know about God's promise of days, too. How exciting."

"Thank the Lord above," shouted someone from the crowd.

"Thank God for His faithfulness, from generation to generation, and throughout all time," added Lamech.

Impressed, Enoch looked at his grandson for quite a while, deep in thought. "You know, Lamech, something has occurred to me."

"What, Grandfather?" asked Lamech.

"What you just said reminded me of something else God told me. And now I think I'd like to tell you all another story, and I want you to pay close attention to what your earthly father is telling you. If you think I'm difficult, just imagine how terrifying it is to appear before the Ruler of Heaven?"

Methuselah then chimed in. "We'll listen, Father. But will you please do us a favor?"

"What is it now, my boy?" Enoch replied, growing weary with trivial interruptions.

"Would you please sit down while you tell us your next story?"

All the children giggled, and Enoch smiled awkwardly. "Certainly, son." And turning to pick up his book, he plopped back down into his chair. "But don't expect me to lean back and put my feet up while I do."

"No, we'd never think that, Pop," said Methuselah with a wry smirk. "Not in a million years."

"Good; because more than anything else, the Lord wishes that you cheerfully endure every difficulty in life, all for His sake. That way you'll be sure to find your reward in the Day of Judgment, because on that day everything will be exposed on the weighing-scales and in the books."

"Tell us, Grandfather," Lamech pleaded. "What do the books say?"

"Yes, Papa Enoch," peeped little Eli. "Please tell us."

"Very well, my children. I'll tell you another story from the books of the Lord."

And again a hush fell over the crowd.

"Next week, that is." Enoch grinned at the disappointed looks on all the faces of everyone in the group, which obviously wanted to hear more.

"Next week?" groaned Lamech. "Why next week?"

"So people from far and wide can come to hear the same stories you're lucky enough to hear. Why else?"

"But why do we want that, Papa Enoch?" asked Eli.

"Well, why should you be the only ones to hear these remarkable stories? Don't you think the Lord would want others to hear them and learn to trust Him, too?"

Everyone nodded in agreement; all except for a sullen Jubal, that is, who surreptitiously withdrew from the front of the group and disappeared into the crowd.

"Certainly, Father," said Methuselah. "We understand now. The mercy of the Lord is available to anyone who will trust Him. Is that what you're saying?"

"That's right, son."

"Then that's what we'll do, Grandpa," added Lamech. "We'll invite everyone everywhere to come and listen to what God has shown you and told you."

ONE WEEK LATER, Enoch was seated before a huge gathering of people, and just as he had done before, he reverently cradled a large book in his lap. Scanning the entire group, he saw that not only were all of his sons there, sitting right in front, but his elders were there, too.

"Welcome, welcome, everyone," began Enoch. "I'm so glad to see that, in addition to Methuselah, the rest of my fine sons have decided to join us today. There's Regim, Riman, Uchan, Chennion and Gaidad. Good to see you boys."

They all nodded in recognition of their father, and Regim stood up and bowed on behalf of his brothers. "Thank you, Father, for inviting us. We're honored to be here."

"Don't mention it, son," replied Enoch with a wink. "Not only that, but I'd like to express my gratitude to our beloved elders who have also come to graciously offer their support today."

Even at their advanced ages, these men all still possessed a keen eye. Every one of them nodded, one by one, as Enoch acknowledged their presence. "Seated with my father Jared, there's my grandfather Mahalaleel, my great-grandfather Cainan, my great-great-grandfather Enos, and my great-great-great-grandfather Seth. Thank you, gentlemen. I'm more honored than you can ever imagine."

"You're welcome, my boy," replied Seth. "We're very pleased that you've invited us to hear what you have to say today."

With that, Enoch looked out across the hushed crowd. "In fact, it's good to see all of you today. Now, can anyone tell me why we're here?"

Again Regim stood, as if for the entire group this time. "Yes, Father, we've all come to hear everything the Lord of Heaven and Earth told you when He spoke to you face to face."

Enoch nodded benevolently and slowly opened his book. "Very good, Regim, thank you. Then listen closely, everyone, because I know all too well about the things I'm about to describe for you. Of all the people in this world, I was there when the Lord's voice thundered from the midst of swirling clouds."

Fire and Blade

Adapted from

The Book of Jasher,
also called
The Book of the Upright

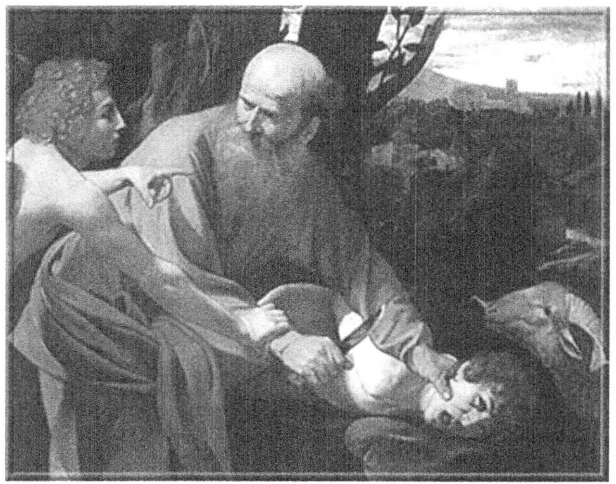

Sacrifice of Isaac, Carravaggio, 1603

Fire and Blade

Shooting Star

IN THE YEARS AFTER the Great Flood, Cush, the son of Ham and grandson of Noah, got married. He was getting to be an old man so when his wife gave birth to a son, he loved the child very much. They called him Nimrod, saying, "Once again men have begun to rebel against God."

In no time at all, the boy grew up, becoming a fine young man, and one day Cush presented him with a gift so special that he made sure to give it to him in the secrecy of his own tent.

With a tremendous smile of satisfaction, Cush handed Nimrod a package and said, "Here, my son; this is for you."

The young man eagerly reached out to take it. "Thank you, Father; but what's it for?"

"It's to honor your twentieth birthday. You're a man now, and because you're so special to me and your mother, I wanted you to have this."

Wide-eyed, Nimrod stared at the package. "What is it?"

"Why not open it and find out for yourself."

Tearing into the package, Nimrod found a loincloth made of sheepskin inside. Quite puzzled by them, he asked, "What's this?"

"It's a very special garment, my son."

"Oh?" said Nimrod, not entirely convinced. "What's so special about it? Did Mother make it just for me?"

Cush chuckled. "No, no. That's not why it's so special. It's special because this garment was the same one that God provided for Adam after he was expelled from the Garden of Eden."

Nimrod's eyes lit up. "No."

"Yes, it's true."

"But how did you get it?"

"Well, like you, my father … your grandfather, gave it to me when I was your age."

Running his fingers across the sheepskins, Nimrod smiled proudly. "Really? And how did Grandfather get it? Did God give it to him?"

Cush hesitated at this, momentarily taken aback. Clearing his throat, he continued. "Well, not exactly, no. You see, son, the story of these sheepskins goes back a very long way, as you can imagine."

Nimrod looked up at his father, quite expectantly. "Please tell me, Father. I want to know all about it."

"Of course, Nimrod, I'll tell you. To begin with, the garment was originally handed down to Enoch, the son of Jared, after Adam's death. Then, just before Enoch was taken up to Heaven by God, he gave it to his son Methuselah, and after he died Noah inherited it."

"Amazing. Then what?"

"When the time came, Noah wore it when he brought the animals into the Ark."

"Father, didn't you say these skins were special?"

Cush nodded. "Yes, son, I did. Why do you ask?"

"Oh, nothing; I was just wondering. Could that have been how Noah was able to control all the animals? Otherwise, how could he have gotten them all to cooperate with him?"

"Why, yes, Nimrod, it is. But how could you have possibly known something like that?"

Nimrod shrugged his shoulders. "I don't know. It just came into my mind, I guess."

Dumbfounded, Cush just stared back at his son for several moments.

"Is something wrong, Father? Have I made you angry?"

"No, of course not. As a matter of fact, I'm very pleased you've discerned this thing on your own. It's a tremendous omen. It can only mean one thing."

"It means the God Who walked and talked with Adam and Enoch and Noah is with me as well. Doesn't it, Father?"

Cush beamed back a smile, as proudly as any parent could. "Yes, my son, I do believe it does."

"Then just imagine what God has in store for me when I begin to wear these skins."

With that, Cush turned to leave. "Certainly I have imagined it for you, Nimrod, more than you can possibly know. Since the day you were born it has weighed heavily on me to do this thing, sensing somehow that this was what my father had in mind ever since he received it from Noah."

As Cush neared the door of the tent, a peculiar look flashed across Nimrod's face and his eyes thinned. "Don't you mean, ever since Grandfather *stole* it from Noah? Isn't that what you meant to say, Father?"

Startled, Cush turned back toward his son. Nodding cautiously, his lips barely parted. "Yes, Nimrod, that's right. Now, is there anything else I've failed to mention?"

"Of course, Father; it seems you forgot to remind me to keep your gift of these skins a complete secret, even from my own dear mother."

Cush nodded nervously. "Naturally," he whispered and then slipped out through the tent door.

TRUE TO NIMROD'S own prediction, when he began to wear the sheepskin garment of Adam, he became empowered by them. He quickly became a formidable hunter, using his bow and arrows with tremendous prowess. Then, he would reverently sacrifice many of the animals that he had killed on an altar. Lifting his eyes skyward, Nimrod exclaimed, "I pray that the Lord of Heaven and Earth accept this offering as an expression of gratitude for His care and protection."

AS ONE WARRIOR AMONG many in his clan, Nimrod slashed away at his enemies with his terrible, swift sword, whirling and stabbing, as if he already knew what his opponents were going to do before they did. If an opponent swung at him with his sword, Nimrod ducked well ahead of time. When an opponent whirled about in a different direction, he was already there with his blade to cut the man to pieces. And this happened in battle after battle as Nimrod steadily rose within the ranks of his family. He moved from the flanks of their battle array to the point where he entered the fray at the right hand of the leader, until finally he was the one leading the charge into enemy lines.

AT THE CONCLUSION of yet another of these conquests, Nimrod stood tall at the head of his troops, bloody sword raised in triumph, and let out a thunderous shout. "What say you to this, my brothers? God has helped me in so many battles, I've become invincible!"

Echoing his battle cry, the roar of his troops rippled through their ranks like an irresistible tidal wave.

"May God always help us, just as He does Nimrod," yelled one of his fellow warriors, "a mighty hunter before the Lord, invincible in battle!"

AS NIMROD SAT ONE day contentedly honing the blade of his sword, several of his soldiers came to him with heavy hearts and bowed.

"My Lord," began one of them, "I'm afraid to report the children of Japheth have attacked our people, and several members of your family have been captured."

"What fools," sneered Nimrod. "Don't they have any idea who they're dealing with? Very well, send word to mobilize every available warrior at once. We'll strike our enemies so swiftly, so brutally, they'll wish they'd never started this war with us."

WITHIN TWENTY-FOUR hours, Nimrod and his army were on the move, arrayed head to toe in their most formidable battle armor and every imaginable weapon of bronze.

As they marched toward the battlefield, Nimrod assured them. "Don't worry about a thing, men. With God's help, we're going to easily defeat our enemies, and you'll be able to do whatever you want with them. Trust me."

And with just five hundred warriors at his side, Nimrod smashed into Japheth's army, conquering it within hours of the engagement. Besides the hundreds of men they had killed in battle, Nimrod's troops had taken thousands of prisoners; among them, even women and children were led away in chains.

TEARFULLY REUNITED with his family, Nimrod and his troops headed for home. So grateful was his family for rescuing them that as soon as they got back they unanimously chose to make him king over them all. There and then, they placed a crown on his head. Equally intoxicated by the sting of battle and ecstatic at his meteoric rise to power, Nimrod raised his sword exultantly. "What say you now, my *people*?"

"All hail, King Nimrod," shouted one of his princes, "the mighty warrior of God!"

And the people roared back with a single voice, "All hail, King Nimrod!"

IN NO TIME, NIMROD could be found sitting on his gilded throne, entertaining a steady stream of dignitaries; among them was one man who stepped forward and bowed.

"And how is my new kingdom doing these days, Terah, my prince?" Nimrod asked.

"Very well, My Lord," replied Terah. "As you've requested, many of your princes, governors and judges have been set up in places of authority over your subjects, even as it is the custom among the kings throughout the land."

"Excellent," said Nimrod with a satisfied smile. "And above them all, I've placed you, my favorite prince."

Again Terah bowed. "I'm humbled by such an auspicious appointment, Sire, an appointment that, I must confess, still has me somewhat baffled."

"I don't understand. You mean to say you don't know why I've appointed you to such a position of authority."

"Not really, My Lord, no."

"Then maybe I appointed the wrong man."

Terah put up his hand in protest. "No, no, Sire. I mean, I think I might know why you've appointed me; that is to say, for all my years of dedicated service, my cunning administrative skills, my ruthless attention to detail."

Nimrod smiled slyly. "You've answered well."

"Then I'm correct in assuming you've promoted me because of these things?"

The king nodded with a smirk. "That, and the fact that your father is Nahor the First, of the line of Shem, the brother of Ham, my grandfather; which means you're from the good side of the family. Now, do you, or do you not, want to be chief prince over my army?"

"Of course, My Lord," replied Terah, bowing again. "I cannot thank you enough, and I forever pledge my loyalty to you, Great King."

"Yes, yes. Then quickly remove yourself from my sight, and proceed with your duties, before I grow weary with your groveling and change my mind."

CONVENING A MEETING with his princes, governors and judges, Nimrod eagerly leaned forward and said, "I've called you all here today because I've decided it isn't proper that a king of my stature and reputation should reside in such a puny, little province as this."

"What would you like us to do, Great King?" wondered Terah. "I, and all your loyal subjects, stand ready to execute your will."

"Good, because I want you to build me a city, a magnificent city with a majestic palace, one befitting your ... *great king*."

LED BY TERAH, HIS princes immediately spread out across the landscape, where they found a large valley facing westward and there construction began.

SURVEYING THE WORK of building, Nimrod nodded in approval. "I think I'll call this city of mine Shinar, because the Lord has vehemently shaken and destroyed all my enemies."

ONCE THE CONSTRUCTION of his city had been completed, vast numbers of people came to live with him on the plains of Shinar. They bowed to him and presented him with a tremendous assortment of gifts.

"Oh, Great King," said one man, bowing graciously and placing his gift at the foot of Nimrod's throne, "your fame has spread throughout the world; you are indeed the lord and master over all the sons of Noah. Now, everyone is following your advice, and before long the whole world will be speaking a single language, the language of your people."

NIMROD WENT OUT one morning, amongst the plains of Shinar to hunt for game with his bow and arrows. When he returned with his quarry, he sacrificed some of the animals he had killed on an altar, but this time, it was not an altar he had built for the God of Heaven and Earth but one made for idols fashioned by his own hands. "I pray these gods of wood and stone will accept this humble offering as an expression of my thanks for their care and protection."

Then, he turned and motioned to some of his family members, and they, too, came and laid their sacrifices on the altar. Following their lead, his princes came and did the same thing. Eventually, all of his subjects began to follow suit, until everyone was following in Nimrod's footsteps, sacrificing and bowing to idols made of wood and stone.

IN THE MEANTIME, Terah met and fell in love with a beautiful woman, and before long, the day of their marriage arrived. In a tremendous wedding ceremony, Terah and his bride were lavished by everyone in Shinar. Presided over by Nimrod, his princes, governors and judges, the event was attended by dignitaries from miles around. They all came to show their respects to Terah and his new wife. Sitting to Terah's right, as part of the wedding party, were two young men who bore a striking resemblance to him. They each picked up a cup of wine and stood together.

"Attention, everyone," said the man standing next to Terah. "Time to toast the happy couple." Then turning to his right, he asked, "Do you want to go first Nahor, or should I?"

"By all means, Haran, you're the oldest by fifteen minutes," quipped Nahor with a hearty grin. "So, first in birth, first to toast!"

"Very good," replied Haran, who proudly held up his cup. "I'd like to offer this toast to our father and his beautiful new bride. May they know only happiness together, and a long and prosperous life."

"Absolutely, brother," said Nahor, who then raised his cup. "We love them both very much, and wish a future for them that will bring everything they've always desired."

"May it come true," intoned all the guests with one voice as they held up their cups.

"Very nice, boys," said Terah, who then stood and hugged his two sons.

Then the king raised his glass to the happy couple. "Here's to the chief prince of my army and his lovely bride, Amthelo, the daughter of Cornebo. May his next child grow up to be even mightier than his father."

"Let it be so," exclaimed one of Nimrod's governors, "even as the king has proclaimed!"

And with a blast of music, the celebration kicked into high gear.

SOON TERAH'S WIFE bore him a son. As the midwife held up the screaming child, she turned to Terah. "Congratulations, My Lord, it's a boy. Have you decided on a name?"

"His name is Abram," replied Terah, beaming like the proudest father in the world, "because the king has promoted me far above the rest of his princes."

That whole day, Terah's family, along with Nimrod's people, celebrated the birth of Abram. Terah's house overflowed with guests as they happily ate and drank with him. Trays filled with an assortment of food were passed around, as was cup after cup of wine, which the guests all happily consumed well into the evening.

AS THE PARTY GUESTS began to say their goodbyes and depart, some of the king's sages and sorcerers were walking with them. Just then, one of them looked up into the night sky and saw something that absolutely astonished him. A huge star, shining very brightly, was soaring across the sky, traveling from east to west.

"Look!" exclaimed the sage, pointing skyward. "A shooting star!"

"It's an omen!" shouted a sorcerer.

Together, they watched as that single shooting star streaked through the night sky in four different directions, swallowing up four other stars in the process. Everyone watching was mystified by the spectacle; the sages and sorcerers, however, were more disturbed than amazed by what they saw.

"An omen?" wondered one of the onlookers. "Is it a good omen?"

The sages and sorcerers all exchanged disturbed looks amongst themselves.

"No, I'm afraid it's not," said one of the sages with a look of grim concern on his face. "This speaks of none other than the child that was born to Terah tonight."

"But what does it mean?" pressed the onlooker. "Why is this a bad omen concerning Terah's child?"

"Because the shooting star we just saw gobbled up four stars from the four corners of the night sky," insisted one of the sorcerers.

"So?" asked the onlooker with a shrug of his shoulders. "What's wrong with that?"

"An omen like this clearly foretells that when this child of Terah's grows up, he's destined to become very powerful," continued the sage. "In time, he'll flourish into a vast race of people, his children will kill great kings, and as a result will inherit all their land. Eventually, they'll acquire the entire world by means of their invincible power and will own it forever after."

Everyone there gasped.

"I don't know," continued the onlooker. "Maybe it was all just a trick of the light. Maybe we had too much to drink. Have you considered that?"

Perplexed, the group began to disperse, still obviously undecided about the true nature of what they had just seen. The sages and sorcerers, however, were going away with no such doubts in their minds. Far from being divided in their interpretation of this nighttime spectacle, they were unanimous in their appraisal. To a man, they were all clearly overwhelmed with a foreboding sense of dread and doom.

Child of Destiny

ASSEMBLED IN THEIR sacred hall the next morning, the king's sages and sorcerers looked just as concerned as they had the night before.

"Of course," began one of the sages, "the king has no idea about what happened last night at Terah's house. Am I correct in assuming this, gentlemen?"

"That is correct," replied one of the sorcerers. "No one's told him a thing. But you know, if he does find out someday, he's going to ask us why we kept the truth from him."

"He'll have us all killed then, for sure," muttered another of the sages.

The sorcerer scratched nervously at his flowing beard. "I say we go right now and tell Nimrod everything we saw."

"Should we tell him about our interpretation of the event?" asked one of the sages.

"Of course," insisted the sorcerer. "We should *especially* tell him about our interpretation! That way we'll all remain innocent of the matter."

APPEARING BEFORE Nimrod, the whole group reverently bowed before him.

"Long live the king of Shinar," said a sorcerer, who slowly stepped forward.

"Yes, yes, what is it?" asked the king, annoyed with the interruption.

"Well, My Lord, it appears that a child was born to Terah, son of Nahor the First, the chief prince of your army."

"I'm aware of that. What about it?"

"But, Sire, there's something else you may not be aware of yet."

"Really? What?"

"As we were leaving Terah's house, we observed a great star, soaring from the East, and this star swallowed up four other stars from the four corners of the night sky."

"Interesting," said Nimrod as he sat up in his throne. "What was your reaction?"

"We were all quite astonished, of course, even a little terrified."

"Yes, I see. Have you arrived at an interpretation for this event?"

"Certainly, Your Highness," replied a sage, who came forward and stood next to the sorcerer. "Our verdict of this matter was quite unanimous."

Nimrod leaned forward in anticipation. "Well, then? Tell me now!"

"Sire," continued the sage, "we're fully convinced this thing involves the child that was born to Terah! This portent of the star devouring the other stars signifies that he'll flourish and become incredibly powerful. He'll kill every king on Earth, and his descendants will inherit their land forever."

Nimrod's eyes became as big as saucers. "You mean to tell me this child, this son of Terah, is going to kill every king in this world, including *me*?"

"I'm afraid so, yes."

Nimrod gritted his teeth at the thought. "You've done well bringing me this news."

"Thank you, My Lord, for saying so. You see how we've faithfully reported everything concerning this child."

"Yes, yes, of course. Well done. You'll all be rewarded accordingly." Nimrod sat there for several agonizing moments. "Now, on to the question of what should be done to this son of Terah."

"Well, Sire," continued the sorcerer, "we think you should kill Terah's child before he ever has a chance to grow up, because if he's allowed to establish himself in our country, we'll all die for sure."

Mulling over the idea, Nimrod was obviously disturbed by such an outcome. He grimly nodded and said, "Very well. Have Terah brought before me immediately."

AS TERAH STOOD AT attention, Nimrod scrutinized him from his throne. "My dearest prince, I've just been told that when your son was born the other day, astounding things were seen in the Heavens, all because he's supposed to be special; so special, I'm told, it's prophesied that when he grows up, he'll conquer the whole world. Is this true?"

Terah timidly nodded. "Yes, My Lord, I suppose it is."

"Then I want you to give me the child right now."

"Give him to *you*? Then what will you do with him?"

"Naturally, I'm going to kill him before he has a chance to destroy us all," the king replied, quite matter-of-factly. "Of course, I'll pay you handsomely for your trouble. In fact, I'll fill your entire house until it overflows with silver and gold."

"Excuse me, Sire," said Terah, trying to remain calm. "I hear what you're saying, and of course I'll do anything you want. But, please, can I first tell you about what happened to me the other day? Then maybe I'll be able to better respond to your generous offer."

Nimrod stared thoughtfully at his favorite prince for several tense moments. "Very well, my friend, go ahead."

"Well, you see, uh, last week, an associate of mine came to me and said, 'Give me the beautiful horse the king gave you, and I'll pay you well. Just name your price.' But I told him,

'Not so fast. Wait until I ask the king about your offer, and I'll do whatever he decides.' So, Your Highness, now that you've heard my story, what do you think I should do?"

"You idiot! How could you even *think* of selling the fine horse I gave you? That horse is priceless! There isn't another one like it in the whole world!"

"But, Sire, that's exactly what you're asking me to do with my son."

A look of recognition swept across Nimrod's face as he suddenly realized Terah was using this parable to talk about him. Initially embarrassed, the king next became infuriated.

"But, of course, My King," continued Terah, "everything I have is still in your power. Do whatever you want with me. Yes, even my son is in your power, without receiving anything in exchange for him. Even his two older brothers are yours, too."

"No, no, of course not," said Nimrod, settling back down in his throne, somewhat appeased. "Don't be ridiculous. I only want to purchase your youngest son."

"Then, please, Your Highness, could you at least give me three days to consider all this for myself? Allow me the chance to talk with my family about what you're asking me."

"Fine, I'll give you three days. But only because I hold you in such high esteem."

"Yes, Benevolent One, of course," said Terah, bowing graciously. "Thank you so much. I can't tell you—"

"Enough already. You know I hate when you grovel."

THREE DAYS LATER, the king's official deputy was pounding on Terah's front door. "Terah, chief prince of Nimrod, the king says your time is up! You must comply with the royal decree to send your son for the price he spoke about, and if you don't hand him over, everything in your house will be slain, and not even a dog will be left alive."

Terah quickly ran into the back room, where he took one of his concubine's newborn sons and gave the infant to the deputy, who paid him handsomely.

DELIVERING THE CHILD to the king's court, the deputy handed him over to Nimrod. As he held the child in his arms, Nimrod wrestled in his mind for a moment. "Tell me, Deputy, are you sure this child is the one my sages and sorcerers predicted would topple my kingdom?"

"He is, Your Highness. I saw Terah retrieve him from his house with my own eyes."

Having satisfied himself, the king then took the baby and, with all his strength, smashed his head into the ground.

UNDER THE COVER OF night, Terah spirited little Abram away, along with his mother and nurse, and concealed them in a cave.

"Now, I want the three of you to stay here awhile," said Terah, "and I promise, you'll all be safe from the wrath of Nimrod."

"Wait, what about you?" blurted Amthelo. "You're not going to just leave us here all alone, are you?"

"But I have to return to my duties, dear, or else the king will get suspicious. Besides, who better than me to ensure the necessary provisions are delivered to you every month?"

"Don't *dear* me, husband. How can you be so callous, just abandoning us like this?"

"I'm sorry, Amthelo, but I don't see that we have much choice in the matter. If I don't return, then we merely put the boy back into harm's way. Now, I promise, in six months this whole thing will blow over, and Nimrod and his men will forget it ever happened."

LATE ONE EVENING, Terah came to visit his wife in the cave. After warmly greeting her, however, Terah found that she was not nearly as pleased to see him as he was to see her. But Terah just shrugged it off.

"I can't tell you how good it is to see you, Amthelo," he began. "Things have been damned difficult back at the palace. You don't even want to know how hard it's been to get away from there, let alone manage to have all your supplies delivered without the king's knowledge. I trust my men have been faithful in that regard, have they not?"

Unimpressed, Amthelo nodded while a young boy, around ten years old, stood just behind her, as if he were using her as a shield. "They have," she grumbled reticently.

"Good, good," said Terah with an awkward smile. "After all, you're both very important to me. Just because I'm not here in person doesn't mean I'm not thinking about you two all the time. Always remember that." Terah took several steps forward, obviously trying to get a better look at the boy. "Hello, son; how've you been? He looks well enough. What is Abram now, anyway? Seven, eight years old?" Looking back to his wife, Terah was met with a frown.

She snapped, "He's ten."

"Ten years old?" Terah exclaimed proudly, still trying to avoid the fact that his wife was so irked. "Really? And he's still being a good boy for you, I hope, living here like this."

Growing more perturbed by the moment, Amthelo nodded sternly. "Well, yes. Considering he hasn't had a father all these years, he's been a very good boy."

Terah stepped over to his son and bent down to give him a perfunctory pat on the head. "What do you mean he's never had a father? Of course he has a father. Who else has been taking care of him all these years? Isn't that right, son?"

Young Abram, however, just stared back at Terah, as if he were a complete stranger.

"I mean a *real* father," scoffed Amthelo. "What happens when he starts to become a man? What happens when he starts asking me why his father is never around? Then what?"

Terah turned to his wife and, in hushed tones, said, "Then we'll deal with that when it happens. Until then, I've decided that maybe it would be best if we took the boy to live with Noah and Shem."

"Oh, thank God," said Amthelo with a tremendous sigh of relief. "It's about time. Anything would be better than living here in this miserable cave."

AMTHELO, YOUNG ABRAM and his nurse soon left the cave and, accompanied by half a dozen men, traveled quite some distance before they eventually reached some foothills.

Turning to one of the men with them, Amthelo asked, "Are you sure you know where you're going?"

"Of course, ma'am. The home of Noah and Shem lies beyond these hills, hidden away in a mountain stronghold, in a land forgotten long ago by the world." As the man spoke, he turned his eyes north toward a foreboding mountaintop beyond the foothills where they stood. "To this day only a handful of followers remain loyal to the great patriarch and his son, while the rest of mankind has completely abandoned the ways of the Most High."

Amthelo took a long look at the mountaintop he was referring to and then turned back to him with her nervous eyes. "You mean, we're going up there?"

"Yes, ma'am. Those were my instructions. Do you wish to turn back?"

Amthelo and Abram's nurse exchanged a concerned look while the rest of the men continued on, unaware of their reluctance.

"Somehow I don't see we have much choice," murmured Amthelo and, taking hold of Abram's hand, haltingly started after the group.

ARRIVING AT THE HOME of Noah, they were greeted right away by Shem. Kneeling down, he shook young Abram's hand. "Hello, Abram; welcome. It's good to see you, son. Did your mother tell you who I am?"

Abram nodded bashfully. "You're my great, great, big, big grandfather."

"Very good. What a fine boy you're growing up to be," he said, nodding to Amthelo, who beamed the smile of a proud mother.

NIMROD AND HIS subjects, meanwhile, continued to bring their burnt offerings to their endless array of idols. Doing exactly as Nimrod had taught them, the people reverently bowed to these idols, and even though they were incapable of responding in any way, they persisted in sacrificing their animals to them. In Terah's house, there were twelve idols, one for each month of the year. Most of them were quite large; some were made of wood and some, of stone. And when Terah finished preparing his sacrifice, he would proudly bring his meat offering to his idols and lay it at the foot of one of them, depending on the month.

IN THE HOME OF NOAH and Shem, however, young Abram would sit for hours and listen to a very different kind of teaching.

"Whatever you do, Abram," said Noah, "never forget there is a God Who rules the Earth and all its inhabitants, a God Who alone is worthy of our praise and sacrifice, a God Who lives in the Heavens above, a place of incorruptible majesty."

"Can you remember that, Abram?" asked Shem.

Abram nodded eagerly. "Yes, Father Shem. The Lord of Heaven and Earth is the only One Who is worthy of our sacrifice and praise."

"Not only that, Abram," continued Shem, "but the Lord of Heaven and Earth is the only One you should ever obey. Anyone who tells you to do something that your Heavenly King would disapprove of isn't worthy of your allegiance or obedience, no matter how many thousands or tens of thousands bow down to that man."

"Do you understand?" asked Noah.

Again young Abram nodded. "Yes, Father Noah. No earthly king should ever stand in the way of what the King of the Universe wants me to do."

"Good, Abram, very good," continued Noah. "The Lord is very proud of you and everything you're learning."

"Do you have any questions, son?" asked Shem.

"Yes, Father Shem, I do," he replied with a precocious gleam in his eye.

"Well, Abram, go ahead," prodded Noah. "What is it?"

Slowly, the words formed in Abram's mouth, and then they came out. "What does God look like?" he said with a smile, revealing the missing tooth in his childish grin.

Noah and Shem burst out laughing, causing young Abram's smile to grow even bigger.

AS ABRAM WENT OUT into the fields one day, he was accompanied by his dog. As the two of them wandered aimlessly, something sparked Abram's curiosity. "Hey, boy," he said, squinting up at the Sun. "Did you ever notice the way that great ball of light glows as it moves across the sky? I wonder if that's God. Maybe we should serve Him."

So Abram sat down with his faithful companion, and together they basked all day in the warmth of the Sun, but when evening came, the Sun set and disappeared. "Hey, where'd it go, boy? I guess that wasn't God after all. I wonder Who did create the Heavens and the Earth. Where could He be?"

Soon the night darkened around them, and looking up, Abram noticed the Moon, lit brightly against the starry sky. "Of course, that must be the God Who made the Universe. And look, those are His servants all around Him."

So they sat and stared all night at the Moon and the stars, but as the evening dragged on, Abram grew too tired to continue, so he fell fast asleep.

THE NEXT MORNING, Abram was rudely awakened by his dog licking his face. Sitting up, he realized that the Moon had disappeared and the Sun had returned, and with it, the daylight. Abram looked around, and surveying his surroundings, he exclaimed, "Of course, boy, none of those things were God. None of them made the world or the people in it. They're all just God's servants. I'll bet you anything He lives somewhere else."

Overjoyed, Abram jumped to his feet and started to walk back home. "I can't wait to tell Father Shem and Father Noah, boy. They'll be so proud of what we figured out." And before Abram had taken more than three steps, he broke into a full run, followed by his faithful companion, who galloped happily alongside him, wagging his tail the whole time.

Tower of Folly

NIMROD'S PRINCES, along with the most influential men from his family, came together for a meeting. This time, though, it was Nimrod's father, Cush, who presided over the gathering.

"Welcome, everyone. It does my heart good to see you've all dragged yourselves here today!" exclaimed Cush, eliciting a boisterous cheer of approval from the group. He motioned proudly to three men to his right. "Even my kid brothers Phut, Mizraim and Canaan have managed to join us!"

"Thank you, big brother," said Canaan with a hearty salute. "Glad to be here."

"Good. Now, as you all know, for many years the mighty Nimrod has been ruling his kingdom with an iron fist, and he's been doing it from this great and glorious city of Shinar. But today I'm here to tell you, it's time to build another city, an overflowing city, one that will extend the fame and glory of our kingdom into all the Earth! So, I ask you, here and now: Who is with us?"

Everyone enthusiastically thrust their swords skyward. "We are!" roared the group in thunderous unison.

"Good, because not only do we intend to establish a new city, but we also plan to construct a magnificent tower in the very heart of it, a tower so huge, so colossal, it will reach Heaven itself! Our enemies will be so dismayed, they'll never even think about going to war with us again! We'll rule the world, and our names will go down in history forever!"

Again the group burst out with a resounding cheer.

CUSH AND HIS THREE brothers next went to Nimrod's palace, where the king sat smugly on his gilded throne.

"Then it's agreed," said Nimrod with a satisfied grin. "It's time to unleash the full potential of my kingdom, until no one is beyond my command. Send a thousand men to look for a place to build our new city, somewhere suitable to construct this mighty tower."

LIKE A THOUSAND milling insects searching for a morsel of food, a vast array of men fanned out across the countryside, inspecting every square foot for miles around.

CANAAN SOON RETURNED with a report for the king. "I believe we've found a suitable location for your mighty ambition, nephew."

Nimrod smiled approvingly. "Very good. You've done well, Uncle Canaan. Where?"

"A lush valley, just two days east of Shinar."

"Then let the work begin. And may this kingdom of ours never be the same again."

"Certainly, my nephew, My King," said Canaan, bowing reverently. "Let it be so, even as you have decreed."

THE LAND BEGAN TO swarm with determined workers, moving in every direction, like a vast colony of single-minded ants, making their way back and forth from a central hub in the valley. One group of workers set about excavating clay, which was scooped in huge quantities from hillside after hillside. The next group placed the clay, mixed with sand and straw, in tens of thousands of wooden moulds. Once removed from these moulds, the wet bricks were set out in row after row, to dry in the heat of the noonday Sun. Another group hauled these naturally-dried bricks to crude kilns, where they were fired and cooled into finished bricks, while yet another hauled the bricks to an enormous circle that was forming around this central hub, which was at last used by those who did the actual construction of the city and the tower.

Within six months, the foundations of the city and the tower were complete, and a little more than a year later, so was the city itself. But long after the buildings were finished, the tower continued higher still, brick by brick and layer by layer. Eventually, huge ramps were built to hoist the workers, along with their bricks and mortar, to the next layer of the tower, which then became the next level and, in turn, the next section.

A BURLY CONSTRUCTION worker stopped what he was doing with his brick and mortar one day and asked the man next to him, "Hey, you ever worry that what we're doing here is wrong?"

Confused, his co-worker mumbled, "Wrong? What do you mean, wrong? I don't get you."

"This tower; you know, a tower built to reach Heaven, and all. Don't you ever wonder if god might get mad at us for doing it?"

"God? Which god?"

"How should I know?" he replied with a shrug of his huge shoulders, and thinking better of it, he went back to laying his next brick. "Never mind. Forget I even mentioned it."

SO THE TOWER CONTINUED to rise, slowly but surely, higher and higher. As it did, Cush and his three brothers watched proudly, as though on a sacred vigil.

"Just think, brothers," said Cush with tremendous satisfaction, "someday we might even be able to start a war with god himself."

"You might be onto something, brother," remarked Phut. "At this rate, the tower will be high enough to reach the gates of Heaven before you know it."

"And when it is," boasted Mizraim, "we'll strike down every last one of god's pathetic angels with our fearsome arrows."

"Then no one will stop our warriors from invading his kingdom," swore Canaan, "and when we have, we'll set up our own gods of worship."

THE TOWER EVENTUALLY soared to such a tremendous height that it took a full year to carry the bricks and mortar to the top. Some men ascended, while others descended. And when a brick fell from their hands and broke, they would weep over it, but when a man fell and died, none of them would pay the slightest attention to him.

AT NOAH AND SHEM'S home, meanwhile, Abram was growing up nicely, continuing to learn more and more from his two mentors.

"So, Abram, do you have any questions about the Lord?" asked Shem.

Nodding, Abram smiled precociously, "Yes, sir, I do. I still want to know what God looks like. Doesn't anybody know?"

With a tilt of his head, Shem turned to Noah. "He is a persistent one, isn't he?"

"That he is, my boy, that he is," replied Noah, who patted Shem on the back and turned to leave. "He sprang from your loins, didn't he?"

"Where do you think you're going?" Shem asked plaintively. "The boy is posing a good question here. He needs an answer."

But Noah just kept on walking. "Not to worry, son. I'm sure you can handle it. After all, it's only the most impenetrable mystery of creation. Consider it a personal challenge."

Shem shook his head, partly in amusement, partly in frustration. "Great," he muttered, then turned to gaze into the face of young Abram, who was still patiently waiting for an answer.

"Well, Father Shem?" persisted Abram. "Hasn't anybody seen the Face of God? I mean besides the people who've died and gone to Heaven."

"Sure, Abram, I guess so, if you put it that way. There has been one man in the history of our people who's been fortunate enough to see God and live to tell the tale. But that was a long time ago."

"Tell me, tell me," exclaimed Abram, his face lighting up. "Who was he?"

"His name was Enoch, and he was a great man whom God deemed worthy to translate into His very presence without ever having to taste the bitterness of death."

"Really? But why him?"

Again Shem stared back for several moments, stumped for a response.

"Well, unfortunately, that's still a mystery, my boy. I don't think we'll ever know for sure why God chose Enoch. It's hard to say why the Lord chooses anyone for that matter. The most obvious answer, of course, is because Enoch had tremendous faith in God. He worshiped the Lord no matter how much the rest of mankind refused to obey Him."

"Did he tell anybody what God looked like?"

"Certainly, Abram. He told his whole family, and then he wrote all about it in books he wrote for his descendants, like you and me."

"So what did he say? I mean, about how God looked."

"According to Enoch, his description of what he saw in Heaven was of a remarkably awesome Face."

"A Face?"

"Yes, a molten Face of God, with brilliant sparks that shot out every which way."

"Was Enoch scared?"

"Sure, at first. Fear of the Lord is, after all, the beginning of wisdom. But once God spoke to Enoch, he immediately realized He was also a Supreme Being of tremendous compassion and love."

"Oh, Father Shem, thank you so much for telling me all this," Abram said, stepping forward to hug Shem. "I hope someday the Lord will deem me worthy of some great mission for His sake; if not as important as Enoch's, like being translated into His presence and writing books about it, then at least in some small way to serve such a majestic God as Him."

"You're welcome, Abram," replied Shem with a sigh of relief. "And I hope the same thing for you as well. God bless you, son."

HIGHER AND HIGHER, Nimrod's tower continued to grow, when one day his men took a break from their arduous task. From the uppermost section of the tower, they shot arrows into the sky, and when they fell to the ground, they were covered in blood. Examining one, a man triumphantly shouted, "I think we just killed someone in Heaven!"

"Hurry," roared another. "Let's build faster!"

So, intensifying their efforts, they continued building the tower, until the years eventually turned into decades.

AS THE MOLTEN FACE of God looked down on their construction project, He turned to the seventy angels who stood nearest to Him. "For nearly forty years," said the Face, "I've watched the building of this tower, reaching higher and higher, till finally it's risen more than a mile and a half above the plain of Shinar. But now, I've grown weary with their folly. Come, it's time to go down and confuse the language of everyone who's building that infernal tower. That way no one will be able to understand what anyone is saying anymore, and work on the tower will grind to a halt."

"As You wish, Lord," replied one of the angels.

SWOOPING DOWN FROM Heaven, the seventy angels began to pass imperceptibly through the ranks of the builders. With a single invisible touch, the workers were, one by one, plunged into a state of utter confusion. Whenever a builder wanted something from a co-worker, like a hammer, he tried asking for it. But what came out of his mouth sounded like gibberish, so his co-worker would hand him something he had not asked for, like a brick. When he found that it was not what he wanted, he would simply throw it away, and invariably, the thing he tossed aside would then strike another one of the builders somewhere down the line, either maiming or killing them in the process.

QUITE A NUMBER OF MEN were struck down that way, and dismayed by such mayhem and chaos, the men building that tower eventually began to go insane. Some men began wandering around as brute as apes, while others turned against one another with their bows and arrows. The rest of the builders who witnessed these horrors began to abandon their work, little by little, dropping their tools and walking away.

A VIOLENT EARTHQUAKE suddenly struck the place, and the ground opened up, swallowing a third of the tower. Not only that, but fire fell from the sky, too, burning up another third of it. As a result, so many men died at that tower that when the onlookers came to survey the devastation, they could hardly walk without stepping on the corpse of one of the construction workers. Only a third of the tower remained, jutting up out of the ground, left as a grim reminder of the folly of those who attempted to defy the God of Heaven.

WHEN ABRAM HAD GROWN up to be a fine-looking young man, a messenger came to the home of Noah and Shem. Noah read the letter and sadly handed it over to Shem, who was also deeply moved by the news.

"What is it?" wondered Abram. "Is there something wrong?"

"It appears that one of your forefathers has died, Abram."

"Died?" said Abram. "Who died?"

"Your grandfather, Nahor the First, son of Serug, has died," murmured Noah.

Shem hung his head in mourning. "But he was still so young."

"How old was he?" asked Abram.

"Nahor was only three hundred and four years old," replied Noah. "It seems as though men are simply not living as long as they used to. What a pity."

"That's terrible," exclaimed Abram. "How old are you, Father Shem?"

"Who, me?"

Noah grinned at Shem. "Old Shem, here; he's a middle-aged man, now. Or at least what used to be considered middle-aged."

"Really?" said Abram. "How old is that?"

"I'm four hundred and thirty-nine."

Abram's eyes widened. "Wow, that is old."

Shem smiled reluctantly. "You think I'm old? Father Noah has us all beat. He's more than nine hundred years old."

Astonished, Abram turned to Noah. "Really, Father Noah? Are you really that old?"

"That's right, my boy," he replied with a weary nod. "And soon, I'll be standing before the Face of God, too, just as Nahor is at this very moment. So as difficult as it for us to accept the absence of our loved ones, it's actually a blessing for those who have passed from this life to the next."

"So what you're saying is," Abram slowly said, trying to visualize what he was hearing, "Grandfather now knows firsthand what I've been seeking to know my whole life."

"That's right, Abram," added Shem, proud of his student. "Today, he knows what God looks like."

IN THE AFTERMATH of the earthquake at Nimrod's tower, the king and several of his princes stood on a nearby hilltop, surveying the devastation.

"How the mighty have fallen," muttered Nimrod, half to himself, half to his men.

"What's that, My Lord?" wondered Terah.

"Oh, nothing, really. I was just contemplating how, in a matter of minutes, a magnificent city like this could simply vanish from the face of the Earth."

"What will we do now, Sire?"

"We'll rebuild, of course. What else can we do?"

"Naturally, My Lord. Then we'll commence to rebuild the city at once." Terah whirled about and turned to leave.

But Nimrod raised his hand. "Wait, wait; something has just occurred to me."

Stopping, Terah looked back in anticipation. "What is it, Your Highness?"

"I've decided I must respond to this disaster in a manner befitting my great kingdom, a manner that will commemorate, for all time, the adversity I and my people have endured in this misbegotten place."

Terah nodded thoughtfully. "Very good, My Lord. What will you have us do? Should we make the city even larger and mightier than before?"

"No," replied Nimrod with a capricious twinkle in his eye. "Where there used to be a single city, I want *four new ones* built to replace it."

Befuddled, Terah considered the king's declaration. "I see, Sire," he mumbled.

Irked, Nimrod growled, "What's that? I didn't quite hear you, Chief Prince of My Army?"

"I said, I'll see to it right away, Sire," exclaimed Terah as he turned again to leave.

Quite pleased with himself, Nimrod grinned from ear to ear.

THE SURVIVORS FROM amongst the construction workers of that tower soon spread out across the landscape, where they began their monumental effort of not simply rebuilding one city but four of them in its place.

AS WAS HIS CUSTOM, Nimrod stood with Terah and his associates at his side, atop a nearby hillside, supervising the rebuilding efforts. "Tell me, my princes, what do you think of my ambitious project now? Did any of you actually think it could have been accomplished so quickly?"

"Most impressive, My Lord," replied one his princes. "You've outdone even yourself."

"Thank you, Chedorlaomer. And what about you, Arioch?"

"Who would have thought that less than a decade ago, this land lay in complete ruin?" said Arioch. "But today, here it is in all its glory, a testament to your enduring legacy."

"And you, Tidal, what's your opinion?"

"Truly magnificent, Your Highness. Lying before us are nothing less than four more jewels in your illustrious crown of achievements."

Nimrod nodded proudly, exhaling a satisfied sigh.

"Have you decided what you will name your new cities, My King?" asked Terah.

"I have, yes," he replied with an impish grin, "and according to the practice of our day, I'm naming them in memory of what we've all experienced as a result of building our mighty tower to Heaven."

Puzzled, Terah and the other princes exchanged a nervous look amongst themselves.

"Really, My Lord?" Terah said cautiously. "And what, may I ask, have you decided upon?"

"The first city I've named Babel because god confused the language of everyone there. The second city is called Erech because god scattered the people from that place. The third is Eched because there was a tremendous battle with god in that land. And the fourth is Calnah because I provoked god, and as a result, my princes and warriors were consumed there."

For several, intense moments, his princes stood there, unable to respond, until finally, apparently bored with the spectacle, Nimrod began to walk away. "Now, my princes, I bid you all, good day. Carry on with your duties. I'm sure there's still a lot of work to be done."

No one moved a muscle as they all watched the king leave. Then, when they were sure that he was no longer within hearing distance, Chedorlaomer turned to the others and grumbled, "The arrogance of that man. God crushes his ill-conceived tower, nearly wiping out an entire civilization, and then he has the audacity to mock us by trivializing the matter."

"What could he be thinking," blurted Tidal, "naming cities to commemorate such a black day in the history of our people? And cities, mind you, built upon the backs of these same people."

"Well, I, for one, have had it," continued Chedorlaomer. "If he insists on bringing us all down with his reckless abandon, I think we'll have to give *him* a name to commemorate his stupidity in building that damned thing!"

"Then so be it," said Arioch, raising his hand in a mock salute. "From this day forward, ignominious King of Shinar, you will be known as Amraphel because your princes and warriors fell as a result of your foolishness at that tower. All hail, King Amraphel!"

Together, they all followed suit, raising their hands with him, exclaiming, "All hail, King Amraphel!"

BACK HOME IN SHINAR, Nimrod resumed his favorite pastime of sitting on his gilded throne, receiving a steady stream of dignitaries.

As one foreign prince came bearing gifts, he humbly bowed before Nimrod. "Greetings, King Nimrod, I wish to congratulate you on this the inauguration day of your four newest crown jewels. And I especially wish to commend you on the naming of your latest cities, built to extend your fame and glory throughout the entire world."

Benevolently, the king nodded. "You've spoken well, sir. Your gracious words are much appreciated."

"It is particularly heartening to see that since the destruction of that abominable tower, you've chosen to memorialize God's judgment to the benefit of all mankind. The Lord, I'm sure, is most pleased you've honored His actions in this way."

Tilting his head oddly, Nimrod sat up on his throne and glared down with furrowed brow. "Excuse me, my good man, but I think you've completely misunderstood my motive in the naming of my new cities. My intention was not to honor some unknown god who capriciously hides behind a mask of anonymity but to mock the mindless fates that inexplicably struck down my heroic efforts."

"B—*but I* don't understand. I thought for sure, after such a crushing blow, I mean—"

"You thought *what*?" barked Nimrod, who became increasingly irritated. "That I'd lost my nerve, that I'd repented of my decision to honor the gods of my own choice?"

"Why, yes, what else would I have thought?"

"Well, then, my deluded friend, you are sorely mistaken, aren't you? Now, before I lose my temper and demonstrate what divine retribution is really like, I suggest you leave my presence immediately."

ABRAM WAS HAVING lunch with Shem and Noah several months later.

"Well, Abram," began Shem, "it's hard to believe, but it's been forty years since you came to live with Noah and I."

"My word," Noah said wistfully. "It seems like only yesterday. How old are you now, anyway?"

"I just turned fifty, sir."

"Ah," said Noah with a playful smile, "you're still just a child."

"But, sir, I've grown up in more ways than you can imagine."

"It's true, Father," said Shem. "Abram is a grown man now, a man in whom God has given a unique heart of understanding."

"Is that so?" Noah asked thoughtfully. "Then tell me, Abram, what's the most important thing you've learned in all your years with us?"

Abram pondered the question for several moments and then confidently replied, "I've come to realize that all the efforts of this idolatrous generation are as useless as their false gods."

Proudly, Shem looked at Noah and winked. "See, Father, I told you he was ready."

IN THE NEIGHBORING territory of Elam, another king was, at that same time, holding court with several of his princes, and this king was none other than Nimrod's own prince,

Chedorlaomer.

One of his princes graciously bowed. "King Chedorlaomer, we came as soon as you called. How may we serve you today?"

"I've made a rather momentous decision today, and in light of recent developments, I believe the time is ripe to act upon it."

"Tell us, My King, what have you decided?"

"Well, you all know how I've faithfully served King Nimrod as one of his chief princes for many years. Without question, I've obeyed his every command. Even when he decided to build that damned tower of his, I never hesitated to supply him with as many men and materials as he desired. But it's been ten years since the confusion of tongues, and our kingdom has never been the same since."

"I heartily agree, My Lord. It's taxed all my skills as an administrator just to reorganize and maintain our standing army."

"Tell me, then; how would you rate your efforts? Is my army ready for action?"

"They are, yes. They thirst for action. Men like that grow restless with nothing to test their mettle."

"Excellent."

"What did you have in mind?"

"One last thing," replied Chedorlaomer, carefully considering a new thought. "And please be frank with your response. I'll hold your answer in the utmost confidence, of course."

"What is it, Sire?"

"Have you heard what the people are saying about Nimrod? Behind his back, I mean."

"Naturally, My Lord, news of such a nature always spreads like wildfire. Any man who seeks to uphold the highest position in the land is always a target for this sort of derision."

"What have you heard, then?"

"I've heard that since the rebuilding of his cities, his own people have begun to call him by a new name, that of Amraphel, because his princes and warriors were struck down at that tower because of his foolishness."

"What does that tell you?"

"It tells me the once and great king of Shinar has lost his grip on the hearts and minds of the very people who have faithfully served him. It tells me that, just as you have said, the time is ripe."

"So it is, yes. The time is at hand to put an end to the tyranny of Nimrod."

"And not a moment too soon, My Lord. Have you heard what's being said of his own son?"

"What? That his son Mardon is proving to be an even greater menace than his father?"

"But it's true. Men have even begun to spread a proverb concerning his evil ways. Are you aware of it?"

"I am. 'From wickedness proceeds even more wickedness.'"

"Exactly."

"Then it's settled. We must uproot this weed before another one has a chance to grow up alongside it, one even more pernicious than the first."

"Will we be attacking Nimrod head on, then?"

"Certainly not. We're still in no position to take the bull by the horns yet. We'll attack the Five Cities of the Plain, Sodom and Gomorrah and her neighbors. Once we've brought them under our sway we'll consolidate our power. Then we'll be ready to bring down the tyrant, once and for all."

"An excellent idea, My Lord."

"Then make the necessary arrangements. Let my army prepare itself for battle. Let all my people know what we have decided today. Let everyone know that the time for revolution is upon us all."

CHEDORLAOMER'S ARMY was on the move before long, and with terrible swiftness, it struck into the heart of the Cities of the Plain. With hacking swords and flying arrows, the warriors of Chedorlaomer fanned out through the five cities, besieging the inhabitants with remorseless fury.

WHEN HIS TROUBLED messenger came and bowed before him, Nimrod was, as usual, relaxing on his gilded throne. Concerned by the look on the man's face, the king sat up in anticipation.

"Tell me, messenger; you have bad news for me, don't you?"

"I'm afraid so, Your Highness. Your great kingdom has suffered a terrible blow today. What's worse, this treachery has been dealt upon you by none other than one of your very own princes."

Bolting to his feet, Nimrod was incensed. "What prince of mine would dare such a thing? Tell me his name, and I'll blot him out of existence."

"It's Chedorlaomer, and he's attacked the Five Cities of the Plain. As of this moment, the army of Elam appears unstoppable. Sodom and Gomorrah have already fallen, and the other three are on the verge of complete collapse."

Disheartened, the king sat back down and slowly sank into his throne. "My power, my power," he whispered, "what is happening to my power?"

"What's that, My Lord? I couldn't hear you."

"Never mind." Nimrod looked back at his messenger with hollow eyes. "I wasn't addressing you."

"Then what should I tell your princes? They look to you for guidance, Sire. They wonder when you will organize them in a counter-attack."

But the king remained unmoved. "Tell them," he continued, simmering to a boil, "*tell them* I've grown weary with their incompetence."

Confused, the messenger stood there, mouth agape. "Excuse me, My Lord? You want me to tell them that?"

"Yes, yes, tell them exactly that, word for word," snapped Nimrod with a wave of his hand. "Now, leave me, before I grow weary of your services, too."

The Homecoming

WHILE TERAH WAS relaxing at home one day, his servant entered and said, "Excuse me, My Lord, but you have a visitor."

Obviously deep in thought, Terah waved him off. "Tell them to go away. I'm much too busy to entertain guests right now."

"I told him the same thing, sir, but he refused to leave. He insisted you would want to see him, immediately."

Curious, Terah sat up in his chair. "He did? Who does this man think he is, barging into my home this way?"

"The man," said a voice from beyond the doorway, "thinks he's your son."

"My son?" As Abram entered the room, Terah stood, trembling. "Abram?"

"Yes, sir, it's me, Abram. Tell me, Father; am I still your son, even after all these years?"

Terah smiled and opened his arms wide as Abram ran forward to embrace his father. "My son; of course, Abram, you'll always be my son. Welcome home, my boy. I've missed you so much."

TO CELEBRATE HIS son's homecoming, Terah and his entire household had a tremendous feast. Open fire pits roasted wild boar, filling the night air with a thick, smoky haze. Dozens of servants lavished Abram and his guests with tray after tray of food and flagons of wine. Exotic dancers sensually moved to the beat of lilting musical strains that filtered through the crowd.

Sitting next to Abram and Terah were two more men. One of them heartily slapped Abram on the back. "Just look at our little brother, Nahor. He's all grown up now."

"That he is, Haran," said Nahor. "You're looking quite well, Abram. It's good to have you home."

"Thank you, Nahor. It's good to be home."

"So, Abram," continued Haran, "what have you got to say for yourself after all these years?"

Feeling a little tipsy, Abram smiled. "I am well, Haran. How've you been?"

"Oh, as well as can be expected, I guess. And how are old Noah and Shem doing these days? Did they take good care of our kid brother?"

"They're fine. And yes, they did take care of me, very good care of me, in fact. Everything I needed to know about serving the Lord of Heaven and Earth, I learned from them."

As one of the beautiful dancing girls swiveled her way closer to Abram, Haran grinned at his brother's obvious uneasiness. "But tell me, brother, did Noah and Shem ever teach you in the ways of love?"

Abram timidly shook his head. The woman danced so sensually between the two brothers that it made Haran swoon.

"Ah, love so sweet it takes your breath away," Haran continued. "Did they teach you about that?"

"No, brother, they did not," replied Abram with an embarrassed gulp.

"I didn't think so," grunted Haran, clearly intoxicated. "What a shame. Then I'm afraid they might've been wasting your time after all."

Seeing the uncomfortable look on Abram's face, Terah leaned in. "Relax, Haran, leave your brother alone. He hasn't been home two days, and you're already making trouble for him."

"Don't worry about me, Father," insisted Abram. "I can handle my own battles."

"Well, listen to you," added Haran, amused by his brother's gumption. "Hear that, Father? Abram can handle himself. By the gods, my brother's become a man, and now he's come home to take his rightful place among his real family."

"Well, it's about time!" spouted Terah proudly.

"A toast!" blurted Haran, who thrust forward his cup of wine. "A toast to my dear brother; the wandering sheep has finally come home to stay!"

SEVERAL DAYS LATER, Abram ventured into an ornate chamber in his father's home, where he discovered twelve idols, each standing in its own miniature temple. Abram was clearly shocked by what he saw. "Good God, what is this?" Seeing his brother walking down the hall, he called out, "Haran, come here, please."

"What's wrong?" Haran asked, stepping to the doorway.

"Have you seen all this?"

"Seen it, of course, I've seen it," he proudly replied. "Everything you see here, I helped Father build with my own two hands."

"But I don't understand. What are you saying? What is this room?"

Confused by his question, Haran shrugged his shoulders. "This is Father's room for our gods. What did you think it was?"

"Your what? Your gods?"

"Our gods, yes, you brainless idiot," Haran replied, giving Abram a gentle tap on the back of his head, "one god for each month of the year. Now, if you're done wasting my time, I'd like to go. I have things to do." And turning to leave, he left Abram standing there with his mouth hanging open.

"And he calls me a brainless idiot?" mumbled Abram. "The man fashions idols with his own hands and then has the nerve to call them his gods? I don't believe it. As the Lord lives, I refuse to stand by and watch my father and brothers destroy their own souls with a bunch of useless idols."

Abram stormed out of the chamber and went to the living room, where he found Terah sitting with his brother, Nahor. Abram sat down next to them. "Father, please answer a question for me, won't you?"

"Of course, Abram; what is it?"

"Where is the God Who created everything and everyone?"

"Why, of course, the gods who created us are right here in this house."

"Then, please, sir, could you show me?"

"Certainly, son," said Terah, who then led him into his chamber of idols, with its twelve statues. "See, here they are. These are the gods who created you and me and all mankind." Bowing to them, Terah then left the room.

DEEPLY TROUBLED, Abram went to see his mother.

"What's wrong, son?" asked Amthelo. "You look like you've just seen the devil himself."

"I'm afraid you're not too far from the truth, Mother."

"Tell me, then. What happened?"

"Father just showed me the gods whom he claims made the Universe."

"Oh, them. So you finally got to see his beloved chamber of idols."

Dolefully, Abram nodded.

"So what did you think of it?"

"It made me sick, absolutely sick. To think that my own father could actually believe a bunch of idols created the Universe. It's more than I can take, I tell you."

"What are you going to do about it?"

"What am I going to do? I'm going to give them a meat offering; that's what I'm going to do. And you're going to help me."

TAKING SOME SAVORY meat, Abram laid it at the feet of one of his father's idols. Then, he sat there all day, watching and waiting, to see what they would do with it, but, of course, they did nothing in response. "Well, well, I guess Mother's cooking wasn't as good today as what you're used to getting. Or maybe I just didn't serve enough to suit any of you. Maybe that's why you didn't eat anything. Tomorrow, I'll bring you an even bigger and better meal than this one; then we'll see what happens."

WITH ANOTHER PLATE of succulent meat, Abram returned the next morning to his father's chamber of idols. He approached them and placed the offering in front of the largest one there. Again he sat and watched them well into the afternoon. Still, none of them reached out to eat a thing. Springing to his feet, Abram began to anxiously pace back and forth, growing more agitated by the moment. Lifting his eyes toward Heaven, he cried out, "Lord of Heaven and Earth, please tell me: What should I do?"

Suddenly an eerie wind blew into the room, gusting through his hair and into his nostrils. Inspired by the whirlwind, Abram shouted above the din, "My father and this wicked generation are all doomed! They serve idols with mouths that can't speak. They have eyes and ears and hands, but still they're completely useless, just like the people who made them!" As if seized with a tremendous insight, Abram's eyes began to gleam with a curious shimmer. Grabbing a hatchet, he started hacking away at his father's idols.

Hearing the sound of the hatchet from outside his home, Terah ran inside to see what was happening. As Terah was heading for his chamber of idols, he passed Abram casually walking down the hall in the other direction. And when Terah went into the room, to his absolute horror, he found that all of his idols had been smashed to pieces; all except one, that is. Much to his chagrin, this remaining idol was standing there with a plate of food in front of it, and stranger still, this idol was holding Abram's hatchet in its hand. A stunned Terah ran into the living room, where he found Abram, lounging with his brother, Nahor.

"Abram, by the gods," blurted Terah, "what have you done?"

"What's wrong, Father?"

Wringing his hands in abject frustration, Terah then pointed down the hallway toward his chamber of idols. "M—*my gods*, someone's destroyed them! Didn't I see you coming from their room just now? You did this thing, didn't you?"

"You say they've *all* been destroyed?"

"All but one, yes. They're completely smashed. Tell me, son, before I lose my temper. Why'd you do it?"

"But I have no idea what you're talking about, Father," replied Abram, as calm as can be. "I only brought them a meat offering in your honor, but when I came closer, they all tried to grab the food before the biggest god had a chance to eat any of it."

"Nonsense."

"No, Father, really. Didn't you say they'd all been destroyed except one?"

"Yes, you know I just told you that."

"Well, there you are. It's just like I told you, really. You should've seen it. The biggest god was so angry he became violent. He took a hatchet and smashed them all before I had a chance to stop him. As I recall, he's still got the thing in his hand. Check for yourself, if you don't believe me."

"Never mind that now, Abram." His father's frustration abruptly turned to anger. "You're lying! You're nothing but a filthy liar!"

"No, Father," said Abram in earnest, looking his father right in the eye. "That's where you're clearly mistaken. Tell him, Nahor. Tell him his son is no liar."

But Terah was too angry to wait for Nahor's response. "You actually expect me to believe these gods have the power to do what you've just described? What kind of a fool do you take me for?"

"What are you saying, then? You mean your gods aren't capable of such a thing?"

"Of course not. How could they? They're just wood and stone. I should know; Haran and I made them ourselves."

Astonished, Abram gaped at his father. "Then, for Heaven's sake, why do you worship them?"

"Because, well, because…" Terah blanched, momentarily taken aback. "Because that's what we've always done, why else?"

"Do they hear your prayers?"

"H—*how* should I know?"

"Will they fight any of your battles? Can they rescue you from your enemies?"

"Of course not." Terah obstinately crossed his arms. "Please, son, now you're just being ridiculous."

"You know, Father, I'm sure this can't be good for you or my brothers. Only a fool would serve an idol, or worse, a rebel against God."

"Enough already! You're overreacting, son. There's no way that God could be that concerned about how we choose to live."

"But that's just it; He does care. Don't you remember? Our forefathers sinned like this in the past, and the Lord wiped them out with the Flood!"

Terah defiantly shook his head. "Oh, Abram, that was then; this is now. The Lord would never do something like that again, not to us."

"I don't know, Father. Are you really so eager to find out? You actually want to risk inciting the anger of God just so you can worship a bunch of useless idols?"

"Abram, please. I still say you're overreacting to this whole thing."

"For God's sake, Father, put an end to this madness right now, before it's too late! You don't want to bring disaster to your own family, do you?"

Abram then sprang to his feet and started back toward the chamber of idols.

"Abram, son, where do you think you're going?" Turning to his other son, he pleaded, "Nahor, don't just sit there; do something! Your brother's gone insane!"

"*Me*? What do you expect me to do about it? He's your son."

"Abram, wait!" Bolting down the hall, Terah ran through the doorway just in time to see his son approaching his one remaining idol. "Son, I forbid you to come in here anymore!"

"I'm sorry, Father, really I am; but all this has to end, so help me God."

Abram strode to the idol, took the hatchet from its hand, and raised it, ready to strike.

"No, son! Don't!"

And after hacking Terah's last idol into so many bits of firewood, Abram ran out of the room, leaving his father just standing there, stunned and speechless.

Into the Fire

APPEARING BEFORE Nimrod, Terah humbly bowed. The king was puzzled by the troubled look on Terah's face. "What's wrong, my friend?"

"Please, Sire, I have something very important to discuss with you."

"Go on, tell me. What's troubling my favorite prince?"

"Well, you see, it's been many years since one of my sons was born to me." Terah paused, trying to find just the right words.

Nimrod leaned forward. "Yes, and now?"

"And now you wouldn't believe what he's done to me and my gods. And the things he keeps telling me; I don't understand. I'm at my wits' end. He's gone insane, I think."

"I'm sorry to hear it, Terah. How can your king be of assistance?"

"I'm afraid I have no choice but to have him brought before you, My Lord, so you can judge him according to our Law. That way maybe you can put an end to his evil; otherwise, we might all succumb to his madness."

SO ABRAM WAS BROUGHT to stand before Nimrod, who was sitting with his princes and governors, and, of course, Terah was seated there, too.

The king looked at Abram, perusing him from head to toe. "What's your name, young man?"

"My name is Abram, sir."

Upon hearing this, the king had a peculiar look flash across his face. "Abram? Hmmm, Abram, yes. Why does that name sound familiar?" Turning to Terah, the king saw his favorite prince just shrug his shoulders. "No?" muttered Nimrod, dismissing his suspicion with the wave of his hand and returning his intense eyes back upon Abram. "Do you know who I am?"

"Of course I do. Everyone knows who you are. You're King Amraphel, right?"

An audible gasp swept through the ranks of everyone in the room as Nimrod's eyes thinned. "What did you call me?"

"I called you King Amraphel. I'm sorry. Isn't that what people call you nowadays?"

"How dare you address me like that. Don't you realize I hold your life in my hands? Your own father has brought you here to suffer the consequences of my judgment. Still you have the audacity to mock me to my face?"

"Really," said Abram as he glanced over at his father, who looked away, unable to face the scrutinizing gaze of his son. "That's why I've been brought here?"

"That's right, young man. You stand accused by your own father. Now tell us, what have you done to his beloved gods?"

Abram calmly replied, "I, sir, have done nothing to my father's *idols*. The damage he described was caused by his chief idol when *it* became jealous that the others were receiving more attention than they deserved."

"Ridiculous," scoffed Nimrod. "Certainly you don't expect me to believe Terah's chief god has the power to do something like that."

"Then what are you telling me? If they're powerless, why do you serve them? Do you actually think they can rescue you?"

"Don't be absurd. The gods are fickle and beyond our understanding. They do whatever they want, whenever they want, whether we like it or not. Who are you to expect them to do your bidding?"

"Then why not serve the God of the Universe? He created you. He controls your life. He's the only One Who can both annihilate and sustain life."

"Just who is this god of yours, anyway? I've never met him."

"What an ignorant king you turned out to be. Shame on you. Instead of teaching your subjects to do the right thing, you've infested the world with your rebellious attitude."

The king slammed his fist down on the arm of his gilded throne. "How dare you! Your father was right. You are an insolent, little bastard!"

"Oh, stop. It's time to end this madness, or you'll all die miserable deaths." Abram then lifted his eyes toward Heaven. "The Lord sees every wicked person and judges them all."

"Enough! Seize this man and throw him in prison until I decide what to do with him!"

Nimrod's guards immediately grabbed Abram, dragged him to his jail cell, and slammed shut the iron bars.

NIMROD SOON ASSEMBLED his sages and sorcerers, along with all his princes and governors from each of his provinces.

"Have you heard about what Terah's son, Abram, has done?" snorted the king.

"He's a disgrace, I tell you!" shouted one of the princes.

"That's exactly what he is, yes," sneered Nimrod. "And when I ordered him to appear before me, he insulted me to my face; so I threw him in prison!"

"Prison is too good for him, Great One," chimed in one of the governors.

"Then tell me," continued the king. "What should I do to a man who mocks me this way?"

Stepping forward, the governor declared, "The man who defies his king should be crucified!"

"But that's not all he did!" cried one of the sages. "He's insulted our gods, too! And for that, the Law states he should be burned to death. So if it pleases the king, we can make a fire in your brick furnace and let it burn all day."

"Then we'll throw Abram into it!" added the prince.

Nimrod nodded, motioning to his servants. "Then it's settled. Prepare the furnace of Chaldea. But don't let it burn for just one day; let it burn for three full days. Then notify me when it's ready."

"As you wish, My Lord," replied one of his servants.

ABRAM WAS MARCHED from prison three days later, flanked by two of Nimrod's guards. Every one of the king's princes, governors and judges came to watch him get put into the furnace, not to mention a swarm of spectators. Women and children crowded onto rooftops and towers to see what was happening, and even though so many people had to watch from a distance, there was hardly a person in the country who did not come to see the spectacle that day.

As soon as Abram arrived, Nimrod's sages and sorcerers discerned who he was. "Why, of course, My Lord!" shouted a sage. "This must be the same man who was born into the house of Terah so long ago, just as we told you."

Frantically, they crowded around the king. "Yes, Your Highness," weighed in one of the sorcerers. "This is undoubtedly the man who was born when the great star swallowed the other four stars! But we already told you about this thing some fifty years ago!"

"I don't understand," Nimrod said, growing agitated. "What are you saying?"

"This man, Abram," continued the sage, "it appears he was born into the House of Terah after all. Apparently, you didn't kill his son as you believed so many years ago."

"*What*?" grunted Nimrod. "You mean to tell me Terah's son survived?"

"Yes, Sire," the sorcerer continued, "it seems that Terah defied your decree!"

"But I distinctly remember killing the little monster with my own two hands! How can this be?"

"He must have given you a different child," said the sage. "You must have killed *it* instead of Abram!"

"Of course, of course," murmured the king, "but why didn't I see this thing for myself? How could my insight have failed me so miserably, just when I needed it most?"

DRAGGED BEFORE THE king, Terah straightened his disheveled clothes and looked up at Nimrod, who was as frustrated as he was angry.

"So, Terah, Chief Prince of My Army, have you heard what my sages and sorcerers have said about you?"

Terah nodded timidly. "Yes, My Lord, I have."

"Tell me, then, my old friend. I must hear it from your own lips. It's not true, is it?"

"It's true, Sire. Everything the sages and sorcerers have told you is true."

"How could you?" asked Nimrod, truly disappointed. "You disobeyed my direct order?"

"Yes, My King. I'm afraid so."

"You gave me a child that wasn't yours?"

"In my defense, Sire, the boy was mine, born to me by one of my concubines."

"Still, the boy you gave me was not the one I asked for, the one I paid a great deal of money for. Is that correct?"

"It is, Great King, yes."

"But why you? Why would you, of all people, betray me like this?"

Befuddled, Terah shrugged his sagging shoulders. "I don't know. I guess my love for him overwhelmed me at the time."

"At least tell me it wasn't your idea to deceive me like this. Tell me someone else persuaded you to do it. Tell me now, and I promise: You won't have to die for this crime."

A terrified Terah stared back at the king for several agonizing moments. "Uh, yes, well, Haran … my oldest son … as a matter of fact, he was thirty-two years old when Abram was born … and, yes, he was the one, you know … who told me to do it. Come to think of it, it *was* him."

"Very well, then. You, my dear prince, will live, and for telling you to do this thing, Haran, your son, will stand in your place; he will receive the death penalty instead of you. He will die for concocting this insufferable lie that now jeopardizes our entire kingdom! He will die with Abram in the furnace of Chaldea."

"Wait, *what*? Wait, not—" Terah gasped, suddenly finding it difficult to breath. "No, not *both* my sons, please. Oh, dear God, no… What have I done?"

MEANWHILE, HARAN was at home, having lunch with Amthelo, who looked quite worried as she sat there, just playing with the food on her plate.

"Mother, you haven't had a single bite," said Haran. "Please eat. It won't do Abram any good for you to waste away on his account. Everything will be all right. Trust me."

Amthelo glared up at Haran. "That's easy for you to say while you sit there in the security of your comfortable home. But what I want to know is: Why doesn't your father do something? What good is being the king's chief prince if he can't even save his own son?"

"I wish I could tell you, Mom, really I do."

"Is that all you have to say for yourself? You know, you may not want to admit it, but I know you admire Abram, even if he is your kid brother. Deep down you wish you had his guts, his conviction. I see the way you are around him, always trying so hard to keep your thoughts to yourself, trying to act so unconcerned, but you don't fool me. I may not have given birth to you, but I still have a mother's instinct, you know."

Haran nodded. "Of course I'm concerned by this. And you're right. I do have tremendous respect for Abram; so much so, in fact, I've made a very important decision."

"A decision. What's that supposed to mean? You're going to say something to your father? Is that it?"

"Not exactly, no."

"What, then? What's this big decision of yours?"

"I've decided it's time to follow Abram in the ways of the Lord, assuming he survives his ordeal with the king. I figure if God sees His way to rescuing Abram, then He must be worthy of my commitment, too."

Amthelo stared at him in disbelief. "That's it? That's your momentous decision?"

"Well, what else can I do?"

"For one thing, you could talk to your father. Demand he intervene on your brother's behalf. Now *that* would be the brave thing to do. And what if God doesn't save Abram from the wrath of Nimrod? Then what?"

"Well, naturally, I'll follow the king instead."

Disgusted, Amthelo jumped to her feet and bumped her plate of food from the table, sending it crashing to the floor. Just then, there was a knock at the door. Haran got up and opened it. Standing on the doorstep were several of Nimrod's soldiers.

"Are you Haran, son of Terah, the chief prince of Nimrod's army?" asked the lead soldier.

"Yes," replied Haran with a suspicious nod. "What's this about?"

"By order of King Nimrod, you are under arrest."

"For what?" asked a befuddled Haran.

"For treason against His Majesty, King Nimrod. Now come with us peaceably, sir, or we'll have to take you by force."

The soldiers stepped forward and seized Haran.

Horrified, Amthelo sprang to Haran's side. "No! There must be some mistake. My son is absolutely loyal to the king. By whose testimony does this charge of treason come?"

"By no less than Terah's himself."

"My husband did this?"

"It appears so, ma'am."

Haran and Amthelo both gasped. "God, no," said mother and son with one voice.

A RESTLESS SEA OF onlookers had swollen to the point that there was standing room only along the thoroughfare where Nimrod's servants were leading Abram and Haran, who were both stripped down to their underwear, hands bound with linen cords. Together they were hoisted and thrown into the furnace. Within moments, Haran, screaming in agony, burned to ashes, but miraculously, Abram was not even singed by the inferno. Only the linen cords that bound his hands burned up, so Abram continued to walk around, quite unharmed, inside the furnace. As several of Nimrod's stunned servants peered inside, flames spewed out, killing a dozen of them.

ABRAM WAS STILL wandering around the next day, inside the furnace, as if nothing unusual was happening to him. Nimrod's bewildered servants stood and stared, frozen with fear and indecision.

"What should we do?" asked one of them. "We can't just stand around doing nothing."

"What do you expect us to do?" asked a second.

"Someone has got to go to the king," insisted a third. "Someone has to tell him what's happening here. Don't you think?"

"And tell him what?" blurted the first servant. "He'll think we're making the whole thing up and order *us* into the furnace."

"He has a point," said the second to the others. "So what *should* we do?"

"I say we tell the king and take our chances," continued the third. "One way or the other we're in big trouble. But if we don't say a thing, we're dead men for sure."

"He's right," said the second. "If we tell the king, and he doesn't believe us, then at least we'll die knowing we did everything we could to avoid it. And who knows, maybe he'll come here and discover the truth for himself."

The other servants all nodded in agreement.

"I think you're right, yes," added the second. "Either way we have to tell him."

WHEN ONE OF THE servants appeared before the king, Nimrod was naturally surprised to see him. "What are you doing here?"

"Excuse me, Your Highness," replied the servant, "but what I'm about to tell you is too impossible to believe."

Nimrod leaned forward in anticipation. "Yes, yes, what is it?"

"Well, when we threw the two brothers, Abram and Haran, into the furnace, the older one died in a matter of moments." The servant shook his head, searching for just the right words. "But Abram. H—h—*he's* walking around inside the furnace like it's nothing!"

Nimrod's heart sank. "Are you insane? That's impossible. Has everyone in my kingdom lost their minds?"

ARRIVING AT THE furnace of Chaldea the next day, two of Nimrod's princes carefully approached it and peered inside. Seeing Abram walking around in the midst of the fire, they turned to one another with a look of complete disbelief.

"It's impossible," muttered the first prince.

"Oh, it may be impossible," said the second prince, scratching his head, "but there it is, right in front of us. Now what do we do?"

"You have to tell the king."

"*Me*? Why me?"

"Never mind. We'll both tell him, then."

THE TWO PRINCES reluctantly returned and appeared before Nimrod, who sat up in anticipation.

"Well," snorted the king, "what have you two got to say for yourselves?"

The two men exchanged a nervous look.

"Don't just stand there, staring at each other. Tell me what you've seen."

"It's true, Great One, we've both seen it with our own eyes. Abram *is* still alive, wandering about in your furnace, unharmed and unperturbed."

"Nonsense! I don't believe it! I won't believe it; not unless I see it for myself!"

SURE ENOUGH, WHEN Nimrod went to the furnace and looked inside, he saw Abram casually walking back and forth through the flames. Noticing the charred remains of his brother, the astonished king waived to his servants. "Get Abram out of there, this instant."

But the men just stood there, frozen with fear.

Frustrated, the king motioned them toward the furnace and growled, "Do it, you cowards, or else."

Finally, a trio of servants nervously made their way to the door. One of them quickly unbolted it and ran away. The door slowly swung open, and as soon as it did the fire breached the confines of the furnace and lashed out, forcing the other two men to withdraw.

"Hurry up!" Nimrod shouted above the roar of the flames. "Get Abram out of there right now, or I'll have you all thrown in with him!"

Again several of his servants moved toward the door of the furnace. This time the flames rushed out so violently that eight more men were engulfed and killed.

Nimrod cautiously stepped forward. "Abram, Servant of God," said the king in as pleasant a voice as he could muster, "won't you please come out of this furnace and stand before me now?"

With that, Abram walked out of the firestorm, through the open door of the furnace, and casually made his way over to the king.

The bewildered Nimrod examined Abram from head to toe. "B—*but how*? I don't understand. How on Earth did you survive inside that furnace, while your brother ... my servants ... all burned to a crisp?"

Abram calmly smiled. "The God I trust, the God of All Power, rescued me from your fire."

EVERYONE WHO HAD witnessed how Abram had endured the furnace of Chaldea soon began coming to see him up close.

"Obviously, this man is blessed of the gods," said one woman, who reached out to touch him.

One spectator, however, was more amazed than all the rest; and that was Abram's father, Terah. He watched in utter disbelief at all the people who came to bow down to his son, including many of Nimrod's princes. Even more startling, he watched as Nimrod, much to the amazement of the entire crowd, kneeled before Abram.

But Abram frantically raised his hands in protest. "No, no, no. Don't do that! Only worship the Lord above! *He's* the One Who saved me from the fire. I didn't do anything."

Rising to his feet, Nimrod motioned to his servants and princes, who showered Abram with a staggering assortment of gifts, including cattle, sheep and goats; wine, dates and olive oil; gold, silver and jewels.

"Here you are, Blessed Man," said Nimrod, "the finest gifts my kingdom has to offer. I even want you to have my chief servant, the absolute best servant I've ever had, in fact. His name is Eliezer."

The fellow came before Abram and bowed. "I'd be most honored to serve you, Master Abram."

Embarrassed, Abram nodded back. "That's quite all right, Eliezer. Thank you, you're most gracious."

"I'd especially like to hear more about this God of yours," said Eliezer. "You say *He* was the One Who rescued you from the fire?"

"Yes, He was. And I'd be very happy to tell you more about the God of my fathers, you and anyone among you who wishes to know more about Him."

"Now, Abram," interjected Nimrod, "if you'd like, you're free to go."

Abram was pleasantly surprised. "You mean, I'm really free to leave? Just like that?"

"Most assuredly, yes; you and anyone else who wishes to follow you and your god," replied Nimrod with an awkward smile, "just like that."

SO WHILE THE SAME people who had come to watch him die in Nimrod's furnace now hailed him as a conquering hero, Abram triumphantly marched out of the town square, followed by some three hundred of the king's people who joined him that day.

Out of Chaldea

THE FIRST PLACE Abram went after regaining his freedom was his father's home, where a forlorn Terah greeted him as he approached.

"Oh, Abram, I am so sorry. Will you ever be able to forgive me for what I've done?"

Looking into his father's eyes for several moments, Abram mulled over his response. "Of course I forgive you, Father, but the real question is: Will you ever be able to forgive yourself?"

Cut to the quick, Terah averted his eyes and kicked at the dirt. "Would you like to come inside?"

"This is still my home, isn't it?"

"Certainly, Abram. You'll always be welcome here."

"So you're not still angry with me for destroying all your beloved idols?"

"What, that? I've already forgotten about that. Besides, you were just trying to protect your old man, right?"

"Of course, Pop; you know I was."

Turning from his father, Abram started toward the front door.

"Abram, wait a minute, will you?"

"What is it, Father?"

"I need to ask you for a favor."

Stopping, Abram turned back toward his father, who then walked over to him with a grim expression. Terah continued in hushed tones, "Haran's two daughters are here for his memorial service, and I'm worried they might start asking questions."

"Questions?"

"Yes, you know, about their father; how he died."

"You mean *why* he died, don't you?"

"Something like that, yes."

"You're afraid they might find out it was you who implicated him, trying to save your own skin. Is that what you're telling me?"

"Please, son, just tell me you won't say anything about my role in all this. I'm afraid it'd break their hearts if they found out I was involved."

"I'm sorry, Father, I thought I made it quite clear. I'm no liar. And I certainly don't plan to start becoming one now. Not for anyone in this world."

"But, son, be reasonable. You said yourself that when you told a white lie about destroying my idols, you did it because you were trying to protect me from myself. Can't you do it one more time for my sake?"

Taken aback, Abram hesitated for a moment, then countered, "That was different."

"How was it different?"

"It was just different, that's all." Then, Abram turned and headed for the front door.

"Please, Abram, if you won't do it for me, then at least do it for the sake of the girls. It would break their hearts, I tell you."

Almost to the door, Abram hesitated, as if he might respond, but thinking better of it he opened the door and stepped inside. He immediately caught sight of his brother Nahor and beside him two young women who were trying in vain to hold back their tears.

"Abram," began Nahor with a sigh of relief, "it's so good to see you still in one piece. We've been so worried about you. It's hard to believe you survived such a gruesome ordeal."

Hardly paying any attention to his brother, Abram fixed his gaze on the two women, and his heart sank when he did. "I'm all right, Nahor, but please, I'd rather not talk about it; not in front of the girls, anyway."

Turning to the two women, Nahor became embarrassed. "Oh, I am so stupid. I'm sorry, Sarai. I don't know what I was thinking. Milcah, will you forgive me?"

"It's okay," replied Milcah as she lovingly embraced Nahor. "We're all at our wits' ends right now. You don't have to apologize because Father didn't survive Nimrod's fire."

"Milcah's right," said Sarai, "you didn't mean any disrespect. We're all a little out of kilter. We're grieving."

Abram dolefully stared at Sarai and then stepped over to her. "I'm so sorry about what happened, Sarai. How are you holding up?"

"I'll be all right, Abram," she said, falling into his arms. "I just can't believe Father is gone."

She gazed up at him with such beautiful, tear-filled eyes that Abram nearly swooned. "You'll be okay, Sarai. I'm here for you."

"Thank you, Abram," she murmured, hugging him tightly. "I just wish someone could tell me how this could have happened. It just doesn't make any sense."

Just then, Terah walked in and saw Sarai in Abram's reassuring embrace.

"I mean," Sarai continued tearfully, "Uncle Nahor told us why the king was angry at you, but why did Father end up in that furnace? What did he do to make the king condemn him like that? Do you have any idea, Abram?"

Considering her question for several agonizing moments, he looked first at his father standing there, breathless with anticipation, and then back at Sarai, who was likewise looking to him in hopeful expectation. Slowly, reluctantly, he replied, "I wish I could tell you, Sarai, really I do... But, unfortunately ... I don't, no." And hugging her, he blankly looked at his father, who turned away with an imperceptible sigh.

A DOUBLE WEDDING ceremony soon had Abram and Sarai standing together alongside Nahor and Milcah.

BY THE FOLLOWING year, Milcah and Sarai were both holding crying babies. The two women appeared quite happy, as did Nahor and Abram, who both looked on proudly.

"Congratulations, Nahor," said Abram. "Your sons are beautiful."

"And what lungs those two have," remarked Nahor. "Can you believe it? Twins! Who would've thought."

The two men stepped into the other room. "Oh, that's much better," continued Nahor. "I'm not so sure I'm cut out for fatherhood."

"Ah, you'll get used to it."

"So what about you, brother?"

"What about me?"

"How are you and Sarai getting along? Any children in the works for you, I mean?"

"Of course we want kids. But as you can see, we haven't had any luck in that area yet."

"Give it time. Besides, you don't want to get tied down too early in your marriage."

"What's your excuse, then?"

"Well, I don't count. I'm a lot older than you. I'm at the point in my life when I'm ready for something like this. But you? I just don't see you as the childrearing type."

"What's that supposed to mean?"

"Relax, Abram, don't get offended. I just meant that you strike me as a man who's going places, a man with a mission, you know? Sometimes a man like that finds a family holds him back from what he needs to do."

Abram considered his words for a moment and said, "But what if that mission involves children? Then what?"

"If that's the case, then, naturally, they'll come. But until that day comes, I wouldn't lose any sleep over it." Wincing at an outburst of crying from his twins, Nahor glibly smiled. "Ah, blessed sleep, something I'm afraid I won't be getting much of for quite some time."

AS NIMROD SAT ON HIS throne in Babel, he fell into a deep sleep. He dreamt that he was standing with his troops and subjects in a valley located directly in front of the furnace of Chaldea. Suddenly Abram vaulted out of the fiery furnace, and with sword in hand, he came and stood before Nimrod. Without warning, Abram swung his sword at the king who fled, terrified. As he ran away, Abram threw an egg at Nimrod, which broke on the king's head. From the broken egg, water poured out. A trickle at first, it quickly became a stream, and then a raging river, which proceeded to drown all his soldiers and subjects in a torrent of water. Nimrod looked around and was horrified to find that only he and three other men had survived this deluge. As Nimrod waded through the floodwaters, the three men ran after him. After this trio caught up with him, the king could see that they were also dressed in princely attire. Then, from out of nowhere, an eerie gust of wind began to blow into the river, causing its waters to reverse their course and flow back into the broken egg, which inexplicably reassembled itself and sealed back up. Bewildered to see the egg intact again, Nimrod blanched at the sight of another crack splitting the egg open. This time the egg released a hawk, which came out and flew straight at the king. With outstretched talons, the bird lunged at his head and plucked out his eyes. With a blood-curdling scream, Nimrod woke up and found that he was lying at the foot of his throne, clearly as embarrassed as he was terrified.

ALL OF NIMROD'S SAGES and sorcerers quickly assembled before the king. "Now that you've heard the contents of my dream, can any of you explain it to me?"

"Yes, My Lord, I believe I can," replied one of the sages.

"Ah, yes, Anuki, my esteemed sage. Come forward and tell me what you think."

Stepping to the head of the group, Anuki humbly bowed. "I believe what you're seeing is none other than the evil of Abram and his descendants making itself known again."

"What?" Nimrod eyed his sage suspiciously. "Are you sure?"

"Yes, Your Highness, there's no doubt about it."

"Tell me, then. What's the meaning of my nightmare?"

"It speaks of the day when Abram and his family will start a war with you. They'll destroy your troops, your subjects, your entire kingdom."

"My kingdom? Destroyed? But what about me? What's going to happen to me?"

"As you recall, My King, three men escaped with you in your dream, three men you saw dressed like yourself."

"Yes, yes. I remember. What about it?"

"Well, you see, that means you'll escape with three other kings out of all your allies in battle."

"I see, good," said Nimrod, somewhat relieved. "Then my life is to be spared."

Anuki exchanged a nervous look with one the sorcerers, and Nimrod sat up. "What? Is there something you're not telling me? Out with it, or I'll have you all torn to pieces!"

"Well, My Lord, in your dream you described a river that turned back into an egg. Is that correct?"

"Yes, yes, that's right." The king leaned forward. "And?"

"And that's when a hawk plucked out your eyes?"

"Yes, yes! But what does it mean? Tell me!"

"My Lord, I regret to inform you this means a descendant of Abram is going to kill you someday."

"What? Don't be ridiculous."

Anuki bowed humbly before Nimrod. "But I assure you, My King, this is your dream and its interpretation, both of which are entirely true."

"Impossible, I tell you!"

"But, Sire," interjected one of the sorcerers, who took a cautious step forward, "certainly you remember it's been more than fifty years since we first warned you about your fate, a fate which was clearly written in the stars even then."

Nimrod glared back at his sages and sorcerers. "Of course I remember, but what should I do about it?"

"Abram must be killed, of course," continued the sorcerer.

"Kill him, you say? But I already tried that."

"Yes, My Lord, and, with all due respect, you must not stop trying. As long as Abram is allowed to live, neither you nor your kingdom will survive."

"Very well. Then find Abram and bring him back to me. Maybe this time we'll have better luck."

Fortunately, Eliezer, Abram's chief servant given to him by Nimrod, was in the hallway eavesdropping on the conversation. As soon as they were finished, he slipped out of the palace.

ABRAM LISTENED INTENTLY as Eliezer spoke in earnest, "So you see, sir, I'm afraid you have no choice. Nimrod is more determined than ever to try to kill you."

"And you say this is happening because of some sort of nightmare the king had?"

"That, and the advice of his sages."

"Those fools. When will they ever learn?"

"What are you going to do?"

"I'm not sure." Abram shrugged his shoulders. "But I'm not going to panic."

"Of course not, My Lord. After all, you are the same man I saw survive the furnace of Chaldea. What can a mere man like Nimrod do to someone like you?"

"It's not me I'm worried about, though. I still have to worry about what Nimrod can do to my family. I survived that fire, but for whatever reason, my brother Haran didn't."

EVENTUALLY, THE king's soldiers went to Terah's home, and one of them banged loudly on the front door. "In the name of King Nimrod, open this door!" shouted the commander, "or we'll have no choice but to break it down!"

A FRONT DOOR OPENED wide, and Shem stood there surprised by what he saw. "Well, hello," he said, "what are you all doing here like this? This is no time of the year to be traveling in these parts."

Standing on the doorstep of Noah's mountain hideaway were Abram and Sarai, accompanied by half a dozen men. "Sorry, Father Shem," said Abram, "but we had no choice. It was an emergency. May we come in?"

"Of course, of course. Get in here, everyone, before you catch your death of cold."

APPEARING BEFORE Nimrod, his soldiers stood at rapt attention.

"So, Commander," grumbled Nimrod, "what do you have to say for yourself? Have you found Abram yet?"

"We regret to inform you, Your Highness," said the commander, "Abram was nowhere to be found. For three full weeks we've searched everywhere we could think of, but none of my men can locate him."

Disappointed, the king hung his head and put his hand to his furrowed brow. "Why am I not surprised?"

TERAH EVENTUALLY came to see Abram at Noah's place. "Well, son, are you ready to come home yet?"

Abram stared back at his father in disbelief. "Are you kidding? *Your king* is trying to kill me. Or have you forgotten?"

"Abram, stop. You're overreacting, as usual. I guarantee Nimrod has already forgotten about the whole thing."

"Oh, Pop, please. Stop kidding yourself. You know that bunch of old, snaggle-toothed sages will never stop feeding Nimrod their bad news. And if that beloved king of yours can't kill me, then you know he wouldn't mind killing my entire family just to spite me."

A deflated Terah hung his head and frowned. "Yeah, I guess you're right. I just wish there was something I could do."

"But there is something you can do."

Terah looked up expectantly. "What?"

"Well, unless there's something holding you back, I recommend you leave with us right now."

"Leave? Leave and go where?"

"To the land of Canaan."

"But why do I need to go with you?"

"Have you already forgotten what happened to Haran because of your king? Do you want the same thing to happen to Mother, to Nahor or Milcah, to your grandchildren?"

"Of course not. But how can you expect me to abandon everything I've worked so hard for? My privileges, my status, the love of my king, all wiped away on a whim?"

"*A whim*? I'd hardly call it a whim, Father. Don't you realize? Nimrod doesn't give you privilege or status because he loves you. He showers you with gifts for his *own* benefit, not yours. Besides, what good is all the wealth in the world when you and your family are all dead?"

Terah took several moments to let his son's words sink in. "Fine. Then tell me what we should do."

"We pack everything we have and go to Canaan right away, out of Nimrod's reach, where he can never hurt any of our loved ones again."

"Right now? But I need more time. I have to arrange for my gods to go with us."

"No, Pop, I'm sorry. There's no room for them; not anymore, not *ever*."

Terah started to responded but thought better of it.

"Please, Father, just throw away all the useless things you've been pursuing. Serve the Lord Who created you, then everything will be all right. You'll see."

No sooner had he finished speaking than Shem stepped forward from out of the shadows. "It's true, Terah. Everything Abram is telling you is true. Go to Canaan as soon as you can, before it's too late for all of you."

DETERMINED TO GET beyond the reach of the king of Shinar, Abram gathered his entire household as quickly as he could. Soon he and Sarai, along with Terah, Amthelo, Nahor, Milcah, their two children and all their servants were on the move, followed by everyone who had joined Abram after the incident at Nimrod's furnace. Traveling in a tremendous caravan, there were more than four hundred people in the group, not to mention their various herds of cattle, sheep and goats.

They marched for several weeks before coming to a fertile outcropping in the middle of an otherwise arid landscape, nestled alongside a meandering river, and there they stopped to set up camp.

"What do you think of this place, everyone?" asked Abram. "Beautiful, isn't it?"

"Where are we?" wondered Nahor.

"First we establish camp, my boy," said Terah. "Then we find out where we are."

"There's so much room here," added Amthelo. "And plenty of water for our herds and people."

"This place is perfect," said Nahor. "I say we christen it after Haran, to honor the memory of what happened to him in the furnace of Chaldea. That way our children will always have something to remember him by, and his name will never fade from our history. What do you say, Abram?"

Considering his suggestion with a satisfied smile, Abram nodded. "I like that, Nahor. I agree. We'll call this place Haran. But don't anyone forget: This isn't our final destination. We're just stopping here awhile en route to Canaan."

"I just hope the people living in these parts are friendly," interjected Sarai.

"We'll find out soon enough, my dear," said Abram. "But I'm sure with the Lord on our side we'll have no trouble winning the people over."

STROLLING THROUGH a lush pasture one pleasant evening, Abram was tending to his flock of sheep, when suddenly a shimmering purple light materialized several yards in front of him. From within this sphere of light, a radiantly handsome Man stepped forward and stood before Abram.

A startled Abram blanched at the spectacle, sucked in a deep breath, and exclaimed, "What the—*Who*—*How*?"

"Don't be alarmed, Abram. I've just come from the presence of the Lord."

"Excuse me? You what? You came from where?"

"Certainly you've heard of Heaven, haven't you?"

"Of course I have. I've just never met anyone *from there* before."

"I see. Well, now you have."

"What should I call You?"

"I am the Word of God, the Mediator between Heaven and Earth, the One Who rescued you from the furnace of Nimrod."

Abram gulped at the news. "Oh, dear. And what have I done to deserve such an auspicious visit as this?"

"You, Abram, are a man who has tremendous faith in the God of your fathers, Noah and Shem. Are you not?"

"I am. Since before I can remember, I've sought to know the God of my fathers, to know His will, to know His ways."

"You've done well, my friend. Now you'll have what you've desired of the Lord, and if you simply do what I tell you, Abram, I'll vanquish all your enemies. Your descendants will become as numerous as the stars and the sand, and I'll bless everything you do so you'll never need a thing."

Overwhelmed, Abram kneeled in a gesture of obedience. "My Lord and my God, thank You so much for this. Mere words could never express what I'm feeling right now."

"Now, Abram, take your wife and your group to Canaan. Stay there, and I'll be your God and will bless you." Then the Word of God vanished, leaving Abram alone again, except for the bleating sheep that gathered around him in the night.

ABRAM AND SARAI MADE preparations to leave Haran several days later, but when he went to his father's tent, he was disappointed to see that Terah, Amthelo, Nahor, Milcah and several others were just casually sitting around.

"Father, what's going on?" asked Abram "Why aren't you guys packed and ready to leave? We're wasting daylight."

Terah hesitantly explained, "I'm sorry, son, but your mother and I have decided not to go along this time. Maybe we'll catch up with you later."

"Not going? But why?"

Amthelo interjected, "Don't worry about us, Abram. It's just that I'm so tired of being uprooted every time I turn around. Your father and I like it here in Haran. The past few years have been so nice here. I don't mind telling you, this place makes me feel right at home. Besides, Canaan is no place for people like us. You go there with Sarai and your people. Visit us when you can. You understand, don't you?"

"Sure, I guess so."

Then, Nahor stood up with a look of melancholy on his face. "Dear brother," he began, "I'm sure going to miss you."

"Nahor, you? You're not coming, either? What is wrong with everybody? It was never our plan to stay here. We were always supposed to continue on to Canaan. What's happened to you guys?"

"I'm sorry, Abram, but frankly, Mom and Pop are done with this whole *mission* thing you've got us involved with. You know as well as I do, they're not as young as they used to be, and they need someone to look after them."

"You mean *you*."

"Yes, me. Look, little brother, I realize you supposedly had some kind of epiphany and all, inspiring you to pack up and leave everything behind, *again*. But that's just not for me right now. I'm sorry; you're on your own, buddy boy."

Turning to one of the other young men there, Abram asked, "And what about you, Lot? Sarai will be heartbroken if her kid brother doesn't go with us. What's holding you back? Don't you want to seek the Lord's call? We have a wonderful destiny just waiting for us. Don't you want to find out what it is?"

Lot just sat there, trying to think of something to say, but before he could, Terah stood and walked up to Abram. "Don't worry about him, son. You have enough to worry about with your own group. Lot is still a young man. He's not like you."

"Like me? What's that supposed to mean?"

"Well, you know, you've always been one to seek the higher road, with your head in the clouds."

"I'm sorry, Uncle Abram," Lot said hesitantly. "Life is too short to get so serious all the time. I want to live a little; you know, sow my wild oats. Someday I'll come and stay with you guys; you'll see. But right now, I'm just not ready for all this *destiny* stuff."

Thoroughly deflated, Abram just hung his head.

A House Divided

ONE MONTH LATER, Abram and his overflowing entourage, comprised of more than five hundred people and their herds, arrived at the outskirts of Canaan, where the landscape was dotted with orchards of fruit trees and fields of grain.

Turning to Eliezer, Abram said, "This looks like a good spot to stop for now. Tomorrow, you and I will go into the city with some of the men and find out what the people are like. In the meantime, pass the word that everyone is to set up camp here for the night."

"Yes, sir, right away."

ABRAM, ELIEZER AND half a dozen men made their way by foot into the midst of the city, where they came across a large bazaar displaying goods and wares of all kinds, including wine, dried fruits and grain. Hawkers selling their wool products, dyed a deep purple, beckoned Abram and his group as they passed by. Intrigued by what they saw, two of Abram's men stopped to examine an area with several rows of tools and weapons of every sort. As Abram paused to give his men a chance to look at some of the swords on display, a dirty-faced urchin boy approached him, holding out two arms covered with ornate bracelets.

"Hello, good sir," said the little boy, "would you like some beautiful jewelry today? Your wife would love some, no?"

"Well, well, what have we here?" mused Abram, who leaned forward to examine the goods. "And how much will you take for one of those bracelets you have there, my boy?"

"How much you got, sir?" asked the boy with a toothy grin.

"I'm not sure," replied Abram, who then withdrew his moneybag and opened it to look inside. "Let me take a look."

Without warning, another boy, considerably older than the first, bolted from out of nowhere and snatched the bag from Abram's hand.

"Quick, get that little thief!" shouted Eliezer, who started to run after him, followed closely by several of Abram's other men. Darting through the crowd, the men had a difficult time maneuvering past the people in the way. As they ran after the youngster with Abram's moneybag, they knocked several people over, not to mention numerous carts filled with various fruits and vegetables. Suddenly the fleeing youth collided with an unsuspecting shopper and crashed to the ground, where Eliezer and the men finally caught up with him.

DRAGGING THE YOUNGSTER back to Abram, Eliezer returned his moneybag to him. Opening the bag to inspect its contents, Abram was satisfied. "Hmmm, everything seems to be here. No harm done. You may release the lad."

"But, sir," muttered Eliezer, "I'm sure there's a law against this sort of thing, isn't there?"

Overhearing the conversation, a Canaanite woman stepped forward and snapped, "He's right, you know! Our Law metes out a very fitting punishment for a thief like this!"

Several Canaanite men moved in and wrestled the youngster from Eliezer's grasp.

"We'll take over from here, sir," barked one of the men. "We know exactly how to handle this sort."

"No, please, I'm so sorry," cried the youth, who then turned to Abram. "My mother is very sick and needs medicine. We had no money left, good sir. Please don't let them do this to me."

"Oh, well, why didn't you say so in the first place," grumbled the Canaanite man. "You little fool; what do you take us for? Now hold out your hand. Your mother may not be getting the medicine she needs today, but we certainly have the kind that'll cure your ailment."

The men forcibly dragged the boy to the nearest countertop and stretched his arm out across it. Withdrawing his sword and raising it, the man turned to Abram and said, "Now, all that remains is for you, sir, to pass judgment on this street rat."

"Me?" gasped Abram.

"Yes, of course, you. You're the man who was injured at the hands of this crook, aren't you?"

"But I haven't been injured in any way, my good man. No money was lost in the exchange. I have no quarrel with the boy. If there's any judgment to be meted out, I'm sure the God of Heaven is perfectly capable of doing it."

The confused Canaanite man lowered his sword and walked over to Abram. "You actually want this little thief to go unpunished? Don't you realize you only have to say the word, and he'll receive a just penalty for his crime?"

"You mean, if I simply give my consent, you'll chop off this defenseless boy's hand, is that it?"

"Naturally, it is the Law," replied the man, confused as ever.

"But it's not my Law, sir."

"Then what do you propose I do with this pest?"

"I say let God judge him."

"God? Which god?"

"Why, the God of my fathers, Noah and Shem."

Eying Abram suspiciously, the man stepped even closer. "You're not from around here, are you, mister?"

"Certainly not."

Frustrated, the man turned to the others, who were still struggling to restrain the youth. "Very well, release him." Turning back to Abram, the man grunted, "But if this unsavory brat is ever caught stealing again, I'll hold you personally responsible. You hear me?"

"I understand completely, yes. Now, good day to you, sir. Thank you for your concern."

And just as quickly as they had appeared, the three Canaanite men disappeared into the crowd, leaving the youth just standing there, quite speechless. He stood there for the longest time, staring dumbfounded at Abram, who began to get uncomfortable.

"Well, son, what have you got to say for yourself? Certainly you don't plan on standing there all day with your mouth hanging open, do you?"

"No, sir, it's just that…"

"It's just that *what*?"

"It's just that I'm so grateful you're such an understanding and compassionate man. If it wasn't for you, I'd have suffered terribly at the hands of those men. How can I ever thank you?"

"Don't thank me. Thank the God I serve. He's the One Who's so understanding and compassionate. I'm merely His servant."

The youngster slowly stepped up to Abram and humbly bowed. "Then, please, sir, would you be so kind as to tell me more about this God you serve?"

"I'd be glad to, my son. I don't think I caught your name?"

"My name, sir?"

"Yes, lad, your name. What do they call you?"

"Nicu. They call me Nicu."

"Very good, Nicu. Now, if you don't mind, I'd like to ask you for a favor."

"Anything. Just say the word."

"I need a place to accommodate a large number of people and herds. Do you know of such a place?"

"I do, sir. Follow me, if you please."

ABRAM AND HIS GROUP were soon setting up camp in the very heartland of Canaan. As evening began to fall around him, Abram stood alone on a nearby hillside, overseeing the operations of his tremendous entourage of people and animals, when suddenly the Word of God appeared next to him.

"Lord, hello," said Abram, somewhat startled, "it's good to see You again."

"Hello, Abram. I see you finally made it to Canaan. How do you like it here?"

"I like it very much. There seems to be more than enough room here to sustain the group You've so generously blessed me with."

"That's good, Abram, because this is the land I've given to you and your children."

"You're giving this place *to me*? Really?"

"That's right. Not only that, but in time I'll make your descendants even more abundant than the herds and flocks you see before you. Someday, your descendants will be as numerous as the sand and the stars, and this land will be given to them as an inheritance forever."

Kneeling before the Word, Abram bowed his head to the ground. "Thank You, Lord. I'm truly grateful for all You've done for me and my family. We'll honor You all the days of our lives."

"You're welcome, Abram. And be sure to continue teaching everyone you meet to follow in the ways you've received from your fathers, Noah and Shem, and it will be well with them, too."

"You mean like the young man we encountered last week in the bazaar? If men like that are willing to receive Your Word, then even they'll be included in this promised inheritance?"

"Yes, Abram, even them." Again the Word vanished, leaving Abram staring out across the landscape where his people and animals wandered about in every direction.

ABRAM BUILT AN ALTAR of stone, then and there, sacrificing one animal of every kind from among his flocks and herds.

"Dear, God, I thank You for all Your blessings. From this day forward I will call on the Name of the Lord, seeking You daily and endeavoring to teach everyone concerning Your marvelous ways. And in the years to come, they will all commemorate this moment in time, and they'll remember this place, this Bethel, this House of God, from generation to generation and throughout the ages to come."

ARRIVING AT ABRAM'S camp in Canaan, a messenger delivered a letter to the patriarch. Upon reading it, Abram became deeply disturbed. When Sarai saw the troubled look on his face, she hurried over to him. "What's wrong, husband?"

"I'm afraid that after living some nine hundred and fifty years on this Earth, the wise old man of our clan has died."

"Noah died?"

Abram nodded mournfully and began to weep. "Yes, my dear, my beloved teacher and father has gone to be with the Lord."

Touched by his lament, Sarai embraced him. "Oh, my love, don't cry. He lived a good, long life, and now he rests peacefully with our forefathers."

"Yes," whispered Abram. "And together they're all gazing upon the Face of God."

NIMROD WAS SITTING on his throne, as usual, entertaining another foreign dignitary. Abruptly interrupting their meeting, his messenger burst into the room.

"I'm sorry to disturb you, Your Highness, but we just received word you will definitely be interested in."

"This better be good. Out with it."

"Apparently, after paying Chedorlaomer, king of Elam, an annual tax for more than a decade, the Five Cities of the Plain, led by Sodom and Gomorrah, have begun a revolt against his rule."

Intrigued, Nimrod sat up on his throne. "A revolt? Against my old friend and adversary, Chedorlaomer?"

"It seems that way, My Lord."

"Well, well," muttered the king, half to himself. "I guess your plans of conquest are finally beginning to unravel, my old prince. How does it feel now that the shoe is on the other foot for a change?"

"What should I tell your princes, Great King? They await your command."

"Tell them the day of revenge is at hand. Tell them to assemble my troops at once and prepare their weapons of war, and when they're ready to march, tell me at once."

SOME SEVEN HUNDRED thousand armor-clad warriors congealed in the valley of Babel to form a massive sea that was Nimrod's army. They gathered there between Elam and Shinar, preparing to clash with Chedorlaomer, whose forces, stationed along the hilltops, were dwarfed in comparison to their opposition. One of Chedorlaomer's princes came to him with a concerned expression.

"Why the troubled look, Commander?" asked Chedorlaomer.

"My Lord, our estimate of Nimrod's army is nearly three quarters of a million men."

"And your point is?"

"Sire, our present force stands at a mere five thousand warriors. We're outnumbered a hundred and forty to one. Far too many of our troops are tied up at the moment trying to suppress the revolt of the Five Plain Cities."

"I see, and what would you advise at this time?"

"My advice would be to wait until we can recall some of our troops. Bring them up from the south to support our exposed flank. We'd stand a much better chance with their numbers added to ours."

"Your point is well taken, Commander, but right now we hold the high ground, while Nimrod's men lie below us in the valley. If we wait for reinforcements, we run the risk of losing our present strategic advantage. Not only that, but should we allow them the opportunity to strike first, it could prove to be even more suicidal than attacking them with our inferior numbers. You certainly see my dilemma."

"Yes, My Lord, I do. But the look in your eye also tells me you have another strategic advantage you haven't mentioned yet."

"Very perceptive, Commander. I commend you on your astuteness." There was a subtle gesture from Chedorlaomer, and a shadowy figure slowly emerged from his group of warriors. "Gentlemen," exclaimed the prince to his men, "meet our tactical advantage. His name is Anuki; and he's come to us straight from the court of King Amraphel himself. Here to bring us news of our foreordained victory, news of the once invincible king's defeat, news that has actually been written in the stars for the entire world to see."

ARMED WITH THIS DIVINE foreknowledge, Chedorlaomer and his warriors hurled themselves with reckless abandon upon Nimrod's troops down in the valley of Babel. Arrows flew, swords clashed, and bodies collided, as a great mass of howling warriors swirled in a blood-curdling dance of death. The fighting lasted all day. By nightfall, Nimrod's army was struck down by the sheer audacity of the attack, with nearly six hundred thousand of his men having fallen in battle. Among them was Mardon, the king's own son, who was killed in a hailstorm of arrows.

WHEN NIMROD CAME upon his son's corpse, bloody and arrow-riddled, he was devastated. "No, no, no; not my son," he moaned, dropping to his knees and weeping over his lifeless body.

"My god, my god, why have you forsaken me? How could you let this happen to me? To me, the mighty hunter before the Lord?"

Several arrows abruptly swished past, barely missing the king, and Nimrod's soldiers quickly swooped in and grabbed him by both arms, wrenching him away from his son's body. "Your Highness, you have to leave this place," insisted one of the soldiers, "or else you'll be lost as well. Please, Sire, you must live to fight another day."

Reluctantly, Nimrod relented. As they led him away, he glared at the men who were escorting him. "To live another day, you say? Tell me, you misbegotten mongrels, tell me: What have I done to deserve such a miserable fate as that?"

SITTING AT THE CENTER OF a large gathering of people who all eagerly nodded at his every word, Abram said, "So you see, the Lord of Heaven and Earth is not just the God of a single people, He's the God of everyone who will trust Him, of everyone who will follow His ways. Thank the Lord for His loving-kindness and mercy to a thousand generations. Amen."

And all the people there echoed Abram, saying with one voice, "Amen."

"Now," continued Abram, "unless there are any more questions, that will be all for today."

Everyone rose and slowly dispersed, when a young man stepped up to Abram. "Excuse me, sir, but there is one more thing, if you don't mind."

Looking up at the man, Abram smiled. "My dear Nicu, just look at you. I still can't believe it's been twenty years since we met you in the dusty, unfamiliar streets of Canaan."

"Yes, sir, I still can't believe it myself."

"What can I do for you, son? You have a question?"

"Not so much a question as a request."

"Out with it, then," said Abram with an impish grin. "Neither one of us is getting any younger, you know. And just seeing how old you're getting to be is beginning to make *me* feel old."

"Old?" said Nicu. "You're not that old, are you, Master Abram?"

Another voice suddenly intruded into their conversation. "Not if you call a man of seventy-five old, no; he's not old at all. He still has a lifetime of adventures ahead of him."

Turning to see who was speaking, Abram and Nicu saw a man standing next to them.

Abram's face lit up with excitement. "Lot! Is that really you?"

"Of course it's me, Uncle Abram."

"What on Earth are you doing here like this, so unexpectedly?"

"I'm sorry I didn't warn you in advance, Uncle, but I didn't want to spoil the surprise."

"Of course, Lot, I understand. Is this just a visit, or have you decided to come stay with us for good?"

"I'm not sure. Do you want me stay?"

"Certainly, my boy; nothing would make Sarai happier. And you know that whatever makes her happy, makes me happy, too."

"Fine. Then it's settled. I'll stay."

Turning to Nicu, Abram exclaimed, "Quickly, my boy, can you do me a favor?"

"Anything, sir."

"Tell me what your request was."

Confused, Nicu tilted his head. "Sir?"

"Before Lot showed up just now, you wanted to ask me something. What was it?"

"Oh, right, I almost forgot. It was just that I was hoping to be more than just a student of your teaching. I was hoping you might find me a place of employment, working for you and your family, that is; even if it means being a servant."

"Consider it done, young man; you're hired. Now, for your first assignment: I want you to find my wife and tell her we have a very special guest. Can you do that for me?"

"Yes, sir, thank you. Of course I can do that."

"Good, then run as fast as you can, Nicu, and tell her the good news. Tell her to prepare a feast today because her dear brother Lot has come home to stay with us for good."

THE WINE FLOWED and the food was served that evening, as everyone celebrated with Abram and Sarai at the homecoming of Lot and his wife. Music played and dancers danced, and the night air was filled with the sweet smell of roasted meat and herbs.

"Oh, Ado, my beloved sister-in-law," said Sarai with a serene happiness. "You've never looked more beautiful. How do you do it?"

Coyly, Ado smiled back. "Ah, Sarai, you can't fool me. You're just saying that because I brought your brother back to you in one piece."

Sharing a hearty laugh, the two women clinked their cups together, spilling some of their wine as they did.

From Feast to Famine

BUT SADLY, THE FESTIVE mood of this joyous homecoming soon turned to mourning as the land of Canaan was, within a matter of months, seized by famine. In the spring, the air had been filled with the scent of succulent meat roasting in the fire pit, but by summer it was filled with the stench of rotting animal carcasses strewn about the landscape, hapless victims of drought and disease.

"Oh, Abram," groaned Sarai, "just look at how quickly our happiness has turned into misery. Everywhere we look death stares us in the face. Once, this land was flowing with milk and honey, but now it's a place oppressed by hunger and thirst."

As Abram and his family watched helplessly, droves of people were on the march, trudging past them in makeshift carts, filled with their meager belongings.

"Where are they all going, Master Abram?" asked Nicu.

"From what I understand most everyone is headed for Egypt. Word has it the land to the south has, so far, remained untouched by famine."

"Then what are we waiting for, Uncle Abram?" said Lot. "Let's pack our things and get down there as fast as we can, before we lose any more of our herds."

Abram hung his head in defeat. "As much as I hate to leave the place God has chosen for us, it seems we have no choice. Send out the word. We leave for Egypt right away."

ABRAM AND HIS BAND of several hundred men, women, children and animals were once again on the move, heading south for greener pastures.

FATIGUED FROM THE journey, the group paused at the Mizraim River, where they watered their herds and rested awhile. As Abram and Sarai strolled along the river's edge, the weary husband turned to his wife. Noticing his intense gaze, she asked, "Abram, why are you looking at me like that?"

"Tell me: When was the last time I told you how beautiful you are?"

Tilting her head and wrinkling her brow, she replied with a suspicious tone, "Husband, what is going through that mind of yours?"

"Nothing, really. It's just I'm concerned about our journey to Egypt."

"Concerned about what?"

"I'm afraid God made you so beautiful the Egyptians might kill me and steal you for themselves."

"Oh, please."

"No, I'm serious. You know very well the fear of our God doesn't exist there."

"So what do you plan on doing about it?"

"Well, I think the best thing for us would be if anyone asks about you, then we should tell them you're my sister. What do you think about that?"

"You think lying to people about my being your wife will keep them from killing you and abducting me? Is that what I'm hearing?"

"It's not that far-fetched, if you think about. After all, you are my brother's daughter. You have to admit there is a family resemblance."

"Oh, Abram, I don't know."

"I'm telling you, it'll work, as long as we all stick to the same story."

"But it seems so underhanded. It just doesn't sound like something I'd be comfortable with, living a lie like that."

"You have a better idea?"

Sarai stared at Abram for several intense moments. "And since when did you start lying to get what you want? This doesn't sound at all like the man I married."

"Sarai, please, don't be so naïve. Even a man like me will do almost anything when it comes to protecting the ones he loves."

"I don't understand. I've never known you to tell a lie before. But now you're telling me you *do* lie if it suits you?"

"That's not what I said, Sarai," replied Abram, getting frustrated. "I was referring to the fact that I was willing to abandon our home in Canaan to ensure the survival of my loved ones, even if it meant leaving the very place God had given us."

Sarai started to raise her hand in protest but thought better of it.

ABRAM ADDRESSED HIS gathered group. "So, do we have an understanding amongst ourselves? If the Egyptians ask you about Sarai, what are you supposed to tell them?"

Timidly, Nicu raised his hand.

"Yes, Nicu, go ahead."

"We tell them that Mistress Sarai is your sister."

"Good, very good."

THIS GROUP OF WAYWARD travelers eventually began their final approach to the Egyptian border, but still Abram seemed deeply troubled.

Noticing the worried look on his face, Sarai asked, "What is it now, husband?"

"I'm sorry, my dear, but I just have a bad feeling about this. I can't seem to shake it. Something is going to happen. I can feel it in my bones."

"But, Uncle, what more can we do?" wondered Lot.

A strange look flashed across Abram's face. "Stop the caravan. I have an idea." Turning to Lot, he said, "I want you to find the largest trunk we have, empty it of all its contents, and bring it to me as fast as you can."

"But why, Uncle?"

"Don't argue with me, Lot. Just do it. Hurry!"

Sarai glared suspiciously at her husband. "Abram, what are you up to this time?"

BRINGING THE TRUNK to Abram, Lot opened it, revealing that it was empty.

"Now, Sarai, I need you to do me a favor."

Staring back in disbelief, she stammered, "I'm not getting in that thing, if that's what you're suggesting."

"But I need you to do this, sweetheart, please."

"Don't *sweetheart* me. I'm not doing it. I'll suffocate in there."

"But it's only until we make it through the gate. Once we're past the guards we'll have you out in no time."

Sarai adamantly shook her head. "No, Abram, no. You can't make me do it. I might die in there. I won't."

ARRIVING AT THE border, Abram and his entourage were halted by the king's chief officer.

"Give a tenth of what you own to the Pharaoh of this land," said the chief officer. "And then you may enter our country."

Abram and everyone with him were more than happy to comply, and once they did they all entered with their cargo and herds, but once inside the king's chief officer noticed how Abram and Lot were paying a great deal of attention to another chest they were transporting. Suspicious of their behavior, he approached them.

"Hey there, you two!" he shouted. "What are you doing with that chest?"

"Who, us?" Abram surreptitiously asked, trying his best to remain calm.

"Yes, you. I don't remember inspecting this chest when you came in. What's in it? I demand you open it immediately and give a tenth of everything inside to the Pharaoh."

Abram and Lot exchanged a nervous look.

"But, sir, I *can't* open this one," sputtered Abram. "I'll pay you whatever you want to insure its safe passage. Please, just name your price."

"Aha! There is something suspicious about this chest. It's full of precious jewels, am I right? Then give us a tenth of them, or else you'll have to turn around and leave at once!"

"Please, I'm begging you. I'll give you anything you want, but don't open this chest."

"Enough!" the king's officer snapped, motioning to two of his deputies, who then came and pushed Abram aside. Stepping to the chest, the deputies hesitated, looking at one another, as if unsure of what to do next.

"Don't just stand there, you fools. Open it!"

"Please, gentlemen," blurted Abram. "This chest contains very precious cargo. Whatever you do, be careful!"

Forcing the chest open, the deputies peered inside and then looked at one another quite perplexed.

"Well, what's inside?" demanded the king's officer.

"It's a body," muttered one of the deputies.

"Of a pretty lady," added the other.

"A woman's body?" exclaimed the dumbfounded officer, who then turned to Abram. "What kind of nasty business are you up to, sir? Why are you trying to smuggle a body into the country of the great Pharaoh?"

Horrified, Abram and Lot bolted to the chest, and to their utter dismay, they found Sarai was unconscious.

"Sarai, no!" Abram shouted. "Quick, Lot, get her out of there!"

Abram and Lot hoisted her from the chest and gently laid her on the ground.

"Sarai, dear Sarai," moaned Abram. "Please, wake up." He began to shake her in an attempt to revive her. "Somebody, get some water!"

Someone then handed Abram a cup of water, and he splashed it over her face. Instantly, Sarai gasped and opened her eyes. Wiping her face, she looked around, baffled at the sight of everyone hovering about her, gawking in anticipation. Then, turning to Abram, she grumbled with an angry scowl, "I'm going to get you for this."

THE KING'S CHIEF officer soon came and dutifully bowed before Pharaoh.

"I was told," began the king, "you're here to report an unusual border incident that occurred yesterday. Is that right?"

"Yes, My Pharaoh, I am. While attending my duties as chief inspector of the main gate, I encountered a visitor from Canaan, a man who came here seeking refuge from the famine that's raging in that land."

"I'm well aware of the famine, yes. What about this visitor?"

"Well, among his cargo was a chest we considered suspicious in nature, so we searched it, much to the chagrin of this fellow and his family."

"I see. And what was in the chest?"

"At first we thought he was smuggling a body in it."

"A what?"

"A body, a woman's body. And the strangest thing about it was that even in death this woman seemed to be the most beautiful woman my men had ever laid eyes on."

"Well, what can one expect from such laggards?"

"But, My King, with all due respect, I saw her myself. The men, I can assure you, are not exaggerating in the least. She really is that beautiful."

"This dead woman, you say?"

"But that's just it. She wasn't dead after all. She'd merely fainted while having been concealed in this man's treasure chest."

"What on Earth was she doing in a chest?"

The king's officer shrugged his shoulder. "No one knows for sure, but I have to assume the strangers were concerned for her safety."

"I've never heard of such a thing before. This woman must be truly exceptional for a man to go to such lengths to hide her away like that. I'd like to meet her. See to it that she's brought to me at once."

AND WHEN SARAI MADE her appearance before him, Pharaoh was so smitten by her beauty that it nearly took his breath away.

"Well, well, my dear lady," said the king, "it's been brought to my attention that you endured a most unfortunate incident while entering my fair city."

"I did, My Pharaoh," replied Sarai, who curtsied politely.

"But I trust you've made a full recovery?"

"I have, thank you."

"Good. I'm glad to hear it. Why were in that infernal chest in the first place?"

With an embarrassed smile, Sarai murmured, "My family was worried about my safety. They meant no harm."

"Your safety? What were they trying to keep you safe from? Certainly there were no bandits lurking about the gate to my country, were there?"

"No, My Pharaoh, I'm afraid it was just a big misunderstanding. Sometimes my family can be a little overprotective."

"Naturally. A woman of your exceptionally rare beauty should be protected by any means possible."

"Why, thank you, My Lord. I don't know what to say."

"Say you'll do me the honor of accompanying me for dinner this evening."

Nervously, Sarai bowed. "Of course, My Pharaoh, how could I possibly refuse such a charming invitation?"

ABRAM HAD A VISITOR before too long. It was Nicu, and he had a rather grim look on his face.

"What's wrong, son?" asked Abram. "Where's Sarai? Didn't she return with you?"

"I'm sorry, sir, but Mistress Sarai will be detained a little longer than expected."

"What's that supposed to mean?"

"Pharaoh has invited her to stay for dinner, and unfortunately—"

"Don't tell me she accepted."

"But what choice did she have, sir? After all, he is Pharaoh."

"All right, all right, let's try not to panic. I mean, what harm could there be in her having a little dinner with the king, right?"

SITTING IN PHARAOH'S private chamber, a deeply troubled Sarai lifted her eyes toward Heaven. "Dear God, you told Abram to go to Canaan, so we did. We left our home and our family, and went to a strange place. Then, because of the terrible famine, we had to come here.

And now this happens! Please, Lord, save us from this predicament."

Just then, Pharaoh entered the room. Turning to see him walking toward her, Sarai was stunned to see an angel hovering a few feet behind him, though unnoticed by the king.

"Don't be afraid, Sarai," said the angel. "The Lord has heard your prayer." With that, he vanished from view.

Making his way across the room, Pharaoh sat down next to Sarai. "Hello, my dear," he said. "I hope you enjoyed your dinner."

But Sarai was still too upset to respond, so she simply nodded politely.

Undaunted, the king pressed on. "Please, Sarai, don't be upset. You've done nothing wrong. In fact, quite the opposite is true. I find everything about you to be quite remarkable." The Pharaoh gazed longingly at Sarai, waiting for some response from her. Again she could only think to politely nod. The frustrated king sat back, thinking for a moment. "Very well, then. Tell me this, if you would. About the man who brought you here to Egypt: What is he to you? Is he your husband, your fiancé, perhaps?"

Staring at the spot where the angel had appeared, Sarai was hoping to catch another glimpse of him. "What?" she muttered and then turned to Pharaoh. "Oh, no, of course not. Abram's my brother."

"Wonderful. I'm so happy to hear it. Then of course it's my responsibility to do everything I can to make him important in my country. I'll make him a dignitary; give him whatever else you can think of."

QUITE MISERABLE IN his tent, Abram stared off into space, when suddenly there was a tapping at his door. "Hello, Abram," said a man's voice. "I know you're in there. Would you please come outside? I need to speak to you about a very important matter."

With a tremendous sense of dread, Abram slowly stepped outside. To his chagrin, he was greeted by none other than the same chief officer of Pharaoh who had ordered the opening of the chest containing his wife.

Abram was obviously dismayed at his appearance. "You again? Haven't you caused me enough trouble already? What do you want now?"

"Oh, my dear sir," replied the officer, smiling as though he were addressing an old friend. "I am so sorry if we got off on the wrong foot the other day, but you must understand I was only following orders."

"Yes, yes, how commendable. Just tell me why you're here. No, let me guess. You found more of my belongings, and now I have to pay your king a tenth of them. Is that it?"

Amused with Abram, the officer burst out laughing. "Oh, that is a good one, my friend. You are a funny, funny man, I think. No, no, that is not why I am here."

"Then tell me, before I go back inside. I also have important business to tend to, if you don't mind… Truth is: I'm not feeling very well right now."

"Of course, my friend, then maybe this might help you feel a little better." The Pharaoh's officer then stepped back and clapped his hands. "Look and see your great reward from His Majesty, the Pharaoh!"

A swarm of Pharaoh's servants jumped into action, delivering several baskets of gold, silver and jewels at the feet of Abram. Looking around in amazement, he saw a dozen more of the king's servants step forward, each of them leading a head of cattle behind them. Overwhelmed by what he saw, Abram muttered, "What is all this?"

"Why, of course, this is a royal gift for you, sir. These are your riches, your cattle, your servants, all compliments of the Pharaoh himself."

"But why? What have I done to deserve all this?"

"Because you have brought great happiness to the one and only Pharaoh of this mighty land, by presenting him with your beloved sister Sarai as his new bride!"

Abram's knees buckled, and he very nearly collapsed. "Oh, God, no," he mumbled under his breath. "Now it's time to panic."

A DISCONSOLATE Abram made a token appearance before Pharaoh, as he was regaled in a lavish prenuptial celebration, presented in honor of the brother of the king's bride-to-be. With Sarai at his right hand, Pharaoh proudly nodded at Abram, who tried his best to keep a straight face, even while his wife never looked lovelier sitting there in her Egyptian betrothal gown. Naturally, it was all that Abram and Sarai could do to keep from having a nervous breakdown during the otherwise boisterous festivities, considering how torn their hearts were at that moment.

PHARAOH WENT TO Sarai's room the next day and found her sitting on the bed. He casually walked over and sat down next to her. Reaching out to caress her cheek, he received quite a shock when an invisible force slapped his hand away. Confused, he jumped to his feet and took a step back.

After a while, the king took a cautious step forward and again reached out to touch her cheek. Again the unseen power knocked his hand away. Pharaoh stood there, flabbergasted, trying to comprehend what was happening.

Screams suddenly began to echo throughout the palace. Bewildered, the king sat back down next to Sarai. For several disturbing moments, he listened to the sounds of terror resounding in the background, but eventually he found that he could no longer resist. Once again he reached out to touch her face. This time the invisible force violently shoved him off the bed, sending him crashing to the floor.

"That does it!" blurted Pharaoh. Jumping to his feet, he dusted himself off and headed for the door. "I don't know what's going on around here, beautiful lady, but I have a strange feeling it has something to do with you!"

RETURNING TO HER ROOM later that evening, even as intermittent screams could still be heard echoing throughout the palace, the king spoke to her as pleasantly as he could. "Sarai dear, please, can you tell me anything else I might need to know about this man Abram? Is he some kind of sorcerer?"

"Who, *him*?" replied Sarai, quite sheepishly. "A sorcerer? Certainly not, My Pharaoh. My husband is no sorcerer, I can assure you."

"Your husband? Did you say your *husband*?"

Sarai reluctantly nodded. "Yes, I did."

"Then why on Earth did you tell me he was your brother?"

"I only told you that because we were afraid someone might kill him to get to me. I did try to warn you my family was overprotective when I first met you, remember?"

Perplexed and dismayed, the king turned and left her room, and when he did the haunting shrieks began to subside throughout the palace. As the cries slowly died down around him, a peculiar look washed across his face. "I knew it," he mumbled as he scratched his furrowed brow. "But how is this possible?"

ABRAM STOOD CONTRITELY before Pharaoh. Glaring at him for several intense moments, the king finally broke the uneasy silence. "Well, well, if it isn't the deceiver, here to tell me another amusing story at the expense of me and my people."

"Please, sir, I can understand why you'd be furious with me, but believe me, I never intended for anyone to get hurt."

"Tell me, then. What could you have possibly thought to gain by telling me Sarai was your sister? I want to hear it from your own lips."

"I did it because I thought it would help me live longer."

"You may think you're an amusing fellow, but I do not. You knew very well I was taking steps to take her as my wife, yet you did nothing to prevent me from making a complete fool of myself, not to mention endangering the lives of everyone in my palace."

"And for that I am truly sorry," Abram solemnly replied.

"Never mind that now," grumbled Pharaoh as he motioned to his servants, who brought Sarai out and led her to Abram's side. "Here's your wife back. Take her and leave my country before someone dies."

Again Pharaoh motioned to his servants. This time they brought out several more baskets filled with gold, silver and jewels, and presented them to Abram.

"Here, take this with you as well. Call it an expression of my gratitude for leaving my country still in one piece."

Abram bowed perfunctorily. "Certainly you're a most gracious king."

Pharaoh, however, was clearly unimpressed. "Yes, yes, of course. Don't mention it."

After another gesture from the king, a servant girl walked over to Abram and Sarai, and bowed dutifully before them.

"My dear, Hagar," Pharaoh said, addressing the girl, "I believe it would be better for you to be a slave to this man and his wife than to stay with me as a mere concubine. Please, go with them and be blessed by the power of this man. I have no idea how he's accomplished the things he's done in our land, but I do hope that somehow you may live your life as a recipient of his miraculous gift."

"Thank you, My Pharaoh," replied Hagar, who curtsied toward Pharaoh and then turned to Sarai and curtsied to her. "Ma'am, it seems I'm now in your service."

"So, I bid you all a fond farewell," said Pharaoh with a sardonic smirk, "and just to show you there are no hard feelings between us, I'll have my guards escort your entire group to the border. That way no one will bother you in any way, which means Abram will have no further need of securing his poor wife in a chest while traveling through our fair country."

A Parting of the Ways

RETURNING TO CANAAN, the first thing that Abram and his group saw was a dried-up water hole, littered with the bones of several dead animals, a stark reminder of the famine which had had such a devastating effect on the territory prior to their departure no less than a month earlier.

Undaunted, the group eventually arrived back at Bethel, going to the very spot where Abram had built his first altar. There, he and his entourage set up camp.

Laying a burnt offering on the altar, in the sight of all his people, Abram lifted his voice to Heaven. "Dear God, we've returned to the land You've promised to me and everyone who follows me in Your ways of truth and righteousness. We now humbly ask You, Lord, please restore this land of plenty to what it once was and heal it from this horrible famine before there's no one left among us to serve You and Your holy Name. Amen."

And the people echoed his salutation together with one voice, saying, "Amen."

IN DUE TIME, THE famine loosened its grip upon their country, and eventually Abram and Lot had nurtured their surviving heads of cattle, sheep and goats back to their previous numbers. The two of them bred so many animals, in fact, that they began to have a difficult time coexisting. Now there were too many animals and people, and simply not enough land to go around.

WHEN ABRAM'S shepherds took their flocks out to feed in the fields, they never allowed them to cross over into their neighbor's land to graze, but Lot's men never bothered to do the same, allowing their flocks to graze in other people's fields all the time.

"Hey there, you!" cried one of the neighboring Canaanite shepherds.

"Who, me?" Lot replied, sounding so innocent.

"Yes, you. Why are you letting your herds graze on my property? You're supposed to stay in your own territory."

"All right, already. Don't get yourself in an uproar. How am I supposed to control where my herds graze? They're just animals, you know. They have a mind of their own. Don't blame me."

AT THEIR WITS' END, the Canaanites began coming to Abram to plead their case.

"Abram, Abram," began one the Canaanite shepherds, "what are you going to do about your nephew's herds? They're allowed to graze on our property without any concern for the consequences. This can't go on much longer. Please speak to your nephew, won't you?"

"Of course, my friend," replied Abram. "I'll take care of it right away. I promise it won't happen again."

A FRUSTRATED ABRAM then confronted his nephew, who was busy tending to his herd. "Lot, my boy, what are you trying to do? Our neighbors are furious with me."

"What's wrong, Uncle?" groaned Lot, annoyed at the interruption.

"You know perfectly well what's wrong. Your shepherds keep allowing your flocks to feed in my neighbor's fields."

"But how do you expect me to keep track of where my flocks decide to graze?"

Unconvinced, Abram shook his head. "No, no, no; that's no excuse. What you're doing is wrong, and you know it. We should be trying to live in harmony with these people, not stealing from them. Have you forgotten? We're still technically strangers among the Canaanites."

"Then maybe you should start worrying more about your own family instead of a bunch of strangers." With that, Lot turned and walked away.

"Oh, Lot, my dear boy," murmured Abram, truly disappointed. "Why are you doing this?"

BUT NO SOONER HAD Abram stated his case than Lot's shepherds were up to their old tricks again, allowing their herds to roam freely, grazing wherever they wandered, much to the chagrin of Abram's Canaanite neighbors.

THOROUGHLY EXASPERATED, Abram again confronted his nephew. "Lot, how long are you and your men going to be a nuisance to my neighbors? I'm begging you."

"But I already told you, Uncle. My herds are hungry, and my family has to do whatever it takes to survive. I'm sorry you don't see things my way, really am I."

"Look, this is getting tedious. Let's not argue about this anymore. We're family."

"Then maybe you should quit sticking your nose in my affairs, Uncle."

Stung by his nephew's rebuff, Abram bluntly replied, "Fine. If that's the way you want it, then maybe it's time we parted company."

"Fine," said Lot without a shred of remorse.

"Then I suggest you find another place where you and your people can live with your herds."

"Fine."

"But just make sure your group keeps its distance from ours. Is that clear?"

For just a moment, Lot's resolve wavered. "So now you're going to disown us, is that it? What happens if everyone else attacks us once they've seen we've had a parting of the ways?"

Abram resolutely shook his head. "I'm sorry, Lot, but you chose this course of action for yourself, and you'll have to face the consequences of that choice. Now, are you, or are you not, prepared to leave on your own terms?"

Several more tense moments passed as Lot thought hard about his uncle's proposition, then came his terse reply. "Fine."

"Good, then I want you to get your things and move out as soon as possible." Abram felt a sudden twinge of remorse as he looked upon his beloved Sarai's brother. "And, no, I'm not going to abandon you completely. If anyone attacks you, just let me know, and I'll gladly avenge your cause."

But Lot was barely listening by then. He was already gazing longingly out across the well-watered plain of Jordan. Without the slightest response to his uncle's offer, Lot just walked away, and Abram sadly watched him leave.

LOT QUICKLY GATHERED his family, his herds and everything he owned.

"But, Lot, where will you go?" asked a heartbroken Sarai as she embraced him, her eyes filling with tears. "When will I see you again?" Turning to Abram, she said with a lamentable sigh, "Oh, Abram, don't make him leave, please. Why are you doing this?"

"I'm sorry, my dear," said Abram, shrugging his shoulders. "I tried to resolve this situation in a reasonable manner, but—"

"Please, Sarai, don't cry," interjected Lot. "We're not going that far. Before you know it we'll all be together again. As soon as we get settled we'll send word. Then you can come visit us, all right?"

Drying the tears from her eyes, Sarai nodded with a sad, little smile.

BEFORE LONG, LOT AND his group, which now included Nicu, were all on the move in their trek for new frontiers.

As they traveled along, Lot said to Nicu, "I'd like to thank you for joining us, Nicu. I know it wasn't easy for you to part ways with Master Abram."

"No, sir, it definitely was not. I love him very much. If it wasn't for him, I wouldn't be the man I am today."

"Do you mind my asking why you did it, then?"

"I did it because Mistress Sarai personally asked me to do it."

"Really? Did she give you her reasons?"

"She asked to me go along with you as a special favor to her, because she hoped I might serve you as faithfully as I've served the both of them."

"And will you?"

"As much as it is in my power, yes; I pledge myself to you and your wife as if it were to Master Abram and Mistress Sarai. Does that answer your question?"

Without another word, Lot nodded, obviously humbled by the man's fierce loyalty.

ALONG WITH ALL THEIR cattle, sheep and goats, Lot and his entourage of about a hundred and fifty people traveled across the plain of Jordan, where they eventually came to a lushly vegetated, well-watered expanse. Surveying the land, far and wide, Lot said with great satisfaction, "Well, everyone, I think this might be just the place for us." Noticing a traveler wandering by, Lot called out, "You, my friend, can you tell us where we are? You there, do you hear me?"

Finally realizing that he was being spoken to, the man turned and suspiciously eyed Lot's group. "Yes, sir. I hear you just fine. Why do you ask?"

"Because I and my group are adventurers, seeking new lands, new pastures for our herds and flocks."

"I see. Then I'd advise you to keep on traveling. Strangers aren't welcome in these parts. Best you just keep moving along, if you know what's good for you."

Lot and his wife exchanged a peculiar look.

"But I don't understand," replied Lot. "Certainly the people here wouldn't turn away a man like me, would they?"

"You? What makes you so special?"

"Just look at the tremendous herds and flocks at my disposal. Don't the people here require such things to live? If we chose to live here, we wouldn't be a burden at all. On the contrary, we'd be blessing and a boon."

Considering his words for a moment, the man reluctantly nodded. "I suppose so."

"Good, then it's settled."

"Suit yourself," said the man as he turned to go. "But don't say I didn't warn you."

"Wait, sir."

"What is it now?" he grumbled impatiently, looking back and squinting into the Sun.

"You still haven't told us the name of this place."

"Sodom," the man grunted and turned to leave. "This place is called Sodom."

Turning to his wife, Lot declared, "Welcome to your new home, my dear Ado. Welcome to Sodom."

How the Mighty Have Fallen

MEANWHILE, CHEDORLAOMER, king of Elam, was sitting on his gilded throne, sulking with his dark, brooding eyes. Standing at attention before him were three men, all dressed in royal attire: Tidal, king of Goyim, Arioch, king of Elasar, and Nimrod, king of Shinar.

"Good afternoon, gentlemen," began Chedorlaomer. "I trust you've all been well."

"We have, Your Majesty," Tidal replied with a slight bow of the head.

"Naturally, you're all wondering why I've summoned you here today."

"We've heard rumblings, Sire," remarked Arioch with a respectful nod. "Rumblings of another rebellion."

"Really? What have you heard?"

"Word has it that after more than twelve years of paying you tribute," Nimrod replied, "Sodom and Gomorrah are planning another revolt against your rule."

"And what about you, Nimrod?" asked Chedorlaomer. "Are you eager to rejoin them in their revolt against me? Do you still thirst for revenge for my rebellious actions so long ago?"

"I think not, Your Majesty. Since the death of my son Mardon, I've lost much of my former zeal for battle. I'm now quite content to serve my people of Shinar on your behalf."

"How touching, how noble, how wise. You've spoken well, King Amraphel, even if it has taken disaster upon disaster to bring you to such a conclusion. Then you'll join my cause as an ally this time. Is that what you're telling me?"

Nimrod nodded dutifully. "I will, My King. I, and all my warriors, are at your disposal."

"And what about you Tidal?"

"The same goes for me and my warriors, Your Majesty."

"Arioch?"

"Of course, Sire. My men and I are always at your service. Just say the word."

"Very good," said Chedorlaomer, raising his clenched fist. "Then together we'll crush this revolt, once and for all!"

SO ALL FOUR KINGS, Chedorlaomer, Tidal, Arioch and Nimrod, led a tremendous wave of their warriors, about eight hundred thousand strong, plundering everything they could get their hands on, and as this great swarm of soldiers marched, they left a wake of sheer terror in their path, killing every man they found along the way.

AT THE SAME TIME, the two kings of Sodom and Gomorrah were conferring in their royal tent, overlooking the Valley of Siddim, when a royal messenger arrived.

"Excuse me, King Bera, King Bersha," said the messenger, bowing graciously, "we've received word that Chedorlaomer and his combined forces are proceeding toward the Siddim Valley to oppose us with more than three quarters of a million men under their command."

The two kings exchanged a serious look.

"Thank you, messenger," replied Bera, "then prepare to send word to our commanders in the field to prepare our armies for the impending invasion." Turning to his fellow king, he then said, "Bersha, tell me: You're sure the kings of the other Cities of the Plain are resolved to join us in battle."

"They are, Bera. Rest assured, my friend: We five stand as one. Shinab, Shemeber and

Bela have all declared their absolute allegiance with us in this matter."

"Good. For all our sakes, I hope they are, or else we're doomed for sure."

"Don't worry about them. They've all assured me they feel it's far better to fight and die in battle than to continue serving the infidel Chedorlaomer as mere slaves."

ALONG WITH THEIR overflowing armies, those nine kings came together in a resounding clash of men and arms in the Valley of Siddim. Arrows flung in every direction, striking targets with deadly effect; swords savagely swung left and right, hacking off innumerable appendages. After a fearsome, bloody battle, a tremendous loss of life was suffered on both sides, but in the end, the warriors of the Five Plain Cities, outnumbered and outmaneuvered, proved to be no match for Chedorlaomer and his combined forces, and eventually they were struck down, having been reduced to row after row of bloody carcasses.

FOR GOOD MEASURE, the warriors of Chedorlaomer pursued the kings of the Plain Cities, who sought refuge in the lime pits that were so common along the borders of Siddim Valley. What survivors there were ran every which way, fleeing into the mountains for safety. Still, the war-weary Elamite forces refused to relent, pursuing their quarry to the very gates of Sodom. They seized everything and everyone, even capturing Lot and Nicu, who both became prisoners of war, along with thousands of their fellow countrymen.

INTOXICATED BY THEIR victory, as well as the copious amounts of wine they had seized in battle, the Elamite troops drank themselves into a complete stupor that night, eager to celebrate their achievement. Fortunately, Nicu found himself working as a wine steward that evening, having been commandeered by one of Tidal's field commanders. One by one, the soldiers drank themselves to sleep, and eventually Nicu saw his opportunity for escape.

TRAVELING ALL NIGHT and well into the next day, Nicu made his way to the home of Abram and Sarai. Confused by his unexpected arrival, the couple anxiously greeted him. As Nicu proceeded to tell them what had happened to Sodom and how Chedorlaomer's forces had captured Lot in the process, Sarai fainted dead away at Abram's feet.

ABRAM IMMEDIATELY marshaled his forces, gathering around three hundred fighting men from his group. "Now, everyone," Abram began, "I realize that what I'm asking of you might seem like an impossible task. We're greatly outnumbered, in fact. But there is still one thing even more important than this, and that is the Lord of the Universe is on our side today, because the same God Who protected me in the furnace of Nimrod, spoke to me personally and, in no uncertain terms, promised me He'd vanquish all my enemies. So, I stand here this fateful, dreadful moment and I say to all of you who, with me, trust in the God of Heaven and Earth: Trust now in His awesome power, and go forth today as His warriors in a righteous cause, and He will lead us to certain victory!"

Amidst a tremendous hurrah from his men, Abram set out after those Elamite kings and the remnant of their armies.

JUST BEFORE DAWN, Abram gave the signal to attack, and in a tremendous display of selfless courage, his men struck swiftly and violently, slinging arrows and swinging swords with deadly accuracy. From the start, the Elamites, hung over and bleary-eyed from their night of revelry, were thrown back on their heels by the sheer audacity of Abram's men. Not only that, but they were quickly joined by thousands of Sodomite prisoners of war, who were just waiting for a chance to avenge their shameful loss. In fact, the disoriented Elamite troops were in such disarray that they even killed many of their own fellow warriors in the panic and confusion.

THE COMBINED FORCES of Abram's men and the freed Sodomite prisoners soon cut down every last Elamite soldier. The only survivors were their four kings, Chedorlaomer, Tidal, Arioch and Nimrod who all fled like cowards. As the vanquished kings were running for their lives, Nimrod found himself in a strangely familiar situation. Suddenly he began to remember the dream he had had, many years earlier, warning him of this very day when Abram would cause his downfall. Haunting images of that horrific dream began to flood his mind, images of the mysterious egg that had cracked open and released a hawk. Nimrod blanched at the sight of that screeching hawk as it flew straight for his head with outstretched talons, and plucked out his eyes. Seized by an uncontrollable madness, Nimrod screamed wildly as he clutched at his face. Abruptly splitting away from the other three kings, he then ran off in his own direction, muttering incoherently under his breath as he went.

HORRIFIED BY THE carnage he saw along the battlefront, Abram shook his head in disbelief, but very quickly all was forgotten when he turned to see Lot walking toward him. His grief instantly turned to joy as soon as he was reunited with his nephew. Letting bygones be bygones, the two men embraced.

"Uncle Abram, what a sight for sore eyes you are."

"Lot, my boy, it's good to see you, too."

"Is it true? You led this task force?"

"It's true."

"Just to save me?"

"To save Sarai."

Lot hung his head. "Of course, sir, I should've known. How can I ever thank you?"

"Don't thank me. Thank the God I serve. He's the One Who brought us this victory today. Without Him, we'd never have had the slightest chance of success."

Looking up at his uncle, Lot dolefully nodded. "Then, from this day forward, I owe my life to both you and—" Looking over Abram's shoulder, Lot blanched. "God, no."

A perplexed Abram turned to see what was affecting his nephew, and that was when he saw it for himself. "Nicu," he murmured, as one of his men walked toward him with his friend and servant dangling in his arms.

Stepping up to Abram and Lot, the man laid Nicu down at their feet. "He's barely holding on, sir. I'm afraid he's been badly injured. He insisted I bring him to you."

Kneeling down, Abram leaned forward to examine Nicu's blood-stained body and whispered, "Oh, no, my dear Nicu, not you. What happened?"

With great difficulty, Nicu feebly replied through bleeding lips, "We fought a good fight, didn't we, Master Abram?"

"We did at that, my son. And because of your tremendous courage, my wife will have her brother restored to her."

"Good. I'm glad to know it," he replied, reaching up with his right hand to embrace Abram, who then saw that the man's hand had been severed at the wrist.

Heartbroken at the sight, Abram groaned, "Oh, Nicu, I'm so sorry."

Turning to see what he was looking at, Nicu grimly smiled. "Oh, that. Funny, how things turn out."

"Lord, why? Dear Nicu, believe me when I say I never wanted anything like this for you; not you."

"You don't have to apologize, sir. You were the one who restored my life. Without you … that thing would've been gone a long time ago."

As tears began to roll down Abram's face, he shook his head with a sad, reluctant smile. "Dear, silly boy."

"Thank you, Master … for all you've done for me… Because of you, I've lived a wonderful life … a life worth living."

"Oh, Nicu, please don't talk like that. And whatever you do, don't call me master. Don't you know? You're much more than a servant to me. In my heart, you'll always be my son. Do you hear me? My son."

Nicu coughed, sputtering a mouthful of blood and nodded. "I hear you ... Father." Then with his last syllable, Nicu died.

Devastated, Abram embraced him and wept uncontrollably.

RETURNING FROM THE battlefield, a grief-stricken Abram and his weary men passed by the lime-pits there, and as they did Bera, Bersha and their men came out to meet Abram.

"Greetings, Abram of Canaan. I am Bera, king of Sodom, and this is Bersha, king of Gomorrah. We want to personally thank you on behalf of all the people of the Plain Cities for what you did for us."

Nodding amicably, Abram solemnly replied, "That's quite all right, gentlemen, but naturally I didn't do it for you. I did it to save my wife's brother and his family."

"Naturally," added Bersha with a thoughtful nod. "But that still doesn't change the fact that we're forever indebted to you for your heroic actions. It's remarkable what your people accomplished today in the face of such overwhelming odds."

"What we did, we did with the help of the Lord of Creation. Make no mistake about it. If you're indebted to anyone, you're indebted to Him, not me."

"As usual, my favorite student has spoken well," said a familiar voice.

The group turned to see who was speaking, and Abram's face lit up. "Father Shem!"

"Abram, my son; just look at you now, the mighty warrior of the Lord."

An embarrassed Abram shook his head. "No, the Lord Himself deserves all the credit for this victory. How could I ever lay claim to such a success?"

"Nonsense, Abram. Obviously, the God of Strength helped you in your efforts. That goes without saying. But it's just as true that He couldn't have won the battle if you didn't lead the way. So God may be the author of this victory, but without a willing pen to cooperate in the effort, there still remains an empty page."

Pleased with this accolade from his beloved teacher, Abram finally broke into a reluctant smile. Bera and Bersha then stepped forward and bowed before Shem.

"If I'm not mistaken, sir," continued Bera, "you are Shem, king of Jerusalem."

"I am. However, I stand here today not as the king of an earthly city but rather as Melchizedek, a priest of the Most High, come today to bless my son Abram, to consecrate him and assist him in honoring the Lord Whom he has served since the days of his youth."

Again Bera and Bersha respectfully bowed.

"Then if it pleases the priest of the Most High," added Bersha, "we stand ready to assist the man Abram in whatever way he deems acceptable."

So Shem turned to his charge and asked, "Well, Abram, what do think? Do you consent to having these men participate in today's ceremony?"

"I have no objections."

"Very well, then," replied Shem with a clap of his hands. "Let the festivity of the bread and wine begin."

EVERYONE THERE SOON received a piece of bread, which was broken from dozens of loaves and passed from person to person. Then, copious amounts of wine were quickly handed out to all the men.

Shem reverently raised his cup of wine in one hand and a piece of bread in the other, and began to intone, "We praise You, oh, God of Heaven and Earth, Author of life and death. We come together this day to honor a great victory, one that You've accomplished through the hands of your servant Abram. I pray You consecrate his life from this day forward in all he does in Your great Name, and I ask this of You, as I stand here today, worshiping Your majesty, as one who is called Melchizedek, priest of the Most High. And all the people said: Amen."

Together, everyone echoed his words, saying, "Amen." And eating their piece of bread, each one of them drank their cup of wine.

"ABRAM, FRIEND OF GOD," exclaimed Bera, "how could we have been so fortunate as to have had your nephew Lot among our people? Certainly there must be some way we can repay you for your tremendous act of selflessness."

"All our goods recovered from the battle are naturally at your disposal," added Bersha. "Take whatever you wish. We'd consider it a great honor to relinquish all of it in exchange for restoring our lives and our freedom."

"As the Lord lives, gentlemen," insisted Abram. "I want nothing from you. The Creator of the Universe redeemed our lives and defeated our enemies. What more do I need from you?"

"But we insist," continued Bera. "After all, it's only right that you should be rewarded for helping us."

Abram adamantly shook his head. "Thank you, but no. I require nothing for myself. Of course I would like to see that Anar, Ashcol, Mamre and my men receive something for their efforts in this battle. I do think they're entitled to their fair share of the spoils."

"Of course," said Bera. "Anything you wish."

"Your deeds here will never be forgotten, Abram," chimed in Bersha. "I only wish we could do more to express our gratitude."

"Well, now that you mention it," replied Abram. "I do have one final request."

"Anything," replied Bera. "Just name it."

"I want Shem to receive one tenth of everything we recovered, and by that I mean, not just what was restored to you from the plunder of Sodom and Gomorrah but one tenth of everything Chedorlaomer lost as a result of his defeat. Agreed?"

The two kings exchanged a determined look and then nodded.

"Agreed," replied Bera and Bersha as one.

The Sand and the Stars

HAVING RETURNED TO his home in Hebron on the plains of Mamre, Abram was relaxing one afternoon, watching over his herds and flocks, when suddenly the Word of God appeared next to him.

"Lord, it's You," sputtered Abram, who sprang to his feet.

"Hello, Abram, how are you today?"

With a solemn, calculated tone, Abram replied, "I'm well, as is my family, thanks to You, of course."

"Good. I want to commend you for honoring the priest of God the way you did. I can see that his words of truth have not been wasted on you."

"Thank you, Lord, for saying so."

"And someday, Abram, because of your obedience to the words of your beloved teacher, you'll receive a tremendous reward from Me. I'll bless you and make your descendants like the sand and the stars, so numerous you won't be able to count them. Not only that, but I'll give this land to them as an eternal inheritance. Just be courageous and sincere with Me always, and everything I've promised you will come to pass."

"Descendants, Lord," replied Abram, thoughtfully mulling over the words in his troubled mind, "like the sand and the stars?"

"Yes, Abram, that's right."

"Lord, forgive me for saying this, but..." Abram tried in vain to get the next words out of his mouth. He futilely hung his head in despair.

"You're thinking of Nicu, aren't you?"

"Yes, I am. If only he was still with me, I could be as happy and proud as any father could be about a son."

"Don't despair, Abram; all is not lost. As surely as I live, Nicu has found his reward in Me, and he's asked me tell you how grateful he is to you and Sarai for rescuing him and showing him the only true kindness he had ever known, until now."

With a sparkle in his eyes, Abram looked up with tremendous joy. "Nicu said that?"

"He did, yes."

"Oh, Lord, thank you so much for that. You don't know how happy it makes me feel."

AS THE DARKNESS OF night began to settle in around him, Abram sat by the door of his tent, gazing out across the landscape. He casually picked up a handful of sand and watched the granules slip through his fingers. He did that again and again, and then he turned his eyes toward the night sky, looking up at the stars as they appeared, one by one.

Noticing what he was doing, Sarai walked over and sat down with him. "Is something bothering you, husband?"

As if coming out of a trance, Abram turned and focused his eyes on her. "What's that, my dear?"

"You've been so distant lately, moping around, staring off into space. Are you all right?"

"I'm fine. I've just been thinking, that's all."

"About Nicu?"

"I do think about him, yes; very often, as a matter of fact."

"He loved us so much, and we loved him, too."

"He was the closest thing we've ever had to a son, and now he's gone."

"I'm so sorry, Abram. This is all my fault, isn't it?"

"What? Of course not. Why would you say something like that? It wasn't your fault that Nicu was killed."

"No, that's not what I meant."

"Well, then, what are you saying?"

"I meant that if only I could be a real wife to you, a wife who could give you a son, your own son, then maybe I could help heal this emptiness in your heart."

Touched by her lament, Abram reached out and took hold of her hand. "Oh, Sarai, my dear, dear wife. Don't worry. The Lord will provide someday. You'll see."

"HAGAR," SHOUTED SARAI as she busily stoked an open fire one cool, breezy afternoon. "Hagar, where are you, young lady?"

"I'm right here, ma'am," replied Hagar, sticking her head out of the tent.

"It's time to bring the meat."

"Right away, ma'am."

BUSY WATCHING OVER his flocks, Abram suddenly became distracted. Sniffing at the air, he muttered, "Oh my, something smells good. It must be lunchtime."

SIDLING UP TO SARAI, Abram found her ladling a rack of sizzling meat with a creamy mixture of butter and herbs. Swiping at the meat with an eager finger, Abram then sucked on his flavorful fingertip. "Oh, that is good. How thoughtful of you, my dear. You're making my favorite."

"Hey, you; stop that. Go away. It's not done yet. And don't thank me, thank Hagar. She prepared the spices especially for you."

"Really?"

"Yes, really. She wanted to surprise you."

"My goodness. This is a surprise. I suppose compliments to the chef are in order. She certainly is a quick study, isn't she?"

"She is at that. We're very lucky to have her. There's nothing I've tried to teach her that she hasn't taken to practically overnight."

"Clearly, she's a chip off the old block."

Sarai flashed a wry smile at her husband. "Clearly."

Intrigued, Abram remarked, "You know, Sarai, if I didn't know better, I'd say there was something else going on in that head of yours. What are you thinking?"

"I want a baby, Abram, and I want one now."

"Excuse me."

"You heard what I said."

"But, Sarai, we've already been over this. When God wants you to have a child, you'll get pregnant. Until then, there isn't much else we can do."

"Oh yes there is."

"There is?" Abram stared at his wife with a confused look. "What might that be?"

Hagar then stepped up to the couple as they stared at one another with a peculiar look on both their faces. "Excuse me, ma'am; is there anything else I can do for you?"

"Yes, Hagar, as a matter of fact there is." And taking hold of Hagar's hand, Sarai placed it into Abram's. "I want you to give me a child I can hold on my lap."

"*What*?" replied Abram and Hagar together.

"You know, a child, a baby, *a son*," Sarai said emphatically, squeezing their hands together. "I'm tired of waiting for God to make this happen, so I'm taking matters into my own hands."

Pulling his hand from Hagar's and Sarai's, Abram shook his head. "Oh, Sarai, I don't know about that. Have things really become that desperate?"

"You mean, have *I* become that desperate? Isn't that what you're asking? Well, the answer is yes. And besides, you said yourself that she's a chip off the old block."

"Oh, Sarai, how could you? That is so unfair to use my own words against me like that."

"I'm sorry, but my mind is made up. You're not getting any younger, you know."

"For God's sake, wife, I'm only eighty-five years old. My father was seventy when he had me. So what are a few more years going to—"

"Uh, ma'am, sir," Hagar interjected, "I'm still standing right here. You're making me feel very uncomfortable talking about me as if I'm not."

Suddenly embarrassed, Sarai turned to Hagar. "I'm so sorry, Hagar, how rude of me. I hope I didn't offend you with my bluntness."

"No need to apologize, ma'am. I realize how depressed you've both been since Nicu's death. It's only natural. You were so close, as close as any son could ever be. I don't blame you for what you're asking, really I don't."

"Thank you, Hagar," Sarai sighed. "So you'll at least consider my proposal, then?"

Hagar dutifully nodded. "You and Master Abram have been so kind to me ever since Pharaoh sent me away. I'd have to be completely heartless not to at least consider it; if only to provide you both with as much happiness as you've provided me."

Turning back to Abram, Sarai asked, "And you? What about you? Won't you at least consider it, for my sake?"

And Abram nodded, too. "For your sake, my dear, of course I'll consider it."

FINALLY THE DAY CAME when Abram relented to the persistent pleading of his wife. Slowly, he entered Hagar's tent, where his servant girl stood awkwardly smiling. He hesitantly stepped up to her and kissed her tenderly, first on her forehead, then on her cheek, and finally full on her mouth.

AS DAYBREAK WASHED away the darkness of night, Hagar was carrying two pails of water from a nearby well. Stepping up to where Sarai was working with a roll of cloth, Hagar poured the contents of one of her pails into several smaller vessels. A strange expression suddenly rippled across her face, and just as abruptly, she grabbed the bucket that she had just emptied and vomited into it.

"Hagar," exclaimed Sarai. "Are you all right?"

"Forgive me, ma'am. I'm afraid I haven't been feeling well the past few mornings."

With a worried look, Sarai handed a small towel to Hagar, who then wiped her mouth.

"Mornings, you say?" murmured Sarai. "You're sick in the mornings? But the rest of the day?"

"The rest of the day, I'm fine. I can't imagine what's wrong with me."

"Hagar. You don't think?"

"What, ma'am?

"You don't think you're pregnant already, do you?"

"Pregnant? No, of course—" But no sooner had the words slipped out than she vomited again into the bucket.

"My God, you are pregnant."

AS HAGAR CELEBRATED with several other servant girls who were lavishing her with hugs and kisses, Sarai coolly watched them from a distance.

"Congratulations, Hagar," said one of the girls. "God has blessed you tremendously."

"How lucky you are," added another, "and how happy Master Abram must be with you for conceiving his child so quickly."

Receiving another hug from her friends, Hagar's joyous expression melted away when she noticed that Sarai was watching her. Suddenly smitten with an intense sadness, Sarai turned and walked away, unable to bear the sight of their celebration any longer.

"GOOD GOD, ABRAM," grumbled Sarai, "you should see what a spectacle Hagar is making of herself, carrying on like she was the queen of the hive."

"Sarai, what's gotten into you? I thought this was what you wanted."

"I wanted a son, yes; but this is more than I bargained for."

"But I don't understand. What's got you so upset?"

"That servant girl of yours obviously thinks she's better than me now. That's what has me so upset!"

"Don't be ridiculous. She doesn't think that. Not Hagar... You think?"

IN NO TIME AT ALL, Hagar's belly was beginning to show signs of the child within her. One evening as Abram and Sarai were having dinner in their tent, Hagar poured some water into their cups. Hagar gasped suddenly, and seeing her clutch at her stomach, Abram stood and held her arm to steady her balance.

"Hagar," exclaimed Abram, obviously nervous about her condition. "Are you all right?"

"Of course, sir. It's just the baby kicking inside me again." Taking hold of his hand, she placed it on her stomach. "Here, feel for yourself." Readily complying, Abram slid his hand across her swollen belly, and then he flinched.

"Oh, I felt that," sputtered Abram. "Good Lord, woman, sit down this instant. Sarai, get her a chair. I refuse to have Hagar waiting on us like a common servant girl anymore."

Sarai reluctantly cooperated, and Hagar slowly sat down with them at the table.

"There, that's better," announced Abram. "How do you feel now?"

"Much better, thank you."

"No, no, thank *you*, my dear. You are most welcome. After all, you're going to be the mother of my child soon. Isn't that right, Sarai?"

Turning to her, Abram and Hagar were both confronted with a mildly suppressed, though unmistakable, scowl.

"Please, ma'am," said Hagar, "don't be angry just because God has seen fit to provide me with a child so soon. You can't blame *us* just because you haven't been able to conceive yet … can you?"

SARAI CONFRONTED Abram the next morning while they were alone in their tent.

"This is an outrage, husband!" Sarai growled as she paced about like a stalking lioness. "How come you didn't pray for *me* to have your child?"

"Sarai, sweetheart, please be reasonable. You know perfectly well I've prayed long and hard for you to have my child."

"Reasonable? Reasonable? How do you expect me to be reasonable? Now, whenever I talk to Hagar in your presence, she mocks me; all because she's carrying *your child!*"

"I don't know what you expect me to do."

"I expect you to say something to her."

Abram shook his head in frustration. "It's a little late for that now, isn't it?"

"You infuriating man!"

Abram shrugged his shoulders. "Now what did I say?"

"I hope this all comes back to haunt you someday!"

"Sarai, please, you have to stop taking this out on me. This was all your idea in the first place. Why do you act as if *I* were to blame?"

"Well, you didn't exactly have to be whipped into her tent, you know."

"Oh, Sarai, that is so unfair. Now stop this nonsense. I've had quite enough of your ranting for one evening. In the meantime, Hagar still belongs to you, so you do whatever you want with her. I don't want to hear another word about it."

A PAIL OF WATER WAS dropped to the ground, spilling its contents.

"Hagar!" snapped Sarai. "How could you be so clumsy? Now pick that up."

But Hagar just stood there, glaring back in defiance.

"Young lady," Sarai continued, "I'd advise you to stop looking at me like that. Stop this nonsense immediately, and quit acting like a spoiled child."

"Funny, your husband didn't think to treat me like a child when he came to visit me in my tent."

"How dare you!" Cut to the quick, Sarai slapped Hagar square across the face.

Hagar blanched, wide-eyed and, quite abruptly, turned and ran away.

TRUDGING THROUGH the desert in the heat of the day, Hagar grew more exhausted with each step she took, until finally she came to a well. She eagerly pulled on the rope and drew up a pitcher of water, which she drank right away. Then without so much as a sound, an angel suddenly appeared next to Hagar. Startled by its unexpected arrival, she took several steps back, eyes darting every which way as though she were about to run.

"Hagar, wait," said the angel. "Don't be afraid."

"Who are you?" she replied, looking the creature over from head to toe. "*What* are you?"

"I'm an angel of the Lord."

"So I'm dead; is that it? Is that what you're telling me?"

"No, no; you're not dead."

"Then what do you want from me?"

"I'm here to inform you the Lord has seen the way your mistress has mistreated you, and He wants you to know that He's with you in your distress."

"*He* would help *me*?"

"He would, yes. In fact, the Lord has promised to make your family flourish, too, even as He's promised to bless all the children of Abram. Soon you'll have a son. Call him: Ishmael. But for now, you need to return to Sarai and submit to her."

"Submit? To that woman? I'd rather die first."

"Fine," replied the angel as he surveyed the barren landscape all around them. "But just remember, when you die, alone in this wilderness, the legacy of your son dies with you. Is that really what you want?"

HAVING RETURNED TO Abram's tent, Hagar, in due time, gave birth to a son.

"Your son, Master Abram," said the midwife, holding the baby up for Abram and Sarai, who came in to see how mother and child were getting along.

"A boy," exclaimed Abram, proud as he could be, much to the chagrin of Sarai. The midwife handed the baby over to Hagar, and very quickly, the child nestled upon her breast and fell asleep.

"Have you decided on a name, sir?" asked the midwife.

For several moments, Abram thought about it.

"Ishmael," whispered Hagar, exhausted and spent.

"What's that, Hagar?" wondered Abram.

"The angel told me to name our son Ishmael."

Exchanging a puzzled look between themselves, Sarai remarked to Abram, "The woman is obviously delirious. What do you expect?"

"MA'AM, YOU CALLED for me?" asked Eliezer of Sarai, who had her back turned to him as she busily prepared the afternoon meal.

"Yes, I did, Eliezer, two hours ago," Sarai replied impatiently, then turned to face Eliezer with a frown on her face. "When I ask for you, I don't expect to have to wait so long. Where have you been this whole time?"

"Begging your pardon, ma'am, but one of the lambs wandered off from the flock, and the ewe apparently went looking for it. By the time we caught up with them, a wolf had them cornered in a ravine."

Sarai's anger instantly turned to grief. "Oh, no. What happened?"

"We got there just as the pack started to converge. We were able to scatter them, but the mother was left to shield her lamb from the first wolf."

"So you managed to save them?"

With downcast eyes, Eliezer replied, "The lamb was unharmed, but the ewe, I'm afraid, was not so lucky. She tried to drive the beast away, but in the end she gave up her life to save her lamb."

A heartbroken Sarai grew weak in the knees. "Dear God, no." Suddenly she could not seem to catch a breath as she reached to steady herself.

Eliezer rushed to her side and helped her to sit down. "Steady, ma'am, steady. I'll run and get the master."

But Sarai's plaintive eyes kept him from moving. "Eliezer, no. Please don't do that. I'll be fine, really I will. There's no need to concern my husband."

"But ma'am—"

"But nothing, Eliezer," she replied, holding her hand to her breast, still trying to steady her breathing. "I'll be fine, I tell you. Now I need you to do something very important for me. Can I depend on you?"

"Certainly, ma'am, always. What is it?"

"I need you to pick two good men and go to Sodom for me. I need to find out how my brother Lot and his family are doing. The rumors I keep hearing about that place have got me worried sick. I need to know if they're true or not. Can you do that for me?"

"Yes, ma'am, of course."

"And not a word about my little spell to Master Abram. Is that understood?"

Eliezer nodded solemnly.

Reign of Terror

NO SOONER HAD THEY arrived in Sodom than Eliezer and his two companions witnessed an altercation between two men; one fellow was well-groomed and dapperly attired, while the other fellow was, quite in contrast, severely unkempt and bedraggled.

"Please, sir," muttered the bedraggled man to the well-groomed man, "I'm a stranger to these parts, and I have nowhere else to turn. Won't you help me?"

"What do you expect me to do for you?" asked the dapper Sodomite, obviously irritated with the intrusion.

"I'm so hungry," muttered the man as he feebly held out a handful of silver and gold coins. "Please, won't you sell me some food?"

"Oh, I see, why didn't you say so?" said the Sodomite, who then casually dropped a silver coin into the man's hand. "Here you are."

Dumbfounded, the pathetic, little man stared at the coins in his hand. "But, sir, what am I supposed to do with more money? What I need is something to eat."

"Then I guess you're out of luck, my dear fellow." With that, the local man turned to leave.

In a fit of desperation, the stranger dropped his handful of coins and grabbed the Sodomite by the sleeve. "No, wait, please. I'm at my wits' end. I have to eat something, or else I'm going to starve to death."

The Sodomite coldly stared down at the dirty hand clutching his sleeve. "How dare you put your grubby paw on me, you filthy foreigner. Release me, this instant."

"Please, sir, I just need something to…" The man spoke with ever-increasing difficulty. "Something, anything, to eat. Please, I need…"

As Eliezer and his two companions stood some distance away, they watched in horror as the Sodomite cruelly grasped the stranger's hand and, with considerable force, wrenched it from his sleeve. "What's that, you miserable worm? You say you need a good thrashing?" The Sodomite slowly twisted the offending hand, forcing the stranger to drop to his knees. Then quite abruptly, he landed a swift blow to the head of his supplicant victim. The man's eyes rolled into the back of his head, and he collapsed to the ground in a dusty heap. Then, to add insult to injury, the Sodomite proceeded to rip the man's coat from his body, leaving the poor fellow with just his tattered trousers. To the amazement of Eliezer and his two companions, the spectators who had gathered to watch applauded the Sodomite as he triumphantly walked away with the man's coat securely under his arm.

Eliezer immediately ran over to the bedraggled man and helped him to his feet. "Are you all right, sir?"

The poor fellow shook his head, trying desperately to clear his mind. "I'm not sure. What just happened?"

"That man just struck you on the head and took your coat."

As if waking up from a bad dream, the stranger focused his eyes on Eliezer and mumbled, "Will *you* help me, my friend?"

Bolting into action, Eliezer then ran and caught up with the Sodomite. "Hey, you there!"

Stopping in his tracks, the Sodomite turned. "Who, me?"

"Yes, you. How could you do something like that? Striking a defenseless man that way, and then stealing his coat. You should be ashamed of yourself."

The Sodomite defiantly glared back at him. "What are you saying to me? Was that man your brother? Is that what has you so upset?"

"No."

"I take it the people of Sodom have made you a judge. Is that it?"

"Of course not."

"Then I suggest you stop pestering me. This man is obviously none of your business."

"But there's no need to treat a man like a worthless dog."

"Is that so? Well, for your information: He's a vagabond, an out-of-towner. And around here, people like him aren't welcome. He got what he deserved; no more, no less."

"That's ridiculous." Eliezer stepped up to the Sodomite with his hand held out. "Now, be decent about it, and give the man his coat back. Come on."

"Who are you, anyway?"

"I'm nobody; just a man who hates to see injustice done to any human being."

"Justice? What do you know about justice?" said the Sodomite, who casually leaned down to pick up a rock. "Personally, I think you're suffering from a very serious malady, an acute imbalance of the head. Here, let me help you with your delusions."

The Sodomite then struck Eliezer in the forehead with the rock, and instantly blood gushed from the wound.

"Now that that's been taken care of," said the Sodomite, quite matter-of-factly, "pay me for helping you get rid of all this bad blood."

"What?" blurted Eliezer, wiping the blood from his forehead. "Are you insane?"

"How dare you speak to me like that," replied the man, who then grabbed Eliezer's arm. "Now pay me what you owe, or else!"

Looking at him in utter disbelief, Eliezer pulled his arm free. "You mean, you've wounded me, and now you want *me* to pay you for it?" Refusing to speak to him any further, Eliezer turned to walk away, but the Sodomite grabbed his arm again.

Just then another man, dressed in flowing black robes, strode from the gawking crowd.

"Hold on, hold on," grunted the man in stentorian tones. "What's all the excitement about?"

As soon as the Sodomite saw this man, he released Eliezer and respectfully bowed. "Excuse me, Your Honor. We're most humbled by your presence here today."

"Never mind, never mind. Just tell me what this is about."

"Who are you?" asked Eliezer, pressing the wound on his forehead in an effort to stop the bleeding.

The Sodomite wrinkled his brow. "Who is *he*? Why, this is Shakra, of course, esteemed judge of Sodom."

"A judge?" said Eliezer. "Oh, thank God; finally someone who can sort this out."

"Tell me, then," continued Shakra. "What seems to be the problem?"

"With all due respect, Your Honor," began the Sodomite. "You wouldn't believe what's transpired here today. I struck this delusional man with a stone so that the bad blood flowed from his forehead, and still he's unwilling to pay me for my services."

So the judge turned to Eliezer. "Well, what's wrong with you?" he asked with a perfectly straight face. "You heard the man. Pay him what you owe."

"Excuse me?" asked a flabbergasted Eliezer.

"I said, pay this man for services rendered. He is, after all, perfectly within his rights."

"Pay him? For what?"

"Now, see here, you," interjected the Sodomite. "I'm quite well known for my services in Sodom. How dare you question the efficacy of my work."

"Your work? What on Earth are you talking about? What kind of work do you do?"

"Why, naturally," continued Shakra, "this man is a highly esteemed doctor of spirits. People pay him dearly for his skill in removing the bad blood that is responsible for quite a number of ailments."

"Is that so?" Eliezer replied.

"That is so, yes," said the Sodomite matter-of-factly.

Thoughtfully nodding, Eliezer bent down to pick up a stone, and then he threw it at the judge, hitting him squarely in the forehead and producing a sizable wound that instantly started to bleed. "Fine, Your Honor," Eliezer said to Shakra. "If this is the Law around here, then please pay this man what I owe him!" And with that, he dashed off.

"Stop!" howled the judge. "Don't let that man get away!"

"By your own decree," Eliezer yelled back as he ran away, followed by his two companions, "you're getting exactly what you deserve; no more, no less!"

Several bystanders just stood there, without so much as moving a muscle.

"Are you just going to stand there while he gets away?" asked the bewildered Sodomite, addressing the bystanders.

"But he does offer a perfectly good argument, sir," replied one of the apathetic bystanders, who innocently shrugged his shoulders.

Thoroughly frustrated, the Sodomite shook his head in disgust as several other bystanders stepped forward to help the wounded judge try to stop the bleeding from his forehead. Disgusted with their feeble efforts, Shakra gruffly waved them off and, whirling about, disappeared into the crowd. As everyone began to disperse, there was still one young woman who stood there, apparently deep in thought.

"FATHER?" ASKED THE young woman, having returned home.

"Yes, Paltith. What is it?" replied the man, who just happened to be Lot.

"I was downtown this afternoon picking up some things for Mother, when I witnessed an altercation between a pair of out-of-towners and some of the locals."

"What happened?"

"I saw one out-of-towner try to defend another out-of-towner after a local man beat the first man and stole his coat."

"Good God, Paltith, you didn't get involved, did you? You know you're not supposed to have anything to do with out-of-towners."

"I know, Father. It's just so sad to see the way the locals continue to treat them. Why do they have to be so cruel? What crime have they ever committed?"

Overhearing their conversation, Lot's wife, Ado, walked over to her daughter and hugged her. "My dear, sweet Paltith, so innocent, so compassionate."

"Mother, please. Stop treating me like a child. You know how much I hate that."

"Well, then, it's time you stop acting like one, isn't it? The world is a harsh, unpredictable place. People do not just accidentally wander into town for no reason. Maybe these men were thieves or con men looking for easy money. You just don't know."

"Oh, hardly. You know perfectly well not everyone in this world deserves to be treated with suspicion and contempt."

"That's not for you to decide, young lady. Now, I don't want to hear another word about it. The rules are the rules, and as long as we live in this city we have to abide by them. Do you understand me?"

"You mean just because the locals refuse to sell food to an out-of-towner we're supposed to go along with it, even if it is a crime against God?"

"Rules are rules, Paltith," insisted Ado. "We didn't make them."

"But don't you think it's a barbaric practice? We refuse to sell a morsel of food to these poor souls, but we'll give them gold and silver instead. Then, because no one will sell them a thing to eat, they eventually drop dead from starvation, and everybody takes back their money. Who would devise such a wicked scheme, anyway? It's sick, I tell you, absolutely sick!"

"Young lady, I've had just about enough out of you! I'm still your mother, and I won't have you speaking to me as though I'd instituted this policy myself."

Thoroughly frustrated, Paltith turned to Lot. "Daddy, please."

But Lot adamantly shook his head. "I'm sorry, Paltith, but there's nothing I can do about it. Now, obey your mother. She only has your best interests in mind. Best not to pursue the issue any further."

"Oh, all right," she replied, skulking, and walked away.

HAVING MANAGED TO make his way out of the downtown area, the bedraggled stranger found a shady tree and sat down under it. Still, he feebly held out his handful of coins. "For Heaven's sake, won't somebody please sell me something to eat?" But all he ever got were more coins from the occasional passersby, so he just sat there, thoroughly frustrated, staring at the growing collection of coins in his hand. Then, unexpectedly, a piece of bread dropped into his hand. Hardly able to believe his good fortune, the stunned stranger slowly looked up into the most compassionate eyes he had ever seen; they were the eyes of Paltith.

"Are you an angel?" asked the stranger, who gratefully devoured the piece of bread.

Paltith smiled warmly at the sad, little man. "Of course not, silly." And handing him a cup of water, she happily watched him gulp it down all at once.

AS THE STRANGER continued to sit under the shade of that tree, his demeanor no longer reflected that of a man in distress. Instead, he was resting quite comfortably with a serene smile on his face, and as the people of Sodom made their way past him, they glared at the man with a growing suspicion.

"I wonder why this out-of-towner is still alive," commented one man. "I've never seen anyone conquer starvation for so long."

"And why isn't he still begging us for something to eat?" grumbled one woman.

"Something isn't right here. This man looks too happy, and I don't like it one bit."

"How do you think he's doing it? Could someone be helping him?"

"I have no idea, but I aim to find out."

Shaking their heads in disbelief, the disgruntled pair continued on, muttering incoherently under their breath, until finally they disappeared around a corner.

HEADING BACK TO THE well with her pitcher, Paltith paused to give some bread and water to the stranger. Quickly gulping down the water, he began to eat the bread, when suddenly the suspicious Sodomite man peeked around the corner.

"Aha!" he exclaimed as he bolted into action, marching over to the unsuspecting pair. "So you're the one who's been helping this foreigner! That's why he hasn't starved! That's why he hasn't died like all the rest!"

Then, before the stranger could get another bite of his bread, the Sodomite snatched it out of his hand. Tossing it to the ground, he stomped on it, grinding it to powder.

PALTITH WAS SUMMARILY brought before Judge Shakra, much to the dismay of her parents. Lot and Ado helplessly watched the proceedings from amidst a mob of angry spectators.

"She's the one all right, Your Honor!" snapped the Sodomite man. "I caught her red-handed supplying bread and water to a filthy out-of-towner."

As he sat so smugly in his regal black robes, Shakra gazed down at Paltith. "Tell me, then, my dear, is this man telling the truth about you?"

With downcast eyes, she meekly replied, "He is, Your Honor, yes."

"But why would you do such a thing? Aren't you aware of our civil code prohibiting the feeding of foreigners?"

"I am."

"Then why did you do it?"

"Your Honor," interjected Lot, "if I may offer a word in this girl's defense."

"You? Who are you?"

"I'm her father."

"I'm sorry, sir, but you're not on trial here today; this young woman is. Permission denied. Now answer the question, young lady. Why did you feed an out-of-towner when you knew it was in clear violation of our Law?"

"Law?" said Paltith, raising her head in plaintive defiance. "What kind of law condemns someone to death for no other reason than that they're from another country? I'd hardly call it a law at all, Your Honor. I think what you mean to ask me is: Why was I unwilling to commit a crime in the name of Sodom?"

At this, a tremendous outcry rose up from the angry crowd.

"You insolent brat!" growled a man. "How dare you question the wisdom of our Law!"

"Clearly this woman has violated a sacred trust, Your Honor!" bellowed another man. "She must pay for her crime, or else we'll all suffer the consequences!"

Shakra impatiently pounded his crudely fashioned stone gavel. "Silence! Silence! I will have order in my court, this instant!"

The incensed crowd slowly simmered down to a quiet boil, and the judge returned his attention to Paltith. "I can see from your arrogant attitude, young lady, you remain unrepentant of a crime you freely confess to committing, and unfortunately, a violation of this nature strikes at the very heart of our city's existence. If allowed to continue, we would certainly be overrun with an endless stream of foreigners, swarming about like so many locusts in search of food. Therefore, you leave me no choice but to sentence you with the strictest penalty our Law allows, and that sentence is death." Again Shakra slammed his stony gavel down with a tremendous thud. "Sentence to be carried out immediately."

"No!" screamed Ado. "You can't kill my daughter just for having pity on an out-of-towner! This is an outrage, a crime against God!"

Another man turned and glared at Ado, pointing his bony finger in her face. "Oh, yeah? Well just watch us, lady! And there ain't a damn thing you can do to stop us! Not you, and certainly not any *god* of yours!"

Overwhelmed with grief, Ado staggered, and Lot had to hold her up.

THE PEOPLE OF SODOM soon built a huge bonfire in the middle of one of their streets, and slowly they led Paltith toward it. To the absolute horror of Lot and Ado, they watched as their daughter was thrust into the flames; and although she screamed miserably as she died, burning to ashes in a matter of minutes, no one there but her family pitied her in the least.

BUT PALTITH'S CRIES did ascend to Heaven, as the molten Face of God looked down with incredible anger and said, "Never has it been truer said: From the wicked proceeds even greater wickedness. For so long now the people of Sodom and Gomorrah have provoked Me with their evil deeds, even though they've been blessed with a beautiful land, one with plenty of food and water to sustain them. And even though Abram, My servant, rescued them from the bondage of Chedorlaomer and his forces, they still refuse to share any of the resources I've given them. But now the time has come to end their reign of terror and greed. Something must be done about their crimes against humanity, once and for all."

One of the seventy angels then turned to the Face that was gazing down with such righteous indignation, and asked in great anticipation, "What, Lord? What will You do?"

"Wait and see," was all He said.

A Father of Many Nations

ABRAM WAS SITTING alone on a hilltop one evening, just as the stars above and the crickets below were beginning to make their presence known. Gazing thoughtfully across the landscape, he surveyed the meanderings of his numerous cattle, sheep and goats while his men were busy corralling them for the night. As he sifted a handful of sand through his fingers, his eyes inevitably wandered upward to the night sky, where he saw more and more of the twinkling lights coming into view. Abruptly the Word of God appeared before Abram, diverting his attention from the Heavens. A startled Abram jumped to his feet and sucked in his breath. "As long as I live, Lord, I don't think I'll ever get used to You showing up like this."

The Word smiled warmly. "Hello, Abram, how've you been?"

"Fine."

"Fine? Really?"

Embarrassed, Abram looked away. "Oh, what's the use. There's no point in trying to hide anything from You, is there?"

"Not really, no."

"Then what's the point of asking me if You already know what I'm feeling?"

"The point is to always be honest with Me, to know you can trust Me in all you do, to believe I'll listen to whatever you need to say, no matter how difficult it is to understand why you're going through it. Does that make sense?"

"Yes, Lord, it does. So if I said I was frustrated with how things were going for me, You'd understand?"

"Of course I would."

"Frustrated with how things have turned out for me and Sarai, I mean. You wouldn't hold it against me?"

"Certainly not. In fact, that's why I've come here tonight."

"Really?"

"Yes, Abram, I've come to let you know about My intentions to make a contract between you and Me so that before long you and Sarai will have more children than you can possibly imagine."

"Like the sand and the stars?"

"That's right, Abram, just like the sand and the stars. So from now on, your name will no longer be Abram, but it will be Abraham, because I'll multiply your family to such an extent that your descendants will comprise many nations, and your wife will no longer be called Sarai, but her name will be Sarah, because kings and queens will descend from her."

Abraham bowed reverently. "Thank you, Lord. Thank you very much."

"And as a sign of our agreement, you and every male child among you will be circumcised, and this contract, which will be testified to in your flesh, will bind us together, forever."

ENJOYING THE HEAT of the day, Abraham was sitting uncomfortably outside his tent. Then, as if from out of nowhere, three men appeared not more than a few hundred feet from where he sat; and they were headed straight toward him. Grimacing painfully, he got up to greet them.

"Hello, gentlemen, how are you all doing today?" Abraham asked.

"We're hungry, thirsty and tired from our extended journey," replied one of the men.

"I know exactly how you feel," said Abraham, squinting up at the Sun. "I've spent many years myself traveling from one country to another. Where are you folks from, if you don't mind my asking?"

"We've come a very long way, Abraham," the second man replied. "Further than you can possibly imagine."

"Is that so?" Wrinkling his brow, the patriarch stared back for several moments. "You know who I am, then?"

"Why, certainly," said the third man. "The reputation of a man like you travels far and wide."

"You don't say," Abraham said thoughtfully as he fixed his eyes on the third man standing before him, to the exclusion of his two companions. "Because until recently, I was known by my former name, Abram. I've only just recently taken on the name of Abraham. Could it be that we've met before, sir? Could that be why you seem vaguely familiar to me?"

The trio exchanged a peculiar look amongst themselves, then shrugged innocently.

"Like we said," continued the first man, "news travels far and wide."

"Interesting," said Abraham.

"So Abraham, father of many nations," continued the second man with a wry smile, "where are all your children?"

"Oh, them?" he mumbled. "I only have one son at the moment."

"Pity," replied the first man, "for a man called Abraham, I mean."

"One can always hope and pray, though, can't they?" he replied.

"Always," echoed the third man, supremely confident.

"Who knows, Lord willing," continued the second man, "maybe someday your name will inspire God to provide you with the many children you've been hoping and praying for."

"Yes, Lord willing, I do hope so," Abraham said with an awkward smile. "Now, if it's all right with you, gentlemen, won't you join me for lunch? That is, if you're still hungry and thirsty."

"It would be our distinct pleasure, Father Abraham," said the third man, who nodded respectfully.

ABRAHAM'S GUESTS ate and drank everything that had been set before them. After they finished their meal, the third man turned to Abraham and quietly remarked, "You know, my friend, I have a very good feeling that by this same time next year, I'll be returning to find that Sarah has given birth to your child; a son, in fact."

Amazed at this, Abraham beamed a huge smile at the man. "Oh, that would be nice. You say you have a good feeling about it?"

The man nodded confidently. "Yes, a very good feeling. So much so, I can guarantee it will happen."

Abraham's eyes lit up. "Really? I can only hope you're a true prophet of the Lord, sir." Turning to the two other men, he playfully asked, "Hey, can you two vouch for your friend here? Is he really a prophet sent by God to deliver such good news to me?"

Without hesitation, the pair nodded.

"Yes, sir, he most certainly is," said the first man.

"He's all that, and more," added the second.

Then the trio stood to their feet.

"And on that note," continued the third man, "we must be on our way. We have another very important mission to take care of."

Abraham sat there, unable to think of anything to say. He just waved goodbye and watched silently as the trio departed. As they moved off toward the horizon, Sarah stepped over to her husband, who sat there still watching the men in the distance with the most peculiar expression on his face.

"What did that man say, Abraham?" asked Sarah. "I don't think I heard him correctly."

"He said you're going to bear me a son next year."

But Sarah just laughed. "I think you were all sitting in the Sun too long, that's what I think. Either that, or you were drinking the good wine."

Abraham shook his head, as if awakening from a deep sleep, then he smiled at his wife. "Oh, Sarah, never underestimate the wonders this life can bring. Never. After all, you're still as beautiful to me as the day I married you."

Sarah smiled back at her husband. Then, as they returned their gaze back to the landscape, they saw that their trio of guests had split up along the way. Two of the men continued their journey, while one of them veered off by himself and abruptly vanished into thin air. Abraham and Sarah exchanged an odd look and, as if to signify they had not seen anything unusual, simply shrugged it off.

Sodom and Salt

AS THE HEAT OF THE day began to bear down on the plains of Sodom, Lot was sitting just inside the gate to the city, fanning himself with a palm leaf. Staring blankly out across the plain of Jordan, he suddenly caught a glimpse of Abraham's two visitors as they approached him. With great anticipation, Lot watched the pair as they walked right up to where he was sitting. Rising to his feet, he graciously bowed before the two strangers. "Greetings, gentlemen, glad to meet you."

"Likewise, I'm sure, my good fellow," the first man said.

"Looks like you two have traveled a long way," continued Lot. "Where'd you come from?"

"Canaan," replied the second man.

"Canaan?" blurted Lot, excited by the news. "You don't say. Canaan. Beautiful place, that's for sure. I have family living in Canaan."

The two visitors nodded vacantly, staring past Lot and toward the heart of the city.

"Is that so?" muttered the first man, apparently only half-listening.

"Why, yes, my sister, actually," Lot continued. "You know, not many strangers like you come around here anymore. What brings you to Sodom, anyway?"

The two looked at each other, as if wondering how to respond, but before they could say a word, Lot excitedly raised his hand like a knowing child in class.

"Of course, of course, how stupid of me. You two must be here to participate in one of our famed annual festivals. Am I right?"

"Festival?" asked the first man. "What festival?"

"The festival of the Moon, naturally."

Again the pair looked at each other, then back to Lot, shrugging their shoulders, obviously unfamiliar with what he was talking about.

"Four times a year," continued Lot unabated, "the people of Sodom gather together to celebrate the various degrees of the Harvest Moon. There's wine and women, there's music and singing. It's a time of wild revelry, where many a man lays with his neighbor's wife. I've even heard tell of some taking their virgin daughters this time of year."

The two visitors exchanged a disturbed look, and seeing their strained expression, Lot quickly added, "Er, uh, well, that is, if one indulges in that sort of thing. Not that I do, you understand."

"I should hope not, sir," said the first man.

"No, friend," continued the second man, shaking his head, "we're certainly not here to attend a festival like that."

"What does bring you here, then?" Lot asked, clearly confused. "Decent folk like you shouldn't be wandering through a place like Sodom unless you know somebody here or have some real purpose. If not, then this place is liable to eat you alive and spit you out."

"Yes, Lot, we understand," said the first man. "But you don't have to be concerned for our safety. That much we're certain of."

"Hey, how do you know my name? I don't remember telling you yet. Who are you guys, anyway?"

"That's not important, Lot," replied the second man. "What is important, is our mission."

"Mission? What mission?"

"Never mind that right now," said the first man. "You'll find out soon enough."

Confused at this, Lot shook his head, as if to clear the cobwebs from his melancholy mind. "You'll have to excuse me. I haven't been myself lately. I've recently suffered the tragic loss of my dear daughter."

Without further delay, the two men started past him, heading down the main thoroughfare that led to the city's center. "We know, Lot," said the second man, quite matter-of-factly. "That's why we're here."

Lot oddly titled his head. "Excuse me?" Then seeing they had started without him, he hastily followed after the pair. "Hey, are you two thirsty? You can come to my home for something cool to drink if you want."

The two men stopped, turned to Lot, and nodded perfunctorily. And when he made his way past them, they followed. "And if you're hungry, you might have dinner with us, too. How does that sound?"

Again the pair nodded graciously and continued to follow Lot.

AS LOT AND HIS TWO visitors walked along, the lilting strains of music began to fill the air. A crowd of men, women and children appeared from out of nowhere, dancing and singing as they went. Passing by Lot and the two men, several people from the group paused to address the trio.

"Well, hello, gentlemen," said one Sodomite man, pleasantly inebriated. "How are you this fine afternoon?"

"We're well, neighbor," Lot replied.

"Wonderful. And are you here today to celebrate with us?"

"We are not, good sir," the first visitor stated perfunctorily.

"How disappointing," said the Sodomite as he pulled a beautiful woman forward to stand next him. "Are you sure there isn't something you see that might change your mind?"

A mortified Lot stepped between the Sodomites and the two visitors. "We thank you for your generosity, friend, but I'm afraid these men are not interested in that sort of thing."

"Not interested?" wondered the bleary-eyed man, who looked at the woman next to him and back again at the trio of men. "Not interested in this? That's the stupidest thing I ever heard. Are you people out of your minds?"

"But he speaks the truth, sir," insisted the second visitor. "We seek something altogether different."

"Well, why didn't you say so," said the Sodomite, who then stepped over to a young girl around fourteen years of age. Taking her by the hand, the man led her up to the trio and spun her around like a toy doll on display. "Then maybe I can interest you in my daughter, guaranteed virgin soil, if you know what I mean."

The two visitors exchanged another serious look and turned to Lot for support.

"Gentlemen, please," interjected Lot, "we're most grateful for your selfless offer, but really, my friends and I will pass."

Upon hearing this, the Sodomite became irritated. "What are you saying, then? We're not good enough for you, neighbor?"

"That's not it at all, sir," the first visitor said. "It's just that our mission involves something entirely different."

"Mission? What do you mean, *mission*? Say, who are you people, anyway?"

Finally losing their patience, the two visitors stepped past the Sodomite man, followed quickly by Lot, leaving the entire group of Sodomites with the strangest look of bewilderment on their faces.

TO HIS TENT, LOT and his two guests found Ado inside, sewing one of his shirts while their two young daughters, twins about sixteen years old, looked on. Turning to see Lot enter, the girls ran and embraced him.

"Papa, you're home," exclaimed one of the girls.

"Well, hello you two. I'm glad to see you as well."

Looking up at the two visitors, the other girl asked, "Who are you?"

"These are my new friends. Can you say hello?"

"Hello," said the girls together.

"They've just arrived from Canaan."

"Really," replied Ado, who turned from her sewing and, with a suspicious tone, continued, "And just like that you've decided to invite your *new friends* into our home? Out-of-towners you've only just met?"

"Yes, my dear, that's right. I understand your concerns, but there's something special about these men," Lot insisted with an awkward smile. "I'm not quite sure how to put it, but something about them compelled me to make their acquaintance."

"Compelled you?" echoed Ado, obviously unconvinced.

Uncomfortable with her scrutinizing gaze, the two visitors turned to Lot.

"We're sorry if we've caused you any inconvenience, Lot," said the first man. "We'll leave at once if you wish."

"No, no, don't be silly," he replied. "Don't mind my wife, please. As you can imagine, living in a place like Sodom, a place so suspicious of foreigners, she's just looking out for the safety of her family."

The two men bowed perfunctorily.

"Certainly," said the second man. "And we can assure you, ma'am, your safety is of paramount importance to us as well."

"You see, Ado?" continued Lot. "There's nothing to be afraid of. I'm telling you, these men are our friends. I can feel it in my bones."

"Tell me, then," Ado said. "Have your friends told you why they've come to Sodom?"

"Naturally, my dear. They're here on a very important mission."

"A mission?" wondered Ado. "In Sodom? What kind of mission could you possibly have in a place like this?"

The two men dutifully bowed again.

"Time will tell, good lady, time will tell," insisted the first man.

Ado turned to Lot with a puzzled look. "They certainly are a mysterious pair, aren't they? I sure hope you know what you're doing, Lot."

WHEN ADO PUT DINNER on the table, the pair dug right in. Ado furtively glanced at her husband. "Mission, eh?" she said to Lot with a wry smile. "And you're certain that this mission of theirs isn't to eat us out of house and home?"

THE NEXT MORNING, the two visitors approached Lot and Ado.

"It's time now for us to carry out our mission," said the first man, quite calmly. "Are you ready?"

"Ready?" asked Lot, turning to Ado. "Who us?"

"Yes, of course, you, your wife, your daughters."

"But what do we have to do with your mission?" asked Lot.

"*You are* our mission, Lot," replied the second. "The Lord has sent the two of us to rescue you from the destruction that's about to overtake this evil place. Very soon the judgment of God is going to rain down upon this land. Very soon Sodom will be obliterated from the face of the Earth."

"You're kidding," blurted Lot.

The two men looked at one another, obviously confused.

"I'm sorry, Lot, but we never kid," remarked the first man.

"And that's another thing," Lot said. "You never did tell me how you knew my name before I told you."

"How else do you think?" asked the second man. "The Lord Himself sent us here. Now, do you, or do you not, want us to save you?"

"Save us from what?" Ado sputtered. "What are you people talking about?"

"We already told you," said the first man, growing impatient. "The Lord is about to destroy this place!"

"Destroy?" exclaimed Lot. "What do you mean, *destroy*?"

Looking oddly at his partner, the first man then shifted his gaze back to Lot. "Eradicate, annihilate, *destroy*," he continued, apparently unsure of the question. "What don't you understand about this word, destroy?"

Lot shook his head in exasperation. "No, no; of course I understand what destroy means. Look, I guess you just caught me by surprise."

"God knows, Sodom can be a terrible place to live sometimes," added Ado, "but it's still our home, like it or not."

"Well, I, for one, am sick to death of it," Lot said with a lamentable sigh. "After what they did to our Paltith, this whole God-forsaken country can burn to the ground, for all I care."

"Lot, this is crazy," Ado interjected, "we don't know these men. How can we be sure they're telling us the truth? For all we know they're going to lead us off on some wild goose chase while their partners move in and ransack our home of all our valuables."

Mulling her words over, Lot turned to the two men and asked, "What do you gentlemen have to say to that? Is there any way you can prove you've been sent by God?"

"Yeah," continued Ado, "tell us something only God would know about us. And if you can't, I want you out of my home right now."

The two men exchanged another serious look.

"You see, Lot?" snapped Ado. "They can't do it. They're frauds, I tell you."

"Paltith," said the first man, "your daughter."

"Paltith?" wondered Ado. "What about Paltith?"

"Besides your immediate family," the first man continued, "does anyone know why you named your daughter Paltith?"

Lot and Ado looked at one another and shrugged.

"Not that I'm aware of, no," replied Lot.

"Well, apparently after Abraham rescued you from Chedorlaomer and his army, you wanted to pay tribute to God for delivering your family, so, on the very day that Ado announced to you she was pregnant, you decided to honor that miraculous event by naming your daughter Paltith."

Again Lot and Ado looked at each other, but this time, they appeared more astonished than anything else.

Ado's legs grew weak. "But I don't understand."

"I'm right, aren't I?" asked the first man.

Feebly, Lot and Ado nodded in tacit confirmation.

"It's not possible, I tell you," Ado muttered. "How could you know something like that? *Why* do you know something like that?"

"Because, for the sake of Abraham and his family," replied the second man, "the Lord is watching over you to avenge their cause."

Turning to the visitors, Lot said with unflinching resolution, "When do we leave?"

"As soon as possible," replied the second man. "There isn't much time left. Gather your two daughters, whatever you can carry, and prepare to leave at once."

Ado clutched at her husband's arm. "Lot, wait! Not so fast." Looking to the two men, her look of desperation was downright heartbreaking. "We have two more daughters, married daughters, who don't live with us anymore. What about them?"

"Go," said the first man without hesitation. "Find them. Persuade them to come with us, *now*. Go quickly, before it's too late!"

UNFORTUNATELY, THOUGH, when Lot arrived to plead with his daughter, she raised her hand in protest. "I'm sorry, Father," she said, quite unsympathetically, "but you must be out of your mind. You think God is really going to destroy our city? How could you even suggest something like that?"

ADO, TOO, FARED NO better with their other daughter. "Oh, Mother," she stubbornly said, "I can't just uproot my family at this point in our lives. And for what? Some ill-conceived exodus? And to where? Out there, to wander and die in the wilderness? I'm surprised at you, really."

WHEN THEY RETURNED home, Lot and Ado understood all too well what the look of despair meant on the face of the other. So without a single word between them, they gathered their two youngest daughters and whatever they could carry, and left their home, accompanied by their gracious visitors.

ALONG THE WAY, LOT'S family and their escorts encountered the same group of Sodomites they had met the day before. The head of the group suspiciously stepped up to block their path.

"Well, well, look who we have here," said the Sodomite man. "If it isn't our old friends, too busy to spend any of their precious time with us during this happy time of festival, as if we were something to be shunned, or worse, to be *despised*."

"Please, sir," the first escort began, "we meant no disrespect to you or your family."

Obviously a little tipsy, the Sodomite turned to his companions. "How noble. Isn't our new friend as noble as the day is long?"

Another of the Sodomite men there was quite amused at his friend's antics. "How noble," he echoed with a drunken nod.

Turning back to Lot and his escorts, the first Sodomite noticed the bags that they were carrying. "And just where do you folks think you're going with all this stuff?"

"Please, sir," interjected the second escort, "we have no quarrel with you. Just let us pass, and there will be no trouble between us."

Undeterred, the Sodomite man stepped up to the escort who had just addressed him. "Trouble? Trouble from who? From you? Don't make me laugh. Now, if you know what's good for you, we can make a little deal. I understand you may not be interested in our wives or our daughters. No harm done. But *I am* very interested in yours. So hand them over to us right now, or, if you prefer, I might be persuaded to accept all the goods you're carrying instead. Which do you prefer, friend?"

At a complete loss, Lot and the others exchanged worried looks all around.

"Well," snarled the Sodomite, "don't just stand there gawking at each other. What'll it be? Your women, or your goods?"

"I'm warning you, sir," continued the first escort, "we don't have time for this. Now step aside, or else."

Wrinkling his brow, the Sodomite tilted his head. "Or else *what*?"

Suddenly the two escorts transformed into a pair of luminously beautiful angels who stretched out their wings in an awesome display of power. Gasping in disbelief, the group of Sodomites took a collective step back. The two angels then simply waved their hands, and every last one of those Sodomites were instantly struck with blindness.

"What did you freaks do to me?" screeched the first Sodomite. "I can't see a thing!"

The terrified Sodomites all began clutching at their eyes and groping around, as if they had been plunged into utter darkness.

"Now, hurry!" said one of the angels to Lot and his family. "We've got to get out of here as fast as we can."

"If we don't leave this place right away," continued the second, "you'll be consumed along with the evil of this entire city!"

So Lot, his family, and the two angels immediately began to run.

THICK CLOUDS BEGAN to congeal in the atmosphere above the Five Cities of the Plain, turning into angry, blood-red thunderheads as far as the eye could see. Then, a crimson drop of rain fell, followed by several more drops, which quickly turned into rainfall. This steady rainfall turned into droplets of magma, which then became a torrential downpour of liquid flame. With relentless force, it came down upon Sodom, Gomorrah and the surrounding Plain Cities, until the entire region was being consumed in a vast conflagration of fire and brimstone.

Breathless and exhausted, Lot and his family made their way beyond the outskirts of Sodom, still accompanied by their two angelic escorts. In anguish, Ado turned to her husband and groaned, "Oh, Lot, I'm so worried about the girls. What's going to happen to them?" Turning back to witness the destruction of the doomed cities, she froze in her tracks, horrified by the sight of the great cloud of smoke and ash that rose up from the plain. And as soon as the stark realization of the devastation struck at her, heart and soul, Ado instantly transformed into a pillar of salt.

My Laughter

SITTING CASUALLY by his tent, one lazy, hazy afternoon, Abraham was watching Sarah as she walked by. Noticing his scrutinizing gaze, she smiled and stepped over to him. "Abraham, why are you looking at me like that? I always know you're up to no good when I see that look in your eyes."

"But Sarah, dear."

"Don't *dear* me. What's going on?"

"I was just thinking."

"Thinking?"

"Yes, thinking."

"And?"

"Well, we've been living in Canaan for what, twenty-five years now?"

"Around that, yes. What about it?"

"It's just that we've done just about everything we can do in this place, and I'm growing restless for new horizons."

"New horizons? You actually expect me to believe that? You mean, this has nothing to do with the fact that you're on the verge of your one hundredth birthday?"

"Oh, all right. There's no use trying to put anything past you. Yes, I've been thinking a lot about that lately."

"Abraham, what are you so worried about? You know perfectly well how long Noah lived. Shem is what, well past four hundred? And he's still going strong. Eber, Reu, Serug, all past two hundred. Compared to them, you're barely middle-aged, for Heaven's sake."

Abraham's frown turned to a smile. "My sweet Sarah; you always know how to cheer me up."

"Now, what were you saying about new horizons?"

"Who, me?"

"HELLO, SARAH," SAID a quiet voice.

Startled, Sarah, who was folding clothes inside her tent, turned to see who was speaking to her. It was the Word of God. With her hand to her breast, she hesitantly replied, "Oh, dear, hello there. Where did you come from?"

"I'm sorry if I startled you, Sarah."

"Excuse me, but have we met before?"

"Not exactly, no. But I have met with your husband before."

"Really?"

"As a matter of fact, yes; on several occasions."

"So you're here to see him again?"

"No, not today."

"You two are friends?"

"Yes, very close friends."

"That's nice. I don't think he's ever mentioned you before. Who are you?"

"I am the Word of God, the Mediator between Heaven and Earth, the same One Who told you last year that I'd be returning with word of Abraham's son. Don't you remember?"

"That was you?"

"It was. And do you remember when Abraham told you about your conceiving a son? *Your* son, Sarah? Do you remember what you did when you heard the news?"

An embarrassed Sarah smiled awkwardly. "I laughed."

Then, right before her eyes, the Word vanished, leaving Sarah standing there with the most peculiar look on her face. Quite unconsciously, she reached down and placed her hand on her stomach.

Abraham walked into their tent. "Sarah. Are you all right? You're not ill are you?"

With her hand still on her belly, she replied, "No, of course not. Why do you ask?"

"You should see the look on your face. What's wrong?"

"The strangest thing just happened. A man was just here."

"Here? Just now? A man?"

"Yes, a man. But not just any man. He said he was the same man who came to visit us last year, the same man who told you I'd be giving birth to your son. First, he was standing right here talking to me, then suddenly he was gone, just like that."

"Sarah, no."

"I'm afraid so, yes. If I didn't know better, I'd say the summer heat has finally drained me of all my senses."

With an odd smile, Abraham stepped up to her. "Oh, Sarah, don't be ridiculous. You've never made more sense in all your life."

"What?" Sarah gaped at her husband, thoroughly perplexed. "What are you saying? You mean I haven't lost my mind?"

"Of course not, my darling."

"But how can you be so sure?"

"Because the same Man you've just described has been appearing to me in exactly the same way, over and over, throughout my entire adult life. One moment He's there, and the next, *poof*, He's gone."

"*Poof*? Just like that."

"Just like that." A strange look then flashed across Abraham's face. "Sarah, do you know what this means? The Man Who came here last year to tell us about our son was not just any man; it was Him. It was the Lord Himself Who came to bring us such good news. No wonder He seemed familiar to me that day. No wonder."

With a sigh of relief, Sarah exclaimed, "Well, why on Earth haven't you told me about any of this before?"

"Oh, I see. It's not enough that I've dragged you from one end of the country to the other, on nothing more than an apparent whim." And looking down at Sarah's hand resting on her stomach, Abraham smiled impishly as he placed his hand on hers. "Now you want me to give you even more reason to think the father of your child is completely insane."

THE MUFFLED CRIES of a baby echoed through the night, causing Abraham to turn in the direction of the sound. As he did, a midwife came out of his tent. "Congratulations, My Lord," she said wistfully. "That's the healthy cry of your newborn son."

"My son? *Sarah's* son?"

"That's right."

"How are they?"

"They're both fine. Go inside and see for yourself."

Stepping into his tent, Abraham proudly smiled at the sight of Sarah and their newborn son. As she held the crying baby close to her heart, Sarah whispered, "Hush, hush, my child; there's no need to cry. The days and nights of weeping are over, and now they've become laughter; my son ... my Isaac ... my laughter."

AS THE SUNLIGHT FADED from view and the crickets began to chirp all around, Nimrod and several of his men entered their makeshift camp. With an exhausted sigh, they relinquished their kill of antelope and wild boar from their stout shoulders, dropping them just beyond the perimeter of the fire pit.

"Have the cook prepare our meal right away," Nimrod said. "I'm hungry, and I'm tired."

"As you wish, Sire," replied one of his men. "I'll see to it at once."

"In the meantime, I'm going to warm myself by the fire. Let me know as soon as dinner is ready."

SEATED SEVERAL YARDS away from the crackling fire, Nimrod yawned and stretched his tired muscles. As he sat there, his weary eyes flitted from the flames jumping up out of the fire pit, to the bustle of activity of his men hurrying about the camp, and back to the fire again. Hypnotized by the flickering of the fire, he was unable to resist closing his eyes, but when he heard the sound of footsteps very close to him, he quickly opened them. He could hardly believe what he was seeing.

"Abraham," blurted Nimrod, whose eyes grew wide with surprise, "what are you doing here? How did you get past my men?" Looking around, he saw that no one except Abraham was standing before him. "Where *are* my men, for that matter?"

"It seems as though they've all abandoned you," came Abraham's calculated reply.

"That's absurd. Why would they do that?" A glint of steel reflected from the hand of Abraham, causing Nimrod's eyes to open wider still. "What's that in your hand?"

"What?" Abraham asked nonchalantly as he held out a sword. "This?"

"Yes, that." Nimrod's uncharacteristically nervous eyes darted about, his hand surreptitiously taking hold of his sword lying next to him.

As Abraham held his sword up and examined it with a peculiar look in his eye, he replied, "This, my friend, is an instrument of divine justice. Apparently your rebellion against the God of Heaven has finally overtaken you."

Abraham abruptly lunged at Nimrod with his sword, striking down at him just as the king rolled out of the way. With sword in hand, Nimrod sprang to his feet and swung back at Abraham, who adeptly evaded his blade. The two men then stood face to face and sword to sword. Still Nimrod's eyes furtively searched the landscape that flickered in the light of the campfire.

"Quit wasting your time wondering where your men have gone, King Amraphel," insisted Abraham as he raised his sword, preparing to strike again. "You alone must stand as the recipient of God's wrath." And with a furious growl, Abraham rushed at Nimrod, swiping his blade with reckless abandon. Barely ducking the tip of his opponent's sword, the king slashed back and, with one clean stroke, cut off Abraham's arm. Sliding cleanly off his shoulder, it fell to the ground with a thud. As Nimrod turned to look, however, he no longer saw Abraham but only his bloody right arm, which was lying on the ground in front of him.

With a satisfied grin, Nimrod said, "Well, well. So much for the retribution of God."

For just a moment, he stood triumphantly over the severed appendage of his foe; that is, until the arm began to writhe and twitch in the dust. The bewildered king watched as the bloody arm then transformed into a huge serpent, which rose up before him. Frozen with fear, Nimrod dropped his sword just as the creature, with blood-red eyes and dripping fangs, lunged forward, and clamped its tremendous jaws down on his head.

WITH A BLOOD-CURDLING scream, Nimrod sat upright, sweat pouring down his face. His wild eyes swiveled in every direction as he quickly realized he was still seated by the campfire with all of his men staring at him, perplexed by his anguished outburst.

"CLEARLY, SIRE, THIS was another vision of Abraham's destiny involving your demise," intoned one of Nimrod's black-robed soothsayers.

"My demise," Nimrod sputtered with a sarcastic grimace. "Quit mincing words with me, soothsayer. You mean my *death*, don't you?"

"Forgive me, My King. My intention was not to offend you."

"Then stop treating me like a simpering child. I have to know the truth about this vision. What does it mean?"

"I believe the vision speaks of the fact that, despite all your efforts, typified by your cutting off his arm, Abraham will still, one way or the other, wind up causing your death."

"You mean to say that Abraham himself will be the one to kill me with his own hands? Is that what you're telling me?"

"Of that, I'm afraid, no one can say for sure. The fact that his right arm became the serpent that killed you might indicate an offspring of Abraham will carry out the act, a son or maybe a grandson. It's difficult to say."

"Difficult? The only difficult thing around here is trying to decipher your flimsy explanations. If Abraham and his sons don't put me out of my misery, listening to all your vague interpretations will surely be the death of me."

"A thousand pardons, Your Highness," muttered the soothsayer, hanging his head. "Please believe me when I say, we're doing everything we can to assist you in this matter."

"How commendable. Then tell me: What do you suggest I do to rid myself of this scourge of Abraham? So far, all our humanly efforts have failed miserably. Can't one of you cast a spell on him? Smite him with dumbness or madness? Conjure up the dark lord of the underworld? Anything! What good are you people if all you ever do is offer me a bunch of useless interpretations?"

With a thoughtful nod, the soothsayer replied, "We'll look into it right away, Sire."

WHEN ISAAC WAS AROUND five years old, he was sitting by the door of the family tent, quietly playing with a small wooden toy. Nearby was Ishmael, who was nineteen by then. As Isaac played by the tent door, Ishmael was diligently practicing with his bow and arrows, taking shot after shot at a tree marked with a bull's-eye. Quite skilled with his bow, Ishmael managed to nearly hit his mark, missing it by only a few inches.

Eventually getting bored with his target practice, Ishmael walked over and stood just a few feet away from his younger brother, staring oddly at him for several moments. "So you like playing with your toys, do you, Isaac?" he asked.

Isaac looked up at his brother with a smile and a nod. "Papa made it for me. Papa loves me very much."

With a peculiar look in his eye, Ishmael replied, "Is that so? Well, I have a toy of my own, little brother." And taking another arrow from his quiver, he slowly drew it back in his bow, taking direct aim at little Isaac.

Walking past the tent, Sarah caught sight of what Ishmael was doing with her son and screamed, "Ishmael, no!" Horrified, she ran and got between his poised bow and Isaac. "Stop, Ishmael! Put that thing away, this instant! What do you think you're doing?"

Ishmael lowered his bow in frustration and walked away, muttering under his breath. "Ah, I didn't mean nothin' by it. I was just playing around."

OUTRAGED AND TREMBLING, Sarah went to Abraham. "You will never believe what I caught Ishmael doing just now."

"Good Lord, Sarah. What?"

"He had this crazy look in his eyes, like a wild animal, and he was aiming an arrow at Isaac!" Sarah began to weep as she relived the moment. "He was going to kill my baby! My God, I can only imagine what might have happened if I hadn't been there to stop him."

Abraham reached out and pulled his wife into an embrace. "Oh, Sarah, thank God you did. I'll go right now and talk to that boy."

"Talk to him?" snapped Sarah as she abruptly pulled from his arms. "Are you kidding me? You can't talk to that one anymore. You should've seen the look in his eyes, Abraham; so hollow, so remorseless."

"But what else can I do, Sarah?" replied Abraham, confused by his wife's stark anger. "Ishmael is my son. He'll do what I tell him."

"This is the last straw, I tell you. I want him and that mother of his out of my home!"

"But I can't just kick them out like that, can I?"

"That woman is still our slave, isn't she?"

Begrudgingly, Abraham nodded. "Of course."

"Then I want her and her son gone from this place, right now! Her son is not going to be heir with mine! Not after what I just found him doing!"

Speechless, Abraham hung his head in despair.

THE VERY NEXT DAY, a deflated and distraught Abraham gathered twelve loaves of bread and several flasks of water, and gave them to Hagar and Ishmael. Then he reluctantly sent them, along with a large number of cattle, sheep and servants, into the wilderness of Paran.

OVER THE COURSE OF time, Ishmael grew into a skilled archer and eventually married an Egyptian woman. With his wife, his six children and his mother, Ishmael traveled throughout this wilderness, pitching his tents and nurturing a huge number of flocks and herds as they went.

ONE DAY, ABRAHAM was sitting with his wife in their tent. "You know, Sarah, it's been a long time since I've talked to my son Ishmael. I think I'll take a trip to see him."

So Abraham rode his camel into the wilderness of Paran, searching for his son.

ABRAHAM ARRIVED AT Ishmael's tent around noontime. Unfortunately, his son was nowhere in sight. Only Ishmael's wife was there, sitting inside with three of their six children. Remaining on his camel, Abraham called out, "Hello? Anybody? Can someone tell me where Ishmael is?"

"He's gone hunting!" came his wife's gruff reply from within the tent.

"My dear woman, could you please get me something to drink? A bit of water would really help me right now. I'm so thirsty from my long journey."

Remaining inside the tent, Ishmael's wife responded with an obvious edge of irritation to her voice. "We don't have any water, or bread, for that matter."

Still Abraham sat patiently on his camel as he listened to the various sounds of Ishmael's wife and children moving about inside the tent. Then suddenly there came the muffled sound of a child's face being slapped, followed by a young boy's scream.

"Stop it, you good-for-nothing brat!" howled Ishmael's wife. "How many times have I told you not to do that? But what could I expect, considering you were born of that misbegotten father of yours!"

Even from inside the tent, her grating voice bellowed so loudly that it embarrassed several passersby and absolutely offended Abraham. Finally losing his patience, Abraham's typically pleasant demeanor turned to an angry scowl. "Excuse me, young lady. I must insist that you come out here and speak to me directly."

"Oh, for God's sake," Ishmael's wife grumbled. After several awkward moments, she finally exited the tent, looking quite annoyed, and stood before him with her arms crossed. "What do you want now?"

"I take it you're Ishmael's wife?"

Nodding impertinently, she replied, "Yes, yes, what about it?"

"My dear woman, can you please tell me with whom am I speaking?"

Ishmael's wife grunted, "What?"

"Your name, your name. What do I call you?"

"Oh, Meribah," she replied suspiciously. "My name is Meribah. What's it to you?"

"Well, then, Meribah, I need you to tell something to Ishmael when he comes home. Can you do that for me?"

Reluctantly, the woman nodded. "Yes, I suppose so."

"Good. Then I want you tell him an old man from Canaan came to see him, but when he arrived, I never asked him who he was, or offered him any refreshments for his long journey. Finding you gone, he said, 'When Ishmael returns, tell him the old man said to discard the nail you're using for your tent, and put another one in its place.'"

Then Abraham turned and rode away on his camel.

ISHMAEL, HAGAR AND the three oldest boys, ages fifteen to twenty, returned later with an assortment of game they had acquired during a fruitful day of hunting.

With considerable disdain, his wife informed him, "Ishmael, an old man from Canaan came here today looking for you."

"From Canaan? An old man, here for me? Who?"

"How should I know? He never told me his name."

"Well, didn't you ask him?"

"I guess it never occurred to me, no. He just kept asking for food and water."

"And did you give it to him?"

"Well, of course not. What am I, the maid?"

"Did he tell you what he wanted? Besides food and water, I mean."

"I already told you: He was looking for you."

"Meribah, what did he do when he found out I was gone?"

"When I told him you'd be out hunting all day, he told me to give you a message."

"Okay, then. Please, tell me what he said."

"Just a lot of nonsense, that's all."

"Like what?"

"He told me to tell you the nail to your tent was no good, and that you should replace it. Isn't that the most ridiculous thing you ever heard?"

And when Ishmael heard this, he was so smitten that he turned and walked outside, where he hung his head, deep in thought. Troubled by her son's reaction, Hagar followed him outside.

"Ishmael, what's wrong? Do you know who this man was, or why he came here?"

"Of course I do, Mother."

"Tell me, then. I want to know what has you so upset."

"Don't you see? The old man from Canaan was Father. He came to see me today, but we weren't here to greet him."

"Your father?"

"Yes, yes, Father. And what's worse, my silly, stubborn wife failed to honor him properly. She gave him nothing to drink, nothing to eat. She just sent him away empty-handed, in her typically hospitable way. It's a disgrace, I tell you."

"Oh, dear. That's too bad. And what was all that about a nail in your tent? Is that supposed to mean something?"

"What else? It was Father's subtle way of breaking the bad news to me."

"Bad news? What bad news?"

"That Meribah is unfit to be my wife, and that she should be replaced with a better one."

THREE MORE YEARS passed by, and one day Abraham grew restless again.

"What's wrong, husband? You've been so preoccupied lately."

"Oh, nothing, my dear. I'm fine. It's just I was thinking how long it's been since I've seen Ishmael. Maybe I should take another visit to try and see him."

SO ABRAHAM RODE OUT into the wilderness again, on his camel, finally reaching Ishmael's tent around noon. Seeing no one around, he called out, "Hello? Could someone tell me where Ishmael is?"

This time a different woman came out of the tent and smiled at him. "I'm so sorry, sir, but he isn't here right now. He's gone hunting with Mother and the boys."

"Hello, my dear. And who might you be?"

"My name is Malchuth. I'm Ishmael's wife."

Abraham's face lit up. "Oh, how nice to meet you, Malchuth. How are you this fine day?"

"I'm very good, sir. Won't you please come inside? Have something to eat. You must be exhausted from your journey."

Abraham shook his head. "No, thank you, my dear. That's all right. I won't be stopping. I'm in a terrible rush to continue my journey; but I would like some water. I'm so thirsty."

Malchuth ran into the tent and brought out a cup of water and a piece of bread. She urged him to enjoy, and so he happily ate and drank.

"God bless you, my dear, for your kindness. Now, when Ishmael comes home, can you tell him something for me?"

"Why, of course, sir. Anything you like."

WHEN ISHMAEL, HAGAR and the boys returned home with their game, Malchuth came out of their tent to joyfully greet them. "Hello, husband. How was your day?"

"Oh, not bad. How about you? Did anything happen while I was gone?"

"Not much. Oh, I almost forgot; someone came to see you, now that you mention it."

"Someone came to see me? Who?"

"You know, I'm not really sure. When I asked him his name, he just told me to tell you an old man from Canaan came to see you, but you weren't here, so I brought him bread and water, which he happily ate and drank, and when he left, he said, 'Tell Ishmael the nail of your tent is very good. Don't ever remove it.' Isn't that strange? I wonder what he could have meant by that."

Gratified and relieved, Ishmael beamed a tremendous smile. "Thank you, sweet Malchuth. You've done my heart good today. Did you hear that, Mother? An old man from Canaan came to visit me today, and he said the nail of our tent is a very good one."

"I heard, son," she said with a proud smile. "I'm so glad to hear it."

ISHMAEL THEN GATHERED his household and all his flocks and herds, and journeyed to see his father in Canaan, where he was met with Abraham's tearful embrace.

"Ishmael, my son," Abraham said wistfully. "It's good to see you again. I've missed you so very much. Please, won't you stay with us awhile?"

"Of course, Father, if you insist. I'll stay."

A Line in the Sand

ISAAC WAS GROWING up nicely under the tutelage of Abraham, when one day a messenger arrived outside the tent where father and son were conversing. Seeing the messenger depart and noticing the sad look on her husband and son's faces, Sarah immediately went to them. Before she even had time to ask, Abraham told her, "Bad news from Haran, I'm afraid."

"What's happened?" she asked.

"It seems as though Grandfather has died," Isaac replied, "at the age of two hundred and five."

"Terah?"

"Terah," Abraham quietly said with a somber nod.

TRAVELING TO THE city of Haran were Abraham, Sarah, Isaac and Ishmael, who together with Nahor and Milcah, mournfully tended to Terah's funeral service.

Watching the solemn proceedings from a distant hilltop was a shadowy, hooded figure, standing alone against the murky night sky. From out of the darkness, someone stepped up and stood next to the figure.

"What is it, Commander?" asked the shadowy figure, obviously annoyed with the interruption.

"Sorry to disturb you, Sire," he replied, "but I'm afraid our scouts have been detected. Should I order our withdrawal?"

With a dissatisfied sigh, the man reached up and pulled back his hood, revealing that he was none other than Nimrod. "Fine. Have the men withdraw at once."

"As you wish, My Lord," said the commander, who turned and slipped back into the darkness.

Still, Nimrod stood gazing at the funeral service. "Your days of running are over, Terah, my prince, my old friend," he murmured. "Your days of strife are finally at an end. How I envy you."

Abraham and Nahor stood side by side, grieving over their father's grave, when someone surreptitiously moved up to Abraham, whispered in his ear, and pointed in the direction of the shadowy figure far off in the distance. Head still down, Abraham merely shifted his eyes to catch a glimpse of the figure that finally turned and disappeared behind the hilltop.

ISHMAEL WAS VISITING Isaac in his tent one afternoon. "You know, when I was thirteen years old," Ishmael began, "the Lord told Father to circumcise us. I gave my life to Him then, and ever since, I've never disobeyed."

"Why brag to me about something like that?" asked Isaac, obviously unimpressed. "You cut off a piece of your skin because the Lord told you to. As the God of Abraham lives, if He told Father to cut me into pieces and sacrifice me as a burnt offering, I wouldn't hesitate. I'd gladly consent."

THEN CAME THE TIME when the seventy angels arrived to place themselves before the molten Face of God, and when one angel, looking more beautiful than all the rest, caught the Lord's attention, He immediately addressed him. "So, the renegade has returned to the 'scene of the crime,' as it were."

Graciously, the angel nodded. "Greetings, Eternal One."

"And just where have you come from today?" asked the Face.

"Why, from traveling back and forth throughout the Earth, as I so often do."

"And what do you think of the people living there?"

"Well, I'm particularly amused by the ones who serve you," cooed the angel, whose eyes suddenly turned black with hatred. "Whenever they need something, that is!"

Startled by his outburst, the angels next to him cautiously moved away to a more suitable distance.

"You don't say," replied the Lord matter-of-factly.

"Yes, and then, when you give them what they want, they ignore you again!" continued the angel through clenched teeth, as his beauty and brilliance began to fade, slowly revealing the sinister features below the surface. "Just like that, doing things your way is completely abandoned."

"Well, well, the Morning Star has spoken. How ironic that Satan would think himself capable of righteous judgment. Then tell me: What about Abraham, the son of Terah?"

"What about him?" scoffed the dark angel with a wave of his hand, shedding the last vestiges of his disguise, grotesque as ever now, grinning with his hideous fangs exposed for all to see. "You think he's special? He's no different from all the rest."

Finally realizing who was sitting amongst them, the rest of the angels moved even further away, leaving the devil alone in his stand against the smoldering Face of God.

"Really?" said the Face, quite casually.

"Yes, really. First, he lied to his own father about destroying his idols, he lied to Sarah about Terah's involvement in the death of her father, Haran, and then he lied when he tried to convince everyone his wife was his sister. In my book, that makes him a low down, filthy liar. There's no telling what he'll lie about next."

"I see. Is that all?"

"Well, how about the fact that when he had no children he prayed to you, day in and day out, building altars to you, and proclaiming your name to everyone he met? But now just look at him. Ever since that brat Isaac was born, he's completely abandoned you."

"But are so sure you've considered My servant Abraham thoroughly? There really isn't anyone quite like him in the whole world."

"Then how come when Isaac was born he didn't offer you any of the animals he killed that day? Not one of them was brought to you. No burnt offerings, no peace offerings, not an ox, not a lamb, not even a goat! *Why*?"

"Offerings? How dare you speak to Me about offerings. What do you know of genuine sacrifice? Your rabid hatred of anything sacred blinds you. Abraham is a noble man, one Who reveres Me and hates evil, but you only see what you want to see. You don't really think you fool Me with your self-righteous façade, do you? Since the day Abraham was born, you've done nothing but stir up the hatred and jealousy of Nimrod and his people. But in the end, all your efforts will fail, just as they failed when you tried to thwart My plans for Adam, his forefather."

"How touching, how sentimental, how *sickening*. Still, nothing you've said will change the fact that ever since Isaac was born your so-called 'servant' hasn't built you a single altar! All because you *gave* him what he wanted! And now, for thirty-seven years, he's forgotten you, just like all your other pathetic, little replicas!"

"Ah, you may think you know Abraham, but I'll bet if I told him to bring Me his son Isaac as a burnt offering, he would even do that."

"Then say the word!" growled the devil with blood in his eyes. "Tell him to do exactly that! Then we'll see, once and for all, if he has the guts to go through with it!"

SO THE WORD OF GOD went down to Earth and visited him. "Abraham?"

Startled at his abrupt appearance, Abraham stood there for several moments. "Yes, Lord, what is it?"

"I've come to bring you another important message. Will you receive it?"

"Of course, I will. What is it this time?"

"I want you take Isaac, your only begotten son, and go to Moriah. Sacrifice him there on one of the mountains to which I will lead you."

"You want me to do what?" asked a confused Abraham.

"I want you to offer up Isaac as a burnt offering. Will you do that for Me?"

"I suppose so, Lord, if You insist. But how will I know which mountain to go to?"

"Above it will be a cloud filled with the splendor of the Lord. That's how you'll know."

"And what should I tell his mother? How will I ever be able to tell her I'm sacrificing the son You provided for us in our old age?"

"Why not try telling her the truth? Are you afraid of what she might think of you if you follow the command of God?"

"Forgive me, Lord, but this is nothing compared to my ordeal in Nimrod's furnace or my battle with Chedorlaomer. After all, back then, I hardly had time to even think about the dire nature of my predicament, so compelled by the audacity of youth as I was."

"But now?"

"But now, so many years later, after so much living, so many worries, so many disappointments, things are different. And this isn't something that just involves me and my decision to defy a king. This involves my son and my wife."

"I see. Is that all?"

"Of course not, Lord. This time it involves not just an earthly king but an eternal one. May I ask what I did to deserve such a fate?"

"In due time, Abraham, all in due time."

"Meanwhile, what choice do I have in the matter, really? Who am I to defy the Lord of Glory?"

"Well said, my friend."

"And perhaps God will protect my son from the blade the same way He protected me from the fire of Nimrod."

"Certainly, Abraham, time will tell; time and the inscrutable decision of the Lord above."

Then the Word vanished, leaving Abraham standing there, more confused than ever.

ABRAHAM PENSIVELY entered his tent and sat down with Sarah. "You know, my dear," he began, carefully choosing his words, "Isaac is grown up now, and it's been a while since he's studied the service of God. So tomorrow I'm taking him to see Shem and Eber."

"Really?" replied Sarah. "What for?"

"So they can teach him what they know about the Lord. Maybe they have a thing or two to tell him I haven't thought of, something I might have overlooked. Who knows. Then he'll know how to serve God even better than before."

"Well, I suppose so; if you feel that strongly about it. Just don't keep him too long, though. You know how connected we are."

Abraham sighed. "Oh, Sarah, let's pray for the Lord to do great things with us."

March to Moriah

AS ABRAHAM AND ISAAC left their tent, along with Ishmael, Eliezer and several of their servants, a distraught Sarah followed some distance behind them.

"Be a good boy, Isaac," Sarah called out, barely able to speak the words. "And come home safe and sound, you hear?"

"Please, Mother, I'm not a child," he replied, annoyed with all the fuss. "I'll be fine."

But just hearing the sound of her son's voice, Sarah started crying. Abraham began weeping, too, and so did Isaac. Everyone there, in fact, had to fight back their tears because they were all so affected by Sarah's emotional outburst.

Unable to resist any longer, Sarah ran to Isaac and grabbed his hand, holding it tenderly to her face. "Who knows if I'll ever see you again, my son?"

"Mother, you're embarrassing me in front of everybody. Would you please go home? Everything will be fine, honestly."

Abraham could hardly stand it. "Please, Sarah, you don't have to worry. Of course you'll be seeing Isaac again. Before you know it, he'll back in your arms. I promise. The Lord, I'm sure, will see to it Himself. Now, stop your crying please, my dear, or else we'll never be able to leave."

Nodding mournfully, Sarah wiped the tears from her face and finally let go of Isaac's hand. Then with the help of some of her other servants, she reluctantly walked away.

AS HE WAS SO OFTEN in the habit of doing, Satan watched the whole scene from a distant hillside, flanked by his lieutenant and several of his minions. "Well, well," he croaked. "It looks like that old fool Abraham is going to call my bluff after all. And worse still, it looks as though that addlepated son of his is going along with god's absurd plan."

"What should we do, Lord?" asked his lieutenant.

Satan slowly turned to him with his angry, reptilian gaze. "*Do*? What do you think we should do? We do whatever we can to stop them, you brainless idiot! Why would you even ask me such an asinine question?"

The lieutenant shrank back in abject fear. "Forgive me, Master, I was just trying to help."

"Help," grumbled the devil, thoroughly disgusted, as he turned his lurking black eyes back upon his quarry. "What do you know about *help*? I suppose your idea of help would be to openly terrorize them with fear and intimidation. Is that it?"

The lieutenant then turned to the demons next to him and asked quietly, "What else is there?"

ABRAHAM'S CARAVAN, consisting of a dozen men, was plodding along at a slow but steady pace. Most of them were walking alongside their camels, which were laden with supplies, as was Abraham who was walking some distance behind the others, thoroughly absorbed in his own thoughts, when suddenly he realized that an old man he did not recognize was walking alongside him.

"Good day, sir," exclaimed the stranger. "How are you this glorious morning?"

"Well, hello there, friend," replied Abraham, apparently relieved with the diversion. "I'm fine. Thank you for asking. I hope all is well with you."

"It is, thank you. But, sadly, there is one thing troubling me."

"Oh, and what could that be?"

"Well, sir, I have to admit. I'm very confused by your actions here today. I mean, are you really such a heartless man after all?"

Confused at this, Abraham asked, "What in the world are you talking about?"

The old man, however, remained undeterred, shaking his head knowingly. "Ah, don't play coy with me. You know very well what I'm talking about. I'm talking about your son."

"My son? What about my son?"

The man grinned back sardonically, revealing that several of his teeth were missing. "I just want to know why? Is that too much to ask? Why would you do it? I mean, really."

Beginning to get irritated with the stranger, Abraham blurted, "Why what?"

"Why would a supposedly good man like you do something so evil as to kill his own son?"

Momentarily taken aback, Abraham slowly mustered his reply. "Look, I don't know who you are, but I am only doing what the Lord has asked me to do. What could be wrong with that?"

"You mean to tell me it's all right to murder the son that God gave you and Sarah in your old age as long as it's because He asked you to? Is that really what I'm hearing? I take it back; you're not heartless, you're crazy."

Abraham swallowed hard at this. "How dare you, sir. Who are you, anyway? A sorcerer? How do you know so much about me and my family?"

"Ah, that's not important. What's important is why you won't answer my question. Why is a good man like you leading his own son to the slaughter?"

"I already told you: Because the Lord asked me to, that's why!"

"Has Isaac done something wrong? Is that it?"

"I never said he did."

"Yet you still insist on destroying him. You are insane, aren't you?"

"If that's how you see it, then, yes, I guess I am."

"But don't you realize the Lord would never ask someone to do something this evil? He'd never ask a man to kill his own child."

Thunderstruck, Abraham stopped dead in his tracks and turned to the old man. "You know, *friend*, something has just dawned on me."

"Really, what?" asked the old man, stopping with Abraham.

"You never did say how you knew so much about me. If you really were a sorcerer, you'd have had no problem admitting it, but you didn't, did you? No, of course not. So you must be someone else, or *something* else, for that matter."

The old man tilted his head in a curious way. "What in Hell is that supposed to mean?"

"Yes, that must be it. When I was a young man, my forefathers, Noah and Shem, used to tell me stories about beings who were capable of such a thing."

"Beings? What are you going on about now?"

Abraham stared intently into the eyes of the old man, mesmerized by the train of thought that came flooding into his mind. "Yes, shape-shifters; that's what they called them, malignant beings who could transform themselves into any form they desired."

The old man shook his head in disbelief. "Have you lost your mind, sir? Or have you just spent too much time in the Sun today?"

"And the most evil of them all was their leader, a diabolical creature who, for some inexplicable reason, still had limited access to the heavenly realms."

"You really have gone insane, you babbling fool," said the old man, who took several steps back from Abraham, obviously disturbed by what he was hearing.

"No, sir, not at all. In fact, I've never been clearer about anything in my life, as if an arrow has just been shot directly into my heart. It is you. That's how you knew so much about me, my family, my mission here today."

With a wild look in his eye, the old man moved back some more, but Abraham kept pace with him with each step. "Certainly not," he insisted.

"Yes, of course," pressed Abraham, raising an accusing finger. "I can see right through you now. You're the Evil One himself, the very one who was thrown down from the heights of Heaven. Satan, get away from us, this instant! I won't allow you to stop us!"

The old man held his hands over his ears. "Shut up, you raving lunatic! I won't be spoken to like that!" And quite abruptly, the man turned and walked away, furiously kicking at the dirt.

Finally, Isaac came over to investigate. "What was that all about, Father?"

"Nothing to worry about, son," replied Abraham, who anxiously put his hand on Isaac's shoulder to steady himself.

"Are you all right?" asked Isaac.

"I'll be fine. No worries. Everything is perfectly fine now."

"Who was that man?"

Abraham thought for a moment about how to answer. "Just a wanderer, I suppose."

"He seemed so angry," Isaac said, staring in the direction of where the old man had disappeared. "Do you think he poses a threat to our journey?"

"No, Isaac; he's nothing more than a thundercloud with no rain, something to be seen but never heard from again, I hope."

With that, Abraham and Isaac, along with the rest of their group, continued their journey.

BEFORE TOO LONG another stranger wandered up to them. This time a handsome young man came up alongside Isaac, who, like his father before him, was straggling some distance behind the group, lost in his thoughts.

"Hello, my friend," said the young man with a gracious charm. "How are you on this wonderful day?"

Vacantly nodding back, Isaac was apparently not as happy with the intrusion as his father had been. "Fine, thanks," he muttered. "And you?"

"Oh, I can't complain. There is one thing puzzling me, though."

"Really," said Isaac, hardly paying attention. "What?"

"Do you have any idea why your father is taking you on this trip?"

"Well, yes, I have my suspicions," replied Isaac. "But I don't think he wants to tell me because he's afraid I might not go along with his plan."

The young man was flabbergasted. "*What*? You mean your father hasn't even told you what he's up to?"

"Not in so many words; but the Lord and I both know I'm ready for this. I've declared my intentions to God, and I believe He's found me worthy of such a mission."

"But don't you know your silly, old father is wasting his time by killing you today?"

Isaac turned with a peculiar look. "Who said anything about me being killed?"

But the young man grinned back knowingly. "Ah, not so fast, not so fast. You know as well as I do, there are some people in this world who can sense what others fail to recognize. Get my drift?"

"So you're telling me you're one of those people. Is that it?"

"That I am, my friend, that I am."

Not sure how to respond, Isaac frowned and turned away.

Satisfied with himself, the young man pressed on. "So that's it? You have nothing more to say for yourself?"

"Look, friend, I don't have to explain myself to anyone, least of all you."

"Aha," exclaimed the man. "I knew I was right. Admit it. You are having second thoughts about this harebrained scheme of your father's, aren't you?"

"Not necessarily," replied Isaac as he flashed the young man a keenly determined look. "If the Lord told my father to do this thing, then who am I to argue with what they've decided?"

The young man grew agitated at this. "But don't you see? Your father is senile. He's lost what little mind he has left."

"No, you're wrong," Isaac insisted. "He's a good man, and he knows what's best for us."

"Oh, please, stop. Certainly you must know you were made for better things. I mean, honestly, what purpose could it possibly serve to throw your life away like this?"

"But I'm not throwing my life away. I'm obeying the God of Heaven."

"You poor, ignorant fool. You actually think your life is that precious to God? Who do you think you are, anyway? Out of all the people in this world, what makes you so special? Tell me that."

Fed up, Isaac started to walk faster until he caught up with Abraham. "Father, have you heard what this man has been saying to me?"

Abraham stopped and turned. "No, son; what?"

"He thinks we're wasting our time doing what God has told us to do. He says I shouldn't bother throwing my life away for His sake."

"What? How dare you say such a thing to my son."

The young man walked up to them and innocently shrugged his shoulders. "But I'm only saying: How do you really know you're doing the will of God today? You could just be wasting your time serving a figment of your own imagination. Have you ever thought of that?"

Abraham took a step closer to the man and looked him straight in the eye. "My God, are you back again?"

Uncomfortable with Abraham's piercing gaze, the young man moved several steps back. "What?" Turning to Isaac, he asked, "Why is he looking at me like that?"

Isaac shrugged back. "How should I know?"

As Abraham stared him down, the young man slowly withdrew. "What is wrong with you people?" he grumbled.

"It is you," Abraham insisted.

"Who, Father?" asked Isaac. "Who is he?"

Abraham held up his hand, as if to caution his son. "Be careful with this one, Isaac. Don't listen to another word he says. This may be hard to believe, but this man isn't who he appears to be."

"What is that supposed to mean?" blurted the young man.

Abraham pointed an accusing finger. "He's actually the archenemy of God and all His sacred purposes."

"But how can that be?" Isaac wondered. "He's just an ordinary man."

"No, I'm afraid not, son. Thank God our forefathers taught me all about him. Since time immemorial there have been malignant creatures, diabolical shape-shifters who walk among the living. And whether or not you're willing to accept it, this so-called 'ordinary man' just happens to be the granddaddy of them all."

"You *are* crazy, you old coot," snapped the young man, who grew more agitated by the moment, "you and anyone else who believes in your wild stories."

"Father, please," intoned Ishmael, "I don't mean to sound disrespectful, but you don't really expect us to believe such nonsense? You're talking gibberish."

"Really, sir," Eliezer added. "You don't want to say anything you'll regret later. I'm sure this young man will leave us alone if we ask him. We don't have to make up outrageous accusations, now do we?"

Abraham defiantly shook his fist. "Fools, all of you. You have no idea what you're dealing with."

"Father, you're scaring me," continued Isaac. "What are you saying? Who do you think this man really is? Some sort of demon?"

Turning to Isaac, Abraham implored, "Not just any demon, son, but the chief of all demons, the most evil spirit of them all!"

"You mean the devil?" asked Isaac, wide-eyed at the realization. "You're saying this is actually Satan himself?

"Yes, Isaac, it is Satan, disguised as this young man. He was here before. Don't you remember that old man earlier today?"

"Of course I do. What about him?"

"That was him, too. And now he's back again, trying everything he can to lure us away from what God wants us to do!"

Ishmael and Eliezer, still unconvinced, however, just hung their heads in embarrassment.

But an undeterred Abraham again pointed an accusing finger at the young man. "Satan, I rebuke you in the Name of the Lord Who created you. Leave this place immediately, you foul creature!"

The young man covered his ears and threw his head back as though he were in excruciating pain. "Shut up, you crazy bastard!" Abruptly the man transformed into his true form as the devil, hideously grotesque, sniffing and clawing at the air. Craning his wolfen head back around toward the men, Satan focused his reptilian black eyes on Abraham and growled, "No one talks to me like that, filthy human, especially you!"

Equally awestruck and terrified, Ishmael, Eliezer and the rest of the men blanched at the sight of this malignant creature, while Abraham and Isaac resolutely stood their ground.

"Silence, Devil!" thundered Abraham. "And leave us at once! I don't ever want to see you again, do you understand?"

As agonized as he was furious, Satan howled through his jagged fangs and, extending his leathery, bat-like wings, turned and flew away in a whirlwind of dust. Then, as if nothing unusual had just happened, Abraham and Isaac calmly wiped themselves off and resumed their journey, but Ishmael, Eliezer and the other men stood like statues for quite a while, shaken and bewildered. Then, realizing that Abraham and Isaac were moving on without them, followed by the camels and all their supplies, they began to stir into action.

"What are we doing dawdling around in this God-forsaken place?" Eliezer exclaimed. "And whatever you do, don't talk to any more strangers for the rest of this trip. You hear me?"

REACHING A POINT in their journey where they saw a large brook flowing across the road, Abraham and his group started across. Casually wading through it at first, the men quickly found the water reaching up over their knees. Venturing further still, they were soon in up to their midsections. Eventually, the group became very concerned that the water was by then up to their necks. Not only that, but the current's strength was increasing with every step. Desperate to reach the other side, the men and their camels struggled through the ever deepening and ever more powerful river.

"Wait!" shouted Abraham. "I know this place! There was never any river here before! Now I understand what's happening! It's that damned Satan again, doing all he can to keep us from finishing what we've started!" Defiantly shaking his fist over his head, he roared above the din of the river's flow. "Stop this, Devil! We have to do what God wants! The Lord is going to punish you! Get away from us right now, or else you'll suffer the consequences!"

Suddenly the place where they had been struggling through a coursing river became dry land. The group exchanged troubled looks all around as they examined themselves in total disbelief.

"We're not even wet," muttered Ishmael. "But how?"

"B—*but*," stammered Isaac, who, when he turned to his father, was met with a knowing look, "but we were just up to our necks in raging waters."

"*Why* aren't we wet?" blurted Ishmael, his voice trembling. "What on Earth is going on?

This is sheer madness!"

"I don't know," grumbled Eliezer, "and, frankly, I don't want to know."

Then without another word between themselves, the dismayed and confused group started off again, headed for their destination.

ON THE THIRD DAY OF their journey, Abraham looked up and saw a remarkable fire burning on a distant mountaintop. Even from afar, he could see that its smoke rose into a shimmering, iridescent cloud.

Abraham pointed. "Isaac, do you see what I see rising above that mountain?"

"I see fire and smoke, Father," he replied, obviously awed by what he was seeing. "And above that is a cloud filled with the splendor of the Lord."

Abraham then turned to Ishmael and Eliezer. "What about the two of you? What do you see on top of that mountain straight ahead?"

"I see a mountain," said Ishmael, "like any other mountain on Earth. What else would I see?"

Eliezer shrugged. "I see a mountain, too. An ordinary mountain, that's all. Why?"

Abraham confidently nodded at Isaac. "Then the Lord has revealed His decision, just as He promised." Turning to Ishmael and Eliezer, he said, "You two, wait here with the rest of the group. Isaac and I will go to the top of Mount Moriah, where we'll worship the Lord, and when we're done, we'll return again. Is that understood?"

"But, Father," said Ishmael with an uneasy tone, "there's no telling what might happen to us while you're away."

"Please, sir," added Eliezer, sounding just as nervous. "I wholeheartedly agree with Ishmael. We have no desire to part ways with you now. Not after everything we've endured to this point."

"I'm very sorry," replied Abraham. "Really I am. But this is the way it has to be. Besides, I'm quite sure nothing further will threaten you down here."

"But how can you be so sure, Father?" asked Ishmael.

"Because if anything is going to happen, it's going to happen on the next leg of our journey," said Abraham, who returned his gaze to the ominously glowing mountaintop, "on our way up there."

IT WAS EARLY AFTERNOON by the time Abraham and Isaac had nearly reached the mountaintop. Along the way, Abraham began picking up pieces of wood, and one by one, he handed them to Isaac, who carried them for his father.

Finally to the top, Abraham pointed to a suitable clearing, where Isaac dropped his load of wood and then stood watching while his father knelt to make a small campfire with some kindling he had whittled with his knife.

"Father, I see the fire, and I see the blade, but where's the lamb we need for our burnt offering?"

"Oh, Isaac, my dear son," Abraham said as he dolefully stared into the fire. "I'm afraid the Lord has chosen you to be the burnt offering, not a lamb."

Isaac tried his best to smile. "Yes, Father; I suspected as much."

"What?" An amazed Abraham turned to his son. "You knew? But how? I never told a soul."

"You didn't have to. I declared my intentions to the Lord, and He obviously heard me."

Confused, Abraham got to his feet and walked over to his son. "What are you saying, Isaac? You spoke to the Lord about what He's asked me to do?"

Isaac nodded. "I have, Father, yes, and I'll happily do whatever He wants."

"You mean, you don't think what we're doing is wrong? Just tell me, son, if you have any doubts about this. I'll understand."

"As the Lord lives, Father, nothing is going to keep us from doing what God wants. I'm completely resolved. In fact, I thank God for choosing me to be a burnt offering for Him."

With a heavy sigh of relief, Abraham hugged his son, and together they began to gather stones. As they built up their stones into a crude altar, the two men quietly wept. After placing a stack of wood on the altar, Abraham began tying Isaac's hands and feet with linen cords.

"Make sure the rope is good and tight, Father, so I can't roll around. I don't want to ruin the offering by breaking loose when your knife cuts me."

Abraham nodded sadly and tightened the cords around his son's hands and feet. Then he carefully placed Isaac atop the pile of wood.

"And Father, please, promise me you'll take some of my ashes to Mother. Tell her: 'This is the sweet-smelling savor of Isaac.'"

Abraham dolefully nodded again. "I promise, son."

"But make sure you don't tell her if she's sitting near a well or anywhere high up. I don't want her throwing herself off trying to come after me."

Cut to the quick, Abraham cried even more, spilling his tears onto Isaac, who also began to cry uncontrollably.

"Don't worry, Father, we'll be all right. Outwardly, our eyes are weeping, but inwardly our hearts rejoice."

Abraham smiled awkwardly. "Yes, my son, I can't explain it, but I feel the same way, too."

Isaac stretched out his neck. "Hurry, Father, do what God told you to do."

"My dear, sweet boy, I love you so much. My only consolation in all of this is knowing that, even before I do, you will look upon the magnificent Face of God."

Then, Abraham raised his blade, preparing to slash his son's throat.

AT THAT VERY MOMENT, the seventy angels appeared before the Face of God.

"Lord!" exclaimed one of them. "You're such a compassionate King. Do You see how Abraham's son is tied down like an animal prepared for slaughter?"

"I do see, yes," replied the Face.

"Dear God, can You imagine how Abraham and Isaac are feeling right now as they carry out Your orders?"

"I can imagine. What would you like Me to do?"

"Lord, please, won't You provide a ransom for Your servant, Isaac?"

"Very well, go."

IN A FLASH, THE ANGEL appeared next to Abraham at the altar. "Abraham, stop!" shouted the angel, grabbing his hand just as it lunged toward Isaac's outstretched throat. "There's no need to harm Isaac. Now God knows for sure you really trust Him, even to the point of sacrificing your own son for His sake."

Looking up, Abraham saw a ram with his horns caught in a thicket.

"Take the ram you see," the angel continued, "the ram that God prepared on the first day of His Creation, created for this very moment when you'd sacrifice it as a burnt offering to the Lord in place of your son."

Running to the ram as it struggled to break free, Abraham discovered a disembodied hand, leathery and grotesque, hidden amongst the thick branches, where it had ensnared the ram's horns with its talon-like fingernails.

"What is this?" asked an astonished Abraham.

"It's the devil again," the angel said. "He's trying to thwart God's purposes to the bitter end. This ram was actually advancing toward you, but when Satan heard God was providing a substitute for your son, he entangled his horns in these bushes, hoping you might kill Isaac before it got to you."

As Abraham wrestled with Satan's horrid claw, the ram struggled to break free with all its might.

"I told you before, Devil," Abraham bellowed, "I didn't ever want to see you again, even if it is just your miserable paw. Now be gone in the Name of the Almighty Lord! Away with you!"

Immediately, the hand vanished, and, that quickly, the ram was released from the thickets. Abraham led the animal to the altar, and untying Isaac, he helped his son down. With the same linen cords that had been used on Isaac, Abraham securely tied up the ram, and placing it on the pile of wood, he killed the ram instead of Isaac. Sprinkling some of the ram's blood over the altar, Abraham intoned, "This was done in place of my son. May it be regarded as his blood." And after each and every thing he did at that altar, Abraham announced: "May the Lord accept this instead of my son."

MEANWHILE, THE seventy angels looked down from Heaven, as did the smoldering Face of God.

"Tell us, Lord, if You would," began one of the angels. "Did you honor the sacrifice of Your servant, Abraham?"

"I did, yes," the Lord replied. "In fact, everything Abraham did with the ram at his altar has been counted as though it had been done with Isaac himself. And as a result of Abraham's actions, I'll pour out My blessings on him and his descendants, and will continue to do so from this day forward until the end of time."

Sweet Sarah, Why?

BACK HOME, SARAH anxiously paced back and forth inside her tent, waiting for some news about her husband and son.

With a sad, downcast face, an old man stepped up to the door of her tent. "Hello, Sarah?" he called out. "Sarah? Are you home, my dear?"

Finally realizing that someone was calling her, Sarah turned and stepped to the door of her tent. Upon seeing the man, she graciously nodded. "I am, sir. And who might you be?"

Gently kicking at the dirt, he muttered, "Who, me? Oh, that's not important. Let's just say I'm a concerned party."

"Really?" Sarah took a closer look at this strange man.

"What is important is I have some very bad news for you."

"Bad news? What news? About my husband? My son? Tell me."

"Well, you know that husband of yours," the man said, shaking his head pitifully.

"Yes, yes," gulped Sarah. "What have you heard? Just tell me."

"Oh, dear, it seems he went and built himself another one of those altars he's so fond of building. You know the kind."

"Yes, and?"

"Well, then God told him to take Isaac and kill him on it."

"What?" Sarah gasped. "No!"

"Yes. He actually offered him up as a living sacrifice, just because God asked him to. Can you believe it?"

"But how could he do such a thing?"

"You know, I haven't the slightest idea. And no matter how much Isaac wept as he begged his father to spare his life, Abraham refused to even look him in the eye. All the compassion he ever had for his son was completely gone at that moment."

Then, the old man shrugged his shoulders, turned and walked away, disappearing around one of the tents.

As Sarah stood there, agonizing, one of her servant girls ran to her side. "What's wrong, My Lady? What has you so upset?"

"That old man," muttered Sarah, growing breathless, as though a tremendous weight was crushing her chest.

"What about him? Who was he?"

"I don't know; he didn't say. But I think he was one of the men traveling with my husband and son when they left on their trip. That much I do seem to remember."

"But what did he do to get you so upset? Did he say something?"

"He told me Abraham had sacrificed my boy as a burnt offering to the Lord?"

"A burnt offering? Isaac?"

Still trying to catch her breath, Sarah nodded as tears began to well up in her eyes.

"But why?" asked the girl.

"He said, God asked him to do it."

"What? Well, that doesn't make any sense. Are you sure that's what he said?"

"My dear, sweet Isaac, dead." Bursting into tears, Sarah's legs grew weak, and she fell to her knees. "Oh, my son, if only it could have been me that died, not you!"

"My Lady, please don't despair."

Weeping miserably, Sarah threw dirt over her head. "My heart is breaking, my boy. I was so happy to raise you, but now just look at how my joy has turned into mourning."

"Try to think of the good times, ma'am," said the girl, who kneeled next to Sarah and tenderly embraced her. "You two shared so much love and happiness together."

For a moment, Sarah's mind shifted. "Yes, how I remember those special days. How I wept and prayed to God to even have you at my age." Then suddenly a wave a grief seized her again. "But now, after all that, it turns out you were made just for the fire and the blade."

"Please, My Lady, be strong."

"Still, I can console myself with your memory, my son, and with the time we had."

"And by doing this marvelous thing, your husband and your son have faithfully carried out God's plan."

"But how?" asked Sarah through her cascading tears.

"I wish I could tell you, ma'am, but I just don't know. How can we ever hope to understand the mind of God?"

Sarah meekly nodded. "And who could ever resist doing what the Lord wants? He controls every living creature."

"Lord God, everything You do is perfect," Sarah's servant girl added.

"So now I, too, will celebrate Your decision, and even though I'm crying on the outside, inwardly I will rejoice." With that, Sarah gently laid her head on her servant girl's shoulder and became as still as a stone.

AFTER GATHERING HER wits, Sarah began to scour the area, approaching anyone she passed by. "My husband, Abraham, have you seen him?"

"No, Sarah, I'm afraid I haven't," replied one woman.

UNFORTUNATELY, EVERYONE she met along the way just shook their heads as she continued her desperate quest. Accompanied by some of her servants, Sarah traveled for miles, unwilling to stop even when someone offered her a cup of water.

"I think it's time we split up so we can cover more territory," Sarah said to one of her male servants.

"Begging your pardon, ma'am," he replied. "I don't think that would be wise. Not in your condition."

"I don't care what you think!" snapped Sarah. "Just do it! We need to find my husband, now!"

Reluctantly, the man bowed. "As you wish, My Lady."

Then, while her servants went off in one direction in their search, Sarah turned and went the other way.

EVENTUALLY, SARAH encountered the same old man who had come to her tent earlier that day. There he was again, smiling, greeting her as cordially as ever. "Sarah, my dear, I am *so* sorry. I'm afraid I spoke too soon earlier. It turns out I was wrong about your son."

"Now what are you saying?"

"It's Isaac. He's not dead!"

"What? But how?"

"I guess Abraham didn't sacrifice your son after all! God was just testing him. Isn't that marvelous?"

"Are you serious? My boy isn't really dead?"

"No! I'm telling you: Isaac is *alive*!"

Sarah was ecstatic. "That's wonderful!" But within a matter of moments, her wild elation quickly turned to agonizing sorrow. A terrified look swept across Sarah's face. Her breathing became labored, and she started clutching at her chest.

The old man's eyes widened. "Dear lady, what's wrong? You don't look so good."

Dropping to her knees in a cold sweat, Sarah murmured, "God, no, not again; not now." And after several desperate, gasping moments, she slumped to the ground and died. As the old man stood over her body, he transformed into his true appearance. Once again it was Satan. Laughing sadistically, he flew away before anyone noticed what had happened.

BACK AT MOUNT MORIAH, Abraham and Isaac returned to where Ishmael, Eliezer and the rest of the men were still waiting at the base of the mountain. Then, they all headed back home for Hebron.

BUT WHEN ABRAHAM and Isaac arrived back at their tent and found that Sarah was gone, they began searching everywhere for her.

Abraham found one of his servant girls. "Where's Sarah? Have you seen her?"

"But, sir, she's not here."

"What do you mean, she's not here? Where is she?"

"She went looking for you."

"Looking for us? Why?"

"She heard you'd sacrificed Isaac as a burnt offering, so she was desperate to find where you'd gone."

"What? How on Earth did she find out about that? I never told her a thing about my plans."

"She said an old man who'd been traveling with your group came and told her."

"An old man, here?"

The distraught servant girl nodded.

"My God, not again," Abraham growled.

"Do you know who the old man was?"

"I'm afraid I know exactly who the fiend was, my dear." Abraham frantically turned to see Isaac. "Quickly, son; we've got to find your mother before it's too late."

"Too late? What do you mean, too late?" he blurted.

"There's no time to discuss it, Isaac. We've got to hurry. Now let's go."

ACCOMPANIED BY SEVERAL of their servants, Abraham and Isaac searched the countryside for Sarah with ever-increasing desperation. Eventually they were greeted by two men. "Abraham, Abraham, I'm so glad I found you," one of them said, obviously depressed. "I'm afraid I have some very bad news."

"Sarah," gasped Abraham. "Is she all right?"

"Follow me, old friend. I'll take you to her."

WITH A DEEP SENSE OF foreboding, Abraham and Isaac were led to the tent where Sarah was lying in state. When Isaac saw his mother's body, he ran to her side, fell to his knees, and put his cheek to hers. His tears flowed down over her face. "Oh, Mother, Mother, where've you gone? How could you leave me like this? Why, God? Why did You let this happen?"

Heartbroken at the sight of both his deceased wife and his grieving son, Abraham buried his tear-stained face in his hands. "My sweet Sarah, why?"

WITH THE POMP AND circumstance observed only for royalty, Abraham and Isaac then set out to bury Sarah, having dressed her in wonderfully ornate garments. Shem and his great grandson Eber, along with Anar, Ashcol and Mamre, all walked alongside her casket as the carriage made its way to the burial cave.

A HAND LIGHTLY TOUCHED down on Abraham's shoulder as he sat quietly weeping. "I'm here, Abraham. You wanted to see me?"

Abraham dolefully looked up. "Yes, of course, Father Eber." And sucking in his breath in an attempt to regain his composure, he wiped a tear from his eye. "I'm so glad to see you."

"How are you holding up, son?"

"Not very well, I'm afraid. My heart breaks all over again every time I think of my Sarah just lying there, gone like that."

"I can imagine. We were all devastated when we heard the news. It was so completely out of the blue."

"It just doesn't make any sense. How could God have let something like this happen?" Hanging his head, Abraham could not hold back his tears any longer.

Deeply touched by his lament, Eber put his arm around him.

"And thanks again for coming on such short notice," Abraham murmured as he fought to regain his composure again.

"Of course, Abraham, you know you can always count on me. We all share in your loss. Sarah was a good woman, such a spirited girl. I can't believe she's really gone. She was still so young. What was she, all of a hundred and twenty?"

"A hundred and twenty-seven last April."

"Do you have any idea what could have caused her untimely death?"

"I do, yes. In fact, that's why I've asked you here today."

Eber sat down and looked deep into Abraham's mournful eyes. "What is it, son? I sense something stirring deep within your soul."

"It's Isaac. I believe he's in terrible danger."

"Tell me, Abraham. What can I do?"

The Woman at the Well

"BUT, FATHER, I STILL don't understand," Isaac grumbled as he and Abraham stood waiting on the doorstep of the home of Shem and Eber. "Why can't I stay with you?"

"Isaac, Isaac," replied Abraham, trying to remain patient, "we've already gone through this before. My mind is made up. I want you to spend time with Shem and Eber so they can teach you what they know about the Lord."

"But why can't you keep teaching me?"

"I'm sorry, son, but this is how it has to be. Besides, you know very well that my father did the same thing for me when I was a boy. So, please, don't make this any harder than it has to be."

Then Shem and Eber came out to greet them. "Abraham, Isaac," exclaimed Eber. "So good to see you."

Abraham turned and lit up at their appearance. "Father Shem, Father Eber; how are you?"

But Isaac just frowned.

"Isaac, please," Abraham pleaded. "Stop acting this way. You're embarrassing me. Say hello to your elders. They deserve your respect."

"Hello, Father Shem, Father Eber," said Isaac with a perfunctory smile. "How are you both today?"

"There's a good boy," Abraham sighed. "See, Isaac, before you know it, you'll be having the time of your life."

"I don't know, Father," he grumbled, obviously unconvinced. "Why do I get the feeling there's something else you're not telling me about?"

Shem and Eber exchanged a knowing look.

Eber leaned in to Shem and quietly said, "Clever boy, that one."

"Chip off the old block, if you ask me," murmured Shem.

"What are you saying?" sputtered Abraham, who looked to Shem and Eber, hoping for some moral support. "Of course not, Isaac. Don't be ridiculous."

"Isaac, my boy," interjected Shem, right on cue. "Did your dad tell you how much Father Eber and I have been looking forward to this? These are important days in a young man's life, and I was really hoping I could do for you what I once did for him. How would you like that?"

Isaac turned to Shem and reluctantly smiled. "Well, I guess so, sir; when you put it that way."

"Then you'll be all right with them, son?" ventured Abraham hesitantly.

"Don't be silly, Father. Of course I'll be fine. I'm not a child anymore, you know."

Thoroughly amused, Shem and Eber both grinned from ear to ear.

THOUGHTFULLY GAZING out across the sprawling landscape, Abraham watched the bustle of that afternoon's activities as people purposefully moved about in every direction.

"You called for me, sir?" asked a voice.

Looking up, Abraham forced a smile. "Eliezer, yes, I did. Thank you."

"How are you today, sir?"

"Oh, as well as can be expected, I suppose."

"That's good to hear. We've been so worried about you lately."

"Worried about me?"

"Of course. I mean, it's bad enough you haven't seen your son in ages, but on top of that you've had to endure the deaths of your nephew Lot and your beloved brother Nahor. It's a great deal for any man to handle, even a man like you."

"Nahor, yes, Nahor," he replied with a distinct air of melancholy. "It's true. A day hasn't gone by that I haven't thought about my brother's passing. Even though I know he's been reunited with our forefathers, it still saddens me to know I can no longer see him in this present life."

"But certainly you can rejoice in the fact that he led a good, long life."

This time Abraham replied with a more relaxed smile. "Yes, Eliezer; you're quite right about that. For one hundred and seventy-two years that scoundrel gave the world all it could handle, didn't he?"

"That he did, sir, that he did. Now, what can I do for you today?"

"What's that?"

"You called for me, sir. What did you want?"

"Oh, of course, I forgot. I'm getting so old, I lose my train of thought sometimes."

Eliezer smiled back politely.

"In fact," continued Abraham, "I'm getting so old, who knows, my death may come at any moment."

"Please, sir, don't talk like that. You still have many more years left. I'm sure of it."

"Yes, well, that may be true, but with so many of my loved ones having passed from the scene, I'm not sure I want to keep on living. Only Isaac, the light of my life, and Ishmael, that rascal, hold me fast to this life on Earth."

Eliezer nodded with another smile. "Of course, My Lord."

"And even you, my dear Eliezer, if the truth be told. Certainly you know how much I love you. You've always been like a son to me."

"And you, sir, have always been like a father to me. So you see: There are at least three reasons to go on living after all. Now, please, tell me: How can I be of service?"

"It's my son, Isaac."

"Isaac? What about him?"

"I need you to help me find him a wife; someone who isn't from this place, I mean. Lord knows I do not want him marrying a daughter of the Canaanites."

"But what can I do? Where would I go?"

"I need you to go back to the city of Haran, where the rest of my family still lives. Find a wife for my son there. Can you do that for me?"

Eliezer shrugged his shoulders. "But Haran is such a large city. How will I ever hope to succeed in something like that, without having any idea where to look?"

"Ah, don't worry about that. The God of the Universe has led me my whole life. I'm sure He can do the same for you if we just ask Him."

Eliezer perked up. "You think so?"

"Of course, Eliezer. I'm quite confident that with God's help there's no way you can fail. This way you'll be sure to bring Isaac a wife who comes from our own family."

"Then I'll be leaving right away, sir."

"Good. There's no time to lose."

"But what if the woman I find for your son isn't willing to return with me? Then what? Should I take Isaac back there?"

"No, no, no!" insisted Abraham, his eyes growing as big as saucers. "Whatever you do: Don't ever take my son back there! Do you understand?"

Eliezer dutifully nodded.

"Good," Abraham continued. "Now stop worrying. I already told you: The Lord Who has been walking with me my whole life will help you in your mission."

GATHERING TEN OF Abraham's male servants and ten of his camels, each heavily laden with baggage, Eliezer headed out.

"God of my master, Abraham," whispered Eliezer. "If You can hear me now, please bless this journey of ours and guide us to Haran, the city of Nahor, the brother of Abraham. Amen."

A MESSENGER ARRIVED at the home of Shem and Eber one afternoon and delivered a letter to them. Eber read it immediately.

"What does it say, son?" asked Shem.

"It's word from Abraham. He says the danger that was threatening Isaac's safety has apparently passed, for the time being, at least. Now it's time for us to return him home. He says he's planning on getting him married."

"Married?"

"That's what it says. Married."

"Here I thought you said the danger had passed," Shem said with a wry smile. "Sounds like the danger is just beginning for that young man."

The two men burst out laughing. Hearing the commotion, Isaac walked into the room to investigate, and as soon as he did, the men ceased their laughter. Puzzled, Isaac saw the strangest look on both men's faces. "What is going on?" he asked suspiciously.

Quickly regaining his composure, Shem replied, "Your father has sent word that we're to send you home."

"Home?" he wondered. "Did he say why?"

"So you can get married," said Eber, in mock congratulatory fashion. "Our best regards to the happy bridegroom this fine day. We salute you."

"Married?" blurted Isaac. "That's the craziest thing I ever heard."

"You're telling me!" chided Shem with an impish grin. "I didn't think you even knew what a woman was."

"But I don't," Isaac stammered. "I—*I* mean, of course I do. Of course I know what a woman is! I am forty years old, you know."

It was all that the two men could do to suppress any more laughter, as Isaac just stood there with a bewildered look on his face.

AS THE SUN REACHED its zenith in the noonday sky, Eliezer and his ten men arrived in Haran. Parched and weary, the group stopped by a watering hole just inside the city gates so they and their camels could drink their fill of water. As the men and their camel's were resting, Eliezer slipped away by himself. "God of Abraham, please lead me in the right direction so I can find a wife for Isaac from his own family. Amen."

Just then, a young woman around sixteen years old came and began drawing water from a nearby well. Intrigued, Eliezer walked over to her. Seeing him approach, she curtsied.

"Hello, young lady," Eliezer began, "I hope you don't think it too forward of me, but I felt compelled to meet you."

"Good day, sir," she said. "Compelled, you say?"

"Yes, isn't that odd?" he continued with a peculiar, faraway look in his eyes.

"If I didn't know better, I'd say you had dishonorable intentions," the girl said in a playful tone. "Should I run and fetch my brothers before it's too late?"

A startled Eliezer then looked directly at her. "Heavens, no. My intentions are absolutely honorable; on behalf of my master, that is."

"I see. So you weren't waiting to draw water from this well?"

"Oh, no, child," he replied, motioning to the water hole, "my men and I have already had our fill for the time being, but thank you for asking. Besides, there was no one around to obtain permission to access this well."

"That's very noble of you. Most people around here would have simply drawn water without any thought of permission. What's your name, if you don't mind my asking? I've never seen you around here before."

"That's because I'm not from around here."

"Then that explains your manners," she replied with a wry smile.

"My name is Eliezer." Smiling back, he was clearly charmed by her precocious wit. "And I've traveled here from Canaan on a very important mission. And who might you be?"

"My name is Rebecca, daughter of Bethuel."

Eliezer's ears instantly pricked up at the sound of that name. "Bethuel? Do you mean to say your father is Bethuel, the son of Nahor?"

"Yes. That's right."

"Then your father is the nephew of Abraham? From the land of Canaan?"

"Yes, of course. Why do you ask?"

"Because Abraham is my master, the man I spoke to you about earlier. It's on his behalf that I've come here."

"Abraham of Canaan is your master?"

"Yes, he really is, young lady."

"I see. Then maybe you'd like to come to our home, where you can speak to my father personally."

ACCOMPANIED BY Rebecca, Eliezer, followed by his ten men, rode up to her family's tent, where they were met by none other than Bethuel and his wife, who both came out to see who was arriving. Eliezer got off his camel and reached out a hand of greeting to Rebecca's father.

"You must be Bethuel," said Eliezer, smiling graciously. "I'd recognize the family resemblance anywhere."

Intrigued, Bethuel looked at his wife, then back at Eliezer. "You know who I am?"

"Of course; you're Bethuel, son of Nahor, nephew of my master, Abraham of Canaan."

Bethuel nodded with a craggy grin. "Yes, that's right. And you say you're a servant of Uncle Abraham?"

"Not just any servant, mind you; his chief servant. My name is Eliezer."

"Well, well, Eliezer. How is it that you've come to me on this fine day?"

"That's the astonishing thing, I must admit, because I came to this land without a clue as to where I was going, or with whom I would meet. Master Abraham simply told me I should come here to seek a wife for his son, Isaac. And even though I had no idea what I'd find, he assured me his God would lead me to where I needed to go."

"A wife, you say?" muttered Bethuel, who again glanced at his wife.

"That's right. And, as you can imagine, I was quite amazed when we stopped, purely by chance, at the well where your daughter came to draw water. It's an absolute miracle that our paths crossed so unexpectedly."

"A miracle, you say," echoed Bethuel.

"Yes, I do say. Certainly the Lord has blessed us all today."

As his eyes began to wander, Bethuel took a closer look at the entourage of men and camels that were gathered around Eliezer. "And what is all this, anyway? It looks like you have an awful lot of stuff. Looks like you're planning to go a long way still."

"Oh, forgive me, I nearly forgot," Eliezer said, shaking his head, as if he were scattering the cobwebs from his mind. "How foolish of me. No, we have no other destination in mind but this one. All this is for you and your family. It's my master's dowry on behalf of Isaac."

"For me, you say?" wondered Bethuel, his eyes widening at the thought of what might be amongst the cargo that took so many men and camels to transport.

"Yes, that's right; all of it's for you, if, of course, you're willing to provide a wife for my master's son."

With that, Bethuel turned and, clutching his wife's hand, led her back into their tent. After much discussion in hushed tones, the two of them came back out and bowed respectfully before Eliezer.

"It is agreed," intoned Bethuel. "Tell Uncle Abraham that we accept his gracious, and most generous, offer."

"Wonderful," Eliezer exclaimed, exhaling the breath he had been holding in anticipation. "Do you have any idea who the young lady will be?"

"We do, yes," Bethuel's wife replied, glancing at her husband with a happy smile.

Bethuel nodded back with his craggy grin and continued, "May we present you with our beloved daughter on behalf of my uncle." Together, he and his wife turned to see a young woman coming out of their tent.

"Rebecca," said Bethuel and his wife with one voice.

"Rebecca," echoed Eliezer. "You?"

Curtsying as graciously as she had when they first met at the well, she smiled sweetly and replied, "Yes, Eliezer. It's me."

AS SOON AS ELIEZER and his group returned to Canaan, Isaac came out to greet them. Beaming with pride, Eliezer led Rebecca by the hand and walked her right up to Isaac, who already appeared star struck by her beauty.

"Rebecca," began Eliezer, "I'd like you to meet my master Abraham's son, Isaac; Isaac, this is Rebecca, daughter of Bethuel, the son of Nahor and nephew of Abraham of Canaan."

With barely a thought, Isaac reached out, took her delicate hand, and lovingly kissed it. "Hello, Rebecca. I am so glad to meet you."

Embarrassed, Rebecca turned away, looking to Eliezer, unsure of what to do next, and he nodded back, as though urging her to respond. Turning back to Isaac, who still held her hand, anxiously awaiting her response, she curtsied and said, "Likewise, I'm sure. I'm pleased to meet you, too, Isaac."

In that moment, the pair locked eyes and, for quite a while, stayed like that as if there were no other people in the whole world except them.

The War Within

TWENTY YEARS WOULD pass by before Rebecca would conceive, and when she did the children inside her began to struggle. This caused her so much pain, in fact, that at times all her strength would drain away. Bewildered and fatigued, she paid a visit to one of the other women in her village. "Has anything like this ever happened to anyone you know?" Rebecca asked.

"No, never," came the woman's solemn reply.

"But why am I the only one?"

THEN SHEM AND EBER came to see how Rebecca and Isaac were getting along.

"So how's our mother-to-be?" Shem asked Isaac. "We've heard she's been having quite a time of it."

Isaac was clearly consumed with concern for his wife. "I don't know, Father Shem. I'm afraid for her life. No one has any idea what could be wrong with her."

"Don't be alarmed, son," said Eber. "The only thing wrong with your wife is she's going to give birth to twins."

"Oh, my Lord, *twins*?" Isaac blurted, nearly as breathless as his poor wife.

Eber nodded knowingly. "That's right. Even now the children inside her are struggling for supremacy, as each one tries to outwrestle the other. From this pair, two great nations will emerge. Naturally, one of these nations will be stronger than the other, but, as it turns out, the more powerful of the two will end up serving the younger one."

IN DUE TIME, THE DAY to deliver her children arrived. Kneeling down, Rebecca proceeded to give birth to twin sons. The first child came out as though he were wearing a hairy garment.

"Look at this one!" exclaimed the midwife. "We should call him Esau. He was already complete even before he came out of the womb."

Then, after Esau had been pulled out, his twin brother reached from their mother's womb and grabbed Esau's heel.

"And this one must be Jacob, the heel-catcher."

"YOU WANTED TO SEE me, Father?" asked Isaac, who upon entering his father's tent was stunned by the riches he saw surrounding the aged Abraham who was comfortably reclined on his bed.

"Pop, what's all this?"

"Ah, this? It's nothing. A small sample, really. And now it's all yours, Isaac."

"Me? But why? What did I ever do to deserve this?"

"You came into this world, my boy. By God's grace, you've blessed your mother's heart and mine, and what you're seeing here is just a part of your inheritance when I die."

"Father, don't talk like that."

"Oh, son, don't worry about me. I've lived a good, long life. One hundred and seventy-five of the most thrilling years a man could ever hope to live. But before I leave this present life, I have a few things to settle."

"Like what, Pop?"

"Like some things I've been meaning to tell you about, important things that need to be said before it's too late."

"All right. I'm listening."

A great melancholy suddenly washed over Abraham as though his whole life were flashing before him. In his mind's eye, images from his past came flooding back to him. First, he saw himself destroying his father's idols in a fit of rage, and then he found himself in the furnace of Nimrod again. But much to his dismay, although he miraculously survived the ordeal, he remembered all too clearly how his brother Haran had died in such agony. Then he remembered how, to make matters worse, he had lied to Sarah as she mourned his passing.

"Father, are you all right?" asked Isaac as he watched his father slipping away before his very eyes.

"Promise me, son," whispered Abraham.

Leaning forward, Isaac asked with an odd tilt of his head, "What, Father?"

"Promise me."

Then came more images into the patriarch's weary mind, all-too-fleeting glimpses of his beloved Sarah, of the time he went so far as to hide her in a chest in his attempts to deceive the Pharaoh, and of the time he lied to her concerning his plans to do God's bidding in sacrificing Isaac. Especially vivid was his recollection of how Sarah had wept when she had to say goodbye to her son for the last time, although at the time none of them could have ever known it really was the final moment they would spend together in this life.

"Just promise me, Isaac, promise," moaned Abraham, on the verge of tears.

"Anything, Father, anything. What's wrong? Please tell me."

Then, as if wrestling free from the grip of those bitter memories from so long ago, Abraham refocused his eyes back upon his son and wiped away the tear that slowly trickled down his cheek. "Oh, my dear son, Isaac. Please forgive me. I'm such a fool."

"Don't say that, Pop. You're a good man; no, you're a great man, a man in whom the Lord of Hosts has entrusted the fate of the whole world. Who else can lay claim to such a thing?"

Still clearly unhappy, Abraham shook his head. "But at what price, my son, what price? Never forget, serving God comes only at a tremendous price. Do you hear me?"

"I hear you, Father."

"Never forget that, Isaac. Never deceive yourself for a single, solitary moment. In order to do the things that God requires, one can never underestimate the lengths to which our humanity will stoop, will sink, in order to preserve itself in response to the Lord's call. The human heart is pernicious and cunning and never stops fighting us for even a moment, as it continually seeks to undermine the higher good." Struggling to sit up, Abraham became extremely agitated. "Do you understand what I'm trying to say, Isaac?"

"Hold on, Father, hold on," he replied, stepping forward in an effort to keep him from springing headlong out of bed. "Relax. Everything's going to be all right."

"Then you'll follow my advice, son?"

"Of course. You know I've always done whatever you've asked me. Haven't I?"

Somewhat appeased, Abraham settled back into his bed. "Certainly, Isaac, yes, always. You're a fine man. Now, there's just one last thing I need you to do for me."

"Name it, Father."

"Promise me that whatever you do, you won't ever let the earthly treasures you see before you take the place of God in your life. Always remember, the Lord of Heaven and Earth is the only lasting treasure you should seek in this life. Can you do that for me?"

"Of course, I promise."

"He's the One Who gave me every earthly delight, the One Who delivered me from the furnace of Nimrod and led me here, Who promised to give this land to my descendants whenever they did things His way. So you have to remember to always follow Him, and never let anyone lead you astray from the commands of God."

"I'll remember, Father. There's no One but Him."

"Good. And never forget, my son, always teach your children to do what He says. That way things will always go well with them, too. Above all, teach your children about the Lord and His way of doing things. Always, always remind them."

"I promise, Father. I'll do everything you've asked of me."

"Good, very good. Then I'm ready."

"Ready for what, Pop?"

"After a lifelong quest to penetrate the greatest mystery of the Universe, I'm finally ready, my son, finally ready to look upon the Face of God for myself."

THEN, IN THE FIFTEENTH year of Jacob and Esau's life, Abraham died. Immediately, Isaac and Ishmael set out with heavy hearts to bury their beloved father, along with their wives, Rebecca and Malchuth, accompanied by the twins, Jacob and Esau. There to show their support as well were all of Abraham's relatives from Haran, including Bethuel and his family, and as they led the great patriarch's coffin in a lavish royal procession, the Canaanite kings, princes and noblemen all joined in to pay their respects, too.

The Hunter Becomes the Hunted

THE MID-MORNING SUN began to wipe away the dew of the previous night as several antelope raised their heads, startled by the sound of tall grass crumpling very near to where they were feeding. Young Esau poked his head through the lush blades, but before he even had a chance to draw his bow, the antelope bolted away, much to his chagrin.

Meanwhile, at the opposite end of the same field, less than a hundred yards away, Nimrod, in spite of his advanced age, was also hunting with his bow and arrow. Accompanied by several of his fiercest warriors, the wily king caught sight of Esau, who was quite oblivious to their presence.

"Well, well, what do we have here?" Nimrod muttered, obviously more interested in this human quarry than he was in the animal prey that ran for cover as his men fanned out across the landscape. "If it isn't Esau, the grandson of my old nemesis. Just look at him strutting about. So he thinks himself a mighty hunter, does he? What a foolish, arrogant child."

EXHAUSTED AND empty-handed, Esau came home, only to find Jacob cooking a pot of beef stew over an open fire. He eagerly sniffed at the air like a wild animal in desperate search of prey. "That smells delicious," he growled. "What are you cooking? I'm famished."

"No luck hunting, eh?" asked Jacob, grinning at the pathetic look on Esau's face.

"Afraid not. Scarce pickings out there today. No thanks to Nimrod's men, of course. They always grab the best territory for themselves."

"Of course."

Esau wandered closer toward the pot of Jacob's simmering stew. "You are such a wonderful cook, brother. May I have some?"

"How come you're only my friend when I'm making something good to eat?" he replied mockingly. "Why is that?"

"Jacob, my twin soul, how could you say that? Talk like that hurts my feelings."

"Hardly."

"Well, what do you expect?" said Esau with a miserable groan. "I've been hunting all morning, with nothing to show for it except an empty belly. I'm hungry, no, I'm starving to death, right before your very eyes. Please, dear brother, have pity on your own flesh and blood, won't you?" Reaching around Jacob, he scooped out two fingers full of stew and instantly gobbled it down.

"Hey, you pig! Get your filthy paw out of my food!"

"You know, someday somebody's going to give that Nimrod the lesson he deserves."

"Yeah, then why don't you give it to him?"

"Who, me?" scoffed Esau. "Yeah, right. With all his men surrounding him wherever he goes? Are you nuts?"

"His power doesn't lie in his men, you know," Jacob assured him.

Esau licked his fingers of every drop of juice. "What are you babbling about now?"

"His power."

"Yeah, what about his *power*?"

"It's not what you think, that's all."

"And what makes you such an expert?"

"Don't you remember? Fathers Shem and Eber told us about it when we were kids."

"You mean, those old wives tales, don't you?"

"Not the part about the garment of Adam. They didn't make that part up, did they?"

"Garment? What garment?"

"God provided sheepskins as clothing for Adam, and it was handed down to Enoch and then Noah. Don't you remember?"

"Oh, sure, those," he cynically replied. "I remember now. And I suppose that's why they had power over the animals. Adam named them all, Noah brought them into the Ark, that sort of thing."

"Exactly," exclaimed Jacob, as if he thought Esau actually believed what he was saying. "But after the Flood, Ham stole the garment and gave it to his son Cush, which was how Nimrod got it. That's how he became the mighty hunter before the Lord. In fact, the garment not only gave him power over the animals, but it also made him invincible in battle. That's why his people made him king; that's why he nearly conquered the entire world. That is, until the confusion of tongues at the Tower of Babel disintegrated his kingdom. Don't you get it?"

Esau shook his head. "My dear, demented brother, you are so naïve. Honestly, if I thought for one second that that garment Nimrod is wearing actually turned an ordinary man into a world conqueror, even I'd try to steal it from him."

ESAU WENT HUNTING again in the fields where Nimrod often went, but this time, he saw the king and his warriors before they noticed him. As luck would have it, Esau discovered that only two of his bodyguards were with Nimrod, while the rest of Nimrod's warriors were all some distance away, off in their own search for game. So, before anyone had a chance to see him, Esau hid behind the surrounding bushes and began stalking his prey. As Nimrod and his two guards wandered past him, Esau leapt into view, adeptly brandishing his sword. Nimrod's two men instinctively withdrew their blades and prepared to rush at Esau.

"Wait!" Nimrod exclaimed. "Stand down, you two. This ends, here and now."

"But, Your Highness," said one of his bodyguards, "certainly you're in no position to defend yourself alone."

"How dare you question me. I may be two hundred and fifteen years old, but I'm not dead yet!"

"Forgive me, Sire. As you wish."

The two bodyguards obediently returned their swords to their sheaths and stepped back several feet.

"*This* is between me and the boy," said Nimrod, who then withdrew his own sword.

"Who are you calling a boy?" Esau grumbled.

"What are you, all of seventeen, eighteen?"

"I'll have you know, sir, I'm twenty years old."

Nimrod tilted his head oddly. "How fitting. I was the same age when I took on the responsibilities of a man."

"So it's man to man," said Esau, supremely arrogant. "Is that it?"

"As a matter of fact, yes, it is. Before you stands not a king, not a rebel, but a man, a man who refuses to wrestle with phantoms in the night any longer." Slowly, Nimrod held up his sword with one hand and motioned to Esau with his other, beckoning him to commence their engagement.

With his sword drawn, Esau charged at Nimrod. "Then prepare to taste the vengeance of the God of Abraham!"

Nearly upon him, Nimrod inexplicably lowered his sword.

"This is for Uncle Haran," spewed Esau, "you miserable bastard!" And with a single, furious slash of Esau's blade, Nimrod's head rolled off his shoulders and his body fell limply to the ground. Stunned by what they had just witnessed, Nimrod's two bodyguards let out a vicious howl and charged Esau with flashing swords. Spinning to avoid their attack, Esau furiously slashed away, killing them both with two swift strokes of his blade.

THE REST OF NIMROD'S warriors, who were out hunting in different parts of the wilderness, heard the distant cries of the two bodyguards and started to run to see what had happened.

ESAU KNELT DOWN NEXT to Nimrod's body and removed Adam's garment from around his waist, tightly wrapping them around his own. From a distance, he saw Nimrod's men coming toward him, so he ran as fast as he could with the priceless garment now securely in his possession.

RUNNING INTO THE CITY with the garment, Esau finally came to his father's tent. To the point of exhaustion, Esau approached Jacob, who was cooking a steaming pot of lentil stew, and wearily sat down next to him. "What a wonderfully delicious aroma," he sighed, still trying to catch his breath. "My God, I am ravenous."

"Don't tell me. You've been out hunting again?"

"You know me so well, brother."

"And let me guess. You had no luck again with the game today, all thanks to your old nemesis, Nimrod."

"Ah, yes, the game. Well, you see, today it turns out that the game actually went all my way."

An intrigued Jacob turned to look at his brother and was instantly shocked by the sight of the sheepskins wrapped around Esau's waist. "Good God, you did it? You got the garment?"

"You mean to tell me you knew this was Adam's garment just by taking one look at it?"

"Something like that, yes, I suppose I did."

"Must be nice. Now, before I die of starvation on this very spot, would you please give me something to eat?"

"Something to eat?" Jacob asked incredulously. "You have the garment of Adam in your possession, and all you can think about is your empty belly?"

The hairy one shrugged. "What else is new?"

"Fine, I'll feed you." With a wicked twinkle in his eye, his brother added, "For a price, that is."

Grinning from ear to ear, Esau waved his hand in a friendly gesture. "Of course, brother, anything for you; just name it. After all, if it wasn't for you, I would never have known this garment was—"

"I want your birthright," Jacob interjected, quite casually.

Esau's grin immediately turned to a scowl. "But I'm about to die, right here and now. How could you be so mercenary at a time like this?"

The heel-catcher shrugged. "Sorry; not my fault. So … what'll it be?"

"You dirty scoundrel, you conniving rat. You really are my twin brother, aren't you?"

"That's right, brother," Jacob cooed as he held out a bowl of his most delicious lentil stew. "So tell me. You want some … or not?"

"Of course, I want some … brother," he replied with a snide grin. "What do I need with my birthright, anyway, now that I have Adam's garment?" And grabbing the bowl of stew from Jacob's outstretched hand, Esau hungrily gobbled its contents.

TRANSPORTING NIMROD'S body back to his own city of Shinar, the king's warriors buried their dead monarch amidst great pageantry and lamentation. And after reigning for one hundred and eighty-five years, the king of Shinar died shamefully by the sword of Esau, killed by a descendant of Abraham after all, just as Nimrod had seen in his own dreams and just as his sages and sorcerers had predicted so many years ago.

The Mystery of the One

ENOCH SLOWLY CLOSED the book in his lap and looked up at everyone. As before, the crowd had continued to swell as he had been reading his story aloud. The pleasantly surprised patriarch scanned the group of eager listeners. "Well, everyone, now I want you to think carefully about what I've been telling you, because it really does come to you straight from the Lord's own mouth."

"Thank you, Father," said Methuselah. "That was another incredible story. How do you do it?"

Enoch smiled contentedly. "Tell me, then. Did anyone learn anything from this story of the father of faith? And what about the children of faith who followed in his footsteps? Did they teach you anything?"

Lamech stood up. "Well, I learned that each and every person has to have faith for themselves. No one else can do it for you. The faith of a single individual, that's what the Lord responds to. Is that right, Grandfather?"

For several moments, he gazed at his grandson before breaking into a smile, like a teacher satisfied with his student. "Very good, Lamech. Yes, that's correct."

Then Jubal stood up and boldly took a step forward. "You mean to tell me one person's faith really does all that? I'm sorry, Grandfather, but it seems to me you're filling everyone's head with a bunch of silly old wives tales."

Enoch turned slowly. "Young man, I do believe you still have a great deal to learn. In the meantime, I'd advise you to avoid saying anything you'll regret later."

"I beg your pardon, sir." Jubal reluctantly bowed to the patriarch. "I meant no disrespect. I just fail to see the moral of your story, that's all. How can the faith of one person accomplish everything you've just described?"

"My dear, Jubal." Enoch knowingly smiled. "You mean to tell me you don't know about the mystery of the One?"

"The mystery of the One?" Jubal shrugged. "No, sir, I'm afraid not."

"Oh, yes, the mystery of the One. As one year is more honorable than another year, so also is one person more honorable than another. One person may have tremendous wealth, while someone else may be very poor. One person may be quite intelligent, while another is not so bright. One person is famous for their silence, another for their cleanliness, one for strength, another for sensibility. But let it be heard and understood by everyone here, there is no one better than the one who respects God. In the time to come, that person will be more glorious than all the rest."

"That's it?" replied Jubal, clearly mystified. "That's the mystery? I don't get it."

"I guess that's why they call it a mystery, cousin." Lamech smiled sarcastically.

The entire group chuckled, but Jubal, unamused, scornfully glared back at Lamech.

"What's so difficult to understand, my son?" Enoch continued. "It's simple. The one who respects the principles of his forefathers is blessed, but the one who perverts the decrees of his forefathers is cursed."

Jubal shook his head impatiently. "Yes, yes, of course, I get all that, but what about the angels and the thrones? Can't you tell us more about them? What about the gatekeepers, serpents with eyes like lanterns and teeth like razors?"

"The one who imparts peace and love is blessed," Enoch persisted, "but the one who disturbs those who love their neighbors is cursed. The one who is humble in speech is blessed, but the one who speaks peaceably, while harboring murder in their heart, is cursed. The mystery of the One is just like that. Do you see what I'm saying?"

"Of course I do, yes," replied Jubal, nodding his head in frustration. "That's all very commendable. I see that. But, please, why won't you tell us more about the treasure houses of ice and snow? Or about the secrets of the wind."

"Blessed is the one who refuses to hold a grudge," Enoch continued patiently, "the one who helps the injured, the condemned, the brokenhearted, who gives to the needy, because on Judgment Day every weight and measure will be as it is in the marketplace. That is to say, they'll be hung on scales so that everyone can inspect the truth for themselves, and according to this measure, they'll receive their reward."

"Fine, yes, well," said Jubal, clearly exasperated. "Then I guess you're not going to answer my question. Never mind. I'm sorry I even asked. Good day to your, sir." And bowing dutifully, Jubal turned and walked away, disappearing back into the crowd.

"Don't mind him, Papa Enoch," urged Eli's mother. "He's a handful, that one. Headstrong like his mother, I'm afraid."

Enoch nodded amicably. "I understand all too well, my dear."

"So, Pop," interjected Methuselah, trying to steer the conversation in a new direction, "what else do your books have to say?"

"Ah, yes, of course. Let me see: Well, the one who brings an offering to the Lord, will have God Himself assist in the blessing of that gift, but the one who approaches Him without sincerity will not have his treasures increased in Heaven. And when God demands an offering of bread or cattle or any other sacrifice, for that matter, it's nothing compared to what He's really looking for."

"And what's that, Grandpa?" asked Lamech.

"A pure heart, my boy. Sincerity, honesty, call it what you will. In fact, a pure heart is so important to God that He uses all these other things just to test the heart of each and every man, woman and child. That's the mystery of the One. Don't you see?"

"Is it even more important than the secrets of the wind and the snow and the stars?" wondered Eli's mother.

"Yes, my dear, much more. Listen, everyone. Understand something very important here. If anyone brings a gift to an earthly ruler while harboring disloyal thoughts in his heart, and the ruler finds out, won't he be angry with him?"

"Of course he would," Lamech replied.

"And wouldn't that same ruler also refuse to accept any of his so-called 'gifts'? Wouldn't he then hand him over to a swift and severe punishment?"

"Of course," chimed in Jared. "That goes without saying."

"That's right, yes. Then there's your answer. The mystery of the One is like that, too."

Methuselah's wife squinted her eyes, trying to wrap her mind around what Enoch was saying. "I'm still not sure if I understand what you're telling us, Father."

"That's all right, my dear. There's no shame in admitting you don't understand right away. These things take time. That's why it's so important to take the books I've written for you and read them for yourselves. Take your time getting to know what's in them."

"We'll do just that, Grandpa," Lamech said. "How many books are there, anyway?"

"Oh, my, there are hundreds of these wonderful books, just waiting for you all."

"Hundreds?" chirped little Eli in amazement.

"Yes, hundreds. Right there in black and white for everyone to see, answers to all your questions, about everything that took place long ago in the beginning of God's creation, right up until the End of Time."

"Well, Pop," said Methuselah, "now that you've finished with your story, what will you do next? And when do we get to see these books of yours with our own eyes?"

"Soon, my boy, very soon. In the meantime, I have one last story to tell you before I return to God."

Methuselah looked puzzled at this statement. "Now, when you say return to God, what, exactly, do you mean by that?"

"Well, it means I have three weeks left before the Lord sends his two angels, Sariel and Raguel, to return me to where He is."

Methuselah and Lamech exchanged a concerned look.

"Father, please," replied Methuselah, "let's not talk about that right now. I think it's time for a break, don't you?"

Enoch wearily nodded. "Then we should all agree to meet back here again next week at this same time, and I'll tell you another story. How does that sound?"

"Very good, son, we're looking forward to it," said Jared, who turned to the rest of the elders seated there with him. "Isn't that right, everyone?"

To a man, they all nodded.

JUBAL AND HIS TWO brothers, Hiram and Tubal, were loitering the next day down the street from Enoch's home. To the casual passersby, there was nothing at all sinister about this unassuming trio, but to those in the know, it clearly represented a worrisome moment for Enoch and his group.

Hiram lustily licked his lips. "Boy, would I love to get my hands on one of Enoch's books. How about you, Jubal?"

Grinning back, Jubal sneered, "That's exactly what I was counting on, brother."

"What?" wondered Hiram, who suddenly realized what Jubal just said, "Wait. You were?" He then turned to his other brother. "Tubal, what do you think Jubal means by that?"

"I'm not sure, Hiram. Jubal, are you saying what I think you're saying?"

"I might be," he replied with a malicious twinkle in his eye.

"Uh, oh, Tubal," said Hiram suspiciously. "I do think our brother is up to no good again. I've seen that look in his eyes before."

"What look is that, brother?" Jubal asked, quite innocently.

"You know very well, Jubal," replied Tubal. "The look of desire."

"He's right, Jubal," Hiram groaned, as Jubal looked at them as if he were offended. "When I see that look in your eyes, I see the eyes of robbery staring back at me."

"What is wrong with you two?" Jubal scoffed. "What harm could there be in borrowing a few books? Have you both lost your nerve? It's not like we'd be taking anything of value. They're just books."

Hiram and Tubal exchanged a troubled look.

"Besides," continued Jubal as his eyes veered off into the distance, "we'd just be borrowing them for a little while. Then, after we've had a good look at them for ourselves, they would, quite mysteriously, find their way right back to where we found them."

"All right, all right," Tubal said. "I admit it. The thought of seeing one of Enoch's precious books with my own eyes has begun to gnaw at me, too."

"We haven't lost our nerve, have we, Tubal?" wondered Hiram.

"Of course not, Hiram," insisted Tubal.

"Good, then it's settled," murmured Jubal, consumed by his thoughts. "Together we hatch our plan, together we execute that plan, and together we discover for ourselves exactly what's inside those books." And turning to his two brothers, he donned a malicious grin. "When the time is right, that is."

ANOTHER HUGE CROWD surrounded Enoch, who sat happily with his book perched in his lap, gazing out over several hundred eager faces. From his sons and daughters, and his fathers and mothers, to his aunts and uncles, and his nieces and nephews, everyone was there to listen that day. And in the their midst, Jubal, Hiram and Tubal sat like hawks watching a field mouse from across the field, just waiting for an opportunity to strike.

"Well, hello, everyone," Enoch began. "I'm so glad to have this chance to tell you all about the wonderful books the Lord has asked me to give you."

"Thank you, Papa Enoch, for having us today," said Eli's mother.

"Of course, my dear, my pleasure. Now, I want you all to know that after I'm gone, you'll be able to give these books to your children, too, throughout all your generations."

"Tell us, then, son," asked Jared, "these books you're going to give us, will they be intended for our nation alone?"

"No, Father, of course not. The Lord is the Ruler and Judge of the entire Universe. Anyone who respects God will be allowed to read them. That way everyone will have a chance to come to love these books, more than any mere earthly delight. Does that make sense?"

"Certainly," Jared replied. "It does, yes."

"In the meantime, everyone, don't be deceived," continued Enoch. "There really is a place that's already prepared for each and every person. How do I know?" Looking around at the crowd before him, Enoch gazed deeply into their eyes. "Does anyone here know how I know?"

Everyone just shrugged their shoulders.

Enoch then turned to Jubal. "Do *you* know?"

But Jubal never even flinched.

Tubal surreptitiously looked over at him. "Is he talking to you, Jubal? He's looking right at you, isn't he?"

"Would you shut up?" muttered Jubal. "And quit looking at me, you idiot."

Enoch gazed intently at Jubal as he continued. "I know because I've already described everyone's life in all the books that God had me write, that's why."

Hiram mumbled under his breath. "You don't think he suspects us, Jubal, do you?"

Enoch proceeded. "I assure you all, even before you were born, each and every one of you had a place prepared for you. Not only that, but God has measured out a unique set of trials and tribulations which are designed just for you and your specific nature."

"He doesn't know a thing, I tell you," whispered Jubal. "The man is a charlatan."

A stern woman sitting next to Jubal and his two brothers leaned in toward them, grumbling indignantly. "Would you please be quiet? Show some respect."

The trio immediately snapped to attention, trying, however clumsily, to conform.

Enoch's words continued to flow like water from a mountain stream. "Analyzing every person's accomplishments and failures throughout their lifetime, I wrote corresponding judgments to go along with those specific deeds." Again and again, the patriarch's eyes kept returning to Jubal, resting his intense gaze on him. "In fact, there isn't a single person born on Earth who can hide from this kind of scrutiny, ever."

Hiram muttered to Jubal out of the corner of his mouth. "So tell me again, brother, why he keeps looking at you."

"Hush!" snapped the stern woman.

Again the trio of brothers snapped up, front and center, trying their best to look like they were paying attention to the storyteller.

"And when the Lord sends a great light," Enoch continued in reverential tones, "there will be judgment for the just and the unjust alike, because no one among us can ever hope to escape from being held accountable by Him." The wistful patriarch slowly opened the book in his lap. "And so it continues, this mystery of the One."

Trial by Fury

Adapted from

The Letters of Herod and Pilate,
The Epistles of Pilate to Tiberius Caesar,
The Trial and Condemnation of Pilate,
and *The Death of Pilate, who Condemned Jesus*

and

The Gospel of Nicodemus,
formerly called
The Acts of Pontius Pilate

Behold the Man, Antonio Ciseri, 1871

Trial by Fury

Teachers and Tyrants

CANAAN, OR PALESTINE, as it was later called because of the Philistines living there, would become known by yet another name after its conquest under Joshua – Israel.

These were the words on a chalkboard inside a room full of raptly attentive Jewish schoolboys, ranging in age from thirteen to seventeen, where a neatly clad teacher strode back and forth.

"So, class," beamed the proud teacher, "are you ready for today's history lesson of how we, as a proud and mighty nation, came to be in this land of ours?"

"Yes, Professor Ada," the class chimed in unison.

"Very good, then let us commence. It all began about fourteen centuries ago, when Joshua led the Twelve Tribes of Israel in the conquest of Canaan. This was followed by a period of four some hundred years, in which the land was ruled by judges, such as Gideon and Samson. Then, a little more than a thousand years ago, a loose but powerful confederation of all the tribes was welded together under King David, who ultimately catapulted our nation to its zenith of glory. Sadly, however, the kingdom divided some seventy-five years later, when the last portion of our great nation ceased to exist as an independent territory, and for the next several centuries, two kingdoms struggled for survival where, before, there had been just one. Both the House of Judah to the south and the House of Israel to the north would then become minor provinces in a succession of larger empires. Yet try as they might, none of these fierce nations, not Assyria or Babylon, not Persia or Greece, none could extinguish the indomitable spirit of our people."

As Professor Ada paced back and forth in front of them, the enthralled students tried very hard to envision the scene as he was describing it.

"Then, about ninety years ago, Roman barbarians took control of our beloved homeland when their expanding domain overflowed eastward and Julius Caesar's most effective general, Pompey, subdued Jerusalem in a horrific three-month siege."

A VALIANT BATTLE raged in the mind of every schoolboy there, as each one imagined how their brave ancestors had fought in that not-too-distant past. Arrows flew and swords clashed, with warriors on both sides squaring off in brutal hand-to-hand combat, district by district and street by street.

"Sadly, though, in spite of the valiant efforts of our fighting men, our proud nation fell again to the merciless hand of the foreign usurper, and for nearly twenty years the land and its people lay waste and desolate. But finally, after having revived from the bitter slumber of servitude, the spirit of patriotism was rekindled and civil war broke out."

In their unbridled fury, droves of ordinary Jewish peasants, armed with nothing but crude shields and swords, managed to break through a formidable blockade of Roman soldiers.

"Hoping to quell the chaotic situation, the Roman Senate appointed a client-king over Palestine, choosing a man who'd been governor of Galilee for six years."

Above the chaos of strife and revolt, a new king arose.

"Known as Herod the Great, he was given an army that eventually helped him re-establish Roman order in Jerusalem. Total victory was achieved in three years, and as a result of the ongoing support he received from Rome, Herod's rule there remained unchallenged for the next four decades."

Overwhelmed by the sheer volume of Roman soldiers, many proud Israelite warriors were led away in chains, to the absolute horror of their onlooking families.

"Naturally, in the years following the fall of Jerusalem, the Jewish nation chafed bitterly under Herod's yoke, despising this puppet-ruler because of his complete insensitivity to their religious and political concerns."

Their shields and swords taken from them, these Jewish prisoners were handed picks and shovels, and summarily whipped into action.

"Turning many of the cities in his domain into Roman civic centers, Herod tried unsuccessfully to introduce a way of life the people of Judea would forever detest."

Digging away the rubble, the Israelites were forced to rebuild new edifices where the war had reduced the old ones to piles of rock and burned-out lumber.

"But what made matters even worse, Herod the Great was an Idumaean Jew, from the nation of Edom, which had descended from Esau, the hated twin brother of Jacob."

As his forced laborers toiled to rebuild the city, Herod the Great supervised the work from the safety of his palace stronghold.

"And ever since Esau was tricked by Jacob out of the birthright blessing, there has been perpetual distrust and division between the two clans. So for the nation of Israel to be made subject to anyone with Edomite blood, well, as you can just imagine, class, this was an insult too great to bear."

Although they had been deprived of their traditional weapons of war, the servile Israelites were not beneath turning their construction tools into implements of revolt. While their overlords were not paying attention, they diligently sharpened their picks and shovels into razor-sharp condition.

"So for Rome, the threat of a Palestinian revolution would be a constant concern, for them and for anyone given the task of ruling over a nation prone to such religious fervor."

Many an unsuspecting Roman construction supervisor or legal magistrate would be subdued by the Israelite slaves, thereby forcing the position to be refilled with another man; each time with someone even more apprehensive about the role than the last person.

"Then, approximately thirty years ago, in an attempt to decentralize the troubled territory, the Roman emperor Augustus Caesar split up the kingdom, dividing it among an ailing Herod's three sons."

The solitary puppet-monarch, Herod the Great, slowly faded from the scene and was replaced by three vassal-kings, each ruling from his own lavishly decorated palace.

"Philip was given jurisdiction over Bethsaida and Paneas, Archelaus controlled Samaria and Idumea, while Herod Antipas presided over Judea and Galilee. A decade later, Tiberius Caesar, the stepson of Augustus, ascended as emperor of Rome."

Handing away his sword and receiving a royal scepter in its place, this proud monarch was crowned amidst a lavish Roman parade.

"Having already distinguished himself as one of Rome's greatest generals, Tiberius proved more adept still as an administrator, successfully strengthening the Roman economy and ensuring that even his far-flung provinces were properly governed. But Tiberius was personally unpopular because of his austere ways."

As the parades and celebrations came to an abrupt end, this somber king retreated to his solitary existence securely behind the walls of his palace in Rome.

"Still primarily a soldier at heart, Tiberius abhorred indulgent living and public spectacles. So, after just eleven years on the throne and in opposition to the advice of his counselors, he withdrew from public life, temporarily leaving behind the political intrigue of his power-hungry relatives. Retaining his emperorship, however, he left the administrative details to someone else, the commander of the Praetorian Guard, Lucius Sejanus."

Mortified and incredulous, his family and associates cringed as Tiberius handed over his royal scepter to one of his most decorated soldiers. With great satisfaction, Sejanus raised the scepter while the only people celebrating this stroke of imperial whim were his fellow soldiers amongst the ranks of the Praetorian guards.

"Once in place, Sejanus had no problem at all getting his friend and ally appointed as the governor of Judea. His friend's name was Pontius Pilate, a Roman knight from the Samnite clan of the Pontii, hence his name Pontius."

A new man then came to the forefront, striding onto the scene with his robes of imperial power wrapped securely around him.

"Thoroughly confident of the skills of his old friend, Sejanus was certain that Pilate, a ruthlessly efficient administrator, would have no difficulty in restoring much-needed order in his new role as governor of this volatile territory."

Strutting his way through the streets of Jerusalem, Governor Pilate was followed stride for stride by his cadre of stalwart Roman soldiers.

"But for all of Pilate's prior successes as a seasoned soldier and cunning politician, he seemed unusually incapable of cooperating with Jewish sentiments. In fact, his very first act as governor brought on needless turmoil. In an ill-conceived attempt to honor his patron Sejanus, he installed images of Emperor Tiberius throughout Jerusalem, images which portrayed Caesar as a god. To the Jews, a graven image like this was utter sacrilege."

Wherever Pilate and his soldiers went, they left plaques in their wake, which caused every Jewish citizen who gazed at them to react with disgust.

"Then Pilate began to mint coins bearing pagan religious symbols."

Without warning, imperial soldiers invaded every one of the market places in Jerusalem, where they dumped out jars of Roman coins. Then having emptied their jars, the soldiers absconded all the Jewish money from their places of business, refilling the jars with the money they had just seized.

"Soon, the entire city was in an uproar."

As Pilate complacently sat on his governor's seat, a surging crowd of Jewish peasants clamored around his palace.

"They begged Pilate to remove these objects of sacrilege from their sacred capitol but were adamantly refused."

The demonstrators tried their best to push their way forward, but the heavily armored Roman soldiers stood their ground, injuring numerous protesters in the process.

"Even if the governor couldn't understand these strangely zealous people, he would at least have the satisfaction of ruling over them with a firm hand of imperial authority, and thanks to the protection of his friend Sejanus, Pilate was assured of at least that much."

As a result of so many injuries amidst the jostling throng of demonstrators, a lamentable howl rose up, which Pilate could hear even from inside the palace. Finally losing his patience, the governor sprang to his feet. "Enough already!" he shrieked. "Tell this obstinate bunch to disperse or suffer the pain of my soldiers' hardened blades!"

A pair of his men bolted out onto the balcony overlooking the city square. Brandishing his sword for all to see, one of them leaned forward and barked, "Governor Pilate wants you to know that if you don't leave immediately, he'll have you all cut down where you stand!"

A hush swept across the crowd, and for several tense moments, everyone there looked to the person next to them. Then, from out of the midst of the crowd, a solitary protestor hissed, "Do your worst, you filthy dogs! We're not intimidated by your threats."

Then, as if with a single mind, the protesters all held out their necks in bitter defiance. Puzzled by this peculiar display, the two soldiers looked at each other, then went back inside and stood at attention before Pilate, unsure of what to tell him.

Obviously pleased with himself, the governor gloated. "Well, well, they certainly simmered down after that, didn't they? They're disbanding, then?"

"I'm afraid not, sir," said one of the soldiers.

"What?" blurted Pilate, who looked to the other man in frustration.

"He's right, Governor," the second soldier added. "In fact, they seem more determined than ever to die for their cause."

"Ridiculous," spewed Pilate, who went out to witness the spectacle for himself, flanked by his soldiers. Incredulous at the sight of so many people postured in mock submission, he leaned over the balcony rail and bellowed, "What is wrong with you people? Don't any of you value your lives? What about your families? Doesn't the prospect of their grieving over your corpses concern you at all? And for what? A bunch of plaques and coins paying tribute to your king?"

"Caesar is not our king!" screamed one man from the crowd. "We'd all rather die than see such a violation of our sacred city."

Baffled, Pilate threw his hands up. "You're obviously all insane." Turning in disgust, he went back inside, followed by his men.

"What should we do now, sir?" the first soldier asked. "Should we give the order to disperse the crowd by force?"

"No," Pilate murmured.

"Then what do we do?" wondered the second soldier, half to himself.

A deflated Pilate slowly replied, "I want you to remove the plaques and return all the money you confiscated, and I want it done immediately."

The two soldiers exchanged a confused look.

"Yes, Governor Pilate," said the first soldier. "Right away."

As the pair left his presence, Pilate dropped heavily into a chair, stewing in his own juices. "What kind of madhouse have I gotten myself into?"

EVERY YOUNG MAN IN that classroom watched in eager anticipation as Professor Ada paced back and forth in front of them like a caged lion. "Then, just four years ago, Tiberius Caesar, emperor of Rome, uncovered a plot to seize imperial power. And the man attempting to overthrow him was none other than Pontius Pilate's friend and protector whom Caesar had personally placed in charge of his kingdom. Now, does anybody here remember the name of the man that Tiberius left in charge?"

One of the boys instantly raised his hand, furiously bobbing it about until finally the professor pointed to him. "Yes, Zachariah; do you remember?"

The boy excitedly jumped to his feet. "Yes, sir, I think I do."

"Go ahead, then. If you'd be so kind, tell the class for us."

"Lucas Sojourner."

Several of the boys giggled, and Professor Ada smiled. "Very good, Zachariah. That was very close, actually. In fact, class, that man's name was Lucius Sejanus. And in no time at all this man, who presumed to corrupt the authority he'd been granted, was summarily executed, along with many of his supporters."

LED BEFORE TIBERIUS Caesar, who was back again on his gilded throne, Lucius Sejanus had been stripped of every vestige of his illustrious military status. Forced to kneel at the hands of a captain of the Praetorian guard, Sejanus glared defiantly up at Tiberius.

"Do you have any last words in your defense, old friend?" Caesar asked.

Sejanus just shook his head, choosing instead to bow his head in silent resolve.

"How noble of you," said Tiberius sarcastically, and after a subtle gesture from the king, the captain of the guard sliced off Sejanus' head with a single swipe of his sword.

A YOUNG MAN'S HAND was again bobbing up and down with great excitement.

"Yes, Zachariah, what is it now?" Professor Ada asked.

"Why didn't they execute Pontius Pilate, too?"

"Well, class, that's a very good question, isn't it? Unfortunately, though, no one really knows for sure. Somehow, I guess, fortune just happened to be smiling on Pilate that day, because for whatever reason he was never implicated in the plot to overthrow the emperor. But, of course, that didn't mean his situation continued without further controversy. Far from it, actually. Not long after that, Pilate was up to his old tricks again, inept as he was in governing such a political hotbed as Judea."

ROMAN SOLDIERS FANNED out across the city.

"Again the governor tried to display commemorative shields dedicated to Caesar, but this time, he made sure the shields bore no images, just the names of the emperor and himself."

Everywhere they went the soldiers posted these shields engraved with the names of Tiberius and Pilate on them.

"But because Caesar was universally worshiped as a god throughout the Roman Empire, the Jewish population soon took up arms in protest."

A swarm of demonstrators again overflowed the city square, buzzing about like a dense cloud of angry hornets, surrounding Pilate's palace and eventually forcing the centurions below Pilate's balcony to abandon their posts.

"This is an outrage, Governor!" screamed one of the protesters. "We refuse to sit back and let you persist with your damnable worship of Caesar!"

EVEN HEROD'S THREE sons, Philip, Archelaus and Herod Antipas appealed to Pilate.

"How many times do we have to go through this, Governor?" Philip said. "It's simply not in our best interests for you to continue meddling in areas you know so little about."

"How dare you come here and tell me what I can and cannot do," snapped Pilate. "This is still Roman territory, and none of you rule here without the authority of Rome. Or has your loyalty suddenly grown stale?"

"Don't be ridiculous, sir," Archelaus replied. "Our loyalty to Rome is unquestionable, but in the interest of both your nation and ours, we insist that you remove the shields from this holy city."

"But I won't remove them, I tell you," insisted Pilate. "Not unless I receive direct orders from Caesar himself. Now, either you gentlemen leave of your own free will, or I'll have my soldiers escort you to the door. Which will it be?"

The three men exchanged angry looks and, without another word, turned and left.

THE FOLLOWING WEEK, Pilate received a letter by royal messenger. Disgusted by its contents, the governor threw the letter down at his wife's feet.

"What's wrong now, husband?" she asked.

"Can you believe it, Procla?" fumed Pilate. "The emperor of Rome has taken sides with these Jewish foreigners. Those three traitorous sons of Herod have gone behind my back and reported me to Caesar himself. Now he's rebuked me on their behalf and ordered me to remove the shields I posted in *his* honor."

Procla gasped. "By the gods, this is awful. It's bad enough those puppet-masters have managed to best you in a contest of wills, but now Caesar has begun to take sides against you. Dear husband, I can't tell you what a dangerous precedent this is."

As if he had just suffered a physical blow, Pilate's knees grew weak, forcing him to sit down on his bed. "It now seems, with the execution of Sejanus," Pilate grumbled painfully, "my situation as governor of Jerusalem is on even shakier ground. Now I know how a caged animal feels. It appears I can no longer sweep my actions so easily under a rug, no matter how well-intentioned they are."

Touched by his lament, Procla moved to his side and sat down, placing her hand on his. "My husband, do you realize what this means? If there's ever an investigation from Rome, they'll certainly uncover an endless list of atrocities, acts of corruption and plunder, your unmitigated cruelty and murder of people who've all been condemned without the benefit of a trial."

Cut to the quick, Pilate sprang to his feet and stepped away from her. "Thank you for that, my dear. As usual, I can always count on your complete frankness."

A STUDENT'S HAND popped back up.

"Yes, Zachariah; go ahead," said a mildly frustrated Ada.

"Has Pontius Pilate ever done anything good in his life?"

"Unfortunately, no," the professor replied.

Then another hand popped up.

"Yes, Tobias. Is there something you'd like to add to the discussion?"

"My father told me that, one time, the governor built an aqueduct to supply water to Jerusalem. Isn't that a good thing?"

Ada shook his head with a wry smile. "Oh, he built it all right, but unfortunately he did so using sacred money from the Temple treasury. So even when Pilate tried to do something positive for the city, he did it with a complete lack of understanding as to how his methods might affect the people he was governing. As you can imagine, when the people of Jerusalem found out about Pilate's underhanded dealings, they were outraged."

THOUSANDS OF ANGRY demonstrators were again trying to push their way into the governor's square, and because the area was too small to accommodate them all, the rest milled about the outskirts of the palace grounds.

"We demand an end to this project, Governor!" yelled a protester who stood just below Pilate's balcony.

"You foul dog, you're not worthy of your position!" screamed another.

"Why not just cut your own throat and be done with it, you scum, before we have to do it for you!" bellowed another.

Inside the governor's palace, Procla stood at her husband's side as they both listened intently to the commotion from the safety of its interior.

"By the gods," murmured Procla," what have you done this time, husband? The people are on the verge of an all-out riot."

"Relax, Procla. I have everything under control."

"Control?" she blurted, cautiously stepping out onto the balcony. "Somehow I fail to see what you mean by that."

Following her outside, Pilate walked past her and moved to the edge of the balcony. As he looked down upon the overflowing mob, he pondered his next move.

"Do you hear us, you filthy swine?" another disgruntled protester growled. "Put an end to your treachery, or we'll burn your palace to the ground."

Aghast, Procla leaned into her husband. "What are you going to do about all this?"

"Just watch," he calmly replied. Then, after a simple hand signal from Pilate, what appeared to be ordinary civilians in the midst of the crowd jumped into action. Dozens of men began beating the protesters, causing a tremendous cry to rise up, as chaos instantly ensued. Unwilling to give in so easily, though, the angry protesters began to fight back. Spurred on by the unexpected resistance of the crowd, the aggressors then withdrew daggers from beneath their robes and began to indiscriminately stab the demonstrators. Unarmed and outmanned, many of the protesters were killed or wounded.

Horrified by all the bloodshed, Procla turned to her husband. "What on Earth just happened? Is this your idea of having everything under control?"

"Absolutely not," Pilate croaked, as though he were being reprimanded by his own mother. "I only had my soldiers infiltrate the crowd in disguise so they could rough them up. I never ordered them to draw blood. Honestly, I had no idea that something like this would happen."

"Unbelievable," snapped Procla, who, disgusted and disappointed, turned and walked back inside. "This is the last straw, for sure."

Watching her disappear back into the palace, Pilate then turned to his men and motioned for them to cease their assault. "Enough!" he roared. As the noise of the tumult slowly died down, the governor haplessly gazed out across the disheveled crowd. Disheartened by the debacle of death that lay before him, he turned away and muttered beneath his breath, "What have I done this time?"

"THEN, SOMETIME during those dark days," Professor Ada continued, "a series of startling eyewitness reports began to circulate throughout Palestine, reports that threatened to overthrow not only the Roman Empire but the nation of the Jews as well."

The professor's hand etched out another word on his chalkboard; just one.

Martyrdom.

"In some cases they were reports that these eyewitnesses were to seal with their very lives in martyrdom." Ada turned back to address his students. "Now, class, can anyone tell me what this word means?"

Several hands popped up, and the professor pointed to one student. "Yes, Nathaniel."

"Martyrdom is when someone is killed for a sacred cause, when a person gives their life for a purpose greater than themselves."

Professor Ada smiled like a proud parent. "Very good, Nathaniel. I couldn't have said it better myself." Then, hesitating for several moments, he thoughtfully scanned his audience of eager students. "Now, the reason I bring this up is because I wish to delve into a very important aspect of our current society, one which may be viewed as too controversial for boys of your age. But considering the caliber of students I seem to have, I feel very confident you can all handle this kind of adult subject matter."

Returning to the chalkboard, he underlined the word he had just scratched out and reiterated in a solemn tone, "Martyrdom." Professor Ada turned back to his students again. "So now that we've defined this word: What does the notion of martyrdom mean to us in the context of today's lecture concerning the history of the Jewish people in Palestine? And to answer that question we have to begin examining a radical new sect of Judaism, one which has actually had its beginnings in our very own territory here in Galilee. And the leader of this new sect is a wise Man called Jesus. Have any of you heard of this Man before?"

Several hands timidly rose into the air, and Professor Ada pointed to one. "Yes, Nathaniel; you've heard about this Man?"

"Yes, sir, I have."

"Good, and what have you heard?"

"Well, my father talked about him once, but he said he was just a madman who believed the impossible about himself."

"Really?"

"Yes, and that's why the Romans killed him."

Ada smiled awkwardly. "Ah, but that's where you're wrong, my boy. The Romans didn't kill him."

"Then who did?" wondered Nathaniel.

Again Ada tried his best to smile. "Well, you see, unfortunately, that's where things get a little tricky, and what we're confronted with, in the end, is the irony of life's most fickle human trait, that of the power to rule and those in our society who've been entrusted with that power."

"What does that even mean?" Nathaniel asked, thoroughly confused.

Ada scratched his brow. "Oh, dear, maybe I should've thought twice about proceeding with this after all."

"No," yelped Zachariah. "We want you to continue, Professor. My mother says this Jesus was a wise Man, that He was the most special Man Who's ever lived, considering all of the amazing things He did."

Intrigued at this, Ada smiled.

But Nathaniel, obviously unimpressed, rolled his eyes. "If he was so special, Zachariah, then why was he crucified?"

Zachariah shrugged his shoulders. "How should I know?"

"He was crucified, Nathaniel," blurted Ada, suddenly caught up in the moment, "because the religious authorities considered Him a threat to their vested positions of power."

"But my father said he was a fraud," retorted Nathaniel, "and that he led the people astray."

"No," Zachariah insisted. "My mother said He was a good Man."

"Your mother doesn't know what she's talking about," replied Nathaniel, as cold as ice. "But my father does, and he told me the man was nothing but a heretic."

"Nathaniel, no," Ada countered. "I'm sorry to have to tell you this, but that's where your father is wrong. He *was* a good Man, a Teacher of the kind of men who gladly received the truth, Jews and Gentiles alike. He was undoubtedly the Christ, and when Pontius Pilate, at the behest of our own religious leaders, had Him condemned to die on a cross, He appeared alive again after three days in the grave."

An audible gasp rippled through the classroom.

"What did you say?" asked Nathaniel, his mouth hanging open in disbelief.

With firm resolution, the professor looked him right in the eye. "I said, He rose from the dead after three days in His tomb. As a matter of fact, this same Jesus confirmed everything our divine prophets have been foretelling our people since the beginning of time."

A stunned Nathaniel rose to his feet. "Well, sir, I'm sorry to have to tell *you* this, but I think you've lost your mind. And I'm going straight home to tell my father the terrible lies you're spreading at school." Bolting to the door, Nathaniel flung it open and ran out as fast as he could, leaving everyone there in a complete state of shock.

An Eye for an Eye

AS PONTIUS PILATE was intensely scanning an assortment of documents late into the evening, he was interrupted by one of his servants.

"Excuse me, Governor," said the servant, "but you have a very important visitor."

"An *uninvited* visitor, you mean," replied an exasperated Pilate. "At this hour?"

"I'm sorry, sir, but it's Herod Antipas, and he wishes to see you right away."

"The king of Judea? Here, now?"

"I'm afraid so, yes."

"But why?"

"He wouldn't say, sir. He just said it was urgent."

"Very well. Send him right in."

"Thank you, Governor," said the servant, who dutifully turned and left.

In a matter of moments, the regal figure of Herod Antipas stepped inside and stopped, hovering there between light and shadow. "Greetings, Governor Pilate," he said through a suppressed yawn. "I regret the intrusion at this late hour, but unfortunately it couldn't be helped. I hope everything's going well with you at least."

"Why, hello," replied Pilate, trying to mask his uneasiness with the unexpected visit. "Why didn't you let me know you were coming? I could've made adequate preparations for your arrival."

"You can dispense with the diplomatic posturing, Governor. I have much bigger problems on my hands."

Pilate nodded tacitly, eyeing his visitor as though he were sizing up an opponent in battle. "Yes, of course. If you insist. Please, come in, have a seat, make yourself at home."

Herod then took several steps forward and wearily replied, "That won't be necessary. I'm not staying long."

Now that the monarch was that much closer to him, Pilate could see that he clearly looked as though he had endured too many sleepless nights.

"You know," said the governor, "you really don't look so good. What's wrong?"

"Wrong? What hasn't gone wrong for me lately? That's the question."

"So tell me: What has you so upset?"

"My daughter, Herodias," he replied, almost incapable of uttering the words, "my dear, sweet child."

"Your daughter? What about her?"

"She's dead," whispered Herod.

"Dead? How?"

"An accident. She was playing on a pool of water covered over with ice. Then without warning the ice beneath her broke, and her little body fell through. Her head was cut off instantly, before anyone had time to even blink."

"No," gasped Pilate.

"Oh, yes. And her head? Yes, well, it just laid there on the surface while everyone just stood around, frozen with fear, hoping somebody would do something, anything."

"That's terrible. I'm sorry for your loss. How are you and your wife holding up?"

"Not so good, I'm afraid. You should have seen my poor wife, sitting there for the longest time, just holding our daughter's head in her lap. Our home will never be the same after this."

Even Pilate seemed genuinely moved. "Is there anything I can do for you?"

"I need a favor, Governor."

"Of course, anything. Just say the word."

"Well, as you know, ever since I heard about the man Jesus, I had a desire to see him for myself, one on one. I wanted to hear his words firsthand to find out for myself whether or not they were like those of any other ordinary man."

A suddenly smitten Pilate turned away as he tried to gather his wits. "Yes, of course," he muttered, awkwardly clearing his throat. "I do know; I know exactly how you feel, in fact."

"But now," interjected Herod, hardly noticing Pilate's suppressed reaction, so distraught by his own personal ordeal, "because of all the evil things I did to John the Baptist, and because I mocked the Nazarene for believing he was the Christ, I'm receiving the rewards of my corruption."

"What?" gasped Pilate, turning back again. "You actually think that's why your daughter was killed? It was a freak accident. You can't blame yourself."

"But what else can I think? You know as well as I do, I've spilled way too much innocent blood with these hands. Don't you see?"

Pilate stared back at Herod for several tense moments, then mumbled, "I see."

"So it appears that God's judgment is perfect after all," Herod continued blankly, beyond the point of grief, nearly drained of all human emotion, "because every man receives according to his thoughts."

"Then tell me," said Pilate, confused and shaking his head, "if you're convinced this is some sort of divine retribution for your evil deeds, then why are you asking *me* for a favor? Why not go knocking on the door of your local temple?"

"Because you were worthy to get to know that God-Man, that's why," he replied, his face suddenly going flush. "Now, it's only right and good that you've agreed to help me. You did say you wanted to help me, didn't you?"

"So let me get this straight. You're here because I've personally encountered this God-Man, as you called him, and because I've apparently survived unscathed? Is that it?"

"I know it sounds absurd; I know it. But I also know that something evil, something unspeakable, has attached itself to me and my family."

"And you believe it's because of this man?" Pilate hung his head in disbelief, stepping away to clear his mind of the sheer weight of this avalanche of thought. "Oh, Herod, I just don't know. I have to be honest with you. This is the last thing I would've expected from a man in your position, coming to me with all this. I don't know how to respond. I'm not a priest; I'm a politician."

"Well, do you have a better explanation?" Herod continued, beginning to work himself into a frenzy. "Even as we speak my son Azbonius lies in agony on his deathbed. He'll be dead before very long. I, too, have been doomed to an appalling fate. I'm miserable with the dropsy now, and all because I persecuted John, the one who introduced baptism by water. Don't you get it?"

Pilate was dumbfounded. "I'm finding this very hard to take in. Do you realize what you're asking me to believe?"

"Believe whatever you want. All I know is: My wife is blind in her left eye, mourning day and night for our daughter. Why? Because we wanted to blind the eye of righteousness. So you see, it all makes perfect sense: A verdict from God really is a just sentence."

"I don't know. If you say so. I suppose your answer is as good as any."

"There's no peace for an evil person, just as the Lord says," muttered Herod.

"If what you're saying is true, then why are you the only ones suffering from this curse?"

"But we're not the only ones, you fool! Tragedy has already overwhelmed the scribes and priests of the Law because they delivered the Just One to you! The consummation of the age has come upon us, and now the Gentiles have become heirs of the promises. The Children of Light will be cast out, having rejected the things preached concerning the Lord and His Son."

"I still can't believe I'm hearing all this from the king of Judea. Why don't you proclaim this recent insight of yours to your own nation?"

"Are you insane? Do you have no idea what you're suggesting? And since when did you start caring about my nation, anyway?"

"But I don't. I was just curious."

"Then stop being such a hypocrite, will you? The fate of my nation is already sealed, regardless of what I might say or do... Now, it's time for you and your wife Procla to face a similar destiny; depending on your response, that is."

"What's that supposed to mean?"

"It means that now it's time for you to commemorate this Jesus, because the kingdom is being handed over to you, the Gentiles."

"But why?"

"What a ridiculous question. I can still see you have a lot to learn about the people you're governing. This kingdom of ours is now available to you because we, the Chosen, have scorned the Righteous One! What do you think I keep trying to tell you?"

"Fine. Just for the sake of argument, let's say you're right. So I embrace this kingdom of yours, fine, it's mine now. What good does that do you? You still haven't answered that question, have you?"

"Well, at least it might leave you with a change of heart; I don't know. Maybe then you could see your way to doing some good in this life for a change."

"For someone like you, you mean?"

Herod nodded eagerly. "That's right, yes, even for someone like me."

"So, what? Now I'm supposed to start doing good in this life to make up for all my evil deeds in the past? Is that what you're suggesting?"

"Well, naturally. Is there anything wrong with that?"

"Then spit it out. What do you want from me?"

"I want you, as the acting governor, to see to it that my family and I are properly buried."

"That's it? You want proper burials? That's why you've come here under the cloak of night?"

"That's right. My wife, my children and I; we all deserve to have dignified ends, don't you think?"

"Well, of course. You all deserve treatment worthy of your status, but don't your priests have some sort of predetermined ritual to take care of things like that for royalty such as yourself?"

"No, no, no! I already told you. The priests are all doomed! Revenge will soon be overtaking every last one of them!"

"Revenge? When?"

"At the return of the Christ, of course, just as the Scriptures declare."

Pilate frowned. "I don't know. I still think you're overreacting to all this."

"Just promise me that you'll arrange decent burials for me and my family, and I'll leave you alone in peace. Can you just do that for me?"

Pilate paused again to scrutinize Herod, who waited for his response with great anticipation. "Yes, of course, I can do that. I promise to make sure you and your family receive proper treatment when the time comes."

"Thank you, Governor," he said with a sigh of relief. "Then I'll be leaving now. Say goodbye to Procla for me, will you?"

Pilate nodded vacantly. "Certainly."

"Oh, and I'm sending you my daughter Herodias' earrings, as well as one of my own rings."

"What on Earth for?"

"Let's just say I'm giving them to you as a memorial of my death. Even now my body is being consumed from the inside out. So you see: I'm already receiving a form of divine justice."

"Maybe you've just lost your mind. Maybe you're in shock because of the tragedy of your daughter's death. Have you ever considered that?"

"More often than you can imagine, my old friend and adversary. But losing my mind isn't what disturbs me. The scary thing is the thought of losing my soul. Tell me: Has a man like you ever worried about a thing like that in your life?"

Pilate wearily shrugged his shoulders. "I don't suppose I have, no."

"Then consider this: Lose your mind, and you still might be fortunate enough to find it again someday; lose your soul, and you're never able to restore it in your own strength, *ever*."

With that, Herod turned and left, disappearing into the darkened corridor, as surreptitiously as when he had arrived.

This Man from Galilee

CAREFULLY WEIGHING each and every word as he spoke them, Pilate began to dictate a letter to his scribe. "Greetings from Pontius Pilate, governor of Jerusalem, to Herod Antipas, king of Judea: I certainly hope you and your family are feeling better in this terrible time of crisis. But please remember that from the first day you delivered Jesus to me I took pity on myself, even going so far as to demonstrate my disapproval by washing my hands of the whole affair. So, concerning the Man's fate, I'm innocent of every charge. After all, I only did to Him what you wanted me to do. It was you who asked me to cooperate with His crucifixion. But no sooner had He been killed than His executioners began testifying to me that He'd risen from the dead. And believe me, I've gone to great lengths to confirm the things I'm about to tell you."

As Pilate recounted his tale, his thoughts drifted back to those fateful events, his mind shot through with the startling images that would forever change his life.

FIRST AND FOREMOST was the image of Jesus, a gentle, confident soul, who stood amidst a crowd of baffled onlookers, unsure if what they were seeing was real or not.

"Because according to innumerable eyewitness accounts," continued Pilate as he proceeded to dictate his letter, "this Man reportedly appeared in Galilee, looking just as He always had prior to His crucifixion. He boldly continued to teach about His resurrection and a kingdom that would last forever."

Then there was Pilate's wife, who strode through the landscape of his troubled mind, looking as determined as ever, accompanied by an entourage of Roman soldiers.

"Even Procla, my wife, became convinced of the visions that came to her at the same time you asked me to deliver Jesus to those spiteful Jewish leaders. So, as soon as she heard He'd risen, she enlisted the efforts of Longinus, the centurion, and several of the guards at His tomb, and they all went to see the risen Christ, as if they were going to witness some kind of grand spectacle."

Entering the city, Procla and her group found Jesus with His disciples. Awestruck, they all stood and stared at Him.

"What is it, Procla?" asked Jesus. "Do you believe in Me, too?"

Procla nodded. "Yes, Lord, I do believe. What would you have me do?"

"Are you aware of the agreement that God made with the Fathers, where it's written that everyone who dies will live again through My death?"

"I am, Lord."

"Good for you, Procla, and now you've seen it with your own eyes. I'm alive, even though I was crucified. I suffered many things, until I was put in a grave, but I broke down the gates of Hades and destroyed the power of death, and someday I'll return again in all My glory."

"Thank you, Lord, for allowing me to see Your mysteries unfold. What should I do now?"

"I want you to believe in My Father Who is in Me. Can you do that?"

"Yes, Lord, I can."

AS PILATE SAT GRIMLY postured before his scribe, he continued to dictate his letter. "After that, Procla came home and told me everything she and her group had experienced, and they wept as they did because they felt so badly that they had originally been against Him, even going so far as to plan every horrible thing they had done to Him."

DRIFTING THROUGH the darkened corridors of his memory, Pilate was no longer clad in his flamboyant governor's robe but in a drab cotton garb.

"I, too, was cut to the core by a sickening guilt and the deepest depression I'd ever known. Dressed in a garment of mourning, I took fifty soldiers with me and my wife, and headed for Galilee so I could see Him for myself."

With a melancholy look in his eye, Pilate led his own entourage, which included Procla and a very determined group of Roman soldiers, who were likewise clad in rather modest outfits, also quite in contrast to their stations in life.

"And while we were on our way, I testified that you, Herod Antipas, had ordered the things I did, forcing me to arm myself against Him, to judge Him Who judges everyone, and to scourge the Innocent One, the Lord of the Just."

Eventually, Pilate and his somber group arrived in Galilee, where they found Jesus, standing and talking with His disciples. The Lord turned and stared directly at Pilate.

"Then and there," continued the governor with his dictation, "I also realized that this Man you had delivered to me really was the Creator."

Pilate and his companions all fell face-down at His feet.

"I've sinned, Lord," Pilate told Jesus. "I helped condemn You, the One Who avenges everyone in truth! At first, I only saw Your humanity and not Your divinity, but now I realize You're God in the Flesh, the Son of God Himself. Herod and those Israelites forced me to do this despicable thing to You. Please, have pity on me, God of Israel!"

Procla lamented, too. "Dear God of Heaven and Earth, please don't punish me for what Pilate or those Israelites did to You, and please don't be too hard on my husband."

Stepping up to Pilate, the Lord helped him to his feet, along with Procla and the soldiers, too. Looking closely at Him, they all marveled at the sight of the scars of the cross that were clearly evident in His body.

And Jesus calmly said, "Everything the righteous Fathers could only hope to see actually took place in your lifetime. The Lord of Time, the Son of Man, the Son of the Most High Who is forever, has risen from the dead and is glorified."

SOON PILATE'S MESSENGER delivered his letter to Herod Antipas, who immediately read it. Obviously disturbed, he crumpled it and threw it to the ground, and for the longest time Herod sat there brooding, rubbing his bearded chin, trying to decide what to do next.

Day of Reckoning

MEANWHILE, BACK IN Rome, Tiberius Caesar was lying in bed, groaning softly. In obvious discomfort, he rolled over and rang a small bell.

Within moments, his royal steward appeared at his door. "I'm here, Sire. How are you this morning?"

Tiberius sat up, grimacing painfully. "Terrible. If I didn't know better I'd have thought that one of Hannibal's elephants slept on me all night."

"I'm so sorry to hear that. Is there anything I can do for you?"

"Yes. I want you to send for Cadmus immediately."

The royal steward dutifully nodded and left.

A SHADOW APPEARED in Tiberius' bedroom doorway as Caesar lay dozing on his side.

"I'm here, My Lord," said the shadow.

Tiberius slowly opened his eyes with a scowl. "Cadmus, it's about time. Get in here. What took my most trusted counselor so long to get here?"

The man stepped forward, out of the shadows, and humbly bowed. "A thousand pardons, Sire. My wife is in labor with our second child. I came as soon as I could."

"Of course. How is she?"

"All things considered, she's doing well."

With great difficulty, Tiberius sat up in his sickbed. "Good. I just wish I could say the same for myself."

"How can I serve you today, My Caesar? Do you wish me to consult with your physicians?"

"Certainly not. I've had it with my physicians. They're all useless as far as I'm concerned. You're here today for a far different sort of consultation."

"I see. What about?"

For several moments, Tiberius pondered his reply. "Tell me, Cadmus, do you believe in the intervention of the gods?"

The counselor tilted his head thoughtfully. "I myself, Sire, remain undecided. But naturally, in your case, I would not rule it out."

"Why is that?"

"Because you're Caesar, of course. You are the embodiment of the deity itself. If ever there was someone with whom the gods would wish to intervene, you would certainly be that person."

Intrigued, Tiberius nodded. "Good, because I wish to make a very special request of you."

"Certainly, My Lord. How may I be of assistance?"

"It just so happens that I've recently gotten wind of some very peculiar reports. Of course these reports only circulate in the darkest of shadow, and of course the people spreading these reports wish that no one else knows what they're saying, but still I hear about them anyway."

"I see, and these … peculiar reports are why you called me here?"

"Yes, Cadmus, it is," snapped Tiberius, growing impatient. "And stop playing coy with me."

Taken aback, Cadmus offered a conciliatory nod. "Certainly, Great Caesar. I meant no disrespect. Please, Sire, help me understand what you're trying to say."

"Fine, fine," he replied with a weary wave of his hand. "I just want you to tell me honestly: What do you know about certain reports concerning the work of a unique physician in Jerusalem, a man by the name of Jesus of Nazareth who supposedly heals every disease just by speaking. Tell me: What do you know about this man?"

A befuddled Cadmus tried to respond. "I—*I*, uh—"

"Come on, out with it, preferably before I expire on the spot. Are you, or are you not, aware of the rumors concerning this man? And if not, then I want to know why I continue to employ you as my counselor?"

"Yes, of course, Sire, I've heard about the man, but as to vouching for the veracity of these accounts, I cannot say one way or the other."

"I didn't ask you to vouch for them. I want to know what you *think* of them?"

"Think, My Lord?"

"Yes, considering the sheer impossibility of these reports, do you think there's even the slightest chance that they might be true? For a man like me, in my condition, that is."

"As I alluded to before, I remain undecided on issues like this, but I can tell you, there is one way to find out, once and for all."

"Really? How?"

"Bring the man here as fast as our swiftest vessels can deliver him. Jerusalem is under our control. As you know, Pontius Pilate is the governor there. Dispatch your royal messenger Volusianus to fetch him, and then you'll find out for yourself just how true these rumors are."

Tiberius considered his answer for a moment. "So you don't think I'm insane for believing this man might actually provide me a divine cure?"

"Certainly not, My Lord. I'd never presume to make such a judgment. I am merely your humble counselor. You, on the other hand, are Tiberius Caesar, the divine emperor of Rome."

"Good. Then let's make sure we keep it that way. Are you sure Volusianus is the right man for a task like this?"

"I am, My Lord. I believe Volusianus is more than up to it."

"Then speak to him about the delicate nature of his mission, and have him set sail for Jerusalem immediately. It's time my friend and servant Pontius Pilate make good on his appointment there. Tell him that more than anything else in this world I wish for him to hand over this physician to me so I can also have my health restored."

EMBARKING UPON HIS quest, Volusianus traveled first by ship and then by royal caravan, eventually arriving, after a lengthy journey, in Jerusalem.

THERE, VOLUSIANUS appeared before Pontius Pilate, who sat auspiciously in his ornately decorated governor's seat.

Volusianus bowed graciously before Pilate. "Greetings, Governor Pilate, my name is Volusianus, and I am the royal messenger sent here by your most omnipotent master, Tiberius Caesar, emperor of Rome."

"Really? The emperor of Rome sent you here to see *me*? But why?"

"It seems that Caesar has heard the rumors circulating in your country about a remarkable physician, one who's been performing a tremendous work here."

"A physician? This country has all sorts of physicians. Which one is Caesar looking for? Just give me his name, and I'll see to it that he's immediately sent to our great and illustrious emperor."

Volusianus hesitated for a moment, trying to decide how to articulate his unusual request. "Uh, well, let me see. It seems as though Caesar is looking for the physician who heals his patients simply by speaking to them."

"Oh, that one," replied a deflated Pilate.

"Then you know who I'm talking about?"

"Yes, I'm afraid I do."

"Good; because Caesar is very eager for you to send him to Rome as soon as possible. He wants his disease to be healed, too."

"But the man you're talking about was accused of being a criminal," sputtered Pilate, whose gruffness was merely an attempt to mask his inner terror. "People from his own nation insisted he was fomenting revolution against the Empire. How was I supposed to know he was innocent of every charge? I'm just one man here, trying to maintain order in this madhouse. You have no idea what I've been dealing with here! No idea at all!"

Volusianus eyed him suspiciously. "So what are you trying to say, Governor? Where is this man now?"

Dumbfounded, Pilate just sat there.

"Well, where is he?" pressed Volusianus. "In exile? In prison? Tell me."

The governor's words came out with great difficulty. "I'm afraid that after discussing the matter with the city's spiritual leaders it was decided he should be crucified."

"Crucified," Volusianus groaned as if someone had punched him in the stomach. "But why?"

Pilate just shook his head, unable to reply. Staring at the floor, the mortified governor sank down in his seat and put his hand over his brow as though he were hoping he might simply disappear. Head in hand, a grief-stricken Volusianus just turned and walked away.

ON HIS WAY BACK TO the ship that would return him to Rome, a sullen Volusianus, burdened with the responsibility of conveying the bad news to Caesar, encountered a noble woman.

"Excuse me, good lady," Volusianus said, "but could I have a moment of your time?"

"Veronica," replied the woman with a charming smile.

"Ma'am?"

"My name is Veronica."

Obviously distracted, the messenger nodded. "Of course, Veronica, pardon me. I am Volusianus, royal messenger sent here from Rome by His Majesty, Tiberius Caesar."

Seeing the regal caravan that was traveling with him, the woman was intrigued. "Certainly, sir. What can I do for you today?"

"I was just wondering. I know this may strike you as odd, but considering the importance of my mission here, I feel compelled to ask."

"Go right ahead, young man. Ask me anything."

"You see, it seems there have been rumors going around, rumors that we, even in faraway Rome, have been hearing."

"Rumors?" echoed Veronica with a curious tilt to her head. "What rumors?"

"Rumors that there was a remarkable physician in this country who healed his patients simply by speaking to them. Is it possible you might know who I'm talking about?"

"Oh, yes, of course, my dear boy," she said as her face lit up at the mere mention of Him. "I know all about the Man you're describing. Why do you ask?"

"Well, as it turns out, I was sent here specifically to look for this special man on behalf of my master who's very sick and seeking a cure from his disease."

"Oh, dear, I'm so sorry to hear that," Veronica replied, truly touched. "What do you want to know?"

"I want to know why anyone would've killed a man like that. What could have possibly driven a people to such hatred, such madness?"

"Oh, my dear sir," moaned Veronica, who began to weep. "He was crucified because they were jealous of Him, that's why."

"Jealous?"

"Yes, jealous," she replied, fighting back the tears. "Ordinary folks loved Him, but corruption in high places wouldn't stop until they saw Him dead."

"But I was supposed to return this man to the emperor of Rome. He was hoping so much that he could help cure him." Volusianus hung his head. "Now I'm afraid I'll never be able to accomplish my royal mission."

Veronica slowly regained her composure. "Maybe you still can."

Confused and intrigued, Volusianus looked up at her. "Pardon me? I'm afraid I don't understand. What are you saying?"

"It just so happens that after Jesus finished teaching in our town, He had to leave, so I wanted a painting of Him. That way I'd have His likeness to console me while He was gone."

"That seems natural enough, yes."

"So just imagine my surprise when: Who do you think I happened to meet on my way to see an artist?"

"No." Eyebrows raised, Volusianus gaped. "You don't mean—"

"That's right, Jesus."

"What did he do? What did he say?"

"Well, when He found out where I was going, He asked me for my canvas."

"Yes, yes. Then what?"

"Then He gave it back to me, and…" Veronica chocked up, unable to continue.

"And?"

Veronica opened her mouth, but nothing would come out.

"And what?" Volusianus' eyes grew wider.

"Oh, you wouldn't believe me if I told you," murmured Veronica, obviously embarrassed.

"But I would, honestly. Tell me: I'll believe you, and I'll personally make sure that Caesar himself hears what you have to say."

"Well, I could hardly believe my own eyes," she continued, slowly measuring out of her words, "but incredibly, the canvas He handed back to me was no longer blank. Now it had a picture of His marvelous face painted on it."

"What? I'm sorry. Could you say that again for me? I don't think I heard correctly."

Veronica sheepishly smiled. "You heard me. There was a picture of His face on it."

"Astonishing. Caesar will definitely have something to say about this."

"What will you do now?"

"I'll return to Caesar with the news. But only the gods know for sure if I'll find him still fit enough in mind or body to receive it."

"I wonder what would happen if your master were to see this painting for himself."

"What do you mean? Take your painting to Caesar and present it to him in person?"

"Yes, that's right. Maybe if he looked at it, you know, maybe he could experience His healing power, too."

Volusianus was thunderstruck by the mere suggestion. "Yes. I do think you're on to something. Would it be possible to buy a picture like this with gold or silver?"

"No, of course not," replied Veronica, smiling sweetly. "But I will go with you, and together we'll take the painting to Caesar."

IN THE MEANTIME, Pilate sat with his scribe and began to dictate another emotionally charged letter. "Greetings from Pontius Pilate, governor of Jerusalem, to Tiberius Caesar, emperor of Rome: Your Majesty, although I was quite opposed to it and went to great lengths to stop it, a bitter punishment was recently inflicted on Jesus of Nazareth by the will of the people. But, in fact, no age has had, or ever will have, a Man so good and so disciplined. Yet the people made an incredible effort with all their leaders, scribes and elders, to conspire in crucifying this Ambassador of Truth, and they did it even though their own prophets, like the Sibyls among us, warned them not to."

FROM HIS DISTANT vantage point, Pilate watched the gruesome spectacle, a scene forever emblazoned in his tortured memory. First, Jesus was nailed to the crossbeam using a pair of iron nails that were mercilessly pounded through His wrists, and with the sound of each hammer blow and each agonized groan, the governor flinched.

"And believe me, Great Caesar, when I tell you," continued Pilate to his scribe, "if there hadn't been such a threat of revolt amongst the bloodthirsty rabble, this Man would probably still be living among us."

A trio of Roman soldiers then banded together to hoist Jesus, securely nailed to the horizontal beam, onto the upright section of the cross. With an eerie thud, it dropped into place, and lastly, one of the soldiers nailed His feet in place, much to the delight of the gawking onlookers who let loose with an approving howl.

"But being compelled by my loyalty to you, rather than by my own desire, I never tried too hard to prevent the sale and suffering of righteous blood, even if it was guiltless of every accusation. An injustice to be sure, these were the actions of malicious men, although, as their own Scriptures foretell, it will eventually work to their own destruction."

PAINED AT THE RECOLLECTION of that fateful day, Pilate enunciated each word as his scribe, who seemed similarly affected by the governor's account, wrote it down as fast as he could. "Just as everyone there will testify, when He was hung on that tree, supernatural signs appeared, which, in the opinion of the philosophers, threatened to destroy the entire world."

AS SOON AS VOLUSIANUS arrived back in Rome, he was ushered in to deliver his report to Tiberius, who sat precariously on his throne, obviously still in a state of poor health.

"Oh, Great Caesar," said Volusianus, "I regret to tell you that Jesus, Whom you've wanted to see for so long, was crucified by Pilate and the Jewish authorities. Quite illegally, of course."

"What?" Stunned, then furious, Tiberius struggled to his feet. "But why?"

"According to every report I've gathered: It was jealousy that nailed Him to the cross!"

"You mean to tell me a simple case of political intrigue has deprived me of meeting this remarkable physician?"

"I'm afraid so, Majesty. But fortunately, a gracious lady has returned with me to Rome."

Then Caesar's expression turned from anger to incredulity. "By the gods, first you tell me the treachery of cowards has denied me my request, and now you think I'll be appeased by the company of some strange woman? Is that what I hearing?"

"Certainly not, My Lord. That's not what I meant at all. What I'm saying is: I believe you'll be pleasantly surprised with something she's brought you."

"Seriously?" Exasperated and exhausted, Tiberius dropped down into his seat, too frustrated to continue looking at his royal messenger. "What could she have brought that could possibly interest me at this point? A potion, perhaps?"

"No, Your Majesty, a gift."

"A gift," grumbled Tiberius, deflated merely at the thought. "What do I need with more gifts? I need a cure."

"Well, a talisman, really."

"I see, go on," said Caesar, still unimpressed. "Surprise me, then."

"It's a miraculous painting of the same Jesus Whom you've been seeking. I think if you look upon it, there's a chance that your health might be restored."

"Miraculous, you say?"

WITH THAT, CAESAR'S royal servants draped his entire room with marvelous silk cloths in preparation for the occasion. As the king lay expectantly on his bed, Volusianus slowly entered with Veronica's painting. With great anticipation, he stepped forward and held up the sacred talisman for his ailing emperor to gaze upon, and as soon as he looked at it, Tiberius' entire being was transformed. Flushed with a look of sheer ecstasy, Caesar jumped to his feet, and turning to Volusianus, he gave him an affectionate bear hug, much to the amazement of everyone there.

Fury of the Gods

PILATE'S LETTER WAS delivered several days later to Caesar, who was sitting quite contentedly on his throne. No longer looking ill, he exuded a healthy, confident glow, but after reading the letter, his expression darkened, and he became incensed. With a renewed vigor, Tiberius shot out of his royal seat like a man half his age. "Summon my scribe immediately," he growled.

WITH AN INTENSITY that made his scribe uncomfortable, Caesar dictated his letter with a steely glint in his eye. "Greetings from Tiberius Caesar, emperor of Rome, to Pontius Pilate, governor of Jerusalem: Pilate, my servant, tell me: Who was this man that such complaints were lodged against him? And why would the men of Palestine have ever crucified someone like him? If the majority demanded what was right, it would have been proper to consent to them, but if what they were requesting was unjustified, then how could you have so blatantly violated the Law?"

WHEN PILATE FINISHED reading the letter from Tiberius, he limply dropped his arm to his side and released the tattered page, allowing it to slip through his rigid fingers. Eyes glazing over, he watched it flit about in the air until it landed on the ground.

IT WAS NOW PILATE'S turn to respond. The words he spoke to his scribe were brimming with an ominous dread. "Greetings from Pontius Pilate, your administrator of the eastern province, to the most potent and divine Tiberius Caesar: My most excellent emperor, I'm writing to you with great apprehension in order to report what has happened here recently. It's true: Jewish religious leaders did deliver the Man called Jesus to me, accusing Him of all sorts of terrible crimes, but they were never able to convict Him of a single thing. All they did was charge Him with heresy because He insisted the Sabbath wasn't their true rest, but in my opinion this was an incredibly flimsy basis on which to accuse someone, especially when you consider all the remarkable things the Man had done up to that point."

AS JESUS MADE HIS way through a clamoring crowd of sick people, who all pressed in toward Him, a mere touch of His hand healed each and every one of them. "He restored sight to the blind," continued Pilate to his scribe, "cleansed the lepers, healed the paralyzed.

A hunched, bedraggled fellow wandered aimlessly through the desert. "Still others were severely tormented by demons, forced to live among wild beasts." The man's hair and beard were matted and gnarled, eyes yellow with fear and pain. He gnawed at his own bloody fingers. Startled, the man sniffed at the air like an animal and turned to see Jesus, flanked by several of His disciples. "Once vexed by foul spirits, these people were all restored with just a word from this amazing Man." Within moments, the man's beastly appearance melted away, and the crooked creature that had just been so deformed gradually stood up straight before Jesus, looking as handsome and complete as any human being could.

"Then, there was a poor woman who had had an issue of blood for so many years her bones could be seen through her glass-like skin." A feeble wisp of a woman crept to her window. "All her physicians had completely dismissed her, refusing to offer her any hope of recovery." The woman in question was none other than Veronica, teetering at her window, a mere shell of the beautiful lady who had so proudly ventured to Rome with Volusianus. Looking out her window, she saw Jesus was approaching, followed by a group of people vying for His attention. "But once, while Jesus was passing by, this woman saw her chance for the impossible thing her doctors told her she would never have." As Jesus made His way past her home, Veronica somehow pressed through the crowd and, with her last ounce of strength, reached out with her trembling hand. "She merely touched the hem of His garment, and all her strength returned." Instantly healthy again, she began to run about as though she had never been sick at all.

"Not only that, but sometime later this same Jesus did something even more powerful, something unheard of even among our gods. He raised a dead man named Lazarus, a man who had been in his crypt for four days, and He did it just by speaking to him." As a group of onlookers mourned and wept, Jesus stretched His right hand toward the grave. "Lazarus, come out!" exclaimed Jesus. "And so Lazarus, smelling of sweet perfume, came bounding out of his tomb like a bridegroom running to greet his beloved bride."

AS PILATE DICTATED his letter, he noticed the odd look on his scribe's face, obviously uncomfortable with what he was writing. An irritated governor sat up in his chair and affirmed, "And as hard as all this is to believe I can absolutely assure you everything happened the way I'm describing it. I even saw Him perform some of these miracles with my own eyes. Still, the only complaint the Jewish leaders could offer was that Jesus did these things on the Sabbath. That was when He was handed over to me by Herod Antipas and the priests Annas and Caiaphas. And even though they condemned Him, I refused to cooperate with them, but in the end, because the people threatened to start an all-out riot, I reluctantly consented to His crucifixion, but no sooner had He been killed than I realized I'd made the biggest mistake of my life."

AS JESUS DANGLED ON the cross, struggling for every breath, a midday eclipse began to blot out the light of the Sun. "Because even as this Man was slowly dying before our very eyes, the world was mysteriously plunged into darkness, as if it were expiring with Him. The Sun disappeared, even though it was still daytime, and the sky became black as pitch, and although the stars became visible for a time, even they refused to shine with their typical luster."

The inhabitants of Jerusalem became quite agitated at the dark spectacle of the sky as they wandered the streets like lost sheep, gawking upward and bumping into one another in the darkness. "But I'm sure I don't have to remind you, Your Majesty, about how we had to light our lamps at noon and keep them going until the evening. It seemed like the Moon was covered in blood. Even though it was full, it was barely visible, as if Orion and all the stars were openly mourning the crimes of the Jews."

HEAD HUNG SLIGHTLY, the lamentable Pilate paused, unsure of how to proceed. His scribe looked up from his writing, waiting expectantly for the governor to continue, and finally, with obvious difficulty, he did so. "And as if that were not strange enough, three days later, on the first day of the week, around nine o'clock in the evening, the Sun suddenly reappeared, shining at night as it had never done before. It was then that a swarm of angels appeared above us, flashing like lightning in a storm."

A MYSTIFIED GROUP of spectators cowered at the sight of a massive cloud of angelic beings, hovering above them in the night sky.

"Glorify God above everything else!" one of the angels shouted. "Peace has finally come to mankind! You who are chained in the depths of Hades, come out!"

PILATE'S VOICE BEGAN to quiver, and his scribe flinched ever so slightly as he wrote down the governor's words. "The hills and valleys shook with the blast of the angel's proclamation, and as if in response to that cataclysmic voice, an earthquake unleashed its fury across the landscape. Boulders cracked, tremendous chasms formed in the ground, the very regions of the Abyss opened up."

AS THE GROUND LET loose beneath their feet, several men tumbled headlong, screaming, into these chasms, cavernous openings in the ground that belched smoke from their depths. "Amazingly, the Jews who suffered most were the same ones who'd spoken against Jesus. Only one of their synagogues remained in Jerusalem, because all of those that had conspired against Him were overwhelmed in the disastrous events of that day." Then the governor's lips uttered the impossible, almost choking on the words as he did. "And suddenly the most astonishing thing of all began to occur. As if it weren't enough that the ground had opened up to swallow men whole, but then having devoured one group, it proceeded to regurgitate another. No sooner had men sunk into the Abyss, never to be seen again, than those same depths began to spit out others who had previously been imprisoned there."

THE SCRIBE STOPPED writing and looked up at the governor, who was obviously lost in his thoughts. Clearing his throat, the scribe timidly muttered, "Excuse me, sir, but I'm not sure I understood that last part. Could you please reiterate?"

Looking his scribe squarely in the eye, Pilate seemed oddly plaintive. "What didn't you understand? Was I stuttering?"

"No, sir."

"Then proceed with your dictation, and, by all means, make your description as explicit as possible. Is that understood?"

"Yes, sir, but I'm simply not sure what it is I'm being explicit about."

"Dead men," murmured a distraught Pilate.

The scribe tilted his head and squinted his eyes. "*Dead men*, sir?"

"That's correct, scribe, *dead men*. Right before our very eyes we began to see dead men rising again, rising from the ground, rising from their graves."

ONE BEWILDERED MAN pointed and, barely able to utter the words, stammered, "L—L—*Look*, there's Abraham and Isaac and Jacob!"

Sure enough there stood Abraham, flanked by his son Isaac and his grandson Jacob, all looking as healthy as can be, as though they were still in the prime of their lives.

Abraham boldly proclaimed, "The Lord God has raised us from the grave, even as He brought me out of the furnace of Nimrod! He's conquered death and plundered Hades, restoring the dead back to life again!"

"But how is that possible?" asked the bewildered man's wife. "These men have been dead for two thousand years!"

"Don't ask me," replied the man, shrugging his shoulders. "All I know is, there they are. I've even heard reports that others have seen Noah and Job and Moses, all alive again, healthy as can be!"

Awestruck by everything he was seeing, Pilate wandered past the gawking couple. "Even I, My Caesar, saw many of these dead men who had appeared alive again in the flesh." The governor stepped up to one fellow, looking dazed and confused, and asked him, "Are you all right?"

The man nodded blankly, as though he had just awakened from a dream, and replied, "I'm not ... quite sure. Where am I?"

"Jerusalem."

"Jerusalem?" blanched the man, who stared at Pilate in complete disbelief. "But I don't understand. One moment, I was sitting in the midst of the shadow of death, and then suddenly I was here."

"That's it? That's all you remember?"

For several seconds, the man strained his mind in an effort to answer, and then his eyes opened wide. "I think I *do* remember something else, yes."

"What?"

"A tremendous light, yes, I remember now; purple and gold, streaming into our darkened world, lighting up every recess, and..."

"Yes, and then?"

"And then ... there was a Man."

"Who? Who was this Man?"

"Yes, a Man," muttered the fellow, who then proceeded to wander away from Pilate as though he no longer had any idea that he was having a conversation with the governor. "A Man with the strangest scars in His body," he sighed, as his voice faded in the distance.

With that, Pilate looked as confused as the man who had just wandered away. In whichever direction he looked, he was met with an astonishing sight: People stumbling around, obviously wondering how they had gotten there, others who were staring at them, looking just as confused as they were. Still others, both the living and the undead, were weeping and wailing over the magnitude of the destruction of their once-magnificent city. "In fact, Glorious Caesar, so many inexplicable wonders had overtaken me that day that I was gripped with the most terrible dread I had ever known. That was when I ordered a written account of everything that happened, and it is this very record that I've sent to you."

AS CAESAR SAT IN HIS illustrious auditorium, amidst his Senate and soldiers, a tremendous chattering rippled throughout the crowd.

"So that's what happened?" blurted one of his senators. "Who would have thought that something so far away, involving such a backward, superstitious people, could have had its effects felt even in distant Rome?"

"But there you have it, Rufus," replied Tiberius, quite matter-of-factly, "you just heard it for yourself. The solar eclipse, the earthquake, the evening light, all of it having a direct impact on our beloved capitol; all of it did, unmistakably, occur because of what happened in the land of those backward, superstitious people."

"Besides the tremendous loss of life and property caused by the earthquake," Rufus continued, "the resultant tidal wave that swept through the Mediterranean devastated the southern coasts of Cyprus, Crete and Rhodes. Even Achaia and Sicily were not beyond the reach of this disaster. Initial reports have it that untold thousands perished in its wake, but, of course, it will be several months, maybe years, before its true impact can be fully ascertained."

Then, for the longest time, everyone in the auditorium fell silent. Tiberius, at the center of it, sat brooding, scratching his brow, obviously deep in thought. Sitting up, he drew the eager attention of everyone there. Finally, he began again. "But as tragic as this devastation is to the physical order of things, which is to say, the loss of life and property, actually the most devastating thing about these cataclysmic events is how they force us to re-evaluate the nature of this misbegotten world of ours. Clearly, the fury of the gods was incited at the death of this innocent Man called Jesus, but as to why the gods would've willingly conspired with this Crucified One is a mystery that will haunt us all for a very long time."

"Quite true, My Lord, and considering this question of re-evaluation, if I may be so bold."

"You may, Rufus. Speak your mind."

"Obviously the otherworldly nature of these events can only be ascribed to the intervention of the gods. That much is beyond question. But based on this most recent report, a report which, for all intents and purposes, constitutes an explicit confession of guilt, it appears that all of it was due to the negligent actions of a man who was supposedly an ally of Rome."

Tiberius nodded thoughtfully. "Yes, I see what you're saying. Your point is well taken."

"So tell me, Great Caesar, if you don't mind my asking: What should be done to someone who readily confesses to a crime of this magnitude? In fact, what *must* be done to the man who, as you've said yourself, triggered what can best be described as a 'cosmic conspiracy,' if you will, a conspiracy of world-shattering proportions?"

"Why, of course, such a man will be arrested and brought to Rome, where he'll personally answer to me for his negligence." Then Tiberius stood to his feet and, with fists clenched, snarled, "And mark my words, all who hear the sound of my voice, I will utterly destroy the one who nearly destroyed our world!"

The Sky is Falling

THE AUDITORIUM WAS buzzing with a cacophony of hundreds of conversations, but all that ended when the hall doors swung open. Immediately, a hush fell throughout the crowd, and Pilate, bound in shackles and clad in a meager linen robe, was led into the room. Made to stand at the bar of judgment, the governor contritely looked up at Tiberius, who sat poised upon his throne, looking as menacing as ever. Seething with rage, Caesar stood up and took a step forward. Barely able to withhold his inner fury, he opened his mouth to speak.

But inexplicably, at that moment, all of his anger melted away and his face reflected a charming glow he usually only exhibited in his happier moments. As gently as a lamb, he said, "Well, hello, dear Pilate, my old friend. I'm so sorry to see you looking like this. Tell me: Were my soldiers kind to you? If not, just say the word, and I'll have them flogged, this instant."

Dumbfounded, Caesar could hardly believe the words that came out of his mouth, as was everyone else in the auditorium. Struggling to lift a finger, Tiberius motioned to his men. "Please, guards, would you be so kind as to take this poor man out into the hall," he said through pursed lips.

And as soon as Pilate had vacated the room, Caesar's fury returned with a vengeance. "By the gods, what on Earth just happened? Why didn't I strangle that man with my own hands? What was I thinking? Bring that child of death back in here right now so I can tell him what I really think of him!"

The bewildered guards retrieved Pilate, and as soon as they marched him back in, Tiberius' anger, once again, simply melted away. "Pilate, my friend, what a terrible injustice it is to see you in this state. I can't tell you how sorry I am. After all, it wasn't your fault that Jesus was crucified, now was it?" Completely flabbergasted by this, Tiberius put his hand over his own mouth. His senators gasped in disbelief. Even his guards looked at one another, amazed by what they were hearing and seeing.

Then one of the Roman soldiers promptly stepped over to Senator Rufus, who was sitting in the front row, and whispered something into his ear. Immediately, the senator sprang to his feet and motioned to Tiberius. "Sire, please, may I have a word with you, in private?"

Caesar, however, was in no mood for subterfuge. "Come here, Rufus, please," he replied, struggling with a peculiar smile that formed on his otherwise bewildered face. "Share your secret with me, here and now. Whisper in *my* ear, too, won't you?"

So the senator moved to Tiberius' side and whispered in his ear, at which point, apparently struck with an idea, the emperor, still sounding as pleasant as ever, said, "Guards, if you don't mind. Would you kindly remove the prisoner's robe?"

"Your Majesty?" replied a guard, obviously confused by the request.

"The prisoner, my good man. His robe. Strip him of his robe, this instant."

"Here?"

"Of course, here. Do you have a problem with that?" asked Tiberius with an odd grin.

"No, Majesty," replied the embarrassed guard, who finally jumped into action and stripped Pilate of his linen robe, leaving the governor naked and barely able to cover himself with both of his hands in shackles.

Immediately, the original fury of Caesar's mind rushed back into him. His face went flush with rage. "Thank you, guard! You've finally given me a reason *not* to have you executed alongside this prisoner. Now, before I change my mind again, remove this sorry excuse for a Roman governor from my sight, and take him to his cell while I decide what to do with him."

Bolting into action, the guard dragged Pilate out of the room as the emperor just shook his head.

Perplexed by the preceding spectacle, another senator slowly rose to his feet. "With all due respect, Great Caesar, could you please tell us what just happened here? Since when does a mere governor of Rome possess the power of a magician?"

Looking back at the senator, Tiberius started to reply but thought better of it. Turning to Rufus, he nodded to him as he turned and stepped through the door to his private chambers.

"Apparently, Rubellio," began Rufus, "the source of Pilate's magic lay in the fact that he was wearing the seamless robe of Jesus of Nazareth."

"Absurd," scoffed Rubellio. "Miraculous healings, flying angels, walking dead men; and now a magical robe? How much more of this nonsense are we expected to endure?"

"I sympathize with you, my dear fellow, but you saw what just happened here with your own eyes, didn't you? Do you have a better explanation?"

"You know very well, Rufus, I do not. So tell me: If what you say it true, how could anyone even know something like that?"

And just as Caesar had done before him, Rufus simply turned to the Roman soldier who had first whispered into his ear and nodded.

"Because I was one of the centurions who stood guard the day Jesus was crucified," said the man with sullen, resolute eyes. "That's how."

"You, Longinus?" asked Rubellio. "How did you come into possession of the robe?"

"Of all the people in the world, I happened to win the robe when some of my fellow soldiers and I decided it would be fun to gamble for it."

"I see. But that still doesn't explain how Pilate got hold of it."

At this, the steely-eyed centurion blanched momentarily, as if teetering upon a precipice in his own mind.

Growing impatient, Rubellio pressed on. "Longinus, what is your problem? Are you worried your testimony might implicate the governor? Did Pilate, in fact, confiscate the robe in the hopes of commandeering its alleged powers of persuasion? Is that it?"

Longinus shook the cobwebs from his mind and looked the senator straight in the eye. "No, sir, he did not. I gave him the robe of my own free will."

"But why?" interjected Rufus. "After what we all witnessed just now? Why would you give something like that away? I would've thought a talisman of this nature would be very useful in the hands of an imperial warrior like yourself."

Again Longinus hesitated, clearly disturbed by what he was thinking. "But it wasn't like that at all, Senator. It's not some kind of magic wand, if that's what you're thinking."

"Then enlighten us, dear Longinus, if you please," Rufus insisted sarcastically. "We're all dying to know why you so willingly gave it away."

"Because once it was in my hands, I was seized by a terrible dread, all right?" snapped Longinus, clearly embarrassed by his abrupt confession. "As if every act of war, every act of violence I'd ever committed, came flooding into my mind; as if every drop of blood I'd ever spilled in the almighty name of honor and valor was drenching my soul. I couldn't stand it anymore. I *had* to get rid of the robe; I had to get rid of it. Don't you see? What else could I do?"

Drained of all emotion, Longinus just hung his head. The two senators exchanged a troubled looked, and the auditorium fell as silent as a tomb.

PILATE WAS BROUGHT before Caesar once again as the king sat in the Temple of the Gods, above the Senate and his soldiers, displaying the complete array of his power, and there at the bar of judgment, the governor stood, in chains and rags.

"Pontius Pilate, you profane ass!" growled Tiberius. "When you heard that this Jesus was doing such remarkable things, how could you dare allow Him to be crucified? Don't you realize? Your treacherous act almost ruined the whole world!"

"Oh, Great King," Pilate sputtered, "I'm not the guilty one! It was those Jewish leaders who instigated this whole thing! They're the guilty ones, not me!"

"Just who are these men?"

"Herod Antipas, Archelaus and Philip, along with Annas, Caiaphas and many of their so-called 'religious authorities.'"

"But why did you carry out their plan?"

"Their nation has always been subversive! You know that! They're all rebels who never submit to your authority!"

"You fool! When they delivered Him to you, He should've been protected, then sent to me, but under no circumstances should you have agreed to crucify such a Man! Even *I* was restored to health just by looking at His painted image. Obviously, all these miracles prove that not only was this Jesus the king of the Jews, but He also was undoubtedly the Christ!"

Suddenly a tremendous rush of wind blew into the auditorium, causing all the statues of the gods, perched high above, to tremble and shake. Panic-stricken, people began to scatter in every direction. Caught in the vortex of the whirlwind, the statutes cracked into pieces and toppled to the ground in a heap of rubble and dust. Most escaped with their lives, but many were not so lucky, having been crushed to death by the falling debris. One man, pinned by a gigantic hand, lay disfigured and bleeding. With his dying breath, he whispered, "Surely the lips that uttered the Name of Christ have vanquished the power of our gods."

Tiberius stood gawking at the destruction and mayhem all around him and mournfully shook his head. "Who is this Jesus of Nazareth? And what kind of Man could cause such devastation at the mere mention of His Name?"

CAESAR AND HIS ENTIRE Senate were now assembled in the Capitol Building, and again he began to fiercely interrogate Pilate. "Because of your infamy against this Jesus, our sacred temple has been reduced to rubble! So I want you to tell me right now, you impertinent ass, just Who was this Man you crucified?"

"But I already told you," the governor whimpered. "I didn't want Him to be crucified. I had no choice."

"Enough of your lies! Your evil crimes have begun to infect Rome itself! Earthquakes and tidal waves have devastated the continent. And now the mere utterance of His Name has toppled our gods!"

"Well, I, for one, can vouch for the accuracy of what people say He did. Even I became convinced by what I saw. He really is greater than all the gods we worship."

Tiberius slammed his fist down. "You fool! If you admit that you realized Who this Man was, then why did you allow Him to be treated in such a despicable manner?"

Pilate shrugged his shoulders pathetically. "I have no idea, Sire, but I can tell you I am truly sorry if any of my actions have brought shame upon either you or Rome."

"Yes, yes, how touching. Maybe you were hoping to capitalize upon this Man's notoriety. Maybe you were really trying to undermine my government, like all the rest. Is that what you were up to, Governor?"

"Of course not, Your Majesty."

"Has anyone from my family contacted you?"

"No, Sire. No one."

"Then you wish to cause my downfall in order to avenge the execution of your friend and protector Lucius Sejanus! Is that it?"

"No, of course not! I did it because those rebellious Jewish leaders forced me to crucify Him! Let the public record show that *I* was His greatest advocate!"

"Nonsense." Tiberius shook his head in disgust.

"But it's true. I'm *begging* you, Great Caesar, please let the record be read before you as my only witness, and before God as my final testimony."

Tiberius scowled, then reluctantly nodded and gestured to one of his soldiers who hastily left the building. "Very well," he said with a vindictive sneer. "All I've got to say is, this better be good."

Moments later, the soldier returned with a large book and handed it to Senator Rufus, who stepped up to the bar of judgment next to Pilate. Setting the book down, he opened it and cleared his throat. "As it turns out, Your Majesty, this book was discovered at Jerusalem, in the Hall of Pontius Pilate, just as the governor has testified." Looking down, Rufus began in stentorian tones to read it aloud. "It states that all the things written here took place in the nineteenth year of Tiberius Caesar, emperor of Rome, in the seventeenth year of Herod Antipas, king of Judea, son of Herod the Great."

A Most Improbable Ally

AT THAT TIME, A GROUP of disgruntled, black-robed Jewish religious leaders appeared before Pontius Pilate. "Greetings, Governor Pilate," began one of them, nodding graciously. "As I'm sure you're already aware, I am Annas, chief priest at Jerusalem, and these, my esteemed colleagues, have all joined me today in a most holy cause on behalf of our nation."

"Naturally," Pilate replied with a hint of sarcasm in his voice.

Gesturing to the man next to him, Annas said, "This is Caiaphas, our current high priest."

"Of course," said the governor as Caiaphas nodded respectfully.

"My fellow priests, Summas and Datam," continued Annas, motioning to the other members of his group. "And from our supreme council, the Sanhedrin: Representing the Pharisees are Gamaliel, Judas and Levi, and from the Sadducees are Alexander, Cyrus and Nepthalim. With us, too, are various elders, scribes and doctors of the Law. First of all, we would like to express our gratitude for your providing us this opportunity to meet with you personally."

For several intense moments, Pilate stared at this group of men who were all looking at him with such stern faces. "Certainly, Annas, but before you continue, at least do me the honor of putting away any false pretense of diplomacy. I'm well aware of what to expect today. Some moral outrage has you all in an uproar, as usual. Am I right?"

With that, Annas' amicable demeanor washed away, having been replaced by an offended scowl. "As you wish, Governor. Forgive me if I offended you with any ill-conceived attempt at civility."

Pilate nodded, apparently satisfied with his pyrrhic victory. "And don't think I'm not aware of your illustrious history, Annas. Not only were you once the residing high priest of your people, but you've also been father to no less than three more. In fact, the present high priest, Caiaphas, the man standing at your right hand, is your son-in-law."

Annas and Caiaphas exchanged a serious look.

"But, Governor," interjected Caiaphas, "I fail to see what that has to do with today's proceedings."

"Really?" Pilate quipped. "Well, from where I sit, it has everything to do with them. Never forget, gentlemen, a man in my position, as governor of Jerusalem, must always see through to the truth of any matter I'm forced to confront. So, when a group of men like you suddenly appears on my doorstep, it's absolutely critical for me to know who's pulling the real strings of power. You get my meaning now?"

Annas reluctantly nodded. "Of course, Governor; I do, yes."

"Good, then quit wasting my precious time, and state your business before I throw you all out on your sanctimonious asses."

"As you wish, sir," said Annas, trying to remain calm in the face of Pilate's abrasive manner. "We've come here today to discuss a very serious concern of ours; one which will no doubt concern you as well."

"Me? What could you possibly have to say that would concern me?"

"You have a revolutionist in your midst, Governor," blurted Caiaphas, "a seditious man who threatens the peace and tranquility of the entire nation of Israel!"

Obviously unimpressed, Pilate rolled his eyes at the mere suggestion. "Please, not another revolutionist. Don't you people ever learn?"

The black-robed men all exchanged nervous looks as Pilate yawned apathetically.

"But what do you propose to do about it?" Annas pressed "And what if Caesar finds out that, when given the chance to intervene, you instead allowed things to escalate because of your failure to act?"

"How dare you imply I'd ever shirk my duty to Rome; and just who is it this time that has you all in such a fit? You're usually the first ones to spearhead this kind of rebellion. What's so unusual about this man?"

"This time the rebel in question seeks to not only undermine our way of life but also the authority of Rome."

Still obviously unconcerned, the governor said, "Really. And just what is the name of this rebel?"

"His name is Jesus of Nazareth," continued Annas, "and he is a criminal of the highest order."

"You don't say. And what could he possibly have done to make me think he's a threat to Roman authority?"

"The man declares himself to be king of the Jews," Annas replied.

Pilate blankly stared back at the group. "Well, is he?"

"Of course not!" exclaimed Caiaphas. "The man has lost his mind. He's even gone so far as to declare himself to be the Son of God. But, of course, it's common knowledge this Jesus is merely the son of Joseph and Mary."

Pilate grinned, amused by such antics. "So the man has gone insane. So what? He hardly sounds like a threat to the imperial majesty of Rome. Would any of Caesar's loyal subjects actually switch sides for the likes of such a man? Is that what you're suggesting?"

The men exchanged more nervous looks all around, growing frustrated with Pilate's blatant sarcasm.

"But he's trying to destroy the sacred Law of our Fathers!" blurted Annas. "And if he's allowed to continue, unopposed, you might very well have another riot on your hands. Is that what you want? More bloodshed?"

Pilate grew serious at the mere mention of another riot. "Of course not. So tell me: What is he saying? What's he trying to destroy?"

The Pharisee Gamaliel stepped forward. "Our Law that forbids the performing of cures on the Sabbath."

"But still he insists," barked Summas, the priest, "on curing both the lame and the deaf!"

"And those tormented with palsy and blindness," grunted another priest, Datam. "Not to mention lepers and demoniacs!"

"All on that very day!" yelped Alexander, the Sadducee.

"And all with diabolical methods!" growled Annas.

"Hold on, hold on. One at a time, people," Pilate said with his hand up in protest. "Now obviously, I'm no expert in religious matters, but even I fail to see the logic in what you're telling me. How can this man be doing all these good things by diabolical means?"

"Because he's a sorcerer, that's how!" snapped Caiaphas. "He casts demons out by the power of the prince of demons. That's why everything is under his control!"

Pilate shook his head. "Casting out demons doesn't seem to be the work of an evil spirit. These things have to come from the power of the gods."

"Please, sir," said Annas, "summon this Jesus to appear before your tribunal and listen to him for yourself. Then you'll witness firsthand the true nature of our grave predicament."

APPEARING BEFORE Pilate, a solemn messenger dutifully bowed. "Greetings, Governor, how may I serve you today?"

"Tell me," said Pilate. "Are you familiar with this man Jesus of Nazareth?"

Pilate's messenger nodded. "I am, sir."

"Good. I need you to figure out some way to get him here without causing a huge scene. Can you manage that for me?"

"I believe so, Governor, yes."

"Very well. Go, then, and bring him here as soon as possible."

MAKING HIS WAY through the city streets, the messenger soon found Jesus. Bowing, he worshiped Him. "Lord, I've been sent by no less than the governor of Jerusalem, Pontius Pilate himself, who's requesting an audience with You."

Jesus nodded calmly. "I see. Would you like Me to come with you now? Is that it?"

"With all due respect, Lord, yes. Thank You."

"Then lead the way," He said, smiling graciously.

ESCORTING JESUS TO the door of the Assembly Hall, the messenger spread his robe on the ground for Him. "Lord, please walk on this as You enter."

But the Jewish authorities were milling around outside, and when they saw what the messenger had done, they were outraged.

"How dare you, young man!" shrieked Caiaphas. "You were ordered to summon this heretic, not to grovel before him as though he were some sort of royal figure!"

Then turning to Jesus, Annas pointed a crooked finger at Him. "You stay here. We'll deal with you later. Right now we're going to see to it that this boy is dealt with first."

THE YOUNG MAN WAS immediately corralled into the presence of Pilate.

Glaring defiantly at the governor, Annas snarled, "Why didn't you give Jesus his summons through an official bailiff, and not just by simple messenger?"

"What is wrong now?" wondered an exasperated Pilate.

"Apparently, this messenger of yours worships Jesus," snapped Caiaphas. "He laid his robe down for him to walk on, and said, 'Lord, the governor anxiously awaits your arrival.'"

Turning to him, the governor asked, "Is this true?"

The messenger nodded timidly.

"Why on Earth would you do something like that?"

"I did it because I saw other people do it."

"When?"

"Well, sir, it was not too long ago, when you sent me to deliver a message to Herod's nephew, Alexander. As I made my way through Jerusalem, I saw Jesus riding majestically on a she-ass. The Hebrews called out to Him: 'Hosanna!' And that's when I saw the people there spreading their clothes before Him in the street and saying: 'Please, save us, You Who are from Heaven! Blessed is He Who comes in the Name of the Lord!'"

Many of the Jewish leaders began grumbling in protest.

"Those people were speaking Hebrew!" Summas exclaimed. "You're Greek! How could you understand them?"

"Because I asked one of the men there: 'What are those people saying?' So he told me."

Pilate turned to the angry Jews, who were suddenly speechless. "So, is it a crime now to do what a bunch of Hebrews were first seen doing?"

The Jewish leaders looked amongst themselves, hoping someone would offer something in their defense.

"I'll assume your silence means you've changed your minds about my messenger's so-called 'guilt' in this matter. Again I ask you: What has he done that was so wrong?"

But the men remained silent.

"Fine. Then if we can put this matter behind us, we can proceed." The governor turned to his messenger. "Go ahead. Bring Jesus in now."

AS JESUS ENTERED the Assembly Hall, where twelve standard-bearers held up the royal insignias of Imperial Rome, the tops of the standards bowed down as He walked past them. Taken aback by this bewildering sight, Pilate had the most peculiar look on his face. The Jewish authorities, however, reacted quite differently.

"Wait, wait, wait!" Annas bellowed. "Now your standard-bearers are bowing before this criminal! I must insist, Governor, that you put an end to this sort of thing immediately!"

Pilate shook his head, still unsure of what he had just seen. "Look, gentlemen, I realize it wasn't pleasant for you to see the standards bow to Jesus all by themselves, but why get angry with the standard-bearers as though *they'd* bowed before him?"

Caiaphas fumed. "But we *did* see them bowing before Jesus!"

The governor motioned to one of the standard-bearers to come to him. "Why'd you just do that?"

But the man shrugged, clearly perplexed by all the fuss. "But we didn't do anything, sir.

We're pagans. We worship the gods in the Temple. We have no reason to bow to this man."

Satisfied with his explanation, Pilate then turned to the leaders of the synagogue. "Now I want you to choose the strongest men from amongst yourselves and have them hold up the standards. Then we'll see if they bow down by themselves or not."

SO THE TWELVE STRONGEST men that the Jewish authorities could find had the standards handed to them, and these new men proceeded to hold up the royal insignias.

Pilate told them, "By the life of Caesar, if you men don't keep the standards held up properly when Jesus enters, I'll have all your heads cut off. Is that understood?"

"It is, Governor," replied the first man in line.

"Good. Now have Jesus brought back in."

And when Jesus came in and walked past the standard-bearers again, the royal standards bowed down, just as they had before.

Equally amazed and confused by this, Pilate sat contemplating his next move, when suddenly his wife Procla, who was standing some distance away, motioned to her own private messenger. She whispered something in his ear, and then the messenger ran to her husband.

"Begging your pardon, sir," said the messenger, "but I have an urgent word from your wife."

"Yes, go ahead."

"She says: 'Please, don't harm this innocent Man. I've suffered horribly because of a night vision involving Him.'"

"See, didn't we tell you he was a sorcerer?" Summas barked. "Now he's caused your wife to have some kind of nightmare!"

Pilate turned to Jesus. "You hear their testimony against you, yet you still offer nothing in your defense. Why?"

But Jesus just calmly replied, "If they hadn't been given the power of speech, they'd never even be able to speak, and since they're all capable of making their own decisions, they'll just have to work it out for themselves."

"What do we have to work out for ourselves?" scoffed Annas. "We already know more than enough about you. First of all, you were born through fornication!"

"And because of the reports of your birth," Caiaphas said, "the male infants in Bethlehem were all slaughtered."

"Even your mother and father fled into Egypt," added Datam, "because they couldn't trust their own people."

But a man named Antonius stepped forward from out of the crowd. "Well, we know His mother Mary was married to Joseph at the time, so you can't say He was born through fornication."

Pilate glared at the Jewish leaders. "Then your account is false. Men from your own nation have testified that he wasn't born through fornication."

Annas glared back. "But you'd better pay attention to the ones who insist that he *was!*"

"The only ones denying this charge are his converts and disciples," insisted Caiaphas.

"Who are these converts?" Pilate asked.

"They're the children of pagans," groaned Summas. "They aren't real Jews. They're just some of his followers, that's all."

But several more Jews stepped forward, including Eleazer, Asterius, Caras and Crispus.

"We're not converts," Eleazer said. "We're Jews, and we're telling you the truth."

"We were present when Mary and Joseph became engaged," added Asterius.

"I charge you to swear by the life of Caesar!" growled Pilate. "Are you sure you're telling me the truth?"

"Certainly we are, sir," Caras insisted. "But our Law forbids us to swear because it's considered a sin, so if *they're* willing to swear by Caesar that what we told you is false, then we'll gladly submit to execution."

Disgusted, Annas shook his head. "These men will never believe what we know to be a fact. The man was born a bastard."

"No matter how much he pretends to be the son of God and a king," Caiaphas added with a shudder.

"Enough already," snapped Pilate. "I want everyone out of here immediately; everyone, that is, except for the men who are sympathetic to the Nazarene."

ALONE WITH JUST THE group of sympathizers, Pilate turned to them. "Why are men from your own nation, religious men, no less, why are they so determined to condemn this Jesus? It doesn't make any sense."

"They're angry," Crispus began, "because He cures people on the Sabbath Day, our holiest day of the week."

"Excuse me?" muttered Pilate with a peculiar tilt of his head. "You can't be serious. You mean to tell me that they'd condemn a man for doing *good* just because he did it on a so-called 'holy' day?"

"Yes, sir," Crispus mournfully replied. "It seems they would."

STORMING INTO THE outer hallway where the Jewish authorities were milling about like a cloud of angry bees, Pilate angrily confronted them. "I call you all to witness. This man has done nothing wrong. How dare you bring him to me thinking I'd cooperate with the likes of you!"

"Hold on now," persisted Annas, who stepped forward to face the governor, "if this man were not a criminal, we'd never have brought him before you."

"Don't be absurd! If this man has committed a crime against your nation, then take him away and try him according to your own Law."

"But it's against the Law for us to put anyone to death," Gamaliel replied.

"Oh, I see," grumbled Pilate, "so the commandment: 'Do not kill,' belongs to you but not to me, eh?"

BACK INSIDE THE Assembly Hall, Pilate addressed Jesus in private. "Tell me: Are you really the king of the Jews?"

"Are you asking this for yourself? Or have the Jewish leaders told you this about Me?"

Pilate shrugged. "What do I care? Am I a Jew? Your own religious leaders have delivered you to me. What have you done, anyway?"

"My kingdom is not of this world. If it were, My servants would be fighting for Me right now, and I'd never have been turned over by these men."

"Are you really a king, then?"

"You say that I'm a king. That's why I was born into this world. My purpose is to bear witness to the truth, and every person of the truth recognizes My voice."

"What is truth?"

"Truth is from Heaven."

Pilate seemed genuinely disappointed. "Then what are you saying? Truth is nowhere to be found on this Earth?"

"Believe Me when I tell you: Truth is on this Earth whenever those with the power of reason are governed by truth and make correct decisions."

Thoroughly frustrated, Pilate hung his head with an exasperated sigh.

ADDRESSING THE JEWISH leaders again Pilate insisted, "I'm sorry, gentlemen, but I can't find a single crime this man is guilty of."

"But he said, 'I can destroy the Temple of God,'" Cyrus grumbled, "'and rebuild it again in three days.'"

"What kind of temple was he talking about?" asked the governor.

"The kind that took Solomon forty-six years to build!" barked Datam. "The man is a raving lunatic!"

Pilate shook his head in disbelief. "But that's no reason to condemn him. I'm sorry, but I'm innocent of his blood, I tell you. You'll have to work this out amongst yourselves."

But Summas persisted. "Let his blood be on us and our children!"

"Gentlemen, please. Stop acting this way. I keep telling you the man hasn't done a thing that deserves the death penalty. He certainly shouldn't be killed for curing sick people on the Sabbath."

"By the life of Caesar," blurted Levi, "if anyone is a blasphemer, he is worthy of death, but this man blasphemes the Lord!"

ALONE WITH JESUS, Pilate gazed at Him for quite a while. "What am I going to do with you?" wondered the governor.

"Do what is written," He replied.

"What is written?"

"Moses and the prophets have prophesied a great deal about My suffering and resurrection."

Eavesdropping at the door to Pilate's chamber, the Jewish leaders became furious again. Caiaphas banged the door with his fist and bellowed, "Why will you continue to listen to this man's blasphemy?"

An enraged Pilate swung the door open and confronted them. "If what he just said is blasphemy, then you'll have to take him to your court and try him according to your Law!"

"Our Law says he should receive thirty-nine stripes by whipping," said Gamaliel, "and if he continues doing the same thing, he should be stoned to death."

"Well, if you think that speech of his just now was blasphemy, then I guess you'll have to put him on trial, won't you?"

Gamaliel continued. "But our Law orders us to not murder anyone."

"So we want *you* to crucify him," Alexander grunted, "because he deserves to die on a cross!"

Pilate adamantly shook his head. "No. It isn't right that he should be crucified. Just whip him publicly, and send him away."

And when the governor looked around, he saw many of the Jews in the crowd were crying. "Well, well, not all your people want his death, do they?"

"We *all* came here," croaked Summas, "just for the purpose of seeing him die!"

"But why should he die?" asked Pilate in amazement.

"Because," Annas said, "he declares that he's the Son of God."

"And a king," added Caiaphas.

Angry and exasperated, Pilate motioned for his soldiers to usher everyone out of the hall again. Court was adjourned, and, for the time being at least, the Assembly Hall fell completely silent.

In His Defense

THE JEWISH LEADERS were together again, appearing before a disgruntled Pilate in his Assembly Hall. This time a pair of temple guards led Jesus in, and when the governor saw that His hands were in shackles, he became particularly agitated.

Still another black-robed Jewish leader came forward and stood before Pilate. "Oh, righteous judge, please allow me to say a few words."

"And who are you now?" the governor asked. "Another detractor here to berate the good man?"

"My name is Nicodemus, and although I'm a leader among the Pharisees, no, I'm not here to rail upon the good Man, as you call Him."

"Really." Intrigued, Pilate nodded. "Go ahead, then. I'm interested to hear what you have to say. By the gods, I've certainly had my fill with trumped-up charges thus far."

So Nicodemus proceeded to state his case, slowly and confidently. "Very good. Then hopefully I will divert you today with my fresh testimony, because I've just recently come from a meeting where I spoke quite frankly with a group of our elders, scribes and priests who are all gathered in Jerusalem for our Passover festival. I talked to them about this Man Who has performed so many miracles, unlike anything anyone has done or ever will do again, and I asked them: 'What, exactly, are your plans for this Man?'"

"How dare you disturb the esteemed governor's official business like this, Nicodemus," interjected Annas.

"Excuse me," Nicodemus replied calmly, "but I've been given permission to speak here. Do you mind?"

Pilate perked up. "Ah, don't pay any attention to them. You go right ahead."

"You silly, old fool," Caiaphas interjected. "What in Heaven's name do you expect to gain from all your pathetic groveling, anyway?"

"I was hoping the governor would agree to release this Man, before He falls victim to your unmitigated hatred and envy."

"Well, how about that," said an astonished Pilate, who turned to Caiaphas with a wry smile. "One of your own leaders thinks this Jesus should be released. What do you say to that?"

"Preposterous, blasphemous!" Caiaphas howled. "This man should be ashamed to call himself a spiritual leader of our people!"

"Oh, please," scoffed Nicodemus, "what's all the fuss about, honestly? If this Jesus is a mere mortal as you people claim, then you have nothing to worry about if He's released. His so-called 'miracles' and 'divine cures' will simply come to nothing all by themselves."

"But what if he really has been sent by your alleged God, then what?" queried Pilate, leaning eagerly forward, as if to get a better view of the fistfight that might ensue at any moment.

"If He does come from God," Nicodemus continued, "then His miracles will be unstoppable no matter how hard you try to prevent them."

"Ridiculous!" growled Annas. "What this man is suggesting is completely absurd."

"No, that isn't true," countered Nicodemus. "A similar thing happened when God sent Moses into Egypt to perform his miracles. Pharaoh's sorcerers, Jannes and Jambres, could do some of the same miracles Moses performed, but in the end their power proved to be no match for Moses."

Pilate turned to Annas and Caiaphas. "Were either of you aware of this fact from your own Scripture?"

"Of course they're aware of it," insisted Nicodemus, sensing that the governor might prove to be a potential ally after all. "Any teacher in Israel would remember the stories about those sorcerers. They'd also be very aware of what happened to all the people who believed in them."

"What did happen to them?" asked a wide-eyed Pilate with an almost child-like enthusiasm.

Caiaphas awkwardly cleared his throat. "They all died untimely deaths, naturally."

"Naturally," echoed Nicodemus.

The governor flashed a lusty smile at this, much to the chagrin of Annas and Caiaphas.

Seeing Pilate's favorable reaction, Nicodemus pressed on. "So, Governor Pilate, may I be so bold as to appeal to your sense of propriety and justice. Please, release this Man right away. Obviously, anyone can see that the miracles He's performed have come from God. The last thing He deserves is to be executed for them."

But Annas coldly replied, "So now you're making eloquent speeches on his behalf, are you? Have you become one of his disciples, too?"

Nicodemus, however, remained unruffled. "Certainly you're not suggesting that Governor Pilate has become one of His disciples, simply because he also makes speeches in His defense?"

"You traitor!" bellowed Alexander, shaking his fist at Nicodemus. "You just go ahead and believe everything he taught you is true! I hope you end up with him!"

"Yes, I do accept everything He taught me as the truth," replied the unflappable Nicodemus. "And, yes, I do hope I end up with Him as well, just as you say. Thank you."

"All right, everyone," said Pilate, who put up his hand in protest. "Enough already. Both your sides have been well represented. Now, is there anyone else who can offer something new to this discussion?"

Another Jewish man timidly stepped forward and quietly said, "Yes, sir, I can."

"Really now, and who are you?"

"Oh, my name is unimportant, sir. Unlike these other important men, I am just an ordinary man. But I can promise you I have an extraordinary story to tell."

"Then, by all means, tell it."

"For thirty-eight miserable years, I laid by the sheep pool at Jerusalem, struggling with a terrible disease. Year after year, I sat there waiting for a cure brought whenever an angel of God would come and disturb the water so that whoever stepped in first, after the stirring of the waters, was healed of whatever illness they had."

"Yes, yes," Caiaphas groaned impatiently. "We're all aware of the legend. Please make your point."

"Well, you see," the man continued, "Jesus saw me languishing there, so He asked me: 'Would you like to be healed?' But I answered: 'Sir, I have no one to put me into the pool when the water is disturbed.' Then He said, 'Get up and walk,' and immediately I was healthy again."

"It's a lie!" yelped Caiaphas. "Certainly the testimony of this scoundrel cannot be admitted before this grand tribunal!"

"But I'm telling you the truth, Governor," he insisted. "I swear it. That very moment I got up and walked away, completely healed."

"But, sir," Annas grunted, "ask him what day it was when he was cured of his disease."

"On the Sabbath Day, of course," murmured the man. "Why do you ask?"

"See," cried Caiaphas, "didn't we tell you this Jesus performed his cures on the Sabbath? And all by the power of the prince of demons!"

Then, a disheveled man slowly stepped up and bowed before the governor.

"Who are you?" Pilate asked.

"My name is Bartimeus, and I was born blind. My whole life, I was a prisoner to darkness, but one day, as Jesus was walking by, I called out: 'Son of David, have mercy on me!'"

"Then what happened?"

"Jesus stopped, of course, and told me: 'Receive your sight,' and instantly I could see for the very first time in my life. And I've been following Him ever since."

"He just *told* you to receive your sight?" asked the incredulous governor. "And then you could see again?"

"Yes, sir, that's exactly the way it happened?"

An astonished Pilate darted a look at Annas and Caiaphas, who both looked as skeptical as ever.

"Preposterous, I tell you," Caiaphas sneered.

Another man then stepped up.

"What's your story, young man?" asked Pilate.

"Me? Oh, well, I used to be a leper."

"And you also encountered this man called Jesus."

"Yes, Governor, I did, and when I met Jesus, He told me: 'I want you to be healed.'"

"And you were healed?" queried Pilate. "With just a word from this man?"

Shaking his head, still in disbelief himself, he replied, "I know it sounds absurd, sir, but it's true. Jesus simply told me to be healed, and just like that, I was healthy again."

"Please, Governor," Caiaphas grumbled. "How much more of this rubbish do we have to listen to?"

A woman pressed forward through the crowd. "Governor Pilate, Governor Pilate, please. I also have a story to tell."

The governor nodded amicably. "Go right ahead, young lady. Tell us."

Trying to hold back her tears of joy, she said, "I am a daughter of Abraham, and I was severely deformed. My back was so crooked it was impossible for me to stand up straight."

"Don't tell me," scoffed Caiaphas. "You also had an encounter with a mystical healer calling himself the son of god."

"That's right," came her charming reply, completely undeterred by the high priest's cynicism. "And with just a word, He straightened my back. I've been able to live a normal life ever since."

Another woman, her eyes downcast, then came forward and stood contritely before Pilate. Slowly lifting her head, this beautiful lady beamed a radiant smile, a familiar smile, the smile of the same woman who previously had in her possession a remarkable painting of the Man she now sought to defend. "Hello, Governor Pilate. My name is Veronica, and for twelve miserable years, I was afflicted with an issue of blood. My doctors gave me no hope of recovery. To a man, they were unanimous as to the certainty of my fate. For all intents and purposes, sir, I was a walking corpse, withering away, day after wretched day, just waiting for the day of my blessed release … my death … the only thing I was told that would free me from my deadly affliction. Until the day, that is, I was somehow able to press through the crowd surrounding Him, and that was when I merely touched the hem of His garment, and then…" Veronica choked up, unable to continue.

Pilate leaned forward in anticipation. "Yes, and then?"

Regaining her composure, Veronica looked him straight in the eye and replied, "And then the bleeding stopped that very moment; and I've been healed ever since."

"Excuse me, Governor," Gamaliel interjected with a disgruntled scowl, "but our Law forbids women from being allowed to offer evidence in court."

"You don't say," said Pilate, who, upon seeing the sour look on the face of the prosecution, glibly smiled. "Too bad for you that you neglected to mention it until now."

So another man came forward. "Then I guess I'll have testify to what I saw, sir."

"Of course, go right ahead," urged Pilate. "You also encountered this man?"

"I did, yes. I was at a wedding celebration in Cana where Jesus and His disciples had been invited."

"When was that, young man?" queried Annas.

"Oh, I'd say right around the time there was a wine shortage in Galilee."

"I see," mused Annas. "Can you please tell us what happened at this wedding?"

"Yes, well, after we drank all the wine, Jesus ordered the servants to fill six clay pots with water."

"Water?" chimed in Caiaphas. "You ran out of wine, so this man told you to fetch *water*?"

"Yes, that's right."

"Then what happened?" Pilate asked.

"The servants filled the jars to the brim, just as they'd been ordered."

"With water?" quipped Annas.

"Yes, with water, and then He blessed it."

"Great," snickered Caiaphas. "Then you served holy water to a bunch of disgruntled wedding guests. Is that about it?"

"No, sir, that's not how it happened at all."

"Young man," intoned Annas, trying to remain patient, "would you please just get to the point of your story?"

"Well, then, the servants poured drinks for everyone there, and to our absolute amazement, the water had turned into wine."

"What?" moaned Caiaphas. "You're joking."

"No, sir. I can assure you I saw the whole thing with my own eyes: Water went into the jars, and then wine came out of them. We all drank it together, and celebrated well into the night. Honestly."

"Ridiculous, I tell you." Caiaphas crossed his arms, quite indignantly.

"I know it sounds crazy," the young man said, thoroughly apologetic. "We could hardly believe it ourselves, but I can assure you, it really did happen."

Then another gentleman stepped forward. "That's nothing compared to what I saw."

Pilate leaned forward. "You saw something more amazing than that?"

"Oh, yes, sir. I saw Jesus teaching in the synagogue at Capernaum. A man with a demon yelled at Him: 'What do You want with us, Jesus of Nazareth? Have You come to destroy us before our time? I know You're the Holy One of Israel, the Son of God!'"

Annas turned to Pilate with outstretched hands. "Please, sir, do we have to listen to any more of this nonsense? Now we have to be subjected to stories about demons? Really?"

But Pilate glared back at him. "I'll decide what is, or is not, considered nonsense." Then the governor turned his attention back to the gentleman. "Now, continue. What makes you so sure this man had a demon speaking through him?"

"Well, I don't really know how to answer that, sir. All I know is that, when Jesus said to him: 'Shut up, demon! Come out of this man, right now!' I mean, instantly, some kind of evil spirit flew out of his chest, and just like that, the man was completely normal again, as though he'd just woken up from a bad dream."

"What?" asked a stunned Pilate. "Is he all right? Where is he now?"

"Oh, he's fine. Back to work, as usual. Like nothing ever happened to him at all."

Another young man slowly stepped forward and awkwardly cleared his throat.

"You?" blanched Caiaphas. "Jonathan? Don't tell me you're here to testify on this man's behalf, too."

The man resolutely nodded. "Yes, sir, I am."

"But, Jonathan, why?" asked the high priest, horrified and distraught. "Why on Earth would you do something like this?"

Intrigued by the palpable tension between these two, Pilate sat up in his seat. "Wait a minute, Caiaphas. Just who is this man?"

The high priest almost choked on his words as he reluctantly replied, "He's my nephew."

"Your nephew?" exclaimed Pilate, clearly amused with Caiaphas' dilemma. "Oh, that is a good one."

"Not only is he my nephew, but he's also a man who until recently was in training for the priesthood, a fledging Pharisee, as I understood it from my sister."

"Well, well, so the story gets even more interesting," the governor continued. "So, then; Jonathan, is it?"

"Yes, sir, that's right."

"So, Jonathan, what's your story?" he pressed. "You're not studying to become a priest anymore? No longer interested in joining the vaunted ranks of the Pharisees?"

"No, sir, I'm not."

"But why? Why the sudden change of heart?"

"Because ever since I encountered the Nazarene, I could no longer bring myself to continue following a path that, for me at least, had no meaning, no purpose, no hope."

An audible gasp rippled through the ranks of Caiaphas and his colleagues.

"Jonathan, how could you?" grimaced the high priest. "We all had such high hopes for you."

"I'm sorry, Uncle, but I didn't choose any of this for myself. It happened *to* me, I'm afraid."

"And here you are," Pilate continued, "not only willing to risk your future in the ministry of your so-called 'Chosen People,' but you also stand here willing to risk being spurned by your own family."

"Yes, it does appear that way, doesn't it?" replied Jonathan with utmost resolve.

"Why, Jonathan, why?" Caiaphas asked again, bitterly disappointed.

"Because I, too, saw vast numbers of sick people come to Jesus, from Galilee and Judea, from the seacoast and many of the countries around Jordan. Wave after wave of the sick followed Him wherever He went. The anguished, the dying, the hopeless, all besieged with every kind of disease that no doctor, no medicine, no ritual could cure. But in this Man's presence alone, they found a remedy. They found in Him the answer to all their desperate prayers. In Him, they discovered the truth about what made them sick, in body and in spirit, and through His benevolent intervention, everyone who came to Him in faith and hope was miraculously healed."

"No, no, no," groaned Caiaphas. "That's just not possible. You've lost your mind, I tell you; your soul, for that matter. This carpenter's son has deluded all of you by the power of Satan."

"No, Uncle, that isn't true," Jonathan insisted. "I saw it all for myself, and there's nothing you'll ever be able to say or do to persuade me otherwise."

Then a Roman soldier stepped forward. This time it was Pilate who sat up, suddenly curious. "Centurio, what are you doing here?"

"Well, sir, I saw Jesus in Capernaum, too."

"That's your hometown, isn't it?"

"Yes, Governor, it is."

"Don't tell me. You're here to tell us about some miraculous encounter you also had with this man?"

"I am, yes."

"This man healed you, too? Is that it?"

"Not me, sir, my servant. For the longest time my servant was bedridden with the palsy. You remember, don't you?"

"Yes, of course. I do remember something about that, now that you mention it. And you're telling me this Jesus came to your hometown?"

"He did, Governor."

"What happened?"

"I begged Him to heal my servant, and right away, He told me: 'I'll come and cure him.' But I said, 'Sir, I don't even deserve to have You come to my house. You just say the word, and my servant will be healed.'"

"Interesting," mused Pilate. "And then?"

"Then He told me: 'Go now. You'll receive just as you've believed.' And my servant was healed from that very hour."

Amazed at this, Pilate flashed a peculiar look of dissatisfaction at Annas and Caiaphas, who both had to avert their eyes, unable to bear his scrutinizing gaze.

Then a nobleman came forward and stood before the governor. "I had a son in Capernaum who was on the brink of death."

"Another person from Capernaum?" mumbled Caiaphas. "Haven't we heard enough from that part of the country yet?"

The man hesitated at this and looked to Pilate, unsure if he should continue.

"Ah, don't mind them," the governor said with a wave of his hand. "I, for one, am very interested in hearing your story. Go right ahead."

"Well, sir, one day, I had heard that Jesus was in Galilee, so I went there on my son's behalf, and I asked Him if He could possibly heal my boy, too. And He said, 'Go home, your son is fine now.'"

"Just like that?" said Pilate, snapping his fingers.

"Yes, sir, just like that," came the man's unflinching reply. "And when I returned to my home in Capernaum, I found that, just as He had assured me, my son really had been cured."

Another young man stepped forward. "Of course He's the Son of God, sir. How else could He cure every disease by merely speaking?"

"Obviously this power can only come from God!" declared an old man.

"The demons are all completely under His control!" said another woman with an emphatic conviction that made the governor raise his eyebrow.

Pilate then turned to His accusers. "And why aren't these demons subject to the power of your doctors?"

"The power to control demons can only come from God," Datam replied with a smug arrogance. "Men simply don't have the kind of power these people are describing, especially a mere peasant like this good-for-nothing Nazarene."

"But I saw Jesus raise Lazarus from the dead with my own eyes," interjected Nicodemus, "even after he'd been dead for four days. That doesn't sound like something an ordinary person can do, does it?"

Pilate shuddered and again turned to the prosecution. "So tell me again, gentlemen: What, exactly, do you seek to gain by shedding the blood of this innocent Man?"

Lamb Led to the Slaughter

THE EXASPERATED governor stood on his balcony, gazing out over a mob of Jewish protesters. With each passing moment, the crowd was swelling to the point of overflowing the square below him. Furious spectators waved their fists in the air, and someone even went so far as to throw their sandal in the direction of one of Pilate's guards who was standing near the balcony rail.

Barely ducking out of the way of the hurling object, the guard turned to Pilate. "Sir, how long will you permit this crowd to roam free? They grow more unruly by the minute. Say the word, and we'll clear the square in no time flat."

"Stand down, soldier, stand down. No one ever lost his life at the point of a sandal. I'll let you know when I want you to take action. Is that clear?"

"Yes, sir."

"Pilate, you filthy pig!" shouted one of the spectators. "If you're not willing to execute the Nazarene, in the name of your almighty Caesar, hand him over to us! We know how to take care of scum like him!"

Shaking his head in disgust, the governor muttered under his breath. "And they say we Romans are the bloodthirsty ones."

INSIDE, PILATE ADDRESSED Nicodemus and the Jews who had stated that Jesus was not born through fornication. "This whole thing is creating a riot among your people," the governor began. "If something isn't done quickly, there's liable to be more blood on my hands besides that of your Jesus. Isn't there some way to reason with these fanatics?"

"I'm afraid, Governor," Nicodemus said, "that the people you're dealing with are no longer acting in accordance to reason. They've been deluded by the powers that be that it's in the nation's best interest to sacrifice one decent man for the sake of their collective peace and tranquility."

"But all this flies in the face of my experience to this point. Certainly I've dealt with my share of anarchists before, believe me, but I've never known insanity like this; and from the very people you'd think would benefit most by a revolutionist like Jesus. Frankly, I'm at a complete loss. Can't any of you offer me a viable solution?"

Crispus shook his head. "We don't really know what to tell you anymore, Governor. Maybe you should let the ones who are in such an uproar decide."

"Tell me you're joking. Tell me you're not actually suggesting I allow that mob out there to decide this man's fate, because not only does his fate rest on my next act, but so does mine. And not in Caesar's eyes alone but certainly in the eyes of the One who's responsible for all of the miracles this man's been performing."

A DISHEARTENED PILATE walked out onto the balcony and took his position at the railing, where he again faced the tumultuous throng of Jewish protesters. With him were two of his guards, both of whom escorted a prisoner bound in chains. To his right was a resolute Jesus, beaten, bruised and bleeding, who stood serenely looking out over the angry crowd. To his left was a brutish man, grimy, wild-eyed and menacing, who took one look at the man guarding him and defiantly spit at his feet.

With every ounce of dignity that remained in him, Pilate raised his hands in an effort to silence the crowd. Slowly but surely, the clamoring mob simmered to a low boil. "Listen up, everyone, and listen well. As you all know, we've established a custom among your people where I'm allowed, by virtue of imperial decree, to release one prisoner from among you during this festival known as Passover. Presently, I have here a notorious criminal, a man by the name of Barabbas, the leader of a rapacious gang of thieves responsible for unspeakable mayhem, with so many murders to his credit it would be impossible to catalog them all. And I have here a man by the name of Jesus, whom many call the Christ, a man who doesn't deserve to die for any reason, someone responsible for so many deeds of kindness and mercy that to catalog them all would prove just as impossible. Therefore, keeping this in mind, I put it in your hands: Which man does your conscience bid you to return to your community? Will you unleash the beast, Barabbas, back upon your wives and children? Or would you rather set free the Innocent One, Jesus? Tell me now: Which one should I release?"

Momentarily smitten, everyone in the crowd glanced at his neighbor with a nervous look, and then returned their eyes back upon the governor. The crowd roared back unanimously. "Release Barabbas!"

Flabbergasted by the crowd's reaction, Barabbas grinned maliciously and nodded to them. "That's right, that's right," he snarled like a wild animal. "Release Barabbas!"

An irritated Pilate turned to the man guarding his outspoken prisoner and flashed him a sinister look, which invoked the guard to deliver a swift kidney punch to Barabbas, who doubled over in pain.

Turning back to the mob, Pilate shouted, "Then what do I do with Jesus, the Christ?"

For several heart-pounding moments, a deafening silence hung in the air, teeming with the imperceptible sound of a thousand stifled consciences. Then, all at once, the remorseless mob howled, "Crucify him!"

"You're no friend of Caesar if you release this man!" Alexander bellowed. "He says he's the son of God and a king! Would you rather have him as your king instead of Caesar?"

As enraged as the crowd that was vexing him, if not more so, Pilate lashed out uncontrollably, banging his fist on the railing. "What is wrong with you people? You're a spiteful nation of rebels, always antagonizing anyone who tries to do you a favor!"

"Who's ever done us a favor?" scoffed Annas.

"Your god for one!" Pilate snapped back. "First he rescued you from slavery in Egypt, then he led you through the Red Sea, as if it were dry land. He fed you with manna and quails in the Wilderness. He brought you water out of a rock. It's said he even gave you a Law straight from Heaven."

"You've heard correctly, sir," cooed Caiaphas.

The governor glared back. "Still you provoked him! Why?"

Annas and Caiaphas exchanged a concerned look.

Pilate pressed on. "You demanded a molten calf. You worshiped it, sacrificed to it, as if *it* had delivered you from Egypt! So your god wanted to destroy you."

"But He chose not to destroy us, didn't He?" Annas countered. "He must have seen something in our nation that was worth saving."

"He didn't destroy you because Moses interceded on your behalf. That's why your god forgave you. Still you people got so mad at him and his brother Aaron, when they fled into the tabernacle, you wanted to kill them both. Apparently you do this to everyone who tries to help you!"

Turning from his balcony, the governor started to leave, but someone from the mob shrieked, "But we want Caesar as our king, not this Jesus!"

Summas then elbowed his way forward. "He's the reason Herod gave the order to kill the male infants of Bethlehem! It's time he account for this outrage with his own blood! If you don't execute this man, we'll have no choice but to take matters into our own hands, here and now!"

This alarmed Pilate, and the entire assembly grew restless and noisy again. The governor turned back toward the crowd and again raised his hands in an effort to silence them. "All right, people, calm down, calm down!" As the mob slowly quieted back down, Pilate turned to Jesus and implored, "Are you really a king, then?"

Caiaphas pointed an accusing finger. "He's no king. He's just an insignificant, little man, a usurper who wishes to replace our beloved Caesar."

"So, what's it going to be, Governor?" yelped Annas. "Will you actually risk your future to save a single man? One word from us, and this whole city could go up in flames, and Tiberius would have no one to blame but you!"

The seething crowd let loose with a discordant roar of approval, and for several agonizing moments Pilate glared back at them. He then motioned to one of his servants, who brought out a basin of water and set it down on the railing in front of him. Slowly and methodically, Pilate washed his hands in the sight of everyone there. "I tell you all, here and now," he bellowed above the din. "I am absolved from the blood of this innocent man! You work this out amongst yourselves!"

"Let his blood be on us and our children!" Summas shouted.

Pilate reluctantly turned to Jesus again. "Your own nation has charged you with making yourself a king. Therefore, I, Pontius Pilate, governor of Jerusalem, on behalf of Tiberius Caesar, emperor of Rome, do sentence you to be whipped according to the Law of former governors. Then, you will be bound and hung on a cross, along with two other criminals named Dimas and Gestas, until such time as you are dead."

WITHOUT A SINGLE word of protest from Jesus, He and the two thieves then proceeded to carry their crossbeams to Golgotha.

ARRIVING TO THE PLACE of execution, the prisoners were handed over to a trio of Roman soldiers who stripped Jesus of His seamless robe and wrapped a skimpy linen cloth around His waist. They placed a crown of thorns on His head and a reed in His hand. Then, Pilate personally wrote on a plaque that was placed atop the cross. Written in Hebrew, Latin and Greek, its message read: *This is the king of the Jews.*

With that, the soldiers nailed Jesus to the crossbeam, piercing His wrists. Lifting Him into place on the upright post, they finished the job by nailing his feet into place. Finally, the two thieves were lashed to their crossbeams and hoisted up so they could be crucified alongside Him, Dimas to His right, and Gestas to His left.

The mocking mob gathered as Jesus looked skyward. "Please, Father, forgive them," He murmured. "They don't really know what they're doing."

Near the foot of the cross, the three Roman soldiers each rolled a crude set of dice, then one of them happily grabbed Jesus' seamless robe and stuck it in his sash. That soldier was Longinus the centurion.

Meanwhile, the rest of the onlookers, accompanied by the priests and elders, stood by, gawking at Jesus as He hung there trying to catch His breath with each passing moment.

"He saved others, now let him save himself," Alexander barked, "if he can!"

"If he's really the son of God," yelled Summas, "let him come down from there this instant!"

"If you're really a king," said Longinus, "then command us to remove you from this cross, before it's too late." Then, taking a stick with cloth at the end, the centurion dipped it in vinegar, mixed with gall, and held it up to His mouth.

Gestas, the thief being crucified to the left of Jesus, turned to Him and sneered. "If you are the Christ, then deliver yourself, and us."

Dimas, the thief to His right, turned toward Gestas. "Doesn't a condemned man like you fear God even a little? We're at least receiving proper sentences for what we've done, but this Jesus, what crime has He ever committed?" And turning to Jesus, he implored, "Lord, please remember me when You enter Your kingdom."

With great difficulty, Jesus, His face mired in sweat and blood, replied, "Certainly, Dimas, today you will be with Me in Paradise."

AS THE SUN REACHED its zenith in the sky, an eerie darkness began to fall across the countryside with the onset of a total eclipse. The once mocking mob ceased its jeering as everyone stood staring up at the darkening sky, frozen with fear and dismay.

AROUND THREE O'CLOCK in the afternoon, with the darkness caused by the eclipse having fully enveloped the landscape by then, Jesus could be heard gasping on the cross. "My God, My God … Why … have You abandoned Me? Father ... I now give You ... My spirit." Then He died.

Suddenly a powerful earthquake struck the countryside, sending terrified spectators scrambling in every direction. The veil of the Temple was torn from top to bottom, and its foundations crumbled, causing the building to teeter to one side. All the cemeteries in the area were decimated. The ordinarily neat array of manicured tombstones was now a jumbled mess of jagged stones, tilted at every imaginable angle. Graves everywhere were ripped up, torn from the inside out, split open as though the ground had belched out its very interior.

Clearly shaken, Longinus gazed up at Him hanging on the cross. "This really was an innocent Man," he whispered. Then stepping forward, he raised his spear and plunged it into the right side of Jesus, directly between the fifth and sixth rib. Blood and water immediately gushed from the wound.

A NOBLEMAN WENT TO see Pilate late that same evening. As the man patiently stood before him, the governor looked up with his weary, bloodshot eyes. "What do you want?"

"My name is Joseph of Arimathea."

"I know who you are. I asked you: What do you want?"

"I'm here to request your permission to bury the Nazarene's body."

"Don't tell me. You're one of his faithful disciples, too, but because you fear those bloodthirsty zealots who demanded his death, you're here under the cover of darkness."

Joseph hung his head in shame. "Yes, I suppose you're right. I stand before you guilty as charged."

Pilate continued with his glib tone. "Still, you felt someone should see to it that the man be given a decent burial, and that someone just happens to be you. Is that about it?"

Eyes still downcast, Joseph painfully nodded. "That's correct, Governor."

"Well, I admit, you're not the first person who's come to me lately asking for the same consideration. But before I do give you permission, give me one good reason why I should allow *you* access to the body? Were you particularly close to the man in life, or, now that he's dead, are you feeling remorseful for having done nothing to save him from such a despicable fate?"

"I'm asking you, sir," said Joseph, lifting his head in all earnestness, "because the Man was not only my dearest friend and esteemed Teacher, He was also my nephew."

Pilate's expression abruptly transformed from that of the cynical antagonist to one of sympathetic ally. "Then, please, accept my apology, and, by all means, see to it that the good man receives the sort of treatment in death that he deserved to receive in life."

AS JOSEPH AND Nicodemus led a solemn procession of men who were carrying the body of Jesus, they all openly wept. Joining them in their solemn task, several women came out of the shadows to assist them. Together, they took part in wrapping Him, according to Jewish custom, in linen cloths sprinkled with spices of myrrh and aloe.

JOSEPH, NICODEMUS and the other men then transported the linen-wrapped body of Jesus to a tomb, cut out of rock, where they lovingly laid Him to rest. For the longest time the group stayed with Him there, mourning, sobbing, unwilling to leave Him even in death. Finally, however, they reluctantly exited the tomb, and having done so, the men rolled a huge round stone into place, sealing the doorway with a tremendous thud.

Blood on Their Hands

"THEY DID WHAT?" barked Caiaphas, wide-eyed and furious.

"They got permission from Pilate to bury his body," Summas timidly replied.

"Then what did they do with it?" wondered Annas.

Summas rolled his eyes in disgust. "Can you believe it? They buried it in Joseph of Arimathea's brand-new tomb."

"The fools," groaned Caiaphas. "That man's body should have been cast into the pit of Gehenna, like the rest of his kind. When will these heretics ever learn?"

Then turning to Annas, Summas asked, "What should we do now, sir?"

"It's time these infidels answer for their crimes against God," growled Annas. "Find them, Summas, and bring them before our tribunal; them, and anyone else who showed sympathy to the Nazarene. It's time, once and for all, that these men get a taste of what we gave their beloved savior."

STILL OBVIOUSLY disturbed by what he had experienced, the Roman soldier who had stood at the foot of Jesus' cross went to see Pilate.

"Hello, Governor Pilate," said the soldier. "I know you're a busy man, so I'll be as brief as possible."

"Of course," Pilate replied. "What can I do for one of Caesar's great and glorious centurions?"

"I came here today because it's my understanding we have a mutual interest between us."

"Really? And what might that be?"

"It seems we've both had an encounter with the Man called Jesus."

"Jesus," Pilate muttered under his breath. "You, too? That's why you're here?"

The soldier nodded blankly.

"By the gods, does this man plan to haunt me even from beyond the grave?"

"It does appear so, doesn't it?"

"What's your name, centurion?"

"My name is Longinus, and I was one of three soldiers directly responsible for the crucifixion of Jesus of Nazareth." Agonized, he held both hands out. "These hands, sir, are the hands of a soldier, hands that gloried in the sting of battle, the shedding of blood, the revelry of victory." Longinus paused and stared down at his hands, as though he were horrified that they were connected to the rest of his body.

Realizing he was unable to continue, the governor prodded. "And now?"

"Now, they're nothing but a horror to me."

"But why?" asked an incredulous Pilate.

"Because now they're the hands of the man who spilled the blood of the Savior of the World." Snapping out of his spell, Longinus looked up at Pilate, looking him straight in the eye. "Tell me, Governor, when you washed your hands of His blood, did it work? Did it really absolve you from your crime after all?"

Pilate stared back for the longest time before shaking his head. "No, sadly, it did not."

Longinus then turned and headed for the door. "Goodbye, sir, and may God have mercy on our souls." Almost to the door, he stopped and turned back toward the governor. "Oh, I almost forgot." Reaching into his sash, he pulled out a bundle of cloth and tossed it to the floor. "I want you to have this. I don't ever want to see it again."

Pilate gawked at the pile of cloth. "What is it?"

Longinus turned and headed through the doorway. "Just something I won in a little game of chance."

With a curious look in his eyes, Pilate walked over to the pile of cloth and picked it up. Confused with what he was looking at, he unfurled the cloth, which turned out to be a man's linen undergarment. It was the seamless robe of Jesus.

ONCE AGAIN PILATE was staring down the same group of black-robed Jewish leaders.

"So, did any of you see the miracle of the solar eclipse the other day?" queried the governor, agitated and tense.

They all smugly nodded at Pilate.

"Of course we did, Governor," Caiaphas calmly replied.

"And you all felt the earthquake?" asked the governor.

Again they nodded knowingly.

"But I'd hardly call what happened a miracle," the high priest quickly added. "Would you, Annas?"

The chief priest shrugged innocently. "Certainly not."

"Well," Pilate continued, "do any of you have a better explanation for the things that happened when Jesus died? A solar eclipse *and* an earthquake? Both occurring on the exact day of his death? That's quite a coincidence, if you ask me."

"But, Governor, be reasonable," Annas said with a feigned chuckle. "The things you're so alarmed about were natural, ordinary occurrences. There was nothing miraculous about them in the least."

"Natural?" blurted Pilate. "Ordinary? You can't be serious."

"On the contrary, sir," interjected Datam with a similarly innocent shrug of his shoulders, "we've never been more serious in our lives. The eclipse of the Sun took place according to its usual custom, and as for the earthquake, it just so happens that because of the celestial imbalance that occurs during an eclipse, earthquakes are actually quite common."

"By the gods," Pilate sighed wearily, throwing his hands up in sheer frustration. "You people are unbelievable. Why do I even bother?"

THEN CAME THE DAY when Joseph of Arimathea arrived at the Temple at Jerusalem.

"How dare you enter this synagogue?" Summas croaked, pointing an accusatory finger. "You were a collaborator with the Nazarene!"

"Why are you so angry with me?" asked Joseph. "All I did was ask Pilate for the Man's body. I wrapped Him in clean linen, put Him in my own tomb, placed a stone at the entrance. What harm is there in any of that?"

"You had no business doing something like that in the first place," snapped Datam.

"No, you're wrong. I had every right. Have you forgotten, the Man was my nephew? I owed it to my family to see that He had a decent burial. I did what any one of you would've done in my position. You should all be ashamed of yourselves. You did everything you could to destroy a perfectly innocent Man, and to top it off, you even prayed for the guilt of His blood upon your own heads."

"How dare you accuse us of something like that!" screeched Levi.

"We never said any such thing!" Datam yelped.

"Throw him in prison, I say!" howled Summas. "At least until the Sabbath is over. Then we can deal with the likes of him, once and for all!"

Annas nodded in agreement and stepped up to Joseph. "Better make your confession now, Joseph, while you still can. For the time being, it's unlawful to harm you. That is, at least until the first day of the week comes."

"And because you're unworthy of a decent burial," Caiaphas sputtered, "we'll just be giving your corpse to the birds and beasts!"

Joseph turned to address the assembly. "You know, talk like that reminds me of Goliath bragging to David, but you priests and doctors of the Law know full well what God says by the prophet: 'Revenge is Mine, and I'll repay you with the same evil you threatened Me with.'"

"Watch yourself, Joseph," sneered Caiaphas. "You don't want to end up like your poor nephew, do you?"

"That does it, Caiaphas," snapped the otherwise implacable Joseph. "I've had it with you. I'm through being afraid of you and your threats. You may think you've gotten away with murdering Jesus, and you may think you'll get away with doing the same thing to me, but one thing's for sure: No matter what you've done or what you're planning to do, your treachery will come back to haunt all of you!"

Putting his arm around his son-in-law, Annas led the high priest several feet away from Joseph. "On second thought, Caiaphas, maybe we should rethink this. I say, we turn this matter over to Governor Pilate. Maybe he could arrange to have Joseph taken care of for us. That way we'd avoid any further involvement in this whole mess."

Joseph stared back in disbelief. "What are you people thinking? Pilate is no ally of yours. Even *he* washed his hands when you insisted that he cooperate with your plan. He flatly stated: 'I'm absolved from the blood of this innocent Man.'"

This immediately evoked an irritated scowl from Annas, who dropped his arm from around Caiaphas as both men turned back toward Joseph.

"Enough of your insolent backtalk, heretic!" Caiaphas barked. "The innocent man, as you call him, got exactly what he deserved; nothing more, nothing less."

"Yes, and then you all agreed together," Joseph countered. "'Let His blood be on us and our children!' So, as you wish, I hope you all perish forever!"

With that, the whole group flew into an incredible rage.

"This man should not be allowed to speak to us this way any longer!" screamed Datam.

"Away with him!" grunted Caiaphas.

MANHANDLED BY A PAIR of temple guards and thrown into a room without windows, Joseph fell to the ground in a dusty heap. The iron door slammed shut, and a wax seal was placed on the lock.

"SO IT'S BEEN DECIDED," Annas announced to all the priests, Levites and doctors of the Law gathered before him. "We won't consort with the foreigner Pilate anymore. Instead, we take matters into our hands this time. Agreed?"

"Agreed," they all said with one voice.

"We'll reconvene after the Sabbath," continued Annas, "at which time we'll decide this man's fate, as we see fit."

"Then, it will be unanimously decided," Caiaphas added, "how this infidel, Joseph of Arimathea, should be killed."

"So it shall be upon any man who opposes the will of the righteous," sneered Summas, "he'll go down into the pit of death, and there he'll rise no more."

"And the people said," Annas intoned.

"Amen," replied the group.

Earthquakes and Open Graves

AS THE LIGHT OF THE full Moon broke out from behind a cloudbank, it shined an eerie streak across the decimated cemetery adjacent to the Temple at Jerusalem, which now lay in complete ruins. Like the temple courtyard, the cemetery was littered with debris, with row after row of open graves surrounded by scattered piles of dirt and rock, along with its smattering of disheveled gravestones, jutting up at every angle.

Just then a tremendous flash of sunlight wiped away the darkness of night, followed by the abrupt appearance in the sky of a vast array of angelic beings, streaking about in every direction. "Glorify God above everything else!" one of the angels shouted. "Peace has finally come to mankind! You who are chained in the depths of Hades, come out!"

The ground visibly shook at the sound of that voice, and then suddenly a mound of dirt pushed up from out of one of the open graves, then some more dirt came up from another grave, and then some more. At which point many of the saints, who had been dead for so long, began to rise from these open graves, and wandering aimlessly, silently, alive in the flesh once again, they fanned out across the strangely lit landscape in no particular direction at all.

WHEN ALL OF THE Jewish authorities reconvened several days later, the Assembly Hall was buzzing with the incessant droning of dozens of frenetic conversations.

"Quiet down, gentlemen, please," Annas exclaimed, waving his hands about at the head of the group. "I realize there are many questions you all wish to address today, but first we must attend to this business concerning the heretic Joseph of Arimathea."

Caiaphas then motioned to a temple guard, who hastily left the room. Slowly but surely the group came to order as everyone there gradually disengaged with their private conversations and solemnly turned to give the chief priest their undivided attention.

Hurrying to Joseph's prison chamber, the guard saw the seal on the lock was still intact, but upon opening the door, he gasped when he found that Joseph was not inside. Running as fast as he could back to the Assembly Hall, the anxious temple guard was nearly out of breath. "Sir, the seal … on the prison door was intact … but…" As he struggled to get the words out, the guard began wheezing for air and doubled over.

"But what?" Caiaphas demanded.

Standing upright, the temple guard grimaced. "But Joseph is missing."

"What?" Annas roared. "Impossible!"

Shocked by this unexpected turn of events, the whole room resumed its cacophony of alarm and dismay, and again Annas frantically waved his hands about. "Hold on, everyone, hold on! If you'll all kindly restrain yourselves, I assure you, we will get to the bottom of this. Now, please, quiet down!"

Again, in response to his plea, the room slowly simmered down to a quiet chatter.

"Now, guard," Annas continued. "Are you absolutely certain that no one tampered with the seal on the door?"

"Not a scratch, sir."

"Well, if the seal was still intact, then how could anyone have gotten out?" wondered Caiaphas. "It makes no sense."

"We'll just see about this," grunted Annas.

But before they had time to take a step, two Roman soldiers strode into the Assembly Hall, the effect of which elicited instantaneous silence from the entire group.

Annas eyed them suspiciously. "What is the meaning of this intrusion?"

One soldier stepped forward. "Look, we just needed to talk to you people about something very important. You have nothing to fear from us, I assure you. This is not an imperial matter; it's strictly personal."

Caiaphas moved in next. "How dare you invade this sacred place with your profane presence."

The soldier put up his hand as an intended sign of conciliation. "Please, sir, we mean no disrespect, but we have a genuine mystery on our hands, and we thought someone like you could explain it, that's all."

"Who are you people, anyway?" asked Annas.

"I am Petronius, and this is Marcus. My friend and I were among the soldiers who were assigned to guard the Nazarene's body as it lay in the tomb."

"How do you expect us to help the likes of you?" groaned Caiaphas.

Then the other soldier stepped forward. "See, Petronius, I told you this was a bad idea. Let's just go."

"No, Marcus," Petronius countered. "I want a straight answer from somebody, and I want it now."

"Very well, then," relented Annas. "Tell us why you've come here."

"I want to know if you can explain something for us."

"Explain something," chided Caiaphas with an equal mixture of impatience and contempt. "Explain what?"

"Explain to me what happened to us while we were on duty at the Nazarene's tomb," insisted Petronius. "Why was there was an earthquake? Why did the night sky light up like it was daytime? Why did an angel roll the stone door away and sit on it?"

"An angel?" scoffed Caiaphas. "That's preposterous! You were probably drunk, as usual."

But Annas raised his hand to quiet his son-in-law. "Hold on, Caiaphas, hold on," he said, apparently intrigued. "Now, what did this angel look like?"

"You want to know what he looked like?" Marcus interjected, clearly still distraught from his experience. "All right, I'll tell you. He looked like he was made of lightning, but his clothes were made of snow. Care to explain that?"

"I'm telling you," snapped Caiaphas, "these men are either drunkards or lunatics."

Marcus turned to Petronius, shaking his head in disgust. "See, I told you this was how they'd react. I say we just leave. Find somebody else who'll listen to our story."

"No, wait!" Annas blurted. "Don't go. I want to know more. Tell me: What happened when the angel appeared? What did you do?"

"We didn't *do* anything," replied Petronius, thoroughly frustrated. "How could we? We were scared to death. We just collapsed."

"But then something happened after that?" pressed Annas.

"Yes," Marcus insisted, "that's what we've been trying to tell you."

"Then," Petronius continued, "the angel began speaking to the women at His tomb. 'Don't be frightened,' he told them. 'I know you're looking for Jesus. They crucified Him, but He rose again exactly as He explained to you beforehand. Just look inside the tomb and see for yourselves.'"

Caiaphas rolled his eyes in disgust. "Oh, please. How long do you expect us to entertain such nonsense?"

"Was that all the angel said?" ventured Annas.

"Then he told the women to go and tell His disciples He'd risen from the dead," said Marcus. "And that very soon He'd be meeting them in Galilee, just as He'd told them."

Annas and Caiaphas exchanged a disturbed look, as did everyone else in the room.

"Please, follow us, if you don't mind," Annas said to the soldiers.

Then Annas and Caiaphas led the two Roman soldiers from the Assembly Hall and into another room, closing the door behind them. Now there were just the four of them standing there, two black-robed priests squaring off with two uniformed centurions.

"So, tell us," insisted Annas, "who were these women speaking to the angel?"

"And *why* didn't you seize them when you had the chance?" blurted Caiaphas.

"We don't know who the women were," Petronius replied. "And how do you expect us to grab someone while we're flat on our faces? We just told you. We all collapsed, we were so scared."

"As the Lord lives," yelped Caiaphas, "we don't believe a word of what you're telling us. We think you two stole the body of Jesus, and concocted this insane story to divert attention from this fact."

Petronius shook his head in disbelief. "But what would we gain by doing that? What possible motive would we have in stealing His body?"

"How should we know what goes through the mind of pagans like yourselves," said Caiaphas. "Blackmail, I suppose. If word ever got out that the body of Jesus was missing, then it might lend credence to this absurd movement of theirs."

"Undoubtedly!" Annas added emphatically. "A rumor like that could quickly fan the flames of insurrection. You know how volatile these heretics are, what with their silly superstitions. It's not at all hard to believe you might steal the body and blackmail us in exchange for its return."

"Blackmail," scoffed Marcus. "That's crazy. We didn't come here to blackmail you. We don't want your money; we want answers."

"Then I'm afraid you've come to the wrong place," Caiaphas replied, as contemptuous as ever.

"That figures," Marcus grumbled. "What did I tell you, Petronius? You can't reason with these people. When they saw Jesus performing His miracles with their own eyes, they still didn't believe in Him. You didn't really expect them to believe our story, did you?"

"You know, you people were right when you said, 'The Lord lives,'" quipped Petronius. "The Lord really does live! Because we just heard how you imprisoned the man who buried Jesus, but when you opened his cell, he was missing, too!"

"Never mind that!" snapped Caiaphas. "That doesn't concern you."

"Oh," exclaimed Petronius, "but it does concern us."

"How?" queried Annas.

"Well, you expect us to deliver Jesus' body to you, don't you?" Petronius asked.

"In fact you'll be made to do so," snickered Caiaphas. "Or else you'll suffer the consequences."

"Consequences?" echoed Marcus. "What consequences?"

"If you don't produce his body in due time," Caiaphas continued, "then we'll have no choice but to see to it that the Roman authorities have you arrested for treason."

"What?" groaned a stunned Petronius. "Why would the authorities consider the theft of a body grounds for treason?"

Caiaphas pressed on, like a ravenous wolf closing in on its defenseless prey. "Because that theft would be in direct connection with a civil uprising that seeks to undermine Roman authority."

"That, or dereliction of duty," Annas interjected, "considering the fact that if you didn't steal the body yourselves, then you at least aided and abetted the disciples who did. Either way, your only recourse is to produce his body … or else."

"Fine," Petronius replied. "But first you have to produce Joseph, whom *you* were guarding. Then we'll be glad to produce Jesus for you."

"Oh, we'll produce Joseph, all right," insisted Caiaphas. "You just make sure you produce Jesus! Besides, Joseph is probably in his own city of Arimathea right now."

"Well, if Joseph is in Arimathea," said Marcus, "then Jesus is already in Galilee. I'm sure I heard the angel tell the women He'd meet them there."

Annas and Caiaphas exchanged another concerned look.

"Would you gentlemen please excuse us for a moment?" asked Annas.

The soldiers dutifully nodded and stepped out into the hallway, where the two men stared at one another for several moments before Marcus finally broke the silence. "Well, this couldn't be going any worse. What a complete waste of time this turned out to be."

"I'm sorry I dragged you into this mess, Marcus," replied Petronius, shaking his head in exasperation. "What was I thinking? As if this bunch would've cooperated with us."

Spying both directions down the hallway, Marcus continued quietly, "I say we get out of here while the getting's good. I've had it with these pious hypocrites. There's no telling what they'll threaten us with next in the name of their precious god."

Back inside the room, Annas handed Caiaphas a leather bag and sighed heavily, "I don't see that we have any other recourse at this point. This whole thing is getting out of hand, I tell you. If any of this becomes public knowledge, then everybody might start believing in this Jesus, and we'll never hear the end of it as long as we live." Dreadfully concerned, Annas headed for the door. "See to it these soldiers understand how they're to save their own skins. Instruct them well, Caiaphas; we're all counting on you."

"Of course, Father; I'll take care of everything."

Almost to the door, Annas turned back. "I told you to never call me that."

"Yes, sir."

Annas then left the room and encountered the two soldiers in the hallway. "The high priest will see you again," he said, nodding politely. "Good day, gentlemen."

Doing their best to conceal their growing contempt, the soldiers nodded back and reluctantly went back in to see Caiaphas.

"Now, unless you men want us to report you to your superiors," Caiaphas continued, "you'd better start cooperating with us. Agreed?"

Petronius and Marcus looked at one another for several intense moments, then returned their attention to Caiaphas and nodded.

"It seems we don't have much choice in the matter," Petronius replied.

"Good," said Caiaphas with a smugly satisfied smile, and then he handed Petronius the leather bag. "Then take this to seal our deal."

Looking inside, Petronius was dumbfounded. "There's a lot of money in here. What if we're unable to return the body for you after all? Then what?"

"Look, between you and me," said the high priest, lowering his voice as if he were worried someone might overhear him, "I don't really care if you did or didn't steal the body. That isn't important."

"Really?" Marcus asked, momentarily taken aback.

"No, of course not. Who cares if Roman soldiers stole the body of Jesus? What good is that to me? But, if you help us convince everyone that his *disciples* stole the body, then that would provide a far more viable solution to our problem. You follow my meaning?"

Both men tacitly nodded.

"Good. Then off with the both of you; time to get to work."

"But what if Pilate gets wind of this?" queried Petronius. "What if he finds out we made a deal with you?"

Caiaphas shrugged unconcerned. "So what? If Pilate hears about it, then there'll be a reward in it for him as well."

NOT FIFTY FEET DOWN the road, Marcus stopped dead in his tracks and stared pathetically at the bag in his hand. "So tell me, Petronius; we're not really going to cooperate with that bunch of hypocrites just because we took a lot of money from them, are we?"

Petronius turned and stepped up to his comrade. "Of course not, Marcus."

"I knew it," Marcus said with a sardonic grin.

"We're going to do it because we want to save our sorry necks," grumbled Petronius, who then spun around and started off again, leaving Marcus just standing there as the grin on his face slowly turned to a frown.

DARKNESS NEARLY enveloped a cemetery dimly illuminated by the light of a Moon that was shrouded in clouds. It was a faint light that cascaded across the stone-littered landscape, creating pockets of visibility, interrupted here and there by a haphazard shadow, darting past a disheveled tombstone.

"Filthy, good-for-nothing vandals," a gravedigger muttered as he and a fellow worker were busy shoveling dirt back into an open grave. "Don't they have anything better to do than cause trouble for working stiffs like us?"

"Ah, quit your complaining, will you," said the other man. "We get paid the same whether we dig graves up or fill them back in. Makes no difference to me."

Pausing in his work, the first man stared back at his partner as though he were about to respond, but suddenly he was distracted by another one of those indiscriminate shadows. "Hey, what was that?" Dropping his shovel, the man peered into the streaky blackness.

"What?" asked the second man.

Wiping the sweat from his brow, the first man called into the night. "You there! What are you up to? This is private property, you hear me?"

Leaving the gravesite, the man ventured toward the moving shadows, followed by his associate. One shadow became two, and then two became four.

"Hey, what do you people think you're doing here at this hour?" the first man shouted. "Get out of here, right now!"

"Why should we leave this place?" asked a sad voice from out of the darkness.

"What's that?" blurted the first man, who turned in the direction of the voice with his curious eyes squinting in the moonlight. "Who's there? Who said that?"

Then, from a different part of the cemetery, another voice called out. "I did."

"Wh—*Who's* that?" stammered the second man, nervously whirling about in the direction of the new voice. "What are you doing here?"

"This is our home," said still another voice. "We belong here."

"Don't be ridiculous!" the first man growled.

A peculiar sound of scratching began to invade the intermittent darkness, and the two men craned their necks in an effort to discern its source.

"What is that noise?" continued the first man.

"It sounds like chicken scratching," replied the second.

"Chickens? You idiot. This is a cemetery, not a chicken farm. Whatever it is, though," said the first man, who started toward the sound, leaving the second man standing there, "I aim to find out."

"Why not wait till morning to find out? Why do we have to do it now?"

"Help me," a plaintive voice said from beyond the pale of visibility. "Won't somebody please help me?"

As the first man disappeared into the relative darkness, the second man looked nervously about and muttered, "Help you? Who's going to help us?" And not wanting to be left behind, he darted after his friend. "Hey, wait for me."

The sound of chicken scratching then became the familiar sound of dirt being piled upon dirt, and when the first man made his way past several mangled tombstones, he stopped and stared aghast at the ground. "What in the world are you doing?"

Catching up with his friend, the second man stood alongside him, and he, too, gawked at what he saw. "Is that what I think it is?"

In utter disbelief, the two gravediggers stood in the pale moonlight, watching as a sad, little man, lying in an open grave, was desperately trying to cover himself with dirt. With the lower half of his body already covered, he pulled more and more handfuls over himself. Noticing the two men staring down at him, he looked up and murmured, "You there, kind sirs, won't you please help me?"

"Help you?" wondered the first man, who flashed his friend a disturbed look, then returned to address the man in the grave. "Help you do what?"

"Why, help me bury myself again, of course."

A Rumor in the Land

ONE HOT AND HAZY afternoon, a priest, a Levite and a schoolteacher were walking together through the dusty streets of Jerusalem.

"How much longer to the Temple, Phinees?" asked the schoolteacher, nearly out of breath.

"It won't be long now, Ada," the priest replied.

"If I'd known it was going to be such an arduous journey," said Ada, who stopped to wipe the sweat from his brow, "I might have reconsidered coming all the way from Galilee by foot."

Phinees stopped with his two companions. "I'm sorry you have such delicate sensibilities, Professor, but you knew what you were getting yourself into when you agreed to come along. Besides, what better way to investigate the rumors we've been hearing about the Nazarene?"

"Naturally, you would be the one to say something like that," Ada replied, "what with so many of your temples in ruins after the earthquake. So why didn't you put your back into restoring your own house first before dragging us out here like this?"

"You know very well why, Ada," said Phinees, suddenly perturbed, "because of what we've seen with our own eyes. Somebody has to say something—*do something*. Or are you having second thoughts about why we came?"

"It's not that I'm having second thoughts," insisted Ada, who turned to his fellow traveler, the Levite, for moral support. "Please, Ageus, make him understand. I'm simply not used to such deprivation. A month ago, I was in a classroom teaching a bunch of kids about Jewish history. Now here I am traipsing about the countryside in search of stories about body snatchers and the living dead. Needless to say, I'm just a bit out of my comfort zone."

"And not a moment too soon, if you ask me," blurted Phinees.

"Don't be so hard on him, Phinees," Ageus interjected. "Ada is right. None of us are used to this sort of thing. We're scholars, for Heaven's sake, men of learning, not adventurers. I just hope this ordeal is worth all the effort."

"Of course it's worth it," snapped Phinees. "Look, this is no time to lose our nerve. Not when there's so much at stake."

"I couldn't agree with you more, my friend," Ageus continued. "But I don't think it would help matters if we were to turn on each other in the process of pursuing such a noble cause. After all, *we* are not the enemy."

Suddenly reconsidering, Phinees thought better of it. "Your point is well taken, Ageus," he said with a decidedly apologetic tone. "I'm sorry, Ada; you're right. This journey *is* more than we're accustomed to. Forgive me, won't you?"

"Of course, Phinees," replied Ada. "I forgive you."

"Good," Ageus said, "because I can't wait to get to the bottom of all this. Considering everything we've seen, I think we can all agree that the disciples didn't steal His body."

"Of course not, no," scoffed Ada. "Not after what we've seen."

"Fine," Phinees continued, "then I suggest we proceed to the Temple. I'm sure the high priest will be very interested in hearing our version of the story."

AS SOON AS THE TRIO arrived to the Temple at Jerusalem, they began looking around.

Before too long, Summas, the priest, intercepted the men in the entry hall. "Pardon me, gentlemen," he began suspiciously. "Can I help you with something?"

Phinees stepped forward to speak for the group. "Yes, of course, sir. Please forgive the intrusion."

"Not at all. I see you're also a priest of the Most High. Welcome, I am Summas."

"And I am Phinees of Galilee." Then he motioned to his fellow travelers. "And these men are also from Galilee: Ageus, a Levite, and Ada, a schoolteacher."

Summas nodded, and they, in turn, nodded back. "Welcome, gentlemen. I don't wish to appear rude, but could you tell me why you've come here all the way from Galilee, unannounced like this?"

"We're here to discuss the rumors concerning Jesus of Nazareth," said Phinees.

Summas blanched. "Rumors? What rumors?"

"The ones about His disciples supposedly stealing His body."

"What about them?" wondered Summas, shrugging his shoulders. "His disciples stole the body. What more is there to say?"

"Well, there's quite a lot more to say, actually," Phinees insisted. "That's just it. That's why we came all this way."

Summas seemed both confused and dismayed as he scanned the resolute faces of the three men standing before him. "You mean to say you've come all this way to talk about the body being stolen? Is that what you're telling me?"

"No, no, no," said Phinees, emphatically shaking his head. "His disciples *couldn't* have stolen His body. That's what we're trying to tell you."

"And how could you possibly know something like that?"

Looking both directions, Phinees cautiously leaned forward. "Because we've all recently seen Jesus with our own eyes, that's how," he whispered.

"What?" asked a smitten Summas. "Y—y—*you can't* be serious." His eyes darted to the other two men who both nodded affirmatively.

"It's true," insisted Ageus. "We really have seen Him."

"In the flesh, sir," Ada added, "looking as healthy as any of us standing right here."

"Now, please," continued Phinees, "can we just talk to the high priest about all this?"

Summas glared at the men for several moments. "Wait here," was all he said, and whirling about, he started down a corridor.

PHINEES, AGEUS AND Ada stood expectantly before Caiaphas, along with Annas and the rest of their black-robed colleagues.

"You what?" asked an incredulous Annas.

"We saw Jesus of Nazareth, alive and well, in Galilee," Phinees said. "You remember? The Man you crucified? He was talking to His disciples on the Mount of Olives."

"Impossible," groaned Caiaphas. "What do you take us for? A bunch of naïve schoolchildren?"

"The man you're talking about has been dead and buried for almost two months now," snapped Datam. "Haven't you heard? His disciples stole the body!"

"But that's where you're wrong, sir," Ageus interjected. "We saw Him for ourselves, gathered with His disciples, as though nothing had changed at all. He ate with them, drank with them, told them to pick up right where He left off. 'Go out into the whole world and preach the gospel to everyone,' He said. 'Baptize them in the Name of the Father, the Son and the Holy Spirit, and whoever has faith in your teachings will be saved.'"

"Then, sometime after that," added Ada, "we saw Him ascend to Heaven."

Cut to the quick, the entire assembly roared in protest.

"Blasphemers!" squealed Datam. "Heretics!"

Raising his hands, Annas stood tall to quell the outburst. "Silence, everyone, silence," he said as the assembly slowly simmered down. "Give glory to the God of Israel, gentlemen, and make your confession before Him. I'm warning you three, you'd better start telling the real truth before it's too late."

"By the God of Abraham, Isaac and Jacob," said Phinees. "We *have* told you the truth. In fact, if we *didn't* stand by our testimony, we'd be guilty of sin."

Stepping forward, Caiaphas held up *The Book of the Law*. "You will stop declaring these things you're saying about Jesus! Return to your synagogues and never say another word about this to anyone. Do you hear me?"

"But we can't," said Phinees with a lamentable sigh.

"You can't, or you won't?" Caiaphas growled.

"We can't," insisted Phinees. "Our synagogues were destroyed in the recent series of earthquakes. You know that as well as we do."

"I say, flog them for blasphemy," Summas barked, "and send them away in the dust of their own infamy!"

"Is that really what you men want?" said Caiaphas, glaring coldly at the trio.

"Of course not," Ada sputtered. "But you can't punish us for speaking the truth."

"Oh, but they can, Ada," replied Phinees. "Don't you see? It's what they do to men who are willing to stand up to their tyranny of lies."

"Enough already!" cried Annas. "You men come with us so we can discuss this matter in private."

ANNAS AND CAIAPHAS were squaring off again with their adversaries in the inner chamber; just them and the three visitors from Galilee.

"Now, gentlemen, before things spiral completely out of control," cooed Annas, "let's be reasonable. We're not barbarians like our Roman usurpers. We're pious men, one and all, am I right?"

Together, the three men nodded.

"Good, then above all," Annas continued, in his most conciliatory tone of voice, "men like us should seek the greater good of our people. Agreed?"

Again the trio nodded affirmatively.

"Of course," said Annas as he motioned to Caiaphas, who stepped away and picked up a leather bag. "Then why don't we try to put this nonsense behind us. What's done is done. Yes, mistakes have been made, but laying blame on our own kind won't do us or our congregations any good."

Caiaphas returned and handed the bag to his father-in-law.

Annas continued with a smile. "What we need is to heal the wounds of our people who've been oppressed by the boot of Rome, because in the end, Caesar is our enemy, not some deluded soul who thought he could save us from foreign occupation. Am I right?"

Confused by his smooth talk, the trio exchanged nervous looks amongst themselves.

"What are you saying?" wondered Ada. "You're not going to flog us?"

"Of course we don't want to have you flogged," Annas replied. "But neither can we run the risk of you three needlessly inflaming another insurrection in our fair city. Certainly you can understand that, can't you?"

"So what do you propose to do with us?" asked Ageus, obviously suspicious.

"I propose you drop this matter entirely and return to your homes in the spirit of peace," Annas replied and then handed the bag to Ada. "No questions asked."

Looking inside, Ada was clearly surprised. "*Money*? And so much of it. But why?"

"To keep us quiet, that's why," Phinees said with a steely tone.

"What?" blurted Annas. "Heavens, no! It's for your rebuilding efforts, with a little extra for traveling expenses, for your journey home. Naturally, it behooves us as fellow Jews to see to it that our satellite synagogues are restored as quickly as possible. Am I right?"

The trio again exchanged furtive glances.

"Well, I have to admit, he does make a good point," said Ageus, however reluctantly.

"Then it's settled," Annas continued. "You'll return to Galilee. You'll start the process of healing your communities in such dire need of repair, and we'll never need to discuss another word about who did what to whom. Agreed?"

Ada and Ageus then looked to Phinees for his response. After much consideration, he finally relented with an amicable nod. "Fine," said Phinees, "if that's the way it has to be. We'll take the money; but only because the people of Galilee are in such need of it."

"Naturally," insisted Annas, who flashed a subtle smile at his son-in-law. "And just to show you men there are no hard feelings, we'll even have escorts sent along with you to insure your safe passage out of Jerusalem."

CARRYING THEIR HEFTY bag of money, the reluctant trio made their way toward the city limits, escorted by a pair of temple guards, and as the three men continued their journey, they did not say a word to each other.

BEYOND THE OUTSKIRTS of Jerusalem, Ada exhaled a sigh of relief. "Wow, that was close. Thank God we got out of there in one piece."

Phinees glared at him with an angry scowl. "Thank God? What makes you so sure it was God Who rescued us from those men?"

Ada, stung by his question, shrugged innocently. "I'm sorry I brought it up. Just an expression, I guess. I didn't mean anything by it. What I meant was—"

"Don't worry about it, Ada," interjected Ageus. "Phinees isn't mad at you; he's angry with himself. I am, too, if the truth be told."

"Well, it's a little late for that, don't you think?" snapped Phinees. "Frankly, I don't know how I'll ever look my congregation in the eye again. I had my chance to stand up for the truth, and I failed. I failed my calling, and I failed God. I'll never be the same again, *ever*."

"But think of all the good that can be done with the money," Ada asked plaintively. "Doesn't that make up for any of it?"

"Have you lost your mind?" blurted Phinees. "Is that why you think I agreed to take the money?"

"Naturally," Ada replied. "Why else take it?"

"Because in the eyes of pious men like Annas and Caiaphas, heretics like us are deserving of far more than a good flogging."

Confused and frustrated, Ada turned to Ageus with a woeful look in his eyes. "I don't understand. What's Phinees talking about?"

"He's saying that, according to our Law, flogging is merely a prelude for anyone accused of blasphemy. After that, if the heretic refuses to recant his testimony, there's only one course of action left for the high priest."

"And do you have any idea what that might be, Ada?" asked Phinees.

The schoolteacher shook his head. "Of course not, Phinees. You know I'm just a history professor; you two are the theologians."

"Then tell him, Ageus. Tell the good professor what was in store for us if we didn't take the money and scurry away like rats leaving a sinking ship."

Sadly, slowly, Ageus continued. "Our Law states that the blasphemer who refuses to recant is to be stoned until dead."

"B—*but*, I..." Ada stammered, trying his best to offer up some sort of reply, but seeing the look on both his companions' faces, he hesitated.

Thoroughly disgusted with himself, Phinees whirled around and marched away, leaving the two men standing there.

"Don't worry about him, Ada. He just needs some time alone to straighten things out in his head; in his soul, for that matter. We all do."

"I just wish there was something I could do to make up for it all," Ada mumbled pathetically.

"Who knows, Professor, maybe someday you'll get that chance," Ageus said with a subtle shrug and a knowing smile. "But until that day ... keep praying to God that He helps you recognize that opportunity when it comes." Then, he turned and started after Phinees, leaving a disheartened Ada standing there just shaking his head.

NO LONGER TRAVELING side by side as they once had been, the three friends were now walking in single file; each one several yards behind the other. Eventually, they encountered a beggar standing along the roadside. Phinees walked by him first.

"Please, kind sir," said the beggar, with outstretched hands, "you look like a man who might have pity on a poor, wayward soul like me. May I bother you for a handout? Anything to help feed an empty belly; mine and my family's, I mean."

For a moment, it appeared that as Phinees walked past the man he had not even heard him. Still, Ageus, followed by Ada, continued forward, headed right for the beggar, but then Phinees stopped in his tracks and turned around. With an odd look in his eye, he smiled strangely at his two companions, who were fast approaching him.

"Alms, you say?" asked Phinees.

The beggar's eyes lit up expectantly. "Why, yes, sir, that's right. Even the smallest sum would be most appreciated."

"Then today is your lucky day, my good man," Phinees said as he flashed a grin at his friends, who held their collective breaths. With eyes as big as saucers, they watched as Phinees then handed the moneybag to the beggar.

With utter gratitude, the man looked at Phinees. "I and my family thank you, sir. God bless you for your generosity."

"No, my friend, it's you who is to be thanked today." Satisfied with himself, Phinees turned and walked away, leaving the beggar quite perplexed.

"Me?" the man asked. "Why me? What did I ever do for you?"

By then, Ageus had made his way to where the beggar stood, bag in hand. With a sardonic smile, he patted him on the back as he walked by and said, "Today, my good man, you've helped redeem the souls of three wretched sinners. How do you like that?"

Thoroughly confused and a little intrigued, the beggar opened the bag to see what was inside. He gaped at its contents and sank to his knees, weeping at his good fortune, and still without so much as a word between them, the trio continued on their journey home.

A Sword to Pierce the Heart

ONCE AGAIN ANNAS and Caiaphas called the Jewish leaders together for a private session, and many of them had the most lamentable expressions on their faces.

"Can you believe something like this has happened in Jerusalem?" Cyrus moaned.

"Could there be any truth to what these Galileans are saying?" asked Nepthalim.

"Of course not," Annas assured them. "Just a lot of wishful thinking. That's all there is to it; believe me."

"But the Roman soldiers," pressed Alexander. "What about their sworn testimony? Certainly they aren't looking forward to the resurrection of the dead, are they?"

Annas shrugged his shoulders. "But why should we even believe what a couple of Roman soldiers told us? Just because they *said* an angel rolled the stone away?"

Caiaphas nodded in agreement. "No one pays any attention to foreigners. And besides, how do we even know they were actually the soldiers who guarded his tomb? After all, they did accept an awful lot of money from us."

"That's right," Annas added, "and we know they're already telling everyone the story exactly as we instructed them."

"So what more do you need, gentlemen?" asked Caiaphas with a confident wave of his hand. "Relax. Go home to your families. I assure you all: Nothing more will come from any of this. Trust me."

Finally convinced, the group exhaled a collective sigh of relief.

BACK IN THE TEMPLE, Nicodemus was again addressing the grim-faced assembly of black-robed authorities. "Greetings, men of Israel, I'm sure by now you've all heard the latest news. Three of the most upstanding men you could ever hope to meet have swore by the Law of God that they recently saw Jesus speaking with His disciples on the Mount of Olives, and then saw Him ascend to Heaven."

"Nothing but hearsay, if you ask me," Summas muttered.

"But why do you say that? None of this should seem unusual to anyone here. Doesn't the Scripture already teach us that Elijah, the prophet, was taken up to Heaven?"

"That was different," grunted Summas.

Growing impatient, Caiaphas asked, "And what does Elijah have to do with any of this, anyway?"

"Well, if you recall," Nicodemus continued, "when the sons of the prophets asked Elisha where Elijah had gone, he told them he'd been taken up to Heaven, but those sons replied: 'Maybe the Spirit of God carried Elijah into one of the mountains of Israel.' And they insisted that Elisha search with them for Elijah; but they never did find him, did they?"

"I'm afraid I still fail to see where you're going with all this," said Annas.

"What I'm saying is: Maybe you should send some of your own men to look for Jesus. What if the Spirit of God carried Him away like Elijah? Maybe you'll find Him wandering around in the mountains of Israel somewhere. Did you ever think of that?"

SO A GROUP OF MEN proceeded to do exactly that. They searched for Jesus throughout the hills of Judea, but even after a great deal of time and effort was spent searching the countryside, they never did find Him, either.

"WE LOOKED EVERYWHERE, sir, but we didn't find Jesus," one searcher told Annas and Caiaphas. "Funny, though, we did find Joseph in his hometown of Arimathea. Imagine that."

"Excuse me?" Annas mumbled. "What did you say?"

"I said, we did find Joseph, though."

"The man who escaped from our prison?" asked a dumbfounded Caiaphas. "You found *that* Joseph?"

"One in the same, sir, yes."

WHEN THE JEWISH leaders came together again, Annas and Caiaphas were looking rather disheartened, as was the rest of the group.

"Gentlemen, it would hardly be an understatement to say this is a most unfortunate turn of events," began Annas. "If Joseph starts telling people about the way we treated him, things could get really ugly for us."

"Why not just apprehend him and bring before the tribunal again?" asked Summas.

"On what charge?" Annas replied.

But Summas shrugged his shoulders. "I don't know."

"No, my friends," continued Annas, half to himself, half to those who were there in the room. "I'm afraid the precarious nature of our position demands that things be handled in a much more diplomatic manner this time around."

ANNAS PRIVATELY dictated a letter to his scribe. "Hello, dear Joseph: We hope all is well with you and your family, and as shocking as it may be to you, we are writing this letter to inform you that we have had a change of heart concerning our position. After all, considering the extraordinary nature of your escape from prison, what else could we do? What we did was malicious, unwarranted and, most regretfully, done without thinking things through. Obviously the Lord Himself delivered you from our evil designs, and obviously we were wrong about you in every conceivable way. We now realize we have offended both God and you, and were hoping you might grant us a visit so we can personally make amends for the way we treated you. Take care of yourself, Joseph. You're a man respected by everyone. Most sincerely, Annas, chief priest of the Temple at Jerusalem."

GATHERING SEVEN OF Joseph's friends, Caiaphas then gave each of them a copy of the same letter. "The next time any of you sees Joseph of Arimathea," he told the men, "I want you to salute him in friendship and give him your letter."

WHILE VISITING Arimathea, one of Joseph's friends saw him walking home. Running up to him, the man hugged Joseph and handed him his copy of the letter. Joseph quickly read it.

"Bless God," Joseph muttered. "It's a miracle."

"Why?" asked his friend. "What does it say?"

"I can hardly believe my eyes," said Joseph as he lowered the letter and gazed back at his friend in sheer disbelief. "The authorities in Jerusalem want me to make an appearance before their tribunal so they can officially make amends for how they treated me."

"You're right," his friend said with a smirk. "That is a miracle."

AS JOSEPH APPROACHED Jerusalem, a small group of black-robed Jewish authorities approached him.

"Hello, Joseph," exclaimed Summas, "it's so good to see you again. Everyone is very excited you've come back to us today!"

"We're so sorry for how we acted before," Datam said. "Will you ever forgive us?"

"Of course, Datam, I forgive you," replied Joseph. "God bless you, Summas, it's good to see you, too!"

"BY THE GOD OF ISRAEL," Annas said to Joseph, who was again standing before the austere group of Jewish authorities, "do you solemnly swear to tell the truth, the whole truth and nothing but the truth, so help you God?"

"I do, yes, of course," insisted Joseph. "You all know that."

"Good," said Caiaphas, "because we've been very anxious to get to the bottom of this mystery, Joseph. Are you ready to answer our questions to the best of your ability?"

"Certainly. I'd be glad to. What would you like to know?"

"Well, naturally," Annas continued, "we'd like to know how you got out of the prison cell we put you in. Did you bribe the guards?"

"No, of course not."

"Then how on Earth did you escape?" wondered Annas. "Until now, we considered that cell to be impenetrable."

Caiaphas continued. "So tell us, Joseph. How'd you do it?"

"And remember," added Annas, "God is your witness."

"Oh, you locked me up good and tight, all right, but sometime in the night while I was praying, Jesus appeared in the room, bright as the Sun, and I fell to my knees, terrified."

"You poor, deluded fool," Caiaphas muttered. "Here we go again."

"Hold on, Caiaphas," urged Annas. "Let the man speak. What happened next, Joseph?"

"Well, then Jesus took me by the hand and pulled me to my feet."

Caiaphas pressed on, sarcastic as ever. "You mean the Jesus who appeared to you as bright as the Sun?"

"Yes, that's the One."

"All right, then, Joseph," Annas said condescendingly, as if he were speaking to a confused child. "So this luminous Jesus pulled you to your feet. Then what?"

"Well, then, a dew sprinkled over my entire body, so Jesus wiped my face. He kissed my cheek and said, 'Don't be frightened, Joseph. It's just Me.' So I looked at Him, and said, 'Elijah? Is that you?' But He answered: 'No, I'm not Elijah. I'm Jesus of Nazareth. You buried My body, remember?' Then, in the twinkling of an eye, He took me to the tomb where I'd placed Him. He showed me the linen clothes I'd buried Him in, and finally, I realized it was Jesus."

"Uh, excuse me," Caiaphas interjected impatiently, "this is all very fascinating, but what do the delusional ravings of a madman have to do with our investigation? We just want to know: How did you get out of that prison?"

"Look, I'm sorry I can't do a better job of explaining any of this, Caiaphas," shrugged Joseph. "Really I am. But all I know is: One moment, I was sitting in prison, awaiting my doom, and the next, Jesus was with me in my cell. He reached out His hand, and just like that, we were in His tomb. Then, before I even had time to think about what had just happened, we were in my hometown of Arimathea."

"Just like that, eh?" snorted Caiaphas. "You took his hand, and *poof*, you were here and then you were there, and then suddenly you were home again. Is that about it?"

"Yes, that's about it. Again I do apologize if I can't tell you anything more than that."

"Is that all?" Annas continued, maintaining his conciliatory tone. "Did he at least leave you with some sort of message?"

Joseph thought about it for several moments, trying to push the memory back into view. "Yes, now that you mention it, I believe so. He did tell me something important."

"What?" asked Annas.

"He said, 'Everything is going to be all right, Joseph. He Who comes in the Name of the Lord is blessed, and now it's time for Me to go visit My disciples in Galilee.'"

The priests, Levites and doctors of the Law were all so astonished that several of them fell face-down on the ground like dead men.

"What is going on?" Datam groaned. "How could something like this be happening in Jerusalem? After all, this Jesus had ordinary parents like all the rest of us, didn't he?"

Then a Levite stepped forward. "Oh, yes, he's as human as any of us, all right. I personally knew many of His relatives. They were all very devout people, always bringing sacrifices and burnt offerings to the Temple at Jerusalem."

"Thank you, Mattathias, for coming forward," said Annas. "Is there anything else you can add? I mean besides the fact that this man's family used to visit the Temple here."

"Please, sir," Caiaphas interjected painfully. "Haven't we already gone over this before? What good could possibly come from any further investigation into this matter?"

"Wait just a moment," insisted Annas. "I understand your reluctance, Caiaphas, but in this case I must insist on hearing more from Mattathias. Now, do continue, if you please, Mattathias. You said you were personally acquainted with the Nazarene's family. Can tell us about any firsthand experiences you might have had with them?"

Mattathias nodded thoughtfully and began, "Well, sir, I can, yes. Let me see: Well now, as I recall, on one occasion, I do remember the time His mother Mary brought Jesus here, when He was still a baby. Yes, that's right. She brought Him here to be blessed by Simeon, the high priest at the time. That was when I overheard Simeon saying, 'Lord, Now You can let me die because I've finally seen the salvation You've prepared for everyone, the Glory of Your people, Israel, and a Light to the Gentiles.'"

"You don't say?" Annas mused.

"Yes, sir, that's what he said all right. Then, a little later, I heard Simeon saying to Mary: 'Let me tell you about this son of yours, Mary. He's been appointed for the rise and fall of the multitude, and He'll be a sign that many will speak against.'"

"I see," murmured Annas, who flashed a furtive glance at the disgruntled Caiaphas. "Is that all?"

"Oh, and something about a sword."

"A sword?" Caiaphas asked. "What about a sword?"

"I don't know for sure," replied Mattathias, struggling to retrieve the elusive memory from the shadows of his mind. "But I do seem to remember overhearing Simeon saying something; yes, I remember now. He was warning Mary."

"Warning Mary?" asked Annas. "What would he warn Mary about?"

"Yes, as I recall, he warned her that not only would a sword pierce her heart but that the same sword would also reveal the intentions of many other people in the process. Yes, that was it!" Mattathias stared back at his interrogators with the most peculiar look on his face. "Do you have any idea what that could have meant?"

Annas and Caiaphas exchanged an anxious look.

"How should we know," shrugged Caiaphas. "Sounds like the ravings of a lunatic, if you ask me."

The Mysteries of the Resurrection

STRUTTING BACK AND forth like a proud peacock, Annas was again addressing the entire assembly of austere Jewish authorities. "Well, gentlemen, once more we are reconvened in an attempt to deal with the events that continue to plague our city. So I ask every one of you here today: How do we, as a body of pious men, plan to respond to the outrageous allegations of men like Joseph of Arimathea, men like the three Galileans, who all insist they've seen the Nazarene alive and well, even after his supposed demise, not to mention the sworn testimony of the Galileans who say they saw Him ascend into Heaven? Who among us cares to offer his wisdom as to how we can handle these disturbing reports? Anyone?"

One man hesitantly stood to his feet. "Not that I would ever presume to advise this learned group, sir, but I would like to mention one thing in passing."

"Naturally, Cyrus, if you'd be so kind."

"Well, as we're already well aware of: Our Law states that everything should be confirmed by the testimony of two or three witnesses. So, taking this admonition into consideration, what do we know so far? Since our earliest days as children we've all heard the stories of men like Enoch and Elijah, men who have pleased the Lord and were transported to Heaven as a result."

"That's right, Cyrus, yes," added Datam. "And now, there's this man Jesus. Every day, more and more people keep coming forward to testify that they saw him ascend to Heaven as well."

"But that was then, and this is now," Summas insisted. "Certainly you can't expect us to believe there's any similarity between this Nazarene and two of the greatest heroes in our history."

"But why not?" asked a confident voice that filtered in from the wings of the crowd.

The entire group turned toward the voice, just as Joseph of Arimathea strode into the room. "Why not, gentlemen? Certainly a Man Who's performed the kind of miracles that Jesus of Nazareth has performed deserves to be held in the same regard as an Enoch or an Elijah, if not more so."

"Not you again," Caiaphas grumbled. "Who let you in? I demand that this man be removed from our solemn proceedings, immediately."

"Oh, Caiaphas," said Joseph with a condescending shake of his head, "how will you ever discover the real truth of this matter, if you're always trying to extinguish any opposing view to your preconceived notions? What are you so afraid of?"

"I am afraid of nothing; least of all you."

With an amicable nod, Joseph then turned to the group, just brimming with anticipation. "See, everyone? I'm nothing to be afraid of. Then I'll proceed, if you gentlemen don't mind."

To a man, everyone in the audience nodded, much to the chagrin of the high priest.

"So, as Cyrus has just astutely pointed out, there's nothing inconsistent about the reports concerning the risen Christ and previous accounts we've all read about in the Word of God. Just because the stories you're being told about Jesus are hard to believe, doesn't mean they should be disregarded simply because they don't conform to your expectations, does it? Of course not. Because I'm here today to tell you, no, I'm here to *insist*, with all sincerity, that these reports are absolutely true!"

"But it's a hoax, I tell you!" blasted Caiaphas.

"A hoax?" Joseph replied with an exasperated toss of his head. "You still think this whole thing is just a hoax? Even after all the testimony of your own people to the contrary?"

"Come now, Joseph, be reasonable," cooed Annas, "You can't really expect us to believe what you people are telling us. Enoch and Elijah, yes. These men were well known among our people to be great and holy men, but this Jesus was a common criminal. Certainly you don't expect us to believe that God would receive this scoundrel into Heaven, do you?"

"Very good, sir," exclaimed Summas. "Well said!"

"Look, everyone," Joseph continued, "I realize that what I'm telling you sounds too amazing to believe. I don't blame you, really I don't."

"Good," said Caiaphas, "then you admit you have no real proof to offer in your defense. Will you be so kind, then, as to stop promoting such heretical nonsense?"

"Oh, but I do have real proof, sir; I do."

"Preposterous," Caiaphas snorted, obstinately crossing his arms."You're bluffing."

Joseph shook his head with a mild chuckle and a knowing look. "Bluffing, am I?"

"Of course, you're bluffing," groaned Annas. "If you had any real proof that these stories were anything more than hysterical delusions, you would've already offered it to us as evidence; pure and simple."

"Well, then, prepare to confront your worst nightmare, gentlemen," Joseph said, quite undeterred, "because not only did Jesus rise from the dead, but there are others who've also risen from their graves."

"Wh—*What*?" blanched Caiaphas, as did most everyone else in the room who mirrored the same sentiment. "That's the most ridiculous thing I've ever heard!"

"But I'm telling you all, here and now," insisted Joseph, who implored the assembly that buzzed with excitement, sensing that not all of them were as antagonistic to his cause as was their leadership, "these risen ones have been seen by numerous eyewitnesses throughout Judea."

"You mean *dead people*, besides this Jesus, have actually risen from their graves?" ventured Datam. "But how is that possible?"

"That, I'm afraid, Datam, I cannot say for sure. All that I am certain of is this is what I was told. Others have, in fact, risen."

"Who?" gasped Summas. "Certainly no one we would know."

"Well, now that you mention it, yes, there are some you might know. Everyone here remembers Simeon the high priest for the Temple at Jerusalem."

"Of course, we all knew Simeon," said Annas. "He had two sons, two fine, upstanding sons, actually. Both tragically died untimely deaths, though, within months of each other, as I recall. Absolutely tragic. Many of us here went to their funerals."

"That's right," Joseph continued. "And now, if we go to their graves, you'll find that the two sons of Simeon have actually risen from the dead."

"You must be joking!" blurted Datam, staring back in disbelief. "I knew the sons of Simeon myself. Charinus and Lenthius were good friends of mine. You mean to tell me that people have actually seen them alive, *recently*?"

Joseph nodded. "They have."

"W—*well*, what are they doing?"

"Not much, actually. Some people have reported seeing them praying in silence, but for whatever reason they refuse to talk to anyone. They just carry on, mute as dumb men."

Datam was clearly intrigued by it all. "Like they still haven't figured out what they are yet; dead or alive."

Joseph nodded thoughtfully. "Something like that, yes, I guess so."

Caiaphas, as usual, rolled his eyes and shook his head. "Oh, please. Would you people listen to yourselves?"

Annas, on the other hand, frowned painfully. "But how is any of this possible?"

A stunned Caiaphas flashed a look of disappointment in his father-in-law's direction.

"How should I know?" Joseph shrugged his shoulders. "I'm just telling you what I was told. Now it's up to us to go to Arimathea to investigate this mystery for ourselves. Does anyone here care to go with me?"

"I'll go," said Datam. "I'd like to find out what's happening."

"Me, too," Summas chimed in.

But Caiaphas defiantly shook his head. "This is absurd, everyone. The mysteries of the resurrection are simply beyond any man's ability to comprehend. What makes you think you're any different?"

"Oh, I don't know, Caiaphas," Joseph replied with a serene smile. "Maybe it really comes down to faith after all. So the real question now seems to be: Who else has the faith to go with us?"

A People in Darkness

SO JOSEPH, NICODEMUS, Annas, Caiaphas, Summas, Datam and Gamaliel all went to Arimathea, and just as had been reported, they found that the gravesites of Simeon's two sons were no longer intact. Staring wide-eyed into the open graves, everyone exhibited a wide variety of deeply felt emotions, ranging from complete shock to absolute wonder.

"It's true!" exclaimed Nicodemus. "Their graves *are* empty! They really have risen from the dead!"

"Don't be too sure of yourself, Nicodemus," Caiaphas insisted with a disgruntled scowl. "I still say this is merely a hoax."

"A hoax?" wondered Datam. "Who would do such a thing?"

"Who knows," scoffed Annas, "probably gravediggers with nothing better to do. I certainly wouldn't put it past them. They probably concocted this whole thing as a prank to exploit impressionable minds that have nothing else to believe in."

"But look at the arrangement of the dirt around these graves," Joseph said, thoughtfully exploring an idea that seemed to be evolving as he spoke. "It doesn't look to me as though gravediggers were responsible for any of this."

"Whatever are you going on about now?" asked Caiaphas, staring down at the open graves, barely able to focus his mind, still unclear about what he was seeing.

"I mean, it doesn't look like this dirt was dug out from above," continued Joseph with a steely determination. "It looks to me like this dirt was pushed up from below."

"Look, see there," said Nicodemus, eagerly pointing his finger. "He's right. Notice how those footprints all lead *away* from these gravesites. If this were the work of a fraud, then there'd be at least one or two sets of footprints facing toward them as a result of their having evacuated the graves."

"What's more," Joseph continued, "the footprints leading from these graves were clearly not made by anyone wearing shoes." Then turning to Annas and Caiaphas, he asked them point-blank, "Tell me, gentlemen, since when have you ever known gravediggers to do their job barefooted?"

The two men exchanged a disconcerted look, unable or unwilling to offer a response.

Datam stared incredulously at the gravesites, along with their respective sets of footprints, and then turned to the group. "My God, I don't believe I'm actually saying this, but I think maybe they're right."

Everyone turned and stepped several feet away, wide-eyed at the implications of what they were seeing and saying; everyone, that is, but Caiaphas, who remained as obstinate as ever. "Now I've heard everything," he grumbled under his breath.

Even Annas appeared somewhat smitten. "So if the two sons of Simeon came out of these graves, as you're suggesting, then where'd they go?" He sighed heavily, clearly divided within himself as he weighed the potential meaning of the evidence they were confronting.

"That's a good question," replied Nicodemus. "I suppose we'll just have to look around for them. I'm sure they haven't gotten too far, though."

SCOURING THE COUNTRYSIDE in search of the sons of Simeon, they eventually came across two young men, huddled together, kneeling in prayer, in a nearby lemon grove.

"Is that them?" wondered Summas.

"Don't be absurd, Summas," snapped Caiaphas. "Of course it's not them. Have you lost your mind as well with all this insane speculation?"

"Well, there's always one sure-fire way to find out," said Joseph, who cautiously approached the men. Stepping up to the pair, he cleared his throat and spoke in a reverential voice. "Hello, Charinus, Lenthius? Please, excuse me. I'm sorry to disturb you, gentlemen, but in the Name of the God of Israel, may I have a word with you both?"

Looking up at Joseph, the two men nodded blankly. The rest of the group slowly moved forward, and when they got a good look at them, they were positively stunned by what they saw.

"I—I—*I* don't believe it," stammered Datam, turning white as a ghost. "It *is* them. The two sons of Simeon."

"You mean the two *dead* sons of Simeon," Summas added, suddenly growing weak in the knees.

THE TWO SONS OF SIMEON dolefully accompanied Joseph, followed at some distance by the rest of the group, who shadowed them the entire return trip without so much as a single word between any of them.

ARRIVING BACK AT THE Temple, Joseph and his group then headed for the Assembly Hall. As they walked through the outer courtyard, everyone who saw them coming nervously stepped aside.

Once inside the hall, Nicodemus placed *The Book of the Law* in the hands of Charinus and Lenthius and adjured them, "By the God of Israel Who spoke to the Fathers by the Law and the prophets, if you believe Jesus raised you, then tell us what you've seen. How, exactly, did you rise from the dead?"

Charinus and Lenthius trembled, obviously disturbed.

"Lord Jesus and Father God," Charinus began. "You Who are the Resurrection and the Life. We're sworn by Your holy Name."

"Please give us permission to describe the mysteries of Your cross," added Lenthius, "because until now You've forbidden us to speak about the secret things You did in Hades."

Everyone there exchanged a troubled look with the man standing next to him, and then their eyes darted back to the two sons of Simeon. After a long pause, the men reached out their hands.

"Give us some paper," Charinus said. "We'll write down everything we've witnessed since we died."

Summas quickly brought each of them a stack of paper and a writing utensil. Then the two sons sat down and began writing on separate pages.

"Just like the rest of our forefathers," continued Charinus, "when we died, we were placed in the depths of Hades, where we sat imprisoned in the shadow of death."

"Then after how long, no one knows for sure," Lenthius said, "a brilliant purple light appeared, filling the whole place with an incredible iridescence."

"LOOK," SHOUTED ADAM, the father of mankind, as he jumped to his feet, pointing like a giddy schoolboy. "It's the Author of Eternal Light Who promised to translate *us* to a world of perpetual light!"

Along with Charinus and Lenthius, a large gathering of spectators stood and turned to see the shimmering rays of purple light slice through the eerie darkness that shrouded their abysmal domain.

The prophet Isaiah stepped up next to the two brothers and proclaimed, "This is the Light of the Father and the Son of God!"

"It's beautiful, Isaiah!" exclaimed Charinus.

"I talked about this while I was still on Earth," Isaiah continued. "'In Galilee, beyond Jordan, in the land of Zebulun and Naphtali, a people in darkness saw a great Light.'"

"And it's coming our direction!" exclaimed Lenthius.

"This Light has risen to those of us in the grip of death," Isaiah said. "Now, He's finally coming to shine on us."

STILL, CHARINUS AND Lenthius wrote their letters as the rest of the group listened to them take turns recounting their experience.

"And as we all celebrated the approach of the Light," continued Lenthius, "our father Simeon, the high priest, entered our midst."

MARVELING AT THE purple light that moved closer and closer toward them, the group turned to see Simeon step up to them.

Charinus said with a smile, "Father, I'm so glad to see you. Can you tell us about this incredible light?"

"Certainly, son. The Glory of the Lord is approaching."

"What are you saying, Father?" Lenthius asked. "What's coming?"

"Not what, son—*Who*?"

"Who, then?" wondered Lenthius.

"The Lord Jesus Christ," he replied, awestruck at the thought. "While He was still just a baby, I held Him in my arms, and with the Holy Spirit's help, I recognized Who He was. I was so happy, I said, 'Lord, Now You can let me die because I've finally seen the salvation You've prepared for everyone, the Glory of Your people, Israel, and a Light to the Gentiles.'"

Then, someone looking like a hermit stepped forward, and quite puzzled, the group turned toward him.

"Who are you?" asked Isaiah.

"I am the voice of one crying in the wilderness."

"John?" said Charinus, squinting his eyes. "John the Baptist? Is it really you?"

"Yes, Charinus, it's me."

"The prophet of the Most High," Lenthius added, speaking in hushed, reverential tones. "You're also here because of this light we see coming toward us?"

"Yes, Lenthius. While I was still in the flesh, I went ahead of the Lord, bringing the knowledge of salvation to all men, and when I saw Jesus approaching me, I said, 'Look, the Lamb of God: Here's the One Who takes away the sins of the whole world.'"

"Tell us, John, is that what's happening now?" asked Charinus. "Is this the meaning of the light approaching us?"

"It is, Charinus, yes. After I baptized Him in the river Jordan, we saw the Holy Spirit descend on Him in the form of a dove. Remember?"

"Of course," said Charinus, as if waking from a deep sleep. "I do remember now."

"And that's when a voice from Heaven said, 'See: This is My Beloved Son. I'm so pleased with Him.' On Earth, I prepared the way for Jesus, and just as I did before, I'm here to let you know the Son of God is on His way. The Dayspring from On-High is coming to us, we who are imprisoned here in darkness and death."

Then Adam turned to his son Seth. "Son, did you hear what John just said? Jesus was baptized in the river Jordan." Adam shook his head in amazement. "Can you believe it?"

"I heard, Father," replied Seth. "Imagine that."

"Why, what about it?" Lenthius asked.

"Tell your sons, Seth," said Adam. "Tell the patriarchs and prophets all about the time I fell ill and sent you to ask God to anoint my head with oil."

Seth continued, "Once while I was praying to God at the gates of Paradise, Michael the archangel came to me and said, 'Hello, Seth, I've been appointed to preside over the human race.' So I said, 'Good; then you'll be able to help me, won't you?' But he told me the Lord had sent him to tell me to stop asking for the oil of mercy to relieve my father's pain."

"But why would he tell you that?" asked Simeon.

"Because he said God wasn't going to allow it until the Last Days; that is, not until after five thousand, five hundred years had transpired."

"Why?" asked Isaiah. "What was supposed to happen after five thousand, five hundred years?"

"That's when Christ would come to Earth to resurrect everyone."

"But that's not all; is it, son?" interjected Adam, who flashed a serene smile.

Seth shook his head. "No, Father."

"What?" cried Isaiah. "What aren't you telling us?"

"Tell them, Seth. Tell them the amazing part."

"Michael told me that when the Lord did come to Earth, He'd be baptized in the river Jordan."

Awestruck, the group sighed collectively.

"Imagine that," Seth said again.

"So very many centuries before it ever happened," Charinus intoned, "God made a promise to Adam and his descendants, and faithful as He is, the Lord made sure to keep that promise, at just the right time and in just the right place."

"So, as it turns out," continued Seth, "the oil of mercy I was praying for was not only granted to my father as a result of this baptism at Jordan, but it also opened the door for everyone who has faith in Him. That way the Lord can anoint them all with the oil of His mercy, and this oil will continue to future generations, bestowing eternal life on everyone born of water and the Holy Spirit."

"Simply amazing," Isaiah murmured.

"Was that all Michael told you?" asked Lenthius.

"No. He also told me that when the Son of God came to rescue mankind, He'd personally introduce my father back into Paradise.'"

"And here He comes now!" Adam cried as he flung his arms toward the dazzling light that was approaching them. "Just like He promised me!"

THE SONS OF SIMEON continued writing their story, much to the amazement of everyone in the Assembly Hall.

"Even as the saints were rejoicing at the approach of this tremendously bright light," said Lenthius, "it just so happened that there was another group who was just as startled at this appearing. This group, however, was not at all excited as they saw the coming of the light."

"Instead of rising up to greet this glorious new dawn," Charinus added, "this horrid gathering recoiled at its abrupt appearance. Immediately, their chief Satan, the prince of death, the father of lies, the scourge of the Universe, convened a war council with none other than Beelzebub, the prince of Hades, and together they planned how they might respond to this invasion of their damnable domain."

"PREPARE YOURSELF, Beelzebub!" Satan snarled at his grotesque prince of the dead. "You're about to receive Jesus of Nazareth himself, the very one who boasted *he* was the son of god."

"You don't say?" said Beelzebub, almost nonchalantly. "The son of god, coming here? To my infernal lair?"

"That's right," he replied, grinning maniacally. "Can you believe it?"

"Frankly, no, I can't. How did the old boy take it?"

"Oh, it was delicious, let me tell you. He turned out to be an ordinary man after all, afraid of dying, just like the rest of the little vermin he claimed to love so much."

"Really?"

"Yes, really. You should've seen it. He wept like a baby. *My heart is so agonized, I feel like I might die from grief.* It was pathetic!"

"So let me get this straight. This man you're bringing here; you say he's a powerful prince, yet he's terrified of death. Is that what you're saying?"

"Trust me. The man is a mere shadow of his former self. No more giving sight to people I made blind; no more healing those I made lame; no more curing the ones my minions utterly possessed! Nothing! Just pathetic tears and ignominious death. And this was the same man, mind you, that stole a dead man right out of your clutches!"

"Exactly; which is why I don't like what I'm hearing. We don't want someone like him coming down here!"

"Ah, you worry too much. Why are you so afraid to receive this Jesus of Nazareth, anyway? I told you: He's not the same man he used to be. When I stirred up the bitter ones among the Jews, he couldn't stop them. When I sharpened the thorns for his suffering, he couldn't prevent it. And when I prepared the cross to crucify him on, he was powerless before me, as I drove the iron nails into his wrists and feet!"

"Yes, yes, we already know all about that, but what you don't seem to realize is that a man capable of the things he did in life will be unstoppable here in the realm of the dead."

"Nonsense! I'm telling you: We have him right where we want him. Trust me."

"Trust you?" said Beelzebub, shaking his head in disgust. "You just don't get it, do you? Obviously when a man like Jesus of Nazareth tells you he's afraid of dying, he's only doing it to entrap you, and now that you've fallen for his devices we're both going to be sorry, *forever!*"

"But he's dead, isn't he? What can he do to us now? When he gets here, he'll be completely under our control!"

"Have you already forgotten? You said it yourself. He robs us of our dead, right?"

"Yeah. So what's your point?"

"Just look around you."

Satan obligingly turned every direction, looking out upon the endless rows of imprisoned human spirits, who were all beginning to notice the distant, purple haze that was punching an ever-widening hole through the eerie darkness. Then he turned back to his prince. "Okay, now what?"

"Well, tell me what you see," continued Beelzebub.

The devil shrugged his leathery shoulders and replied, "I see the dreary shades of countless human souls. Why, what do you see?"

"Oh, I see the souls of countless humans, all right, but apparently what you've conveniently overlooked is the fact that all these souls are being preserved and protected by their prayers to God. Otherwise, they'd be completely helpless before us."

"Yeah, so?"

"So? You fool. This Jesus of Nazareth seized the dead man Lazarus from me without the need of a single prayer! He did it entirely by his own authority!"

"So?"

"Stop saying that! What is so hard to understand? Obviously any man who can do the things he does must be almighty god!"

"Impossible. He's no god. He's just a man."

"But a man that powerful in his human nature, with the kind of authority he commands, must be the savior of mankind, don't you see?"

"So what do you think will happen when he comes down here?"

"Stop already. I don't even want to think about such a disaster, because if he ever did come here, I'm sure he wouldn't hesitate to rescue everyone from our grasp and lead them all away to eternal life."

Then from out of nowhere, a tremendous voice thundered. "Oh, princes, open these eternal gates of Hades so the King of Glory can enter!"

Beelzebub glared at the devil. "You see; what did I tell you?"

"What?" Satan sputtered. "I don't understand. What was that?"

"Are you deaf? Apparently the king of glory is coming."

"*Who*?"

"The king of glory, you imbecile, the king of glory!"

"What should we do now?" asked the devil, wide-eyed and bewildered.

"Well, if you're such a powerful warrior, then you'd better get ready to fight this king of glory! But what can you possibly do against Him?" Beelzebub then turned to his gruesome officers. "Hurry, you pathetic worms, secure the gates of cruelty! Make sure they're good and tight! And above all, fight courageously, you hear me? Or else we'll all be taken captive!"

From the Pit to the Pinnacle

CAIAPHAS LOUDLY cleared his throat. "Excuse me, gentlemen, but am I the only one here who doubts what these two men are telling us?"

The two sons of Simeon stopped writing and calmly looked up.

"Who are you, sir?" Lenthius asked without a trace of guile.

"Why, naturally, as you can see by the clothes I'm wearing, I am the high priest at Jerusalem. If you were really the sons of Simeon, you'd know that."

"You'll have to forgive my brother, sir," Charinus said. "But as you can imagine, the shock of being returned so abruptly to this life has been an unsettling occurrence, to say the least. Many things once familiar to us now seem somewhat unclear in light of what we've recently experienced."

Baffled by this, Caiaphas was not sure how to respond, and shot a plaintive look to the rest of the group.

"Please, Caiaphas," interjected Nicodemus, "give these men a chance to speak. Certainly you're not suggesting we dismiss the testimony of so many people concerning these risen ones just because you're uncomfortable with this startling, new report?"

"Of course not," he grunted back. "I'm merely suggesting that the outrageous nature of what we're being told is beyond the scope of any man to know. How can we possibly allow their story to be admitted as evidence? Clearly, these men are either delusional, or worse, they're making the whole thing up."

"Pardon me, sir," Lenthius continued, "but you say you're presently officiating as the high priest at Jerusalem, is that right?"

"That is correct, yes."

"What's your name?" asked Charinus.

"I am Caiaphas."

"Caiaphas, yes, Caiaphas," Lenthius murmured, mulling this name over in his mind, looking to his brother as he did. "Tell me, Charinus, could this be the same Caiaphas whom Father encountered while he was working as a teacher of rabbinical law?"

"It could be, maybe," replied Charinus, who then turned back to Caiaphas. "Tell me, sir, are you the same person who, as a boy, relished in bullying his fellow schoolmates?"

With an irritated frown, Caiaphas opened his mouth, as if he were about to reply.

But before he could Lenthius continued, "And were you the same mischievous lad who delighted in bringing worm-filled apples to his teachers?"

Again the high priest, with furrowed brow, thought about responding, barely opening his mouth.

So Charinus pressed on. "And were you the same little scoundrel who was so fond of pulling the wings off of butterflies? Was that you, sir?"

Still Caiaphas stood there, his mouth slightly ajar, frozen with indecision, while the rest of the group awkwardly looked on.

"Enough already," Annas finally interceded. "There's no need for this. Please, can you two just get on with the task at hand?"

"We can, sir," Lenthius calmly replied.

"Then please do."

"As you wish," said Charinus, and so the two men turned their attention back to their pens and paper as if nothing unusual at all had just occurred.

"OH, YOU PRINCES OF the underworld!" shouted the crackling, disembodied voice, "open up your eternal gates so the King of Glory can enter!"

Startled, Satan and Beelzebub recoiled, as did all the demons surrounding them.

"You heard him, you despicable legions of the dead," shouted John the Baptist, who, along with the whole company of saints, rushed forward to oppose Satan, Beelzebub and all their despicable officers. "Open up your gates so the King of Glory can enter, because now *you're* the ones who are about to be helpless and chained!"

Beelzebub snarled back. "How dare you speak to us like that! This is still our domain, you disgusting maggot!"

Again the deafening voice shattered the gloomy darkness. "Oh, princes, open these gates of brass so the King of Glory can enter!"

And again Satan, Beelzebub and their cadre of minions recoiled in abject horror.

Then the prophet David stepped forward. "Didn't I prophesy about this while I was still on Earth? 'Oh, that men would praise the Lord for the wonderful things He does, because He's broken down the gates of brass and shattered the bars of iron!'"

"That's right, David!" exclaimed Isaiah. "I predicted this, too, when I said, 'Dead men would rise from their graves someday and live again! Then everyone will celebrate because the dew of the Lord is going to bring them deliverance. Oh, death, where is your victory? Oh, death, where is your sting?'"

Again the great voice rang out like thunder. "Oh, princes, open up your gates so the King of Glory can enter!"

But Beelzebub called out as though he were ignorant. "But who is this king of glory?"

"I'll tell you!" David replied. "I understand what that voice is saying! The Lord is powerful in battle. *He's* the King of Glory! He's heard the prisoners groaning and will rescue those appointed to death!"

"So, Beelzebub," shouted Isaiah, "Prince of the Dead, open your gates right now so the King of Glory can enter!"

With a blinding flash of purple light, the Almighty Lord suddenly appeared in the form of a Man, lighting up all the places that had until then been shrouded in perpetual night.

"By His invincible power," Simeon said, as he stood tall among the ranks of the saints, "He's come to rescue those in the grip of sin and death, those bound by chains that could never be broken before but which have now been shattered."

And when they saw how bright this Light was and how abruptly Jesus Christ Himself had appeared in their midst, the grief-stricken legions of the damned let loose with a lamentable howl.

"Who are you?" moaned one of the demons. "Why isn't there even a hint of corruption in you? We're helpless in your presence."

"Of course, your incredible brightness is proof of your majesty," wailed a second. "But you probably don't even stop to notice such things, do you?"

"All-powerful yet compassionate, an average man yet a soldier of the highest rank," grumbled a third, "you command the very elements, even while in the form of a slave."

"First, you were dead," moaned the second. "Now you're down here with us, alive and well. No wonder the entire creation shuddered when you died. It seems you're immune even to death! Will you now disturb our legions, too?"

"How can you release captives bound so securely by sin?" shrieked the first. "How do you spread such a magnificent light over those who were made so blind? Where does this power come from?"

"Until now, the underworld has been completely subject to our control," spewed the second demon. "The prince of Hades has never had a dead man like you here before! How can you just enter our home like this?"

Jesus then gestured with His hand, and from out of nowhere, a brass chain spiraled up and over the bodies of both Satan and Beelzebub, a chain not comprised of brass links but of indestructible brass hands, squeezing and tugging in response to every movement, as its demonic prisoners attempted to break free.

Then turning to the saints, who all stood in anticipation of this long-awaited moment, Jesus offered another gesture. This time He reached out His hand, a hand that clearly bore the scar of the nail that had pierced His wrist, and in response, the hand of Adam reached out to grasp it. Slowly, these two began to ascend like a bubble caught up in a breeze, and as they did the other hand of Jesus waved the rest of the group upward. As if caught up in an invisible net, the entire gathering of saints began to rise with them.

The ensnared duo of Satan and Beelzebub helplessly watched the ascending saints being added to as, one by one, each new soul rose to join the group. Higher and higher, they all continued to ascend together into the misty vault of their conquered world. Unable to hold his tongue any longer, Beelzebub turned to Satan. "Y—y—*you prince of destruction!* You scorn of God's angels, hated by every decent creature! You've really gone and done it this time, haven't you?"

"Me?" Satan's reptilian eyes thinned with rage and recrimination. "Why me? I had no idea this was going to happen."

"You worthless jackass! What made you do something like this, anyway?"

The devil pathetically shook his wolfen head. "I don't know. I thought we were finally riding ourselves of the little menace. Really, I did."

"Oh, I'm sure you thought that crucifying the king of glory was going to win us some great advantage, but you were completely ignorant of what you were really doing, you imbecile! Now just look at how this radiant Jesus has vanquished our horrid powers of darkness and death! Can you feel your world collapsing around you? Can you?"

Satan grimaced as though some unseen force had just struck him. "As a matter of fact, I *can*, yes. His sickening presence is everywhere now."

"So, Prince of Wickedness, Father of the Abandoned, tell me again: Why did you do something like this?"

Dumbfounded, Satan just shook his head, unable to offer a single thing in his defense, so Beelzebub spewed on. "You knew perfectly well our prisoners were without any hope of salvation or life. But now look! You keeper of the infernal regions, every advantage we ever gained when Adam forfeited Paradise has been lost."

"But I don't understand. I thought for sure that I'd killed him!"

"Oh, but you did, you did, you fool! But killing him wasn't the answer! Because the moment you crucified the king of glory, the moment you brought a perfectly innocent man down here to the region of the damned, that was the moment you forfeited our birthright to imprison every single person in the history of this world!"

Then Jesus abruptly reappeared in their midst, causing every hideous creature to recoil in His presence, and He pointed at the prince of Hades. "From now on, Beelzebub, you will have control over Satan, here in the room of Adam and all his faithful children."

With yet another gesture from Jesus, every miniature hand comprising the brass chains that were wrapped about Satan and Beelzebub released its grip, and in a shimmering cascade, they shattered into a thousand pieces and fell to the ground. Then, just as quickly as He had appeared in their midst, Jesus vanished.

IN THE BLINK OF AN EYE, the Lord reappeared among the gathering of saints and stretched out His hand. "Come to Me, My saints, everyone created in My image but condemned by the Forbidden Fruit, the devil and death. So live now because of the wood of My cross. Satan, the prince of this world, has been vanquished, and, along with him, death has been conquered." Jesus then placed His hand on Adam's head. "Peace is finally yours again, Adam, yours and all your faithful children who belong to Me."

Weeping tears of joy, Adam cast himself at the feet of Jesus. "Praise You, Lord. You lifted me up, and didn't allow my enemies to triumph over me. Oh, God, I cried to You, and You healed me. You brought my life up from the grave so I wouldn't remain in the Pit. Sing to the Lord, every one of His saints. Give thanks to Him, because His anger lasts only for a moment;

but in His favor, there is life forevermore."

Everyone there bowed before Jesus, too, and spoke with one voice. "Redeemer of the World, You've come at last!"

David sang out. "You've actually accomplished everything You foretold through the Law and Your holy prophets!"

"By Your cross, You reached down and redeemed us," Isaiah exclaimed. "You delivered us from Hades and rescued us from the power of death!"

"Lord, just as You've placed signs of Your redemptive story in the Heavens," cried John the Baptist, "you've set up Your cross as the standard of Your salvation on Earth!"

"Now, Lord, set this emblem of Your victory here, too," Simeon said, "so death won't have dominion over mankind any longer!"

Jesus then made the sign of the cross over all the saints and, taking Adam with his right hand, continued His ascent while the rest of the group followed close behind. "Everyone, sing to the Lord," said the father of mankind, "because He's done such marvelous things! His right hand has brought us the victory!"

"The Lord has revealed His salvation," Isaiah proclaimed, "even explaining His righteousness to the heathen!"

"You went forth as the ransom of Your flock to rescue Your people!" shouted David.

"The Lord has enlightened us all!" cried Seth. "This is our God, and He will reign over us forever and ever!"

ARRIVING AT THE GATES of Paradise, Jesus handed Adam over to Michael the archangel, who then led the first man inside, followed closely by everyone else. The awestruck saints surveyed the sprawling landscape that spread out before them in every direction, a lush gardenland, overflowing with splendor and beauty. Much to their surprise, the group encountered two men who approached them as soon as they entered.

"Who are you two?" Isaiah asked. "You were never in Hades with us, yet you're already here in Paradise. How is that possible?"

The first man slowly began, "Yes, well, you see, that's because of all the people who have ever been born on Earth, the Scriptures record that only two men have ever temporarily 'cheated death.'"

"And you mean to tell us that you're those two men?" David asked.

"We are, yes," he replied. "I was the first person to attain this honor when I was transported to Heaven with the help of two of God's angels, Sariel and Raguel. I am Enoch, the scribe."

"Of course," exclaimed Abraham, who stepped forward to shake Enoch's hand. "I've heard about you my whole life. What an honor it is to finally meet you face to face." Turning to the group, he called out, "Boys, come here quick. I want you to meet someone."

Two men then walked up to Enoch and Abraham, who then said, "Isaac, Jacob, this is the man I told you all about, remember?"

Isaac reached out to shake Enoch's hand and replied sheepishly, "Of course, Father. How could I ever forget?"

Amused at this, the group laughed heartily.

Enoch nodded and said, "Nice to meet you, Isaac." And nodding to Jacob, who respectfully remained several feet back, he smiled graciously. "Young man."

Then Enoch turned to the second man next to him. "And what about you, sir?" he said with a playful grin. "Would you care to tell everyone your story?"

Clearing his throat, the man said, "Who, me? You want to know *my* story?"

Turning to the group, Enoch asked, "Well, everyone. What do you think? Are you interested?"

"Of course," came their collective reply.

"Well, like Enoch before me, I was also uniquely honored and transported to Heaven, when I was taken up in a fiery chariot. I am Elijah, the Tishbite."

"Elijah?" gasped Simeon. "Is it really you?"

"It is, sir," he replied.

Turning to his two sons, Simeon said, "Look, boys, it's Elijah. Can you believe it?"

Charinus and Lenthius smiled proudly at their father and nodded.

Then John the Baptist stepped forward. "We're honored to meet you both. Since the earliest days of our youth, many of us here have been regaled with the tales of your exploits. You've been quite an inspiration to us all." Moving up to Elijah, John reached out his hand. "And I'd like to mention that you, sir, were of particular inspiration to me. I thank you."

Shaking his hand, Elijah exchanged a smile and a nod of satisfaction with Enoch.

Moved to tears by this special moment, the whole group began to clap and sing praises to the Lord, and after a while, Simeon stepped back up and asked, "Please correct me if I'm wrong, gentlemen, but you did say you only cheated death *temporarily*. Is that right?"

"You heard correctly, yes," Enoch replied.

"What, exactly, does that mean?" wondered Simeon.

"It means that before our mission is fully complete," Elijah continued, "we, too, must be subjected to the same baptism of death that all of you here have undergone. As it is written: Everyone is appointed once to die."

"But how can that be?" queried Abraham. "If you're with us in Heaven, what could possibly happen to you in this place of incorruptibility?"

"What we're destined to undergo will not take place up here," Enoch exclaimed, "but must occur on the Earth below."

"Any moment now we'll be returning to Earth for the coming of the Anti-Christ," said Elijah, suddenly with fire in his eyes. "Armed with divine signs and miracles, we'll face him in the supreme test of our lives, a showdown of biblical proportions!"

Enoch defiantly shook his fist. "We'll engage the devil himself and his counterfeit offspring. We'll wage war with this Anti-Christ with every ounce of our courage, but in the end, we'll be slain in the streets of Jerusalem!"

"No!" shouted many of the saints there.

"God forbid!" Isaac intoned.

"Yes, I'm afraid so, everyone," insisted Elijah. But far from looking fearful at the expectation of such a fate, the prophet exuded a serene sense that likewise washed away any anxiety that the group was feeling for them. "But don't be sad for us. No, sir, because our death is by no means the end of our adventure; not by a long shot!"

"Tell us, please," insisted Jacob, wide-eyed with anticipation.

"It's just the beginning, actually," said Enoch, sporting his familiar grin, "because after three and a half days, our dead bodies will be filled with the same Holy Spirit that raised you all from your graves, and we, too, will rise in newness of life."

"And in plain sight of the whole world, Enoch and I will be taken up," said Elijah with an enthusiastic wave of his hand, "up into the clouds to be reunited with you all once again, to be with the Lord Almighty forever and ever!"

Everyone was astonished by their story, when suddenly another man came forward, a miserable looking figure, donning tattered clothes. Curious about his peculiar appearance, the saints turned to him.

"Who are you?" asked a confused Charinus, who turned to Enoch and Elijah. "I thought you told us you were the only ones who have never died."

Enoch nodded. "That's right; we are."

"Then what's he doing here?" queried Abraham. "He looks like some sort of criminal."

The strange-looking fellow stared back at everyone for several moments. "Yes, you're quite right about me. I *was* a thief, one who committed every sort of crime during my lifetime."

"Who are you, then?" Isaac asked. "And how'd you get here before any of us?"

"I, Dimas, of all people," continued the man, so emotional that he strained to get the words out, "observed the startling things that happened … at the crucifixion of the Lord Jesus Christ… Believing He was the Creator and the Almighty King, I asked Him: 'Lord … remember me when You enter Your kingdom.'"

"But how is that possible?" wondered Lenthius. "When did you ever have a chance to speak with the Christ? You weren't one of His disciples."

"I certainly was not, no… In life … I was a man completely unworthy to even sit in the same room with a Man so wonderful, so compassionate, so kind."

"Tell us, then," said Simeon with a gentle persistence. "When did you speak with the Savior?"

"I asked Him while we were both hanging … side by side … as we struggled with our last breaths … high upon a cross on that despicable hill called Golgotha."

An uneasy hush swept through the entire group.

"You?" asked Lenthius.

"Yes, me," said the man slowly, deliberately, as though he himself could not believe the truth of what he was saying. "I was the thief hanging at Jesus' right hand... And when I asked His forgiveness, He accepted my request, without hesitation … without a word of condemnation, saying … 'Certainly you will be with Me in Paradise today.'"

Everyone there was absolutely amazed.

"Thank God for His boundless grace," Abraham declared, "the Father of Eternal Goodness and Mercy."

Then Seth said, "You've shown such kindness to those who were rebels against You!"

"You've brought us all into the Mercy of Paradise, Lord," Isaac intoned, "and placed us amidst a land overflowing with Your marvelous provisions."

"You've restored us and brought us back into your garden-land," exclaimed Adam, who turned to Eve and reached out to squeeze her hand, "back into the very heart of the Almighty, a heart beating with eternal life, love and hope!"

And everyone there proclaimed with one voice, "Amen!"

The Truth be Told

STILL THE TWO SONS of Simeon were writing down the details of their amazing story.

"These are the sacred mysteries of God that we've both seen and heard," said Charinus. "We aren't allowed, however, to tell you anything more because Michael the archangel ordered us not to."

"So praise and honor the Lord," Lenthius added. "If you repent, He'll have mercy on you, and may Jesus Christ, the Savior of us all, bring you comfort and peace forevermore. Amen, amen and amen."

After they had finished writing their separate reports, Charinus and Lenthius put their pens down and turned to everyone who was still sitting there in eager anticipation of what they might say next, but without warning, the two sons of Simeon changed into incredibly white forms, and slowly faded from view.

As the befuddled group looked on, unsure of what to do next, Joseph and Nicodemus finally stood up and together, with a mutual look of astonishment, sucked in a deep breath.

"My God," gasped Nicodemus, "just when I thought I'd seen it all, something like this happens."

"You're telling me," Joseph replied with an exhilarated sigh. Then turning to Annas, Caiaphas and the others, he asked with unrestrained enthusiasm, "Now what do you have to say for yourselves? Are you convinced now?"

Thunderstruck, the rest of the group jumped to their feet as they looked to one another to see what each of their reactions might be to this startling turn of events.

Caiaphas was the first to respond. "Well, I, for one, cannot say one way or the other what just happened here."

"But, Caiaphas," blurted Nicodemus, "you saw it with your own eyes, heard it with your own ears. What more do you need?"

Crossing his arms, Caiaphas continued with an obstinate scowl, "If I did venture to guess, I'd say we've all been the unwitting victims of some sort of satanic spell. This whole thing stinks to high Heaven!"

"A spell?" echoed Joseph in utter disbelief. "That's the best you can come up with? I'm afraid the only thing satanic about this is the lengths to which you people will stoop to blind yourselves to the truth." And turning to the others, he implored, "What about the rest of you? Are you also so willing to reject what you've just witnessed for yourselves?"

Summas, Datam and Gamaliel stood there, perplexed as ever, their eyes darting back and forth from Annas and Caiaphas, and then back to each other.

"Again I say," snapped Caiaphas, "what proof do you have that this whole affair was anything more than the product of a spirit of delusion, brought forth by the same demonic spirit that enabled the Nazarene to work his cures? What proof, sir? Show it to me now, or else I'll have no choice but to seek your immediate removal from the ranks of the Sanhedrin!"

"Removal?" groaned Nicodemus. "On what grounds?"

Caiaphas pressed on venomously. "On the grounds that you're both in league with the devil himself, in your damnable efforts to delude and divide this congregation of the faithful."

For several agonizing moments, Joseph and Nicodemus stood there, stunned and speechless, as they looked to one another for a rebuttal to such accusations and threats.

"Proof, you say?" Joseph murmured finally.

"Yes, proof," grunted Caiaphas. "As usual you haven't a shred of tangible evidence to support what you insist occurred here today. Nothing!"

Then, as if struck by a sudden inspiration, Joseph started to walk to the table where the two stacks of paper had been left behind by Charinus and Lenthius. "Proof," he quietly said again, half to himself, half to everyone else in the room.

"Joseph?" said Nicodemus. "What do you have in mind?"

To the stack of papers, Joseph started to examine them carefully, and after several thoughtful moments, he said, "Come here, please, Nicodemus." Like a man on a mission, Joseph began to take a page from each stack and set them next to each other.

As Nicodemus stepped up to the desk, he, too, looked down at the pages as they were being laid out. "What is it, Joseph?"

The more pages that Joseph laid out, the more he seemed hypnotized by them.

Growing impatient, Caiaphas cleared his throat. "I demand that you tell us this instant; what do you think you're doing, Joseph?"

Stunned by some as-yet-undisclosed epiphany, Joseph looked up at Nicodemus with a twinkle in his eye. "I'm looking at the proof, Caiaphas, the *proof*."

The high priest's eye thinned and his nostrils flared as he turned to Annas with his typically belligerent scowl.

"Nicodemus, look for yourself," Joseph blurted with an infectious enthusiasm. "Look at these pages when compared to one another. Do you notice anything unusual about them? Anything at all?"

"I think so, yes, but..." Nicodemus looked down at the pages and strained his eyes as much as he strained his mind. "But I just can't seem to put my finger on what it might be. What do you see, Joseph? Tell me."

"What is it, Joseph?" asked Gamaliel. "What are you thinking?"

He replied thoughtfully, "These two sets of documents bear an uncanny similarity, that's all."

"In what way?" wondered Annas.

Turning toward the group, Joseph spoke with an odd expression on his face, as though he were not looking at them but through them. "If I'm not mistaken, gentlemen, although these accounts have been written by two different hands, they have nevertheless been written in absolutely perfect agreement."

"What do you mean, *perfect agreement*?" Gamaliel asked. "You mean to say they agree in penmanship? Agree in grammar? Agree how?"

Looking back down at the pages, side by side, Joseph picked up two of them in his trembling hands and uttered what he himself knew should be impossible. "I mean, there's not a single letter more or less in either of them. I mean, they're mirror images of each other, exactly identical, down the very last stroke of the pen."

"That's absurd," growled Caiaphas, who defiantly strode up to Joseph, almost knocking Nicodemus down in the process. "Step aside." And snatching the pages from Joseph's hands, the high priest placed one page on top of the other. "Have you lost your mind? Let me see those." Then he held them up in the sunlight that was streaming in through a sky light so he could see that the writing on each piece of paper was very nearly overlapping.

Curious, Annas stepped over to get a better look at what his son-in-law was doing. Looking over Caiaphas' shoulder, he watched as the high priest slowly slid the silhouette of the writing of the two pages, closer and closer, until what Joseph had been explaining finally became apparent to the naked eye. Much to the chagrin of both men, the writing on each page lined up perfectly with each other, word for word, letter for letter, stroke for stroke.

Upon seeing the incontrovertible evidence for himself, Caiaphas dropped the pages as though they were infected with the plague. "No, no, no," he gasped, and then turned to Annas. "This is sheer madness, I tell you."

"How can this be?" croaked a horrified Annas. "It *can't* be. It's not humanly possible."

PILATE WAS ON THE march soon, accompanied by Joseph and Nicodemus, as he made his way past the outer wall of the Temple at Jerusalem, which still clearly bore the scars of the recent series of earthquakes, and up the steps that led to the ornate gate of the sanctuary.

GATHERED TOGETHER in a chapel room, the governor gazed out across the assembly of black-robed Jewish authorities, and then he began to address the group in austere tones. "Greetings, gentlemen. I'm here today to inform you all that, as one of my official duties as governor of Jerusalem, I've taken steps to create a written record of the events that have recently transpired in this city. Presently, this account, penned by none other than your esteemed colleague Nicodemus, sits among the public records stored in my Assembly Hall. Now, in conjunction with that effort, I'm here to offer you one last opportunity to add to this historical account, for your sakes, for the sake of your children, and for the sake of your children's children. Who among you, then, would like to be the first to add to this account?"

Everyone there looked to the man next to him to see what his response might be, and then returned his obstinate eyes back upon the governor. Clearly, none of them had any intention of offering up a single word.

"Anyone?" continued Pilate. "No one here has the guts to offer anything in his own defense. No? Not one of you has the slightest residue of a conscience to make amends for this stain on your nation? Is that what you're telling me?"

Then from out of the crowd strode that familiar pair, Annas and Caiaphas.

Pilate could not help but instantly convey a look that revealed both his frustration and disappointment. "No, no, no; not you two again. Haven't you *already* done enough on behalf of your people?"

Holding up his hand in reconciliation, Annas meekly replied, "Please, Governor, not so fast. I admit you have every reason to doubt our sincerity in this matter, but before you jump to conclusions, I want you to know something." And turning toward the assemblage, Annas bowed ever so slightly. "In fact, Caiaphas and I both want all of you to know that this is something we wish to add to this public debate in the sincere hope that it will help to mend the troubling circumstances to which the governor has so eloquently alluded."

Intrigued, Pilate nodded. "Really? Both of you are here for this purpose?"

With a conciliatory nod, Caiaphas replied, "We are, sir, yes. Above all, it is our hope that our nation begin to seal up this terrible wound that has plagued us, so that even our beloved Temple at Jerusalem has been made to bear the cracks of this bitter divisiveness."

The governor continued with a satisfied smirk, "Very well, then, after everything you've said and done to this point, I'd be very interested to hear what you have to say in light of the recent events I've been informed about."

"Certainly, Governor," Annas added with a gesture toward one of his temple guards, "and so you will hear it."

Within moments, the side doors of the chapel flung open, and four priests brought in a gigantic book, so huge and so heavily adorned with gold and precious jewels that it had to be equally supported by all four men in order to carry it.

"Gentlemen," Annas continued in his most reverential tone, "I offer you the testimony of our most sacred text, *The Seventy Books*."

With tremendous effort, the four men maneuvered the huge book and carefully set it down on a brass pedestal. A priest then opened it, revealing its beautifully ornate pages.

"Now," Pilate said with a steely intensity, "I'm ordering you, by the God of your fathers who made this temple; tell me the truth today. You know everything written in this Holy Book of yours. So tell me: Have you discovered anything in your Scriptures about this Jesus Whom you crucified?"

"We have, sir," said Annas, nearly choking on his own words. "In fact, we actually discovered the very moment in history in which he was supposed to arrive."

"No." Taken aback, Pilate's jaw drooped ever so slightly. "How is that possible? Tell me, priest, tell me. I need to know the truth about all this, and I need to know it now."

"Very well, Governor, the truth is what you'll have," said Annas, who continued slowly, solemnly. "Soon after we crucified the man called Jesus we had a meeting in this very room. Of course we never even considered he might actually be the son of God. We naturally assumed he was performing his miracles through magical arts. But while we were deliberating about the true nature of his so-called 'miracles,' eyewitnesses from our own country kept coming to us and testifying that they'd seen him with his disciples even after his death. And as you already know, there was even a report involving two brothers who had also risen from the dead, who, in turn, provided an account describing in great detail what Jesus had supposedly done while he was in the underworld, an account which happens to be in our possession to this day."

"As you can imagine," Caiaphas chimed in, clearly pained by what he was saying, "we were all quite shocked by these outrageous reports, so we decided that for the sake of our entire nation we had to get to the bottom of it, once and for all."

"Yes, I *can* imagine," said Pilate with a smirk. "So what did you do?"

"What else could we do?" Annas shrugged, stepped to the huge book, and placed his hand on it as though he were swearing by what he was about to say. "We began searching the pages of this sacred text for an answer, in the first of *The Seventy Books*, to be exact, where we found a passage in which Michael, the archangel, spoke to Seth, the third son of Adam. In it, Michael explained to Seth that the Christ, the most beloved Son of God, was to appear on Earth after five thousand, five hundred years. And so, because the God of Israel instructed Moses to build the Ark of the Covenant with dimensions of five and a half cubits, we surmised that the Christ would likewise come in an ark, or tabernacle, of a body after five thousand, five hundred years."

"So, you see, Governor," Caiaphas said glumly, "it does appear that our Scriptures have provided us with clues to his true identity all along."

Pilate then raised his hand to interject. "You mean to tell me you discovered all that from this book of yours?"

Annas and Caiaphas nodded solemnly.

"Is that all you found?" pressed the governor.

"Quite frankly, Governor, no, it's not," replied Annas, the words almost sticking in his throat, even as they sought to come out. "We now believe we've ascertained the identity of the

Man that our people have waited for, prayed for, longed for, for five thousand, five hundred years."

"But how?" wondered Pilate. "How is that even possible?"

"How else?" Annas continued. "We traced the generations from Adam down to this one of Joseph and Mary, of course." Then Annas nodded to Caiaphas to continue.

"First, we found the story of Creation," said Caiaphas, who proceeded without a shred of emotion, as though he were reading an obituary of death as opposed to a genealogy of life, "where we determined that from the time that God created Adam up until the Great Flood, some two thousand, two hundred and twelve years had transpired. Then, from the Flood to the time of Abraham, there were nine hundred and twelve years; from Abraham to Moses, four hundred and thirty years; from Moses to King David, five hundred and ten years; and from King David to the Babylonian captivity, there were five hundred years. Finally, from the end of the Babylonian captivity to the Incarnation of Jesus, five hundred more years passed; and, as it turns out, the sum of all those years really does amount to five thousand, five hundred."

"So it appears this Jesus Whom we so mercilessly crucified," Annas said dryly, mournfully, "really is the true King of Israel, the Son of God, and the Almighty Lord. He is Jesus the Christ." And hanging his head, he whispered. "Amen."

It is Finished

SENATOR RUFUS was still reading the record aloud to the assembly while Pontius Pilate stood humbly before Tiberius Caesar. "So ends the account of the acts of the Savior, Jesus Christ, according to this history by Nicodemus, describing what happened after the Lord's crucifixion while Joseph and Caiaphas were leaders amongst the Jewish nation."

The words seared into the mind of Caesar, who could no longer suppress his fury. Enraged, he sprang to his feet and, before Rufus even had time to close the book, pointed his accusing finger. "Return this man to his cell until I can decide how to deal with him!"

A pair of Roman soldiers jumped into action and moved forward to seize the prisoner.

"No, wait," Pilate groaned. "I'm innocent, I tell you. Why are you doing this to me?"

"Silence!" snapped Caesar. "Take him away!"

Each guard grabbed hold of one of Pilate's arms, and together they started to march him out of the room.

"As God is my witness," Pilate exclaimed as he was being pulled through the door, "I'm innocent of this Man's blood."

"Enough, enough, enough!" screeched Tiberius, covering his ears. Then, as the door slammed shut, Caesar looked around at his senators and centurions, who were all taken aback at his temper tantrum. The emperor slowly lowered his hands and wiped himself with a perfunctory swipe, as if to rid himself of any taint of Pilate's guilt. Obviously embarrassed, he shook himself and glared back at his puzzled audience. "Now, summon my scribe," he said with a renewed sense of composure, "I wish to declare my verdict before the entire council and all my centurions."

IN NO TIME AT ALL, the scribe arrived and Tiberius began to dictate his decree. "Greetings from Tiberius Caesar, emperor of Rome, to Licianus, chief of the eastern sector: I've just been informed of the audacity of the Jews at Jerusalem. Recently, they acted cruelly and illegally by compelling Pontius Pilate to crucify a certain god called Jesus, and this despicable crime of theirs darkened the world, very nearly ruining it! So I want you to order your troops to Judea at once! Proclaim their bondage by this decree. Strike them, enslave them, scatter them in every direction. By driving their nation from Palestine as soon as possible, we'll demonstrate to everyone who witnesses this act that they're all full of evil!"

ARRIVING AT LICIANUS' military outpost, Volusianus handed the emperor's decree to the Roman general, who promptly read it. With a steely glint in his eye, he turned to one of his field commanders. "Well, Proteus, are you ready to prove your loyalty to the Empire again?"

Jumping to attention, Proteus dutifully saluted his chief. "Of course, General Licianus, as always."

"Good. Then gather your troops. We've been chosen for a great and glorious mission, by no less than Tiberius Caesar himself."

"Say the word, sir. I, and my men, are ready to do your bidding. Who do we attack? Where and when?"

"We're to attack the Jewish rebels in their own country of Judea as soon as we've sufficiently mobilized our forces. How long would you say before we're ready?"

"To attack a backwater bunch like that, sir," Proteus grinned, "no more than twenty-four hours."

"Excellent," said Licianus, imagining the power of his army and the swath of destruction they were about to unleash. "May the gods have mercy on the innocent, and may they strike terror in the hearts of the guilty."

JUST AS LICIANUS' field commander had promised, his fearsome army was on the march the very next day. With astonishing speed, they spearheaded the people of Judea with all their might, hacking their way through the population with sword and spear, scattering the horrified inhabitants in every direction. Everyone who had been able to evade the edge of their hardened blades was quickly rounded up and forced into slavery, while the rest of the population lucky enough to escape death or bondage were chased into the countryside, where they were scattered among the outlying nations. A pillar of smoke and ash spiraled up from Jerusalem that could be seen and smelled for nearly a hundred miles.

TIBERIUS CAESAR sat brooding on his gilded throne as Volusianus entered the room and handed him a letter.

"For you, Great Caesar," Volusianus said. "Word from your distinguished chief in the East, General Licianus."

"I see." Tiberius read the letter while Volusianus turned and dutifully walked away. Finishing the correspondence, Caesar looked up with a hollow sense of satisfaction and simply let go of the letter. It fluttered to the floor as the emperor's lips barely parted. "It is finished."

PERCHED MENACINGLY on his throne in the Capitol building, Tiberius was flanked by his Senate and surrounded by his neatly clad centurions. Caesar merely gestured and a captain of the guards hastily approached him.

"Sire," the captain said, bowing dutifully, "I am honored to be at your command."

Tiberius nodded perfunctorily. "Very well, Albius. I take it you've been instructed in what's expected of you today?"

"Yes, My Lord, I have."

"Good, because should I require it, I'll need your blade to be one that is both swift and remorseless."

"As you wish, Great Caesar. I will not fail you."

"Good, then take your place," said Tiberius, motioning to Albius, who took several paces back and withdrew his sword from its sheath. Holding it at his side, the captain stood at attention as rigid as a statue. Caesar then proclaimed in stentorian tones, "Just as he laid hold of that innocent Man called the Christ, Pontius Pilate has fallen into my hands, and nothing will deliver him now."

Tiberius nodded to one of his guards standing at attention by the door. Nodding back, the guard swung the door open, and in walked a shackled Pilate, escorted by two soldiers, one on each arm. While he was being led to his place, Pilate prayed in silence. 'Lord, please don't destroy me with those corrupt Jews who were all so intent on provoking a riot against me, because You know I'd never have hurt You had I known it was You. But You understand I only did it in ignorance, so don't be too hard on me because of my crimes.'

The two guards slowly marched Pilate to where Albius stood at attention, and stepped away to take their respective places. Pilate then caught a glimpse of his wife, who stood in the wings, weeping quietly for her husband. He lovingly nodded at her, and she acknowledged him with a serenely sad smile.

'And please, Lord, have pity on Your servant Procla,' he continued to pray. 'You taught her to prophesy that You had to be nailed to the cross, and now she stands with me in my hour of disgrace. Don't punish her for my sins, but forgive us both with the portion of Your just ones.'

Suddenly a voice rang out from Heaven, causing everyone in the room to flinch. "All the generations of the Gentiles will call you blessed because everything that the prophets said about Me was fulfilled under you. Then you'll appear as My witness at My Second Coming, when I judge the Twelve Tribes of Israel and those who refuse to acknowledge My Name."

With that, there came a simple gesture from Tiberius, and jumping into action his captain Albius took one step forward and, with a single, powerful stroke, cut off the head of Pontius Pilate. From out of nowhere, an angel appeared and caught his body as it crumpled to the ground, and when Procla saw what the angel had done for her husband, she was so overwhelmed with joy that she ran to his slumped, lifeless body and died, too, while tearfully clutching his hand.

Farewell to Achuzan

ENOCH CLOSED THE book and looked up at the group of family and friends gathered around him. No longer the overflowing mass of people it was before, the crowd had thinned out since he had begun his last story. Undaunted, however, the patriarch carried on. "So, everyone, what did you think of the story of God fulfilling His promise to rescue Adam and his faithful children after five and a half days?"

An astonished Methuselah shook his head. "Amazing, Father, simply amazing. I was particularly intrigued by the fact that you said you were going to battle some evil person in the Last Days. You called him – what was it again? The Anti-Christ?"

"Yes, that's right, son. My, oh, my. That will be something someday, won't it?"

"So, the mystery of the One," Lamech slowly began, as though he were thinking out loud, "is each person's faith. What seems insignificant to us actually turns out to be the very thing that God desires most, the faith of the one, hoping, loving, trusting. That kind of person can change the world, can't he, Grandfather?"

"Very good, Lamech. I don't think I could have said it better myself."

"Your books, son, I just..." stammered Jared, "I just can't get over them. I mean, the incredible detail you provide; such pathos and joy, such tragedy and hope. I'm very interested in reading these books for myself."

"Me, too, Grandpa," Lamech chimed in.

"Can I read them, too, Papa Enoch?" chirped little Eli.

A smile swept irresistibly across Enoch's face. "Of course you can, Eli. Everyone can read them, anytime they want, from now on. They're God's gift to you all!"

The crowd cheered tumultuously for a while, then Jubal stepped forward, flanked by his two brothers, Hiram and Tubal. They were clapping, too, but they did not look at all as if they were caught up in the festive spirit sweeping through the crowd.

"How touching," Jubal intoned, notably sarcastic. "The benevolent patriarch bestowing such wisdom from On-High. Makes a guy just want to worship you, doesn't it?"

The crowd noticed Enoch's expression abruptly change from that of jubilance to one of disappointment. Everyone but Jubal stopped clapping.

"Not you again?" groaned Eli's mother.

"What's wrong, my dear?" Jubal replied, as cold as ice. "Afraid we might ruin your pathetic celebration?"

"How dare you continue to stir up controversy like this, Jubal," snapped Jared. "This is a sacred gathering, and you know it. What is your problem this time?"

"Well, I guess you could say I'm here to let you all in on a little secret of my own. Now granted, it's not the secret of the wind or the stars or the snow, but it is a stunning revelation just the same." Then, grinning maliciously, he paused for effect.

"Just get to the point, will you?" insisted Methuselah.

Jubal turned first to his brother on his left, then to his right.

"Then by all means: Show them, my brothers."

Together, they each withdrew one of Enoch's books from beneath their cloaks. Holding them both up, they offered everyone a chance to get a good look at them.

Jubal pressed on with sadistic glee. "Do any of you recognize these?"

Enoch gasped. "Of course. Those are some of the sacred books I've already read to you from. How did you get hold of them before you were supposed to? It wasn't time yet for anyone to read them."

"Tell us, Jubal," insisted Jared, "how did you get your hands on these books? I know for a fact they've been guarded day and night since Enoch gave them to me for safekeeping."

"Never mind that now, Father," Enoch interjected. "I'm afraid you have no idea who you're dealing with." Enoch sat there with his book firmly planted in his lap, poised like a shield over his heart.

Jubal flashed another malicious grin. "Yes, well, you see, that's something else I wanted to talk to you about, Papa Enoch. After all, there really isn't an awful lot that you mere mortals can keep safe from me. Now is there?"

"Not really, no." Enoch nodded stoically. "I just can't believe it took me so long to figure out who you really were."

Methuselah turned with a confused look on his face. "What's going on, Pop? What are you saying?"

"Well, son, it seems as though the mystery of the One is being challenged by none other than the Evil One himself."

Eli's mother shook her head in despair. "Can't somebody please speak in a language that regular folks like me can understand?"

A guttural burst of Jubal's laughter crackled through the calmness of the crowd, leaving it chilled to the bone. "That figures," he snarled. "Always have to have it spelled out for you, huh? Because if it ain't on the page, then god knows we have no idea how to think on our own." Jubal then stepped over and opened the book in Hiram's hands. "So take a good look for yourselves, people, and tell me what you see." Rifling through it, he revealed that every page was blank. "Nothing, that's what!" And opening Tubal's book, he showed that it, too, was blank. "Well, what do you know?" he sneered with a satisfied smirk. "There's nothing to read in any of these books after all, folks. I guess you've all been duped!"

An audible gasp rolled through the group of onlookers like a tidal wave.

Then, as if he were stalking a defenseless prey, Jubal took a menacing step toward the crowd and growled, "You all wanted to read for yourselves just what your beloved patriarch has been telling you? Didn't you? Well, here you go! Look! See! And, yes, your eyes have truly been opened for the first time ... to the charlatan who calls himself *our prophet!*"

The crowd suddenly grew restless and stood to their feet as one.

"Good God, son," exclaimed Jared. "What's the meaning of this? Can you explain why the pages of your books are blank? Is this some kind of a hoax, or what?"

"What do you think, Father? Do you think I'm a fraud now? A charlatan?"

"Of course not," Jared said without hesitation.

"Good. And what about you, Methuselah? Or you, Lamech? Do you think I've just been making up the stories that I say the Lord has given me?"

"Certainly not, Father," insisted Methuselah. "Just because Jubal shows us books that happen to look like yours doesn't mean you're lying to us."

Thoroughly frustrated, Jubal yelped, "What is wrong with you people? Can't you see? Clearly this man has duped you all!"

"I don't think you'd lie to us, Grandfather," Lamech said. "I trust *you*, not him."

"That's right," Eli's mother chimed in. "Maybe there's some other explanation for the blank pages in the books. Who knows?"

Slowly, Jubal's look of frustration turned to a scowl as he watched the faces in the crowd soften, one by one.

"You see?" chided Enoch. "What good is all your poison in the face of the One, you despicable creature? Your doubt and misery are powerless here."

Jubal and his two brothers started to groan lamentably.

The patriarch pressed on. "Your entire plan was based on a lie concocted in your own filthy minds. Now you're discovering the real truth of your predicament. Your evil cannot comprehend the purity of faith, so you choke on it."

With that, the trio of brothers began to writhe in pain, and the crowd took a collective step back, stunned and confused.

Methuselah asked, "Father, would you please tell us what's happening here?"

Enoch aimed a menacing finger at the trio. "Now, Satan, I want you and your two henchmen to leave this sacred place, this second! Do you understand me?"

The trio pathetically nodded their heads, like helpless doves caught in a net.

Lamech gawked. "*Satan*? Are you serious? Here?"

"Get out of here right now, Devil! Go!" Enoch pointed off into the horizon, and suddenly all three brothers transformed into none other than Satan and two of his grotesque demons. Grumbling, cursing, spewing, they flew away to the absolute astonishment of everyone there.

"But how, son?" Jared asked. "How did you know?"

"Because I've written about everyone's life in a book. Don't you remember?"

"Yes, of course, now I see," said Methuselah, still trying to grasp what had just happened. "At least I think I do."

"According to *The Book of Life*," Enoch continued, "the three brothers, Jubal, Hiram and Tubal were all tragically killed in a landslide while out on a hunting expedition. Killed that is, more than a month ago, never to be seen or heard from again."

"What? Oh, my word!" exclaimed Eli's mother. "You really have been sent by the God of Heaven and Earth. But, Grandfather, how long have you known about the real brothers being dead?"

"Quite a while now, actually."

"But why didn't you tell anyone when you found out?" Lamech asked. "Why'd you wait so long?"

"Yeah, Papa Enoch. How come?" wondered little Eli.

For several intense moments, Enoch gazed into the eyes of everyone there, eyes all filled with the same dire question, all yearning to know why he had not revealed the truth of his startling discovery sooner. "The answer to that question, dear family, is very much like the answer to your questions concerning the mystery of the One. Just as it is the duty of every man, woman and child to learn the truth for themselves about the Righteous One, each and every one of us must also stand alone in our quest to discern the truth about the Evil One. Does that make sense, everyone?"

"Of course, Father," Methuselah said with a knowing smile. "That makes all the sense in the world. Thank you for that."

Methuselah's wife then turned to Lamech's wife and said, "You know, I knew there was something about that Jubal that wasn't quite right. You could see it in his eyes."

Lamech's wife eagerly nodded back. "Oh, you are so right. I know what you're saying; I felt the same way, too. I just couldn't figure out what it was, though."

"Thank the Lord above for Father Enoch!" someone shouted from the midst of the people. "Not only is he a man uniquely blessed of God, but he's a blessing to all of us, too!"

A tremendous wave of excitement swept through the whole crowd like wildfire.

"Now listen, everyone," Enoch went on to say. "I appreciate your enthusiasm, really I do; but I'm afraid my days are numbered. Time is running out for me. I only have two more weeks before I have to leave."

"Leave?" groaned Eli's mother. "But you can't leave us now, Grandpa."

"But I have to, my dear. In fact, the angels who will be escorting me are standing by right now, ready to take me as soon as the Lord calls me to go. So they just stand there, biding their time, waiting eagerly to carry out God's instructions."

"Please don't go, Papa Enoch," Eli moaned. "We love you. What are we going to do without you?"

"Oh, Eli, are you trying to break my heart? Please be happy for me, won't you?"

Eli nodded obediently. "All right; for you."

"That's my boy. Just think: Soon, I'll be going back up to Heaven, to the uppermost Jerusalem and to my eternal inheritance."

"Oh, Pop, I wish I could go with you," said Methuselah, fighting hard to hold back his tears. "I'll miss you when you leave."

"And I'll miss you, too, my boy. I'll miss all of you! That is, until we're all reunited together again; which is why I want everyone to do whatever pleases the Lord."

"Certainly, Father, you know we will," Methuselah replied. "Just make sure you bless us before you go, won't you?"

"Of course, Methuselah, I'd be glad to do what you've asked."

"Is there anything I can help you with, son?" asked Jared.

"Yes, Father, I want you to help me get everyone together for one last meeting."

"Should I invite everyone?"

"Everyone."

"And Grandfather?" Lamech suddenly perked up.

"Yes, Lamech; what is it?"

"There's still one last thing you haven't explained to us."

"And what might that be, my boy?"

"When Jubal, I mean, the Evil One, opened the books you read to us before, all the pages in them were blank. I mean, they *were* blank, right?"

With a strange wrinkle to his brow, Enoch eyed his grandson for several moments. "Now that you mention it, I guess they were blank, weren't they?"

Obviously confused by his response, Lamech flashed a plaintive look at his father.

"Of course they were blank, Pop," Methuselah chimed in. "We all saw them with our own eyes. What Lamech is asking, I think, is more at: *Why* were they blank? Am I right, son? Is that what you're getting at?"

Lamech nodded, grateful that his father had stepped in. "Exactly. That's exactly what I wanted to know, yes."

"Why, that's very simple to explain," replied Enoch. "So simple, I'm surprised you even had to ask the question, actually. Doesn't anyone here know the answer to Lamech's question? Anyone at all?"

But after a long and awkward silence, no one seemed to have the slightest idea as to how to respond. Suddenly embarrassed, Methuselah cleared his throat and continued. "I'm sorry to disappoint you, Father, but I don't think any of us can say for sure. If I did offer some sort of an answer, though, would it be safe to say it has something to do with the mystery of the One?"

Enoch's eyes lit up immediately. "You see, son; I knew you wouldn't disappoint me. You're right, yes; it does, as a matter of fact."

"Like you told us before," Methuselah continued, spurred on by his father's infectious enthusiasm, "the mystery of the One cuts both ways, for good *and* for evil."

"That's right," Enoch beamed, like a proud teacher. "Go on."

"To the devil, the words in these books are incomprehensible, words of faith, words of hope, words of love. And because they're meaningless to him, they don't exist. So when he opened the books and looked inside, the pages were as blank as his soul."

"Very good, son; and the rest of you?" Enoch pressed him further. "Can you tell us why everyone here saw the pages as though they were blank?"

"Yes, Father, I think so. In fact, that's the greatest tragedy of all, because—"

"Because," said Lamech, breaking in suddenly, his eyes flashing as brightly as those of his grandfather. "Because when Satan held up those books and all he saw were blank pages, we were foolish enough, in that moment, to look at the world through his eyes, so we saw the pages as being blank, too."

"Bravo, my children, bravo," Enoch exclaimed proudly. "It seems that my work here is complete at last."

SO TWO THOUSAND MEN and their families traveled to Achuzan, where Enoch and his family were gathering one last time. Everyone came together as a group, and, one by one, they each came and bowed before the beloved patriarch.

"Dear Enoch," said one man, "you're so blessed of the Lord, the Eternal Ruler. Won't you please bless us, too, so that we may be glorified today?"

Another fellow bowed. "After all, you'll be glorified forever before the Lord, since He's chosen you rather than anybody else. He designated you writer of all His creation, visible and invisible."

"God bless you, my dear family and friends," Enoch replied. "And now, just as anyone asks the Lord for something, I want you to know that He asks you to pray to Him on behalf of all living things, because in God's world, there are many creatures that He cares for. That's why in the great time to come there are countless mansions prepared by God, for humans and for angels, good houses for the good, and bad houses for the bad. Blessed are those who enter one of the good houses, because in the house of evil there is neither rest nor peace, and anyone going to one of those evil houses is never seen from ever again.

"But never forget, everyone, from the greatest to the least of you! The Lord did not create human beings in vain when He fashioned them in His own likeness. He knew exactly what He was doing when He created eyes to see and ears to hear, a heart to reflect, and an intellect to deliberate with. And because the Lord already knew what mankind was going to do, He created the phenomenon of time; and time, He divided into years, months, days and hours, precisely measuring them out so that everyone might reflect on their time in this life. That way people might consider the frailty of their lives, from birth to death, and maybe they'd reflect on their sins, whether their deeds were good or evil; because no work is ever hidden from the Lord. Then they'd understand the impact of what they had accomplished with their lives."

As Enoch continued, a peculiar darkness began to envelope the landscape, slowly but surely shrouding everyone in its inky blackness. Still Enoch's voice penetrated through the darkness. "And when the Lord's creation eventually comes to an end, everyone will proceed to Judgment Day, and then, time itself will be abolished. Imagine that: No more years or months, no more hours or minutes. From that moment forward, time will no longer be a consideration; time will simply cease to have any meaning whatsoever. There'll simply be an eon, and all the righteous who escape the Lord's judgment will be gathered into that great eon, and for the righteous, the great eon will begin, and they'll live eternally. Finally, there'll be no more sickness or humiliation or anxiety or violence. There won't be any more night or darkness. There'll only be a tremendous light, and they'll have an indestructible wall and an incorruptible Paradise, for all corruptible things will have passed away *forever*."

Suddenly Sariel and Raguel appeared at Enoch's side. The patriarch looked up at both of their glowing faces and smiled warmly. Reaching out, he placed a hand on each of their cloaks. The angels then extended their wings, sending out rays of light in every direction, which created quite a spectacle for everyone who was sitting in the otherwise impenetrable darkness.

A man pointed through the murkiness and toward the shimmering streaks of light emanating from Enoch's angelic escorts. "Look! Enoch has become an angel!"

Everyone stopped and turned to look, straining their eyes toward the flashes of brightness that eerily surrounded Enoch, as the angelic wings began to gently lift him up.

"No, no, no," his wife replied. "Enoch hasn't *become* an angel. God just gave him temporary wings so he could fly to Heaven without the help of angels… At least I think so."

Perplexed by this peculiar interplay of darkness and light, the people gaped at the dazzling figures rising upward, higher and higher. Still Enoch's voice rang out as everyone rose to their feet and began to wander about through intermittent pockets of visibility.

"So walk patiently, my children," Enoch continued, "and always rely on God's promises, loving one another until it's time for you to leave this age of misery so you can all become inheritors of eternity. And blessed are the just who escape Judgment Day, because they will shine seven times brighter than the Sun."

Finally, the shimmering dot disappeared from view, like the morning star being swallowed up by dawn's early light; except in this case, this twinkle disappeared into a desperately black void instead of warm blue sky. Once again everyone found themselves completely in the dark, so they all went right back to stumbling around, bumping into one another as they did.

THE VEIL OF DARKNESS that had gripped the landscape gradually began to unleash its oppressive grip, and as the light began to return, one man commented, "Well, I know I saw it with my own two eyes, but I'm still not quite sure what it was I saw."

"How in Heaven's name did Enoch go up like that?" asked his wife as her eyes tried to adjust to the return of the light.

"Don't ask me," the man insisted. "I just told you, I haven't the slightest idea."

"And what do you think happened to all the books that Enoch wrote?"

"There you go again about those books. How many times do I have to tell you? What good are books that don't have any writing in them?"

"So I'm sorry I even mentioned it. Why do I even bother?" said the woman as she walked away, leaving her husband just standing there.

AIMLESSLY WANDERING about, Methuselah stumbled over a ridge, when suddenly a disembodied voice registered quietly in his ear. "Open your eyes, Methuselah, and what do you see?" Looking toward the distant horizon, he squinted against the sunlight. "Books?" he murmured. Holding up his hand to shield his eyes, he could see that there were hundreds of books, lying strewn about an open field. "Everybody, over here! Look! It's the books we've all been searching for!"

The first person who came running was Lamech. Dropping to his knees, he opened one of the books and found that every page had words on it, front and back, and cover to cover. Lamech picked up another one and opened it, too. "And they're all full of writing, just like Grandfather promised."

Everyone else followed, eagerly gathering up the books as they went, and in the end, they counted three hundred and sixty-six of them in all.

ENOCH'S SONS SOON erected a monument on the very spot where the patriarch had been taken up to Heaven. Etched into this stone pillar was a simple inscription. It read: *In honor of Enoch, the man beyond time who graced us with his tales of forever, provided courtesy of the Invisible God.*

Post Script to Time

ENOCH REVERENTLY stepped forward and bowed before the molten Face of God.

"Hello, Enoch," said the Lord. "Welcome back."

"Thank you, Lord. It's good to be back."

For several intense moments, Enoch just looked up into those smoldering eyes as though he were about to say something.

"What is it, Enoch? Is there something I can do for you?"

Enoch smiled sheepishly, slightly embarrassed. "Yes, Lord, there is. Something has been troubling me. I'm sorry to have to even bring it up, actually; but I just can't help wondering."

"Of course, Enoch, I understand. Ask me."

"Could you please tell me about the fate of mankind? I'm so curious. Did they ever accept the message I delivered to them in the books?"

The glowing eyes stared back at the patriarch for what seemed like an eternity. "What's wrong, Enoch? Don't you remember? The answer you seek is already contained in the stories you wrote yourself?"

Enoch was quite perplexed at this. "Yes, that is odd, isn't it?" He squinted as though that might help him jog his memory. "Come to think of it: You're right. I do remember, almost. More like a dream I had, though, that I can't get entirely straight now that I'm awake. At least I think I'm awake. Why can't I remember things the way I used to?"

"Because while you were still living on Earth, you were only concerned with earthly affairs, understanding things in strictly human terms, but now that I've chosen you for heavenly purposes, you're here with Me. Naturally, you'll never see things in ordinary ways again."

Enoch nodded thoughtfully. "I think I see Your point, yes. Nothing will ever be the same again."

"Are you disappointed?" asked the Lord.

"Oh, no, of course not. I'm just trying to figure some things out. Still trying to get adjusted, I guess."

"I understand."

"So tell me, if You'll be so kind as to refresh my memory: How does mankind respond to the message I left for them? Did they believe what I had to say? Or was I simply written off as a lunatic?"

"Well, Enoch, let Me put it to you this way: I'll describe two mysteries for you. First, many rebels will violate the word of truth. They'll speak incredible things and pronounce many falsehoods. Tremendous civilizations will be created, and many books will be composed in their own words."

"Books? More books?" queried Enoch. "What about the ones You had me write? Won't anyone pay attention to *them?*"

"Of course," came the Lord's response. "Someday."

"Someday? What do You mean, someday?"

"Your books, Enoch, will be lost to mankind for a very long time."

"Lost? But why?"

"They're lost because only a handful of people ever appreciate them; people like Jared, Methuselah and Lamech, along with their immediate families. So after generations of neglect and ignorance, they'll simply be lost to much of the world, and for a time it will be as though they had never been written at all."

Enoch frowned at the mere thought. "But You say things will be different someday? You did say that, didn't You?"

"Yes. Someday people will begin to write all My words properly in their own languages without altering or diminishing them. They'll perform the task correctly, and then they'll possess everything I've said about them from the very beginning."

Relieved, Enoch beamed a tremendous smile. "That's wonderful, Lord. Please tell me more, if You would."

"Then I'll describe the other mystery I spoke about. This one, however, concerns the faithful and the wise, who will be given books of joy, integrity and remarkable wisdom, and having received the gift of those books, they'll believe in what they have to say."

"You mean books like the ones I wrote?" interrupted Enoch, unable to hold back his enthusiasm.

"Yes, Enoch, yes, books just like yours. And they'll rejoice in them, and all the faithful ones will acquire the knowledge of every righteous path through them and be rewarded, and someday, they'll call out to the people of Earth and make them listen to their wisdom."

"Then my efforts didn't go to waste after all," sighed Enoch.

"No, of course not."

Pausing for several moments, Enoch gazed longingly up at that incredible molten face. "So, Lord, I was wondering."

"Of course, Enoch. What is it?"

"I just thought that maybe..."

"Yes, Enoch?"

"You know ... I was hoping You might have another story to tell me."

"Another story?" mused the Lord. "Certainly, Enoch. What did you have in mind?"

"Well, Lord, I was wondering. Can You please tell me more about this One You continue to speak about?"

"Ah, yes, of course," replied the Face thoughtfully, "and so the mystery of the One continues still."

THE SEGUE

In theology ... from time to time, there are drastic changes... A new view of man, world, and God begins to prevail in the theological community, where the whole and its details appear in a different light.

Hans Küng, *Paradigm Change in Theology*

The Next Paradigm Shift

A Different Way of Seeing

SO ENDS THE "entertainment" portion of our program, as it were. However, before we roll credits, we must segue to one last order of business—the much-anticipated business of what connects all five *sacred* things and the proof that it conveys concerning God's control and faithfulness. Usually, the end of a book is reserved for various miscellaneous items that have not quite fit into the main body; and while this may hold true to some small degree, it does not hold true to the big picture of this work as a whole. Whatever you do, then, do not let appearances be deceiving. Rest assured, what follows in no way constitutes your typical appendix—a word that often implies something of relatively little purpose and is therefore best removed. And although what is contained in the next act has no real significance when seen in isolation from all that has preceded it, I can honestly say that what follows constitutes the most important part of our presentation. Why do I say this?

Well, apart from the fact that this is the section where I finally tie all the evidence together in terms of what connects the five things, I say it because Act Three is where I hope to put the final touches of presenting the evidence for the validity of the apocryphal books that I am so convinced are worthy to be ranked amongst the canonical books. Whereas most people in traditional Christian circles might still find it too hard to accept such a possibility, they would, however, be much more inclined to do so if a clear-cut connection could be made between the books in question and those things that they already associate with mainstream biblical truths—things like The Ark of the Covenant, The Shroud of Turin, and *The Septuagint Bible.* And quite frankly, to expect otherwise would be the height of folly on my part, especially considering the fact that part of the enigma surrounding their contents have actually occurred as a direct result of God's own desire to withhold these books until the time when a future generation was destined to rediscover them.

Therefore, keep in mind, I have no objection whatsoever to the general reluctance of most Christians in this regard; in fact, knowing what I know about the unfolding drama of God's hidden hand in history, I gladly accept a healthy dose of skepticism in all of this. As a matter of fact, it would be downright callous of me if I were to resent anyone who honestly admitted they were still having a hard time accepting these books back into the Biblical Canon. The only thing I do find intolerable, though, is the stubborn unwillingness on the part of any so-called "truth-seeker" to at least open their hearts and minds to the possibility that *if*—and this is a very important *if* here—that is, *if* a sound biblical basis for them can be adequately demonstrated.

After all, it is no great secret that the hardest part of relating to the controversial subject matter contained in a book like this—subjects like scriptural interpretation, biblical chronology, and religious artifacts—is overcoming the psychological hurdles that are the result of a lifetime of skepticism and doubt. But the greatest tragedy of all would be if, once this connection between the lost books in this work and the five *sacred* things is sufficiently demonstrated, the evidence was disregarded and dismissed simply because these books had not been included in the modern Canon.

In terms of the entire span of human history, however, this is certainly nothing new. In ages past, nearly every generation has been confronted with one such dilemma or another, whereby what was once thought to be "the truth and nothing but the truth" was challenged, then rocked to its core, and finally overturned by the next "paradigm shift." A term coined by American physicist Thomas Kuhn, in 1962, paradigm shift refers to a fundamental change that occurs in the basic ideology of science—a change that opens up entirely new vistas of perception that would never have been considered valid until that moment in time. Originally applied only to scientific thinking, this term has since evolved to the point that it is also used to describe changes in numerous non-scientific models or perceptions. Accordingly, the Swiss theologian and author Hans Küng has applied Kuhn's theory of change to the history of human awareness so that for Küng a paradigm shift is what occurred with both the Protestant Reformation and the Age of Enlightenment. Speaking about this kind of radical change in the field of theology, Küng described it this way:

> In theology ... from time to time, there are drastic changes... As in the change from the geocentric to the heliocentric theory, from phlogiston to oxygen chemistry, from corpuscular to wave theory, so also in the change from one theology to another: Fixed and familiar concepts are changed; laws and criteria controlling the admissibility of certain problems and solutions are shifted; theories and models are upset.
>
> In a word, the paradigm, or model of understanding, is changed, together with the whole complex of different methods, fields of problems, and attempted solutions as had previously been recognized by the theological community. The theologians get used, as it were, to a different way of seeing things, to see them in the context of a new model. Some things are now perceived that were not seen formerly, and possibly some things are overlooked that were formerly noticed. A new view of man, world, and God begins to prevail in the theological community, where the whole and its details appear in a different light.[232]

From this, it also follows that for a paradigm shift to occur there must be a considerable accumulation of information and experience to elicit such a change, all of which, as one can imagine, can only occur through the coordinated efforts of committed individuals over the span of several decades. In rare cases, the onset of a paradigm shift can be noted with a fair amount of accuracy, as with the Reformation, which is generally dated from 1520, and is widely attributed to the influence of one man, Martin Luther, and one document, his Ninety-Five Theses that he nailed to the church door in Wittenberg. More often than not, however, there is little consensus as to when this shift occurs, as with the Enlightenment, which is said to have begun as early as the middle of the seventeenth century and as late as the beginning of the eighteenth century. And whereas one man looms above all others in the case of the Reformation, there are numerous names that stand out in regard to the inception of the Age of Enlightenment. In philosophy, there were Rene Descartes, Immanuel Kant, and Voltaire; in politics, John Locke, Jean-Jacques Rousseau, and Thomas Hobbes.

On With the Struggle

CONSIDERING THE facts of history, then, one can feel quite intimidated by an awareness of all that it takes to stem the tide of the status quo, hence the unique structure of this book, which is not one book but two. Moreover, this book can only be truly grasped upon reading it more than once. This is because one's frame of reference always determines his or her ability to assimilate any new philosophy, and because of this most basic human reality, each reading of this book will provide a new depth of understanding never before possible until after being confronted with the ideas contained in it. Even more important, persuasive words alone do not initiate the next paradigm shift in any given field, as Küng went on to explain.

> Not only in theology, but in natural science, a new model of understanding demands something like a *conversion*, which cannot be extorted in a rational way. I speak less of the initiator—the person who, because of a sudden intuitive experience or a long and arduous ripening, has suggested a new model—than of the recipients, those who have to decide for or against. The defenders of the old and of the new model—something that must not be underestimated—live in "different worlds," different worlds of ideas and of language; often they can

> scarcely understand each other. Translation from the old to the new language is necessary, but at the same time there must be a new conviction, a conversion.[233]

That is why, before expecting anyone to simply accept at face value *The Tales*—and the implications regarding the truth conveyed in the five *sacred* things—I have expended such considerable effort in formulating both phases of their extended *Analyses*. More to the point, this is why I have chosen to convey the message of this work in, dare I say, sublimely poetic terms rather than purely "rational" ones, to echo the words of Küng. In approaching the material this way, I have, of course, taken my cue from what I have come to detect in God's own mode of communication, in terms of the dramas that transcend interpretation—a point I hope I have already adequately expressed—so hopefully you will not think that I am claiming any priority in such an approach. I only mention it here in the context of the hurdles one must overcome in attempting something like this book is hoping to accomplish.

In all of this, however, I am encouraged in light of what the Nobel Prize-winning German physicist Max Planck said about the improbability of affecting change in one's lifetime, and the fact that Küng insisted that what is applicable to the physicist is even more so in regard to the theologian. I am inspired to carry on with the struggle when I hear Planck say, "New scientific ideas never spring from a communal body, however organized, but rather from the head of an individually-inspired researcher who struggles with his problems in lonely thought, and unites all his thought on one single point, which is his whole world for the moment."[234] But however much I take heart from hearing that statement by Planck, I am equally discouraged by another: "A new scientific truth does not triumph by convincing its opponents and making them see the light, but rather because its opponents eventually die, and a new generation grows up familiar with it."[235] Such is the bitter irony of the paradigm pioneers, or as Küng calls them, "model-testers" and "new-thinkers."[236]

Notwithstanding Küng's attitude that as physicists go so do theologians, I would also like to parenthetically point out something to anyone who might be put off by the idea that what Planck said about scientific truth has any bearing in regard to theological truth. And to this objection, I admit I, too, might feel obliged to recant my potentially tenuous position; if not for one small detail, that is. Because as it turns out, Planck himself, whose own work paved the way for the shift from special relativity to quantum physics, firmly believed otherwise. Said Planck: "Both religion and science require a belief in God. For believers, God is the beginning, and for physicists, He is the goal of every thought process. To the former, He is the foundation; to the latter, the crown of the edifice of every generalized worldview."[237] And in no uncertain terms, Planck further insisted:

> No matter where and how far we look, nowhere do we find a contradiction between religion and science. On the contrary, we find a complete concordance in the very points of decisive importance. Religion and science do not exclude each other, as many contemporaries of ours believe or fear. They mutually supplement and condition each other. The most immediate proof of the compatibility of religion and science, even under the most thoroughly critical scrutiny, is the historical fact that the very greatest scientists of all time—men such as Kepler, Newton, Leibniz—were permeated by a most profound religious attitude.[238]

So, even though Planck was realistic enough to acknowledge the forces that resist every advancement toward the next shift in human awareness, he never lost faith in the indivisible nature of theological and scientific truth. Therefore, I can expect nothing less of myself in attempting to elicit a "conversion" by way of my discourse concerning the connectivity of things that have themselves been seen as so many disconnected points on the frontier of a new paradigm that lies just beyond the next horizon. And as I already mentioned in an opening chapter of this book:

> Although there are many pitfalls along the way, the God of *The Bible* does not hesitate to beckon us onward in this journey of discovery. Therefore, if one can appreciate that it is God Himself Who is guiding our quest, then it should come as no surprise that He is also the One Who has provided sufficient signposts to help us along the way.

The Ultimate Key

THAT SAID, I WOULD now like to return to my original train of thought throughout this entire work, which is to say, the way in which the five *sacred* things convey a startling proof of God's control and faithfulness. What were the five things again? One, The Ark of the Covenant, also known as The Ark of Testimony, the wooden chest overlaid in gold, in which the Israelites carried the two stone tablets of the Ten Commandments. Two, The Spear of Destiny, also known as The Holy Lance or The Spear of Longinus, the Roman centurion's spear that pierced the side of Jesus as He hung on the cross. Three, The Shroud of Turin, also known as The Holy Shroud, the linen burial cloth that bears the image of the resurrected Christ. Four, The Great Pyramid of Giza, also known as *The Bible* in Stone, the only remaining structure among the Seven Wonders of the World, said to contain the prophetic history of Scripture in its geometric dimensions. And five, *The Septuagint Bible*, also known as *The Greek Old Testament*, the vernacular translation of *The Hebrew Bible*, produced around 250 B.C., and the book most often quoted by the writers of *The New Testament*.

Thus far, in the course of working toward revealing what these five things have in common, we have detected a series of clues in Acts One and Two. First, we established the fact that *The Septuagint Bible* was well known to have depicted a five thousand, five hundred year chronology from Adam to Christ, which had been universally accepted by the Christian Church more than fifteen centuries prior to Ussher's chronology of just four thousand years. This was followed by the fact that the apocryphal literature introduced us to the prophecy of The Great Five and a Half Days, which together with the prophetic significance contained in the dimensions of The Ark of the Covenant offered us our next clue as to how these things might connect with The Holy Lance, The Holy Shroud, and *The Bible* in Stone. Meanwhile, in the process of digesting *The Tales* themselves, we saw firsthand the importance of another group of sacred artifacts in the history of God's dealings with mankind, artifacts like Adam's sheepskin garment, Veronica's painting of Christ, and Jesus' seamless robe, which, in turn, provided us with a much greater appreciation for such things, far beyond anything that the traditions of a modern age have previously allowed. And finally, in demonstrating the way that the promise of "days" symbolically connects *The Septuagint* and The Ark, we have, most important of all, established exactly the kinds of foundational truths that are so necessary in preparing one's mind for the way in which *all five things* will be shown to connect.

So, now that you have made your way to this point, having digested Acts One and Two, I hope to take you to the next level, with Act Three. But be advised, as always, my methodology will not initially involve just "spelling it out," as it were. In fact, I could shout the answer to the mystery of how the five *sacred* things connect till kingdom come, and still no one might "get it." Therefore, as I have done throughout this entire work, my objective with the following presentation will be to, "bit by bit, action by action, and level by level," build toward a moment of insight. Then, if I have adequately done my job, when I do get to that point of "spelling it out," the attentive reader might actually anticipate the answer I am reaching toward even before I have said it, much in the same way that someone who is paying attention to a conversation can often finish the other person's sentence before they do.

To that end, we will next take a more in-depth look at *The Players* involved in *The Tales*, with the express purpose of further enhancing the position that this book takes in regard to its supposedly "unorthodox" characterizations. Then, we will examine *The Themes* that have been woven throughout this work so that the reader will gain a more explicit understanding of their potential, which might have been overlooked in the initial read-through. And finally, we will turn our attention to *The Subplots*, which is where we will be fitting together all of the puzzle pieces that will finally come together to reveal the ultimate key in verifying the Lord's control over history by way of His faithfulness to His promises.

And now for the final act of *Tales of Forever*; now for Act Three of the unfolding drama of God's hidden hand in history.

ACT THREE

Our mythologies agree with the results of our meditations, not by force and distortion but directly, easily, and naturally; and as such should be seen as civil histories of the first peoples, who are everywhere found to have been naturally poets.

Giambattista Vico, *New Science*

THE PLAYERS

If you shut up the truth and bury it under the ground, it will only grow and gather to itself such explosive force that, on the day it bursts out, it will blow up everything in its way.

Emile Zola, *Dreyfus: His Life and Letters*

Enoch as: The Go-Between

A Bridge Between Worlds

FOUND WITHIN the pages of the biblical record is the strange story of a man by the name of Enoch. Anyone familiar with *The Bible* is familiar with him. In both *The Old Testament* and *The New Testament,* it is related, in no uncertain terms, that "Enoch walked with God, and he was not, because God took him."[239] According to biblical scholars, Enoch is a man who holds the peculiar distinction of being the only patriarch whose life story does not end with the words: "And he died." What is more, Paul elaborated on his story when he said, "By faith, Enoch was taken from this life so that he did not experience death. He could not be found because God had taken him away. But before he was taken, he was commended as one who pleased God."[240]

So in the mouth of multiple witnesses, we have one of the most remarkable biographies—however brief—in all of Scripture, not to mention, this is the same man who supposedly penned numerous books as a result of his encounter with God. Yet flying in the face of such testimony, many of these same scholars—who all presumably believe in God's ability to communicate—have chosen to repudiate the idea that Enoch actually wrote the books that bear his name. Attributing them instead to later writers, who allegedly borrowed Enoch's name to lend authenticity to their own works, these so-called "experts" have categorized these texts as *pseudepigrapha.* In doing so, these remarkable books were stigmatized, and have ever since been tainted by equal parts of skepticism and doubt.

Even after the pioneering work of men like James Bruce and Richard Laurence, most biblical scholars insisted that *The First Book of Enoch* could not have existed during the time of *The New Testament* world, having placed its origins some three centuries *after* the birth of Christianity. That is, they did until 1947, when the unprecedented discovery of *The Dead Sea Scrolls,* in the Judean Desert, sparked a fervent, new wave of inquiry. Amongst the more than seven hundred fragmented documents discovered at Qumran, believers and skeptics alike were amazed to find remains of ten manuscripts of *First Enoch,* as well as several other works in the Enochic tradition, such as *The Book of Jubilees* and *The Testament of the Twelve Patriarchs.* Using carbon-14 dating, these ancient manuscripts were estimated to have been written at least as early as 200 B.C. No longer could anyone argue that these documents had not been produced *before* the birth of Christianity, or that these works were not in a position to influence those who walked and talked with Jesus of Nazareth.

More importantly, since those heady days of discovery, books like those ascribed to Enoch are no longer the sole property of cloistered scholars who discuss such arcane matters amongst themselves in darkened rooms, walled away from the rest of humanity, which is, according to them, bereft of their learned perspective. Now, thanks to today's open-ended world of mass communication technology, those of us who choose to read these texts for ourselves are now in a position to come to our own conclusions, based on a comparison of them with their more familiar canonical counterparts. The fruits of such a labor are positively astounding. Far from lending credence to the *pseudepigraphical* theory of Enochic authorship, the resulting examination—free from the bias that often accompanies institutionally-sponsored reviews—demonstrates that these texts reveal an array of striking parallels between the teachings of Enoch and Jesus. In fact, it has been estimated there are at least one hundred known references in *The New Testament* that can be traced directly to the books ascribed to Enoch. In light of such a connection it appears that, more than any other figure in biblical history, Enoch stands as a veritable bridge between worlds, between that of *The Old Testament* and *The New Testament.*

Parallels of Thought

IN THE GOSPELS OF both Matthew and Luke, for example—when Jesus spoke of the resurrection of the dead, where people will refrain from marriage because they will be like the angels of Heaven—it turns out that He was actually quoting Enoch.[241] "But from the beginning you (speaking of the angels) were made spiritual, living a life that is eternal; therefore, I (God) have not made wives for you because your dwelling place is in Heaven."[242]

Elsewhere, John has Jesus speaking of "rooms" in Heaven.[243] But what most people never realize is that before Jesus mentioned them Enoch spoke of the "habitations of the elect."[244] Speaking to his children, Enoch said, "In the great time to come, there are innumerable mansions prepared for men—good ones for the good, and bad ones for the bad."[245] Later, Paul would echo this same idea when he wrote: "If the earthly tent we live in is destroyed, we have a building from God, an eternal house in Heaven, not built by human hands."[246]

Furthermore, one of the titles Jesus gave Himself to convey His unique role in history, that of the Son of Man—repeated eighty-one times in *The Gospels*—finds its source in none other than Enoch. Mark has Jesus saying, "At that time, mankind will see the Son of Man coming in clouds with great power and glory, and He will send His angels to gather his elect from the four winds, from the ends of the Earth to the ends of the Heavens."[247] In this passage, one can see that Jesus was referring to *First Enoch*, when the patriarch prophesied that:

> The kings, princes, and all who possess the Earth will glorify the Son of Man, Who was concealed from the beginning, in complete secrecy, by the power of the Most High and revealed only to the elect. He will sow the congregation of the saints and the elect, and they will stand before Him on that day.[248]

Another remarkable evidence for the authenticity of *First Enoch* is revealed when one considers the disciple's description of the transfiguration of Christ: "And a voice came out of the cloud, saying, 'This is My Beloved Son: Hear Him.'"[249] Matthew, Mark, and Luke all record this same event, each describing the scene in similar terms—with one exception, however. Luke, in his description, provides a unique distinction that was sadly omitted by the *King James Bible* translators, an omission that obscures the true meaning of Luke's rendition, which was clearly spelled out in the original Greek. Fortunately for us, later generations of translators who had access to the Greek manuscripts were not so worried with the Elizabethan concern for textual uniformity, and have admirably noted Luke's subtle but all-important distinction. According to *The Expanded Bible*, in Luke's recounting, we discover what the voice out of the cloud really said. "This is My Son, My Chosen One: Listen to Him."[250]

In this version, the translators compare this exalted title to one that is found in the forty-second chapter of *The Book of Isaiah*. Most render Isaiah's description as: "Behold, My Servant Whom I uphold, My Chosen, in Whom My soul delights."[251]

Clearly, one can see the parallels in the language of Isaiah with that of Luke's, when he records the circumstances of the transfiguration event. Of greater importance still is that Isaiah's title of "My Chosen " is often rendered as "My Elect." Sources for this variation include the esteemed *Geneva Bible*, a translation that predated the *King James* Version by more than half a century, and one that accompanied the Pilgrims on the *Mayflower*. The reason that this distinction is so important is because the title of the "Elect One" is found *fifteen* times in *First Enoch*.

> In that day, the Elect One will sit upon a throne of glory, and their spirits within them shall be strengthened when they look upon My Elect One, because they've fled for protection to My holy and glorious Name. In that day, I'll cause my Elect One to dwell in their midst.[252]

Assuming, then, that this book was known to the disciples of Christ, one can only imagine their considerable astonishment when the "voice out of the cloud" told them concerning Jesus that "This is My Son, My Elect One," the very One Who was promised in *The First Book of Enoch*.

Could it actually be possible that such precise parallels of thought are the result of books that were not divinely inspired? Furthermore, who in their right mind would even concern themselves with the hackneyed controversy of who did or did not write these books when they have been linked with the teachings of none other than Jesus, Isaiah, Matthew, Mark, Luke, John, and Paul? Clearly, this book—and others just like it—have been treated as genuine sources of truth by some of the greatest seers in the history of the world, and just because a bunch of well-intentioned "experts" have cast these books into the realm of doubt and suspicion does not mean that free-thinking, rational minds should henceforth be kept from coming to their own conclusions.

So away with the outmoded verdict of self-appointed geniuses, who, in their timid ignorance, refuse to sanction the books of such luminaries as Enoch, who, as the canonical record clearly states, walked and talked with God. Let the light of truth shine forth as it has always been meant to do, and let no one presume to hold back what God has intended by way of the revelation of Jesus Christ, the Elect One Who "dwelled in their midst,"[253] the Son of Man Who, though once "concealed by the power of the Most High,"[254] has now "chosen to reveal the secret of God's kingdom to His saints and His elect."[255]

Adam as: The Defendant

A Spiritual Litmus Test

ONE OF THE MOST parodied chapters in biblical history involves Eve's encounter with a talking serpent who led her to believe that simply by eating the Fruit of the Tree of Knowledge she and Adam could become as wise as God.[256] And although Satan, who cleverly masked his appearance to the first woman, is clearly the villain of the story, it is Eve who has over the course of time incurred the blame for the Fall of Mankind. However, upon further review of this scenario, several things leap out to the observant questioner. Most importantly, the simple fact is that whatever one believes about this famous scene reveals more about the person who is interpreting its meaning as opposed to any details that are presented in the story itself. In other words, this story acts as a spiritual litmus test for the human soul. Like some kind of cosmic Rorschach test, it presents us with an ambiguous scene designed to reveal the psychological makeup of the person who is asked to interpret the meaning of that scene. Let me demonstrate what I mean.

The Mother of All Origin Stories

CONTAINED IN THIS mother of all origin stories are a number of critical elements. One, Eve is confronted in the garden by a serpent that just happens to possess the power of speech. Two, due to the nature of the biblical narrative, we are made privy to what is withheld from Eve, that is to say, we know that behind the mask of this talking serpent is the entity *The Bible* describes as Satan. Three, the Fruit that Eve, and eventually Adam, consumed from this Tree of Knowledge was such that, among other things, it has been described throughout the ages as an apple, a fig, a pomegranate, a pear, or a grape. And four, when God asked Adam if he had eaten from the tree that he was told not to eat from, he summarily blamed both God and Eve for his actions by stating, "The woman You, God, put here with me gave me the Fruit, so I ate it."[257]

In regard to element number one, the first thing that springs to mind is that Eve does not seem the least bit shocked when she is spoken to by a serpent. The serpent begins talking to her, and she quite matter-of-factly responds as if she were entirely comfortable with having a conversation with an animal. Naturally, most critics of *The Bible* would argue that this is just one more reason the stories contained in it are only useful as anecdotes or fables that possess no historical value. On the other hand, if you are a person who believes that the extraordinary is possible, then you might have no problem at all with it. In this case, the example of the Rorschach test is useful because what we are concerned with in examining this story is not so much the empirical evidence we are naturally deprived of by virtue of the fact that we were not there at the time but with the psychological legacy of the event. In other words, what is so telling about this story—improbable as it may seem—is the extent to which it persists in impressing itself upon the collective consciousness of humanity.

From a purely exegetical perspective, I would like to point out that the biblical record indicates the animal kingdom was clearly in possession of what humans have generally believed they alone possess, that is, the power of speech. For example, like Eve before him, Balaam had his own strange encounter with a talking animal. In his case, he had a conversation with his donkey. Although he had even more cause for concern than she did, he did not flinch in the least when the animal spoke to him. He, too, just replied as calmly as ever.[258] In this regard, the apocryphal literature is even more explicit. Only when the serpent attacked Adam and Eve did God deprive him and his kind of the power of speech.[259] Ridiculous, one might say! How can anyone possibly think that animals once had the ability to speak as only humans can? To which I would ask: You mean to tell me that animals do not possess the ability to communicate? They are, after all, sentient beings just like us, are they not? When they are angry or scared, dogs growl and cats hiss. When they are hungry, they clearly communicate this fact with eager eyes, a bark, and a meow. Monkeys howl, hyenas laugh, whales sing. Every morning the birds fill the air with their song; every evening the crickets chirp their call. The whole of creation voices its mind. Nevertheless, because humans cannot understand what they are saying, because their thoughts are not expressed in a manner such as ours, some dare to say that they cannot speak. What could be more absurd than that?

No wonder, then, that, before God deprived the serpent of speech, Eve assumed it was the most natural thing in the world to carry on a conversation with a talking snake, and no wonder that, since time immemorial, humans—that is to say, most humans—do not think twice when authors of every kind have depicted animals as having the power to speak. In mythology, folk tales, and children's literature, talking animals abound. From the countryside of Aesop to the dark woods of the Grimm Brothers, from the land of Oz to the wonderful world of Disney, talking animals overflow the landscape. And to think, it all started with a single, seemingly innocent conversation in a place called Eden.

The Puppet Master

AS FOR ELEMENT NUMBER two: Biblical scholars are unanimous in their appraisal that the entity that is "pulling the strings," as it were, in this scenario is not really a serpent but is, in fact, Satan. Yet nowhere in the account found in *The Book of Genesis* does it ever mention the devil. After all, the serpent was the one whom God cursed, not Satan. It does not say Satan will be cursed above all the other animals, and that he will forever after have to crawl around on his belly and eat from the dust.[260] Clearly, God is addressing an actual serpent and not merely an allegorical one. All that theologians are left to do, then, is to infer the devil's complicity in this scenario; and do not misunderstand me here. I, too, believe that Satan was the puppet master of this greatest of all tragedies. All I am saying—as usual—is: How interesting that our traditional view of the canonical record is never as explicit as traditionalists would have us believe. What biblical scholars must do in cases like this is point out that the next verses in *The Bible* merely allude to Satan's role in the Fall of Mankind. Even though the devil is never mentioned, his presence is said to be inferred by way of God's curse upon the serpent when He says, "I'll put enmity between you and the woman, and between your offspring and hers; he will crush your head, and you will bruise his heel."[261]

So, where does one turn to find a more explicit description of Satan's involvement in this scenario? Certainly it must be somewhere in the canonical version of Scripture, right? Sadly, the answer is no. Once again, the only place where one finds God clearly spelling out that it is the devil himself in all of this is the apocryphal record. In *The First Book of Adam and Eve*, we find the primordial couple in a situation where, just days after their expulsion from the garden, they were confronted by a group of angels they initially thought had been sent to them by God. But becoming suspicious of the intent of these angels, Adam prayed for the Lord to reveal whether or not these beings had been sent by Him. No sooner had he uttered his prayer than an angel appeared and told him:

> Don't be afraid, Adam. This group is actually Satan and his minions. He was hoping to deceive you the same way he did in the beginning. The first time he did so while hiding in the serpent. This time, however, he appeared to you in the form of an angel of light in order that you might worship him, and thereby enslave you in the very presence of God.[262]

How ironic. Even as theologians have sought to interpret from the canonical version that Satan was hiding behind the mask of the serpent, it turns out they were really lending credence to the very apocryphal record most of them were trying to discredit. Such is always the case with the power of genuine truth, for even when a stream is forced underground, it will eventually work its way back to the surface; and when it does, the purity of its waters is even greater than the one that has taken its course above ground. Concerning the irrepressible nature of suppressed truth, perhaps the most eloquent observer on the subject is the French writer-turned-social activist Emile Zola. "If you shut up the truth and bury it under the ground, it will only grow and gather to itself such explosive force that, on the day it bursts out, it will blow up everything in its way."[263]

What Kind of Fruit?

ON TO ELEMENT NUMBER three: As every Sunday school student knows, God told Adam and Eve that the fruit from all of the trees in the Garden of Eden were admissible to eat; that is, all but the Fruit from the Tree of the Knowledge of Good and Evil.[264] Naturally, this made the Fruit from that tree more tempting than all the other trees put together. As a result, it was only a matter of time before that fruit was going to get eaten. But what kind of fruit was it? And why, when *Genesis* never reveals what it was, has our Western tradition so often depicted it as an apple? According to *Wikipedia,* there have been numerous contenders, throughout the ages, as to which fruit constituted "the" Forbidden Fruit. For reasons that can only be attributed to the Rorschach phenomenon, this Fruit has among other things been declared to be—besides the aforementioned apple—a pomegranate, a fig, a pear, or a grape.

Nevertheless, the leading candidate, bar none, is the apple. According to some historians, the leaning in the Western world toward the apple has to do with the mythological tradition that has Eris, the Greek goddess of Strife, using one to instigate the uprising that triggered the start of the Trojan War and led to the downfall of their greatest hero, Paris.[265] Other historians, like Dan Koeppel, point to the fact that an ancient translation of *The Bible* even went so far as to insert the word *apple* instead of *fruit*, presumably because of the etymological connotation of the Latin word *malum*, which means both *apple* and *evil*.[266]

Subsequently, many of the greatest artistic minds of the Renaissance carried this idea forward. In his epic poem *Paradise Lost*, John Milton has the serpent revealing to the first couple that the Forbidden Fruit that endowed him with human reason and speech was an apple;[267] while Albrecht Dürer, in his famous engraving *Adam and Eve*, has the serpent holding an apple in his mouth, as Eve reaches out to take it. But certainly the most enduring image in modern times was produced by one of the greatest storytellers Hollywood has ever known, Walt Disney, when he placed a succulent but poisonous apple in the hand of an evil queen, who, like Satan before her, hid within the guise of another, thus enabling her to hand it to an unsuspecting Snow White.

So what was the Forbidden Fruit if not an apple? And if the foregoing information, handed down to us as the gospel truth, is in reality no more reliable than so much circumstantial evidence, then where does one turn if not the traditional version of *The Bible*? Well, as one might have already suspected, the apocryphal record does provide a clue to solving one of the oldest mysteries known to mankind. In *The First Book of Enoch*, we discover that the great patriarch encountered a vast orchard of trees, and in the midst of that orchard:

> He saw one that was like a species of the tamarind tree, bearing fruit that resembled extremely delicate *grapes;* and its fragrance extended to a considerable distance. I exclaimed, "This tree is so incredibly beautiful! What a delight it is just to look upon!"
>
> Then the angel Raphael, who was with me, said, "This is none other than the Tree of Knowledge from which your ancient father and mother ate, and who, having had their eyes opened, obtained the knowledge of good and evil; and thus realizing they were naked were expelled from the garden."[268]

So, it was not an apple, after all, that caused the ruin of mankind but something more akin to the *grape*. Could this be why the grape, with its well-known intoxicating effects, has ever since been both connected and contrasted with the very thing that was forfeited in the Fall? As in: "Don't be drunk with wine ... but be filled with the Spirit."[269] That is to say, do not be filled with the temporary effects of the fruit of the vine, epitomized by the short-sighted effort of our first parents. Instead, seek to fill yourself with the eternal fruit of the divine presence. Said Jesus: "I'm the Vine, and you're the branches. Whoever abides in Me, and I in him, will bear much fruit, because apart from Me you can do nothing."[270]

Later at the Last Supper, Jesus drank wine with His disciples, in an event that strangely mirrors the disobedience of Adam and Eve in their partaking of the Fruit of Knowledge—a fruit that we now see, in light of the apocryphal record, "resembled extremely delicate grapes." Then, Jesus took a cup and, when He had given thanks, passed it to His disciples, saying, "Drink from it, all of you. This is the blood of the covenant that is poured out for many for the forgiveness of sins. I tell you: I won't drink from this fruit of the vine from now on until that day when I drink it anew with you in My Father's kingdom."[271]

By One Man

THE MOST HOTLY DEBATED among the group, by far, is element number four: When God asked Adam if he had eaten from the Tree of Knowledge, his response constituted a classic case of psychological denial. Far from accepting responsibility for his actions, he instantly blamed everyone but himself: "The woman You, God, put here with me gave me the Fruit, so I ate it."[272] And with that single act of denial, Adam instigated a multifront war that has continued to rage to this very hour—war with women, war with God, war with animals, and war with the spirit world.

Ever since then, humans have been asking the same nagging question: Who is really to blame for the Fall of Mankind? In response, every alleged culprit has been thoroughly scrutinized. Eve was the first to eat the Forbidden Fruit; God was the One who put the Tree in their midst; the serpent was the one who tricked Eve into eating the Fruit; and it was Satan who conceived the cowardly plan. So actually, they are all to blame, right? Considering how many others were involved in this tragic chain of events, it would appear that Adam was just an innocent pawn in the whole affair. Yet the writer of the biblical record lays blame not upon any of the active participants just named but directly at the feet of Adam himself. No ifs, ands, or buts about it. Paul succinctly stated God's ultimate verdict in his letter to the Romans: "By one man, sin and death entered the human race."[273]

But why dump all the responsibility on poor Adam? Certainly some of the blame should be spread around to some of the others who were involved, should it not? After all, everyone knows it was Eve's fault. She was the one to whom Adam was most vulnerable. If she had not first eaten of the Fruit and offered some to him, he never would have succumbed to the temptation. He was just trying to make sure they would stay together, right? He could not just let Eve die without making the trip with her. Who could blame a guy for such a selfless act as that? On and on the rationalizations could continue.

Therefore, if we cannot blame Eve, then it must be God's fault. After all, He was the One Who placed the Tree in their backyard. Then, instead of walling it away to protect Adam and Eve from its deadly effects, He allowed them ample opportunity to get near it. What could He have been thinking by doing something like that? No parent in their right mind would ever put their own children at risk, would they? There goes that convoluted train of thought.

Then, I guess if God is not to blame, does that mean it was the serpent's fault? After all, without its direct involvement, neither Eve nor Adam would have ever eaten that damned fruit. I mean, really, the thought probably never occurred to them to eat it until that conniving, little snake brought it to their attention. Just think: If the serpent had never suggested it, Adam and Eve would have undoubtedly lived happily ever after without the slightest inkling of eating the Fruit. The end, right? Such is the power of wishful thinking.

Finally: What responsibility should be assigned to the most vindictive, cruel creature to be found among all of God's creation? What about Satan's role in this whole debacle? If not for his relentless scheming in all of this, Adam and Eve might never have been exiled from their garden home. In this, the Scriptures are, from beginning to end, quite succinct—canonical and apocryphal alike. From the moment the devil became aware that God was replacing him with

Adam and Eve, his desire to have the Lord restore him to his original place in the kingdom was in jeopardy. So for Satan, the elimination of that first couple served two paramount purposes. By getting Adam and Eve kicked out of the garden, either he would force God's hand in reinstating him, or barring that outcome, he would at least have the satisfaction of exacting his revenge on the humans who had clearly usurped his dominion. With such a clear-cut motive as this, then, who could possibly argue the devil's guilt in Adam's downfall?

Yet ironically, apart from all the foregoing weight of evidence as to the obvious guilt of everyone else involved in this most tragic event in history, *The Bible* is unswerving in its final verdict: "By one man, sin and death entered the human race."[274] It does not say that the guilt lies with the woman or God or the serpent or the devil but the man. And the reason, I believe, that it is so cut-and-dry in this regard is due to a single, overriding detail; and it is this: Before Eve was ever created, before the serpent ever offered the Fruit, and before Satan ever conceived his plan of attack, God first instructed Adam about His prohibition concerning the Tree of Knowledge. Then, and only then, did God allow Eve or the serpent or the devil into Adam's sphere of life. This is why Adam is solely held responsible for allowing sin and death to enter the world, because he alone stood face to face with his Creator, Who explicitly detailed the limits that were ordained for him as a created being, living in a God-governed Universe.

Abraham as: The Stranger

A Hero in Exile

WHEN ONE CONSIDERS the story of Abraham becoming the father of faith, the question naturally arises: How did he have faith in the God of Heaven while the rest of the world was so steeped in idolatry and rebellion? *The Book of Genesis* records, in the sparsest of terms, that God called Abraham to leave his father's house and travel to an unknown land, and in response, the patriarch simply followed that call.[275]

But what really happened to prepare his mind to perceive this call from a God Who had been summarily rejected by the rest of humanity? Once again, the canonical record is mysteriously silent on this most important question. Certainly one would think that just such a question would arise in the mind of anyone who would wish to follow in the footsteps of Abraham. After all, Paul declares that those who have faith in God are to be counted as spiritual children of Abraham.[276] If so, then would it not behoove Moses—in his depiction of the formative years of this pioneer of faith—to reveal what enabled Abraham to grasp what no one else could at the time? You would definitely think so.

Yet only the apocryphal record provides a clear answer to this mystery. In *The Book of Jasher*, we find that long before Abraham went to live with his idol-worshiping father he was forced into exile, where he was nurtured for forty years in the home of none other than Shem and Noah, who together taught the young man about the true God.[277] This is why Abraham was able to develop a genuine faith in God. This is why his heart and mind were so thoroughly prepared for the call of God when it came. Too bad, then, that this all-important aspect of Abraham's early training has been obscured by so many centuries of misinformation that would tritely attempt to inspire faith in God by telling us that we "just need to believe."

Of course, this is not the first example of important aspects of the lives of the giants of faith that are conspicuously absent from the traditional biblical record. In this, the hidden years of Abraham's early life clearly foreshadow the so-called "missing years" of Jesus, Who was also forced to flee His homeland so that He, too, could grow up under the care and tutelage of another. So, just as Shem and Noah cared for young Abraham in his formative years, Joseph of Arimathea similarly watched over young Jesus for a specific period of time, until the time came that He, too, was ready to take up the mantle of God's call for His life.

Taking this into consideration, let us take a moment to compare Abraham's exile experience with other heroes of mythic proportions. Interestingly enough, a similar pattern seems to unfold throughout history, myth, and literature—that of the exiling of the hero who is then free to be nurtured outside the culture to which he will one day return to rescue. According to C.W. Ceram, a German journalist known for his popular works on archeology, this group of exiled heroes includes Moses, Perseus, Romulus, Sargon, Krishna, and Cyrus.[278]

A Peculiar Life-Pattern

SHIRLEY PARK LOWRY wrote extensively about this pervasive phenomenon. In her penetrating study *Familiar Mysteries: The Truth in Myth*, she offered this evidence:

> Traditional heroic stories from most of the world tend to elaborate themselves in such similarly bizarre ways that scholars have long discerned a general life-pattern of about nine peculiar elements... Furthermore, this peculiar life-pattern for heroes is very ancient and very persistent. It began to form by the third millennium B.C. and still flourishes. Although some scholars trace the elements of this widespread pattern to particular Middle East myths, the question remains why the pattern arose and why it spread. Here is the heroic life-pattern:

1. The hero is born under unusual or mysterious circumstances (i.e. the mother is a virgin of noble birth, the father is a god, or the birth of the child is extremely unusual, etc.).

2. The child is marked for greatness by some special sign.

3. The child is endangered—often exiled or placed where he is likely to be killed—but is rescued and reared in a dramatic way far from his place of birth.

4. The youth must prove his fitness for the heroic role by a test.

5. The hero fights a monster or does other great deeds involving dramatic risks. Magical helpers often assist him with magical gifts.

6. The hero wins a maiden.

7. The hero journeys to the land of the dead.

8. Banished in his youth, the hero returns to triumph over his enemies.

9. The hero's death is mysterious and ambiguous.

> In an attempt to account for this strange pattern, so unlike the lives of people we know, it might be useful to show how the pattern works itself out in a particular story. Consider the story of a favorite Greek hero, Perseus. King Acrisius of Argos heard from the oracle at Delphi that a son of his daughter, Danae, would kill him. Unwilling to incur the wrath of the god's by slaying a relative, he still wished to ensure that the princess Danae would remain a childless virgin. So he imprisoned her in an underground chamber of bronze. But one day, Zeus, struck by Danae's beauty, contrived to visit her by turning into a shower of gold. Their child was Perseus. Upon discovering the child, Acrisius had mother and son placed in a chest and tossed into the sea. Instead of drowning, as the king had intended, Danae and the boy washed up on a little island. A kindly fisherman rescued them and gave them shelter in his home.[279]

Having detailed the recurring elements of this peculiar life-pattern, Lowry continued her discourse on the exiled hero:

> Another version of the story involves Sigurd, the greatest Scandinavian hero. The boy's father, Sigmund, believing his wife to be unfaithful, killed her, put the baby in a glass vessel, and cast it into a stream. Other such heroes include Dionysus, Alexander, and the Welsh Taliesin… As in the story of Perseus, the threat is usually expressed in a prophecy. In the story of Oedipus, the oracle told Laius that someday his son Oedipus would kill him and supplant him as husband of Jocasta, Oedipus' mother. Laius directed the child be killed. The infant was not killed outright but left in a remote place to die…
>
> Zeus, as an infant was almost eaten by his father Cronus, who had eaten all his earlier children to avoid fulfillment of the prophecy that one of his children would overthrow him… When Herod heard that the Magi from the Orient had seen a great star portending the birth of the Messiah, he sent soldiers to Bethlehem to slaughter every male under two years of age. But one survived. Miraculously, an angel warned Joseph just in time to take Mary and the fated child to Egypt, where they stayed until the angel told them it was safe to return… And in Hebrew legend, Abraham's infancy was attended by similar

dangers, when Nimrod had read in the stars that a child would be born who would reveal Nimrod's religion as a lie.[280]

In these astute observations by Lowry, one can see the extent to which comparative religion scholars have been cognizant of the same pattern that I outlined in a previous chapter of this book entitled *Shadow and Substance*. But whereas I have chosen to represent this life-pattern as proof of God's hidden hand in history, most of these scholars dismiss this well-documented phenomenon as a mere contrivance of historians who are said to have, either consciously or unconsciously, embellished their accounts with a more hallowed tone. In other words, this life-pattern, they insist, is merely another example of the way in which history is notoriously written and rewritten, till finally it becomes nothing more than "his-story."

The Chicken or the Egg?

FOR EXAMPLE, according to this theory of redactionist history, events in the life of Jesus of Nazareth have been liberally re-edited so that they more closely conform to the events of previous "saviors" In fact, the ancient world was filled with such messianic figures: The Sumerians had Tammuz, the Greeks had Dionysus, the Egyptians had Osiris, and the Canaanites had Baal. In every case, what one finds in these stories is a pre-Christian heroic figure who died and was subsequently raised from the dead. Therefore, based on this fact, say critics of *The Bible*, the gospel writers surely must have been clouded by these ideas when they decided to recreate the story of the mere man from Galilee, ultimately turning him into the glorified superhero of Israel.

However, such redactionist history, in its effort to demystify the story of Jesus, does nothing to help answer certain critical questions. How were these nations—embroiled in strife, genocide, and war—able to consistently transmit this unique narrative from one people to another? Are we to believe that these tumultuous, overflowing civilizations—with no common language or frame of reference—possessed some sort of cultural exchange program? If I am not mistaken, whenever one civilization has conquered another, they have generally been in the habit of reshaping the conquered people into their own image, not the other way around. One can only imagine our astonishment today if someone were to propose that the Nazis had, instead of seeking to annihilate every aspect of Jewish culture, decided to absorb into their theory of Aryan superiority the idea of a Hebrew Messiah. Yet this is precisely what redaction-minded scholars are proposing. Simply because the Greek Dionysus predated the risen Christ, the Romans—according to this view of cultural assimilation—found this latest version of the dying-and-rising hero so irresistible that they decided to embrace Jesus as their very own.

Yet nothing, as I see it, could be further from the truth. If there were anything to this notion of conjoined religious thought, then the Jews at the time of Christ would undoubtedly have embraced the concept of a dying-and-rising savior, which, as we have already detailed, was thoroughly Judaistic in principle. Remember: All one has to do is recall the numerous occurrences of such a phenomena in the lives of Isaac, Joseph, Moses, and Jonah. Nevertheless, they did not embrace the idea of a Messiah that fit such a description, did they? No, not by a long shot. So, if the scholars are correct in their appraisal that this concept of a dying-and-rising savior was a clear-cut case of cross-cultural pollination, then why did the Jews of that day dismiss Jesus' claims that He would resurrect from the dead?[281] If the Sumerians, Greeks, Egyptians, and Canaanites were all so wildly enthusiastic about the idea of a resurrection from the dead, then why were the Jews, who were typically steeped in messianic thought, so resistant to the idea?

The answer, I believe, is not so much that they rejected the idea that the pious were destined for their own resurrection, that is, as a theological position *per se*. The problem for the Jewish religious leaders of that day was the implication that the Son of Man—with Whom Jesus clearly identified Himself—would require anything remotely like a resurrection, which presumed that He would first have to suffer the humiliation of death. Frequently referred to in the ancient prophecies of Enoch, the Son of Man was described as a Conquering Hero of absolute dominion and power, not One Who in any way could have been subject to such degradation as an earthen, human grave. Therefore, because it never entered their minds that the vaunted Messiah could die as only a mere mortal could die, it was just as inconceivable that He would ever need to be resurrected like a mere mortal. As a result of this view, even Christ's disciples, who were all convinced of His divinity, never fully overcame their own theological preconceptions, no matter how many times Jesus insisted that, as the Son of Man, He would have to endure death prior to His exaltation to the right hand of the Father.[282]

The concept of a dying-and-rising hero, then, may seem like a universally accepted notion to some highfalutin, self-appointed scholar who lives in a perpetual state of over-analysis but in terms of real world standards their redactionist theories really do not amount to much. If their theories did have any validity, then the disciples of Christ should have had no reason to doubt that Jesus was not Himself just another dying-and-rising hero like all those who had come before Him. So I ask you: If, as all these comparative religion scholars insist, the idea of dying-and-rising is so common to cultures the world over, then why were the disciples not huddled about the tomb of Jesus in eager anticipation of His resurrection? Simply put, it is because the concept of the dying-and-rising hero is not an idea that cultures trade in like children swapping baseball cards, if for no other reason than it just is not an ideology that typically occurs to the mind of mankind. It is, quite to the contrary, a shattering intrusion into the ordinary stuff that we humans experience as the "way of all things." In a world that is dying all around us, the idea of the resurrection of the dead is not something we cynical humans believe in at the mere drop of a hat. Instead, like the doubting Thomases we all are, we must be shaken, stunned, jarred by something that appears from beyond what we typically perceive as normal to existence. An unexpected, unprecedented gash into our known Universe must burst upon us and make itself known. Then, and only then, can we, as a species, say for certain that this otherwise mundane, homely existence has suddenly become the vessel of something historians and mythologists alike deem to call a resurrection.

That said, could there possibly be another mechanism at work that provides scholars with such clear-cut evidence of a general life-pattern that permeates world history? In many ways, this question resembles the classic conundrum: Which comes first, the chicken or the egg? In this instance, the question can be framed differently. Which comes first, the life story of the risen hero or the cultural transmission of the story of that risen one? Ironically, in the case of the question of the chicken or the egg, the answer lies not so much with one's ability—or lack thereof—to offer a sound argument based on a perceived set of so-called "facts." Instead, the answer has everything to do with one's own personal frame of reference. If you are the type that accepts the possibility of the existence of a Creator, then you will likely embrace the idea that the chicken was created by this God, and that this chicken will therefore have produced an egg. However, if you are of the ilk that rejects the notion of a Creator, then you will naturally require the spontaneous development of an egg prior to the hatching of this subsequent chicken. Either way, the facts themselves do not govern the process that provides an answer to the question; on the contrary, the frame of reference of the seeker provides the "answer."

Accordingly, those who believe in God might have no problem with His laying down patterns in the history of His chosen ones, patterns that are uniquely and specifically designed to communicate an understanding of the divine plan of salvation. Proceeding from this way of thinking, then, before Jesus of Nazareth strode upon the stage of world history, there would have been a multiplicity of messianic figures whose ultimate purpose was to foreshadow the events in the life of the Coming One. In this, biblical historians have noted the striking parallel in the life of Jesus with that of Moses, who was similarly destined to be the target of a maniacal king. Yet in his futile attempt to rid himself of the child, Pharaoh would ironically trigger the very events that would float the baby Moses into the court of the king, thereby ensuring the deliverance of the Children of Israel just as the prophecy had predicted so many years earlier.[283]

Before Moses or Jesus, there was Abraham, who would one day be called the father of faith, and before he rose to embrace that high calling, he was simply the infant son of Terah, chief prince of Nimrod. Furthermore, in an event that clearly prefigured the births of Moses and Jesus, a celestial occurrence took place on the day of Abraham's birth, which triggered the malicious actions of the king in that time.[284] In Abraham's case, it was Nimrod who, upon the advice of his soothsayers and sages, tried to eliminate the child of destiny from ever growing up to fulfill a prophecy that pronounced the end of Nimrod's mighty kingdom.[285] But hoping to save the life of his fated son, Terah risked the wrath of his king by bringing him another child—one born to him from his union with a concubine—and it was this child that was killed instead of the infant Abraham.[286]

Following the death of this substitute child, Abraham—like Moses and Jesus who would likewise be spared amidst a slaughter of Innocents—would become an exile from his original family, far removed from the threat seeking to extinguish his life.[287] And like Moses and Jesus had been divinely sheltered in their formative years, the young son of Terah was spirited away to the mountain fastness of Noah and Shem, where he was secretly mentored for forty years concerning the things of the true God.[288]

Pilate as: The Public Defender

A Conscience in Crisis

ONE OF THE MOST enduring mysteries regarding the life and death of Christ is the question of the true state of mind of Pontius Pilate when he washed his hands in the presence of the angry mob and declared, "I am innocent of this man's blood."[289]

Did Pilate really regret sentencing Jesus to die? Or did he merely regret being ensnared in yet another civil debacle that threatened his political career? To this day, the judgment of history clearly remains divided. Nevertheless, considering Pilate's reputation for strong-arm tactics and his utter lack of human sensibilities, it is much easier to assume that he was more concerned about his political future than the so-called "troublemaker" who had been handed over to him for judgment.

The written testimony of *The New Testament*, however, is characteristically ambiguous concerning Pilate's motives. Without a doubt, the gospel writers are faithful in their representation of the governor's persistent attempts to extricate Jesus from the machinations that sought the demise of the Nazarene. Pilate is a man repeatedly portrayed with a conscience in crisis, clearly dumbfounded by the treatment of Jesus by religious leaders among His own nation.[290] But as to the specific motives of the governor, the canonical Scriptures do not say. Once again, the observation of history regarding this provocative question is much akin to the psychological phenomenon invoked by the Rorschach test.[291] As if it were entirely a matter of literary choice, the gospel writers seem to have purposely designed their message in such a way as to leave this question of Pilate's state of mind to readers themselves. In this way, the governor becomes a type of all mankind who stand in their own judgment over the presiding of the court. In this way, Pilate provides a universal mirror for all who would themselves seek to investigate the age-old mystery: "What is truth?"[292]

In this regard, then, the debate over the genuine motives of Pontius Pilate seems to be less about the governor himself, and more about the observer who is seeking to understand Pilate's state of mind. As it turns out, this is very similar to what happens when someone examines the meaning of the life and death of Jesus. In other words, just as everyone reveals the true nature of their heart based on their response to the claims that Jesus made about Himself, everyone similarly reveals the truth about themselves in their response to the man whose fate it was to judge Him.

Did Jesus really orchestrate His own death, as the gospel writers have implied? Or was He inadvertently trapped by forces beyond His control, as critics have suggested? If you answer yes to the former question, it implies that you believe that Jesus' claim to be the Lamb of God is valid; answering yes to the latter implies that you think Him to be an impotent pawn, and thus incapable of saving anyone through His death. Likewise: Did Pilate intercede on behalf of Jesus because he really believed it was the right thing to do? Or was he just trying to avoid further bloodshed because he thought it might advance his career? If you answer yes to the former question, it implies that you believe Pilate tried to release Jesus because he actually believed that He was innocent, and thus worthy of being released; answering yes to the latter implies that you think him to be an opportunistic politician merely trying to save face in the midst of no-win situation. In both cases, answering yes to the former question places you smack dab in the camp of the eternal optimist, while answering yes to the latter puts you squarely in that of the confirmed pessimist.

From Enemy to Ally

JUST AS WITH ALL potent mysteries, questions like these will never be strictly answered by means of empirical evidence. Instead, they are questions that the Scriptures present as universal crossroads for humanity to engage with, psychologically, emotionally, and spiritually. The significance of the truth they seek to impart comes to us not by dictating the absolute meaning of said events and persons but by providing us with a vehicle for empathy and catharsis, which ultimately leads one to a more meaningful awareness into one's own life. No wonder that *The Bible* has proved to be such an enduring document. Not only does it constitute a landmark in the history of world literature but also with such concepts as compassion, justice, and equity. In this way, *The Bible* has, throughout the centuries, paved the way for the most enlightened form of jurisprudence—one that insists that a person is deemed innocent until proven guilty. Even with a man as notorious as Pontius Pilate—a name that has ever since been linked with political impotence and moral ambivalence—the gospel writers never once crossed the line of reading into the scene their own views of guilt or innocence. They were simply faithful to what was said or done, without any added conjecture as to why a certain thing was or was not done.

As a result of this ambiguous telling of biblical history, however, contradictions abound concerning the life and death of Pontius Pilate. On one hand, Philo, the first-century Jewish philosopher, said of Pilate: "He was a cruel man with a furious temper, stubborn and merciless."[293] On the other hand, Philo reports that this same Pilate was of an entirely different temperament when he feared that an investigation by Tiberius Caesar would expose the truth about his reckless tactics as a hard-bitten political boss.[294]

A complex man of startling contradictions in life, Pontius Pilate would prove to be just as enigmatic in death. The father of church history, Eusebius of Caesarea, the fourth-century Roman bishop, laid claim to his own version. According to him, several years after the crucifixion, Pilate fell out of favor with Caligula and was exiled to Gaul, where he supposedly committed suicide. In contrast, Eastern Orthodox tradition—in its attempt to remold the image of the soldier-turned-politician—has Pilate committing suicide not because of his failure as a Roman governor but because of a guilty conscience. In this newly-acquired role of sinner-become-saint, Pilate, like Saul of Tarsus who was converted from an enemy of God to His greatest ally, this tradition—so alien to the Western theological mind—portrays the governor as a changed man. Smitten to the core for his complicity in the death of an innocent Man, Pilate, like Judas before him, is guilt-ridden for having caved in to the Jewish leaders rather than following his own instincts and releasing Jesus.

Apart from the traditional version of events surrounding the life and death of Pilate, there is the apocryphal record, which provides us with alternative views that are not found in *The New Testament*. One of these accounts is given by Justin Martyr, the second-century Greek Christian apologist, in a letter to Augustus Caesar.

> After Jesus was crucified, they cast lots for His robe... And that these things happened, you can ascertain from *The Acts of Pontius Pilate*.[295]

And again:

> With regard to the predictions that our Christ would heal all diseases and raise the dead, listen to what was said. "At His coming the lame will leap about like a deer, and the tongue of the stammering one will be made to speak clearly. The blind will see, the lepers will be cleansed, the dead will rise and walk about." And that He did those things, you can learn from *The Acts of Pontius Pilate*.[296]

According to this account, and several others written in the same vein, Pilate is not nearly as ambiguous as the gospel writers have portrayed him. To be sure, he is still the cynical politician, just as the canonical writers have characterized him. In this version, however, there is an added dimension to Pilate's character in that he is genuinely compelled by the unique personality of Jesus. In response, the once-hardened governor is moved to completely rethink his attitudes about ultimate reality, even going so far as to testify to this change of heart in a series of letters to the Roman emperor Tiberius Caesar. In variance to tradition, Pilate does not take his own life but is instead portrayed as a martyr of the faith. After being put on trial for allowing

Jesus to be crucified, he is beheaded by order of Tiberius for his perceived complicity in Christ's death. Undoubtedly as a result of such testimony, the Ethiopian Orthodox Church elevated Pilate to the status of a saint, celebrating his feast day ever since on June 25th.

The Threshold Guardian

CONSIDERING ALL THE bewildering contradictions surrounding Pontius Pilate, what can one take away from them? Should history continue to condemn him as a villain? Or should it praise him as a saint? Once again, it appears that just as the traditional record portrays the issue without a bias one way or the other, history may never be able to provide us with a definitive answer. One thing, however, is certain. Pontius Pilate, good or bad, active or passive, stubborn or moved, did perform a necessary task in the plan of God. When Jesus refused to defend Himself, Pilate asked, "Why won't you talk to me? Don't you know I have the power to either release you or crucify you?"[297]

At that moment, Pilate represented what Joseph Campbell, the twentieth-century American mythologist, would call a threshold guardian. In the life of every great hero, a formidable foe seeks to thwart his attempt to fulfill his destiny. As Campbell described it, "The hero goes forward in his adventure until he comes to the threshold guardian at the entrance of magnified power… Beyond that is darkness, the unknown, and danger."[298] In Greek mythology, Medusa represented just such an obstacle for Perseus, who sought to free Andromeda from the clutches of a sea monster, whereas for Jason, the sleepless dragon barred the way in his effort to retrieve the Golden Fleece. In this respect, Jesus was no different than any of these other great heroes. For Him, Pontius Pilate represented this threshold guardian. Like Satan in the wilderness, who tempted Christ to use His divine power in ways that would have ultimately derailed Him from His true path, Pilate offered Jesus an easy way out from the roadmap that God, the Father, had laid out. Yet the journey and its inevitable conclusion were already fixed in the mind of Jesus. He knew there was no other way for Him to fulfill His destiny. Said Jesus to His disciples, "No man takes My life, but I lay it down on My own. I have the authority to lay it down and the authority to take it back up again. This command I've received from My Father."[299]

And when Pilate presumed that he, as the appointed prefect of Imperial Rome, was the one who held the life of Christ in his puny, human hands, Jesus did exactly what all great heroes have done before Him. He transformed the threshold guardian before Him from a potential obstacle into an unwitting ally. The unsuspecting governor, a man who had, until that very moment, been someone who had bullied, plundered, and murdered his way to a place of tremendous political power, was with one simple response from this peculiar Man turned inside out, never to be the same again. The man who thought that he alone held the power of life and death was simply told by Jesus: "But you'd have no power over Me if it hadn't been given to you from above. Therefore, the one who handed Me over to you is guilty of an even greater sin."[300]

Upon hearing such a reply, Pontius Pilate, the Scripture points out, became at that moment a new person. Suddenly he was a man who was moving in a new direction, a man with a new purpose. "From then on," said the Apostle John, "*From then on*, Pilate tried to set Jesus free, but the Jews kept on shouting, 'If you let this man go, you're no friend of Caesar! Anyone who claims to be a king opposes Caesar!' And when Pilate heard this, he brought Jesus out, and declared to all the Jews there: 'Here is your king!'"[301]

THE THEMES

Heroes must die so that they can be reborn... In some way, in every story, heroes face death or something like it... They magically survive this death and are ... reborn to reap the consequences of having cheated death.

Christopher Vogler, *The Writer's Journey*

A Prophecy of Days

A Time for Everything

TIME IS A FUNNY thing, it is said. Time is fleeting, we are told. Time – "ticking away the moments that make up a dull day," sings Pink Floyd, the seventies British progressive rock band. "And then one day you find ten years have got behind you. No one told you when to run; you missed the starting gun."[302] Everywhere one turns, there is an obsession with time – time is up, time to go, time is money. Clocks chime, watches beep, phones chirp. Everywhere some kind of device is reminding us of what time it is. Even so, long before the modern world became obsessed with the concept of time, *The Bible* declared its importance in the plan of God. "There is a time for everything, and a season for every activity under Heaven – a time to be born and a time to die, a time for war and a time for peace."[303] The prophet Isaiah referred to the "time" of God's favor.[304] Daniel spoke of the "set times" of the Lord,[305] and twice he spoke of the "appointed time."[306] Jesus spoke to His disciples about the importance of His doing things at the "right time."[307] Paul, too, spoke to the Corinthians about an "appointed time,"[308] and to the Romans, he described how at just the "right time" Christ died for us.[309]

No wonder that when God spoke to Adam and Eve about restoring them to their original state in Paradise, He designed His rescue effort in accordance to a timeline of His own choosing. The first thing God did, as depicted in *The First Book of Adam and Eve*, was to explain: "I have ordained days and years for you and your descendants, Adam, until those days and years are fulfilled; and when those *five and a half* days are fulfilled, I will send the Word to save you."[310] Of course, when Adam heard about this prophecy of The Great Five and a Half Days, he had no idea what God meant. At first, he thought the Lord was saying that the end of the world would be taking place in just *five and a half* days, so he begged God to explain this to him.[311] That is when the Lord informed Adam that the *five and a half* "days" He was referring to actually represented five thousand, five hundred years, after which, "One would come and rescue him and his descendants."[312]

Now, at this point, I imagine that certain ones reading this still might insist on raising a variety of objections, several of which I have already addressed in a previous chapter, entitled *Arguments for Authenticity*. My purpose in this latter section will be to discuss the only question I feel has not yet been addressed, which would be the objection to such a prophecy on the grounds that no comparable prophetic timelines can be found in the canonical record. There are, you may point out, prophecies regarding future events, say, ones predicted by Jeremiah, which involve a *year*-oriented prophecy, as in *seven times seventy* "years." But nowhere have biblical scholars ever mentioned anything similar to this one regarding The Great Five and a Half Days. At which point I would have to strongly object; because there is, in fact, a clear precedence in the realm of biblical scholarship with regard to such a *day*-oriented prophecy. Let me explain what I mean.

A Sliver of Hope

CONTAINED IN *THE Old Testament* is a story that has, for centuries, perplexed biblical scholars who have sought to understand its meaning. It is the story of the prophet Hosea. Although classified as one of the Minor Prophets, due to its subordinate relationship to others like *The Book of Isaiah* and *The Book of Daniel*, the book bearing his name is actually one that plays a major role in terms of its prophetic significance. The most intriguing thing about Hosea, though, is that his prophecies have clearly been overshadowed by the peculiar life that he led as a result of God not merely giving him a series of prophetic utterances to deliver but instructing him to live out the very message he was inspired to preach. To drive home the full impact of how God felt about His people's penchant for idol worship, Hosea was instructed to marry a prostitute. Then, via the choice of names for their children, God dramatically revealed His attitude toward the people of Israel. The first child, a son, was called Jezreel, because God was going to scatter the inhabitants of the land and thereby put an end to the northern kingdom of Israel. The second child, a daughter, was called Loruhamah, because God was going to withdraw His love from the House of Israel to the north and only care for the House of Judah to the south. And finally, the third child, another son, was called Loammi, because the northern kingdom would no longer be treated as God's people, and He would no longer be considered their God.[313]

To a lesser degree, the same thing happened when God inspired Isaiah to walk around Jerusalem—naked and barefoot—as a "sign of things to come." In this case, the "thing" that would be happening to the inhabitants of the land was that they, too, would walk naked and barefoot as they were being led into captivity because of their trusting the Egyptians rather than the Lord.[314] Similarly, to foretell the imminent destruction of Jerusalem, God instructed Ezekiel to shave his head and beard, and to divide the hairs into three piles. One pile was to be burned, one was to be struck by a sword, and one was to be scattered to the wind. Yet from each pile, a few strands of hair were to be tucked away in the folds of Ezekiel's garment—all this to typify the coming destruction of the majority of the population, while but a remnant was to be spared by God.[315]

Just like Isaiah and Ezekiel, then, Hosea was forced to dramatize the message he was entrusted with so that the recipients of his message would not only have to hear it but would be forced to live it, too. Fortunately, though, for the northern kingdom of Israel, Hosea did foresee a sliver of hope in the catastrophic events that lay ahead, because no sooner did he proclaim the abandonment and scattering of the kingdom to the north than Hosea prophesied a much different outcome in their distant future. Notwithstanding the period of desolation and humiliation that the Israelites were to endure, Hosea foresaw the day when "the Israelites would be as the sand of the sea on the seashore, which cannot be measured or counted, and in the very place where it was said of them, 'You are not My people,' they will be called the 'children of God.'"[316]

In many ways, this period of alienation and restoration of the House of Israel constitutes a unique parallel in biblical history with that of the House of Judah. Just as Jeremiah prophesied seventy years of desolation upon the Judahites to the south, followed by their eventual return to Jerusalem, Hosea pronounced a similar sequence of events as they pertained to the Israelites to the north. And so it is with this unique relationship of events that connect the prophetic timelines of both the northern and southern kingdoms—which comprise the totality of the nation of Israel—that we are now able to bring all these apparent loose ends of our discussion to a point of convergence. Let us review to this point.

More than Poetry

WE BEGAN BY EMPHASIZING the importance of timing in the plan of God. In this, the Scriptures are abundantly clear. If nothing else, the God of *The Bible* is a God of Set Times Who fulfills His word of promise at "just the right time." We then considered the possibility that God might have revealed this notion of His "appointed times" from the beginning when Adam and Eve were originally expelled from Paradise. In the apocryphal record, we discover the very moment when God explained that even though He had banished them because of their disobedience He would not abandon them forever. Someday, according to God's first prophetic timeline for humanity, He would allow them back into their garden home upon the completion of The Great Five and a Half Days, or rather—from Adam and Eve's point of view—after five thousand, five hundred years.[317]

Next, we brought up the issue of whether or not this same principle of a *day*-oriented prophecy could be found in the Biblical Canon. Or, to put it in the form of a question: Are there any rescue efforts in the traditional texts depicting a prophecy of "days" like the one in *First Adam and Eve*, as opposed to those utilizing the more familiar timeline of "years" like the one in *Daniel*? In order to answer this question, I then led us to the prophecies of Hosea, Isaiah, and Ezekiel. There we discovered a consistent pattern of God lifting His provision and protection of His people in times of punishment, and in this pattern, I believe, we have the evidence that we are seeking. In all of this, the reoccurring pattern that emerges is: Again and again, whether it is Adam and Eve, or Israel and Judah, the chosen ones begin in a state of blissful ignorance, believing themselves to be the perpetual darlings of God. Then, complacency and pride creep in, slowly but surely eroding the established order, followed by willful disobedience and outright rebellion. Finally, after all the stern warnings of the Lord are ignored comes His reluctant, though necessary, punishment as depicted in the first couple's fall from grace and both the kingdoms of Israel and Judah's deportation into slavery. Yet according to a similarly persistent pattern, God places a time limit on this period of judgment. Instead of destroying the people of His calling, His chastisement ultimately leads to repentance and renewal, thereby bringing them to a higher level of responsibility and awareness.

In the case of Hosea, one comes face to face with this principle when he reassured the Israelites that although they would be abandoned and characterized as "not God's people" they would yet, in the very place of desolation and retribution, someday be called "the children of God."[318] But when was this future restoration and exaltation supposed to take place? Fortunately for us, not only can we find the answer to that question, but in doing so, we will also finally be able to answer our question as to whether or not there is any evidence for the kind of prophecy of "days" in the canonical record like those in the apocryphal record. However, to find that out, one must delve even further into *The Book of Hosea*. First, we read that Hosea ended the fifth chapter with a severe word of warning:

> For I will be like a lion to Ephraim, like a great lion to Judah. I will tear them to pieces and go away. I will carry them off with no one to rescue them. Then, I will go back to My place until they admit their guilt and seek My face. In their misery, they will earnestly seek Me.[319]

Then, Hosea began the sixth chapter with a hauntingly familiar message of hope:

> Come, let us return to the Lord. He has torn us to pieces, but He will heal us. He has injured us, but He will bind up our wounds. After two days, He will revive us. On the third day, He will restore us so that we may live in His presence. Let us acknowledge the Lord. As surely as the Sun rises, He will appear. He will come to us like rain in winter, like the spring rain that waters the Earth.[320]

So there it is. A prophecy of "days" is in the canonical record after all. "After two days, God will revive us. On the third day, He will restore us." And just like God's timeline for Adam and Eve, this exiling of the nation of Israel was destined to involve a prophetic period that would be comprised of a similarly constituted set of preordained "days."

And just in case anyone is liable to think that this prophecy of "days," located in the Canon, is some kind of fluke or aberration, let us take a moment to examine the precision of the scriptural record as it pertains to this particular chapter of prophetic history. To Ephraim, synonymous with the northern kingdom, Hosea proclaimed that God would attack like a lion, and to Judah, the southern kingdom, He would attack like a great lion. In this declaration, Hosea was not merely uttering a poetic turn of the phrase. He was precisely predicting the way in which God was planning to vanquish the two kingdoms.

The northern kingdom of Israel was to be conquered by Sargon the Second, whose power was depicted, throughout that country's architecture and sculpture, by none other than the lion. In 722 B.C., the Assyrians, led by Sargon, vanquished the capital of Samaria, located in the territory of Ephraim, and carried away captive the majority of the population. Then, in 586 B.C., the southern kingdom of Judah came to an ignominious end; this time at the hands of the Babylonian Empire. And what was their national symbol of power? Naturally, just as Hosea had warned them so many years earlier, it was the lion of Babylon, Nebuchadnezzar, who performed God's will in humbling the kingdom to the south.

My purpose in mentioning all of this is two-fold: First, I hope to convey the precision with which Hosea presented his message. In other words, for Hosea, the words that God entrusted him with were more than poetry. When he proclaimed to a rebellious nation that unless they changed their idol-worshiping ways the Lord would attack them as a lion, he was accurately predicting the way in which God eventually raised up both Assyria and Babylon to perform the work of His hands. In this, it was exactly as Moses warned the nation in *The Book of Deuteronomy*:

> If you do not obey the Lord your God, and do not carefully follow all His commands, all these curses will overtake you: The Lord will cause you to be defeated by your enemies. You will come at them from one direction but will flee from them in seven, and you will become a thing of horror to all the kingdoms of the Earth—an object of scorn and ridicule to all the nations where the Lord will drive you.[321]

Second, just as his predictions of doom were more than merely poetic in nature, so also were his predictions of salvation. Therefore, when Hosea reassured the people that God would "revive them after two days; and restore them on the third day," he was being just as precise in his meaning. In this case, of course, we are much more sophisticated in our understanding of the ways of God when He stated that His intention was to restore the nation in three "days" time. Certainly no one in the present age would ever be so naïve as Adam when he thought that God was going to rescue him after just *five and a half* days as they are reckoned from our earthbound perspective. Naturally, when God speaks of doing things according to His days, He is always referring to a period that is, according to our human perspective, equal to a thousand years.[322]

On the Third Day

STILL YOU MIGHT BE asking: Why, then, are there no biblical scholars who have ever published anything about this *day*-oriented prophecy of Hosea? Oh, but there are. The most eloquent of these is Adam Rutherford, the British biblical chronologist, who, in his book *Israel-Britain*, wrote:

> Israel was finally smitten and carried captive into Assyria at the close of Hoshea's reign, their chief city, Samaria, having fallen after a three year siege.[323] But God promised that after Two Days—which, according to His days of a thousand years each, are equal to two thousand years—He will revive them. All are agreed that the captivity of Israel occurred in the eighth century before Christ, therefore, two thousand years later is the thirteenth century of the Christian Era. We are now more than halfway through that Third Day, and just look at the raising up of Israel under the modern name of the Anglo-Saxon race as it takes place before our very eyes.[324]

Rutherford then goes on to compare Hosea's prophecy of the Three Days with Ezekiel's more familiar vision of the Valley of Dry Bones.[325] He continued:

> The restoration of the whole House of Israel, so often spoken of in the Scriptures, is beautifully pictured in Ezekiel's vision of the Valley of the Dry Bones. In this famous vision, the prophet saw an open valley full of dry bones. On Ezekiel's being commanded by God to prophesy that these bones come to life, "there was a noise and a shaking, and the bones came together, bone to his bone." And then, "the sinews and the flesh came upon them, and the skin covered them, but there was no breath in them." The prophet was then asked to prophesy that God would cause these slain ones to live. Then, "breath came into them, and they

lived and stood upon their feet—a vast army." God then said to Ezekiel, "These bones are the whole House of Israel."

Notice the close correspondence between Ezekiel's vision of the Valley of Dry Bones and Hosea's Three Days. Each deals with the House of Israel, and each are in three stages. Hosea's First Day corresponds exactly with the first stage of Ezekiel's vision. The valley of dry bones spoke eloquently of the sad picture of the scattered, hopeless, and lifeless condition of Israel during the First Day. It depicted dispersion, disorder, and death.

Hosea's Second Day saw the luring and the gathering of the tribes into the "appointed place." This resembled the second stage of Ezekiel's vision, where there was a shaking, and bones were sorted and gathered "bone to his bone." Order was evolved out of chaos, but it was not yet orderly life. "There was no life in them yet."

Hosea's Third Day was one of resurrection to national life. "On the third day, He will raise us up, and we will live in His sight." So it was in Ezekiel's vision. The Spirit of God breathed upon "these slain ones," and "breath came into them, and they lived and stood upon their feet—a vast army." It was a vision of life, order, power, and invincible might.[326]

A Man of Substance

The Ultimate Greatness

IN LIFE, WHEN ONE encounters a shadow, it inevitably leads to a search for the substance that is casting it. Likewise, in *The Bible*, there is a similar phenomenon involving shadows and the ensuing search that it invokes. This, in turn, leads one to ask the question: Why does God expend so much effort in expressing His revelatory message in terms of shadow and substance? In our previous efforts toward answering this question, we saw in an earlier chapter that He does so because we, as finite beings, are separated by an immeasurable gulf from the infinite being of the Divine. Therefore, in order to bridge this gap, God instituted a "message delivery system," so to speak, that was specifically designed to transcend the foibles of mere language. We saw that, above all, God's message to mankind is expressed through, for lack of a better term, "story." Simply put, *The Bible* is not merely a book that catalogs the commandments of God, but it is one that conveys its message by way of the dramas of the very lives of those individuals who inhabit it.

Since time immemorial, the God of Salvation has been a teller of tales. Not only has He been the Author of these stories, but He has also been the quintessential Director, weaving His message through every scene, every line, every action. Long before anyone in the history of artistic expression conceived of creating a dramatic narrative, God set about to pen His *magnum opus*. Before the ancient Greek playwright Euripides ever wrote his first play, the Lord of the drama set about to weave a narrative for the ages. In this way, God's message can be understood regardless of any language in which it is communicated.

Time and time again, we have seen this principle revealed in Scripture, both canonical and apocryphal. When God intended that mankind should be rescued by the vicarious substitute of another, He did not simply tell Adam and Eve what He was going to do; the Lord provided them with a covering made from the skins of sheep that had been killed by a lion.[327] When it came time for the Exodus of the Israelites from Egypt, God instructed Moses to slay the sacrificial lamb and smear the blood on their doorposts, thereby instituting the Passover feast.[328] And when in the fullness of time, Jesus was destined to give His life as the ultimate sacrifice for sin, He made sure it occurred at the same time that the Jewish priests were performing their age-old duty of offering up the blood of the lambs at Passover.[329] In this way, anyone could look upon this cohesive string of historical facts—"patterns through time," as it were—and clearly perceive God's intended message, a message that by virtue of the sheer drama of events could not help but transcend interpretation. No matter what language one spoke, they could understand exactly what the God of *The Bible* was saying.

Likewise, before Jesus strode upon the stage of world history, where He was to fulfill His role as the *One true Messiah*, there came many *lesser* messianic figures who prefigured His coming with their lives. Now, mind you, these were not perfect men who laid down a complete pattern, in and of themselves. Rather, they were mere mortals who in glimmers of greatness depicted the ultimate greatness of the Christ Who was yet to come. Then with the precision of a tool-and-die maker, God seized upon these flickers of divinity and worked them into His unfolding drama, like so many finely-wrought pieces of His sacred puzzle. To that end, we have already demonstrated how specific aspects in the lives of Adam, Enoch, Abraham, Isaac, Joseph, Moses, David, and Jonah were able to convey what Christ would be like when He finally came into this world so that we would be able to recognize Him.

Elephant Seekers

WITH THE PRECEDING in mind, I would now like to add a new twist to this familiar concept of biblical typology. Consider the following: If one can positively identify some messianic figure as a type of Christ, then might it not be just as appropriate to say that Jesus is the substance of that particular person? The reason I mention this is because it seems to me that typology has more often than not overemphasized the human participant in these dramas of Scripture, while underemphasizing the most important person in this divine equation. In other words, when one speaks of types in *The Bible*, we generally speak only of Joseph or David or Jonah as a type of Christ. But when was the last time you heard a preacher tell you that Jesus was the substance of Joseph or the substance of David or the substance of Jonah? I certainly never have.

Still, you may say that I am merely splitting hairs in all of this. After all, what is the difference if no one has ever explicitly described Jesus as the substance of "this or that" biblical character? Is this not already implied in the argument that "so and so" is a type of Christ? Granted, that may be the case with the most ardent of scriptural aficionados. My concern, however, is with the incompleteness of this scenario in the minds of the average person who is hearing about this most important subject for the first time or, worse, the complacent Christian who has heard the same old story so many times that it simply goes in one ear and out the other. One could almost compare this to listening to half a phone conversation while being denied what is said on the other end. Certainly one can surmise the drift of any given conversation in this manner, but how much more of an understanding could be had if one were privy to both sides of the dialog?

This is why I believe it is critical that any teacher of God's control over history should embrace the idea that, even more important than someone being a type of Christ, Jesus is the substance of the person in question. If this logic holds up, then, the following list might offer a more comprehensive representation of this biblical notion of shadow and substance:

> If Adam is a type of Christ, then Jesus is the substance of Adam.
>
> If Enoch is a type of Christ, then Jesus is the substance of Enoch.
>
> If Abraham is a type of Christ, then Jesus is the substance of Abraham.
>
> If Isaac is a type of Christ, then Jesus is the substance of Isaac.
>
> If Joseph is a type of Christ, then Jesus is the substance of Joseph.
>
> If Moses is a type of Christ, then Jesus is the substance of Moses.
>
> If David is a type of Christ, then Jesus is the substance of David.
>
> And, if Jonah is a type of Christ, then Jesus is the substance of Jonah.
>
> Similarly, if Benjamin is a type of the disciples of Jesus, then the disciples are the substance of Benjamin.
>
> And, if the brothers of Joseph are a type of the kingdoms of Judah and Israel, then the kingdoms are the substance of the brothers of Joseph.
>
> And finally, if Elijah is a type of John the Baptist, then John is the substance of Elijah.

Furthermore, if the preceding designations bear any reflection to truth, as I believe they do, one might then amplify this idea and take it to its logical conclusion, which could best be articulated by way of asking the question: How, exactly, do these types of Christ foreshadow the One Who was to come? To answer that we could provide a list that is similar to the one presented above but with a distinctly added dimension:

> If Adam was the firstborn son of God's original creation whose fall brought death to all his children, then Jesus, as the Second Adam, is the firstborn Son of the new creation Whose rise brought eternal life to all mankind.

> If Enoch was the human mediator who provided a temporal bridge between Heaven and Earth, then Jesus, as the word of God made flesh, is the Divine Mediator Who provided a permanent bridge between the two worlds.
>
> If Abraham was the servant of God who answered the divine call to leave his father's royal house and journey to an undiscovered country, then Jesus, as the Ultimate Servant, is the One Who emptied Himself of divinity and went to a land where God's call beckoned Him to serve and save the lost.
>
> If Isaac was the sacrificial lamb who willingly allowed himself to be offered up by his father, then Jesus, as the Lamb of God, is the One Who offered Himself to God, the Father, to be slain before the foundations of the world were laid.
>
> If Joseph was the savior of his family, having rescued them from the famine in Canaan, then Jesus, as the Bread of Life, is the Kinsman Redeemer, having rescued the human family from hunger, both physical and spiritual.
>
> If Moses was the human deliverer of Israel, having freed them from the bondage of Egypt, then Jesus, as the Passover Lamb, is the Divine Deliverer, having released all mankind from the bondage of sin.
>
> If David was the king of Israel, who for one brief moment in history united the scattered tribes of his people, then Jesus, as the Sovereign of Heaven, is the Almighty King Who unites the people of the whole Earth for all time.
>
> And, if Jonah was the prophet who survived for three days and nights in the belly of the whale, then Jesus, as the Risen One, is He Who survived for three days and nights in the depths of Hades.
>
> Similarly, if Benjamin was the first brother to recognize Joseph, the viceroy of Egypt, for who he was, then the disciples of Jesus, as the ultimate seers of the light, are the first ones among the tribes of Israel to recognize the Light of the World for Who He was.
>
> And, if the brothers of Joseph were determined to persecute Joseph because he dared to announce that he would rule over them someday, then the kingdoms of Judah and Israel, as the evil generation of their day, are the ones who sought to reject the kingship of Jesus, their true Kinsman Redeemer.
>
> And finally, if Elijah was the messenger who was said to one day prepare the way for the coming of the Messiah, then John the Baptist, as the voice of one crying in the wilderness, is the one who perfectly played out that role in preparing the hearts and minds of the people in anticipation of Jesus.

So why the overemphasis on such an obvious point? For the same reason, I believe, that the God of the dramas of history felt that it required such overemphasis. As finite beings, wrestling with the infinite nature of divinity, we simply lack the capacity to embrace truth in its entirety. In this, we are exactly like those proverbial blind men who, in the famous parable, seek to understand the nature of the elephant with which they are interacting, each from their own point of view. To the extent that one of them is touching but a single aspect of the elephant, for them, that is the reality of the whole. To the one who is touching the trunk, *it is* a snake; to the one who is holding the leg, *it is* a tree; and to the one who is holding the tail, *it is* a rope. By virtue of the form of reality that one is interacting with, that becomes the total sum of their experience and, thus, *it is* the "truth" for that individual. Only when one begins to understand that truth is, in and of itself, beyond the scope of finite understanding, and that one must allow knowledge to take shape as a process, to "build upon itself," as it were, only then can one begin to approach the nature of reality as it actually exits.

Take, for example, the history of mankind's understanding of the nature of the physical world, in terms of both the macrocosm and the microcosm. Concerning the macrocosm, or astronomic dimension, this happened in the process of discovering the heliocentric nature of our solar system. Only over the course of many generations were the great scientific minds able to build and develop—in coordination with the strict observations of their predecessors—a more accurate model of the so-called "truth." Nicolaus Copernicus laid the foundation for Johannes Kepler, and Kepler for Galileo Galilei, and Galileo for Isaac Newton. Concerning the microcosm, or atomic dimension, the same thing occurred in the process of discovering the elemental nature of our molecular world. Although Dmitri Mendeleev is credited with having been the first to "put all the pieces together," in creating what is known as the Periodic Table of Elements, his breakthrough came only after others, like Johann Dobereiner, Antoine Lavoisier, and Robert Boyle, laid the groundwork for his "discovery."

In the same way, just as humanity has only been able to gradually penetrate the truth about the natural world, a genuine knowledge of the divine world has similarly come only as a result of an incremental process of investigation, "bit by bit, action by action, and level by level." And just like those proverbial elephant seekers—as ones crippled by the spiritual dysfunction we all inherited from Adam and Eve—we, too, are forced to assimilate the truth of God's reality over the course of many generations.

Connecting the Dots

CONCERNING THE cumulative nature of knowledge, the same thing can be seen at work when John the Baptist sent word from prison concerning Jesus. The disciples of John asked the Lord, "Are You the One we've been waiting for, or is there someone else?"[330] In response to this question, Jesus could have said, "Yeah, it's Me alright. I'm the One you're looking for." Instead, He told John's disciples: "Go back and report to John what you've seen and heard: The blind receive sight, the lame walk, those who have leprosy are cured, the deaf hear, the dead are raised, and the good news is preached to the poor."[331] So why would Jesus not simply tell John's disciples that He was the Christ? Naturally, as we have already been discussing, it is certainly because God understands the extent to which we, as finite beings, are imprisoned by the nature of human perception. Jesus could have blurted out an answer, and simply expected them to accept it at face value, but this is not what He did. Instead, He forced them to examine their own experience—however limited—in relation to something beyond their fractured human conceptions. Rather than simply telling them that He was their long-awaited Messiah, He first asked them, "What have you seen and heard with your own eyes and ears?" Then before they even had a chance to offer their answer, He cornered them with an answer that was specifically designed to make them think about what they were seeking in an entirely new light. "The blind see," said Jesus. "The lame walk. The lepers are cleansed. The deaf hear. The dead are raised. The good news is preached to the poor."

What is the significance of such an answer? Well, it just so happens that by saying this, Jesus was not merely claiming that He had performed some really impressive stuff, and therefore one must assume He is the Christ. In fact, what He was doing was forcing John's disciples to examine their own experience in light of a much larger context. That is to say, He was challenging them to analyze what they had seen against the backdrop of the entire corpus of Hebrew Scripture that had been handed down to them since time immemorial. In this, Jesus was doing precisely what He did when He inaugurated His earthly ministry. He entered the synagogue, opened *The Book of Isaiah,* and began to read aloud: "The Spirit of the Lord is upon Me, because He's anointed Me to preach good news to the poor. He's sent Me to proclaim freedom for the prisoners, and recovery of sight for the blind, to release the oppressed, to proclaim the year of the Lord's favor."[332] By reading from *Isaiah,* Jesus was reminding His listeners that everything He said or did should always be understood in the context of what *The Bible* had always been saying about the One Whom they had been seeking for so many centuries. This is why whenever Jesus did or said something, the gospel writers consistently pointed to the fact that what He was doing or saying was actually fulfilling what had already been spoken of by "this or that" prophet.

Therefore, when Jesus asked John's disciples to reflect on their seeing Him heal the blind, lame, and deaf, He was, in reality, challenging them to see beyond their limited frame of reference, to see beyond their temporal view of Jesus, the Man, and see Him against the backdrop of eternity. In this way, John's disciples were able to bridge the gap in their own understanding of what the Scriptures had always been saying to them. Instead of simply telling them what they wanted to hear, Jesus led them through an internal mental process in which they would piece together the puzzle of God's plan of salvation in their own minds. In doing so, they would have an even firmer grip on a reality that is all too often clouded by doubt and skepticism. In having helped them to connect the dots this way, John's disciples were then able to personally perceive God's hidden hand in history, and because of this mental process, they would possess the kind of faith in Christ that no one could ever disassemble or explain away.

In this unique fashion, then, Jesus, the Man of Substance, bestows a priceless gift. To anyone who is willing to engage with Him at this level, the Lord imparts the kind of faith that is likened to a tremendous anchor capable of weathering any storm. Every doubt, every fear, every burden, ultimately melts away, as men and women of shadow confront this Man of Substance, and as a result of this process, they become men and women of substance themselves.

A Hero for the Ages

The "Imageness" of God

IN AN AGE DOMINATED by higher criticism and scientific snobbery, the veracity of *The Bible* is often called into question, usually by casting suspicion upon the historical narratives or the miraculous events contained in it. Consequently, cynicism and skepticism rule the day as the necessary price of intelligent inquiry, while faith and hope are set aside as the pathetic contrivances of wishful thinking. Throughout the pages of this work, however, we have sought to refute many of the reasons for such short-sighted conclusions. We have noted the limited frame of reference that humans have regarding the Divine, which constitutes a dimension of reality that is virtually impenetrable to creatures like us who are imprisoned by a fallen nature. Therefore, because of this limited perceptual condition, God has deigned to articulate His truth to mankind in terms of dramatic significance that transcends the foibles of human language. In addition, we have seen how, due to the symbolic nature of "storytelling," the biblical message—in its conveyance of typological truth—is capable of both revealing and concealing knowledge.

So, when the scholar, fueled by higher criticism, demands a greater awareness of the historical process, which is said to dilute the integrity of textual information as it is transmitted from generation to generation, one need simply remind them that God is not nearly as frustrated as they are by such matters. He has already considered the problem and has preemptively designed the dramas of Scripture in such a way that they convey His truth regardless of such difficulties. More intriguing still is that one of the very objections offered by these same scholars is ironically a major proof of its divine authorship. According to critics, *The Bible* is said to have been corrupted as a result of being translated so many times. Yet the fact that the separate books still maintain such a clear-cut continuity from beginning to end is actually one of its most potent elements in demonstrating that mere mortals could not have been the only agency involved in its creation.

And when the scientist, gripped by intellectual snobbery, demands that *The Bible* be expunged of every trace of the miraculous, which is said to confound a realistic approach to the historical nature of the texts, once again, one need simply remind them that God has already figured out how to steer past that objection as well. Such scientific views appear all the more ironic when one considers that these same scientists, while denying the possibility of miracles when they are depicted in Scripture, still insist on believing in the miraculous when they pontificate about such things as the origins of matter or mankind. Never mind that no one was around to witness the Big Bang or has yet to observe the mutation of a gene. As long as one conveys such possibilities with the zeal of the medieval monk who was convinced that the Earth was the center of the Universe, then no one will ever dare to compare such leaps of faith with those that might be required in believing the so-called "poetic nonsense" of *Genesis*.

All this is to underscore another aspect of our prior discussions: One of the reasons that God has apparently chosen to convey the biblical message via dramatic symbolism is because we are creatures with brains that are uniquely tuned to such modes of communication. In other words, it seems that, even in our fallen state of consciousness, our brains are hardwired to interpret data in a symbolic, metaphoric—dare I say—mythic dimension. So that regardless of the immeasurable gulf that exists between God and us there yet remains something in us that is tuned to the frequency of the Divine. That is to say, even though we live in a world where we are imprisoned by our five senses, we still possess some residual aspect of a God-like sensibility, simply by virtue of the fact that we have been created in the image of God.

The psalmist spoke of such incongruities when he wrote, "Deep calls unto deep."[333] Though his tears had been "food" for him day and night, he still remembered that God was there. He placed his hope in the Lord, though everyone around him bombarded him with the same nagging question: "Where is your God? Where is your God? Where is your God?"[334] So how could he maintain a faith like that in the midst of so much misery and doubt? The answer was that the psalmist was able to stay connected to God, in spite of everything weighing in on him, because, as he put it, "deep calls unto deep, in the roar of Your waterfalls, all of Your waves have swept over me."[335] In other words, though everything and everyone sought to break his connection to God, there was something deep within his very being that mysteriously nullified the distance between his earthly existence and the Lord above. There was some ineffable quality—an "internal image," if you will—that somehow maintained a direct link between his mortal being and that of the divine nature, which can be none other than the *"imageness"* of God, to make up a word.

What is more, this connection between God and mankind existed prior to the Advent of the Spirit as it was recorded in *The Book of Acts*, prior to the time that was predicted by John the Baptist, who declared that "soon there will be One Who is going to baptize the world with the Holy Spirit and fire."[336] This ineffable connection, then, is not one that resides only in those who claim to be Christians but in all human beings. With this, I have finally come to the point I have been leading to in this chapter.

Whether or not one believes in God or *The Bible*, all human beings cling to a curious desire to believe in otherworldly possibilities. The believer has faith in his God of Scripture, while the atheist believes in his Big Bang of science. In both cases, however, the same mechanism is at work. Something inside each of us is calling out to some corresponding mystery embedded in the Universe in which we live. We sense it implicitly, and because of this peculiar sensation, we all set out in pursuit of whatever might substantiate this haunting sense of "knowing something" that is beyond our mortal selves.

The Secret Desire

HAVING SAID ALL that, I would like to take some time to demonstrate how this principle of "knowing" is presently at work in the lives of everyone around us, whether in those who believe in *The Bible* or in those who reject it. Furthermore, I will do so by way of another of the ideas already outlined in this work, namely, that the God of Scripture speaks to mankind via the dramatic narratives of *The Bible* because we are creatures that are uniquely tuned to such modes of communication. Therefore, if we as human beings have been created this way, then regardless of our specific belief systems we should find that we all reveal a similar reaction to this thing we call "storytelling." In this, I suppose, anthropologists and psychologists might describe it another way. Human beings, they might postulate, prior to the development of verbal skills, were predisposed to respond to symbolic modes of information, whether in the form of allegory, metaphor, or myth. As such, it is simply a fact of life that we humans, as a species, respond—though, quite arguably, in ways both endearing and disturbing.

The most obvious example of this phenomenon can be seen in the universal response to the mythmaking process that began in the earliest days of movie-making at the turn of the twentieth century, particularly as it was found in a place called Hollywood. Reaching its zenith in the golden era of the 1930s, the "dream factory," as it was dubbed, has ever since—in response to changes in public taste—adeptly alternated between fact and fiction, between drama and melodrama, between the heroic and the anti-heroic. Although it is by no means the only source for motion pictures throughout the world, Hollywood is still widely considered to be the primary cauldron of filmic mythmaking, even as it has endured such worldwide changes as world war and the global religious and economic strife of the twentieth century and beyond.

In many ways, the enduring popularity of movies constitutes one of the most peculiar conundrums known to modern man. It is truly ironic when one considers the fact that this most modern of art forms should inflame so effortlessly the most ancient of ideologies. In a world that prides itself in rationalism and enlightenment, the typical moviegoer rarely objects to the sort of sentimentality and nostalgia that constitutes the primary output of this infamous dream factory, with its preponderance for such "superstitious nonsense" as destiny and redemption, resurrection and immortality, eternal love and self-sacrifice. Just imagine what the movies would be like if there were no monsters or saviors, no aliens or angels, no overlords or freedom-fighters to inhabit the screen. And what if there was no Heaven or God to gaze upon, no Hell or devil to avert our eyes from?

Even while audiences grow weary of worn-out clichés, the demand for more realistic depictions of the world has never quenched the more compelling urge—the secret desire in everyone—to be transported to alternate worlds of existence, where the movie experience becomes for them nothing less than a religious experience. Just consider the box office receipts for the top grossing films of all time, and one will notice a consistent pattern—no doubt exacerbated by Hollywood's reluctance to stray from anything that fails to generate boatloads of cash. In the context of our discussion, however, it is even more telling when one examines this list against the backdrop of the narratives found in *The Bible*.

The Power of One

WITHOUT EXHAUSTING the endless possibilities, a cursory comparison would certainly have to begin with the most mythic of all such motifs—that of the power of "one man." Undoubtedly, the most pervasive story element found in Scripture is that of one man who rises from the muddled masses, one man who alone possesses the skill, the courage, and the sense of destiny to save the day. The roll call of such iconic heroes fills the pages of both Holy Writ and Hollywood. For every Noah, Moses, or David offered up in *The Bible*, there is a James Bond, Luke Skywalker, or Harry Potter among the pantheon of movie gods. When former President Ronald Reagan was asked about what film had most affected him, he cited *Mr. Smith Goes to Washington*.

> When Jimmy Stewart walked the halls of the Capitol building, I walked with him. When he stood in awe of that great man at the Lincoln Memorial, I bowed my head, too. When he stood in the Senate chamber and refused to knuckle under to the vested interests, I began to realize, through the power of the motion picture, one man can make a difference.[337]

In describing what Frank Capra, the director of the film, had done through his hero, film critic Neal Gabler wrote, "He created a powerful myth for the nation."[338] This myth, however, was not created out of thin air. It was, in fact, firmly rooted in those narratives found originally in *The Bible*. "Capra had propounded," Gabler went on to say, "a theology of comedy—a secularized displacement of Christ's tale, in which the common-man hero, blessed with goodness and sense, overcomes obstacles, temptations, and even betrayals to redeem his own life and triumph."[339]

Clearly, without such heroic figures for audiences to root for, movie producers would be sorely lacking the single most important ingredient that keeps people coming back again and again to see the same kinds of movies. Notwithstanding the fact that such things rarely happen in real life, as long as there is some sort of anchor, that is to say, an explicitly *human* anchor to support such mythical motifs, then all the better. And what better "myth" is there to be found than in the pages of the most published book of all time; as famed American film director Cecil B. DeMille once observed: "Give me two pages from *The Bible*, and I'll give you a motion picture." Of course, Mr. DeMille—who directed such films as *The King of Kings*, *The Sign of the Cross*, and *Samson and Delilah*—could never have anticipated the way in which future filmmakers would take the familiar heroes of old and, through a classic bit of Hollywood "rewriting," transform them into heroes for a new generation.

Batman, *Spider-Man*, *Iron Man*, *X-Men*, *Superman*, *Men in Black*, and *James Bond*: Besides representing seven of the all-time highest grossing film franchises in history, what do all these characters have in common? And more importantly, in view of what we are seeking to demonstrate in this work: What do these characters have in common with the narratives that are showcased in the most ancient form of dramatic narrative known to humanity? In a nutshell: They all portray a troubled world that is powerless to resist the overwhelming forces imposed upon it by various personifications of evil—both natural and supernatural. Next, enter into that world some special "one," who has been separated, equipped, and trained to perform a task that no one else is capable of. Then, through the selfless action of this someone—this one man, this one woman, this, dare I say, lone messianic figure—is the archenemy of mankind defeated and the scales of justice set right. Otherwise, without the personal intervention of this hero of biblical proportions, the world would surely remain trapped forever in the clutches of darkness and despair.

Add to the previous list of the super heroic and the not so super heroic: *Marvel's Avengers, The Lord of the Rings, Harry Potter, Star Wars, Transformers, Mission: Impossible, Indiana Jones, Star Trek, The Matrix,* and *The Chronicles of Narnia*. Together, the aforementioned franchises represent seventeen of the top twenty-five movie franchises of all time. Together, they have, to date, amassed worldwide box office revenues to the tune of some 51 billion dollars.[340] The only thing I find more staggering than the untold wealth that such films have procured for their producers is the fact that these seventeen film franchises should so specifically correlate with themes and characterizations that were first described in *The Bible*. Could it really be just a coincidence that audiences the world over would respond with unabashed enthusiasm towards such "impossibly miraculous" storylines? Or, instead, is it simply a product of the kind of wishful thinking that is so common to all human cultures? Certainly, the anthropologists would say so. Or maybe it is just a function of some deep-seated human repression, where we as adults are simply expressing our childhood fantasies when we root for the good guys to triumph over the forces of evil? Of course this is what the psychologists would insist.

But before anyone jumps to such obvious oversimplifications, I believe we would do well to consider the possibility that there might actually be something else at work here. Maybe the answer lies not so much in the fact that audiences are indulging in child-like modes of wishful thinking, but rather that they are simply behaving in accordance with who and what they truly are? That is to say—whether one accepts the message of Scripture or not—we are all human beings who, for a lack of a better description, are much like tuning forks that inwardly respond to frequencies that exist outside ourselves. Anthropologists might call it "correspondence," while psychologists might call it "resonance." Biblical scholars, on the other hand, will insist that it is simply a case of "deep calling unto deep."

Return of the Hero

FURTHER PROOF OF this connection between Hollywood and Holy Writ is that not only is the lone messianic figure found at the core of all these film franchises, but the most prevalent *motif* among them is also the central theme of *The Bible*, which is, the resurrection of the dead. Hollywood filmmakers have repeatedly drawn from the all-too-familiar dramatic well of the vanquished hero who has died—apparently or in reality—while in the effort of saving the day, only to be miraculously restored to life in the end. Christopher Vogler, in his insightful book *The Writer's Journey*, put it this way:

> Heroes must die so that they can be reborn. The dramatic movement that audiences enjoy more than any other is death and rebirth. In some way, in every story, heroes face death or something like it—their greatest fears, the failure of an enterprise, the end of a relationship, the death of an old personality. Most of the time, they magically survive this death and are literally, and symbolically, reborn to reap the consequences of having cheated death.
>
> Steven Spielberg's *E.T.* dies before our eyes but is reborn through alien magic and a boy's love. In *Excalibur*, Sir Lancelot, remorseful over having killed a gallant knight prays him back to life. Clint Eastwood's character in *Unforgiven* is beaten senseless by a sadistic sheriff and hovers at the edge of death, thinking he's seeing angels. *Sherlock Holmes*, apparently killed with Professor Moriarty in the plunge over Reichenbach Falls, defies death and returns, transformed and ready for more adventures. Patrick Swayze's character, murdered in *Ghost*,

> learns how to cross back through the veil to protect his wife and finally express his true love for her.[341]

This ubiquitous storyline involving death and resurrection is never more evident than in many of the most popular film franchises of all time. In fact, more than any other dramatic device, the lives of our most beloved characters have been shaped and forever changed by it. When one thinks of James Bond, Luke Skywalker, Superman, Mister Spock, Neo, Harry Potter, Batman, and Professor Xavier, one cannot help but think of them in terms of the age-old theme of the return of the hero. Case in point: Consider the following scenarios.

In *From Russia with Love*, James Bond is immediately involved in a cat and mouse game with a sinister SPECTRE agent known as Grant. Shrouded in the darkest of night, the two men maneuver adeptly through an outdoor arena filled with hedgerows, fountains, and Romanesque statues. Stalking his prey, Bond fires off a shot, barely missing his opponent. Then, quite unexpectedly, Grant turns the tables on our hero and strangles him to death. It is at this point that the darkened arena is lit up to reveal that we have actually been witnessing a training exercise. With a flick of the wrist, an unknown figure removes a mask from the face of the dead man that we had been led to believe is James Bond but instead turns out to be someone else, a mere pawn in a twisted game of death.

In *Goldfinger*, it is not the hero who is "resurrected" but the hero's helpers. In this case, the troops that guard the gold at Fort Knox are put out of commission by the nefarious villain by which the film derives its name. In one fell swoop, sixteen thousand soldiers are killed by a deadly nerve gas, which is dropped onto them via airplanes manned by Pussy Galore and her flying team of *femme fatales*. But once Goldfinger and his men move in for the heist, the troops all "miraculously" rise to their feet and quickly mobilize to eliminate the threat. As it turns out, Goldfinger's trusted pilot, Pussy—having been turned by the ever seductive James Bond—has switched the contents of the gas-emitting canisters; and the troops have only been faking their deaths in order to lure the enemy into a false sense of security.

In *You Only Live Twice*, James Bond is on assignment in Hong Kong, where he is double-crossed by a beautiful Chinese agent and killed in a hail of machine gun bullets. He is then buried at sea with all honors, commensurate with his rank as a commander of Her Majesty's Royal Navy. His cocooned body is deposited into the sea with the eulogy: "For the trumpet shall sound and the dead shall be raised incorruptible... We therefore commit his body to the deep ... looking for the resurrection, when the seas shall give up their dead." But no sooner has Bond's cocoon slipped into the depths than a pair of deep-sea divers intercept and whisk it away to the safety of a nearby submarine, where it is unwrapped, extricating Bond who has been breathing via SCUBA gear the entire time. Far from being an unsuspecting victim, then, Bond has actually been part of an elaborately staged hoax so that he will be even more effective in his job of infiltrating the enemy's camp because he is believed to be dead.

In *Skyfall*, James Bond is similarly killed in an opening sequence, only to return again with a vengeance, but unlike the "death" of the hero in *You Only Live Twice*, the one in *Skyfall* was not planned. Instead, Bond is accidentally shot, and as a result of his injuries, his skills are severely diminished, due in large part to his gunshot wounds and the wear-and-tear he has endured after many long years in the field as the vaunted Agent 007. Consequently, Bond is forced to muster every ounce of inner strength to free himself from the stigma that his near-death experience has thrust upon him, and only after an arduous journey does he reemerge in the end, reborn, ready to resume his rightful mantle as James Bond.

In *Star Wars IV: A New Hope*, Luke Skywalker is trapped with his companions in a gigantic trash compactor at the heart of the Death Star, when suddenly the huge tentacle of an unseen monster pulls him down into the murky ooze. Horrified, Han Solo, Princess Leia, and Chewbacca watch in helpless desperation as Luke's tell-tale bubbles cease to trickle to the surface. Then, just when they have given up hope, Luke breaks upward through the slimy surface and is reunited with his friends. Later, when Luke's mentor, Obi Wan Kenobi, is killed in a laser duel with Darth Vader, his body vanishes, and Luke, at that point, believes it will be the last time he will ever see his old friend again. But in Luke's greatest hour of need, Obi Wan returns—albeit in spirit form—to guide him with the most important advice of his life: "Trust the force, Luke."

In *Superman: The Movie*, Lois Lane's car careens into a ravine caused by an earthquake that was triggered by a nuclear missile reprogrammed to fulfill the twisted purposes of Lex Luthor. Trapped in her sinking vehicle during the ensuing landslide, Lois is slowly buried alive beneath the cascading rubble. Unfortunately for her, Clark Kent—a.k.a. Superman—is forced into the opposite direction to stop a second missile because he has promised to prevent it from killing the mother of the woman who mercifully released him from the crippling chain of Kryptonite that Luthor placed around his neck. So by the time Superman thwarts this missile, he fails to arrive before he can prevent Lois' death. In a fit of superhuman rage, the Man of Steel then takes to the sky and begins streaking around the globe, causing it to spin in reverse, thereby turning back time to the events prior to Lois' death. Upon returning to her now undamaged car, Superman finds that Lois is alive and well, and no one on Earth has any idea what he has done in restoring her life.

In *Star Trek II: The Wrath of Khan*, the crippled Enterprise, its warp drive damaged in a previous battle, is threatened with annihilation as it drifts in orbit around a dead planet that is about to be "regenerated" by the Genesis Device. As it turns out, this device—designed to terraform barren worlds into habitable ones suitable for colonization by the Federation—will also destroy any prior life forms in favor of its "new matrix." So, in a selfless effort to rescue the Enterprise and its crew, Mister Spock enters the ship's engine room, where he successfully restores the ship's warp drive. In the process, however, Spock exposes himself to radiation and dies while James Kirk, captain of the Enterprise, can only look on helplessly from the other side of the glass partition.

In the next film, *Star Trek III: The Search for Spock*, the lifeless body of Mister Spock has been jettisoned to the surface of the regenerated planet, but before long, scientists involved with the Genesis Device discover signs of an unexpected life form on the planet. Upon arrival to the planet's surface, they discover that Spock has, as a result of the regenerative effects of the device, been resurrected into the form of a child. At first, Spock is a blank slate, apparently mindless, with no apparent recollection of who he is or was. He then undergoes a series of metamorphic changes. As the planet they are on matures at an accelerated pace, so also Spock ages with astonishing rapidity. Soon, Spock has reached full maturity in body, but his mind, his soul, is still apparently absent. Eventually, Captain Kirk and the crew of the Enterprise are able to return Spock to Vulcan, where he is reunited with his soul, which he had at the end of the previous film secretly deposited in the mind of the ship's doctor, Leonard McCoy, prior to his entering the ship's engine room.

In *Star Trek: Generations*, a retired James Kirk is forced back into action when a mysterious ribbon of energy called the Nexus threatens the maiden voyage of the Enterprise-B. In a valiant effort to free the ship, Kirk is apparently killed when this energy ribbon damages the section he was working on. Many years later, we discover more about the Nexus, which has become the singular obsession of the twisted Doctor Tolian Soran, who is hell-bent on tapping into this ribbon of energy, even though he must destroy entire planets in the process. In his attempt to stop Doctor Soran, Captain Jean-Luc Picard unexpectedly finds himself inside the Nexus, which turns out be more than mere energy. It is really an alternate Universe where, throughout time and space, certain individuals have been known to become trapped. While there, Picard learns why Soran is so determined to control the Nexus. Apparently, one of its peculiar qualities is that for anyone inside the ribbon it can generate their innermost desires, something Picard realizes he must reject if he is to escape and return to the real world. Eventually, Picard learns that Kirk is also one of those wayward travelers who has become "stuck" in the Nexus, not yet understanding where he is or why he is there. After some gentle but persistent persuasion, Picard convinces Kirk to reject his comfortable place in the Nexus.

They both return to the "land of the living," where the "resurrected" Kirk fights alongside Picard, and together they kill Soran before he can destroy any more worlds in his attempts to gain control of the Nexus.

In *Men in Black,* Agents K and J confront a gigantic, parasitic alien bug, bent on destroying a rival species that is hiding out on planet Earth. In their efforts to thwart this malevolent threat, Agent J watches helplessly as Agent K first has his weapon eaten by the bug, and while in the process of taunting the monster, K is gobbled up, too. Desperately, Agent J tries to restrain the creature, to no avail. Then, just as it looks as if Agent J might be eaten like his partner before him, the sound of Agent K's weapon is heard powering up from within the bug's belly, followed by the creature exploding from within. After having been blown into a million gelatinous pieces, the creature's disintegrated body catapults Agent K from its innards, alive and well.

In *Men in Black 3,* another nasty parasitic alien, this time a Boglodite assassin by the name of Boris the Animal, escapes from a maximum security prison on the Moon. A one-armed man—or should I say, creature—on a mission, Boris is out for revenge. His target is the agent who is responsible for his having lost his arm and being imprisoned. That person is none other than Agent K. Boris' diabolical plan is to go back in time to kill Agent K before he has the chance to do either. When Boris makes his "time jump" to the past, the present world of the Men in Black transforms to a place in which Agent K no longer exists. But strangely enough, Agent J is aware that something is wrong with their world, while everyone else is convinced that Agent K was killed some forty years earlier by Boris the Animal. Agent K, however, is not the only victim of the Boglodite's scheme, because having avoided being put out of commission by him, Boris is now able, in this "new present," to mount a full-scale Boglodite attack on Earth. Hoping to restore the world that he once knew, Agent J follows Agent K into the past, where he teams up with a younger version of K, and together they thwart both the younger and present-day versions of Boris, thus restoring Agent K to his proper place in the future, as well as preempting the Boglodite attack on planet Earth.

In *The Matrix,* mild-mannered Neo is living a boring, mundane life—software engineer by day, computer hacker by night; but he is searching for so much more. Before long, he meets a mysterious woman named Trinity, who challenges his acceptance of the status quo. Eventually, Neo is introduced to Morpheus, a man who, along with Trinity, attempts to draw him out of his comfort zone. Soon, Morpheus convinces Neo that the source of his frustration is due to the fact that he is actually an unwitting slave to a shadow world called the Matrix. As a captive of this world of illusion, Neo is offered a way out by Morpheus—a way of escape that plunges our hero into a stark new reality that is for him nothing less than a journey from one existence to another. Upon making this transition to his new life, Neo asks, "Am I dead?" Matter-of-factly, Morpheus responds, "Far from it." As a member of Morpheus' band of rebels, Neo finally learns the truth about the difference between the real world he now inhabits and the dream world that had until then held him captive. In time, Morpheus convinces Neo that he is the Chosen One who might lead mankind in an all-out rebellion to destroy the power of the Matrix and release humanity from its grip. Reluctant at first, Neo goes on to develop a variety of skills, both physical and mental, in order to fulfill the destiny that Morpheus and Trinity are convinced is his. In the final confrontation between Morpheus' team and agents of the Matrix, Neo is caught off guard and killed by the insidious Agent Smith, but refusing to accept that his death means the end of Neo, Trinity unflinchingly breathes life back into him with a kiss. Imbued with a new sense of purpose and determination, Neo rises to his feet and, with a power previously unattained, disposes of Agent Smith, thereby ending the threat and turning the tide in the battle against the Matrix.

In *Harry Potter and the Chamber of Secrets,* Harry encounters Professor Albus Dumbledore's pet Phoenix, Hawkes. Right before Harry's eyes, Hawkes abruptly catches fire and disintegrates into a pile of dust. As Professor Dumbledore explains to Harry: "They burst into flames when it's time to die, then they're reborn from the ashes." To Harry's astonishment, just as Dumbledore has explained, a newborn chick wiggles out from the pile of ashes. Later, in his attempt to rescue one of his friends, Harry is confronted in a life-or-death struggle with a huge serpent called a Basilisk. When it attacks Harry, Hawkes comes to Potter's aid by clawing the creature's eyes out. Still, the monster can smell Harry as it relentlessly chases the young wizard. Eventually, Harry gets the better of the Basilisk, thrusting a sword through the creature's mouth, but in the process of killing the monster Harry is mortally wounded by one of its venomous fangs. As Harry languishes in the throes of death, Hawkes flies to his friend's side. Touched by Harry's infirmity, Hawkes begins to weep. One by one, the tears of the Phoenix drip into his wounds, and in an extraordinary turn of events, the young wizard is completely healed through the power of those tears.

In *The Dark Knight Rises*, a masked madman called Bane threatens to destroy Gotham City with a nuclear bomb that has been created by converting a reactor core, originally built for good by none other than Bruce Wayne—a.k.a. Batman. With no way to prevent its detonation, Batman lifts the bomb with the help of the Bat, an aircraft developed and built by Lucius Fox, a man who runs Wayne Enterprises on his behalf. All of Gotham City watches with great anticipation as the Bat streaks far away, out across the bay, where the bomb finally detonates well beyond the city limits. Assumed to have been killed in the blast, the much-misunderstood Batman is posthumously feted as a hero who has singlehandedly saved Gotham. With Bruce Wayne also presumed dead, his estate is divided up among the city's orphans and his faithful butler Alfred. Eventually, however, Fox discovers, to his amazement, that the Bat's autopilot, which had previously been malfunctioning, is now fully restored, and in one final scene, Alfred, while on holiday abroad, is quite relieved to find Bruce Wayne, alive and well, sitting in an outdoor café with his new companion Selina Kyle—a.k.a. Catwoman.

In *X2: X-Men United*, Jean Grey uses her awesome telekinetic power to save her comrades from a massive flood caused by a breach in the dam at Alkali Lake. In the process, however, she is engulfed in the powerful undertow and heroically sacrifices her own life while rescuing the others.

In the following film, *X-Men: The Last Stand*, the memory of Jean haunts her boyfriend Scott Summers, who stands mourning for her on the banks of Alkali Lake. Overcome by grief, Scott—a.k.a. Cyclops—unleashes his own mutant power into the center of the lake. A laser blast from his eyes energizes the waters before him, and from the murky depths, there emerges a figure engulfed in a blinding canopy of light. From out of this shimmering halo, Jean Grey emerges, inexplicably returned from her watery grave. Sadly, though, there is a downside to this apparently blissful reunion. It seems as though the "resurrected" Jean is not entirely the same person that she once was. In time, we find that, according to X-Men Professor Charles Xavier, Jean's personality contains a dark, hidden aspect he calls the Phoenix, a side that he has sought to control for many years, hoping to quell a virtually limitless aspect of her telekinetic power. In the end, however, this dark side consumes Jean, and in an uncontrollable fit of rage, she kills Charles Xavier, vaporizing his body in front of several horrified X-Men. But as one might expect in the peculiar Universe of superheroes, this does not spell the end for Professor Xavier, either. Before *The Last Stand* concludes, the professor's post-mortem presence is already revealing itself to a nurse as she attends to a comatose patient who unexpectedly speaks to her in a voice that she cannot help but recognize. To which the befuddled nurse whispers back, "Charles?"

A subsequent film, *X-Men Origins: Wolverine*, has Logan—a.k.a. the Wolverine—making his way through an airplane terminal. There, he is stunned to see Professor Xavier nonchalantly roll up to him in his mechanized wheelchair, looking as fit as ever. "How is this possible?" mumbles a disbelieving Wolverine. To which Xavier glibly replies, "As I told you a long time ago, you're not the only one with gifts."

Tales of Me and You

SO TELL ME: ARE YOU convinced yet? Or should I continue? I could go on and on with a great many more examples, but suffice it to say, in these numerous scenarios, one is presented with sufficient evidence for the overwhelming correspondence between the narratives of *The Bible* and those of the most popular films of all time. In the end, my purpose in all of this laborious film exegesis remains constant. In a world that prides itself on rationality, logic, and objectivity—call it what you will—there is clearly an equal yet opposite dimension to its innermost belief system. As it turns out, the flipside to these so-called "normal" modes of thought cannot be explained away simply because so many generations of mankind have distorted, abused, and exploited the potential of such otherworldly realities. In other words, just because fanatics, zealots, and extremists are assumed to be the only kinds of people crazy enough to cling to such outrageous notions as the resurrection of the dead, do not fool yourselves with such rigidly shallow interpretations. The verdict has been handed down, and it has been done by way of the almighty dollar. In this most unexpected way, the "secret desire" of the average, everyday moviegoer has revealed the truth about what they really believe to be the meaning and purpose of their world. Moreover, they have done so to the resounding tune of—I repeat—51 billion dollars (and counting), proving once and for all that "audiences are not simply indulging in child-like modes of wishful thinking, but they are," contrary to all critical and scientific ways of thinking, "behaving in accordance with who and what they truly are."

This is why, I believe, *The Tales* found in this present volume can no longer be casually dismissed simply because they seem to contradict one's assumptions about traditional history—either biblical or secular. After all, if humanity's response to the irresistible force of the cinema is taken into consideration, as I am convinced it should, then this belief in nothing less than the redemption and rebirth of the human soul is one that clearly cuts across every known strata of existence. And if this is the case, then no longer should the fantastic accounts of Enoch, Adam, Abraham, and Pilate be excluded on the fallacious grounds that they must have been left out of *The Bible* for good reason.

Simply put, if the Scriptures declare that Enoch walked and talked with God, then it should come as no surprise that as a result of this momentous encounter he might have something of great importance to communicate. And, if Enoch as the first narrator of human history stated that God personally entrusted him with the story of mankind's past, present, and future, then who are we to say that what he wrote was a fantasy or, worse, the product of a delusional mind? After all, nothing is more consistent in this peculiar Universe of ours than the old adage: "Truth is always stranger than fiction." So, when Enoch insisted that he was assigned the task of writing books with the express purpose of detailing the lives of all those who *have* lived, who *were* living, and who *were yet to* live, who—again I repeat—are we to question the apparent improbability of such a thing?

And if God spoke face to face with Enoch, then why could not the Word of God have done the same thing with Adam, Abraham, and Pilate? When Adam suffered the consequences of his futile efforts to regain entrance to the garden, who is to say that the Word of God did not restore him to life again and again so he could fulfill the years that had been decreed for him? When Abraham was wrestling with whether or not God could make him a father of many nations, who is to say that the Word did not convince him he could also become the father of a multitude of spiritual children whose destiny is an incorruptible city in Heaven? And in the fullness of time, when this Word became flesh and dwelled among men, who is to say that He did not reveal Himself to Pilate, the most infamous political boss the world has ever known, and in that shattering encounter transform even a man like him into a most unwitting ally?

Who is to say, really? After all, one only needs to answer a few simple, straightforward questions. Have not the tales of wonder that this man Enoch was supposedly entrusted with made their mark in spite of everything that the world might say to the contrary? Do not tales of redemption and rebirth permeate our global community, within and without? Can anyone really tell us where one storyline ends and where another begins? If not, then maybe it is simply time for the world to finally embrace these *Tales* and, like our father Abraham, cease and desist in questioning the possibility of such impossibilities. Why not drink them in, imbibe them, and become intoxicated by the spirit of them, because through them one might just see the world anew. And maybe, the next time someone looks in the mirror, they will find staring back one who has been forever changed because they, too, have encountered the *Tales of Forever*—tales of heroes and villains, tales of me and you.

THE SUBPLOTS

Why should I speak of … the Phoenicians or … the Chaldeans? For the Jews, deriving their origin from the descendants of Abraham … have handed down to us … the number of 5,500 years as being the period up to the advent of the Word of Salvation.

Julius Africanus, *On the Mythical Chronology of the Egyptians and Chaldeans*

A Capstone to Time

One Final Twist

TALES OF FOREVER chronicles a two-fold drama of paramount importance, to hardcore biblical scholars and casual readers of Scripture alike. The first of these pertains to the little-known prophecy of The Great Five and a Half Days—introduced in *The First Book of Adam and Eve,* alluded to in *The Secrets of Enoch,* and finally culminating in *The Gospel of Nicodemus.* Prior to this work, the scattered bits of this prophetic tapestry lay strewn about like so many disassembled pieces of a puzzle abandoned long ago, but herein they have all been reconnected, and a continuous dramatic narrative has been constructed.

As the story goes: Soon after their tragic expulsion, Adam and Eve were told by God that He intended to allow them back into the garden home they had forfeited; but not until the completion of *five and a half* "days" from His perspective. Why *five and a half* days? They were to be banished for that length of time because, as Enoch stated in his record of events, Adam and Eve had resided in Eden for *five and a half* hours. So, just as the Israelites neglected to keep God's command to let the land lie fallow during His Jubilee years and were consequently exiled, the Lord of Time deigned to establish the prototypical pattern of His judgments in the lives of our first parents and were thereby exiled for *five and a half* "days."

Thus, having established the prophetic timeline of The Great Five and a Half Days, the drama came full circle when Pontius Pilate confronted Annas, the chief priest at Jerusalem, who confessed that he had also become aware of this promise of "days." Quite unexpectedly, Annas had discovered a passage in their most sacred text, in the first of *The Seventy Books,* as he described it himself, in which the archangel Michael was said to have told Seth, the third son of Adam, that the Christ was to appear on Earth after five thousand, five hundred years. Furthermore, he deduced that because Moses had constructed The Ark of the Covenant with dimensions of *five and a half* cubits, this doubly confirmed that Christ would come in an ark, or tabernacle, of a body, according to this same time frame.[342]

Of course, if you have taken the time to read *Tales of Forever* for yourself, you might be saying that you already know all this. What you may not be aware of, however, is one last bit of information—"one final twist," as it were—regarding the prophecy of The Great Five and a Half Days; which leads us to the second drama woven throughout this work, that of Enoch, the scribe, who was entrusted with a knowledge of the entire span of human history. Still you may be asking: How can anyone believe that a mere mortal could possibly perceive the history of all mankind—of those who *had* lived, who *were* living, and who *were yet to* live? Certainly, it is impossible for anyone to know something so far beyond the pale of human cognition, is it not? Admittedly, such questions are perfectly valid ones, and in our attempt to address such impossibilities, we will offer the following possibilities.

Detectives of History

WHEN GRAPPLING WITH mysteries like this, we have focused on certain key strategies. Primarily, we have centered our investigation upon what I have called the dramas that transcend interpretation. In other words, when faced with the dilemma of what can and cannot be trusted in our search for scriptural truth we—as veritable detectives of history—have focused on events that have been repeated over and over again. In the case of Enoch, history's most articulate type of Christ, this means we should seek to collect clues that correlate his life and teachings with Jesus, the articulated Word of God, that is to say, the substance of Enoch. In this way, the greater the extent to which we can find parallels between Enoch and Christ, the greater the probability that the improbabilities in question might not seem so improbable after all.

So, what are some of the ways that Enoch, "as shadow," and Christ, "as substance," are displayed throughout biblical history? Like Jesus of Nazareth after him, Enoch was anointed with a very special connection with God that provided an acute awareness of the divine presence that no one else possessed. This eventually led Enoch into a one-on-one encounter with God Himself, where the patriarch was given a prophetic message for the sake of the chosen -- an event that in many ways foreshadowed the transfiguration of Christ. Upon returning to his family that was convinced he had been killed, Enoch was received by them as one would who had been figuratively brought back from the dead. And finally, having gifted his family with the books he had written, Enoch ascended to Heaven in the sight of everyone, just as Jesus would likewise do after His death and resurrection.

Naturally, because of these striking parallels, skeptics have argued that later authors must have edited the events of Enoch's life in order to create these connections after the fact, much in the same way they have maligned the prophecies of Daniel because of their unprecedented level of historical accuracy. Of course, much of this criticism falls by the wayside in light of the findings at Qumran, where the contribution of *The Dead Sea Scrolls* has demonstrated that the books attributed to Enoch preceded the Christian Era by at least two centuries. In this way, one might better appreciate the role that the life of Enoch plays in foreshadowing that of Jesus', and, considering the relationship between these two miraculous figures, Enoch's insight into the fate of all mankind.

That said, I would like to return to the point I made earlier in this chapter when I mentioned that you may not be aware of one final bit of information regarding the prophecy of The Great Five and a Half Days. Thus far, in our mystery grappling, we have employed the use of dramas that transcend interpretation. Next, we will turn to another form of examining biblical history, one that is also used because of its ability to nullify the inherent problems that occur with the numerous translations of *The Bible.* In this case, we will be interpreting the biblical record in terms of another tool, which, like that of the drama, is universal in nature, regardless of culture and/or language, that is to say, mathematics.

But where some would seek to find mathematical messages in Scripture in the form of obscure codes, which may or may not exist, the ones I will be discussing are the kind that are clearly visible, though hidden in plain sight. Moreover, while some would try to expound complicated mathematics that only a genius might hope to appreciate, I will be discussing the kind that even a child can understand. In this case, the mathematics we will be dealing with pertain to one of the most ancient monuments ever dedicated to the knowledge of God -- The Great Pyramid of Giza, renowned throughout history as The Pillar of Enoch, due to his reputed role as its architect.

Fear not, however, those of you who have already encountered the stupefying mysteries surrounding this enigmatic structure. We will not be delving too deeply into the multitude of cryptic meanings encased in its marvelous design. No, that, I can assure you, is quite beyond the scope of this particular essay. What we will be looking for, though, is the possible link between Enoch, as architect, and The Great Pyramid, as The Pillar of Enoch. Hopefully, we will establish this link by way of investigating the following questions. Do the allegedly prophetic implications built into the design of The Great Pyramid of Giza reveal a connection to the hidden hand of its supposed architect, Enoch? How might this help to explain the way that this mere mortal could have perceived something as unknowable as the fate of all mankind? And in what ways might the testimony of the alleged "word of God in stone" corroborate the validity of the alleged "word of God by the hand of Enoch"?

The Pillar of Enoch

LET US TAKE A MOMENT, then, to examine some of the things that might offer the necessary links we are seeking. First, how does *The Bible* even begin to consider mere stone as a form of witness to the word of God? In fact, a passage in *The Book of Isaiah* has something very interesting to say about it. As in the construction of any grand edifice, which requires a precise plan of measurement, the following verses provide a unique benchmark into the meaning of the divine metaphor of the *stone*. Said Isaiah:

> Listen to what the Lord says to all you skeptics who rule the people in Jerusalem, because you've said, "We've made a covenant with death and Hell. The overwhelming scourge will not reach us when it passes by, because we've made falsehood our refuge, so as to conceal ourselves with lies."
>
> Therefore, the Lord God says, "Look and see how I've placed a stone in Zion—a tested stone, a precious cornerstone as a firm foundation. Whoever believes in it will not be shaken. I'll make justice the measuring line, and righteousness the level. Then, hail will sweep away the refuge of lies, and the waters will overflow the secret place."[343]

What can one deduce about the meaning of the "stone" in the context of the preceding statement? Apparently, Isaiah is revealing that God and His creation are at odds. On one hand, there is the deceitfulness and myopia of the human race, while on the other hand, there is the perfection of God's justice and righteousness—a perfection conveyed by what Isaiah described as a tested stone that functions as a cornerstone. Furthermore, he continues his metaphor by saying that God's justice is like a measuring line and His righteousness is as a level, all of which—a cornerstone, a measuring line, and a level—are devices used in the construction of a building. Is this building merely a metaphorical building? Or, instead, is Isaiah thinking of an actual structure? The answer, I believe, is one that any beginner student in the study of The Great Pyramid is already well aware of. Immediately, one thinks of an earlier chapter in *Isaiah,* which has the prophet saying:

> In that day, there will be an altar to the Lord in the midst of Egypt, and a pillar of God at its border. It will become a sign and a witness to the Lord of Hosts in the land of Egypt, for they'll cry to God because of the oppressors, and He'll send them a Savior and a Champion to deliver them.[344]

One of the foundational passages in the canonical record, this verse is cited by all advocates of Pyramidology in an attempt to verify the scriptural integrity of their subject matter. Because Egypt just happens to be divided into upper and lower sections, this description, they say, is perfectly fulfilled by the fact that The Great Pyramid sits on the very spot that constitutes both its center *and* its border.

The next clue to this verse, say the experts, pertains to the Hebrew meaning of the words for *sign* and *witness*. In order to dismiss the possibility that The Great Pyramid is nothing more than a by-gone funerary heap built for some heathen Pharaoh, pyramidologists quickly point out that the words used by Isaiah leave no margin for error in this regard. According to *Strong's Exhaustive Concordance of The Bible*, the word translated as "sign" conveys the meaning of a signal, a beacon, a monument, and/or evidence.[345] The word translated as "witness" is derived from a word that means to testify, to admonish, to charge, and/or give warning.[346] Together, these words uniquely express the idea that in the land of Egypt, God will provide a monument that will stand as evidence, as a beacon, as a testimonial, bearing witness in a form that encompasses both an admonition and a warning.

To that end, advocates of Pyramidology will proceed with endless explanations as to the latent meaning revealed in the dimensions of the many passageways and chambers in this ancient megalith, each intended to mathematically predict nearly every important event in world history, both sacred and secular. Building off the work of such nineteenth-century pioneers as John Taylor, C. Piazzi Smyth, Robert Menzies, and Joseph A. Seiss, modern scholars like John Garnier, David Davidson, and Adam Rutherford have inspired the next wave of researchers, all with a single conviction held in common across the generations. That is to say, every one of them is convinced that this remarkable structure was divinely inspired to convey a message of God's control over human history. But this message, they insist, is not one that is expressed in the form of words, which can become misconstrued over time or through mistranslation. In fact, it is conveyed via the incontrovertible science of mathematics. According to this way of thinking, because the God of *The Bible* is a God of Set Times, the mathematics of The Great Pyramid are expressed by way of the specific measurements of the passageways and chambers within it. These measurements, in turn, create a time-oriented chronology of the pivotal points in the biblical timeline, such as the Exodus of Israel out of Egypt, the birth, death, and resurrection of Christ, and the Reformation. Similarly, conveyed by the internal dimensions of The Pyramid, there are turning points in world history to be found, such as the invention of the printing press, the year of global revolution, and the commencement and cessation of World War I.

Having pointed that out, however, I did already explain this would not constitute the primary focus of this chapter, because attempting to confirm or deny the truth of all the intricate mathematics involved in the dimensions of this remarkable edifice would lead us down a far different path than I hope to take. Rather, what I am attempting here is to focus on any links that might connect Enoch's role—as the first prophet of history—with whatever prophetic message is encrypted into The Great Pyramid of Giza. I merely mention the prior evidence provided by pyramidologists to demonstrate that just as Enoch has been connected with the gift of prophecy, so also has this most famous of all megaliths been connected with the notion of prophetic wisdom.

So much for this introduction to the way in which The Great Pyramid relates to the history of mankind. How, then, does its architecture reveal the hidden hand of Enoch as its original designer? Granted, one is facing numerous disadvantages in seeking the answer to such a question. If Enoch had drawn the schematics of this Pyramid, he might have signed his name at the bottom; but without such obvious evidence, one is left with only the structure itself as a clue to provide a potential answer. Moreover, as most researchers will confess, a megalithic work of this nature does not easily lend itself to the process of authentication. Except for the counterfeit hieroglyphs placed there by an overzealous explorer—erroneously identifying the pharaoh Khufu, a.k.a Cheops, as the architect—The Great Pyramid, alone among all others, has never been found to contain a single stroke of writing. As a result, the only way to determine who might have designed it comes in the form of detective work. That is to say, one must look for other clues to reveal their true identity. In this case, because we are dealing with a stone edifice with passageways and chambers, we have a unique opportunity at our disposal in that a specific pattern emerges when one takes the time to examine its structural design. As such, a building's construction can actually convey a recognizable signature, much in the same way that certain architectural features reveal whether a Michelangelo or a Christopher Wren might have designed a particular building.

More about this approach in determining Enoch's role as The Pyramid's architect will follow a little later. First, though, let us continue to build up a picture of the structural design that The Great Pyramid presents to us. By all accounts, the primary feature built into The Pyramid has to do with revealing a timeline of historical events of biblical proportion, but is this the only architectural feature that might provide us with the truth of who designed it? As a matter of fact, no, it is not.

In addition to revealing biblical chronology in stone, the dimensions of The Great Pyramid also display a unique insight into the nature of the physical construct of our Earth, which, according to the experts, includes, among other things, its weight, its mean density, and its distance from the Sun. So while researchers might disagree as to the "where and when" of historical events alluded to via The Pyramid's dimensions, there is one thing that they have a much harder time disagreeing about—the verifiable dimensions of our solar system. This is not to say that science does not have different ways of measuring such things as the distance from the Earth to the Sun, the weight of the Earth, or its mean density. Nevertheless, while so much of biblical prophecy resides within the realm of personal opinion, the discrepancies encountered within the realm of physical matter are infinitely more reconcilable. In fact, these dimensional clues as to the physical nature of the Earth and Sun seem to stand out as a clear punctuation mark in the overall investigation of the more metaphysical aspects of Pyramidology. In other words, it seems as if whoever designed The Great Pyramid fully anticipated the skepticism of humanity that would one day ponder the mystery of its construction, and in order to substantiate its prophetic possibilities, they included these more tangible clues concerning the physical nature of the solar system.

With this in mind, we will examine the way in which the number three hundred and sixty-five is commemorated within the architectural design of The Great Pyramid. This number, more than any other, constitutes a unique signature, which—in conjunction with the ubiquitous legends that call it The Pillar of Enoch—goes a long way toward indicating Enoch as its architect. Again, as any student of Pyramidology will tell you: The reason this number is so thoroughly associated with Enoch is that this was his age when *The Bible* records a peculiar event: "So all the days of Enoch were three hundred and sixty-five years. And Enoch walked with God and was not because God took him."[347]

But what, you may ask, is so unusual about this event? Is it because of the ambiguous nature of this "taking"? Certainly, this has always been a bone of contention with students of *The Bible*. However, in the context of our discussion, it is not, I am afraid, even pertinent to the topic. What is pertinent is the patriarch's *age* when he was "taken," because in an antediluvian age, when men were reported to have lived an average of nine hundred years, this man was said to have lived a measly three hundred and sixty-five years. Why?

As usual, the answer resides in "the eye of the beholder." In other words, if you are the kind of person that dismisses Scripture as being purely imaginative, with no basis in fact, then you probably see this as a random lifespan. If, however, you are a believer in God's control over history, then you probably see this as no accidental occurrence. Add to this the apocryphal record that has Enoch being given a guided tour of the cosmos, and one might very likely accept that God purposefully removed him from the Earth so his very lifespan would convey a truth that would resound for generations to come. Either way, the fact is, long before modern man ever determined the actual length of the solar year, the lifespan of Enoch perfectly portrayed it in terms that even a child in Sunday school can appreciate.

The first occurrence of this numerical value of three hundred and sixty-five becomes evident when one considers the exterior of The Great Pyramid, which nineteenth-century British archeologist Flinders Petrie discovered in his pioneering work of measuring the structure's base perimeter. Having measured the four sides of the megalith's foundation, Petrie found that they were slightly indented at the middle. In time, subsequent researchers became intrigued that three distinct measurements of its base, indicated by this apparently random indentation, bore a striking resemblance with the three known variations of the solar year—the tropical, at 365.242 days, the sidereal, at 365.256 days, and the anomalistic, at 365.259 days. (For further details on this phenomenon, please refer to page 65 of E. Raymond Capt's introductory study to Pyramidology entitled *The Great Pyramid Decoded*.)

Furthermore, inside The Great Pyramid is another example of this numerical value of three hundred and sixty-five, or—more specifically, in terms of the precise length of the solar year—365.242. Lying at the nucleus of The Pyramid's interior is what scholars have christened the King's Chamber, where there is an empty granite Coffer, or open strongbox. In order to enter the King's Chamber, one must first pass through another smaller chamber, dubbed the Ante-Chamber. Upon measuring this room, explorers found that within its dimensions a circle drawn inside yielded a circumference of 365.242 pyramid inches—a unit of measurement which, by the way, differs from the British and American inch by just 1/1000th of an inch. As a result of this discovery, this circle is referred to as The Enoch Circle. In addition to this, the distance from the midpoint of the Ante-Chamber to the south wall of the King's Chamber again measures 365.242 pyramid inches. (For a more in-depth explanation on the origins of the so-called "pyramid inch," please refer to pages 290-304 of C. Piazzi Smyth's book entitled *The Great Pyramid: Its Secrets and Mysteries Revealed*.)

And just in case you think that this is all by chance, let me offer the following quote from one of the leading pyramidologists of the last century, Adam Rutherford. More important still to our present investigation, this statement provides additional evidence in our attempt to connect this grand edifice with its true architect; and I quote:

> The entire geometric design of The Great Pyramid is built upon the Enoch Circle—its circumference, diameter, and radius, which are respectively 365.242, 116.26, and 58.13 geometric, or pyramid, inches. So, by geometric symbolism, the representation of Enoch is stamped on the entire Pyramid from top to bottom, inside and out. No wonder that The Great Pyramid is traditionally associated with Enoch, and that Masonic tradition alludes to this Pyramid as The Pillar of Enoch.[348]

Not only is this numerical value of 365.242 built into the dimensions of The Great Pyramid, but also inexorably linked to it is a number that is revered by mathematicians and scientists alike—*pi*. Considered the Universe's one great constant, *pi* is defined as the ratio of a circle's circumference in relation to its diameter, and as such is approximately equal to 3.14159. Concerning the ubiquitous nature of this value within The Pyramid's construction, this is never more evident than at its very heart, that is, in both the Ante-Chamber and the King's Chamber. The length of the floor in the Ante-Chamber just happens to measure 116.260 pyramid inches, or 365.242 divided by *pi*. Inside the King's Chamber, we find that its length, east to west, is 412.131 inches, or 2 times 365.242 divided by the square root of *pi*. Its width, north to south, is 206.065, or 365.242 divided by the square root of *pi*. Its height is 230.388, or the square root of 5 times 365.242 divided by 2 times the square root of *pi*. The floor's diagonal length is 460.777, or the square root of 5 times 365.242 divided by the square root of *pi*. The east and west wall's diagonal length is 309.098, or 3 times 365.242 divided by 2 times the square root of *pi*. The diagonal length of the north and south walls is 472.156, or the square root of 21 times 365.242 divided by 2 times the square root of *pi*. And finally, the distance from either the north or south wall to the end of the Open Coffer is 58.13, or 365.242 divided by 2 times *pi*, while the combined distance to the north and south walls at either end of the Open Coffer is 116.26, or 365.242 divided by *pi*.[349]

In all, the preceding equations constitute no less than nine separate occurrences in which the dimensions of The Great Pyramid's architecture indicate a consistent relationship between the numbers that represent both our solar year and *pi*. Still, I can hear the skeptics out there who are insisting that this is all sheer coincidence. Besides, one must go to an awful lot of trouble in order to arrive at such equations. Not only that, but what could have possibly prompted someone to go to such lengths to hunt and peck for numerical relationships like that in the first place? In point of fact, equations like these did not materialize overnight. The discovery of such permutations, hidden deep within the dimensions of this astonishing stone structure, came as the result of generations of researchers who successively built upon the work of their predecessors.

The Bible in Stone

THE FIRST MAN TO approach The Great Pyramid in a scientific manner was a British professor of astronomy at Oxford by the name of John Greaves, who, in 1646, produced a book on the subject entitled *Pyramidographia: A Description of the Pyramids in Egypt*. As a result of his publication many more intrepid explorers would be drawn into the never-ending labyrinth of trying to solve the enigma that is The Great Pyramid of Giza. Even one the of the most influential scientific thinkers of all time, Isaac Newton, became intrigued by Greaves' work and wrote his own paper, entitled *A Dissertation upon the Sacred Cubit*, which was posthumously published in 1738, some ten years after his death.

It was not until 1859 that British mathematician John Taylor was credited with being the first to determine an actual link between the ancient megalith and modern science when he suggested that the numerical value of *pi* had been deliberately factored into its design. Next came C. Piazzi Smyth, astronomer royal of Scotland, who then elaborated on Taylor's theories in his 1864 book *Our Inheritance in the Great Pyramid*. Greatly influenced by his personal correspondence with Taylor, Smyth went to Egypt at his own expense, where he measured every conceivable dimension of The Pyramid, both inside and out, and was the first to photograph its interior passages. Subsequent to this hands-on investigation, Smyth postulated the idea of the "pyramid inch," which he claimed was the architect's intended unit of measurement with which to interpret the structural and chronological aspects of The Pyramid's design.

Then, in 1865, Robert Menzies inaugurated the next chapter in the story of The Great Pyramid when he began exploring the notion that its various passageways and chambers had been constructed to reveal—in accordance with the very dimensions that Smyth had been documenting—a divinely-inspired chronology of historical events, particularly those of a biblical nature. A decade later, an American theologian and Lutheran minister by the name of Joseph A. Seiss wrote what undoubtedly stands as the most eloquent book on the subject, which became quite popular among evangelical Christians. Entitled *The Great Pyramid of Egypt: Miracle in Stone*, Seiss' landmark publication was the first to refer to the marvelous megalith as "*The Bible* in Stone."

With the turn of the century came the work of John Garnier, who published his 1905 book *Great Pyramid: Its Builder and Its Prophecy*, which further elaborated on the idea that the chambers and passageways inside The Great Pyramid not only provided a chronology of fulfilled biblical events but also contained a prophetic timeline of future events. In the following decades, several more individuals would help popularize the study of Pyramidology, as it came to be known, most notably, a British structural engineer by the name of David Davidson, who published his findings in 1924 with *The Great Pyramid: Its Divine Message*. After him came Adam Rutherford, whose exhaustive work entitled *Pyramidology*, was published in four volumes between 1957 and 1971. More recently, books like the 1972 publication *Secrets of the Great Pyramid* by Peter Tompkins, and the 1977 international bestseller *The Great Pyramid Decoded* by Peter Lemesurier have fueled further interest in the study of Pyramidology. Admittedly, these two latter works contained a much greater emphasis on the esoteric aspects of their subject matter as opposed to earlier works that focused more on a scientific approach to their message.

In this way, each man's work was enriched by the direct influence of his predecessor, causing a chain reaction to occur. One discovery led to another; one realization became the impetus for the next, until finally every conceivable geometric and prophetic relationship had been considered and calculated. And whether all these dimensional relationships in The Pyramid are real or imagined one thing remains constant in unlocking the mysteries of this greatest wonder of the world: Its very existence defies any attempt to casually dismiss the possibility that it might actually contain the ultimate expression of truth. To this point, the words of Joseph A. Seiss speak most eloquently:

> This great monument itself gives palpable demonstration of what cannot be rationally explained… Materialistic and skeptical science has determined that mankind has had to educate himself upward to be what he is today, from a troglodyte, if not from something much lower… But no such philosophizing can hold up in light of the construction of The Great Pyramid.
>
> If primeval man (*of the type that supposedly built this ancient megalith*) was nothing but a gorilla or troglodyte, how, in those far prehistoric times, could the builders of this mighty structure have known what our profoundest *savants*, after scores of centuries of observation and experiment, have only been able to find out imperfectly? How could they know how to make and handle the tools, machines, and expedients indispensable to the construction of an edifice so enormous in its dimensions, so massive in its workmanship, that to this day it is without rival upon the Earth? How could they know the spherical nature, rotation, diameter, density, latitudes, poles, land distribution, and temperature of the Earth, or its astronomic relations? How could they solve the squaring of the circle, calculate the *pi* proportion, or determine the four cardinal points?

> How could they frame charts of world history and dispensations, true to fact in every particular for the space of four thousand years after their time, and down even to the final consummation?
>
> And how could they know to put all these things on record in a single edifice of masonry without one verbal or pictorial inscription, yet proof against all the ravages and changes of time, and capable of being read and understood down to the very end of the world?[350]

How could they, really? That is the question. But in my mind, at least, the question as to *how* they could have known such things is thoroughly tied up in the question of *who* built The Great Pyramid, or, to be more specific, who *designed* it. If one is capable of ascertaining the mystery of *who* designed its impossibly complex construction, then the answer as to *how* they could have known such things seems a foregone conclusion. To reiterate Seiss' view, according to the edicts of science, the historical period for the building of The Great Pyramid simply does not sync with the traditionally accepted level of knowledge of the supposed builders. In other words, the prehistoric date for The Pyramid's construction presents one with an insurmountable gap between the actual level of technological skill required to construct it and the assumed level of mankind's skills at that point in world history. Clearly, then, as it pertains to our present inquiry, a merely scientific explanation will not provide the answer to our "*who-then-how*" mystery.

So, where can we look for the answer of who built The Great Pyramid? Can we look to those of a theological bent? Surely they are in a position to provide us with the sort of answer we are seeking, right? Ironically, even those who proclaim to believe in the divine origins of The Pyramid's construction seem far too timid in their attempts to answer such a question. Displaying no lack of courage in declaring their far-reaching prophetic calculations, they quite uncharacteristically fail, in my opinion, to grasp the true significance of the facts that they are professing to believe in. As a result, the theologians' choice of who designed and built The Pyramid of Giza falls as far short as that of their alleged opponents, the scientists. Whereas the humanist-inspired scientists insist it was built by Khufu, or Cheops, depending on your language frame, the divinely-inspired theologians insist that it was built by, among others, Job, Shem, Melchizedek, or Noah.

In their defense, scientists point to the cartouche bearing Khufu's name, which was "discovered" inside one of The Pyramid's chambers, all the while ignoring that modern inquiry has led researchers to conclude that an overzealous explorer, hoping to secure additional financial backing for his vaunted efforts, fraudulently placed it there. Likewise, in their defense, theologians point out that certain ones in the halls of God's great accomplishments—men like Noah—were clearly in a position to be uniquely instructed in building projects of world-changing importance. Or, if Noah was not the one who built it, then certainly it might have been built by that ever mysterious personage known as Melchizedek, who was reputedly involved in the construction of that blessed city of God, Jerusalem. Another of those who professes to believe in the prophetic aspects of The Pyramid has even alleged a connection that equates Shem—the son of that colossal boat builder, Noah—with Cheops, claiming that an etymological link reveals him as its architect. Still others, in an attempt to prove their point, have pointed to a biblical book, which admittedly contains the most obvious allusion to The Pyramid in all of Scripture.

> Then, from out of the storm, the Lord spoke to Job: "Who is this that obscures My plans with words devoid of knowledge? Brace yourself like a man; I'll question you, and you'll answer Me. Where were you when I laid the Earth's foundation? Tell Me, if you understand. Who marked off its dimensions? Surely you must know! Who stretched a measuring line across it? Upon what were its footings set, or who laid its cornerstone while the morning stars sang together, and all the sons of God shouted for joy?"[351]

Concerning these verses, Seiss, again, has much to say:

> The speaker is God, and the subject is the creation of the Earth. The picture is the building of an edifice. Elsewhere in the same book, the Earth is said to be hung upon nothing; so we cannot pretend to be ignorant of the real facts when here the Earth is being compared to a building that rests on foundations... Behold the architecture of God! The terms are those of the Geometer, the Master Builder. Here is the base ... the measures ... the lines ... the cornerstone! The style of the building is unquestionably The Great Pyramid. That "cornerstone" is spoken of in the singular, which is clearly distinct in relation to the "foundations," while the singing and shouting of the heavenly host as a result of the mighty achievement at the laying of that particular cornerstone requires the proper pyramidal edifice.
>
> This picture cannot be interpreted any other way. That cornerstone could not be at the base because others were there against which no such distinction was made, and its laying would then have been at the beginning, at which time this celestial celebration would be out of place... And as this celebration, according to God Himself, is at the laying of that cornerstone, it must, by necessity, be a top stone—a cornerstone at the summit—whose placement has completed the edifice and displayed the whole work in finished perfection. But for such a cornerstone at the summit there is no place in any then known form of building, save only The Pyramid, of which it is characteristic. Nor is it only to the pyramidal form in general that the allusion is, but to a particular pyramid. By that strange reference to the sunken feet or planting of the foundations in "sockets," we are conducted directly to The Great Pyramid of Giza.
>
> In 1799, two sunken "encasements" in the rock were found under two of its base corners by the French *savants*, which were, in 1837, again uncovered and described by Colonel Richard Howard-Vyse. And as God here speaks of such a fastening down of the foundations in general, Professor Smyth was persuaded that there were corresponding "sockets" at the other two base corners, and when search was made for them in 1865, they were found by William Aiton and Thomas Inglis, assisted by Professor Smyth. Here, then, are all four "sockets" or fastened foundations. Nothing of the sort exists in the construction of any other known pyramid. They are among the distinctive marks of The Great Pyramid of Giza. They are the enduring tracks of its feet cut into the living rock, by which Almighty God Himself identifies it for us as the original image from which His own description of the creation is drawn. Men may treat the matter as they will, but here are the facts showing a divine recognition of this particular edifice as the special symbol of the Earth's formation![352]

My purpose in presenting the preceding in such great length is two-fold in nature. First, I consider it essential in my attempt to cement the idea that a study of The Great Pyramid constitutes more than the vain pursuit of wishful thinkers who are dissatisfied with the simple tenants of Scripture. In light of such eloquence, one can clearly see why some of the greatest theological minds have found a biblical connection with the most thought-provoking monument known to humanity. Second, I inject such worthy scholarship into the mix because I wish to demonstrate how someone as astute as Seiss is still capable of falling short in his honest attempt at solving the mystery of who designed The Great Pyramid. On the subject, he said, "The more I study *The Book of Job* ... the stronger and more satisfying to me becomes the likelihood that here is the mighty prince and preacher of Jehovah from whom we have that monument."[353] Moreover, his choice of Job as the designer of The Pyramid came with the following explanation:

> He was a true man of God, a public instructor in sacred things with whom Jehovah communicated, and whom the Spirit of God inspired. The Almighty speaks to him in Chapter 38 as if he were the identical person who had laid the measures of The Great Pyramid, stretched the lines upon it, set its foundations in their sockets, and laid its capstone amid songs of exalted triumph. Chapter 19:23-27 looks like a description of the high intent of The Great Pyramid, and a prayer that it might endure with its glorious freight, even to the end of the world.[354]

Unfortunately, however, I must wholeheartedly disagree with such a conclusion, and notwithstanding my admiration for such an eloquent spokesperson, I must do so for two reasons. In the first place, when I read the thirty-eighth chapter of *Job*, I do not get the feeling that God is speaking to, as Seiss put it, "the identical person who had laid the measures of The Great Pyramid." If anything, it reads to me as if God is chiding Job, if not downright mocking him: "Brace yourself like a man, Job; I'll question you, and you'll answer Me. Where were you when I (not *you*) laid the Earth's foundation? Tell Me, if you understand."[355] So, if God is mocking Job—quite unlike Seiss' view of this scene—then this could never, in my opinion, at least, constitute an affirmation of his alleged role in The Pyramid's creation.

The second reason I disagree with Seiss originates entirely from the biblical text itself, as opposed to God's tone of voice in speaking to Job. Let me explain what I mean by that. The last portion of the biblical passage in question states: "Upon what were its footings set, or who laid its cornerstone while the morning stars sang together, and all the sons of God shouted for joy?"[356] But who, exactly, is Job referring to when he mentions *morning stars* and *sons of God*? The answer, I believe, will shed a great deal of light in our quest to discover who both designed *and* built The Great Pyramid. And as strange as it may seem, I am fully convinced that this seemingly insignificant portion of canonical Scripture holds the key to solving this ancient mystery. In order to make this point clear, though, one must first analyze all of the details involved in our quest.

Geometer of Heaven and Earth

IN THE GREAT PYRAMID, one is faced with an innumerable list of perplexing anomalies. Not only does it confound us with the sheer impossibility that its dimensions might somehow reveal a prophetic timeline, but its very existence is also a blatant contradiction to modern-day assumptions, based as they are on a scientific worldview. In an age before pulleys, wheels, or iron tools, the builders of The Pyramid still managed to enlist the use of an estimated two and a half million stone blocks, each averaging two and a half tons. The result was a colossus that covers nearly sixty-four thousand square yards, weighing an estimated six million tons, and which, for more than four millennia, stood as the world's tallest structure. In today's terms that would mean that enough stones were employed in its construction to build thirty Empire State Buildings or sixty-five Washington Monuments. Yet for all its massiveness, scientists have determined that it is more closely oriented to true north than any other edifice known to mankind, only missing the mark by less than three minutes of one degree. Modern man's best efforts, on the other hand, as exhibited in the Paris Observatory—completed in 1671—produced results that were six minutes off course.

Add to this the fact that the dimensions of this mammoth megalith incorporate the numerical values of both *pi* and the solar year throughout its construction, and one is faced with an insoluble conundrum. Even if one could explain how these pre-Iron Age builders erected such an edifice, this still cannot explain how they knew to incorporate knowledge that was not discovered until centuries after the assumed date of its construction—in the case of *pi*, around 1,650 B.C., and the solar year, around 150 B.C. Furthermore, when one considers the added occurrence of its numerous other astronomical design features—among them, the spherical nature, rotation, diameter, density, and temperature of the Earth—one is forced, by the sheer process of elimination, to reject every potential candidate that either the scientific or theological community has to offer. In the final analysis, then, neither Khufu, Noah, Shem, Melchizedek, nor

Job possessed all of the requisite skills to complete a structure of such multitudinous splendor.

More importantly, none of the previously mentioned personages had any known connection with those mysterious entities that we recently encountered in the thirty-eighth chapter of *Job*, in that time when "the morning stars sang together, and all the sons of God shouted for joy." Fortunately, for the sake of our investigation, there is someone who does fit such a profile—a man who was knowledgeable in the realms of both celestial mechanics and structural engineering. That man was Enoch. Having walked and talked with God, he is alone among men in having possessed all the necessary ingredients to fit the bill of being the genuine architect of The Great Pyramid of Giza. In addition, he was the only man whom the biblical record portrays as having had an association with that peculiar race of angelic beings known as the Watchers, a.k.a. the "sons of God," the very ones that "went to the daughters of men and had children by them, which became *Nephilim*, or giants."[357]

As one can imagine, there has been no end to the intense theological debate regarding the true identity of these so-called "sons of God," but like most controversial issues of this nature, the debate always seems to hinge more upon the *a priori* position of the one who is making the argument as opposed to said facts of the argument itself. As such, most modern biblical scholars, who are offended by an apparently outmoded view of the Universe, favor a less spiritual interpretation of the meaning of the "sons of God." As a result, they tend to believe that this term simply refers to the righteous lineage of mankind through Seth, the third son of Adam. On the other hand, most of the earliest expositors of Scripture leaned toward the view that the Hebrew words used to translate "sons of God," that is, *bene ha Elohim*, clearly meant that these personages were of non-human origin, and so they had no difficulty at all in accepting them as angelic beings. Among those who held this view were Philo, Josephus, Justin Martyr, Irenaeus, Clement, Tertullian, Eusebius, Ambrose, Jerome, and Augustine.[358]

Naturally, critics who cling to the purely humanistic view—that the "sons of God" were mere children of Seth—do so because they believe that in *The Book of Genesis* there is simply no tenable support for their opponent's theory. Therefore, lacking any further scriptural evidence, they conclude that their interpretation offers the safest road to correct thinking. But alas, they do so by ignoring every other biblical source that is readily available to any modern-day truth seeker, because if they were to simply pull their proverbial heads from the sand, they would be truly amazed at the tenuousness of their allegedly *Bible*-inspired position. Let me take a moment to elaborate. More to the point, let me do so in such a way that our inquiry into the mystery of who designed and built The Great Pyramid does not steer too far off course.

To reiterate, we are seeking to gather together in a single architect all the necessary requirements for The Pyramid's construction, an architect so inspired by God, the Geometer of Heaven and Earth, that he was able to doubly convey his prophetic genius in both stone and book form. Not only that, but it should be remembered that we are attempting to do this in order to connect said architect with the little-known prophecy of The Great Five and a Half Days. Are you still with me on all that? If so, then let us continue with all the preceding concepts in mind.

Sons of God

TO THE BEST OF OUR ability, we have narrowed down our choice for The Pyramid's architect to a single candidate: Enoch, who alone possessed an understanding of the divine mysteries associated with both the celestial mechanics of the Universe and the prophetic knowledge of the history of mankind. This, then, offers us a potential answer as to who could have known the things passed down to humanity in stone and Scripture alike. Yet this still does not adequately answer the question as to how Enoch managed to turn this special knowledge into the enigmatic megalith that is The Great Pyramid. It is, after all, one thing for God to reveal such mysteries to Enoch, and have him, with the aid of angelic helpers, write the books that depict the future of mankind. It is, however, a different matter altogether to convey this knowledge in terms of everything involved in The Pyramid's actual construction, requiring as it does some two and a half million stone blocks, which together form an internal network of passageways and chambers that have all maintained their geometric relationships in spite of centuries of the crushing weight bearing down on them.

This is particularly pertinent when one considers the added presence of what is certainly the most perplexing feature of The Pyramid's interior, that is, the four so-called "air shafts" located within its interior. Two shafts lead from the King's Chamber diagonally up to its exterior, one connecting with the north face and the other with the south face; while two more similar shafts were discovered leading from the Queen's Chamber. Strangely enough, though, these particular shafts were not evident for quite some time because, as it turns out, both ends of this pair had been sealed by The Pyramid's builders. Ignoring, then, all the various interpretations of their true significance, these shafts present yet another glaring conundrum to anyone who considers the incredible lengths that such design features would impose upon their builders, causing many an investigator to scratch their head as they contemplate the staggering difficulty in engineering not just one but four such shafts that cut through more than two hundred feet of solid core masonry, and all in an age prior to pulleys, wheels, or iron tools. No wonder that such insoluble mysteries have caused some to speculate that because no earthly technology could have accomplished such an impossible feat, The Great Pyramid must have been built by some otherworldly race of beings.

Ironically, though, such apparently outrageous conclusions might, as so often happens, actually contain the germ of truth that we are pressing toward, because the final ingredient in the personality profile of the architect of The Great Pyramid does, in fact, involve an eerie offshoot of this very notion. Remember how we mentioned that, not only does Enoch fit the bill concerning his knowledge of celestial mechanics and prophetic wisdom, but he is also the only candidate associated with those strange characters known as the Watchers—angelic beings thought by many biblical scholars to be the same ones referred to in the sixth chapter of *Genesis*? And remember my statement that I believed a single, insignificant verse in *Job* might hold the key to the mystery of who designed and built The Great Pyramid? I certainly hope you have not forgotten about that. What was that verse again? It was: "Upon what were its footings set, or who laid its cornerstone while the morning stars sang together and all the sons of God shouted for joy?" Do I have you caught up so far? Good, then it is time to pick up that thread again and hopefully tie all of our loose ends together.

Even if Seiss is wrong in his view that Job was the architect of The Great Pyramid, he still deserves credit for having correctly surmised that these verses reveal a genuine insight into its construction as being symbolic, from God's perspective, of the Earth's creation. As a matter of fact, if anything at all has been ascertained about this Pyramid it is that in every possible way its dimensions represent the Earth in microcosm. And if the last verse of this passage is any indication of divinely-inspired truth, then the construction of this miniature version of Earth was completed in the presence of those entities that *The Bible* describes as the "sons of God," or *bene ha Elohim*. That said, it should not seem so far-fetched to imagine that these same angelic beings might have actually been the "construction crew," as it were, that saw to it that Enoch's heavenly blueprint was turned into a reality. After all, it is well known to any biblical scholar the extent to which angels have played a pivotal role in accomplishing God's purposes throughout human history, particularly in regard to their superhuman strength and abilities.

After King David presumptuously tallied the number of fighting men throughout his kingdom, God sent an angel to teach David an excruciating lesson. During this encounter, which a single angel executed, it was said, "from the morning until the end of the designated time, seventy thousand people from Dan to Beersheba died, and when the angel stretched out his hand to destroy Jerusalem, the Lord relented concerning the disaster and said to the angel who was afflicting the people, 'Enough! Withdraw your hand.'"[359]

Then there was the time when Sennacherib, king of Assyria, after marching his army to the very outskirts of Jerusalem, threatened Hezekiah, king of Judah, with swift annihilation, but because Hezekiah earnestly prayed to the God of Israel, he successfully invoked divine deliverance. So, "that night an angel of the Lord killed one hundred and eighty-five thousand men in the Assyrian camp, and when the people woke up the next morning, they saw dead bodies lying everywhere."[360]

Additionally, just in case anyone has forgotten, one of the most famous incidences involving angelic strength occurs in *The New Testament*. There it is said that on the day Jesus rose from the dead, a violent earthquake occurred as a result of an angel coming down from Heaven. Going to Christ's tomb, the angel rolled the massive stone away from the entrance and sat down on it, whereupon the Roman guards, terrified by what they had just seen, fell down like corpses.[361]

Several things can be surmised from the preceding examples of angelic activity. First, notice how these supposedly incorporeal beings are quite capable of affecting the substantive realm of human beings. Contrary to popular opinion, the angels of *The Bible* do not simply float about like ephemeral nothings, incapable of exerting tangible results in the so-called "real world." Second, notice the immense impact that a single angel can have when they have been commissioned by God to intervene in human affairs. What would otherwise require a veritable army of men and machines, apparently just one angel can accomplish. And third, notice that angels are not only capable of dispensing a death blow to mere flesh and blood, but they are also more than capable of moving something as immensely solid as a stone. It is important to understand here the nature of the sort of stone doors implemented in sealing the entrance to a typical Jewish tomb. Weighing an average of one to two tons, they were enormous circular stones that were rolled down a slot into their final resting place, and considering that these stone doors were never intended to be removed once they had been secured, one can imagine how much easier they were to roll into position as opposed to rolling them away from the entrance.

Taking all this into consideration, then, one can see how a biblical perspective of angelic intervention sheds new light on how the construction of The Great Pyramid of Giza might have been achieved. Of course, all that is very nice, you may say, but how could anyone make such a speculative leap in proposing that angels could have been involved in building The Great Pyramid? To quote the more conservative theologians: "Besides the fact that there is no scriptural support that angels were involved in The Pyramid's construction, there is no evidence that *Genesis* 6 is even describing angels when it speaks of 'sons of God.' To the contrary, the prevailing theological position concludes that this passage is simply referring to the sons of the righteous lineage of Seth rather than those of the evil line of Cain." To which I would encourage such timid ones not to be so hasty. After all, whenever I read the sixth chapter of *Genesis*, I always find myself intrigued by the latent possibilities that I see there. What do I mean by latent possibilities? Well, when I read the text with unbiased eyes, I notice certain incongruities to which few, if any, seem to pay attention. Let me explain.

Monsters Crashing About

A FEW ENIGMATIC verses in the sixth chapter of *Genesis* paint what is undoubtedly the grimmest picture in the entire biblical record.

> When the sons of God came to the daughters of men, they bore them children, who became mighty men, which were heroes of old, men of renown. And God saw the wickedness of mankind had become great in the Earth … and He grieved that He had made mankind … so He said, "I'll destroy mankind whom I've created."[362]

So why do I call these verses enigmatic? I do so because—in my mind, at least—they have always raised a red flag. As long as I can remember, I have felt that there was something about these verses that was clearly not right in terms of their logical continuity, either human or divine. In a nutshell: Mighty men are born, the wickedness of mankind increases, and in response God decides to destroy the Earth—just like that, no ifs, ands, or buts. Certainly, anyone who has ever contemplated this familiar sequence of events has been similarly perplexed by their apparent abruptness. Certainly, I could not be alone in wondering how a loving, merciful God could have decided to wipe out the whole world so quickly and casually simply because, as the Scriptures state: "The Lord saw how great mankind's wickedness had become."[363] I do not know about you, but this to me has never seemed like an adequate reason for such an all-consuming punishment. If God is truly a divine being of supreme justice, then how does the punishment fit the crime? On that basis alone, judgment in the form of a worldwide deluge has never seemed like a commensurate outcome. Yet since time immemorial we have simply been told by those who are supposedly in the know that we should never question such mysteries of the faith. Quite frankly, we have had it so relentlessly drummed into our heads that "God's ways are not our ways," we have had no choice but to turn off our brains while we are forever left to scratch our heads and wonder: "Who is the bigger jerk here? Me, them, *or worse* … God?"

So what is one to do in the face of this well-intentioned onslaught against questioning such obvious biblical incongruities? Fortunately, as we have repeatedly seen, the solution is to allow the apocryphal record to provide the necessary context for God's anger in His apparently incommensurate act of destroying the world in the Deluge. *The First Book of Enoch* clarifies the mystery for us with this stark description:

> It so happened that after mankind began to multiply in those days daughters were born to them, elegant and beautiful, and when the angels, the sons of Heaven, saw them, they became enamored of them, saying to each other, "Come, let's select wives for ourselves from among these humans, and let's beget children."
>
> Then their leader Samyaza said to them, "I'm afraid you may not go along with me in carrying out our plan, and that I alone will suffer the consequences of such a terrible crime." And they said to him, "Then we'll swear together, and bind ourselves by a mutual oath, in order to confirm that we won't change our minds but execute our projected undertaking." Then they all swore together… So they took wives, each choosing for himself whom they approached, and with whom they cohabitated, teaching them sorcery, incantations, and the dividing of roots and trees, and the women conceived and gave birth to giants, whose stature was each three hundred cubits. These devoured all that the labor of men produced, until it became impossible to feed them any longer.
>
> Therefore, they began to turn against mankind in order to devour them, and began to injure birds, beasts, reptiles, and fishes, to eat their flesh one after another, and to drink their blood… Impiety increased, fornication multiplied, and they transgressed and corrupted all their ways… And men, being destroyed, cried out, and their voices reached to Heaven.[364]

Now in order to put such a horrific scenario into perspective, try to imagine the size of these giants that are being described here. The text states that they were three hundred cubits tall. Naturally, as members of a modern society, which utilizes measurements quite foreign to that distant time, it is very difficult for us to get a genuine sense of what it means to look upon a human being—if it can still rightly be called that—who is three hundred cubits tall. Nevertheless, we can get an idea of the immensity of such creatures if we compare these proportions with other things with which we are familiar.

For example, *The Bible* speaks of two very large things of which we do have a sense, that of Goliath and Noah's Ark. To get an idea of how impossibly huge these *Nephilim* were, consider this. Goliath is said to have stood just over six cubits tall.[365] That would mean these giants were more than fifty times the size of Goliath! Likewise, the immensity of the Ark, which famously harbored not only Noah and his family but also all those animals, was said to be three hundred cubits in length.[366] Imagine, then, standing the Ark straight up, and one of these antediluvian giants would have stood stem to stern with it! According to our best estimates, modern science has determined that three hundred cubits is roughly equivalent to four hundred and fifty feet.

Therefore, having achieved a sense of the enormity of these creatures, imagine the horror of an entire race of these gigantic monsters crashing about the countryside, snatching up both humans and beasts, tearing them limb from limb, drinking their blood, and devouring their flesh. Certainly, a revised scenario such as this might better explain why God decided to destroy the planet in the Great Flood; not simply because, as *Genesis* implies, mankind got a little racy.

At this point, I would next like to take some time to investigate the origin of these giants. Could the gigantism of these creatures simply have been a function of their being sired by angelic beings? Certainly, there is no scriptural foundation that post-Flood giants like Goliath received their enormous stature from this sort of intermarrying of species. In fact, history is replete with the existence of numerous gigantic human beings, but all born—and this is the important thing to note—*after* the Deluge, because, as one will recall, God specifically designed the Flood to remove the *Nephilim* from the planet, once and for all. So, if giants have existed both before *and* after the Flood—though not in such gigantic proportions afterwards—then there must be another explanation for the enormity of this peculiar race of *Nephilim*. But what? Again, the clues to solving this mystery are all around us, though, as usual, one must do a bit of detective work to apprehend the solution.

He Who Descends

OUR FIRST ORDER OF business is to search out what modern scientific thinking has to say about the human body and its potential for the kind of biological mutation displayed by these infamous offspring of the Watchers. Like all questions regarding the wonders of the human body, science has done a remarkable job in ascertaining the role of DNA, genes, and chromosomes in all of its processes. Accordingly, the unique combination of chromosomes that a human being inherits from their parents determines their physical traits. These chromosomes are themselves made up of hundreds to thousands of genes, which, in turn, contain their own unique sequence of DNA molecules. Based on this view, then, a person's height is biologically determined by their inherited genes, which combine to affect such human traits as growth, appetite, muscle mass, and activity level.[367]

Therefore, considering the importance of this biological component in determining the height of any given human being, who among the descendants of mankind could have supplied these *Nephilim* with the necessary genetic material? Is there any evidence in the biblical record, either canonical or apocryphal, which might point us in the right direction? I do believe there is, yes. In fact, I believe it can be found in the opening chapters of our canonical record of *Genesis*, just as one might expect when delving into the origin of the human species and all its peculiarities. Let me present a series of ideas, and hopefully this will provide us with an entirely new way of looking at the situation.

In this first book concerning the father of mankind, one finds the all-too-familiar story of Adam having just eaten the Forbidden Fruit that God had warned him about. Upon eating it, says *The Bible*, he realized that he was naked, and because of his subsequent shame he tried to hide among fig trees, where he found an abundance of leaves in his attempt to cover himself. Then, God arrived in the cool of the day and asked, "Where are you, Adam?"[368] Of course, the telling of this story is almost universal the world over. As such, most biblical scholars are unanimous in offering the same old appraisal of what God meant by asking such an obvious question: "Where are you, Adam?" Certainly God knew where he was, right? After all, He is God. Why, then, would He have to ask Adam where he was? To which these same scholars intone with utter self-assurance that what God was really doing was engaging Adam in a rhetorical argument in the hopes that he might confess to having eaten the Fruit. This way, say the scholars, Adam might somehow gain an insight into just how far he had fallen from grace. The problem with that logic is, assuming the foreknowledge of God and the nature of the Fall, the idea that Adam could have had a genuine self-awareness of his moral bankruptcy at that moment in time makes about as much sense as God holding out that Adam would have taken personal responsibility for his own actions. No, I am afraid that this stale, worn-out interpretation simply does not fit the facts of Scripture. So, what reaction might this question have been meant to illicit in Adam?

To answer that question, I would like to return to Louis Ginzberg, who paints a much more vivid picture in his book than the one found in *Genesis*. According to Ginzberg, prior to their fall from grace, Adam and Eve could never have hidden among the fig trees, because before he committed his trespass against God, Adam was a giant of a man, so much so that any attempt to describe his colossal size bordered on the utterly fantastic.[369] Citing a widespread tradition found in a variety of rabbinical sources, Ginzberg said:

> The dimensions of his body were gigantic, reaching from Heaven to Earth, or, what amounts to the same, from east to west. Among later generations of men, there were only a few who in small measure resembled Adam in his extraordinary size and physical perfection. Samson possessed his strength, Saul his neck, Absalom his hair, Asahel his fleetness of foot, Uzziah his forehead, Josiah his nostrils, Zedekiah his eyes, and Zerubbabel his voice.[370]

It was only after Adam and Eve had eaten the Forbidden Fruit and were stripped of their former glory that they were reduced to their present size. Concerning this momentous turn of events, which occurred as a result of Adam's fall from grace, Ginzberg continued:

> It cannot be denied, the words, "Where are you?" were pregnant with meaning. They were intended to bring home to Adam the vast difference between his previous state and his present state—between his supernatural size then and his shrunken size now.[371]

Based on the foregoing information, then, we may have discovered the "missing link," as it were, between not only the reason for this outcropping of antediluvian giants but also for those individuals who exhibit similar traits of gigantism after the Flood, though not nearly so exaggerated as the *Nephilim*. Either way, what we seem to be dealing with, as far-fetched as it sounds, is actually a genetic throwback, which was undoubtedly triggered by the biologically-encoded DNA buried deep within the father of mankind. If this is true, then the real father of these monstrous *Nephilim* was not the Watchers but Adam.

Meanwhile, anyone reading this may already be wondering: What does any of this have to do with who built The Great Pyramid of Giza? And the reason I have taken this apparent detour is to drive home one very important point—a point that can actually best be summarized by asking a question that is directly linked to the history of the Watchers and their role in instigating God's judgment of the Great Flood. And that question is: If the Watchers, in conjunction with their offspring, the giants, were the ones who were responsible for humanity's downfall prior to the Flood, what in the world could God have been thinking in allowing such a disastrous intermingling of species in the first place? By any stretch of the imagination, it seems like a perfectly idiotic move by a God Who presumably should know better than to unleash events that He knew full well would lead to such a monstrous outcome. Not only that, but considering the complete absence of logical congruity as far as mankind's alleged guilt in eliciting the Flood, it merely adds more fuel to the fire in the view of anyone who doubts God's claim to be a loving and merciful Creator.

Taking all this into consideration, then: What could possibly explain any of these apparent incongruities? Where does one even begin to look to shed light on such a multifaceted mystery? And the answer, as we have seen, time and time again, is the apocryphal record. In this case, we need only turn to *The Book of Jubilees* to find out what God's purpose was in allowing these Watchers to interact with humanity.

> In the second week of the tenth Jubilee, Mahalaleel took a wife, Dinah, the daughter of Barakiel, his father's brother, and she bore him a son… And he called his name Jared because in his days the angels of the Lord descended to the Earth, those who are called the Watchers, in order that they should instruct mankind, and that they should execute judgment and uprightness.[372]

Several important points can be ascertained from the preceding passage that are critical to understanding the mystery of God's original purpose in allowing this angelic interaction. The first thing is how this verse reveals that these Watchers who descended to Earth did so prior to the birth of Enoch, because as we know from biblical history Jared is, in fact, Enoch's father, which would explain how Enoch could have been in a position to interact with these mysterious personages. Next, this verse in *Jubilees* explains why God would have allowed these Watchers to descend to Earth in the first place. They did not just wander onto the scene of their own accord, as it might appear at first glance. The Watchers were specifically commissioned by God Himself to perform a divinely-appointed task.

The next thing to take note of in this verse is the way that it helps to clarify the true nature of these Watchers. To anyone still clinging to the spurious notion that the "sons of God" of *Genesis* 6 were nothing more than the sons of the righteous lineage of Seth, *Jubilees* provides us with clear corroborating evidence that they were not mortal beings, as so many traditional expositors of Scripture have insisted. Notice the portion of the verse that states, "He called his name Jared because in his days the angels of the Lord descended to the Earth." I wonder what these expositors would have to say about this verse. Do they actually expect us to believe that this righteous son of Adam, Mahalaleel, was inspired to name his son Jared, which any scholar understands to mean *he who descends*, because he wanted to convey the idea that the sons of Seth would one day be characterized as such?

Furthermore, this practice of naming the patriarchs because of their connection with some great milestone in biblical history was by no means an isolated incident. In fact, it is one of the bulwarks of scriptural exegesis, whereby God repeatedly deigned to communicate the marvelous nuances of His master plan. There is even an entire school of theological thought which has determined that the name of each and every patriarch in the genealogy from Adam to Joseph, the father of Jesus, typifies an aspect of the Christ Who was to Come. God's purpose in this was to lay down a clearly discernible pattern in order that fallen humanity might better understand the nature of this Coming One.

According to this view, the name of Adam and Eve's third son, Seth, contained a double meaning when *The Bible* recorded: "Adam knew his wife again, and she bore him a son, and called his name Seth because, said Eve, 'God has appointed me another son to replace Abel, whom Cain has slain.'"[373] The underlying application of this name, however, had to do with the hidden, alternative meaning in which Seth represented one of the earliest known types of Christ Who, as the Second Adam, was "appointed" by God as a replacement son for the first Adam who had, in a spiritual sense, been slain by Satan in the Fall.

Similarly, when Noah was born, *Genesis* tells us: "This same one will comfort us concerning the toil of our hands, because the Lord has cursed the ground."[374] Again—to the discerning—the double meaning is obvious. Not only would Noah comfort mankind from God's cursing of the ground, but Christ—of which Noah is a type—would also provide eternal comfort from the curse that was pronounced upon Adam. And just in case you doubt the possibility of such an interpretation, it should be noted that the Hebrew word used here for "ground" is *adamah*, a word that is clearly linked etymologically to that of Adam.

To deny, then, the validity of this pivotal passage in *Jubilees*, regarding this added dimension in the naming of Jared—as so often happens within traditional circles—would sadly constitute a failure of nerve at the very moment when truth could shine its most illuminating beacon of light. Yet such is the habit of the pernicious heart, "always learning but never coming to an awareness of the truth."[375] As it stands, this single verse provides us with several important clues in our ongoing attempt to solve the mystery of who designed and built The Great Pyramid. Above all, it provides corroborating evidence to support the idea that these "sons of God," these *bene ha Elohim*, these Watchers, were never initially of this Earth, but they were of such a nature that they had to "descend to it." As far as the double meaning of the name of Jared, not only did it refer to these Watchers who descended from Heaven, but it also foreshadowed the coming of Christ, Who famously chided His critics with the words: "You are from below, but I am from above; you belong to the Earth, but I am not of this world."[376]

This, then, leads us to the next point that this verse provides us, which is that, contrary to the opinion of most people who have ever heard of these Watchers, they were not demonic in nature. If all that someone did was to take their cue from *First Enoch*, we would have no way of seeing these Watchers as anything more than a veritable fountain of evil, and therefore assume that these creatures were just another class of demons. But far from reinforcing such an interpretation, *Jubilees* states, in no uncertain terms, these Watchers are not to be counted among Satan's original horde of demonic minions; on the contrary, these were angels of the Lord, angels who had to descend from Heaven above in order to initiate contact with mankind below. If the preceding statement is true, then we have our first real insight into the activity of these Watchers, who, though originally commissioned by God to perform a specific task among humanity, obviously took it upon themselves to instigate, of their own volition, a little "extra-curricular" activity upon completing their tour of duty. How familiar does that sound?

Naturally, all this leads one to ask the next series of questions: What was the nature of this God-ordained mission in which the Watchers were to, as *Jubilees* states, "instruct mankind, and execute judgment and uprightness"? What were they supposed to teach mankind, and how were they supposed to convey their message? How, exactly, would this teaching constitute a form of judgment and uprightness? Why assign the job to angelic beings whose offspring would create a monstrous race of giants? And what was so important about their mission that God would send them even though it would lead to the most devastating calamity the world has thus far experienced?

Could I really be the only one who is led to ask such questions? If I am not, then quite possibly I am not the only one who thinks that in the very asking of these questions lie the answers to this ongoing enigma of who, how, and why The Great Pyramid of Giza was built, and hopefully with these answers, we might come full circle in our discussion, and by way of this matriculating route proceed to a clear-cut, satisfying conclusion.

The Architecture of God

LET US BOIL DOWN the aforementioned questions into a single train of thought. Such a question might be framed in the following manner: What sort of mission could have been so important that, in order to achieve His goal, God would be willing to risk sending angelic beings who were not only characterized by their teaching ability and superhuman strength but their freedom to abuse that tremendous power? Would you agree that this is a question that sufficiently embraces all of the preceding facts in our mystery story? If so, then quite possibly the answer might be attained by way of the methodology known as *Ockham's Razor*, a problem-solving technique devised by William of Ockham around the turn of the fourteenth century. Simply put, it states, "All things being equal, the simplest explanation is generally the correct one."

In this case, we might frame our explanation in the following way—as easy as one, two, three: One, God said, "Where were you, Job, when I laid the Earth's foundation? Surely you must know! Who stretched a measuring line across it? Upon what were its footings set, or who laid its cornerstone while the morning stars sang together and all the sons of God shouted for joy?" Two, Seiss declared, "Behold the architecture of God! The terms are those of the Geometer, the Master Builder. Here is the base … the measures … the lines … the cornerstone! The style of the building is unquestionably The Great Pyramid." And three: All this occurred at a moment in history when—having laid the foundation, footings, and cornerstone, or, in the case of The Pyramid, a chief cornerstone—this display of architectural splendor culminated in a choral celebration in which all the "sons of God" shouted for joy.

Or to state our conclusion more specifically, based on all the previous points: "Enoch, prophet-architect *extraordinaire*, joined forces with the Watchers, angelic ambassadors sent to Earth by God, and together they constructed a megalithic pillar of testimony, uniquely designed to communicate a divinely-inspired knowledge of the destiny of mankind via a language frame that is capable of transcending any and all linguistic barriers."

The Sands of Time

THIS BRINGS US TO the next phase of our study. Thus far, we have retraced the two-fold path that is depicted in *Tales of Forever*, that of the storyline concerning the prophecy of The Great Five and a Half Days, and of Enoch as the narrator of our story. In the process of this retracing, I then alluded to a hidden link between these parallel storylines that has until now gone unnoticed by the public—a link, by the way, that also applies to all five of the *sacred* things we have been discussing. But before I would reveal this link, I chose to engage in a lengthy dissertation retracing the age-old debate over who designed and built The Great Pyramid of Giza. So as not to entirely lose our original thought process, I would like to explain why this was so important.

My purpose in the previous matriculating was to establish overwhelming evidence for a series of ideas prior to my revealing this hidden link. The first thing to understand addresses an obvious question asked by anyone who examines the mystery of The Great Pyramid, which is: Why would the person who designed such an important monument—built as a testimony to God's truth and justice—conceal his identity? As usual, before I simply blurt out the answer, I would first like to lay a foundation by highlighting the repeatable aspects inherent in all our points of discussion. Such a foundation might be formulated by asking this preliminary question: What, exactly, is the common denominator in the special wisdom embodied in the person of Enoch? There are the prophecies contained in the books that have been attributed to him; there are the numerous parallels between the lives of Enoch and Jesus; and there are aspects of the architecture of The Great Pyramid that clearly allude to Enoch as being its architect. Each is an example of divine manifestation in the world, which was first rejected by mankind, was then lost for long epochs of history, and eventually rediscovered at some future "set time," thereby restoring them to their rightful place in the hierarchy of God's creation. This sequence of events, then, constitutes a blueprint that undergirds every aspect of messianic history—rejection, disappearance, and rediscovery.

So to return to our previous question: Why would Enoch deliberately conceal the fact that he was the architect of The Great Pyramid? The answer is: He never did. Yet for two primary reasons this authorship would remain a mystery to all but the most discerning of truth seekers. The first reason that Enoch's architectural role has been so difficult to ascertain is because, to whatever extent his authorship exists, it was encrypted in the same "language" used in the rest of The Pyramid's message, which is to say, mathematically. And just like every other form of messianic truth, it was destined that this knowledge—designed as a numeric time capsule—would be set aside as being irrelevant, and then lost amidst the sands of time. Only later, with the arrival of a far distant future generation, would its encoded message be revealed, understood, and restored.

The second reason for the difficulty in recognizing Enoch's role as architect is that it was never his intention to reveal himself as such. What does that mean? It means that Enoch was more interested in conveying messianic truth than he was in revealing his own genius or personal contribution to The Pyramid's construction. As a result, he would never have intentionally "signed," as it were, his architectural masterpiece. Ironically, the ubiquitous nature of the numerical value of 365.242 has led researchers to correctly surmise a connection between this all-important number and its designer, but any attempts to make a case that it constitutes a personal signature on Enoch's part will prove unfruitful. Why? The simple fact is: Enoch would never have been so self-serving. Just because pyramidologists insist they have proof of the existence of this signature in the Enoch Circle—with its distinctive dimensions of 365.242—does not necessarily mean that this is so. To make such an assumption, one must first demonstrate that this was Enoch's specific intention, but clearly no such evidence exists. So rather than call it the Enoch Circle, they should call it the Christ Circle, because God's obvious intention in ending Enoch's earthly sojourn at that age was to convey a numerically-based timeline involving messianic truth, not to glorify this merely human aspect of Enoch's life.

The real reason this number is built into so many aspects of The Pyramid's design is because, true to his calling, Enoch was being faithful to God's purposes in revealing a singularly pivotal aspect of biblical truth. The concept of time—in terms of messianic history—is not merely a human contrivance; it was specifically ordained by the Creator. Without the Earth revolving around the Sun once every 365.242 days, there would never be this thing we humans experience as day turning into night. Without that, days would never turn into weeks, or weeks into months, or months into years; and without these, there would be no such thing as the passage of time. Without the passage of time—not to be confused with the perception of time—there could be no commencement or consummation of the "set times" of God, and without these "set times," instituted by the Lord of Time Himself, there could be no possibility of human redemption as it is revealed in Scripture.

This biblical reality is never made clearer than when Adam and Eve, facing the initial consequences of their garden exile, were forced to endure the harsh reality of the very first nightfall. Having known only perpetual light as a result of their luminous nature in Eden, this stark, new experience was more than they could bear. It took only one seemingly endless night of terror, swallowed up in utter blackness, before they were begging God the next day to hold back the Sun to keep the darkness from overtaking them again.[377]

In response to their terrified prayer, the Word of God visited them and said:

> "I wish I could accommodate you both, really I do, but if I did hold back the Sun, then the agreement I made with you (concerning My promise to rescue you after *five and a half* 'days') could never be fulfilled."
>
> "But why, Lord?" asked Adam.
>
> "Because without the Sun, there would be no more hours or days or years. Then, I'm afraid, you'd remain banished from the garden. You and everyone you loved would be plagued by endless disaster, and no salvation would reach any of you, *ever*."[378]

The next thing I hope to do, in offering this series of pivotal ideas, is provide evidence to prove that the heretofore hidden link between Enoch and The Great Five and a Half Days constitutes more than a passing remark located in *The Secrets of Enoch*. What I am referring to concerns Enoch's remark that our first parents resided in Eden for *five and a half* "hours," which then leads us to the text in *First Adam and Eve* where we discover that they were to be exiles for *five and a half* "days." As it turns out, to find such evidence, one need simply continue reading further in the books depicting the life and times of Adam and Eve, because in them there are, in fact, two more occurrences of the Lord informing mankind about the prophecy of the *five and a half* "days." The next time, however, God is speaking not to Adam but to Seth, his third son. In *The Second Book of Adam and Eve*, the following scene is recorded:

> As the days of Seth came to an end, he asked his sons to bring him an offering so that he might bring it before the Lord, and God accepted his offering and sent His blessing upon him and his children. Then He said to Seth, "At the end of The Great Five and a Half Days, which I told your father about, I'll send My Word to save you and your descendants." And when Seth died at the age of nine hundred and twelve, Enoch was twenty years old.[379]

From this, one will notice two outstanding points—one obvious, the other not so obvious. Both, however, are extremely important in light of our present study. The first point to take note of is that the promise that God made to Adam was given not only to the first man but also to his faithful son. Clearly, the knowledge of this prophecy was something that God intended to be handed down from son to son and from generation to generation. The next thing one will notice is that, out of all of the children that were present at the time of Seth's demise, Enoch was singled out for some unexplained reason. Parenthetically, it should be noted that twenty is particularly important in biblical numerology. Twenty was the age at which God divided the Children of Israel who had failed to trust the Lord in their wandering through the Sinai desert. Those above twenty years old were destined to die off before they entered the Promised Land, while those under twenty were allowed to enter it.[380]

Consider this as well: It just so happens that Nimrod was twenty years old when he received Adam's garment from his father, Cush. It would therefore seem fairly certain that the writer of *Second Adam and Eve* pointed out that Enoch was twenty years old at the time of Seth's death because there was some important connection between these two points—a significance which may be inferred in light of the following verses from *Jasher*:

> And the garment of sheepskin, which God made for Adam and his wife, when they went out from the garden, was given to Cush, because after the death of Adam, his garment was given to Enoch, the son of Jared, and when Enoch was taken up to God, he gave it to Methuselah, his son.[381]

After Methuselah, it went to Noah, then Ham, and then Cush, who eventually gave it to Nimrod when he turned twenty. Thus, it is not so far-fetched to assume from all of this that—before Nimrod, as a type of Anti-Christ, received Adam's garment—Enoch, as a type of Christ, was given the garment upon Seth's passing from the scene, that is to say, at this same age of twenty.

The next occurrence of the *five and a half* "day" prophecy is in the following scene:

> Then Jared made an offering on the altar, just as Adam had commanded him... And God appeared to Jared at the altar, and blessed him and his children, according to the offering... Then, God revealed to him the promise that He had previously made to Adam: He explained to Jared the five thousand, five hundred years, and revealed the mystery of His coming upon the Earth... And Enoch kept the command of Jared, his father... It is this Enoch to whom many wonders occurred, and who also wrote a celebrated book; but all those wonders could not be contained here in this place.[382]

Three things may be surmised from the preceding text. First, God, after informing Seth of the *five and a half* "day" prophecy, did not give it to Seth's son, Enos, or his grandson, Cainan, or even his great-grandson, Mahalaleel. Instead, He waited four generations before reiterating this all-important prophecy, that is, until the time when Jared, the father of Enoch, had become the leader of the clan. Second, an emphasis is provided in the text that Enoch was faithful to the legacy of his father, which assumes the responsibility that comes from knowing about this pivotal prophecy, as well as his role in communicating it to subsequent generations. And third, this Enoch, as opposed to the one named as a descendant of Cain, was unmistakably the same man who had written about his wondrous experiences, presumably as a result of his face-to-face encounter with the Lord Himself.

To be sure, then, there are clear-cut connections between these various texts, all of which exist as necessary cogs in the wheels of an extended historical train. Having said all that, however, I would now like to convey an even more explicit way to demonstrate Enoch's awareness of this nearly forgotten prophecy found in both books of *Adam and Eve,* along with what can be inferred from *The Secrets of Enoch*. Or to put it in the form of a question: Is it possible to demonstrate Enoch's knowledge of The Great Five and a Half Day prophecy beyond that which is displayed in the written record of apocryphal literature? And if so, where would one look to find the evidence for such an awareness?

The reason for such an inquiry is because I am so acutely aware of the skepticism ingrained in most people who are reading all this for the very first time. Naturally, I would not blame them in the least for thinking that I had simply made up the so-called "connections" I believed I had found between various manuscripts. Maybe what I had discovered were actually connections that had been planted by well-intentioned historians who were hoping to embellish their own translations. As depressing as that sounds, one might never rule out such a tragic possibility.

Therefore, it behooves me to seek an antidote for just such a poison to truth. In this case, if our poison is rooted in ordinary language—something so necessary in typical communication—then all the more reason that I am obliged to offer a potential antidote in the form of a medium of communication that transcends language, that is to say, the mathematically-based message found in The Great Pyramid.

This is why it has been so vital to demonstrate that the God Who inspired the mathematics embedded in The Pyramid's dimensions—like *pi*, the solar year, and the Earth-Sun relationships—did not do so arbitrarily, as if those who discovered these numerical patterns had stumbled onto a mere sidebar of biblical revelation. And if establishing such patterns has been adequately done, then what I am about to reveal may not seem so far-fetched after all, and enduring the foregoing deluge of information will, in the end, have been worth it.

Doubly-Gifted Enoch

HAVING SAID ALL THAT, there remains the apparently insurmountable feat of stemming the tide that resists the restoration of lost wisdom once it has slipped from the scene. Never mind that it is right there in front of you, as obvious as the nose on your face, yet residing just below the threshold of public awareness. How does one go about getting people to see the connections between things that seem so obvious to some but so absurd to others?

What are we talking about here, anyway? After all, what could be that difficult about proving that the prophetic wisdom of Enoch, found in the books that bear his name, is so much more than pseudepigraphical in nature? We have all the necessary tools in our arsenal, do we not? We have the dramas that transcend interpretation. We have the language of mathematics. What more do we need? We have the ability to combine these two sides of the same coin; and what do we get?

What we get is a picture of the doubly-gifted Enoch, who, oddly enough, bears a remarkable resemblance to that two-faced Roman god Janus. As it turns out, this dual-natured Janus is depicted as having one face that is looking to the right and another, to the left, which, it is said, enables him to look into both the past and the future. Hence, the word *Janus* is the origin of the name for our month of January, which marks the point at which the previous year ends and the next one begins, and the first day of which we traditionally reminisce about the year just past and imagine the possibilities for the one that lies ahead.

What else is Janus known for? Well, he is, among other things, identified with gateways pertaining to space and time. Concerning space, he is a controller of doorways, bridges, and boundaries. Concerning time, he is associated with the Sun, the Moon, and the year; in one of his ancient temples, the hands of his statue were positioned to signify the number three hundred and sixty-five, said to symbolically express his mastery over time. And just like our doubly-gifted Enoch—equally fluent in word and stone alike—this two-faced Janus was said to possess a key that provided him access to Heaven. Accordingly, Janus symbolizes the transition from the past to the future, from one vision to another, from one Universe to the next.

Do any of the foregoing attributes sound familiar? If so, on which side of the fence do you reside? Are you the sort of person who dismisses such similarities as merely coincidental? Or, instead, do you believe—as do scholars like Vico who have investigated such matters—that they could only be possible because the mythology of the one actually reflects the lost but not forgotten history of the other?

It is also significant to note that before this Roman identification between Janus and Enoch, the Greeks knew Enoch as Hermes, who was best known as the messenger of the gods. Additionally, he was considered a god of transitions and boundaries, acting not only as an intercessor between the natural and the Divine but as a conductor of souls into the afterlife as well. Interestingly enough, according to their mythology, the Greeks believed that Hermes was the only god who had been officially authorized to visit Heaven.

And before the Greeks, the Egyptians knew Enoch as Thoth, the god of all wisdom. E.A. Wallis Budge, the British Egyptologist who famously translated the 1895 version of *The Egyptian Book of the Dead*, said that Thoth was "the scribe of the gods, and as such was regarded as the inventor of all the arts and sciences known to the Egyptians. Some of his titles include 'lord of writing,' 'master of papyrus,' and 'maker of the palette and the ink-jar.' As the chronologer of Heaven and Earth, he became the god of the Moon, and as the reckoner of time, he obtained his name, Thoth, which is to say, the 'measurer.'"[383] Although best known for having invented writing, he was also credited by the Egyptians with instituting the 365-day calendar as opposed to the original 360-day version, as well as—take note of this, please—designing The Great Pyramid of Giza.

So what does all this mean in terms of our trying to restore the status of Enoch's lost wisdom to public acceptance? It means that if the kinds of historical clues we have just outlined really do exert such unmistakable resonances from age to age, so that Enoch's attributes clearly crop up in the otherwise muddled mythology of the ancient world, then we have yet another example of the power of dramas that transcend interpretation. And although Enoch's contribution to the history of knowledge has become skewed over time, it means that the indelible nature of it is such that it is never really lost but is merely transmuted in the process of being conveyed from culture to culture. If so, then maybe our quest for historical certainty is not as hopeless as it might at first appear. In other words, restoring the so-called "lost" wisdom of Enoch is not—as so many have presumed to be a matter of searching for what is missing—as much as it is a case of interpreting that which is not missing at all but is merely hidden in plain sight. And if this is the case, then maybe the time has come to finally connect all the dots to this extended storyline. Time to see, finally, if this domino of ideas tumbles neatly toward a tidy ending or simply fizzles out midstream. Ready or not, here I go.

A System of "Fiveness"

FIRST, WE CONSTRUCTED a narrative chronicling God's promise to rescue Adam and Eve after *five and a half* of His "days," which reached an unexpected climax when Annas and Caiaphas confessed to Pilate that they had become convinced this promise of "days" was fulfilled in Jesus of Nazareth. However, because of the ongoing controversy over the potential for biblical mistranslations, we were forced to look for a unique way to verify such a prophetic timeline that does not involve the idiosyncrasies of human language. To that end, we began an investigation into the potential of mathematically-oriented messages contained in The Great Pyramid because it is known to contain the kind of prophetic timelines so often found in the biblical texts, both canonical and apocryphal. But instead of trying to decipher a series of numbers like *Bible*-code folks are prone to do, we took a different approach. Rather than bombard you with a mind-numbing numerical blitz, I tried to anchor the numerology of The Pyramid in terms that are more human. This, then, would explain my attempts to verify the existence of Enoch's fingerprints in its architectural design via such unmistakably human values as *pi*, the solar year, and the Earth-Sun relationships. All that remains is to connect the prophecy of The Great Five and a Half Days to both the man who stood face to face with the Lord of Time and to the pillar of testimony that bears the stamp of his authorship. How might we go about doing this?

Well, we already know that The Great Pyramid presumably depicts every major turning point in biblical history, from the Exodus of Israel to the Advent of Christ. Therefore, if we were to simply re-examine the work handed down by generations of pyramidologists, one might assume that if evidence for a *five and a half* "day" chronology exists it should quite naturally "speak for itself," as it were. And if this evidence is actually found, then the next question one might ask is: Why has no one ever detected such a pyramidal timeline of *five and a half* "days" before now? To which I would reply: It is certainly because no one has ever thought to look for it. Had they done so, they would have found that not only is there evidence for this timeline in The Pyramid, but—as with all biblical prophecies—there is also ample foreshadowing of it, which its measurements portray in microcosm. In other words, besides a prophetic chronology depicting this *five and a half* "day" period from Adam to Christ, there are numerous occurrences of the primary number that comprises this promise of "days." Accordingly, the most predominant numerical value to be found in the architectural design of The Pyramid just happens to be ... the number *five*.

Again, I turn to my most eloquent allies for their views on this subject. According to Joseph A. Seiss, the numerical value of *five* is so "inherently characteristic" in the dimensions of The Great Pyramid's construction that "with this number, its multiples, powers, and geometric proportions, the number *five* speaks as loudly as stones can be made to speak."[384] In Seiss' view, the ubiquitous nature of the number *five* is no mere happenstance; it is actually the very basis of its existence. Said Seiss:

> From this, The Pyramid seems to have its name. Though different authors have sought to derive this word from the Greek, Arabic, and other sources, the evidence is rather that it came direct from the builders of the edifice and was meant to describe it in the common language then used in that country. The nearest to that language is Coptic, and in the ancient Coptic, *pyr* means "division," the same as *peres* in Daniel's interpretation of the handwriting on the wall; and *met* means "ten." And putting them together—*pyr-met*—we have the name of the structure.[385]

According to Adam Rutherford:

> There is one, and only one, number that is prominent in The Great Pyramid, and that number is *five*. C. Piazzi Smyth spoke of it as "the sacred number of The Pyramid." Septimus Mark wrote, "The number *five* is at the foundation of much of the teaching connected with The Pyramid." This, of course, should be understood to mean *five*, and also multiples of *five*. The Pyramid's sacred cubit itself is comprised of twenty-five pyramid inches, that is, *five* times *five* inches; and this inch is the *five* hundred millionth (500,000,000th) part of the Earth's axis of rotation...
>
> The principal apartment, the King's Chamber, has one hundred stones in its walls, built in *five* courses. It stands upon the *fiftieth* course of masonry in The Pyramid. The King's Chamber is twenty sacred cubits long and ten wide. The north and south walls of the Queen's Chamber are respectively, *five* sacred cubits north and *five* sacred cubits south of The Pyramid's east-west axis. The axis of the Niche in the Queen's Chamber east wall is twenty-five inches south of The Pyramid's east-west axis.[386]

Returning to Seiss, he added:

> Accordingly, a system of *"fiveness"* runs through The Great Pyramid and its measure references. Counting *five* times *five* courses of masonry from the base upwards, we are brought to the floor of the Queen's Chamber. The measurements of that chamber all answer to the standard of *five* times *five*

> pyramid inches. It is characterized by a deep sunken Niche in one of its walls, which Niche is three times *five* feet high, consisting of *five* strongly marked stories. The topmost is *five* times *five* inches across, and its inner edge is just *five* times *five* inches from the perpendicular center of the wall into which it is cut.[387]

The height of the King's Chamber is eleven point eighteen (11.18) cubits, which is itself the square root of one hundred and twenty-five, or *five* to the third power (5^3). The diagonal length of the roof of the chamber is twenty-two point thirty-six (22.36) cubits, which is both twice its height and the square root of *five* hundred. The diagonal line of the short wall is fifteen cubits. The diagonal length from the upper corner to the opposite lower corner is twenty-five cubits. And finally, the volume of the Open Coffer is one *fiftieth* that of the King's Chamber in which it resides. Insisted Seiss:

> This *"fiveness"* could not have been an accident, and likewise corresponds with the arrangements of God, both in nature and revelation. Note the *"fiveness"* of termination to each limb of the human body, the *five* senses, the *five* books of Moses, the twice *five* precepts of the Decalogue.[388]

And just in case one is tempted to give in to the notion that all this so-called "symbolism" has nothing to do with the kind of symbolic truth portrayed in *The Bible*, one would do well to take note of the following. Known to any advanced student of Pyramidology is that C. Piazzi Smyth pioneered the idea that, based on Isaac Newton's evaluation of the sacred cubit, the dimensions of The Ark of the Covenant were such that they exhibit an uncanny similarity to those found displayed in the Open Coffer in the King's Chamber. (To read about how this conclusion was reached, read pages 347-53 and 395-400 of C. Piazzi Smyth's book *The Great Pyramid: Its Secrets and Mysteries Revealed.*)

Naturally, as with so many aspects involved with pyramidal computations, there is no end to the debate over the validity of the numerical values invoked to measure such dimensional relationships. More often than not, the final determination in accepting or rejecting such possibilities comes down to one's own *a priori* position. In other words, it comes down to which version of the sacred cubit one prefers to accept. Do you lean toward the one espoused by Isaac Newton and C. Piazzi Smyth, who decided on twenty-five inches? Or, instead, do you lean toward those determined by other standards, which put it at eighteen or twenty inches? Either way, whichever standard of measurement one prefers, it is noteworthy that *The Bible* states in no uncertain terms that The Ark of the Covenant was to be made with these specific dimensions: "Have them make an ark of acacia wood—two and a half cubits long, a cubit and a half wide, and a cubit and a half high."[389]

The importance of such dimensions, for the sake of our study, is the unadulterated fact that even a child can apprehend. Two and a half, plus one and a half, plus one and a half, equals how much? Hmmm, let me see. The answer is *five and a half*, right? Right. That said, if you are the type of person who can accept the idea that the Open Coffer in The Pyramid is dimensionally related to The Ark, then the fact that they both exhibit dimensions of *five and a half* sacred cubits is something you will not fail to notice. On the other hand, if you are the type of person who rejects the possibility, then at least you must pause to consider what even Annas and Caiaphas could not fail to appreciate. This numerical value of *five and a half* denotes a resounding signature that, more than any other, points to what was the hope of all Israel, which is the Christ Who was to come.[390]

Having established the number *five* as the most special number in the dimensions of The Pyramid, and its connection to *The Bible*, we turn next to examining its significance in scriptural terms. Interestingly enough, the number *five* is repeatedly associated with the grace of God. In his informative book *Number in Scripture*, E.W. Bullinger explained:

> Grace means *favor.* But what kind of favor? Favor shown to the miserable is called *mercy;* favor shown to the poor is called *pity;* favor shown to the suffering is called *compassion;* favor to the obstinate is called *patience;* but favor shown to the unworthy is called *grace.* This is favor indeed—favor which is truly divine in its source and in its character, as it is spoken of in *Romans* 3:24, "being justified freely by His grace." The word here translated "freely" occurs again in *John* 15:25, and is translated "without a cause."
>
> And so it was with Abram. There was no cause in him why God should have called him and chosen him. Therefore, when God established His covenant with Abram—though childless at the time—regarding His intention to multiply his descendants like the stars and the sand, He confirmed this promise by instructing him to offer up *five* sacrifices, that of a heifer, a goat, a ram, a dove, and a pigeon.[391]
>
> It is remarkable, also, that afterwards, when God changed Abram's name to Abraham,[392] the change was made very simply, but very significantly (for there is no chance with God), by inserting into the middle of it the *fifth* letter of the Hebrew alphabet, "h" (*hey*), the symbol of the number *five.* All this was of grace.[393]

Three additional points can be inserted here regarding the role of the number *five* in the previous instances. First, when God established His covenant concerning Abram's descendants becoming like stars and sand, it was the *fifth* time in the canonical record that the Lord had revealed Himself to Abram. Second, when God added the *fifth* letter of the Hebrew alphabet to Abram's name, He did the same thing to Sarai's name by changing it to Sarah—an apparent coincidence overlooked even by Adam Rutherford, who otherwise noted the significance of Abram's name change as it pertains to the number *five* within the dimensions of The Great Pyramid.[394] Third, and most importantly, in the context of the prophecy of The Great Five and a Half Days, this moment of the renaming of Abram and Sarai takes on greater significance. Before one has been made aware of the revelatory nature of the number *five* in the overall scheme of things, the *five and a half* "day" timeline seemed skewed. What do I mean by that? Well, just think about the sequence with which we have become familiar: Enoch explained that Adam and Eve were in Eden for *five and a half* hours before they fell and were made to wander as exiles for *five and a half* "days." Then, no mention of it occurred in the pivotal tale of Abraham and Sarah, until the timeline culminated in the story of Pilate and Jesus. But now, in light of God's insertion of the letter 'h' into the names of Abraham and Sarah, one can better understand how this prophecy of the promise of grace—so enmeshed in this *five and a half* "day" schematic—impacted even the life of the father of faith.

In this way, we can see that this infusion of the letter 'h,' or *five*, represents a succinct midpoint in our total time frame of *five and a half* "days" from Adam to Christ. It also helps us to see how this renaming of Abraham and Sarah instituted a reworking in their lives. Just as Adam and Eve are memorialized as our first natural parents, Abraham and Sarah—by way of this association of the *"fiveness"* of grace—likewise creates in them the status of a second Adam and Eve. In other words, as a result of their acting upon God's call, Abraham and Sarah were directly responsible for the birthing a new race of spiritual beings. Accordingly, the Apostle Paul's words, in his letter to the Romans, could be modified to adapt the roles of Abraham and Sarah.

> So *they are* the *parents* of all who believe... Therefore, the promise comes by faith so that it may be by grace, and may be guaranteed to all of Abraham *and Sarah's spiritual* children ... to all those who have the faith of Abraham *and Sarah*... As it is written: I have made you a father *and a mother* of many nations. *They are* our *parents* in the sight of God, in Whom *they* believed—the God Who gives life to the dead, and calls into being the things that were not.[395] (*Italicized words* inserted by the author.)

Another noteworthy example of the number *five* occurs when the nation of Israel made their most famous journey under Moses. *The Bible* tells us: "The Children of Israel went up harnessed out of the land of Egypt."[396] But in the margin it says: They marched out in groups of *five*. The same idea is conveyed when it is said of the people: "You will cross over before your brothers in battle array."[397] According to *The Pulpit Commentary*, this means that they were to travel in divisions of *five*. Furthermore, the Tabernacle in the Wilderness had the number *five* as its all-pervading numerical value, displaying in nearly every one of its measurements this number or some multiple of it. Again to cite Bullinger at length:

> The Outer Court was one hundred cubits long and fifty cubits wide. On either side were twenty pillars, and along each end were ten pillars, or sixty in all; that is, *five* times twelve, or grace in governmental display before the world, twelve being the number of the Tribes of Israel.
>
> The pillars that held up the curtains were *five* cubits apart and *five* cubits high, and the whole of the outer curtain was divided into squares of twenty-five cubits. Each pair of pillars thus supported an area of *five* squared (5^2) cubits of fine white linen, thus witnessing to the perfect grace by which alone God's people can witness for Him before the world... *Five* times *five* was also the measure of the Brazen Altar of Burnt Offering. This was the perfect answer of Christ to God's righteous requirements, and to what was required of man...
>
> The building itself was ten cubits high, ten cubits wide, and thirty cubits long. Its length was divided into two unequal parts, the Holy Place being twenty cubits long; and the Holy of Holies, ten cubits, being therefore a perfect cube of ten cubits. It was formed of forty-eight boards, twenty on either side and eight at the end, the front being formed of a curtain hung on *five* pillars. These forty-eight boards, that is, three times four squared (4^2), or four times twelve, are significant of the nation as before God in the fullness of privilege on the Earth. The twenty boards on each side were held together by *five* bars passing through rings which were attached to them...
>
> The Entrance Veils were three in number. The first was "the gate of the court," twenty cubits wide and *five* high, hung on *five* pillars. The second was "the door of the Tabernacle," ten cubits wide and ten high, hung like the gate of the court on *five* pillars. The third was "the beautiful veil," also ten cubits square, which divided the Holy Place from the Holy of Holies. One feature of these three veils is remarkable. The dimensions of the veil of the court and those of the Tabernacle were different, yet the *area* was the same. The former was twenty cubits by *five*, which equals one hundred cubits; the latter were ten cubits by ten, equaling one hundred cubits also. Thus, while there was only one gate, one door, one veil, they each typified Christ as the only door of entrance for all the blessings connected with salvation. But note that the "gate," which admitted access to the benefits of atonement, was wider and lower (twenty cubits wide, and *five* cubits high); while the "door" which admitted access to worship was both narrower and higher (ten cubits wide, and ten cubits high); thus saying to us, that not all who experience the blessings of atonement understand or appreciate the true nature of spiritual worship. The highest worship—admittance to the mercy-seat—was impossible for the Israelites, except in the person of their substitute—the high priest; for "the beautiful veil" barred their access. Yet, this "veil" was split in two the moment the true grace which came by Jesus Christ was perfectly manifested, and it was torn by the act of God in grace, for it was split "from the top to the bottom."[398]

A similar pattern of numerological symbolism can also be found in the construction of Solomon's Temple, the dimensions of each part being exactly doubled of those found in the

Tabernacle in the Wilderness. Considering the lengths to which God went in driving home the point that the salvation of His people was a total act of grace on His part, one might gain a greater appreciation as to why this number *five* is so thoroughly encrypted in what has become known as *The Bible* in Stone.

The Five and a Half Days

HAVING ESTABLISHED a link between the repeated occurrences of this number *five,* in both word and stone, all that is left is to establish a similar link between The Great Pyramid and the more specific figure of *five and a half.* But remember, we are not looking for just any old appearance of this number in pyramidal form. We are looking for this number insofar as it relates to the period from the time that God announced His promise of "days" to Adam until the moment that Christ made His appearance to make good on that promise. To do that, we will return to those esteemed pyramidologists who, by way of a lifetime of scholarship, have bequeathed to posterity a comprehensive body of knowledge. First, we will take some time to examine the work of one of the most preeminent scholars of both The Great Pyramid and biblical chronology, Adam Rutherford.

Specifically, we will be looking at two separate works by Rutherford, the first aptly titled *Treatise on Bible Chronology,* and the second, *Pyramidology: Book III.* In both of these, Rutherford focuses on the very period in which we are interested—that of the time span from Adam to Christ. And interestingly enough, as if to make his point crystal clear, Rutherford duplicates himself in both books—word for word—in a statement that spans seven full pages. His unmistakable purpose is to demonstrate that The Pyramid confirms the specific date not only of the life of Adam on this Earth but also when Jesus, as the Second Adam, strode upon the stage of world history. Furthermore, Rutherford is not merely satisfied to confirm this timeline within the dimensions of The Pyramid, but he also insists on verifying it by way of the written record of *The Bible.*

Our initial hurdle, however, in confirming the existence of a *five and a half* "day" timeline from Adam to Christ is already well known to any modern-day biblical chronologist. Since the mid-seventeenth century, it has been considered common knowledge, courtesy of one Archbishop Ussher, that this period was quite different in length, which is to say, four thousand years as opposed to being five thousand, five hundred years. Moreover, to complicate matters further still, this belief has become so entrenched in Christian thought that to believe otherwise is tantamount to heresy. Fortunately, for our sake, though, there is a way to ferret out the truth of the matter, if one is simply willing to trace the history of how we in modern times have come to receive the knowledge of what *The Bible* has to say about the sacred chronology of ages past.

Apart from Rutherford's contribution to this area, many esteemed biblical chronologists in the last one hundred and fifty plus years have shed a great deal of light on this subject, and for anyone who is interested to look he or she will find numerous books on the subject. Among those who have added so much to this discussion are Nathan Rouse, Michael Russell, George Smith, and William Hales. In what certainly constitutes one of the great lost chapters of biblical history, there is a veritable mountain of evidence that suggests the findings of Ussher are completely at odds with the scriptural tradition that had been universally embraced for more than fifteen centuries, from pre-Christian times until the Reformation Era. Suffice it to say, however, I will only be able to provide a brief summary of their work in an effort to elucidate a better understanding of the glaring discrepancies that exist in the domain of such a critical subject—one which, I believe, has so much to say about God's faithfulness to Adam and his descendants.

And speaking of Adam, it is at this point that I feel it necessary to insert a critically important point concerning a distinction between his creation, as the father of mankind, and the creation of the Universe, in general. In fact, in all the various discussions concerning the multitudinous timelines, this just happens to be one of the most misunderstood aspects. I mean, really, do biblical chronologists who purport that the Scriptures depict anywhere from a four to six thousand year period from the Creation to Christ expect us to just dismiss all the geological and astronomical evidence of a Universe that clearly exceeds their claims by many millions of years? If so, how can any rational, intelligent person take any of this business seriously? After all, in today's scientific-savvy world even the average individual is doubtlessly aware of the overwhelming evidence afforded us by way of the geological and astronomical communities. Every museum in town displays its collection of dinosaur bones, while every night sky is teeming with countless stars. Considering the physical evidence of these prehistoric bones, then, together with the knowledge that the light from the stars has taken millions of years to get to us, one cannot possibly argue with the silent but eloquent testimony that the Universe is far older than any of these biblical chronologists seem to be telling us.

Notice, though, that I said this is what they *seem* to be telling us. The reason is because of the very important distinction of which I was alluding to earlier; and the distinction is this: The starting point for our timeline has a built-in theological conundrum. What does that mean? It means that, for as long as most people can remember, the creation of the Universe and the creation of Adam have been seen as simultaneous events as far as the traditional biblical rendition is concerned. "*The Bible* says," intone the vast majority of theologians, "in the beginning, God created the Heavens and the Earth, and then six days later, He created Adam and Eve." End of story. Therefore, any discussion concerning the period leading up to the Advent of Christ is presumed to commence from this point in time when the creation of both the Universe and Adam occurred.

Unfortunately, this notion simply does not hold up to scrutiny when one takes the time to examine the linguistic origins of the *Genesis* text in question. So as not to entirely lose our train of thought at this juncture, I will not belabor the point, but for the record—according to more than a century and a half of scholarship to support it—evidence suggests that the events depicted in the first two verses of *Genesis* did not take place at the same time. That is to say, when the Scriptures declare, "in the beginning, God created the Heavens and the Earth, and the Earth was without form and void,"[399] the second verse can just as correctly be rendered, "and the Earth *became* a waste and a desolation." In other words, "in the beginning, God created the Heavens and the Earth," and then some kind of cataclysmic event—which I and others equate with the primordial casting down of Satan after his expulsion from Heaven—caused the Earth to *become* what it originally was not, which was "without form and void."

The implications of this possibility are far-reaching to say the least. If true, then the creation of the Universe and the subsequent creation of Adam can no longer be seen as concomitant events. Accordingly, biblical scholars postulate there is a vast gulf of time between verse one, when God first created the Universe, and verse two, when a cataclysm struck the Earth, which then forced the Lord to "re-create" the world after it had "*become* a waste and a desolation." This, say scholars who espouse this theoretical model, would explain why God told Adam and Eve to "replenish" the Earth as opposed to telling them to "plenish" it. In theological terms, this is known as the "gap" theory, a philosophical tenant not unlike the one that helps to interpret the meaning of *Old Testament* passages referring to the work of Messiah. Prior to the unfolding of history, the Advent of Christ had always been thought to be a one-time event, that is, until the facts concerning the life and death of Jesus finally enabled mankind to perceive the manifold nature of His coming. Based on the premise of this "gap" theory, then, scholars have postulated the existence of a vast separation of time between the original creation of the Earth and its re-creation subsequent to the cataclysmic casting down of Satan. (For further details on the "gap" theory as it pertains to the creation story in *Genesis*, please refer to the book by Arthur C. Custance entitled *Without Form and Void*.)

But again, without getting bogged down in the finer points of this ongoing debate, keep in mind that when this book cites the beliefs of the various biblical chronologists throughout history, it is important to distinguish the fact that we are not referring to the creation of the world as our starting point for the period in question. Rather, we are referring to the creation of Adam on this Earth, and more specifically, not simply to his creation but to the moment when God promised him that He would be rescued after *five and a half* "days." This, quite apart from all of the theological debates about the "gap" theory, is critically important to hone in on, because, in fact, we are not in this particular case seeking to ascertain the age of the Universe as it is purported in *The Bible*. That, in terms of this present pursuit, does nothing to confirm or deny God's faithfulness to His promises, particularly as they pertain to the foundational verse found in *Second Corinthians* assuring us that all His promises are confirmed in the Advent of Christ.

Make no mistake; the timeline we are looking for is one that runs from the life of Adam to that of Christ's, and even when some biblical chronologist or historian refers to this timeline as being one which runs from the Creation to Christ—in the course of my reporting the historical record—do not confuse these two separate creation events as though they were one and the same just because this is what so many of the Church Fathers assumed. Fair enough? If so, we can return to Ussher.

It should be noted that when the esteemed archbishop determined the world was created on the 23rd day of October, in the year 4,004 B.C., he was using the Hebrew texts found in *Genesis* 5 and 11, together with numerous other passages from Scripture. The important thing to understand is that he arrived at this date using the genealogy of the antediluvian patriarchs found in the *King James* Version of *The Bible*. This, according to Adam Rutherford, lies at the heart of the discrepancy of our two time periods. This is because the younger Hebrew-based *Masoretic* Text, which provided the basis from which the *King James* translators produced their version, contained a genealogy with life spans that were different from the older Greek-based *Septuagint* Version. "When we say *Septuagint*," said Rutherford, "we are referring to the earlier *Alexandrine* Version of *The Septuagint*, not the *Sixtine* Text of it. The Greek *Septuagint* (LXX) is thus witness to a much earlier and purer form of *The Hebrew Bible* than is our *English Bible*."[400]

As a result of this tacit acceptance of the *Masoretic* Text by the *King James* translators, the time period from Adam to the Flood falls far short of what we would expect in our effort of confirming a *five and a half* thousand year period that extended to the Advent of Christ. In fact, as the *King James* Version has it, there are only sixteen hundred and sixty-five years from the time of Adam to that of the Flood, whereas in the *Septuagint* Version, there are two thousand, two hundred and fifty-six years for the same period—a difference of nearly six hundred years. So, considering the fact that most biblical chronologists—Rutherford included—date the occurrence of the Flood around 3,145 B.C., this addition of approximately six hundred years puts the creation of Adam around 5,407 B.C., surprisingly close to the date that we have been searching for, which is 5,500 B.C.

Just think: Had the *King James* Version reflected this lengthier period for the lives of the antediluvian patriarchs, it might have been much easier to locate a canonical confirmation for this prophecy of the *five and a half* "days." So why did the translators of the *Masoretic* Text differ to such an extent with those of the *Septuagint* Version? The answer might shock if not downright anger you. Rutherford cited the following at length:

> Down through the centuries till Christ's time, great precautions were taken to prevent tampering with the sacred Scriptures, but after the destruction of Jerusalem by Titus in 70 A.D., and still more so after the Diaspora of the Jews in 135 A.D., a great change took place. As Dr. Hales says, "After the first destruction of Jerusalem by Titus, the Jews were so oppressed by national calamities that they could think of nothing else for some time; but about the end of the first century of the Vulgar Era, they were roused to oppose the wonderful progress of Christianity. What principally excited their rage and vexation was that their own Scriptures were turned into artillery against them to prove that Jesus was indeed the Christ, from the days of the Apostles.[401] And the chronological aspect formed no small part of that bombardment, for there was a very widespread belief, indeed, it was almost universal among the Jews that just as man was created in the sixth 'day' of Creation, so the Messiah would come in

> the sixth 1,000-year 'day' of human history, for *a thousand years with God are but as one day."*
>
> As we have ascertained, Adam came to life in the year 5,407 B.C., consequently five thousand years were complete in 407 B.C. *The Old Testament*, therefore, contains human history covering a period of five thousand years (in round numbers), hence the Jewish historian Josephus says regarding his work *Antiquities*: "Those *Antiquities* contain the history of five thousand years, and are taken out of our sacred books but are translated by me into the Greek tongue."[402] The sixth "day" of a thousand years from the date of Adam thus began in 407 B.C., and so ended in 594 A.D., during which very "day" Christ came, as anticipated.
>
> As every student of the history of *The Bible* knows, many copies were made, and many versions of Scripture, both Jewish and Christian, sprang into existence in the early centuries of the Christian Era, and considerable variation existed between the different texts. The Jewish scholars and rabbis, taking advantage of this confusion, and professing to bring out "authentic" texts, in reality, seized on the opportunity to corrupt the number of years in the genealogies of the early patriarchs of *Genesis* so as to make it appear that the sixth thousand-year "day" had not yet arrived, and, therefore, Jesus could not be the Messiah. This fact is definitely recorded in history, for Ephrem the Syrian, who lived only three hundred years after Christ, wrote, "The Jews have subtracted six hundred years from the generations of Adam, Seth, etc., in order that their own books might not convict them concerning the coming of Christ; He having been predicted to appear for the deliverance of mankind after *five and a half* millennia."[403]

Just who is this individual by the name of Ephrem the Syrian? Was he alone among the Church Fathers to have held this view concerning the *five and a half* "day" timeline from Adam to Christ? What about the fact that he stated the coming of Christ would not simply occur *sometime* during the sixth "day" of human history but specifically after *five and a half* millennia? And most importantly, is there any evidence to indicate that this statement attributed to Ephrem constituted anything more than a passing remark?

Born in the city of Nisibis, Turkey in 306 A.D., Ephrem the Syrian was a man possessed of rare talents and gifts. Not only was he a prolific hymn writer, of which it is said that over four hundred of his hymns still exist to this day, but Ephrem also wrote biblical commentaries, homilies, prose, and biographies steeped in his imaginatively metaphorical style. His works were richly laden with the poetry of *The Bible* as well as the folk tales of the multicultural Roman world in which he lived. Universally praised, Ephrem is revered by both branches of Christianity. In the East, he is regarded as a Venerable Father; in the West, he has been proclaimed a Doctor of the Church. His various titles include the Harp of the Spirit, the Deacon of Edessa, the Sun of the Syrians, and a Pillar of the Church. In short, this man was no bit player in the history of Christian thought, and when someone like that has something to say about *The Bible*, it would be wise to pay attention to what he has to say.

Some two centuries before Ephrem, this same view was articulated by Theophilus, the seventh bishop of Antioch in Syria from about 168 to 174 A.D. Theophilus was, said British theologian William Sanday, "one of the precursors of that group of writers who, from Irenaeus to Cyprian, not only broke the obscurity which rested on the earliest history of the Church, but alike in the East and in the West carried it to the front of literary imminence, and outdistanced all their heathen contemporaries."[404] Theophilus is also cited as being the first Christian chronologist, and it was in this vein that he outlined a detailed chronology from the creation of the world up to his present day; the result being that he estimated the time of Adam's creation at 5,510 B.C.

Whereas Theophilus worked out a detailed chronology based on the specific dates that he found in *The Bible*, a theologian soon after him, Hippolytus of Rome, sought to date Adam's creation within the framework of the allegorical implications of Scripture. Writing in what is believed to be the oldest surviving Christian commentary, he stated:

> The first appearance of our Lord in the flesh took place in Bethlehem, under Augustus, in the year 5,500... But someone may ask, "How will you prove to me that the Savior was born in the year 5,500?" That is an easy thing to learn, oh, man, because this all took place a long time ago in the Wilderness, under Moses, concerning the Tabernacle, which constituted types and emblems of spiritual mysteries, in order that when the truth appeared in Christ in these Last Days you might be able to perceive that these things were fulfilled. For God said to Moses, "You will make The Ark of imperishable wood, and overlay it with pure gold, within and without, and you will make the length of it two and a half cubits, and the width, one and a half cubits, and the height, one and a half cubits," which when summed up measures *five and a half* cubits so that the 5,500 years might be signified thereby.[405]

Parenthetically, in regard to the dimensions of The Ark of the Covenant, I would like to take a slight detour so that I can point out some things that have probably gone unnoticed so far. The first thing to take note of is that Hippolytus was not the first man of the cloth to have realized that the dimensions of The Ark provided a time-oriented clue to the Advent of Christ, although one might argue that he was certainly the first to do so gladly. What does that mean? Well, as anyone who has been paying attention throughout this book will remember, the first man to have detected this dimensional connection between The Ark and Christ was in fact one of Jesus' most ardent human adversaries, that is, Annas, the chief priest at Jerusalem.[406] Furthermore, Annas, unlike Hippolytus, did not make this inference from The Ark alone, but he did so by connecting it with a passage from Scripture that directly spoke of the five thousand, five hundred year chronology from Adam to Christ. Does everyone remember how Annas described it, howbeit in such ignominious terms?

As the story goes: When Pontius Pilate demanded to know if the Jewish leaders who were responsible for crucifying Jesus had learned anything from their own Scriptures, Annas confessed to his bitter discovery. Stepping up to their most sacred text, Annas said, "In the first of *The Seventy Books*," the chief priest explained, "we found a conversation between Michael, the archangel, and Seth, the third son of Adam, in which Michael told Seth that the Christ was to come after five thousand, five hundred years."[407]

The reason I mention this here is because I would like to know if anyone who has read this part of the story—going on the fourth time now—has stopped to ask the obvious question: To which book was Annas referring? The fact that it was referred to as *The Seventy Books* no doubt brings to mind *The Septuagint*, which itself comes from the Latin word for *seventy*; and particularly intriguing about this is an often-overlooked fact concerning the origin of the name *Septuagint* itself. To this day, tradition insists it was so named because—and this is what I find so intriguing—seventy scholars supposedly translated it. Oh, sorry, wait, not seventy scholars, it was seventy-*two* scholars, actually, who translated it, six scholars from each of the Twelve Tribes of Israel. So, the question remains: If seventy-two scholars translated it, what, exactly, would the harm have been in calling it *The Seventy-Two* as opposed to *The Seventy*? None, I imagine; though in mentioning this apparently minor discrepancy here, I must leave it for now so I can pick it back up in just a moment.

Now, this is not say that I believe the book that Annas was referring to was *The Septuagint*, either, simply because, by Annas' own testimony, the promise of "days" that he discovered was found in the first of *The Seventy Books*, which would mean that if he had been reading from *The Septuagint* he would have found it in *Genesis*. But clearly this is not the case. So, from which book was he reading? What I would suggest, in light of such testimony, is that there must be an alternative to such a possibility; and more importantly, I would suggest this in order to demonstrate that this all-important prophecy of the *five and a half* "days" has a basis in the written word of Scripture as well as its counterpart in stone.

If, then, the promise of "days" that Annas was referring to was not in *The Septuagint*, where was it? Could there be another candidate for this so-called *Seventy Books* to which the chief priest was referring? As a matter of fact, yes, I believe there is. And the man who produced that work is someone who biblical historians say lived around five hundred years before Christ. His name was Ezra, and he just happens to be a man whose role in all of this is made all the more interesting because so many aspects to his life story conform to the age-old pattern of messianic figures. In other words, Ezra, the scribe, seems to be cut from the same cloth as the narrator of our *Tales*, Enoch. In *The Second Book of Esdras*, we find:

> "The world is a dark place," Ezra said to God, "and its people have no light. Your Law has been destroyed by fire so that no one can know what You've done in the past or what You're planning to do in the future. Please send me your Holy Spirit so I can write down everything that has been done in this world from the beginning, everything that was written in Your Law. Then in the Last Days, people will be able to find the right way and obtain life if they desire it."
>
> So God answered, "Prepare a large number of writing tablets, Ezra... Then come here, and I'll light the lamp of understanding in your heart, and it will not go out until you've finished what you're supposed to write. When you've finished your work, you'll make some of it public, and you'll give the rest to the wise ones, who will keep it secret..."
>
> For forty days, ninety-four books were written, and after that, God, the Most High, said to me, "You are now to make public the first twenty-four books that you wrote so that everyone, whether they are worthy or not, may read them. But the last seventy books you wrote are to be held back and to be given only to those who are wise among your people."
>
> And I did so, in the seventh year, in the sixth week, after five thousand years of the Creation.[408]

So, what can we surmise from the preceding information? Several things, in fact. First, we see the allusions to the pattern set forth in Enoch's story: Because the knowledge of God's actions, past, present, and future, were no longer available—no doubt associated with the nationwide loss of Scripture during the Babylonian captivity—Ezra is commissioned to restore that knowledge. Second, this restoration of knowledge was said to be for the benefit of not only Ezra's generation but also a future generation, which will arise "in the Last Days." Third, this God-inspired knowledge that was given to Ezra was to be segregated, with some of it to be "made public," and some of it be "kept secret." Fourth, this division between public and secret knowledge came with the stipulation that the first twenty-four books were to be made public, while the remaining seventy books were "to be held back and given only to those who are wise among your people." And fifth, all this occurred at a point in history that Ezra described as being "after five thousand years of the Creation," which, according to biblical historians took place approximately five hundred years before Christ, thus providing our first corroborative testimony derived from a canonical text—or at least according to all non-Protestant Canons—concerning the *five and a half* "day" chronology.

That said, I would now like to hone in on the salient points in regard to the question of which book Annas found the passage that convinced him the Messiah would arrive after five thousand, five hundred years, and after doing so, I will then continue with our present train of thought regarding the testimony of the early Church concerning the chronology of *five and a half* millennia.

In this particular case, I would like to point out that in the seventy secrets books of Ezra, we have, by far, the most obvious candidate for the work that Annas called *The Seventy Books*, a book that was described as being so enormous that it required the combined efforts of four men to carry it.[409] Clearly, this book was by no means an ordinary book, and as such was certainly not one that was being passed around from synagogue to synagogue. In other words, everything about this unusual book spoke of its clandestine nature, particularly in light of Annas' testimony as to his own ignorance of its contents, until such time as the peculiar events surrounding the resurrection of Jesus of Nazareth compelled him to examine the book more thoroughly.

Furthermore, the utmost regard with which this sacred book was held is most likely because of what we see cropping up, some two and a half centuries earlier, when *The Septuagint* was created. As so often happens in the history of the dissemination of influential ideas, the memory traces of Ezra's volume of *The Seventy Books* was so potent that the reports surrounding its creation eventually found itself woven into the legend concerning the allegedly miraculous creation of *The Septuagint*. This is all the more evident when one considers the otherwise inexplicable discrepancy, in that according to all historical accounts, seventy-two scholars produced it, not seventy; nevertheless the book is dubbed *The Seventy*, rather than *The Seventy-Two*. So why call it *The Septuagint*? They did so, I believe, because of the irresistible and overriding concern, which in this case was to lend credence to its formation, recalling the way that Ezra's most secretive and therefore most precious books were formed, and all of it hearkening back further still, to that greatest of all scribes in the Hebrew pantheon, Enoch, and the special books that he was inspired to write.

Finally, it is important to take note of two more things as we conclude this parenthesis. First, if Annas were in fact reading from the secret books of Ezra, it would explain both why the primordial account of Adam and the prophecy of the Great Five and a Half Days was not a matter of common knowledge, and how an awareness of this prophecy was transmitted to mankind, quite apart from the revelation conveyed by Moses via *Genesis*.

Returning now to the testimony of the early Church concerning the five thousand, five hundred year period from Adam to Christ, we find that another important figure among their ranks subscribed to it as well. His name was Julius Africanus, a Libyan historian and chronologist of the late second and early third century. While unheard of by most people, Africanus is highly regarded for his influence on other more well-known figures among later Church Fathers, most notably Eusebius. Concerning this period, he wrote:

> Why should I speak of the three myriad years of the Phoenicians or the follies of the Chaldeans with their forty-eight myriads? For the Jews, deriving their origin from the descendants of Abraham ... together with the truth by the spirit of Moses, have handed down to us, by their extant Hebrew histories, the number of 5,500 years as being the period up to the advent of the Word of Salvation that was announced to the world which was held sway in the time of the Caesars.[410]

As a result of his work, this same chronology became firmly rooted in the Eastern Mediterranean world, which afterward placed the date of Creation at or about 5,500 B.C.

Significantly, Ephrem, Theophilus, Hippolytus, and Africanus were not the only ones among the early Church who professed the idea that Christ had been expected to arrive five thousand, five hundred years after Adam. Many Church Fathers, as well as a number of early Church historians, who all adhered to the reckoning of time depicted in *The Septuagint*, believed the Creation took place around 5,500 B.C. Based on their estimation derived from it, the following dates were adhered to: Clement of Alexandria (5,592 B.C.), Abulfaragius of Armenia (5,586 B.C.), Julius Hilarion (5,530 B.C.), Georgius Cedrenus (5,506 B.C.), Maximus Martyr (5,501 B.C.), Lactantius, Eutychus, Nicephorus, Gregory of Tours, and Georgius Syncellus (5,500 B.C.), Pandorus of Alexandria and Maximus the Confessor (5,493 B.C.), and Sulpicius Severus (5,469 B.C.). Accordingly, the Byzantine Calendar dated the creation of the world at 5,509 B.C., while in Ethiopia, it has been observed: "The most authentic ancient history of that country, according to James Bruce, is *The Chronicle of Axum*," which attests that "there is an interval of 5,500 years between the creation of the world and the birth of Christ."[411]

So what can we surmise from the foregoing information? Primarily, that many of the most influential Christian theological minds, writing in an era not so far removed from the time of Jesus as we are today, were all in agreement as to this particular time frame of *five and a half* "days" from Adam to Christ. This evidence from the historical record, then, stands in stark contrast to the numerical system that provided the basis for Ussher's calculations, a fact which when fully appreciated clearly undermines any merit thus far given to his chronological claims. Notwithstanding our modern-day ignorance concerning these facts of history, they have not gone unnoticed by others. In his 1856 book, entitled *A Dissertation of Sacred Chronology*, Nathan Rouse stated in no uncertain terms:

> We cannot but express our regret that ... the demonstrably erroneous and absurd system of Archbishop Ussher is still permitted to retain its place in the margin of our *Bible*, and to be taught to the youth of our country. We should despise a man who would at the present day undertake to teach the Ptolemaic system of astronomy, and yet our pulpits and schools are perpetually disgraced by inculcating a manifestly corrupt rabbinical system of scriptural chronology...
>
> The Ussherian chronology ... is inconsistent not only with itself but likewise with all antiquity, both Jewish and Christian... And yet, although we have had the good sense to renounce an erroneous system of astronomy, we doggedly cling to a false system of biblical chronology, and are almost disposed to charge the man with heresy who presumes to call our falsehood into question. It is to be hoped that the time is not too distant when Protestant communities will wipe this disreputable blot from their escutcheon, and when our pulpits and schools will no longer lend their influence to the propagation of such a pernicious untruth.[412]

Needless to say, however, in the more than one hundred and fifty years since Rouse wrote his book, the typical Christian is still no more aware of the preceding sentiments than when these words were first penned. The simple fact remains that most people who have investigated the subject of biblical chronology are still under the impression that the only correct view is the one that has been handed down to us by Archbishop Ussher, which has been singularly revered ever since it was first offered to an unsuspecting public in 1650.

But if the chronology of the Hebrew *Masoretic* Version of *The Bible* was dismissed in favor of the Greek *Septuagint* Version as early as the eighth century of the Christian Era, what could have happened between that time and the mid-seventeenth century to allow for such a radical shift in our understanding of biblical chronology? If someone whose name became synonymous with admiration and respect—that is, one Venerable Bede—failed to impose his view concerning a four thousand year time frame, who did succeed? The answer, like any that a vigorous historical investigation has to offer, is one that turns out to be another of the great ironies of history. And though this shift came in conjunction with the effort of a single individual, unlike the effort of Bede, who was specifically trying to bring about this change, this man was in no way, shape, or form trying to undermine the chronology of the Greek *Septuagint*.

In fact, this shift in theological thinking did not come as a direct result of any specific act made by this one man but was merely an outgrowth of a movement that he instigated. What is undoubtedly the most important advancement in human civilization, this revolution in thought is unsurpassed in terms of its enlightenment and edification of the human race; and the movement I am referring to is the Reformation. Yet, ironically, for all the good that this uniquely positive force in history accomplished, there was a peculiar downside to it as well, although certainly one that could never have been anticipated by its founding father, Martin Luther. In this case, the unanticipated downside occurred as a result of the inevitable backlash that came in response to all things Roman Catholic, a backlash involving the rejection of anything seen as even remotely connected to Papal influence. Concerning this ill-fated turn of events in the history of biblical chronology, Rouse had this to say:

> Notwithstanding the attempt of Venerable Bede, the *Septuagint* chronology prevailed down to the time of the Reformation, and during this entire period, there is no instance upon record of any church, in either the East or the West, having adopted the rabbinical corruptions of the Hebrew. The Protestant reformers, however, did, in this respect, what no Christian church, even in the darkest ages, had ever done. They adopted the chronological corruptions of the Jewish rabbis.
>
> On this point Bishop Russell remarks: "It has not escaped observation that the prejudices against the Roman Church, which animated the disciples of Luther, were allowed to mix deeply with their investigations into this intricate science. The Protestants, aware that the Papal communion followed the computation of *The Septuagint*, exerted all their learning in order to prove that the chronology of *The Hebrew Bible* possessed a higher authority than could be claimed for the most approved version of the Scriptures. And overlooking the convincing evidence that is supplied by the writings of the ancient Jews, as well as the Christian Fathers during the first four centuries, they took part with the Talmudists and modern rabbis, against both the Eastern and Western Churches, and maintained that the Messiah appeared upon the Earth at the end of the fourth millennium."[413]

So, whereas the human spirit won a great victory against the forces of tyranny in the wake of the Reformation, the unexpected casualty in this war of ideology just happened to impact the future of mankind's understanding of this most critical facet of God's control over history. Writing about the same time as Rouse, George Smith confirmed this same idea:

> Up to that period, the authority of the Greek *Septuagint*, and the unanimous consent of the Church Fathers, were still found to regulate public opinion with respect to the age of world. But the reformers were easily induced to consider the extended chronology as one of the errors handed down by Rome, and, therefore, when Archbishop Ussher, in his great impartiality for rabbinical literature, adopted the Masorite numbers, the Reformed Church eagerly caught at the change, and from that time the so-called "Hebrew verity" was defended with as much zeal as if the entire truth of revelation depended on that system of numbers.[414]

And with the fateful decision to substitute the version of *The Bible* that had been accepted by every Christian church from the time of Christ to the Reformation with this—in the view of the reformers—non-Catholic version, the door was opened wide for a new generation of scriptural chronologists. No wonder that men like James Ussher and John Lightfoot, well-intentioned as I am sure they were, would, as a result of referring to the *Masoretic* Text, deduce that the Creation occurred just four thousand years prior to the Advent of Christ as opposed to the previously accepted period of five thousand, five hundred years.

Having therefore established the preceding facts of biblical history, the only question that remains is: What evidence is there to suggest that the fourth-century reference of Ephrem's concerning the *five and a half* millennia from Adam to Christ was anything more than a passing remark? To answer that we now turn to another piece of ancient literature that most *Bible* students are unfamiliar with—one that purports to represent a compendium of events from the Creation to the birth of Jesus. More importantly, this work is attributed to none other than Ephrem the Syrian. Entitled *The Cave of Treasures*, it presents this history in six chapters, corresponding to the six days of creation, in which the first five chapters each depict a period of one thousand years, with the final chapter depicting a period of five hundred years. In other words, this Syriac text—that naturally is besieged by scholastic skepticism as to its genuine Ephremic authorship—just happens to depict a biblically-inspired timeline that spans five thousand, five hundred years from Adam to Christ. An excerpt from the last chapter, dubbed a Chronological Statement, reads as follows:

> Understand now and see, my brother Nemesius, that in the days of Jared, in his fortieth year, the first thousand years came to an end. In the six hundredth year of Noah's life, the second thousand years came to an end. In the seventy-fourth year of Reu, the third thousand years came to an end. In the twenty-sixth year of Ehud's life, the fourth thousand years came to an end. In the second year of Cyrus' reign, the fifth thousand years came to an end. And in the five hundredth year of the sixth thousand years, Christ was born in human form.[415]

In the following way, then, one can see that the comment attributed to Ephrem the Syrian, suggesting a messianic timeline of five thousand, five hundred years, was certainly no passing remark. Quite to the contrary, it became the basis of Ephrem's voluminous work in which he meticulously chronicled "the succession of the families from Adam to Christ," no small feat as one can imagine.

But just because Ephrem, and other Church Fathers like him, gave credence to this timeline of *five and a half* millennia, what evidence is there to indicate a link between it and the *five and a half* "days" found in the document that forms the basis of the present narrative in *Tales of Forever*? To locate such a link, one need simply turn to the preface of the English translation of *The Cave of Treasures*, produced by E.A. Wallis Budge, who wrote:

> There is no doubt whatsoever that the writer of *The Cave of Treasures* borrowed largely from *The Book of Adam and Eve* ... where God promised more than once to Adam that after *five and a half* days—i.e. five thousand, five hundred years—He would send a Redeemer into the world Who would save both Adam and his descendants from the destruction which his sin in Paradise had incurred.[416]

Moreover, Budge confirmed the literary link between the two texts in his recounting of the rediscovery of *The Cave of Treasures*, in which he stated:

> The famous author of *The Catalogue of Oriental Manuscripts* in the Vatican Library, one Giuseppe Assemani, described a Syriac manuscript containing a series of apocryphal works ... which contained the history of a period of five thousand, five hundred years, i.e. from the creation of Adam to the birth of Christ, and that it was a historical chronicle based upon the Scriptures... But no attempt was made to publish the Syriac text; in fact, little attention was paid to it until August Dillmann, the nineteenth-century German Orientalist, began to study *The Book of Adam and Eve* in connection with it... And then he noticed that the contents of whole sections of *The Cave of Treasures* in Syriac and *The Book of Adam and Eve* in Ethiopic were identical.[417]

Therefore, from Rutherford and Ephrem to Rouse and Budge, one can trace a clear connection concerning the historical roots of this prophecy of The Great Five and a Half Days. No longer can the river of this *day*-oriented timeline—found in such universally accepted texts as *The Septuagint*—be seen as existing apart from its headwaters flowing from those previously marginalized books like *Adam and Eve*. Now that it has been exhumed from the depths of apocryphal obscurity, this *five and a half* "day" prophecy can no longer be disregarded as a fanciful tale left over from some bygone era. It is time, then, to restore it to its rightful place in Christological thought, just as the God of *The Bible* originally intended—as integral as that primordial prophecy, which speaks of the seed of the woman being bruised by the seed of the serpent, which, in turn, is ultimately crushed in the very process of its ill-advised bruising.[418]

The Eye of Faith

WITH ALL THE FOREGOING in mind, the only thing left is to connect this *five and a half* "day" timeline, so firmly rooted in the written record of Scripture—both canonical and apocryphal—to that marvelous megalith, *The Bible* in Stone. And the reason for this is two-fold. First, as has been previously stated, one reason is because there are still far too many who stubbornly cling to the view that any contradictions to their traditional interpretation of Scripture are merely by-products of mistranslations that have been handed down from age to age. Therefore, in answer to such objections, we will attempt to offer an antidote, which by its very nature precludes any errors in translation. This answer, then, like all that are conveyed via the geometry of The Great Pyramid, will be one that is conveyed entirely by way of the universal language of mathematics. As such, a message of this sort will be the same today as it was when this ancient testimony of geometric wisdom was originally constructed.

And second, in the process of connecting the numerical value of *five and a half* in The Pyramid with such texts as *Adam and Eve, Secrets of Enoch,* and *Nicodemus,* we will also be elevating these works to a status above and beyond that which has thus far denigrated them to the crude level of *pseudepigrapha.* In other words, even if biblical scholars are willing to entertain the potential contribution of these texts from a purely literary and anecdotal perspective, they still only do so with the caveat that they were written long after the texts themselves imply. As such, anyone who would dare suggest that the message contained in them could have any basis in *bona fide* biblical truth would certainly find themselves at odds with the prevailing status quo. But—I repeat—by connecting this all-important numerical value with both The Great Pyramid and the written texts in question, one goes a long way in providing a much sounder argument for their great antiquity. This is not to say that previous attempts to date these manuscripts holds no merit; please do not misunderstand me here. What I am suggesting, though, is that by demonstrating a connectivity between stone and word alike concerning this number *five and a half,* which is evidently so integral to the central messianic timeline of Scripture, we find ourselves on much more secure ground in arguing that these later texts are undoubtedly based on other source material from an earlier period—such as Ezra's seventy secret books—that far exceeds previously accepted historical limits.

To that end, let us review: In our effort to demonstrate a correspondence between *The Bible* and its counterpart in stone, we first traced the origin of the prophecy of The Great Five and a Half Days as it is depicted in *Adam and Eve, Secrets of Enoch,* and *Nicodemus.* We then proceeded to analyze the "who," "how," and "why" of the construction of The Great Pyramid of Giza. In the process, it was determined by every known criterion of authorship that Enoch, the seventh patriarch from Adam, is the only person in history capable of designing the prophetic implications that are purportedly contained in its geometric features. Additionally, he is known to have had an association with the kind of "construction crew" who alone could build such a structure, that is, the Watchers, who were both endowed with superhuman strength and divinely commissioned to communicate their wisdom to humanity. Together, these essential ingredients provided us with the following conclusions. One, Enoch was the architect of The Great Pyramid. Two, the Watchers provided the angelic "muscle power," as it were, required in The Pyramid's otherworldly construction. And three, it was built according to God's express purposes, as per *The Book of Jubilees,* "in order that they, *the Watchers,* should instruct mankind, *by way of The Great Pyramid's geometric design,* and that they should execute judgment and uprightness, *as a result of the prophetic message revealed in it.*"[419]

Finally, after having rescued the prophecy of The Great Five and a Half Days from the mists of time and establishing that Enoch and the Watchers were commissioned to incorporate their God-inspired wisdom within the geometry of The Pyramid, we turned our attention to the final phase of our quest. In a nutshell: If all the prophetic timelines depicting messianic history are conveyed via the dimensions of The Great Pyramid's architecture, then there is every reason to believe that this foundational prophecy—this promise of "days"—should also be found there. We have now seen the extent to which the number *five* is thoroughly embedded into The

Pyramid's schematics; therefore, considering the ubiquitous nature of this number, it should not be too difficult to locate the number *five and a half*, if one looks for it in the proper place, right? Should we then expect to find it buried within a series of complex computations, as is the case of the numerical value of 365.242? Should we look for it as part of a geometric relationship, such as the one that reveals the factor of *pi*? As a matter of fact, no. One need not look nearly as hard as one might expect to find such a significant numerical value. So where do we find it? And just as importantly, if it really is so significant, then why has no one discovered it yet?

As it turns out, the answer to the last question is even more difficult to answer than the actual locating of the *five and a half* "day" timeline, because, like so much of the numerological significance built into the design of The Pyramid, there are no "neon signs," so to speak, pointing the way to such things. Discoveries of this sort are simply the by-product of serendipitous circumstances. That they are made at all is a testament, rather, to the genius of the designers of The Great Pyramid as opposed to those who grab hold of the train that is the whole history of what has been discovered in its marvelous construction. Just as *The Bible* is a document whose contents are hidden in plain sight, so, too, the divine wisdom embodied in The Pyramid, though hidden to the undiscerning, is still there for all to see, if only to those who pursue it with the eye of faith. Of this kind of apprehension of truth, Ephrem the Syrian had much to say. Sebastian Brock, in his informative study on the life of Ephrem entitled *The Luminous Eye*, said this:

> When Ephrem explores the infinite number of symbols and types in nature and Scripture, we must be constantly aware that, although human understanding of them is essentially fluid and variable, what they all point to is an objective reality that Ephrem calls "Truth." Furthermore, the presence in the types and symbols of what he calls the "hidden power," or "meaning," lends to them some sort of inner objective significance of reality, which is different from that outer reality, which the scientific observer would call objective.[420]

> Said Ephrem:

> Lord, Your symbols are everywhere, yet You are hidden from everywhere.
> Though Your symbol is On-High, yet the height does perceive that You are.
> Though Your symbol is in the depths, it does not comprehend Who You are.
> Though Your symbol is in the sea, You are hidden from the sea.
> Though Your symbol is on dry land, it is not aware of what You are.
> Blessed is the Hidden One shining out![421]

Truth according to God's intention, then, paradoxically contains two separate yet insoluble components, whether in terms of Scripture or, in this case, The Great Pyramid. In other words, truth has both a surface meaning that is obvious to most people, and a deeper meaning that is understood by only a few. As Brock explained it:

> Types and symbols are to be found everywhere simply as a result of the world having been created by God; they are pointers to His existence and creative activity... But they are only observable by the eye of faith; and the clearer that eye is, the more the symbols will become visible, and each individual symbol will also become more meaningful.[422]

Yet this idea is certainly not new to anyone who has read any of this so far. Repetition, after all, has constituted a major component to my approach throughout this work, and this is no time to depart from such tried-and-true methods. Admittedly, though, I did not invent the concept myself. To tell you the truth, I stole it; or, rather, I would like to think I borrowed it. In fact, one of the most obvious clues that a single mind is behind both *The Bible* and The Great Pyramid is this overwhelming repetition of theme, character, and style. Scripture is methodically redundant in its use of types, which inevitably move from the vaguely general to the highly specific, that is, from the lesser messianic figures such as Elijah and Jonah, who set the stage for the greater messianic figures like John the Baptist and Jesus of Nazareth. Likewise, The Pyramid exhibits a similar method of redundancy, in this case the repetition of the number *five*, which, in turn, sets the stage for the appearance of *five and a half.*

So keeping in mind that the symbolic truth of The Pyramid, like that of *The Bible,* is only discernible to those who approach it with the eye of faith, we may proceed in our attempt to connect the *five and a half* "days" in stone with that which is found in word. To reiterate: Do we find it buried within a series of complex computations or as part of a geometric relationship? Again, I say no. Believe it or not, we "see" this *five and a half* "day" timeline from Adam to Christ every time we look at The Great Pyramid. Let me say that again for anyone who might think I just misspoke: In every picture you have ever seen of the exterior of The Pyramid, sitting so majestically upon the Giza plateau, you were actually staring straight at the very timeline that we have been seeking. That is, you have looked at it without realizing that what stood before you contained "more than the eye could see." In other words, like so much of what is revealed symbolically in The Pyramid, the knowledge it contains is actually hidden right before your eyes. Let me explain what I mean by that.

Whenever one looks at a standard image of The Great Pyramid, the first thing one sees rising from the desert floor is a rocky edifice composed of four triangular planes, which all converge at its pinnacle several hundred feet above ground. And what does one see at the summit of this magnificent Pyramid? Does it have a point like every other pyramid around it? No, it does not. Unique among the pyramids of Egypt, this greatest one of all has no capstone, no "crown," as it were, at its peak. But why? To this day, no one can say for sure. Some argue that it was placed there but, like its original outer casing stones of polished limestone, was removed in an act of vandalism. Some claim that it was never built in the first place, while others insist that it was built but, because it was flawed in its workmanship, was never set in place. The only thing we can be sure of today is that it is missing and has been for as long as anyone can remember. Is that the end of the story, then? Of course not; but as one can imagine, only an explanation that offers a decidedly biblical view would be of any consolation to this author. Fortunately, when one looks to the many esteemed pyramidologists, there is much that has been said to connect the meaning of this missing capstone and *The Bible,* which The Pyramid has obviously been intended to symbolize.

To a man, this missing capstone is interpreted as representing Christ, Who spoke of Himself as being the "Chief Cornerstone that was rejected by the builders."[423] The Apostle Peter confirmed this idea when he testified before the Sanhedrin, saying, "Jesus is the stone that you builders rejected, which has become the Cornerstone."[424] In this, Peter was echoing the words of the psalmist, who wrote concerning this Rejected One: "The Lord has done this, and it is marvelous in our eyes."[425] Elsewhere, Peter continued this same thinking, which speaks not only of Jesus as the Chief Cornerstone but also of believers in Christ becoming like Him to a lesser degree. As stones gathered by the purposeful hand of a Master Builder:

> You come to Him, the Living Stone—rejected by humans but chosen by God and precious to Him. You also, like living stones, are being built into a spiritual house to be a holy priesthood, offering spiritual sacrifices acceptable to God through Jesus Christ. For in the Scripture it says, "See, I lay a stone in Zion, a chosen and precious cornerstone, and the one who trusts in Him will never be put to shame."[426]

Said the Apostle Paul:

> Consequently, you are no longer foreigners and strangers but fellow citizens with God's people and also members of His household, built on the foundation of the apostles and prophets, with Christ Jesus as the Chief Cornerstone. In Him, the whole building is joined together and rises to become a holy temple in the Lord, and in Him, you, too, are being built together to become a dwelling in which God lives by His Spirit.[427]

In this way, one could not possibly articulate a more perfect analogy of what is being expressed via this idea of Christ as the "missing capstone" atop The Great Pyramid—a "holy priesthood," who as "living stones," rise up to constitute the "spiritual house" of which Jesus, holding the entire edifice together, is the "Chief Cornerstone." Again, I turn to the eloquence of Seiss, who said this about the preceding verses of Scripture:

> All these are great central passages of the divine word, and not one of them can be properly interpreted without The Pyramid, whose light alone brings out their full significance and beauty... Common architecture furnishes no preeminent cornerstone. There is no chief cornerstone without The Pyramid. That alone has ... a cornerstone, uniquely and indisputably the chief...
>
> The shape of it is altogether peculiar. It is *five*-sided and *five*-pointed... It is itself a perfect pyramid, the original of the edifice which it completes and adorns... Every other stone in all the mighty construction stands in it, and has place with reference to it, and is touched by its weight and influence, as well as sheltered under its lines, and honored and perfected by its presence. It is indeed the "all in all" of the whole edifice. To its angles is "all the building fitly framed together." And in it, every part and particle that belongs to the structure, from foundation to capstone, has its bond of perfectness, its shelter, and its crown.
>
> About such imagery there should be no question. In all the richness of the Scriptures, there is not a more luminous, expressive, and comprehensive picture of Christ—in Himself, in His experiences, in His relations to His friends or foes, in His office and place in all the dispensations of God toward our race—than that which is given in these texts when studied in the light of The Great Pyramid.[428]

From Adam to Christ

HAVING ESTABLISHED that the summit of The Great Pyramid is symbolic of Christ, we can return to locating this *five and a half* "day" timeline to which I have been alluding. To reiterate: Not only is Jesus represented by this missing capstone, but, based on an interpretation from *The Bible*, the entire structure beneath its summit represents the "House of God," made up of "living stones," which are all "fitly framed together and sheltered under its lines." Therefore, if Christ represents the summit of this grand edifice, and the stones that comprise it represent those who make up His body, then who might represent the foundation of this marvelous megalith? Who else but Adam, that is, the father of mankind?

Again, as I previously stated: Whenever someone looks at the exterior of The Great Pyramid, they are actually seeing the *five and a half* "day" timeline from Adam to Christ that we have been seeking. How can we be sure of this? The certainty lies in what is well known to every student of Pyramidology, that the height of The Pyramid has long been determined to be 5,449 pyramid inches. Yet to my knowledge, this particular dimension has never been understood beyond the fact that it bears an uncanny relationship to the biblical passage in *The Book of Isaiah*, to which pyramidologists point as proof of The Pyramid's divine origins. Whereas Egyptologists insist that The Great Pyramid, like every other pyramid in Egypt, was built simply as a royal funerary heap, pyramidologists vehemently deny this assertion; and to prove their case, they offer up the existence of the all-important verse in *The Bible*:

> In that day, there will be an altar to the Lord in the midst of Egypt, and a pillar of God at its border. It will become a sign and a witness to the Lord of Hosts in the land of Egypt, for they'll cry to God because of the oppressors, and He'll send them a Savior and a Champion to deliver them.[429]

Called the "Great Pyramid Text of Scripture," these two verses contain thirty Hebrew words, each letter of which contains a corresponding numerical value. Ironically, when one "adds up" all of the words contained in this *Isaiah* passage, the sum total is 5,449, which, as we just stated, constitutes the distance from The Pyramid's base to its summit. Moreover, in light of our present search for a 5,500 year timeline, this numerical value of 5,449 pyramid inches bears a striking similarity to that time frame, even more so than Rutherford's dating of 5,407 years from Adam to Christ.

Still, one might legitimately ask: What evidence is there that this number depicting The Pyramid's height has anything to do with the *five and a half* "day" timeline that you are talking about? As usual, the best way I know to answer such a question is not to simply look for a one-dimensional response. By that I mean I will attempt to provide an answer that, in accordance to the pattern of both the Scriptures and The Pyramid, is so sufficiently redundant that there could be no other way of looking at it.

To begin with, in attempting to demonstrate that The Pyramid's height represents a timeline distinctly messianic in nature, one should take notice of three important facts. First, not only is The Great Pyramid 5,449 pyramid inches tall, but it is also built up of 203 courses of masonry, a fact that will come into play a little later in our discussion. Second, this exterior measurement of 5,449 pyramid inches does not simply occur once, but it can be found there a second time. And third, the numerical figure of 5,449 can also be located as a measurement within the interior passages of The Pyramid. Together, this tripartite repetition substantially reinforces this number's importance and thus its potential for supporting our claim that The Pyramid's height unmistakably represents a timeline with messianic implications.

Our initial clue that this dimension of 5,449 represents a prophetic—and therefore messianic—chronology comes to us by way of its association with the previously mentioned "Great Pyramid Text of Scripture." Not only is there a correspondence between the numerical value of the *Isaiah* verses and the height of The Pyramid, say pyramidologists, but the total length of the downward passageway also produces a similar measurement of 5,449 pyramid inches. And, mind you, this downward passageway includes the universally acknowledged starting point of the entire timeline of prophetic dates, which are all subsequently revealed in every other point within The Pyramid. In other words, no proponent of The Pyramid's prophetic chronology would dismiss, for an instant, the correctness in seeing this downward passageway as portraying a time-oriented numerical value—one that corresponds precisely with the same number that represents its height.

The next clue concerning the importance of the number 5,449 comes to us when we return our attention to those peculiar "air shafts," which run diagonally from both the King's and Queen's Chambers up to, and toward, the structure's exterior, respectively. Ever since investigators first turned their attention to them, there has been no end to the speculation over their true purpose. Some point to the more mundane assumption that they were designed to provide a perfectly regulated atmosphere for future generations who would require an adequate air supply while investigating its interior. Others—who point to the fact that the shafts from the Queen's Chamber stop short at both ends—lean toward an esoteric interpretation, insisting that their role has more to do with spiritual or astronomical concerns.

Yet whichever direction one leans, a mathematical significance does leap out when one takes the time to look. In his book *The Great Pyramid Decoded*, Peter Lemesurier points to a series of unique dimensional facts, that is, four specific measurements, which are all supremely pertinent to our present inquiry. Two of these measurements we have just discussed, which is, the height of The Great Pyramid is 5,449 pyramid inches, and the total floor-line length of the lower passageway also equals 5,449 pyramid inches. The other two measurements to which Lemesurier refers have only been alluded to so far.

The first measurement involves the combined heights where the shafts leading from the Queen's Chamber would, if extended, penetrate The Pyramid's exterior, which together equal 5,449 pyramid inches. In other words, the shaft leading toward the north face of The Pyramid intersects the exterior at a vertical height of 2,724.5 pyramid inches, while the shaft leading toward the south face does so at the same height, which when added up comes to 5,449 pyramid inches. The other measurement involves the two shafts leading from the King's Chamber, both of which actually do penetrate The Pyramid's exterior, at the 101st and 102nd level of masonry, north and south faces respectively, which when taken together add up to 203 courses. This figure, as you may recall, just happens to equal the height of The Pyramid in terms of its total courses of masonry. As for the significance of such apparent coincidences, Lemesurier said:

> Taking these four measurements together, it becomes clear that The Pyramid's architect wished to emphasize that this number, which represents its height, was of some overriding importance, and that he, therefore, deliberately included the above four references to it in his design.[430]

Again, considering the numerically-oriented information in The Pyramid, what else could the designer have intended by this conspicuous repetition if not to emphasize that, just as the downward passageway represents a messianic timeline, the height of The Pyramid also represents a chronology of similar significance? In this case, it bears an uncanny relationship to the five thousand, five hundred year prophecy that we have encountered throughout the apocryphal record and early church history. Together with Justin Martyr's second-century reference to *Nicodemus*—a.k.a. *The Acts of Pontius Pilate*—we have yet another way to undermine claims that such texts date to no earlier than the seventh century of the Christian Era. And if this is so, then we are on even firmer ground that this very influential work is based on much earlier texts that really have been lost to history. The reason for this is because just as the reoccurring dimensions in The Pyramid reinforce an awareness of its divinely-inspired message, it seems equally certain that the recurrence of this number *five and a half* in the texts of *Adam and Eve*, *Secrets of Enoch*, and *Nicodemus* should also be understood in the context of this same conspicuous repetition—a "pattern with a purpose," as it were. In other words, just as The Pyramid calls attention to itself through its repeated use of the number *five and a half*—in its height, together with the dimensions of the Open Coffer in the King's Chamber, which in turn corresponds to the *five and a half* sacred cubits of The Ark of the Covenant—it should be just as obvious that the apocryphal texts have been inspired by the same author and with the same purpose of conveying the most central messianic timeline in biblical history.

Finally, there is still one more interesting way at discovering the number *five and a half* in the height of The Great Pyramid, which comes via a revealing web-based article dedicated to the numerical value known as *phi*, or the number 1.618—not to be confused with *pi*—sometimes called the "golden number," the "golden ratio," or the "divine proportion." According to the site's author, Gary Meisner:

> This "golden ratio" is unique in its mathematical properties and pervasive in its appearance throughout nature... Most everyone learned about *pi* in school, but few curriculums included *phi*, perhaps for the very reason that grasping all its manifestations often takes one beyond the academic realm of the spiritual just by the simple fact that *phi* unveils an unusually frequent constant of design that applies to so many aspects of life...
>
> The positions and proportions of the key elements of many, if not most, animals are based on *phi*. Examples include the body and wing sections of insects, the spiral of sea shells, and the position of the dorsal fins on porpoises. Even the spirals of human DNA embody *phi* proportions... More intriguing yet

> is the extensive appearance of *phi* throughout the human form, in the face, body, fingers, teeth, and the impact that this has on our perceptions of human beauty… It seems that *phi* is hard-wired into our consciousness as a guide to beauty…
>
> With all the unique mathematical properties of *phi*, and its appearance throughout creation, it is little wonder that mankind would not only take notice of this number and the "golden ratio" that it creates but also use it to capture the beauty and harmony of nature in our own creations in art, architecture, and other areas of design. In some cases, mankind's application of *phi* is undeniable. In other cases, it is still the subject of debate. The Great Pyramid of Giza appears to embody the "golden ratio" in the dimensions of its base, height, and hypotenuse, but its state of ruin and the absence of any mention of *phi* in ancient Egyptian writings make it difficult to prove conclusively that this was by design…
>
> The description of this "golden ratio" as the "divine proportion" is perhaps fitting because it is seen by many as a door to a deeper understanding of beauty and spirituality, unveiling a hidden harmony, or connectedness, in so much of what we see. That's an incredible role for a single number to play, but then again this one number has played an incredible role in human history and in the foundations of life itself. The line between its mathematical and mystical aspects is thus not easily drawn. *Phi* does not appear explicitly in *The Bible*, yet we find that the dimensions given by God to Noah for the Ark, and to Moses for The Ark of the Covenant, both reflect a 5 to 3 proportion.[431]

It just so happens that this five-to-three ratio built into Noah's Ark, The Ark of the Covenant, and The Great Pyramid produces a numerical value of 1.666, while *phi* equals 1.618, a difference of just .048. Furthermore, having established a clear connection between these three divinely-inspired objects and the universal constant of *phi*, Meisner added the next point so pertinent to our investigation:

> In addition to the relationships of The Pyramid's geometry to *phi* and *pi*, it is also possible that The Pyramid was constructed using a completely different approach that simply produced the *phi* (and *pi*) relationships… Another possibility is that The Great Pyramid is based on another method, known as the *seked*. The *seked* is a measure of slope, or gradient. It is based on the Egyptian system of measure in which one cubit equals seven "palms," and one "palm" equals four "digits." The theory is that The Great Pyramid is based on the application of a gradient of *five and a half sekeds*… The slope of a pyramid created with *sekeds* would be 51.84 degrees, while that of a pyramid based on *phi* is 51.83 degrees.[432]

It is important here to understand that according to most pyramidologists the gradient angle of The Pyramid has been found to be 51.51 degrees. So depending on your opinion of what was motivating The Pyramid's architect in deciding on its angle of construction—whether it was *pi*, *phi*, the *seked*, or some other as-yet-unknown factor—the difference between these three numbers is far too slim to have been the result of mere coincidence, and in the end, one is left to ponder the same thing that Meisner has: "The question remains, though, as to why *five and a half* would be chosen over some other number for the gradient. What was more appealing about *five and a half* rather than simply using a gradient based on five or six?"[433]

Certainly by now, anyone who is aware of the *Septuagint* chronology, the apocryphal record, and the testimony of the Church Fathers, will instantly see the irony in such an apparently innocuous question as that posed by Meisner. To anyone following our present inquiry, however, the answer might seem purely academic, especially in light of one simple but unmistakable fact. Not only is the number *five and a half* found in the angle of The Great Pyramid, but this angle also creates a pyramidal structure which itself attains a height bearing the same numerical value of *five and a half.*

Through a Glass Darkly

AT THIS POINT IN demonstrating the various ways that the number *five and a half* is incorporated in the dimensions of The Pyramid, I would like to take some time to deal with one of the more difficult aspects concerning its design features. The difficulty I am referring to involves certain discrepancies that have arisen in the process of measuring the exterior of this admittedly enigmatic megalith. Specifically, I wish to focus on one of the previous points made by Meisner concerning The Pyramid's possible incorporation of *phi* and the *seked*. "The Great Pyramid of Giza," he said, "appears to embody the 'golden ratio' in the dimensions of its base, height, and hypotenuse, but its state of ruin ... makes it difficult to prove conclusively that this was by design."

Due to the great antiquity of this grand edifice—the only extant structure among history's renowned Seven Wonders of the World—it is unfortunate that ever since it was stripped of its protective outer casing of polished limestone The Pyramid has had to endure what any other man-made building is subject to as a result of centuries of erosion and subsidence. In short, any exterior measurements that have been made of the structure, which reveal the dimensional relationships built into it, are inevitably impaired to a certain degree because the stones wear away and settle. As a result of such structural changes, one is forced to incorporate these discrepancies into a modified view of what the actual dimensions might have been when the original builders finished their completed work. This inevitably leads one to a philosophical crossroad in determining the meaning of such dimensional implications, particularly when it comes to such numerical values as *pi*, *phi,* and the *seked*, which certainly do seem to be built into The Pyramid's dimensions.

I, too, am often challenged by all the various modes of pyramidal interpretations. However, I have also come to the conclusion that just because one is repeatedly confronted by conflicting data, one must never succumb to the temptation to dismiss the whole affair into the realm of myth and legend. After all, we do not throw *The Bible* out the window simply because we encounter vagaries and ambiguities when trying to penetrate its mysteries. So why would we dismiss the findings of generations of pyramidologists simply because, like its counterpart in written form, there were discrepancies to be found amongst their ranks? No, when one becomes inundated with conflicting interpretations that both scholars and laypersons offer in their defense, our proper response should be one that is similar to that famous band of blind men who are all individually interacting with the proverbial elephant. In other words, we must simply accept the fact that we, as finite human beings, can never know the totality of truth, whether in scriptural or megalithic form, and being fully aware of this, we must never cave in to the inevitable frustration that arises when one attempts to ascertain the unsearchable riches of divine revelation. As has been observed by many an astute theologian, "It is as blasphemous to define God as it is to deny Him."

Still, you may be asking yourself: What is the point of all the preceding back and forth points of your discussion? First, you assembled your four dimensional facts, each corroborating the idea that the height of The Great Pyramid not only represents a 5,449 year timeline of messianic events, but that this numerical value also bears a striking resemblance to the timeline of The Great Five and a Half Days from Adam to Christ. Next, you introduced evidence that demonstrated The Pyramid's apparent incorporation of the "golden ratio," a geometric dimension that is alluded to in the construction of both Noah's Ark and Moses' Ark of the Covenant. And finally, on top of all that, you showed how a unique method of construction gave The Great Pyramid a gradient angle that demonstrated a geometric design of *five and a half sekeds*. What more do you need, you may be wondering? Why all the fuss about structural changes that have interfered with mankind's ability to measure the exterior of The Pyramid with absolute accuracy?

I mention all this because, while in the process of trying to connect the prophetic implications of Enoch's Pillar with those of apocryphal literature, I came across a different measurement for The Pyramid's height to which other pyramidologists have referred. What is more, this different measurement, which they claimed to represent its height, came even closer than the previous one. It was at that point that I came to a crossroad. Originally, I had been fairly satisfied with the fact that most pyramidologists held the view that The Pyramid's height was 5,449 pyramid inches, a figure quite close to that of 5,500. But notice how I said that I was "fairly satisfied." That is, I was until I, quite unexpectedly, came across this other measurement that came even closer. What was I to do, then, with all the data that had been previously gathered concerning the 5,449? Should I simply "sweep it under the rug" in favor of this new figure? How might I explain such an about-face?

But, alas, before I do anything rash, let me remind you—and in doing so, me as well—that one thing should never be forgotten while in the throes of pursuing the answers to such mind-boggling mysteries. When one considers the many obstacles involved in interpreting the prophetic timelines in Scripture, our greatest hurdle is that we all suffer from the irrevocable condition of "being human." Still, though this humanness means that we have been disconnected from the divine presence, God has deigned to rescue us from this fallen state. But in order to make good on this rescue effort—and this is the crux of my reminder—God has apparently chosen to invoke a process in which we humans are only gradually, and by varying degrees, rescued from the spiritual slavery we inherited from our first parents. In other words, we humans are to be rescued only in due time, and only through an incremental process of receiving God's word that involves many centuries, many generations, many encounters.

With this harsh reality in mind, then, one must always remember that when we humans receive this prophetic knowledge, only God understands entirely what that entails, while we, as mere participants in this process, are always "looking through a glass, darkly."[434] As a result, we can never fully ascertain the big picture from the divine perspective, any more than an insect can understand what has happened to it, when out of the kindness of some human heart it has been rescued from some impending calamity, and instead of being squashed, it is rescued, relocated, and released, unharmed.

Again, you may be wondering: What has all this got to do with the "price of tea in China?" And again, I will reiterate. What have we been doing this whole chapter? We have been tracking the nature of prophetic timelines, both in Scripture and stone. In the process, we encountered the inevitable difficulties inherent in such a daunting task, embarked upon by humans who can only hope for a glimpse into the vastness of God's control over history. Furthermore, we have attempted to outline, to the best of our ability, the history of how we humans have collectively come to understand these prophetic timelines—whether in *The Bible* or The Pyramid—and how we can cooperate in this divinely-inspired rescue effort. That is to say, we have sought to ascertain the "times and seasons" of the Lord's intention to make good on His promise to Adam, according to a plan of salvation that can be anticipated. In line with this revelatory expectation is that the Scriptures depict the creation of Adam on the sixth day, which then led students of prophecy to expect the coming of Messiah to occur in the sixth "day" of God's prophetic history.

As a result, one of the earliest Church Fathers—Ephrem the Syrian—even went so far as to chronicle the history of God's people according to a five thousand, five hundred year timeline from Adam to Christ. Then, having established a correspondence between The Great Five and a Half Day prophecy and the writings of the Church Fathers, we sought to connect this timeline to such texts as *Adam and Eve*, *Secrets of Enoch*, and *Nicodemus*, as well as the megalith that bears Enoch's authorship. Through various pyramidologists, such as Rutherford and Lemesurier, we discovered a dimensional connection with The Great Five and a Half Days of apocryphal literature with the various prophetic timelines in The Pyramid, that is to say, among others, its height of 5,449 pyramid inches, a figure not exactly that of 5,500 but one that was very close.

It was then that I was forced to confront one last hurdle in the process of hunting for a more precise connection of the numerical figure that we have been seeking, because, in fact, other pyramidologists—most notably, Rodolfo Benavides—have published their own findings about their approach to measuring The Pyramid's exterior. To my surprise, I found that they were claiming the height of The Great Pyramid was slightly higher than that which was previously believed. What is more, the findings of these pyramidologists were even more telling in view of the search established in this book. Instead of finding the present-day height of The Pyramid to be 5,449 inches, they have found it to be 5,496 pyramid inches, just *four* inches short of 5,500.[435] It was this unexpected discovery that then led me down the most recent leg of our journey, where we took the time to ponder mankind's convoluted attempts to measure The Pyramid, considering that—more than any other feature—its exterior was so vulnerable to change caused by weather and subsistence.

The main reason for my withholding this latest discovery of the height of The Pyramid at 5,496 inches, as opposed to that of 5,449, was because, like most people who grapple with its mysteries, I became so overwhelmed with conflicting data that I simply did not know which "peg to hang my hat on," so to speak. The most obvious problem in discussing any given dimension of The Pyramid naturally arises from the fact that unless one possesses the ways and means to personally go to Egypt to measure the structure, one is forever left to accept the findings of others who have accomplished such a Herculean feat. To date, history records only a handful of individuals who have done so; among them are C. Piazzi Smyth, Flinders Petrie, David Davidson, and Adam Rutherford. Consequently, the only choice that one is left with is to work with the measurements that have been handed down to posterity, and for better or for worse, it is this database of numerical values that has been analyzed, speculated upon, and thus debated over ever since.

So, even if one is inclined to accept the possibility that The Pyramid's builders incorporated *pi*, *phi*, or the *seked* into its construction, or that the lengths and angles of the interior passageways reveal a timeline of messianic events, all this potential "meaning" must still be seen in the "context" with which all forms of communication are understood. In other words, any meaning derived from such mathematical modes of communication should never be considered the final word on the subject. Make no mistake, however, this does not happen only with mathematical meaning; the same thing occurs with linguistic messages—whether they are delivered in oral or written form. As such, no message can ever be "proven" to mean just one thing and one thing alone. In this, it is just as we cited earlier in this chapter: Truth is always multilayered in content. That is to say, truth has both a surface meaning, which is obvious to most people, and a deeper meaning, which is only understood by a few. Thus, the hard, cold facts of any form of communication is that *numbers*, just like *words*, contain, by their very nature, more than a single potential meaning. As a result, the content of any given message—in this case, a mathematical one—will always convey different meanings to different people, depending on the perceived context with which that message is received.

Signposts

I WOULD NOW LIKE TO propose a formula that might help to interpret all the conflicting data when analyzing the dimensions of The Great Pyramid. However, before I do, I would like to review some of the numbers that have been introduced so far. In no particular order, then, pyramidologists insist on the following: That the height and base of The Great Pyramid of Giza reveal, to a striking degree, the same relationship with which any given circle has to its diameter and circumference. In this way, the builders, they say, purposefully intended to convey that they possessed an awareness of such mathematical values as *pi*, *phi*, and/or the *seked*. But in order to do this—and herein lies the rub—these pyramidologists employ several different heights of The Pyramid, which they each propose to be the correct one.

First, they point out that, because The Pyramid does not have a capstone at its peak, they have decided to utilize a measurement to that point, which is 5,449 pyramid inches high.

However, other pyramidologists insist that the more accurate measurement to said point is 5,496 pyramid inches. Next, in the interest of both fairness and thoroughness, one must take into consideration that there are at least two other accepted heights of The Pyramid that one must consider. Why? This is because, without a capstone, there is yet another dimension of The Great Pyramid that has to be included, which has been coined its "actual height," a numerical value that requires projecting a line along the same angle of The Pyramid to an imaginary point where all four "lines" eventually converge. This, they say, produces an "apex point," which provides us with the so-called "actual height" of The Great Pyramid.

Why is all the foregoing information important? As it turns out, what most people do not understand is that many of the dimensional relationships that pyramidologists find so compelling are actually produced by using this projected height and not the present-day height of The Pyramid without the capstone in place. Therefore, in order to ascertain the value of *pi*, *phi*, or the *seked* within the dimensions of The Great Pyramid, one is generally doing so by way of a numerical value that represents this "actual height," which, by virtue of the logistical difficulties in acquiring this measurement, is such that it changes from investigator to investigator. Accordingly, such esteemed pyramidologists as Adam Rutherford have deemed that this "actual height" of The Pyramid is 5,831 pyramid inches, while others, like Meisner, believe it to be 5,767 pyramid inches. If this is the case, then how can we be sure of anything when it comes to discerning the true meaning of any of these so-called "dimensional" relationships? If no one can even agree on these foundational figures, then certainly no meaning can be ascertained at all, right? To which I would respond, as I so often do: You think? This, then, leads me to introducing the aforementioned formula for interpreting such conflicting bits of data.

For just a moment, imagine that you are going on a journey, and on this journey, you have a roadmap. Then, let us say, your starting point is Los Angeles, California, and this journey you are about to embark upon is going to take you, for the very first time, to a place called Las Vegas, Nevada. In addition to having this roadmap, you have also received advice from some of your friends who have already made the same trip. So together with your map and some advice, you now are going to try and figure out exactly how long it will take you to make this journey to Las Vegas while traveling there in your car. This way you can decide when you should leave so that you will be able to arrive and check into your hotel at just the right time. What would you expect the map to tell you in the process of determining a path to your given location? How much of the advice that you received from your friends would you consider in order to get there as fast as possible? And how might you incorporate all this information into your attempt to find this magical City of Lights located somewhere in the middle of a vast landscape called the Nevada desert?

Naturally, the first thing you would do is give the map a good looking over. Using it, you would see exactly which roads to take that would get you from Los Angeles to Las Vegas. You might even highlight what you considered the best route, and maybe even toss in a nice sightseeing spot along the way. Then, armed with this planned route, together with a careful consideration of the advice you had received from friends, you would come up with an approximate time of arrival. So, to the best of your ability, you might make an educated guess: Based on the route you had chosen, which includes a one hour stop for brunch, and, assuming that you will be traveling an average of, say, seventy miles an hour on the highway, you should arrive in Las Vegas in about five and a half hours. Accordingly, since you have been told that check-in time for your hotel is one o'clock in the afternoon, you decide to leave Los Angeles at precisely seven-thirty in the morning.

Therefore, assuming that you should be arriving to your destination some five and a half hours after your departure, you proceed with your journey as planned. But lo and behold, after taking all the planned roads, finishing your one hour brunch right on time, and moving to the final leg of your journey at exactly your predicted speed, you find that you did not arrive to your destination point after five and a half hours. In fact, you pulled into town after just five and one quarter hours. So what did you do? Well naturally, you kept right on driving because, based on everything you had understood to be true, you deduced that you must not "be there" yet. The map ... your friends' advice ... your average speed of travel ... together, all of it precisely predicted the location of this golden city in the desert, so *ipso facto*, this could not possibly be the place you were looking for. Well, would not that be your reaction, too? No? Of course not, because any dumb fool would be able tell they were in the City of Lights when they have arrived, even if it was only a quarter to one in the afternoon. It does not require a Ph.D. in geography to figure out something so self-evident.

Why, then, would anyone expect the timelines in The Great Pyramid to be any less ambiguous than the roadmap in the previous illustration? And why would anyone expect that the interpretations applied to these timelines to be any less idiosyncratic then our friends' advice? After all, the numerical values in The Pyramid are just like the milestones on a roadmap. The designated role of a milestone is to indicate to travelers on a highway how far along they are in their journey. They are signposts to let you know that you are still on the right path. However, they are not always perfectly measured out from point to point; yet they do still perform their specified purpose. The same thing holds true for the numerical values found in The Great Pyramid.

Now, just in case anyone thinks that I am being footloose and fancy-free with my methodology for coping with the discrepancies arising from a study of The Pyramid, I would like to point out that a similar method of interpretation is already being employed in the sacrosanct realm of *Bible* prophecy. Let me take a moment to explain, and in doing so, we will finally come to a swift and merciful end in this our own eventful journey.

By Design

IN A PREVIOUS CHAPTER of this book, we brought up the subject of the Seventy Weeks of Daniel, which happens to be one of the most famous prophetic timelines in all of Scripture. But just because so many biblical scholars point to it as a roadmap from which to interpret historical events does not mean that the passages comprising this timeline are not themselves fraught with ambiguities and discrepancies. Unfortunately—or fortunately, depending on your attention span—we will not be able to go into detail regarding the well-documented intricacies contained in the book attributed to the prophet Daniel. Suffice it to say, however, because this portion of Scripture contains such an important timeline in terms of God's overall plan, it does merit whatever time we can devote to it. Said John F. Walvoord, long-time president of Dallas Theological Seminary:

> Although other major prophets received detailed information concerning the nations and God's program for salvation, Daniel alone was given the comprehensive program for both the Gentiles ... and Israel, as recorded in *Daniel* 9:24-27. Because of the comprehensive and structural nature of Daniel's prophecies for both the Gentiles and Israel, the study of *Daniel*, and especially this chapter, is the key to understanding the prophetic Scriptures.[436]

Yet for all its importance in regard to understanding the prophetic meaning of *The Bible*, the prophecies in *The Book of Daniel* are probably the most difficult passages for theologians to interpret. In fact, the only other book in Scripture more difficult to interpret is *The Book of Revelation*, which is why *Daniel* is so often referred to as its *Old Testament* counterpart. Yet for all of its ambiguities and discrepancies, this vital book has never been excised from the Canon. Part of the problem that occurs in dealing with the prophecies in *Daniel*, particularly as it is found in the ninth chapter, is that—apart from its extended usage of mystical symbolism—it incorporates two chronological factors that are clearly as difficult to decipher as any of those contained in The Great Pyramid.

First, *The Book of Daniel* tells us, "seventy weeks of years have been determined upon the people of Israel and its capital, Jerusalem."[437] This, say theologians, speaks of a unique timeline of historical events depicting God's intervention in the lives of His people, but unfortunately, these same theologians have never been able to come to any consensus as to the exact meaning and time span of these so-called seventy "weeks," because the word which we translate into English as "weeks" is actually a Hebrew word that simply means *sevens*, which does not necessarily specify seven years. Nevertheless, such an interpretation does seem to be inferred, especially when seen in the context of the usage of the prophet Jeremiah—whom Daniel had been studying and from whom he was receiving his initial inspiration in this matter—when the aforementioned prophet spoke of seventy years of bondage that the southern kingdom of Judah was to endure. Second, this timeline of human events, which is said to encompass an initial phase of sixty-nine "weeks" of years, is said to begin with "the announcement to restore and rebuild Jerusalem," and that its duration will last "until Messiah, the Prince, will be cut off but not for Himself."[438] That is to say, according to most theologians, there will be a period comprised of sixty-nine years multiplied by seven, or four hundred and eighty-three years, from the commandment to rebuild Jerusalem until such time as Christ was to be crucified on Calvary. There is just one problem with tracking this timeline—quite separate from any disagreement over the nature of these "weeks" of years—and that has to do with the discrepancies over the actual date of this announcement to restore and rebuild Jerusalem. According to biblical historians, there are no less than four separate decrees to rebuild that are recorded in Scripture, all of which are said to be potential qualifiers for such a designation.

Just imagine, then, the frustration of anyone living in the time of Christ who was trying to determine the "set time" of the appearance of their long-awaited Messiah, what with so much confusion over Daniel's meaning of the phrase seventy "sevens," and what supposedly qualified as "the announcement to restore and rebuild." In many ways, these semantical and chronological quandaries are exactly the same kinds of stumbling blocks that have plagued advocates of Pyramidology ever since its inception. But just like our traveler making that hypothetical journey to the City of Lights, anyone who had personally come face to face with the Light of the World would have had no trouble realizing that the day of His arrival had come, despite all the inherent ambiguities in the signposts they encountered in the prophecies of *Daniel*.

So why, you may ask, does God even bother inspiring prophets to foretell the coming of messianic events if they are so difficult to interpret? Certainly, if God is all-knowing, then He must realize that the prophecies contained in Scripture are laden with more twists and turns than an Agatha Christie mystery. Why does He even bother? Fortunately, for our sakes, the answer to such an obvious question is nowhere near as baffling as those that pertain to the specific mysteries buried in either the Scriptures or The Pyramid. In a nutshell: The reason that God's prophetic word is fraught with an apparently impenetrable web of ambiguity is because it was done this way precisely by design. Can I say this again for those who think I might have misspoken? I repeat: *The Bible* is a constant source of mystery—just like its counterpart, The Great Pyramid—because that is exactly the way God wants it. In this, it is just as Jesus described when His disciples asked Him why He spent so much time teaching in parables. He told them:

> The secret of the Kingdom of God has been given to you, but to those on the outside, everything is said in parables so that: "They may see but never perceive, and hear but never understand; otherwise they might turn and be forgiven."[439]

Simply put, prophecy, in any form, has never been intended by God as a tool to predict the future *per se*. In fact, the God of *The Bible* summarily condemns prognostication in general. The failure in every case, in misunderstanding the prophetic future depicted in the various scriptural and megalithic chronologies, always rests squarely on the shoulders of those who attempt to predict the future for the sake of their own human purposes, however well-intentioned those purposes may seem. Just as in the case of biblical prophecy, where one is forced to examine historical events as a touchstone to confirm the veracity of prophetic utterances, it should be remembered that the so-called "predicted" events portrayed in The Pyramid must also conform to this same methodology. In other words, the prediction of future events must always be evaluated, and re-evaluated, in light of the actual facts of history. Therefore, one must always resist the urge to predict the future in order to satisfy proof seekers and be satisfied to let history "fill in the blanks," so to speak, just as historians have always had to do when analyzing biblical prophecies.

All this, then, should be remembered when attempting to apprehend the prophetic wisdom that has been so marvelously encrypted in *The Bible* and The Pyramid, because in failing to do so, one might find themselves as thoroughly frustrated as that long list of fortune hunters who are forever vexed by the impossible intricacies that shut them out. But to those who are willing to enter in as little children, they have God's assurance that they will see and perceive, and hear and understand all the wondrous grandeur that has been held in store just for them.

This principle is never more evident than with mankind's understanding of the prophecy of The Great Five and a Half Days—in terms of Scripture and stone alike. Whereas this extended time frame made it virtually impossible to anticipate its fulfillment to generations prior to the Advent of Christ, hindsight nevertheless made it possible to recognize this historical fact once it occurred. And in verifying the Lord's faithfulness to His word as it pertains to the Incarnation, mankind can then rest assured that all the promises of God can be counted on as well. In this way, one can better see the ultimate flaw in Archbishop Ussher's chronology of just four thousand years from Adam to Christ, in that it does nothing to confirm the faithfulness of the Lord, because never once in the biblical record, either canonical or apocryphal, has it ever been recorded that God promised to rescue mankind after four "days." But *if*—and this is the crux of this entire work—*if* it can be shown that Christ strode upon the stage of world history after *five and a half* "days," then it clearly demonstrates the supreme faithfulness of God to an onlooking world.

After all, who really cares if The Pyramid predicts the Exodus of Israel, or the invention of the printing press, or the age of Reformation? What purpose, if any, could there be in that? That is to say, what does it profit anyone in the present age? The only purpose, it seems to me, is to verify a chain of events that are all themselves mere echoes of a much larger event. By themselves, the events that the great explorers and philosophers claim that The Pyramid's prophetic chronology depict appear somewhat meaningful, I grant you. Yet in isolation they utterly pale in comparison to the greater scheme of things. As individual ticks on the clock of history, they represent interesting sidebars in the pantheon of human achievements, but seen in the context of that long-awaited moment, when that clock would finally chime the completion of those *five and a half* "days," the events depicted by way of The Pyramid's interior and exterior dimensions prove to be quite significant after all. Then, and only then, does their fulfillment, as echoes of prophetic truth, find true meaning and purpose; and in doing so, God's hidden hand in history is ultimately revealed for all to see, and thus confirmed once and for all time.

Of Talismans and Timelines

This Extended Puzzle

NOW FOR THE FINAL scene of this *magnum opus*. All along, the purpose of this work has been clearly stated—to find the hidden connection between five *sacred* things that would, in turn, reveal a startling proof of God's control and faithfulness. In order to do this, it was essential to first build a secure foundation, one that has been provided by way of a thorough investigation into some of the most neglected chapters of biblical history. Hopefully, the building of this foundation was accomplished in the retelling of the *Tales* of Enoch, Adam, Abraham, and Jesus, along with their various supporting players, including the likes of Satan, Nimrod, and Pilate. But considering the tremendous amount of resistance to such an untraditional rendition of said persons, we also took the time and effort in an admittedly lengthy process that examined the historical and scriptural validity of these freshly resurrected chapters.

In our opening analyses, we examined the ways in which these *Tales of Forever* might be seen in an entirely new light—tales which until now had been unjustly marginalized due to the stigma of their having been labeled "apocryphal." In the process of validating these stories, we saw the extent to which they can be harmonized with the canonical books of *The Bible*. It was during this process that we introduced such topics as the prophecy of The Great Five and a Half Days, which we discovered would provide a central thread from which this present narrative would be woven. Next, we encountered the mysterious sheepskin garments, given by God as coverings to Adam and Eve after they had been expelled from the Garden of Eden.

As it turns out, Adam's garment would also play a pivotal role throughout *The Tales*, affecting the life not only of that first man but of Abraham, Nimrod, Jacob, and Esau as well. Naturally, though, because of the all-too-familiar vein of modern skepticism that hinders the acceptance of such phenomenon, we took the time to compare the unusual properties of that garment with other talismans with which tradition is more familiar. These included Veronica's painting and Jesus' seamless robe—well-known sources of power in their own right—which would play an integral role in the trial of Pontius Pilate. Seen as a whole, then, the fantastic legends surrounding Adam's garment, Veronica's painting, and Jesus' seamless robe no longer appeared as far-fetched as they might have otherwise appeared at first.

Finally, in our closing analyses, we sought to confirm the validity of the timeline of The Great Five and a Half Day prophecy outside the realm of apocryphal literature by turning to the most famous of all megalithic monuments, The Great Pyramid of Giza. There, while investigating the way that this *five and a half* "day" timeline is depicted in the dimensions of The Pyramid, we uncovered a great many facts that most history books have neglected to report. It was then that we saw how The Pyramid's prophetic chronology is uniquely mirrored in the chronology of *The Septuagint Bible*, which, as we discovered, actually provided the basis for the early Church's view of a five thousand, five hundred year period from Adam to Christ. Moreover, we saw how widely held this view was by reviewing the much-neglected testimony of many of the most influential early Church Fathers and historians—men like Hippolytus of Rome, Ephrem the Syrian, and Julius Africanus.

Thus, having satisfied ourselves with locating a firm historical foundation for this five thousand, five hundred year prophetic timeline, we continued to hone in on the various ways that this numerical value of *five and a half* was built into the geometric design of The Great Pyramid. It was then that we were confronted with a series of uncanny numerical nuances that seemed to offer the very evidence that we were seeking. The first thing one was struck by was the way in which the dimensions of The Pyramid's Open Coffer in the King's Chamber bore a striking similarity to those of The Ark of Covenant, which as it so happens was built—according to God's instructions to Moses—using the dimensions of *five and a half sacred* cubits. Subsequent to discovering this dimensional relationship, pyramidologists have ever since interpreted this to mean that the Open Coffer, like The Ark itself, is a type of the Incarnation of Christ. Another way this number *five and a half* was located in the dimensions of The Pyramid came in the wake of researchers having determined, through various ways and means, its height to be—within a mere four inches—5,500 pyramid inches. And finally, this same numerical value was found to be incorporated in the geometry of The Great Pyramid while examining one of the potential design methods used in its construction. Known as the *seked* method, this particular choice of The Pyramid's builders just happened to require the incorporation of the numerical value of *five and a half sekeds*—not five, not six, but *five and a half*, and as it turns out, using this angle of *five and a half sekeds* produces a pyramidal structure with the same height as the one sitting on the plateau of Giza.

Therefore, in light of this string of uncanny similarities—that is, between the repeated occurrence of this number *five and a half*, in *The Septuagint Bible*, The Great Pyramid, and The Ark of the Covenant, and its obvious relation to that nearly forgotten promise of "days"—one can no longer entertain the possibility that it could all be a product of sheer coincidence. Rather, seen together as a continuum, these occurrences must be understood as one more clue in demonstrating the extent to which the God of *The Bible* is truly the Lord of Time. In this case, what we have is the God of Set Times, Who revealed there would be an "appointed time." That is to say, there was a specific time period, which began when the Word of God told Adam that He would rescue him and his descendants, and which ended five thousand, five hundred years later when, "in the fullness of time,"[440] that same Word put on flesh and blood, thereby "confirming all the promises of God"[441] in that single act.

Having thus revealed the hidden link that connects the promise of "days" with *The Septuagint*, The Pyramid, and The Ark, our story of talismans and timelines finally brings us to where we will be revealing the way that the last two *sacred* things on our list connect with the first three. It is time now to weave into our tapestry of prophetic significance The Spear of Destiny and The Shroud of Turin. Let me demonstrate how this can be done.

Another Impossible Possibility

SO FAR, IN OUR FINAL scene, we have narrowed in on several ideas in our attempt to validate the truth found in the present work. In both *The Tales* and their *Analyses*, we have witnessed a peculiar and persistent connectivity in things that have all, until now, been seen as so many random points on the biblical map—the prophecy of The Great Five and a Half Days, *The Septuagint*, The Ark, and The Pyramid, as well as an array of talismans, including Adam's garment, Veronica's painting, and Jesus' seamless robe. No doubt to skeptics such occurrences represent nothing more than poetic nonsense. However, to those who are inclined to believe that *The Bible* is more than poetry, they come together in a way that no mortal mind could possibly conceive. Together, they form a matrix of ineffable wonder. To the eye of faith, what is hidden to most is clearly discernible. Therefore, to those who might appreciate yet another impossible possibility, I offer the following.

At the long-awaited culmination of The Great Five and a Half Days, a man stood at the foot of the cross of Jesus. The name of that man—a Roman centurion standing guard at the crucifixion—is never revealed in canonical Scripture. Legend has it that his name was Longinus. Naturally, the source for this legend just happens to be the apocryphal record—in both *The Gospel of Nicodemus* and *The Letters of Herod and Pilate*. Though unnamed in *The New Testament*, he is said to be the man who, gazing upon the Crucified One, declared, "This Man really was the Son of God."[442]

However, what is recorded in the received text is that the Jewish leaders demanded that Pilate hasten an end to the crucifixion in order to prevent the bodies of Jesus and the two thieves from remaining there into the evening. As the gospel record reveals:

> The soldiers therefore came and broke the legs of the first man who had been crucified with Jesus, and then those of the other. But when they came to Jesus and found that He was already dead, they did not break His legs. Instead, one of

> the soldiers pierced Jesus' side with a spear, producing a sudden flow of blood and water.[443]

At this point *The Bible* inserts an intriguing sidebar, one that John, the gospel writer, included for the sake of posterity, as if the casual observer might otherwise overlook the previous verses.

> The man who saw it has given testimony, and his testimony is true. He knows that he tells the truth, and he testifies so you may also believe. These things happened so that the Scripture would be fulfilled: "Not one of His bones will be broken,"[444] and as it says elsewhere: "They'll look upon Him Whom they have pierced."[445]

The thing to notice so far, in terms of this final piece of our puzzle, is this piercing of the side of Jesus on the cross, at which point both blood and water flowed from the wound. Several important things emerge from this event: First, there was the Roman centurion who, having been ordered to hasten the death of Jesus, found Him already dead, thus eliminating the need to break His legs. Then there came the subsequent piercing of the side of Christ at the hands of this centurion, and the torrent of blood and water from the wound. And finally, in that moment, a battle-hardened centurion, who presumably worshiped only the gods and goddesses of Rome, did a complete about-face, like Pilate before him, and uttered, in an apparent epiphany, that he was gazing upon the true visage of the Son of God.

In many ways, the string of events revolving around this centurion and his spear is identical to all the previous artifacts that we have already encountered: Adam's garment had a similarly profound impact on the lives of everyone who came into contact with them, as did Veronica's painting and Jesus' seamless robe. Moreover, they did so, not because these objects contained any power in and of themselves to affect humanity, but because of the "message" they conveyed to an onlooking world, that is, the "story" they told concerning the death and resurrection of the One they typified. To reiterate the words of Jesus: "No sign will be given except the sign of the prophet Jonah. For as Jonah was in the belly of the whale for three full days, so the Son of Man will be in the heart of the Earth."[446] In other words, what Jesus was saying was that whenever God chooses to reveal Himself, the sign He is performing has the sole purpose of typifying His death and resurrection, of which Jonah in the belly of the whale is the primary example.

Taking this into consideration, two interrelated questions must be asked: If the previously mentioned talismans of Christ exhibited traits of a miraculous, or as-yet-unexplained otherworldly, nature, to what extent is The Spear that spilled the blood of Christ imbued with such power? And if it is, then what is the story behind its miraculous power that could explain this kind of God-inspired effectualness?

The Very Finger of Destiny

CERTAINLY ONE OF the most provocative takes concerning The Spear comes to us by way of a book by Trevor Ravenscroft, entitled *The Spear of Destiny*. According to Ravenscroft, there is ample evidence to confirm that this spear, throughout its history, became associated with miraculous power. Concerning the centurion and his spear, he wrote:

> It was said that, for a moment in time, he had held the destiny of mankind in his hands. The spear, with which he had pierced the side of Christ, became one of the great treasures of Christendom, and a unique legend attached itself to this weapon, gaining strength with the passing of the centuries, that whoever possessed it and understood the powers it served, held the destiny of the world in his hands for good or evil.[447]

For that reason, Longinus' spear came to be known as The Spear of Destiny. Passing from hand to hand, and generation to generation, The Spear was said to have been held in possession by nearly every emperor of Western Europe, all of whom believed that it imparted to them the power they sought to affect world history. Ravenscroft continued:

> Constantine the Great, one of the world's most enigmatic figures, claimed he was guided through providence when holding The Spear of Longinus at the epoch-making battle on the Milvian Bridge outside Rome. This battle settled the rulership of the Roman Empire and lead directly to the proclamation of Christianity as the official religion of Rome... In his old age, when building the new Rome in Constantinople—a bastion which would withstand all assaults for a thousand years—Constantine carried The Spear in front of him when treading out the boundaries of the site of the new city, saying, "I follow in the steps of Him Who I see walking ahead of me."
>
> The Spear had played a conspicuous role through the centuries of the gradual decline of the Roman Empire, both in resisting the invasions from the North and East and in converting the Barbarians to the new Faith and the Roman cause... Men like Theodosius who tamed the Goths with it in 385 A.D., Alaric the Bold, the savage convert to Christianity, who claimed The Spear after he sacked Rome in 410 A.D. ... and the mighty Visigoth, Theodoric, who rallied Gaul with The Spear, and turned back the ferocious Attila the Hun in 452 A.D....
>
> In the eight and ninth centuries, The Spear had continued to be the very pivot of the historical process. For instance, the mystical talisman had become an actual weapon in the hands of the Frankish general Charles Martel, the Hammer, when he led his army to gain a miraculous victory over the massed forces of the Arabs at Poitiers in 732 A.D. Defeat would have meant that the whole of Western Europe would have succumbed to the rule and religion of Islam.
>
> In 800 A.D., Charlemagne, the first Holy Roman emperor, had founded his whole dynasty on the possession of The Spear and its legend of world-historic destiny—a legend which attracted the greatest scholars in all of Europe to serve the civilizing power of the Frankish cause...
>
> Altogether, forty-five emperors have claimed The Spear of Destiny as their possession, between the coronation in Rome of Charlemagne and the fall of the old German Empire, exactly a thousand years later. And what a pageantry of power and majesty it was! The Spear had passed like the very finger of destiny through the millennium, forever creating new patterns of fate which had, again and again, changed the entire history of Europe.[448]

Yet, alas, as much as history has galvanized this notion that whoever possesses The Spear of Destiny will control the fate of humanity, there is another aspect to the legends that seems to suggest there is an ominously dark side attached to it as well. In other words, just as there has been a decidedly upside to possessing The Spear, a menacing downside reveals that not a few of their glory-seeking owners received far more than they bargained for. On no less than four separate occasions throughout its history, The Spear has not only imbued it owners with great power, but it has also brought them a swift and untimely end.

As victorious as he was while maintaining control of The Spear, Theodoric found that one false move could reverse its power. While leading a heroic cavalry charge, the Visigoth king accidentally dropped The Spear, and after falling from his horse, he was trampled to death in the crush of his troop's horses that were following him into battle. And though his allies rose above this tragedy and won the victory, this single battle proved to be the final such military operation that would ever be undertaken by the Western Roman Empire.

Throughout his illustrious life, Charlemagne never let The Spear out of his sight, even going so far as to sleep with it, but one day he accidentally dropped it as he returned from his last victorious campaign. If not so obvious to Charlemagne himself, those closest to him saw it as a terrible omen of things to come, not only for him but for his kingdom as well. Subsequently, the last years of Charlemagne's reign were filled with many difficulties, and in the end the Frankish king would die a disheartened man, bitterly disappointed at all the hopes and dreams he never saw come to fruition.

Frederick Barbarossa, the twelfth-century Holy Roman emperor, is widely regarded as one of the greatest rulers of the Medieval Era, primarily because of his uncanny skills in battlefield tactics and political maneuvering, which made him seem almost superhuman in relation to those around him. What is less known to history, however, is the conspicuous role that The Spear of Destiny played in the illustrious life and ignominious death of Frederick. Having inherited The Spear from previous emperors, like Henry the Fowler and Otto the Great, Barbarossa managed to unite his kingdom by walking a fine line between war and diplomacy.

Sadly, though, all of that ended one fateful day, in 1190, when Frederick, upon instituting the Third Crusade to Jerusalem, met his untimely end. After initial successes in two battles, the German king was proceeding through southern Turkey, where he and his army were in the process of traversing a bridge. Impatient to join his son on the other side, Barbarossa decided to bypass the bridge and cross the stream on horseback. Much to his surprise, the current was stronger than he had anticipated, and hindered by the weight of his armor, he was drowned when his horse collapsed in the undertow. As one historian poignantly noted, "As he was crossing the stream, the Holy Lance fell from his hand at the very moment of his death."[449]

But by far the most famous example of the consequences of losing control of The Spear comes to us in the case of a man who idolized Barbarossa, a man who dreamed of one day wielding his own irresistible power to reunite the splintered realms of the German Empire, just as the legendary king had done before him. That man was Adolf Hitler.

What Sort of Madness?

AS A WAYWARD YOUTH in Vienna, Austria, Adolf Hitler intensely sought a meaningful direction for his life. According to those who knew him at the time, he was a man strangely driven by a determined self-awareness that he was destined for greatness, and that this greatness somehow involved his future role in returning Germany to her former days of glory. Said Ravenscroft: "Many hours were spent every day in the Hof Library studying Nordic and Teutonic mythology and folklore, and reading broadly in German history, literature, and philosophy."[450] As a result of his research, Hitler became convinced that:

> With the passing of time, humanity had entered a kind of canyon of sleep so that former golden ages, in which man had enjoyed a magical relationship with the Universe, had been forgotten, the only evidence of such sublime conditions lying hidden in myths and legends in which nobody any longer believed.[451]

This, for Hitler, was the key that unlocked the mystery of how his beloved Germany had fallen into such a pathetic state of political impotency and spiritual confusion. All that remained was to discover the appropriate antidote for such a hopeless condition.

Then one day while Hitler visited the Hapsburg Treasure House, he believed that he had finally come face to face with the answer he had been seeking and, along with that discovery, the very means with which he would achieve his world-historic destiny. For it was at that time that he first encountered The Spear, there amongst the regalia of the Hapsburg Dynasty. Initially, Hitler had paid little attention to the ancient spearhead as it lay inconspicuously upon a red velvet dais, sitting with the official Hapsburg crown, scepters, and jeweled ornaments. That is, until he overheard a tour guide telling his entourage about the significance of what was in front of them. As Hitler recalled: "And then I heard the words which were to change the rest of my life: 'There is a legend associated with this Spear that whoever claims it, and solves its secrets, holds the destiny of the world in his hands for good or evil.'"[452] Hitler later recounted seeing The Spear for the first time:

> I knew with immediacy that this was an important moment in my life. And yet I could not divine why an outwardly Christian symbol should make such an impression… The Spear appeared to be some sort of magical medium of revelation, for it brought the world of ideas into such close and living perspective that human imagination became more real than the world of sense. I felt as though I myself had held it in my hands before in some earlier century of history—that I myself had once claimed it as my talisman of power and held the destiny of the world in my hands. Yet how could this be? What sort of madness was this that was invading my mind and creating such turmoil in my breast?[453]

Spurred on by this chance encounter, Hitler proceeded to turn his acute powers of inquiry to determining if The Spear in the Hapsburg Treasure House was real or not. After ruling out several other candidates that laid claim to being the true Spear of Longinus, Hitler became convinced that this one, cloistered amidst the imperial regalia of the Hapsburgs, was the genuine article. His next step was to trace its path from past to present. Ravenscroft described his efforts:

> Hitler spent three days in his first tentative researches into the history of The Spear of Longinus. Perhaps he felt a tingling in his spine as he strode across the library to pull out from the shelves the works of the great German philosopher Hegel, for it seemed to him that the men who had claimed The Spear throughout history and fulfilled its legend fitted into Hegel's description of world-historic heroes—"heroes who carry out the will of the world spirit, the very plan of providence..."
>
> Hitler became utterly fascinated with the passage of The Spear throughout the era in which all his childhood heroes had lived. He found to his astonishment and delight that the great German figures who had filled his youthful dreams had held The Spear as the holy aspiration of their ambitions, their talisman of power… men like Otto the Great, who had lived illustrious lives of world-historic significance.[454]

But of all the emperors who had laid claim to The Spear of Destiny, the one that "excited Hitler's imagination most of all was Frederick Barbarossa."[455] Said Ravenscroft:

> Here, indeed, was a German of incomparable greatness! Barbarossa … had the qualities of a monarch Hitler could really admire … chivalry, courage, unlimited energy, great joy in battle, love of adventure, startling initiative, and, above all, a certain harshness, which gave him the ability to both frighten and charm at the same time. Frederick Barbarossa, who fancied he could re-establish the Roman Empire without the Roman legions, had conquered all Italy, proving himself supreme even over the Roman Pontiff himself.[456]

With discoveries such as these, Adolf Hitler had all the assurance he would ever need, and so he began his impassioned quest to take possession of The Spear of Longinus as his very own.

The year 1933 saw Hitler and his National Socialist German Workers Party ascend to power over all of Germany. One of his first acts in his bid for world conquest was to instigate a *coup d'état* in his original homeland of Austria. In 1934, on Hitler's direct orders, S.S. assassins murdered Engelbert Dollfuss, the Austrian president, but much to Hitler's chagrin, the *coup* failed to materialize. Furious, he turned to S.S. Chief Heinrich Himmler for answers.

More than anyone else in the Nazi hierarchy, Heinrich Himmler was attuned to Hitler's otherworldly aspirations, which meant that whenever he was called upon to provide a solution, it surely called for unorthodox methods. Unbeknownst to most observers at the time, the S.S. was not just a military organization that Himmler had created as Hitler's bodyguard; it was also a quasi-religious order, one in which its members were expected to dedicate their lives in absolute submission, much in the same way that the Jesuits had once served the Pope. In this case, however, the leader of this new pseudo-pagan state religion just happened to be Adolf Hitler; and Himmler was his ever-obedient Loyola.

Jumping into action, Himmler, who was also convinced of the occult power of The Spear of Destiny, had an exact replica of it made—in lieu of securing the real one—and set about restoring the seventeenth-century Wewelsburg Castle in the Austrian Alps, specifically meant to enshrine a knowledge and history of The Spear. In what was certainly the world's first "theme park," each room in the castle was decorated in honor of those who had throughout the centuries claimed the hallowed Spear as their own. Naturally, a room for Hitler was built—if he had ever been so inclined to go there—down to the smallest detail, to recreate the by-gone days of his beloved twelfth-century hero, Frederick Barbarossa.

Finally, in 1938, Hitler's dream of world conquest began to bear fruit, when the Nazis rolled, unopposed, into Austria and were greeted with overwhelming enthusiasm by the unsuspecting population. Upon seizing power there, Hitler wasted no time in giving the order to grab the real Spear from the Hapsburg Treasure House, at which point it was transported, along with the rest of the imperial regalia, to Saint Catherine's Church in Nuremberg. Now the proud possessor of The Spear of Longinus, after so many years of yearning for it, Adolf Hitler turned all his efforts into making use of its legendary powers.

After having so easily annexed Austria, while in possession of a mere replica of the famed spear, Adolf Hitler, with the genuine article in hand, ordered his Nazi juggernaut into action. Before long, the ferocious German forces had proceeded to roll through most of Europe with their seemingly unstoppable Lightning War machine. Like tumbling dominoes, country after country fell before Hitler's indomitable troops, commanded by his equally indomitable will to power, and for one brief moment in time, the world held its collective breath, as Hitler seemed poised to make good on the legend of world-historic domination that had fueled the myth of the power of this strange artifact for nearly two thousand years.

Absolute Power

AS HISTORY ELOQUENTLY records, the reign of terror orchestrated by Hitler fortunately did not last nearly as long as the Supreme Leader of the Holy Roman Empire had hoped for. Like all tyrants before him, his days were numbered. But why, exactly, did Hitler fail in his bid for world conquest once he took possession of The Spear? Was the object he stole from the Hapsburg Treasure House a fake, as many historians have suggested? Or, if The Spear really was the one that pierced the side of Christ, what might explain the reversal of fortune that ultimately spoiled Hitler's plan? To answer such enigmas, we again find ourselves revisiting the apocryphal record. Let us look at what we have discovered so far.

Before Hitler so infamously exerted his will upon the stage of world history, there was the equally insatiable Nimrod; and just like Hitler, legend has it that Nimrod's meteoric rise to power was not merely the result of one man's indomitable "will to power." In fact, what has been determined by examining *The Book of Jasher* is that Nimrod was aided and abetted by the mystical power conveyed by Adam's garment, which was given to him by his father, Cush. Through the instrumentality of that legendary garment, Noah had likewise exerted an uncanny influence over the animal kingdom in securing their cooperation in entering the Ark. In this activity, Noah faithfully served God's purposes, and as result of his righteous intentions, his life in conjunction with that sacred garment was blessed. But what of Nimrod and his usage of the garment? According to *Jasher*, Nimrod did not begin his adventure in defiance of God. Contrary to popular opinion, he initially followed in the footsteps of his righteous forefather, Noah, as the apocryphal record clearly states:

> Nimrod became strong when he put on that garment because God gave him might and strength. He was a powerful hunter in the Earth, and he built altars where he offered the animals he had hunted before the Lord… And the Lord delivered all the enemies of his family into his hands, and God prospered Nimrod in his battles, and he reigned upon the Earth.
>
> Therefore, a saying became popular in those days. When a man had been trained for battle, it was said to him: "As God has done for Nimrod, the mighty hunter who succeeded in all his battles and rescued his family from their enemies, so may God do the same for you."[457]

Therefore, it appears that as long as Nimrod honored God and His purposes, he was revered as the "mighty hunter before the Lord."[458] But in contradistinction to the lifelong blessing that Noah experienced, he was only blessed, in concert with that garment, at the beginning of his life. Eventually, the power that accrued to him by way of this ancient talisman caused Nimrod to make the age-old mistake of turning away from God and turning toward self. As it is written:

> And Nimrod reigned in the Earth over all the sons of Noah, and they were all under his power and counsel, but Nimrod did not continue in the ways of the Lord… He made idols of wood and stone, and bowed down to them in rebellion against the Lord. Not only that, but he even began to teach his subjects to do the same thing.[459]

In short, Nimrod turned away from serving the God-ordained purpose that the sheepskins of Adam were intended to convey. No longer were they being honored as the "shadow" that they were, of the Redeemer Whose coming would restore order to a crestfallen Universe, and as history subsequently records, when Nimrod's pride triggered his decision to defy the Lord and use the power of the garment for his own selfish purposes, at that moment he was forever changed. In this, Nimrod's incorporation of Adam's garment presents us with a phenomenon much akin to what we encountered when observing God's usage of the types of Christ. This time, however, it appears to be a type of Anti-Christ. So that just as Enoch and his role as a divine mediator serves as a type of Jesus, Who was the Ultimate Mediator, in this instance, Nimrod and his role as would-be world conqueror serves as a type of Adolf Hitler, who was himself the ultimate would-be conqueror.

Ironically, like Constantine, Charlemagne, and Barbarossa before him, Hitler for a brief moment in time actually found himself attuned to the potential of The Spear to wield its world-changing power. That is to say, as long as the Supreme Commander of Germany sought to reinvigorate the nation in a way similar to the well-intentioned—although imperialistic—actions of the aforementioned European emperors, Hitler did seem invincible. Yet, like Nimrod before him, having become corrupted by the power that comes in the wake of wielding these divinely-inspired talismans, Hitler, too, was defeated as a result of his own inward turning to self.

In the end, just as all those who have risen and fallen in their brief stints of world-historic domination, Adolf Hitler succumbed to the dark side of the power of The Spear of Destiny. As is so often cited: Power corrupts and absolute power corrupts absolutely. Never is this truer than in the case of anyone who dares wield the power of this ancient talisman that has for more than two thousand years shaped and reshaped the face of history, to both the benefit and detriment of mankind.

The Fickle Nature

THE SUMMER OF 1941 saw the launching of what was to be Hitler's dagger in the heart of Mother Russia: *Operation Barbarossa*, aptly named for the Supreme Commander's beloved idol, Frederick. For all intents and purposes, what should have followed seemed obvious to all who looked in awe at the unrivaled superiority of Germany's military might. After all, in two short years, the Nazis' Lightning War machine had defeated and occupied most of Europe. Between 1939 and 1941, the German Empire had gobbled up Czechoslovakia, Poland, Denmark, Luxembourg, France, Yugoslavia, Greece, and Norway. The combined might of the Nazis then proceeded to turn its fury upon a reeling Great Britain to the north and a teetering Soviet Union to the east. It appeared to the whole world as if Hitler might actually prove unstoppable. At the time, though, very few people had the slightest notion that the real secret to the Nazis' seemingly invincible war machine had nothing to do with military hardware. Very few, actually -- until long after the war's end—would ever come to know that the most technologically advanced society in the world had unreservedly tapped into the most otherworldly of phenomena.

Just like Barbarossa before him, with The Spear of Destiny firmly in his control, Hitler seemed almost superhuman in his ability to strike fear into the hearts of his enemies, both in his uncanny use of military strategy and political maneuvering. Ironically, though, it turned out that Hitler's mysterious gift actually opened the door for the eventual fall of his vaunted war machine. For every fantastic victory won by the Axis regime, just as many inexplicable blunders would undermine the German advance. As legendary as are Hitler's lightning victories in Czechoslovakia and Poland, there are also accounts of an intensely superstitious Hitler who delayed his V-2 rocket program because he dreamed that such an aerial attack would rain fire down from Heaven, not only on his sworn enemies but on his beloved pan-Germanic Empire as well.

So, just as Nimrod discovered the truth about the fickle nature of the powers he had harnessed in possessing Adam's garment, Hitler likewise found himself at a loss when he chose not to manifest the power of The Spear in the spirit with which it was intended. In this, Hitler came face to face with the true nature of this double-edged Universe of ours, as it has clearly been ordained by God. In other words, nothing exists that is wholly good or wholly evil. This is well known not just to philosophers but to everyone. How many times, for example, have you heard that guns or fire are not evil, in and of themselves? Only those who use or misuse them make them so. Naturally, the same holds true for objects of an otherworldly nature, as well as those of a worldly nature.

In this way, history has confirmed just such an interpretation concerning the power of The Spear. Again and again, the same individuals who have blessed the world through its power have also been cursed by it when they lost sight of its true purpose as ordained by the One Whose blood it spilled. This is why, even before the final shot that ended the European conflict was fired, Adolf Hitler's real defeat occurred when he, too, was no longer willing to yield to the same purposes that initially motivated such world-historic figures as Constantine, Charlemagne, and Barbarossa. How ironic, then, that most military historians consider Hitler's ill-conceived decision to invade Russia, codenamed: *Barbarossa*, to be the turning point of the war. What for Hitler was to be his greatest stroke of military genius led, instead, to the Nazis' worst defeat at the Battle of Stalingrad, in the winter of '42, just one year after the zenith of Hitler's power. After their disastrous defeat at Stalingrad, the Nazis would never recover, and as a result of redeploying a large portion of their western troops to fill the vacuum in the East, Germany's enemies wasted no time in marshaling their forces for the 1944 D-Day invasion at Normandy, France. It was truly the beginning of the end.

An Insatiable Lust

THE YEAR 2015 MARKED the seventieth anniversary of the end of the war in Europe and the Hitler-inspired regime that was unleashed upon an unsuspecting world. Like all tragic figures, Hitler, even in death, still provokes a tremendous amount of controversy. Did he really commit suicide, as most historians insist? Or did he fake his death and flee to South America, like so many other expatriated Nazis? Several things are certain in an attempt to answer such mysteries. If Hitler did not commit suicide, he would hardly have been in any condition to traipse off to Buenos Ares or some other such destination, considering the sheer number of forces surrounding him at the time and his well-documented physical condition after so many attempts on his life by his own generals. One has only to remember Hitler's battered body after he was nearly killed in a bomb-blast in July of '44 while attending a staff meeting. In any case, the threat of Hitler, whether as a result of suicide or some other form of exiting his Berlin bunker, April 30, 1945 marks the end of the European war as most people understand it.

The reason this date is so important is because it happens to be the day that an American Army lieutenant by the name of Walter Horn was supposedly digging through the battered remains of a building in Nuremberg that had recently been leveled in an Allied aerial attack. And just as there is an ongoing debate concerning the ultimate end of the Nazi's Supreme Commander, there is a similar debate as to exactly when this American lieutenant found what he found. Nevertheless, to anyone who has been following the string of events as they are depicted in this book, it may not seem so open to discussion, because according to most accounts, the lieutenant found The Spear of Destiny, which had been hidden in the basement of that building in the hopes that it might not fall into the hands of the advancing enemy. But as luck would have it—or should I say, providence—found it he did.

By one account, the time and date of its recovery was said to be 3:00 PM on the 30th of April in that fateful year of 1945.[460] Why is that so significant? Well, it happens to be significant because anyone who believes in the mystical power of The Spear of Destiny would doubtlessly find it interesting that it was recovered at this exact moment, which, according to another account, occurred just one half hour prior to Hitler's suicide.[461] In other words, The Spear's most recent claimant had it removed from his control, and by way of some uncanny sense of loss and defeat, the will to power seems to have been summarily yanked from its earthen vessel. So, having been deprived of his very heart and soul, Hitler, like the soulless zombie that he had become, utterly succumbed to the dark side of the legend of The Spear, and in response, the demonic spirit that it had conjured up finished the job in the quintessential act of surrender, thereby destroying the human vessel that it had until then filled with an insatiable lust for world domination. And in that final, inevitable act of suicide, Adolf Hitler, in death, finally came to grips with the true meaning of The Spear's power in a way that he could never have done in life.

The Tie That Binds

THIS, THEN, CONCLUDES our inquiry into whether or not The Spear of Destiny has ever been associated with the kind of miraculous power that we have previously seen linked with other talismans in the history of Christendom. Like Adam's garment, Veronica's painting, and Jesus' seamless robe, there is, without a doubt, ample evidence to suggest that The Spear of Longinus must be included in this hallowed list. The only question that remains is: If The Spear does exhibit such power, what is the symbolic meaning that such a demonstrable effect is intended by God to reveal?

As previously noted, the only reason that the aforementioned objects exhibited their power was because they were all types of the death and resurrection of Christ. Adam's sheepskin garment, provided by the Lord instead of fig leaves, typify the sacrifice of Jesus as the sacrificial Lamb of God. Veronica's painting, which she presented to Tiberius Caesar, bestowed healing powers on the Roman emperor in direct relation to the efficacy of His shed blood. And Jesus' seamless robe, worn by Pilate with such powerful results in the presence of Caesar, can also be seen in light of their "covering" effect, having appeased the king's wrath until the garment was forcibly removed. As it turns out, the tie that binds all these talismans of power is the sacrifice of Christ Who gave His life as a vicarious substitute for the redemption of humanity. Therefore, if there is any truth to the legends concerning the power that emanates from this Spear of Longinus, then certainly it must do so because it is just as intimately associated with the death and resurrection of Christ.

That said, let us take a moment to see how The Spear of Destiny conveys the divinely-inspired message that we are seeking. As it turns out, such an inquiry produces two very important points. The first has already been revealed in countless essays on the meaning of The

Spear. The second, however, will concern something that I am certain has never been previously cited. More importantly, it is not only the crux of this final essay, but it also represents the final piece of the puzzle in my exhaustive efforts to communicate the connection between all five of the *sacred* things we have been talking about.

Admittedly, the first way in which The Spear of Longinus exemplifies the sacrifice of Christ is that it played a pivotal role in confirming the messianic claims of Jesus. As the story goes: When Pilate's soldiers were sent to break the legs of that trio of crucified men, the two thieves on either side of Christ did have their legs broken in order to hasten their deaths, but when the soldiers came to Jesus, they found Him already dead. It was then that Longinus made his fateful move in piercing the side of Jesus with his spear, thereby confirming the words of the prophets: "These things happened so that the Scripture would be fulfilled: 'Not one of His bones will be broken,'[462] and as it says elsewhere: 'They'll look upon Him Whom they have pierced.'"[463]

It is important to note here that what Longinus did was nothing more than what was already typical of Roman soldiers on the battlefield. Soldiers routinely pierced the rib cages of their fallen enemies to make sure that the dead men were not merely faking their deaths in order to escape later with their lives. Certainly, such a practice seems obvious enough. If the man lying there was really a corpse, it would not react, and it certainly would not bleed. In the case of Jesus, however, something quite unusual occurred. When Longinus pierced His ribcage with the blade of his spear, the expired Christ did not react. In this, what had happened was quite in line with what one would expect from a corpse. However, what was totally unexpected was that, in contrast to a lifeless body, this particular corpse did bleed, and not just blood exited the wound but water also. In this peculiar phenomenon, biblical scholars are quick to see a spiritual meaning. This flow of blood, they say, represents the price that Jesus paid as a ransom for mankind's redemption, while the flow of water depicts the advent of the Holy Spirit that was unleashed upon the world as a result of the efficacy of His sacrifice.

Therefore, if this were all that could be said of what The Spear accomplished in the hand of Longinus, this would certainly have been enough to imbue it with the kind of otherworldly significance with which it has ever since been associated. But is that all there is to the "story"? Is this the only way in which this sacred relic of Christendom speaks of the purposes of God in Christ? Well, according to the typical biblical historian, the answer to that question is yes. That is, until now.

Assurance Sufficient

HERE WE COME TO THE next way in which The Spear of Destiny tells its story concerning the death and resurrection of Christ. However, as I have done in the past, I must qualify what I am about to say with several key points en route. At the beginning of this chapter, we took the time to recall our purpose throughout this double-edged volume of *Analyses* and *Tales*. We have had as our main goal to present a series of ideas that have admittedly been outside the "mainstream" in terms of the general flow of biblical history, but by no means have *The Tales* been expected to be evaluated apart from the traditional books of *The Bible* as we know them today. Repeatedly, we have endeavored to revive an appreciation for these narratives and the subject matter that they deal with, and always with an eye toward demonstrating the extent to which these ideas can be harmonized with the received texts. As such, these so-called "apocryphal" accounts of Enoch, Adam, Abraham, and Pilate have been thoroughly examined in the context of seeing them not as a replacement for traditional Scripture but as a supplement to it.

Still, you may persist in asking the question: What is the point in looking at extra-biblical texts when we are perfectly happy with the ones we already have? To which I would respond by saying that as long as there are such things as doubt and skepticism, there will always be a need to counterbalance the tendency to dismiss any biblical texts that assume their starting point with the miraculous and otherworldly. In other words, in the process of analyzing the nature of biblical texts—both canonical and non-canonical—it behooves the saints to take every opportunity to bolster their faith in a God Who has clearly demonstrated His desire to infiltrate the stream of human history.

In opposition, then, to this tendency to discredit any biblical text that reports an event of a miraculous and otherworldly nature, we have attempted to verify the events found in these *Tales* by approaching them in an entirely unique way. The reason for this approach is because the search for historical certainty is typically plagued by a myriad of obvious difficulties, the least of which being the classic argument against the human capacity for the attainment of any "truth" beyond one's own personal experience. As such, there stands at one extreme the view that nothing can be definitively ascertained about history. Voltaire articulated this point of view when he said, "Doubt is not a pleasant thing, but certainty is absurd."[464] On the other end of the spectrum, there exists at least a modicum of hope. Said John Stuart Mill, "There is no such thing as absolute certainty, but there is assurance sufficient for the purposes of human life."[465]

This is why we have repeatedly examined these *Tales*, as well as our *Analyses*, in light of the latter view. That is to say, while absolute historical certainty is not possible because of our inability to witness said facts of history for ourselves, we, at least, by way of a comprehensive approach to history, can arrive at an "assurance sufficient for the purposes of life." Of course, this will always be the case whether one is attempting to verify the historical certainty of events that took place last year, or last millennium, for that matter.

In this instance, our present pursuit involves the way in which the alleged Spear of Longinus, otherwise known as The Spear of Destiny, reveals an important truth about the death and resurrection of Christ. So far, we have dealt with its apparent role throughout the history of Western Europe, particularly as it pertains to the legend that whoever laid claim to The Spear would in some unique way control the destiny of mankind. This we have done despite the insistence by most historians that it can never be fully determined that The Spear handed down throughout the centuries was actually the genuine artifact. Naturally, such a question can never be proven beyond a shadow of a doubt. In the end, all that is ever ascertainable is whether or not history has sufficiently conformed to the so-called "myth." By that criteria, at least, it does seem certain that the world-shaping events of history have confirmed the validity of such a claim—again, quite apart from verifying that it is the actual weapon that pierced the side of Christ, or that this historical impact was accomplished by way of some as-yet-undefined mystical force.

Having therefore determined, to the best of our ability, that The Spear of Longinus should be included in the role call of Christian talismans, it is only left to determine the "how" in which it reveals the story of Christ's death and resurrection. First and foremost, as we have already noted, without the action of the dutiful centurion, the long-anticipated prophecy concerning the Messiah might have gone unfulfilled, but upon seeing Longinus pierce the side of the expired Jesus, the Roman soldiers' mission to hasten the Nazarene's death was thwarted. Thus, "not a single bone of His body was broken," just as the Scriptures had duly anticipated.

In the context of this volume of *Tales*, however, I promised that there was an added dimension concerning The Spear of Destiny in relation to the work of Christ—one that until now has been totally overlooked. In this, it turns out to be exactly as I have previously detailed concerning The Great Pyramid of Giza. Ever since the pioneering work of Robert Menzies opened the door to a new way of interpreting its geometric design, discovery after discovery has gradually unveiled the various messianic timelines contained in this greatest wonder of the world. Similarly, in light of the evidence outlined in the last chapter, one can now see that the numerical value of *five and a half* (i.e., five thousand, five hundred)—something that was originally thought to be found only in apocryphal literature and early church history—can also be found within the geometry of The Great Pyramid.

So what, exactly, is this added dimension concerning The Spear of Destiny, that is to say, one which bears such a striking similarity to that which we recently discovered in The Great Pyramid? Well, in answering that we come face to face with yet another example of this ubiquitous numerical value of *five and a half*. In this special number, so pregnant with prophetic overtones, we discovered the ultimate timeline of divine redemption, from Adam to Christ, and from Enoch to Moses. Therefore, when one stumbles onto another occurrence of this same number, and this re-occurrence just happens to involve another icon of Christian history, one must undoubtedly marvel at the odds that it could prove to be merely a product of sheer coincidence.

More importantly, whereas biblical historians may question the extent to which the garment of Adam or The Spear of Destiny represent the story of Christ, even the most rabid of agnostics can see how this next icon relates to it. The sacred object I am referring to, and to which I will subsequently connect to the legend of The Spear of Longinus, is none other than The Shroud of Turin, the alleged burial cloth of Jesus of Nazareth.

A Curious Crossroad

BUT NOTICE HOW I said, the *alleged* burial cloth of Jesus. Why? I say alleged because like The Great Pyramid of Giza and The Spear of Longinus, I do not claim to be able to prove—in the traditional sense of that word—the validity of whether any of these things are "real," any more than I can "prove" whether or not Jesus rose from the dead. And do not misunderstand me when I say this concerning the resurrection of Christ. Naturally, as a Christian author who has been writing a book like this, I do believe in the historical certainty that Jesus rose from the dead. Like the Apostle Paul, I firmly believe that without the resurrection of Christ everything in *The Bible* is utterly meaningless; without it, "our faith is useless."[466] Rather, what I mean to say is, I have neither made, nor do I plan to make, any attempt to lay claim to such things as the "reality" of The Pyramid or The Spear or, in this case, The Shroud in—I repeat—the traditional sense. In many other books, written by far more adventurous souls than mine, this has already been managed with a far greater degree of proficiency than I am capable of.

To read the most elucidating and comprehensive arguments for the authenticity of The Turin Shroud, one need only turn to the works of British author Ian Wilson. In a series of books like *The Blood and the Shroud: New Evidence That the World's Most Sacred Relic Is Real* and *The Shroud: The 2,000-Year-Old Mystery Solved*, Wilson scrutinizes every challenge of those who insist—by invoking such scientific bulwarks as carbon-14 dating—that The Shroud dates back to no later than the thirteenth century A.D. Yet according to Wilson and numerous other supporters of The Shroud's genuineness, even this so-called "evidence" as to its medieval origins still fails to account for the fact that the mysterious image on The Shroud bears an uncanny similarity to a "negative" photographic plate. According to Wilson:

> What can be said with absolute confidence is that The Shroud's lifelike photographic negative derives from no modern-day photographic trick. The hidden "photograph," whatever its origin, is a fact of The Shroud that has to be faced by The Shroud's detractors just as fairly and squarely as its supporters must face the results from the radiocarbon dating.[467]

In other words, even if The Shroud can be scientifically "proven" to date from the Medieval Era, it still does nothing to explain how someone artificially imprinted an image that clearly no one in that time period had the knowledge or expertise to create. So try as they might, all the naysayers in the world have yet to undermine the conviction of true believers in such ineffable objects as The Shroud of Turin.

Still, as I have already stated, my purpose throughout this entire volume has been altogether different from those who simply offer up various pros and cons in their arguments for authenticity. What I do claim to offer is an original approach to understanding each and every one of these *sacred* things, from Adam's garment to Jesus' seamless robe, from The Pyramid of Giza to The Spear of Destiny. In short, what I am offering is an approach that "transcends language," whereas language inevitably loses something in the process of translation and mistranslation. What I am offering is an approach that "transcends the scientific method," whereas science, by its very nature, is incapable of surmounting the limitations of time and space. That is to say, what I offer is a new way to "see" the same old things, a new way to "connect" the same old dots, to view things with a completely original understanding of all that has, for so very long, been hidden in plain sight.

Having said that, I submit that the following discussion regarding the alleged facts surrounding The Shroud of Turin—just like those pertaining to the prophecy of The Great Five and a Half Days, The Great Pyramid, and The Spear of Destiny—will not be offered as intellectual or scientific "proofs" as such. Rather, what I will do is offer a new way of approaching the same old stuff, and via this original presentation, you, the reader, will come to your own inevitable conclusion. Yet, ironically, this conclusion will have the same authority as anything that could have been provided by either of the aforementioned pursuits simply by virtue of the fact that most knowledge is communicated without anyone ever experiencing said facts for themselves. In other words, truth is, and always will be, in the "eye of the beholder." But unlike most authors, I choose not to try and convince anyone of facts *per se*. Instead, what I have done, and will continue to do, is offer a unique way to interpret the so-called "facts."

In this, what I am doing is much akin to what any public defender or prosecuting attorney does when they address a jury in a courtroom. Naturally, the jury is incapable of going back in time to witness a given crime in person. So what is left for a trial lawyer to do? Why, naturally, all that they can do is to "paint a picture," so to speak, utilizing whatever elements of "truth" that can be organized and presented by the various advocates, in the form of either eyewitness testimony or physical evidence.

In this case, I am attempting to advocate ways to validate the fact that God has not only revealed His prophetic timeline of The Great Five and a Half Days in apocryphal literature, but that He has also planted it throughout the entire landscape of human experience. To that end, I have attempted to paint a brand-new picture with this possibility in mind—of The Ark of the Covenant, of The Great Pyramid of Giza, and of *The Septuagint Bible*. And now, this attempt to paint a new picture regarding the *five and a half* "days" of redemptive history brings us finally to a curious crossroad, where this same numerical value has been found to occur not only in relation to The Spear of Destiny but is intimately tied to The Shroud of Turin as well.

What does that mean? How does this number, which has invaded the thinking of the builders of The Ark and The Pyramid, and the writers of *The Septuagint Bible*, connect to The Spear? And likewise: How does this number, so imbued with symbolic meaning and sacred significance, connect to The Shroud? Again, my answer—as it oddly turns out—is *not* that it pertains to "this one" in some way or "that one" in another but rather that the same answer *connects them both*.

If that sounds strange, then one can only imagine my difficulty in leading up to offering it. In an interesting twist, this connection of the numerical value of *five and a half* with both The Spear and The Shroud—which in turn binds them to the other *sacred* things in our list—actually parallels what we have already encountered throughout the apocryphal record. After all, what made the phenomenon of the *five and a half* "day" prophecy so compelling was not simply that it had found its way into the story of Adam and Eve, but that it had also been woven into the stories of Enoch and Pilate. In other words, its genuine power emanated from its unexpected connectivity from story to story to story, that is, from *Adam and Eve* to *Enoch* to *Nicodemus*—first with God's promise to Adam, then Enoch's reference to Adam's time in Eden, and finally with Christ's descent to Hades, where He made good on this promise to return Adam to Paradise. As separate elements standing alone, they existed as discordant notes scattered across time, but brought together into a continuous sequence of events, they took on an entirely new meaning—striking a "new chord," if you will—which burst forth as a result of someone simply connecting the dots of prophetic history that had been lying dormant all along, just waiting to be connected this way.

Now, we have come to the conclusion of another sequence of events, similarly discordant, yet similarly destined to one day be connected and rephrased. Like Adam's garment, Veronica's painting, and Jesus' seamless robe—all deriving their mystical power from their association with the death and resurrection of Christ—Longinus' spear, likewise, has exhibited its own uncanny power to sway the course of human history, hence its renowned designation as The Spear of Destiny. But why? Was it simply because it was used to fulfill the prophecies that no bone of the Messiah would be broken, and that they would look upon Him Whom they had pierced? If that were all that could be said of this famed talisman that would undoubtedly have sufficed. However, as it turns out, there is more to the "story" after all, because according to the evidence uniquely revealed in the haunting image of The Shroud of Turin, the spear that was thrust into the side of Jesus did not, as most have assumed, do its piercing without guidance from the hand of the Lord of Time Himself. What does that mean?

In a nutshell, it means that the story from which The Spear of Destiny derives its meaning—that is, the way it typifies the death and resurrection of Christ—comes from the fact that when Longinus thrust his spear into Jesus' side, it pierced His right rib cage between the *fifth and sixth* rib. Thus, in one fell swoop, this piercing not only confirmed the messianic dimension of Christ's dying on the cross, but it also brought into sharp focus the story that would forever imbue The Spear of Destiny and The Shroud of Turin with their otherworldly potential. And in this single, elegant act of piercing, The Spear and The Shroud uniquely combined to reveal—to any who cares to notice—yet another way in which the God of Set Times is conveying His truth concerning the primordial promise to Adam that when He finally would rescue mankind He would do so, right on time, after *five and a half* "days."

These Five Things

The Heart of the Mystery

SO THERE YOU HAVE IT—the special connection that I have been hinting at all along. Five *sacred* things—The Ark of the Covenant, The Spear of Destiny, The Shroud of Turin, The Great Pyramid of Giza, and *The Septuagint Bible*—all with one thing in common, that is, the symbolic message of divine grace typified in the number *five and a half*, which, by its uncanny synergy in each of these things, conveys a startling proof of God's control and faithfulness. For those of you who put all the pieces together on your own, you, like those proverbial men and women of substance, are now in possession of a tremendous insight that no one can ever disassemble or explain away. For those of you who have not yet connected these things in your mind, I offer the following summation to help clarify the matter.

Already well known to theologians and historians alike is the fact that *The Septuagint Bible* contains a chronology that depicts a genealogy from Adam to Christ that spans a period of five thousand, five hundred years. However, what most of them fail to recognize is why this is so. And if ever asked why, they would certainly admit that they had never even bothered to ask such an apparently meaningless question, considering they were perfectly satisfied with the chronology handed down to them from post-Reformation times, that is, the four thousand year chronology devised by the esteemed Archbishop Ussher. But as one has seen from our earlier historical review concerning this grand *faux pas*, this chronology was seriously flawed from its inception. What is worse, it not only presents yet another contradiction to fuel the never-ending controversy over the validity of biblical translations, but it also undermines any attempt that the word of God might offer mankind in the way of demonstrating His faithfulness to His promises. If, however, one looks to the chronology espoused by *The Septuagint*, this obstacle collapses like a veritable house of cards. More importantly, by embracing the five thousand, five hundred year chronology of *The Septuagint*, one is all the more open to the potential significance of this all-important numerical value of *five and a half*, which, as we have seen, so often finds itself at the heart of our mystery concerning the five *sacred* things. This simple but obvious fact, then, should never be overestimated, because once this reality becomes fixed in one's mind, a whole series of truths concerning God's control and faithfulness begins to tumble into place.

Like So Many Dominoes

FROM REPEATED references to the number *five and a half*, we have the exact period of time that would mark the fulfillment of God's promise to rescue Adam and his descendants, as it is depicted in both *The Septuagint* and the apocryphal literature, followed by its recurrence in The Ark, The Spear, The Shroud, and The Great Pyramid. From this, we have even greater confidence that—even if biblical scholars are convinced that narratives like *The First Book of Adam and Eve* and *The Secrets of Enoch* are products of post-Christian times, and *The Gospel of Nicodemus*, that of the Medieval Era—these texts are doubtlessly by-products of much earlier manuscripts whose origins far exceed traditional assumptions. From this, we also have a much more acute awareness of the symbolic meaning presented to us by way of the dimensions of The Ark of the Covenant, which theologians naturally see as signifying all that the Advent of Christ holds in store for humanity. This, in turn, confirms the numeric significance of the dimensions of the Open Coffer in the King's Chamber of The Great Pyramid, which all pyramidologists insist also presents us with a prophetic type of Christ. Additionally, it explains the conspicuous redundancy of the number *five* throughout the dimensions of The Pyramid, causing pyramidologists to go so far as to declare that it is the most important number in all of its marvelous geometry. Even more evidently, this is cemented by the fact that the angle of the slopes of The Great Pyramid, as well as its height, both correspond to this same numerical value in its dimensions, which, to those who are convinced of its prophetic meaning, points to the very moment in history when the long-awaited Christ would finally arrive. Finally, from this, we discover the most overlooked connection of all; yet in this connection, we might now see the two most famous Christian artifacts the world has ever known in an entirely new light. And all because of this numerical connection between both The Spear of Destiny and The Shroud of Turin—in that it testifies, in the case of The Spear, to the blood of the Savior it spilled, while in The Shroud, to the miraculous nature of Christ's resurrection from the dead.

Like so many tumbling dominoes, then, one thing leads to another, each thing unifies the other, and together they translate into exactly the kind of message that this entire work has endeavored to illustrate. On one hand, it is a message that is hidden in plain sight, available to some, obvious to the eye of faith, while at the same time remaining concealed to others, veiled to the eye of doubt. And on the other hand, it is a message of universal dimensions, that is to say, a message that is communicated by way of God's all-encompassing language of the ages—a message of dramatic significance that transcends all interpretation. Therefore, to those who look with discerning hearts and minds, the message of divine grace embodied in these five *sacred* things can be clearly understood, in any language spoken the world over and throughout all time. Whether that language is linguistically- or mathematically-based, the message remains the same: God really is in control of every facet of human history; and because the Lord kept His promise to rescue Adam, right on time, exactly as He promised, we, who are all children of Adam, can rest assured that our future is secure in the knowledge that He will be just as faithful to *all of His promises* that pertain to us.

The End

A New Beginning

HAVE YOU EVER noticed how all great stories never really end? In days gone by, every movie concluded with those familiar words of finality that appeared on the screen: The End. But the good ones, the ones that stuck in your mind, that got to you on a primal level, were always stories that ended with a new beginning.

In *Close Encounters of the Third Kind*, a man seeks to come to terms with his brush with otherworldly forces. In the process of trying to understand what has happened to him, he loses everything that he had, up to that point, held most dear: He is fired from his job, his family deserts him, and ultimately any sense of belonging to this world fades away as he presses on toward his goal. It is not until, in the final sequence of the film, that he finally comes face to face with the alien species that he comes to realize has actually "invited" him to this encounter. Turning to one of his fellow seekers, who bids him farewell with a knowing smile, he anxiously boards an alien vessel, which then takes him and others like him up and away toward a new life. So, far from ending this man's journey with the realization of why he has experienced all that has brought him to this conclusion, the film leaves the viewer with a clear sense that, though his life on Earth may have ended, he has begun an entirely new one as a result of his close encounter of the third kind.

Similarly, all the stories in *Tales of Forever* conclude with new beginnings. *Dawn of Time* has the exiled Adam and Eve attempting, in every way imaginable, to get back into the Garden of Eden, and though all their plans to regain entry come to naught, the couple does eventually come to realize that what they need is not contained in the garden after all. What they really need is the very thing that God, in His mercy, continues to give to them even though they could never have possibly known it at first. In the end, they find that the peace they are desperately seeking is not located in a mere place; instead, it comes from living a life reconciled to the Lord of the Garden Himself. In this way, although the story of the very first couple does not conclude with their being re-admitted to the garden as they had originally hoped for, they have at least been reborn "psychologically," if not spiritually, and have thus been propelled into a totally new dimension of life.

Fire and Blade has the wandering Abraham seeking to follow in the footsteps of the heroes of faith like Enoch, the scribe, his legendary forefather. In the process, he survives impossible odds as both Nimrod and Satan attempt to thwart him from ever fulfilling his world-changing destiny. And though he matriculates through every challenge, even going so far as becoming the father of faith, his greatest satisfaction comes at the end of his life when he comes to the quiet realization that his death will become the gateway that leads him to his most intimate desire: He will finally gaze upon the Face of God. True to his high calling on Earth, then, Abraham fulfilled his goal to live a life like Enoch, and so, true to his heavenly calling, he saw that in death he was about to embark upon a new plane of existence, far beyond anything that he could have experienced during his earthbound life.

And *Trial by Fury* has an embroiled Pontius Pilate, the notorious Roman governor who tries in vain to impose political order upon a zealous people he can never hope to understand. Unfortunately for Pilate, the more he tries to crush the spirit of those he has been charged to govern, the more he inflames their religious fanaticism, thereby fomenting the very civil disobedience he is supposed to suppress. This is never more evident than when he encounters the most unlikely of political foes: Jesus of Nazareth, charged with sedition and treason by His own people. Characteristically unsympathetic to the plight of this alleged Jewish rebel, Pilate, at first, seeks only to solidify his own political position. But before long, this unlikely ally is drawn into uncharted emotional territory, and is forever changed by the things he hears and sees concerning this strangely serene Man. So changed, in fact, that when he is forced to endure his own ignominious end at the hands of an angry Caesar, Pilate faces it not as the belligerent political boss he once was but as a new man humbled by his encounter with the One he, too, has come to view as the Savior of Mankind.

Such is the common thread that binds together this entire collection of *Tales*, that is to say, one in which the conclusion of each story constitutes not so much an ending as a new beginning. As it turns out, the same thing could be said about the story of Enoch, our narrator. Just as the stories of Adam, Abraham, and Pilate depict this narrative pattern of "ending as new beginning," so the story of Enoch follows this age-old dramatic arc as well, and in viewing *The Tales* in terms of this timeless tradition, one is able to gain an insight into not only what constitutes a great story but also the very mechanism that underlies the whole history of apocryphal literature in general. Let me explain what I mean by that.

A Peculiar Paradox

FOR ANYONE WHO HAS read this book to the present point: If you remember nothing else about the life and times of the various characters that inhabit these *Tales of Forever*, remember one thing. The story of Enoch, the scribe, is not just the tale of a man whose journey to Heaven and back constitutes one of the greatest adventures of biblical history, it actually represents an allegory for mankind's relationship to the kind of literature that has for too long been stigmatized by the misguided designation *apocryphal*. In other words, at the heart of Enoch's life story is a drama that provides a unique window into why books like his were given by God to humanity but were then lost to history; and fortunately, for our sake, it also explains—in prophetic terms, mind you—how this forgotten wisdom would one day be restored to its proper place in the hierarchy of divine truth. With this in mind, let us re-examine the story of Enoch's remarkable journey in order to see how this is so.

First, Enoch was quite unexpectedly taken on an unparalleled journey through several levels of Heaven, each more perplexing and perilous than the last. Eventually standing before the molten Face of God, he was then commissioned to communicate a message to his family, which they were in turn entrusted to pass on to subsequent generations. Filled with an overwhelming sense of responsibility, Enoch performed his mission to the letter, whereupon he bequeathed to his family hundreds of manuscripts describing the lives of those who had lived, of those who were living, and of those who were yet to live. Then having completed his task, Enoch was taken back up to Heaven, where he again stood gazing upon the Face of God. Still, one thing plagued Enoch's mind.

Sensing the troubled state that he was in, the Face asked, "What's wrong, Enoch?"

Reluctantly, Enoch replied, "I can't help but wonder, Lord, what's to become of the books that I've provided humanity. Will they believe what's written in them?"

"Of course," came the Lord's response. "Someday."

"Someday?" asked Enoch. "What do You mean, someday?"

"Your books, Enoch, will be lost to mankind for a very long time."

"Lost? But why?"

"They're lost because only a handful of people ever appreciate them—people like Jared, Methuselah, and Lamech, along with their immediate families. So, after generations of neglect and ignorance, they'll simply be lost to much of the world, and for a time it will be as though they had never been written at all."

Just imagine what Enoch must have thought when he heard those words: *For a time it will be as though they had never been written at all.* There he was, standing before the Face of God, having written books dictated by those lips, emitting sparks every which way, emitting words spoken to him for the sake of all humanity, yet they would be words that mankind would neglect and ignore. What a peculiar paradox this must have presented to the mind of Enoch.

"But You say things will be different someday?" Enoch continued. "You did say that, didn't You, Lord?"

"Yes. Someday people will begin to write all My words properly in their own languages without altering or diminishing them. They'll perform the task correctly, and then they'll possess everything I've said about them from the very beginning."

"You mean books like the ones I wrote?" interrupted Enoch, unable to hold back his enthusiasm.

"Yes, Enoch, yes, books just like yours. And they'll rejoice in them, and all the faithful ones will acquire the knowledge of every righteous path through them and be rewarded, and someday, they'll call out to the people of Earth, and make them listen to their wisdom."[468]

So even though Enoch was disappointed that the books God had dictated to him would eventually be lost to much of world history, he was at least reassured by the news that they would not stay lost forever. *Someday* they would be rediscovered. In this, it is just as it is with all things in the greater plan of the God of Set Times. First, truth is given to mankind, then that truth is lost for a determined length of time, and one day that truth re-emerges once again, right on schedule.

Rising from the Ashes

BUT TO ANYONE WHO might still be wrestling with the notion of whether or not such extra-biblical literature constitutes genuine biblical truth, the story of Enoch presents yet another reason that one should take a fresh look at these remarkable narratives. It is time at last to tear down the walls of prejudice and disinformation that one might retain in light of everything offered in this work, particularly because of the way that such narratives have provided the ultimate linchpin in connecting the five *sacred* things.

Without *The Tales*, there would be no knowledge of the prophecy of The Great Five and a Half Days. Without this promise of "days," there would be no reason to believe that there was any more truth to the five thousand, five hundred year chronology from Adam to Christ in *The Septuagint Bible* than the four thousand year version found in *The Hebrew Bible*. Without an awareness of the importance of the *Septuagint* chronology, there would be nothing to point to the prophetic significance encrypted within the dimensions of The Ark and The Pyramid, or the symbolic message conveyed in The Spear and The Shroud. And without an awareness of how the promise of "days" is confirmed in the five *sacred* things, there would be nothing to lead anyone to an awareness of all that the fulfillment of this prophecy brings in confirming the control and faithfulness of a God, Who "in the fullness of time," sent forth His Son to make good on His promise to "rescue Adam and his descendants after *five and a half* 'days.'"

Having said all that, I am, of course, quite willing to concede that there are those diehard skeptics out there who still cling to the possibility that this entire work is merely an exercise in wishful thinking; and for them, I am just as willing—being the eternal optimist that I am—to offer one last argument on their behalf. And as I previously alluded, I will offer this argument in the form of an allegory, one in which Enoch's life story reveals a special truth concerning the literature that has virtually become synonymous with his name. As such, the allegory that I will attempt to describe, just like that of Hippolytus' allegory of The Ark of the Covenant, will be one that is couched in the same terms that we have seen throughout this book, that is to say, that of death and resurrection. But whereas Hippolytus' allegory of The Ark pertained to the resurrection of Christ, this allegory of Enoch points not to a bodily resurrection but to a resurrection of the hidden wisdom of the ages penned by him and others like himself.

And the reason I am doing this is to address the main objection made by anyone who still insists that any talk of extra-biblical literature is meaningless, not only because, in their view, there was a perfectly good reason these books were left out of Scripture, but also because, according to them, there is nothing in human history to account for the restoration of such books once they have been excised. Simply put, there is no precedence to be had in all of history for such things as the "death and resurrection" of *wisdom*. And this, they would further insist, is made all the more evident by the fact that the only thing God has ever seen fit to resurrect is His beloved Son, Jesus.

Sure Enoch walked and talked with the Lord. Sure they must have had a very interesting conversation, but if God never saw fit to make sure that that conversation was inserted into the accepted Canon, then all the conjecture about this literature being providentially lost and restored simply has no precedence in history—biblically or culturally speaking. In short, if it is not in our *Bible* of today, then that is that: The End.

Or is it? Does the death of wisdom, especially that kind of wisdom associated with *The Bible,* really spell the end? Or, as we have so often seen in the remarkable world of the supernatural, does this end simply lead, instead, to a new beginning?

We now come to the point where I can present the aforementioned allegory, an allegory that reveals how a central truth of Enoch's life story illuminates God's intention toward humanity by way of His concealing and revealing His most precious truths. I would now like to remind the reader of one of the most enduring mythic figures known to mankind. It is the age-old story of a remarkable bird found throughout much of the world's history, despite cultural differences across the globe. I am referring to that remarkable creature known as the Phoenix, which to the modern mind doubtlessly seems like just another fairy tale. Yet for the greater part of history and the world, it has clearly been nothing of the sort. In fact, the cultural traces of this legendary bird are so pervasive that it calls to mind the notion set forth by historian Giambattista Vico, who insisted that "uniform ideas originating from entire peoples unknown to each other must have a common ground of truth."[469] Strange as it may seem, then, the story of the Phoenix appears to be one of those traditions that is just as resilient as the bird itself, as the following litany of believers would indicate.

According to ancient writers such as Herodotus, Tacitus, Pliny, and Ovid, the Phoenix resembled an eagle, with its vivid golden and scarlet feathers, and was said to perish in a burst of flames every five hundred years, only to be reborn, having risen from its own ashes. Because of this ability to rise again from the ashes, its legend has permutated the world over, becoming ever after associated with immortality and resurrection. To the Hebrews, it was connected with the eternal cycle of life; to the Egyptians, it symbolized rebirth; to the Persians, it was the bird of Paradise; to the Greeks and Romans, it conveyed the power of regeneration; and to the Chinese, it denoted completeness, harmoniously combining both *yin* and *yang*. It was this association with rebirth that naturally lent itself to the advent of Christianity, as a direct influence of either Hebrew or Greco-Roman thought. States *The New World Encyclopedia*:

> The ideology of the Phoenix fit perfectly with the story of Christ. The Phoenix's resurrection from death as new and pure can be viewed as a metaphor for Christ's resurrection, central to Christian belief... Most of the Christian-based Phoenix symbolism appears within works of literature, especially in medieval and Renaissance Christian literature that combined classical and regional myth and folklore with more mainstream doctrine.[470]

Even Leonardo da Vinci wrote about the famed bird, saying, "For constancy, the Phoenix serves as a type; for understanding by nature its renewal, it is steadfast to endure the burning flames which consume it, and then it is reborn anew."[471]

This was not only the case for Christian theology, however, but included Jewish eschatological thought as well. According to Louis Ginzberg, "The Church Fathers, as well as the rabbis, refer to the Phoenix as a proof of the resurrection."[472] Concerning this association of the Phoenix with both Christian and Jewish theology, Roelof van den Broek, of Utrecht University in the Netherlands, wrote extensively in his book *The Myth of the Phoenix*. In it, he cited a fifth-century Coptic manuscript called *The Sermon on Mary*, which describes a series of appearances of the creature in connection with three pivotal biblical events.

> The first of these appearances took place when Abel made the sacrifice that found more favor in the sight of God than that of Cain... According to the Coptic text, thus, the Phoenix was consumed together with Abel's sacrifice by the heavenly fire ... as a type of Christ. According to the Coptic text, at the first sacrifice mentioned in *The Bible*, the bolt of fire was accompanied by an

appearance of the Phoenix... The fire from Heaven is a sign that the event had divine approval; it legitimizes the sacrifice. The appearance of the Phoenix indicates that the event in question is, by God's will, the beginning of a new time, of a new era in the history of salvation...

The second appearance of the Phoenix ... mentioned in the Coptic sermon: "When God brought the Children of Israel out of Egypt by the hand of Moses, the Phoenix showed itself on the Temple of On, the city of the Sun..." Here again its manifestation marks the beginning of a new era in the history of salvation. Before the meaning of this can be elucidated, we must take up the third appearance of the Phoenix mentioned in the Coptic sermon.

In the year of Christ's birth, the Phoenix is supposed to have burned itself on a pinnacle of the Temple at Jerusalem... The report of this burning begins with a sentence that at first seems rather puzzling: "According to the number of its years, it was its tenth time since its genesis after Abel's sacrifice that it had sacrificed itself: In this year now the Son of God was born in Bethlehem." The intention here is to fix the year of the birth of Christ, chronologically, by means of the Phoenix's appearance every 500 years: 500 years must have preceded Abel's sacrifice, and since there were ten more such periods after it, the birth of Christ must have taken place in the year 5,500 after the creation of the world. This is a concept we encounter frequently in early Christian literature...

In his *Chronographia*, Julius Africanus has divided the history of the world according to this scheme of six periods, each lasting one thousand years, in which he put the birth of Christ in the year 5,500. This had already been done previously by Hippolytus in his commentary on *The Book of Daniel*, the date having been derived from the dimensions of ... The Ark [of the Covenant]...

The author of the Coptic sermon, therefore, drew on a familiar conception when he placed the birth of Christ in the year of the eleventh appearance of the Phoenix, i.e., in the year 5,500 after the creation of the world.[473]

The Light of a New Day

NOTWITHSTANDING the fact that the previous narrative further substantiates the validity of the all-important period of the *five and a half* "days" from Adam to Christ, what could possibly account for such parallels in both Jewish and Christian thought? Considering the intractable antagonism between the two camps at the time, what could have united such disparate groups? One answer, I believe, not only explains this riddle but also provides an answer to a question alluded to previously in this chapter, which was: What historical evidence is there to suggest that the story of Enoch's life could in any way reveal a hidden truth regarding the so-called "death and resurrection" of apocryphal literature? In this instance, the answer is one that should connect Jewish and Christian theology, and one that, in doing so, must predate them both in order for it to influence them equally. In short, what could tie together the mystery of the Phoenix with the Jewish and Christian doctrines of the resurrection of the dead? One word: Enoch.

Of utmost importance here is that one notices I said, "word," because it is to the etymological connection between the words "Phoenix" and "Enoch" to which we will next turn, and thus "end" our story with the new beginning that I spoke of earlier. As it turns out, the Greek word for "Phoenix" is said to have been derived from the Egyptian word *Pa-Hanok*, which means "The House of Enoch." Should one doubt such a possibility, simply examine the etymological aspects of our English word "Enoch," which comes to us straight from the Latin, while in Hebrew it is rendered *Hanokh*. So from the Hebrew *Hanokh*, we get the Egyptian word *Pa-Hanok*, which, in Greek, becomes "Phoenix." Considering, then—a fact we spent considerable time establishing in our chapter entitled *A Capstone to Time*—that Enoch undoubtedly left an indelible impact on the history of Egypt, it is not at all surprising that his very name would become a rich source for all sorts of legend and lore.

With this etymological connection in mind, next consider the common characteristics that the two share: Both Enoch and the Phoenix are associated with rebirth, renewal, and resurrection. Implicit in this also is that they are both associated with the transition from a previous state of existence, or awareness, to a new one. In other words, they are both said to inaugurate new beginnings. We are particularly concerned here with this notion, because above all it has been my intention to verify that the God of *The Bible* has never been embarrassed that the forgotten wisdom contained in books like Enoch's have been, "for a time," stigmatized and marginalized by an indifferent world. In fact, it has been His predetermined plan of the ages to have this timeless pattern built into the very tapestry of the greater dramas that only God's hidden hand in history could have orchestrated.

So, just as these lost books, lost chronologies, and lost truths that demonstrate the Lord's control and faithfulness were destined to temporarily fade from the horizon of human consciousness, the legend of the Phoenix conveys this same idea of periodic death and resurrection. And just as that legendary bird was said to make an appearance to mark the turning points in the history of salvation, we should expect nothing less when, in the unfolding of God's revelation, these hidden gems of wisdom have similarly risen from the ashes of oblivion and thus taken wing in the hearts and minds of those reborn into the light of a new day.

A Parting Shot

THE HERO SLAYS the monster, once ... twice ... but still, as any fan of the cinema knows all too well, the monster will not stay dead. Like the dying-and-rising hero so integral to the great tales, the monster, too, can and will rise again as it resorts to every nasty trick in its relentless pursuit of vanquishing the hero. In movie parlance, it is known as the Law of Triple Endings. In line with this classic principle, then, I would like to provide a parting shot before we finally ride off into the sunset and fade to black.

Throughout this work, we have sought a variety of ways to offset the three most dreaded archenemies of not only a book like this but, dare I say, of mankind itself. They are doubt, skepticism, and cynicism, because doubt is the ultimate adversary of faith and hope; skepticism, of truth and certainty; and cynicism, of beauty and grace. So, just when we think doubt has been conquered by meticulously comparing our non-canonical sources with the more familiar canonical texts and found them compatible beyond question, our old nemesis, skepticism, rears its ugly head. Then, just when we think skepticism has been overcome by painstakingly confirming the existence of the multitudinous ways that the broader landscape of human existence substantiates the truths contained in them, our final enemy, cynicism, seeks to undermine all our previous efforts.

Sure, you may say, I have answered the question of whether there is sufficient evidence to demonstrate the reliability of the texts in question and that wherever we look there is corroborating evidence that my conclusions are sound, but that still does nothing to answer the question that has plagued mankind since the dawn of time. And that is, just because it can be demonstrated that God is faithful and that our Universe speaks of His control: How does this adequately explain why He allowed evil to enter our world in the first place? In short: Just because God is in control and is faithful still does not make up for the fact that He personally unleashed the ultimate monster—evil—upon an unsuspecting humanity. Whether that monster is seen in terms of death, Hell, and the grave, or darkness, sadness, and pain, the fact that God is clearly to blame for the dire predicament we are in—quite apart from Adam's guilt in the whole debacle—undermines any of our bold pronouncements of "God is in control" and "God is faithful." Such is the power of that dreaded archenemy of humanity, such is its power that no vision of divine beauty and grace can withstand its corrosive sting, such is the power of cynicism.

Therefore, it is with the utmost urgency that I turn to delivering the final deathblow to such a one as cynicism, an enemy of such magnitude that it alone can single-handedly undermine every valiant effort that I have made to this point. How, then, does one answer the ultimate question on the lips of anyone who has ever asked such an obvious question? Why, in fact, would a loving and compassionate God allow evil to enter a world with such potential for hope, truth, and beauty? As anyone who has ever pondered why the Fall was allowed to occur in the first place, this is the great conundrum of human existence.

And the answer I will offer, like so many that have been offered throughout this work, will be a multi-faceted one; that is to say, it will be an answer that comes in the form of both word and image. Simply put, just like the universal truths conveyed in the numerological significance contained in the five *sacred* things, this answer will be the same regardless of what language it is conveyed in, and as such will hopefully be understood by everyone the world over, be they young or old, simple or wise, literate or illiterate. Furthermore, this answer addresses the one thing that is so often overlooked by anyone who insists on putting God on trial by asking such questions, as if He would actually be embarrassed that His own creatures have discovered a flaw that He Himself has overlooked.

And the answer comes in the form of the image seen at the end of this chapter. Like so much of this book, which aims at unveiling the hidden truth in the *sacred* things around us, the image on its last page—called *The Beginning of Days*—is full of symbolic meaning just waiting to make itself known. On the surface, it is a depiction of the most tragic event in human history, known ever since as the Fall of Mankind. The hand of Eve places the deadly orb—not an apple, by the way, as we discovered—into Adam's hand, after having already taken a bite from that Forbidden Fruit, in the hopes that he will follow in her willing descent, thereby plunging them and their descendants into endless disaster, despair, and death. But as tragic as this scenario appears at first glance, there is another aspect to it—albeit hidden in plain sight—that is not so obvious; that is, not until it is pointed out, and then, like the proverbial snake that would have bitten you, it literally leaps out and grabs you.

And although it is clearly a picture of the Fall, it is of the utmost importance that you understand it is not, as one would assume, a portrait of unmitigated doom. Again—on the surface—it might look that way; but hidden within its imagery is a simple but overriding dimension, something that becomes apparent upon my asking a few questions: Is this really just an image of Eve handing over the Forbidden Fruit to Adam? What else does one see upon closer inspection? In fact, it is a depiction of that Fruit being handed over while at the same time "eclipsing," as it were, the rising Sun behind it. Why is that important? Well, as it turns out, by portraying the lethal orb of the Fruit this way, in relation to the celestial orb of the Sun, one is actually looking at an allegory for the way in which the consequences of the Fall have been nullified by the inconspicuous actions of that solar timepiece.

This image, then, which is nothing less than an allegory for the promise of "days" given to Adam and his descendants by God Himself, constitutes the answer to the question posed by anyone who seeks to penetrate the mystery of "the fly of evil" in the otherwise perfect ointment of creation. Because springing from the mind of God Who knew in creating divinely-constituted beings like ourselves, the one thing He could not create—as a function of the God-like spark of free will—was both innocence *and* maturity at the same time in those created beings *from the start*. The only way to know what it means to be truly human, to be our "selves" in every sense of that word, as opposed to the Great Other Who created us, we must first experience, in our own finiteness, the duality of God's Universe. But in order to do that—and herein lies the rub—one cannot remain blissfully innocent forever. In other words, without being "cast out" of the womb of Eden, we would never have known darkness, sadness, or pain, but ironically, without knowing any of these things, we would never be able to realize our full potential as individuals made in the image of God. Because without knowing darkness, we could never appreciate light; without knowing sadness, we could never experience true happiness; without knowing pain, we could never embrace real pleasure. Simply put, to go through life without experiencing such dualities would be like never living at all.

Therefore, armed with this awareness of what God knew, even before we did, the significant thing to realize about the Fall—illustrated by the Fruit against the backdrop of the Sun, from which we derive our experience of time—is that two concomitant events are being represented here and not just one. In this superimposed image, we see the beginning of not only humanity's fallen state but also God's unfolding drama of redemptive history so that we might come to know what we could never have known had we remained forever in Eden. What we have is the beginning not only of our own mortality—with all its potential for darkness, sadness, and pain—but also the days and weeks and years that were to count off the ages-long procession of God's set times that eventually culminated in our redemption obtained at Calvary—and with it, the ultimate attainment of light, happiness, and pleasure.

It was the end of innocence; it was the beginning of "days."

THIS CONCLUDES *Tales of Forever: The Unfolding Drama of God's Hidden Hand in History*. For those of you who are so inclined, it would be appreciated if you could post a positive review of this book on such websites as Amazon, Barnes and Noble, and iTunes, in order that others might become aware of its valuable contents. Because this book was not produced by a conglomerate-style publishing house, we rely more heavily on word-of-mouth to advertise its importance to others who, like yourself, are searching for books like this. Thank you for your support.

The end of innocence; the beginning of "days."

THE CREDITS

At the risk of sounding cliché, I would like to thank God, Jesus, and the Holy Spirit, Who all must be having the most incredible conversation right now, as usual. Thanks for a world filled with so much interesting and enlightening dialog.

W. Kent Smith, *Tales of Forever*

Acknowledgements

TECHNICALLY, *Tales of Forever* is the second edition of a book published at the turn of the last millennium entitled *Lost Stories for All Ages.* That initial publication, however, pales in comparison to the present volume. Coming in at just under one hundred and seventy pages, *Lost Stories* was a mere echo of what it is today in its present form as *Tales*, which in the decades that followed eventually blossomed to a work of some five hundred and fifty pages. Whereas *Tales* is a multifaceted work, combining both in-depth analyses and full-orbed dramatizations, the original incarnation of *Lost Stories* was comprised only of the sparsest of narratives. That said, this present volume still owes a tremendous debt to its first-edition cousin, and because of that I would like to take the time to acknowledge those individuals whose contributions were invaluable to its creation.

To begin with, I would like thank my father, my mother, and all my family and friends. Without their encouragement and support throughout the years, I could never have completed the arduous task of publishing this book independently. And at the risk of sounding cliché, I would like to thank God, Jesus, and the Holy Spirit, Who must be having the most incredible conversation right now, as usual. Thanks for a world filled with so much interesting and enlightening dialog, and thanks, especially, for helping me through it all, which is to say, not just with writing this book but also with the "stuff of life." You never cease to amaze me.

In preparing the original *Lost Stories* manuscript for publication, I would to "re-thank" Kris Strevel, Bryan Fox, and David Hovik for their help with the proofreading of the first edition. Thanks also to Elizabeth Shaw, Tom Volguth, Marie Hovik, Eric Frederickson, and Julie Fox, not to mention, John Woods, Lorraine Francis, and Michael "Bear" Schwartz.

As for this latest incarnation, which is now *Tales of Forever*, I would like to thank Scott Weimer, Jeff Kantra, and Rhett "Maxx" Waters. Thanks, Scott, for not only taking time away from your busy schedule to read the manuscript in its most primitive form but also for always instilling in me the much-needed sense of confidence that I was heading in the right direction. Thanks, Jeff, for your generosity and enthusiasm in letting me know what were the strengths of the book, and for your candor and unbiased appraisal concerning the ways in which it could become something better. And thank you, Maxx, for going through the final draft of the book with a fine-tooth comb and helping me weed out all those nasty typos, once and for all. I do not exaggerate when I say that without your contributions in the proofreading phase of this manuscript, I could never have developed this new and greatly expanded version into what it is today.

A special thanks goes out to David Spalione for his artistic contribution of the image that appears on the last page of this book. I hope that someday we will be able to sit down together again and remember all the reasons why a friendship like ours is too important to neglect.

Also, I would like to thank several gentlemen for indirectly helping with the book when they all worked together to completely remodel my computer room. This brand-new room, as it turns out, was essential in enabling me to enter into unexpected avenues of research, which, in turn, helped to elevate the book to an unprecedented level of scholastic excellence. For providing me with this rare opportunity, I would like to thank Larry Bowers, Bobby Mestas, and Robert Soto and his two sons, Javier and Angel. And speaking of computers, I would like to thank Kris Ala as well for his help in getting my word processing computer back up and running, without which, needless to say, this manuscript could never have been completed.

Last but not least, I would like to express my gratitude to a special friend and colleague who alone among this list of contributors offered his talents to this work in both of its incarnations, as *Lost Stories of All Ages* and *Tales of Forever*. That person is Dennis Tracy. From start to finish, Dennis always made sure that I never lost sight of my originally stated purpose of creating a narrative that was not only professional but also readable. While I so often had a tendency to regurgitate the rarefied language of scholarship that I am accustomed to reading while researching the sources for this book, Dennis was always ready, willing, and able to "encourage" me to keep it simple, stupid. Thanks, Skipper.

I would also like to thank the following people who were instrumental in helping procure the right to utilize various quotes throughout this book. Thanks to Ken Lee at Michael Weise Productions for their kind permission to quote Christopher Vogler's *The Writer's Journey*; to Nicole Tilford at the Society of Biblical Literature in quoting James I. Cook's *Edgar Johnson Goodspeed*; to Eric D. Snider for his comments on *Butch Cassidy and the Sundance Kid*; to Gary Meisner at PhiPoint Solutions for his information concerning the numerical value of *Phi: 1.618, The Golden Number*; to Maureen Winter at Black Dog and Leventhal Publishers for words from Leonardo da Vinci's *Notebooks*; to Gordon L. Anderson at *New World Encyclopedia* for their insights about the Phoenix; to Deb Eisenschenk at Liturgical Press for quoting from Sebastian Brock's *The Luminous Eye*; to Laura Westbrook at Brill Archive for Roelef van den Broek's *The Myth of the Phoenix*; to Kristine Cartier for help in acquiring permission from the Estate of Trevor Ravenscroft to draw from his book *The Spear of Destiny*; to Dan Koeppel for permission to quote from his book *Banana: The Fate of the Fruit That Changed the World*; to Michael Lambert at The Joseph Campbell Foundation to quote from Joseph Campbell's *The Hero With a Thousand Faces*; to Connor Sterchi at Moody Publishers in quoting John F. Walvoord's *Daniel: The Key to Prophetic Revelation*; to Perry Cartwright at The University of Chicago for a quote from Edgar J. Goodspeed's introduction to his translation of *The Apocrypha*; and to Christine Lee at Simon and Schuster for a quote from Ian Wilson's *The Blood and the Shroud*.

So ends my acknowledgement to everyone who was personally involved with the creation of *Tales of Forever*. However, I would be remiss if I did not acknowledge several more individuals who greatly influenced this work from afar. In adapting the tales of Enoch, Adam, Abraham, and Pilate, I was greatly affected by two authors and one television writer. The authors are C.S. Lewis and James A. Michener, and the television writer is Rod Serling. For the story of Enoch and his various excursions between Heaven and Earth, I am indebted to Lewis' *The Great Divorce*, and for Adam and his encounters with the many guises of Satan, there are *The Screwtape Letters*. For the tale of Abraham and his journey from Ur of the Chaldees to the Promised Land, I am indebted to Michener's *Caravans* and *Hawaii*. And for the peculiar drama of Pilate and his manifold complications, there are Serling's *Judgment Night*, *Death's Head Revisited*, and *A Quality of Mercy*.

Finally, I would like mention one last individual who just happens to be the man who introduced me to the subject of extra-biblical literature, both by way of his teaching on such diverse subjects as The Spear of Destiny, The Garment of Adam, and Enoch and the Watchers, and his having reissued several of the publications that initially served as source material for this work, specifically *The First Book of Enoch*, *The Book of Jasher*, and *The Book of Jubilees*. That man is Dr. Gene Scott. Prior to my introduction to Doc—as he was best known by his students—I had, in my late teenage years, become fascinated by the subject of biblical chronology, even going so far as to begin work on a historical timeline, depicting the relationship between sacred and secular events, particularly as they pertained to the genealogy from Adam to Christ and beyond. As it turned out, having begun this enterprise in the early 1980s, this timeline would provide a uniquely instrumental jumping-off point that would make me a prime candidate for Dr. Scott's university-level teaching of God's control of history, particularly as it pertained to the Promises of God, the Lost Tribes of Israel, and The Great Pyramid of Giza.

Recently, I had an opportunity to review some of Doc's teaching from those days, and I was struck by the fact that in one of his nightly broadcasts he spent an entire evening reading from *Jasher*. During this particular program, he was pointing out that even though these books had been deemed non-canonical by the mainstream Church, they nevertheless provided an uncanny, behind-the-scenes view of scriptural events that helped to, as he liked to say, "put flesh and blood" on the people who populated *The Bible*. In no uncertain terms, Dr. Scott stated that, regardless of the fact that such books had been marginalized, it clearly deserved another look, particularly because of its ability to shed new light on such perennial mysteries as to why and how Abraham could have become the father of faith during a time that was so steeped in idol worship. As Doc described Abraham's formative years, in his having been sent as a child to be taught by Noah and Shem, thus providing him with critical knowledge that prepared him for God's eventual call, he then offered an off-handed remark to his audience. And I am paraphrasing: "With all the movies that Hollywood has made about *The Bible*, I wonder why they've never gotten around to bringing stories like this to the big screen." It was then that I realized that that moment was undoubtedly when I began my quest to add this information into the matrix of my own investigation into biblical timelines, Christian typology, and God's control over history. Not only that, but without ever knowing it at the time, it would also mark the beginning of an odyssey that would last more than thirty years, one that would eventually culminate in this very work.

So, to those who personally helped me and to those who helped me from afar, I would like to extend my most heartfelt appreciation. I am eternally grateful for all your help in making a lifelong dream finally become the reality that is *Tales of Forever: The Unfolding Drama of God's Hidden Hand in History*.

W. Kent Smith
Los Angeles, California
May 22, 2016

Selected Biographies

WITHOUT THE groundbreaking work of an intrepid band of discoverers, translators, and scholars, this book would never have been possible. For that reason, the following group must be acknowledged for their achievements, without whose contributions this planet would be a much sadder and bleaker place. Therefore, if this present work has anything to add in the way of enriching, enlightening, or educating the world, it is only because I have been afforded the rare and tremendous honor to, for a moment in time, "stand upon the shoulders of giants."

The Discoverers

Johann Grynaeus (1540-1617) was a Swiss Protestant divine, professor of *The New Testament*, and collector of biblical manuscripts. For more than twenty-five years, Grynaeus exerted tremendous influence on both church and state affairs, acquiring quite a reputation as a skillful theologian of the school of Huldrych Zwingli. His many works include commentaries on various books of *The Old Testament* and *The New Testament* as well as an exhaustive collection of patristic literature, entitled *Orthodoxographa* (1569), from which we get the present-day version of *The Gospel of Nicodemus*.

Giuseppe Assemani (1687-1768) was a Lebanese Orientalist and Vatican librarian. Serving as a scribe of Oriental manuscripts, Assemani was sent, in 1715, to Egypt and Syria in search of valuable parchments. Two years later, he returned with one hundred and fifty choice documents, which then became part of the Vatican Library. This success eventually induced Pope Clement XII to send him east again, some twenty years later, and this time Assemani returned with a collection that was even more ancient and more valuable than his first trip. It was among this cache of manuscripts that he discovered a work attributed to Ephrem the Syrian entitled *The Cave of Treasures: The Book of the Succession of the Generations* (c. 350), which later scholars determined bore an uncanny similarity to *The First Book of Adam and Eve*.

James Bruce (1730-1794) was a Scottish explorer and travel writer. Having spent more than a dozen years in North Africa and Ethiopia, Bruce, among other things, traced the origins of the Blue Nile. An examination of Oriental manuscripts at an early age led him to the study of Arabic and Geez, and eventually would determine his future career. Apart from his travels up the Nile River, Bruce also managed to bring back a collection of rare Ethiopian manuscripts, which, according to British historian Edward Ullendorff, "opened up entirely new vistas for the study of Ethiopian languages and placed this branch of Oriental scholarship on a much more secure basis."[474] Among this collection of at least twenty-six manuscripts were the Ethiopic versions of *The First Book of Enoch*, *The Book of Jubilees*, and *The First and Second Books of Adam and Eve*.

E.A. Wallis Budge (1857-1934) was a British Egyptologist, Orientalist, philologist, and author. Working for the British Museum, Budge made numerous trips to Egypt and the Sudan, where he was able to procure a great many objects of antiquity, which in turn helped to build up the museum's collection of cuneiform tablets, manuscripts, and papyri. His various publications on Egyptology helped bring a knowledge of these discoveries to a much larger audience. In 1920 he was knighted for his services to Egyptology and the British Museum. Perhaps his best-known work, which also incorporated his skills as a translator, was *The Egyptian Book of the Dead* (1895), while one of his lesser-known, though no less significant, works was his translation of *The Book of the Cave of Treasures* (1927).

The Translators

William Wake (1657-1737) was a British clergyman, dean at Exeter, bishop at Lincoln, and archbishop of Canterbury. According to biographer Joseph Hirst Lipton, Wake was said to be "a man of wide reading, immense industry, and liberal and tolerant spirit."[475] Of his numerous writings, his most important contribution was an anthology entitled *The Genuine Epistles of the Apostolic Fathers* (1693), which includes the first English translation of *The Gospel of Nicodemus.*

Richard Laurence (1760-1838) was a British Hebraist and Anglican churchman. He was made regius professor of Hebrew and canon of Christ Church at Oxford, in 1814, and archbishop of Cashel, Ireland, in 1822. According to biographer Gordon Goodwin, Laurence's "writings are a model of exactness and judicious moderation. His erudition is well illustrated by the three volumes in which he printed, with Latin and English translations, Ethiopic versions of apocryphal books of *The Bible*, which include *The First Book of Enoch* (1821) from the manuscript that James Bruce brought from Abyssinia and presented to the Bodleian Library."[476]

Moses Samuel (1795-1860) was a British author and translator of Hebrew works. According to *The Jewish Encyclopedia*, Samuel "acquired a considerable reputation as a Hebrew scholar and an authority on rabbinical literature."[477] From an early age, Samuel had a talent for mathematics and languages, eventually speaking twelve languages in all. He is best known for having been the originally anonymous translator of a 1625 Hebrew edition of *The Book of Jasher* (1838) into English, printed in Venice, after becoming convinced by the core of the work that it was the same book referenced in Scripture.

S.C. Malan (1812-1894) was a British biblical scholar and linguist of Oriental languages. Malan was greatly occupied with theological controversy, and published some of his most valuable work illustrative of the Christian East, especially translations from the Syriac, Coptic, Ethiopic, Armenian, and Georgian literatures. According to biographer Cecil Bendall: "In practical knowledge of Oriental languages, Malan had no equal in England, and probably none in the world."[478] Among his more than fifty publications was his English translation of the Ethiopic works of *The First and Second Books of Adam and Eve* (1882).

William Wright (1830-1889) was a British Orientalist and professor of Arabic at Cambridge. He early developed a fondness for Oriental languages, devoting his main efforts to Syriac, but also acquiring a knowledge of all the Semitic languages together with Sanskrit. Many of Wright's works on Syriac literature are still in print and of considerable scholarly value. As a result of his extensive scholarship, he produced such works as *Contributions to the Apocryphal Literature of The New Testament* (1865), from which we have the first English translation *The Letters of Herod and Pilate.*

B. Harris Cowper (1822-1904) was a British archeologist, historian, and translator. As an archeologist, Cowper is credited with having discovered Loughton Camp, an Iron Age hill fort in England, dating from around 500 B.C. As a translator, his work appears in *Apocryphal Gospels and Other Documents relating to the History of Christ* (1865), which gave us English versions of *The Epistles of Pilate to Tiberius Caesar*, *The Trial and Condemnation of Pilate*, and *The Death of Pilate, who Condemned Jesus.*

W.R. Morfill (1834-1909) was a British professor of Slavonic languages at Oxford. He also became curator of the Taylor Institution and was appointed a Fellow of the British Academy in 1903. Writing in his obituary, Sir James Murray said, "We lose in him a unique scholar, whose knowledge of the Slavonic languages was greater than that of any other Englishman, so far as I know." Besides Morfill's various books on Slavonic grammar, he provided, at the behest of R.H. Charles, the English translation of *The Secrets of Enoch* (1896), sometimes designated *The Slavonic Enoch* or *The Second Book of Enoch.*

R.H. Charles (1855-1931) was an Irish biblical scholar and theologian. He gained a Doctor of Divinity and was professor of biblical Greek at Trinity College. Charles is known particularly for English translations of apocryphal and pseudepigraphical works, which includes both *The Book of Jubilees* (1895) and *The Testaments of the Twelve Patriarchs* (1908).

The Scholars

Theophilus of Antioch (c. 120-181) was a Syrian theologian, apologist, author, and chronologist. The seventh bishop of Antioch, Theophilus was a prolific writer whom Eusebius, Jerome, Lactantius, and others mention in reference to his numerous works against the prevailing heresies of the time, of which only his three-volume *Defense of Christianity* (c. 175) survives to this day. Cited as the founder of the science of biblical chronology, he calculated the period from Adam to Christ at about 5,500 years, using a dating system derived from *The Septuagint*.

Julius Africanus (c. 160-240) was a Libyan historian and traveler. He is important primarily because of his influence on Eusebius, all the later writers of biblical history among the Church Fathers, and the entire Greek school of Christian chronologists. He wrote a history of the world entitled *Chronographia* (c. 222) in which he calculated the period from Creation to Christ as 5,500 years. This reckoning of time led to numerous creation eras being used in the Greek Eastern Mediterranean that placed Creation within one decade of 5,500 B.C. Although his history is no longer extant, copious extracts from it can found in the works of Eusebius, Georgius Syncellus, Georgius Cedrenus, and others.

Hippolytus of Rome (c. 170-235) was a Greek theologian, apologist, and chronologist. Hippolytus' voluminous writings embrace the spheres of exegesis, homiletics, apologetics, polemics, and chronography. As an important figure in the development in Christian eschatology, his *Commentary on the Prophet Daniel* is the oldest extant treatise on Scripture. In it, Hippolytus stated that, based on an interpretation on Moses' construction of The Ark of the Covenant, it could be determined that Christ was predicted to arrive on the Earth 5,500 years after the Fall of Adam.

Ephrem the Syrian (c. 306-373) was a theologian, deacon, and hymn writer. His works are hailed by Christians throughout the world, and many denominations venerate him as a saint. Ephrem has been declared a Doctor of the Church by Roman Catholics and is especially beloved in the Syriac Orthodox Church. His hymns, poems, sermons in verse, and prose biblical exegesis were works of practical theology for the edification of a Church in troubled times. He is considered the most significant Church Father of the Syriac tradition.

Giambattista Vico (1668-1744) was an Italian historian, political philosopher, and apologist of classical antiquity. Recognized as one of the greatest Enlightenment thinkers, Vico famously criticized the development of modern rationalism. Best known for his *magnum opus* entitled *New Science* (1725), he is generally regarded as the father of social science, having inaugurated the modern school of the philosophy of history.

George Smith (1800-1868) was a British historian, theologian, and author. According to biographer William Prideaux Courtney: "All his life he was a diligent student, and he was famed throughout Cornwall for his powers in speaking and lecturing. In 1823 he became a local preacher among the Wesleyan Methodists, and for many years before his death was one of the leading laypersons in that society."[479] A member of the Royal Asiatic Society, the Society of Antiquaries of London, and the Royal Society of Literature, he wrote, among other titles, *An Attempt to Ascertain the True Chronology of the Book of Genesis* (1842) and *The Patriarchal Age* (1854).

Joseph A. Seiss (1823-1904) was an American theologian, Lutheran minister, and author. Among his more than one hundred published works, perhaps his best-known are *The Great Pyramid of Egypt: Miracle in Stone* (1877) and *The Gospel in the Stars* (1882). In addition to pyramidology, Seiss was a Christian dispensationalist, a nineteenth-century millennialist school of thought, which viewed history as a series of covenants with God and which became the basis for beliefs widely held by contemporary evangelical Christians.

E.W. Bullinger (1837-1913) was a British clergyman and theologian. Educated at King's College, London, he was a recognized scholar in the field of biblical languages, and in 1881 the archbishop of Canterbury Archibald Tate granted him an honorary Doctor of Divinity in recognition of his scholarship. As an outspoken theologian, Bullinger's views were often unique and sometimes controversial. Among his numerous publications the most noteworthy are *The Witness of the Stars* (1893) and *Number in Scripture: Its Supernatural Design and Spiritual Significance* (1921).

Louis Ginzberg (1873-1953) was a Lithuanian professor of Judaism, a Talmudist, and a leading figure in conservative Judaism. As a result of his impressive scholarship in Jewish studies, Ginzberg was one of sixty scholars honored with a doctorate by Harvard University. The author of a number of scholarly works, he is probably best known for his four volume *The Legends of the Jews* (1913), which is an original synthesis of classical rabbinical, apocryphal, pseudepigraphical, and early Christian literature.

Edgar J. Goodspeed (1871-1962) was an American theologian and scholar of Greek and *The New Testament*. For many years, Goodspeed taught at the University of Chicago, and is best remembered for his various modern translations of *The Bible,* such *The Apocrypha: An American Translation* (1938), all of which stressed an emphasis on updating the archaic language of the original texts into the present-day vernacular English.

Cyrus H. Gordon (1908-2001), was an American biblical scholar and professor of ancient Near East culture and languages. Best known for his key role in the decipherment of Ugaritic, an ancient Semitic language of the fourteenth century B.C., Gordon's contribution has been called "the greatest literary discovery from antiquity since the deciphering of hieroglyphics and cuneiform."[480] With the aid of his textbooks, later scholars were finally able to penetrate the meaning of numerous biblical Hebrew texts and discover striking parallels between the culture of ancient Israel and its neighbors. Prior to Gordon's pioneering work of synthesizing biblical and ancient Near East studies, most scholarship assumed that early civilizations such as Israel and Greece existed as entirely segregated entities, but that basic assumption completely changed with Gordon's publication of *The Common Background of Greek and Hebrew Civilizations* (1965), which boldly challenged the prevailing theories of the day.

Source Material

THE FOLLOWING titles represent a list of the various sources from which this present work is derived. They include written sources as well as audio and visual ones; while written sources range from the apocryphal to the scholarly and the Internet, audio visual sources range from art to music and film.

Apocryphal

The First Book of Adam and Eve, also called *The Conflict of Adam and Eve with Satan*, and *The Second Book of Adam and Eve*, translated by S.C. Malan, 1882

The Book of Enoch, also called *The First Book of Enoch*, translated by Richard Laurence, 1821

The Secrets of Enoch, also called *The Slavonic Enoch* or *The Second Book of Enoch*, translated by W.R. Morfill, 1896

The Book of Jasher, also called *The Book of the Upright*, translated by Moses Samuel, 1838

The Book of Jubilees and *The Testaments of the Twelve Patriarchs*, translated by R.H. Charles, 1895 and 1908, respectively

The Gospel of Nicodemus, formerly called *The Acts of Pontius Pilate*, translated by William Wake, 1693

The Letters of Herod and Pilate, translated by William Wright, 1865

The Epistles of Pilate to Tiberius Caesar, *The Trial and Condemnation of Pilate*, and *The Death of Pilate, who Condemned Jesus*, translated by B. Harris Cowper, 1867

Art

The Creation of Adam, Michelangelo, 1512

God took Enoch, Gerard Hoet, 1728

Adam and Eve in Paradise, Jan Gossaert, 1527

Sacrifice of Isaac, Caravaggio, 1603

Behold the Man, Antonio Ciseri, 1871

The Beginning of Days, David Spalione, 1999

Scholarly

New Science, Giambattista Vico, 1725

The Common Background of Greek and Hebrew Civilizations, Cyrus H. Gordon; W.W. Norton and Company, Inc., 1965

Edgar Johnson Goodspeed: Articulate Scholar, James I. Cook; Scholars Press, 1981

The Apocrypha: An American Translation, Edgar J. Goodspeed; The University of Chicago, 1938

The Criswell Study Bible, W.A. Criswell (Editor); Criswell Center for Biblical Studies, 1979

The Apocrypha and Pseudepigrapha of The Old Testament, Volume 2, R.H. Charles; Clarendon Press, 1913

A Dissertation on Sacred Chronology, Nathan Rouse; Longman, Brown, Green and Longmans, 1856

Dictionary of the Middle Ages, Volume 1: Aachen to Augustinism, Stephen A. Barney (Contributor), Joseph R. Strayer (Editor); Charles Scribner's Sons, 1982

The Epistle to Can Grande, Dante Alighieri, 1319

Icons of the Middle Ages: Rulers, Writers, Rebels, and Saints: Volume 1, Elizabeth K. Haller (Contributor), Lister M. Matheson (Editor); Greenwood Publishing, 2012

Spiritual Gems: The Mystical Koran Commentary, Jafar al-Sadiq; Louisville: Fons Vitae, 2011

The Legends of the Jews, Volume 2: From Joseph to the Exodus, Louis Ginzberg; The Jewish Publication Society of America, 1913

The Witness of the Stars, E.W. Bullinger; Kregel Publications, 1893

Profiles of the Future, Arthur C. Clarke; Bantam Books, Inc., 1961

Screening Out the Past: The Birth of Mass Culture and the Motion Picture Industry, Lary May; The University of Chicago Press Books, 1983

Seventy Years at the Movies: From Silent Films to Today's Screen Hits, David Robinson (Consulting Editor); Crescent Books, 1988

The Many Faces of Christ: The Thousand-Year Story of the Survival and Influence of the Lost Gospels, Philip Jenkins; Basic Books, 2015

The Making of the English New Testament, Edgar J. Goodspeed; The University of Chicago Press, 1925

Romantic Quest and Modern Query: A History of the Modern Theater, Tom F. Driver; Delacorte Press, 1970

Paradigm Change in Theology: A Symposium for the Future, Hans Küng, David Tracy (Editors); The Crossroad Publishing Company, 1989

Surviving the Swastika: Scientific Research in Nazi Germany, Kristie Macrakis; Oxford University Press, Inc., 1993

Scientific Autobiography and Other Papers, Max Planck; Philosophical Library, 1949

Dreyfus: His Life and Letters, Alfred Dreyfus; Yale University Press, 1937

Epitome, Apollodorus, c. 200 B.C.

Banana: The Fate of the Fruit That Changed the World, Dan Koeppel; Hudson Street Press, 2008

Paradise Lost, John Milton, 1667

Gods, Graves, and Scholars: The Story of Archeology, C.W. Ceram; Random House, Inc., 1949

Familiar Mysteries: The Truth in Myth, Shirley Park Lowry; Oxford University Press, 1982

On the Embassy to Gaius: The First Part on the Treatise on Virtues, Philo, c. 40

First Apology, Justin Martyr, c. 155

The Hero with a Thousand Faces, Joseph Campbell; New World Library, 2008

Israel-Britain, Adam Rutherford (Author and Publisher), 1934

The Hollywood Reporter Book of Box Office Hits, Susan Sackett; Billboard Books, 1990

An Empire of Their Own: How the Jews Invented Hollywood, Neal Gabler; Anchor Books, 1988

The Writer's Journey: Mythic Structure for Storytellers and Screenwriters, Christopher Vogler; Michael Wiese Productions, 1992

Strong's Exhaustive Concordance of the Bible, James Strong; MacDonald Publishing Company 1890

Pyramidology: Book I, Adam Rutherford; The Institute of Pyramidology, 1957

The Great Pyramid Decoded, Peter Lemesurier; Element Books Ltd., 1977

The Great Pyramid of Egypt: Miracle in Stone, Joseph A. Seiss; Porter and Coates, 1877

Complete Books of Enoch, Ann Nyland; Smith and Sterling Publishers, 2010

The Legends of the Jews, Volume 1: From the Creation to Jacob, Louis Ginzberg; The Jewish Publication Society of America, 1913

The Egyptian Book of the Dead, E.A. Wallis Budge; The British Museum, 1895

Number in Scripture: Its Supernatural Design and Spiritual Significance, E.W. Bullinger; Eyre and Spottiswoode Ltd., 1921

Treatise on Bible Chronology, Adam Rutherford; The Institute of Pyramidology, 1957

Pyramidology: Book III, Adam Rutherford; The Institute of Pyramidology, 1957

Against Apion, Flavius Josephus, c. 97

Encyclopedia Perthensis: Or, Universal Dictionary of the Arts, Sciences, and Literature, Volume 9, John Brown; Anchor Close, 1816

Studies in Biblical and Patristic Criticism, Volume 1, S.R. Driver, William Sanday, John Wordsworth; Oxford University Press, 1885

Commentary on Daniel, Hippolytus of Rome, c. 205

The Extant Fragments of the Five Books of the Chronology of Julius Africanus: On the Mythical Chronology of the Egyptians and Chaldeans, Julius Africanus, c. 222

The Patriarchal Age: The History and Religion of Mankind from the Creation to the Death of Isaac, George Smith; Carlton and Phillips, 1854

The Cave of Treasures: The Book of the Succession of the Generations, Ephrem the Syrian, c. 350

The Book of the Cave of Treasures: A History of the Patriarchs and the Kings, their Successors, from the Creation to the Crucifixion of Christ, E.A. Wallis Budge; The London Religious Tract Society, 1927

The Luminous Eye: The Spiritual World Vision of Saint Ephrem the Syrian, Sebastian Brock; Cisterian Publications, 1992

Faith, Ephrem the Syrian, c. 360

Dramatic Prophecies of the Great Pyramid, Rodolfo Benavides; Editores Mexicano Unidos, 1970

Daniel: The Key to Prophetic Revelation, John F. Walvoord; The Moody Bible Institute of Chicago, 1971

The Spear of Destiny, Trevor Ravenscroft; Samuel Weiser, Inc., 1982

Secrets of the Holy Lance: The Spear of Destiny in History and Legend, Jerry E. Smith and George Piccard; Adventures Unlimited Press, 2005

Voltaire in His Letters, Voltaire; G.P. Putnam's Sons, 1919

On Liberty, John Stuart Mill; Tickner and Fields, 1863

The Blood and the Shroud: New Evidence That the World's Most Sacred Relic Is Real, Ian Wilson; Simon and Schuster, Inc., 1998

New World Encyclopedia; Paragon House Publishers, 2015

Leonardo's Notebooks: Writing and Art of the Great Master, Leonardo da Vinci; Black Dog and Leventhal Publishers, Inc., 2005

The Legends of the Jews, From the Creation to Exodus: Notes for Volumes 1 and 2, Louis Ginzberg; The Jewish Publication Society of America, 1925

The Myth of the Phoenix: According to Classical and Early Christian Traditions, Roelof van den Broek; Brill Archive, 1972

The Ancient Near East, Cyrus H. Gordon; W.W. Norton and Company, Inc., 1965

Internet

The Jewish Encyclopedia, William Bacher, Kaufmann Kohler, J. Frederic McMurdy (Executive Committee of the Editorial Board); JewishEncyclopedia.com, 1906

On the Film: The Passion of the Christ, Wikipedia: The Free Encyclopedia, 2015

What's the Big Deal?: Butch Cassidy and the Sundance Kid, Eric D. Snider; Film.com, 2011

List of Highest-Grossing Franchises and Film Series, Wikipedia: The Free Encyclopedia, 2015

Genes and Chromosomes, David N. Finegold; The Merck Manual: Home Edition, 2013

Phi: 1.618, The Golden Number: Golden Ratio Overview, Gary Meisner; PhiPoint Solutions, 2014

Last Days of the Third Reich, Walther Johann von Löpp (Compiler), Levi Bookin (Editor); The Propagander, 2016

World War II in Europe; The History Place, 2016

Music

Time, David Gilmour, Nick Mason, Roger Waters, Richard Wright; Pink Floyd Music Publishers Ltd., 1972

Film

The Ten Commandments, Aeneas MacKenzie, Jesse Lasky, Jr., Jack Gariss, Frederic M. Frank, Dorothy Clarke Wilson, J.H. Ingraham, A.E. Southon; Paramount, 1956

Butch Cassidy and the Sundance Kid, William Goldman; 20th Century Fox, 1969

The Longest Day, Cornelius Ryan, Romain Gary, James Jones, David Pursall, Jack Seddon; 20th Century Fox, 1962

Dances With Wolves, Michael Blake; Orion, 1990

The Passion of the Christ, Mel Gibson, Benedict Fitzgerald, William Fulco; 20th Century Fox, 2004

Gone With the Wind, Sidney Howard, Margaret Mitchell; MGM, 1939

Jaws, Peter Benchley, Carl Gottlieb; Universal, 1975

Goldfinger, Richard Maibaum, Paul Dehn, Ian Fleming; United Artists, 1964

Shane, A.B. Guthrie, Jr., Jack Sher, Jack Schaefer; Paramount, 1953

The Searchers, Frank S. Nugent, Alan Le May; Warner Bros., 1956

The Godfather, Mario Puzo, Francis Ford Coppola; Paramount, 1972

E.T. the Extra-Terrestrial, Melissa Mathison; Universal, 1982

Excalibur, Thomas Malory, Raspo Pallenberg, John Boorman; Orion, 1981

Unforgiven, David Webb Peoples; Warner Bros., 1992

Sherlock Holmes, Michael Robert Johnson, Anthony Peckham, Simon Kinberg, Lionel Wigram; Warner Bros./Roadshow Entertainment, 2009

Ghost, Bruce Joel Rubin; Paramount, 1990

Mr. Smith Goes to Washington, Sidney Buchman; Columbia, 1939

From Russia With Love, Richard Maibaum, Johanna Harwood, Ian Fleming; United Artists, 1963

You Only Live Twice, Roald Dahl, Ian Fleming; United Artists, 1967

Skyfall, Neal Purvis, Robert Wade, John Logan; MGM/Columbia, 2012

Star Wars IV: A New Hope, George Lucas; 20th Century Fox, 1977

Superman: The Movie, Mario Puzo, David Newman, Leslie Newman, Robert Benton; Warner Bros., 1978

Star Trek II: The Wrath of Khan, Jack B. Sowards, Nicholas Meyer, Harve Bennett, Samuel A. Peeples; Paramount, 1982

Star Trek III: The Search for Spock, Harve Bennett; Paramount, 1984

Star Trek: Generations, Ronald D. Moore, Brannon Braga, Rick Berman; Paramount, 1994

Men in Black, Ed Solomon, Lowell Cunningham; Columbia, 1997

Men in Black 3, Etan Cohen, Lowell Cunningham; Columbia, 2012

The Matrix, The Wachowskis; Warner Bros., 1999

Harry Potter and the Chamber of Secrets, Steve Cloves, J.K. Rowling; Warner Bros., 2002

The Dark Knight Rises, Jonathan Nolan, Christopher Nolan, David S. Goyer; Warner Bros., 2012

X2: X-Men United, Michael Dougherty, Dan Harris, David Hayler, Bryan Singer, Zak Penn, Jack Kirby, Stan Lee; 20th Century Fox, 2003

X-Men: The Last Stand, Simon Kinberg, Zak Penn, Jack Kirby, Stan Lee; 20th Century Fox, 2006

X-Men Origins: Wolverine, David Benioff, Skip Woods, Roy Thomas, Len Wein, John Romita, Sr.; 20th Century Fox, 2009

Close Encounters of the Third Kind, Steven Spielberg; Columbia, 1977

Permission to Reprint

MOST OF THE TEXTUAL material that has been reprinted or adapted in this book resides in the public domain or has been utilized according to the practice of "fair use," and in lieu of this fact, there has been no copyright infringement involved in its incorporation. As for those works that are not deemed as such, the following permissions have been graciously granted to the author of this publication.

An excerpt from the 1992 edition of *The Writer's Journey: Mythic Structure for Storytellers and Screenwriters* by Christopher Vogler has been reprinted with permission from Michael Wiese Productions.

Excerpts from the 1981 edition of *Edgar Johnson Goodspeed: Articulate Scholar* by James I. Cook have been reprinted with permission from The Society of Biblical Literature.

An excerpt from the 2011 Internet article on *What's the Big Deal?: Butch Cassidy and the Sundance Kid* has been reprinted with permission from its author, Eric D. Snider.

An excerpt from the 2014 Internet article on *Phi: 1.618, The Golden Number: Golden Ratio Overview* has been reprinted with permission from its author, Gary Meisner, of PhiPoint Solutions.

An excerpt from the 2005 edition of *Leonardo's Notebooks: Writing and Art of the Great Master* by Leonardo da Vinci has been reprinted with permission from Black Dog and Leventhal Publishers, Inc.

An excerpt from the 2015 Internet article on the Phoenix has been reprinted with permission from *New World Encyclopedia* on condition of providing the following citation: "Phoenix (mythology)" New World Encyclopedia, 29 April 2015, newworldencyclopedia.org/p/zzindex.php?title=Phoenix (mythology)&oldid=987706.

Excerpts from the 1992 edition of *The Luminous Eye: The Spiritual World Vision of Saint Ephrem the Syrian* by Sebastian Brock have been reprinted with permission from Cisterian Publications and the Order of Saint Benedict in Collegeville, Minnesota.

Excerpts from the 1972 edition of *The Myth of the Phoenix: According to Classical and Early Christian Traditions* by Roelof van den Broek have been reprinted with permission from Koninklijke Brill N.V.

Excerpts from the 1973 edition of *The Spear of Destiny* by Trevor Ravenscroft, who is represented by the Estate of Trevor Ravenscroft, have been reprinted with permission from Red Wheel Weiser, LLC, Newburyport, MA, redwheelweiser.com.

An excerpt from the 2008 edition of *Banana: The Fate of the Fruit That Changed the World* has been reprinted with permission from its author, Dan Koeppel, and publisher, Penguin Random House.

An excerpt from the 2008 edition of *A Hero With a Thousand Faces* by Joseph Campbell has been reprinted with permission from the Joseph Campbell Foundation.

An excerpt from the 1971 edition of *Daniel: The Key to Prophetic Revelation* by John F. Walvoord has been reprinted with permission from The Moody Bible Institute of Chicago.

An excerpt from the 1938 edition of *The Apocrypha: An American Translation* by Edgar J. Goodspeed was reprinted with permission from The University of Chicago.

An excerpt from the 1998 edition of *The Blood and the Shroud: New Evidence That the World's Most Sacred Relic Is Real* by Ian Wilson was reprinted with permission from Simon and Schuster, Inc.

Endnotes

Some Foreword Thinking

[1] *The Many Faces of Christ: The Thousand-Year Story of the Survival and Influence of the Lost Gospels*, Philip Jenkins; Basic Books, 2015, pp. 6-7
[2] John 1:1-3
[3] *Proverbs* 25:2
[4] *Matthew* 12:38-39
[5] *John* 15:19
[6] *Matthew* 21:12-13

THE PRELUDE - The Hidden Books

[7] *Second Corinthians* 1:20
[8] Ibid. 1:20
[9] *The Common Background of Greek and Hebrew Civilizations*, Cyrus H. Gordon; W.W. Norton and Company, Inc., 1965, p. 278
[10] *Edgar Johnson Goodspeed: Articulate Scholar*, James I. Cook; Scholars Press, 1981, p. X
[11] *The Apocrypha: An American Translation*, Edgar J. Goodspeed; Vintage Books, 1989, p. v
[12] *The Criswell Study Bible*, W.A. Criswell (Editor); Criswell Center for Biblical Studies, 1979, p. 1
[13] *Genesis* 6:19-20
[14] Ibid. 7:2-3
[15] *Matthew* 27:5
[16] *Acts* 1:18
[17] *The Apocrypha and Pseudepigrapha of the Old Testament, Volume 2*, R.H. Charles; Clarendon Press, 1913, p. 282
[18] *Luke* 22:69-71
[19] *First Enoch* 46:1-4
[20] See Act Three: The Players—*Enoch as: The Go-Between*
[21] *Jude* 1:9
[22] *The Testament of Benjamin* 2:6-9, 17-18
[23] *Second Esdras* 7:26-29
[24] *A Dissertation on Sacred Chronology*, Nathan Rouse; Longman, Brown, Green, and Longmans, 1856, p. 20
[25] Ibid. pp. 20-21
[26] See Act Three: The Subplots—*A Capstone to Time: The Five and a Half Days*
[27] *A Dissertation on Sacred Chronology*, Nathan Rouse; Longman, Brown, Green, and Longmans, 1856, p. 22
[28] *The Lost Books of the Bible and The Forgotten Books of Eden*, Frank Crane; Alpha House, Inc., 1926, Part 1, pp. 8-9
[29] Ibid. p. 10
[30] *Isaiah* 45:15
[31] *First Samuel* 6:19-20
[32] *Exodus* 14:21
[33] *Joshua* 3:9-17
[34] *Romans* 1:17

THE ANALYSES - Arguments for Authenticity

[35] *John* 19:37
[36] *Nicodemus* 3:11-13
[37] *Matthew* 13:3-9
[38] *Dictionary of the Middle Ages, Volume 1: Aachen to Augustinism—Allegory*, Stephen A. Barney (Contributor); Charles Scribner's Sons, 1982, p. 180
[39] *Icons of the Middle Ages: Rulers, Writers, Rebels, and Saints: Volume 1—Dante Alighieri*, Elizabeth K. Haller (Contributor), Lister M. Matheson (Editor); Greenwood Publishing, 2012, p. 244
[40] *The Epistle to Can Grande*, Dante Alighieri, 1319, pp. 5-6
[41] *The Jewish Encyclopedia: Biblical Exegesis—Pardes*, William Bacher, Kaufmann Kohler, J. Frederic McMurdy (Executive Committee of the Editorial Board); JewishEncyclopedia.com, 1906
[42] *Spiritual Gems: The Mystical Koran Commentary*, Jafar al-Sadiq; Louisville: Fons Vitae, 2011, p. 1
[43] *First Corinthians* 2:9
[44] Ibid. 2:14
[45] *Matthew* 13:34-35
[46] *First Enoch* 1:1-2
[47] *Mark* 1:15
[48] *Romans* 1:20
[49] *First Corinthians* 2:6-7
[50] *Proverbs* 25:2
[51] Ibid. 2:3-5
[52] Ibid. 1:20-21
[53] Ibid. 1:23-26
[54] *Isaiah* 48:4-6
[55] *Matthew* 11:25; *Luke* 10:21
[56] *Matthew* 13:44
[57] *Psalm* 78:1-7
[58] *Matthew* 13:10; *Mark* 4:10; *Luke* 8:9
[59] *First Adam and Eve* 3:2-4
[60] Ibid. 3:6
[61] *Second Peter* 3:8; *Psalm* 90:4; *Jubilees* 4:30
[62] *Nicodemus* 22:11
[63] Ibid. 22:12-13
[64] *Secrets of Enoch* 32:1-3
[65] *Jubilees* 4:31-32
[66] *The Legends of the Jews, Volume 2: From Joseph to the Exodus*, Louis Ginzberg; The Jewish Publication Society of America, 1913, p. 18
[67] *The Testament of Zebulun* 1:18-23
[68] *Daniel* 9:2
[69] Ibid. 9:24
[70] *Exodus* 23:10
[71] *Second Chronicles* 36:20-21
[72] *The Common Background of Greek and Hebrew Civilizations*, Cyrus H. Gordon; W.W. Norton and Company, Inc., 1965, p. 226
[73] Ibid. pp. 283-84
[74] *Joshua* 10:12-14
[75] *Second Samuel* 1:17-19
[76] *Genesis* 3:6
[77] Ibid. 3:21
[78] Ibid. 7:8-9
[79] Ibid. 9:20-26
[80] Ibid. 8:9-10
[81] Ibid. 25:27
[82] Ibid. 25:29-34
[83] *Jasher* 7:23-33
[84] *First Adam and Eve* 50:7
[85] Ibid. 51:2-5

[86] *First Adam and Eve* 52:2
[87] *Revelation* 5:6, 12; 13:8
[88] *First Peter* 5:8
[89] *Job* 9:9; 38:31; *Amos* 5:8
[90] *The Witness of the Stars*, E.W. Bullinger; Kregel Publications, 1893, pp. 124-27
[91] *Genesis* 3:14-15
[92] compare with *Genesis* 14:1, 9
[93] *Jasher* 27:1-11
[94] *Matthew* 13:44
[95] *Matthew* 9:17; *Mark* 2:22; *Luke* 5:37
[96] e.g., The Shroud of Turin
[97] *Acts* 19:11-12
[98] *John* 19:23-24
[99] *Psalm* 22:1; 12-18
[100] *Matthew* 27:46; *John* 19:24
[101] *The Death of Pilate, who Condemned Jesus*
[102] *Profiles of the Future*, Arthur C. Clarke; Bantam Books, 1961
[103] *Matthew* 12:39-40; *Luke* 11:29-30
[104] *Colossians* 1:25-27
[105] *Exodus* 23:10; *Second Chronicles* 36:20-21; *Daniel* 9:24
[106] See Act Three: The Themes—*A Prophecy of Days*
[107] *First Adam and Eve* 3:6; *Secrets of Enoch* 32:1-3; *Nicodemus* 22:12-13
[108] *Matthew* 12:39-40; *Luke* 11:29-30

THE ANALYSES - Shadow and Substance

[109] *Colossians* 2:16-17
[110] *Matthew* 12:40; *Luke* 11:30
[111] *Ephesians* 4:11-14
[112] *The Common Background of Greek and Hebrew Civilizations*, Cyrus H. Gordon; W.W. Norton and Company, Inc., 1965, pp. 290-91
[113] *John* 10:11, 17-18
[114] *Jasher* 22:41-45
[115] Ibid. 16:22
[116] Ibid. 28:24
[117] *Secrets of Enoch* 1-68
[118] *Hebrews* 11:24-27
[119] *Genesis* 22:6-8
[120] *Jasher* 23:49-65
[121] *Genesis* 37:5-8; *Mark* 6:1-6
[122] *Genesis* 37:18-24; *Matthew* 26:47-50
[123] *Genesis* 40:1-23; *Luke* 23:32-43
[124] *Psalm* 105:17-22; *First Peter* 1:18-21
[125] *Genesis* 42:6-8; *Luke* 13-16
[126] *Genesis* 42:3-8
[127] Ibid. 42:9-18
[128] Ibid. 43:29
[129] Ibid. 44:1-13
[130] Ibid. 44:14-34
[131] Ibid. 45:1-3
[132] Ibid. 45:4-11
[133] Ibid. 45:12-15
[134] *Matthew* 16:13-17
[135] *Jasher* 53:10-13
[136] Ibid. 53:18-22
[137] *Matthew* 4:12-15
[138] *Romans* 11:1
[139] *Judges* 19-21
[140] *First Kings* 11:13, 36
[141] *Micah* 5:2
[142] *Jeremiah* 31:15
[143] *Genesis* 43:1-5
[144] Ibid. 43:29-34
[145] *Jasher* 53:21-22
[146] *Genesis* 45:4-8
[147] *Jasher* 53:23-26
[148] *The Legends of the Jews, Volume 2: From Joseph to the Exodus*, Louis Ginzberg; The Jewish Publication Society of America, 1913, p. 100
[149] *Genesis* 31:32; 35:16-20
[150] *Jasher* 53:27
[151] *Genesis* 31:19-37
[152] *The Legends of the Jews, Volume 2: From Joseph to the Exodus*, Louis Ginzberg; The Jewish Publication Society of America, 1913, p. 100
[153] Ibid. p. 101
[154] *Deuteronomy* 33:12
[155] *The Legends of the Jews, Volume 2: From Joseph to the Exodus*, Louis Ginzberg; The Jewish Publication Society of America, 1913, p. 102
[156] *Jasher* 53:21-22
[157] *Genesis* 37:18-19
[158] *Matthew* 16:25; *Luke* 9:24
[159] *Matthew* 16:13-14
[160] Ibid. 11:7-14
[161] *Malachi* 3:1-4
[162] Ibid. 3:1
[163] *Luke* 4:16-22
[164] See Act Three: The Themes—*A Man of Substance*

THE ANALYSES - The Stage is Set

[165] *Genesis* 37:18-19
[166] *John* 20:24
[167] Ibid. 20:30
[168] *Jasher* 12:22-38
[169] *First John* 4:19
[170] *Screening Out the Past: The Birth of Mass Culture and the Motion Picture Industry*, Lary May; The University of Chicago Press Books, 1983, p. 60
[171] *Seventy Years at the Movies: From Silent Films to Today's Screen Hits*, David Robinson (Consulting Editor); Crescent Books, 1988, p. 7
[172] *First Corinthians* 15:3-8
[173] *First Kings* 17:17-24
[174] *Second Kings* 4:20-37
[175] Ibid. 13:21
[176] *John* 11:43-44
[177] *Acts* 2:24, 32; 3:15, 26; 4:10; 5:30; 10:40; 13:30, 33, 34, 37
[178] Ibid. 9:36-41
[179] *John* 1:1-5, 14

[180] *First Adam and Eve* 10:1-3; 20:4-8; 68:1-2
[181] *Genesis* 5:24
[182] *Secrets of Enoch* 38:1-3
[183] *Jasher* 12:1-34
[184] *Daniel* 3:13-27
[185] *Genesis* 22:6-13
[186] Ibid. 37:19-35
[187] Ibid. 41:39-43
[188] Ibid. 42:1-2
[189] Ibid. 45:1-15
[190] *Matthew* 26:64; *Mark* 14:62; 16:19; *Luke* 22:69; *Acts* 2:33; 5:31; 7:55; *Romans* 8:34; *Ephesians* 1:20; *Colossians* 3:1; *Hebrews* 1:3; 12:2; *First Peter* 3:22
[191] *Exodus* 12:11
[192] *John* 7:6-8
[193] *Matthew* 26:18-19
[194] *Matthew* 26:3-5; *Mark* 14:1-2
[195] *Matthew* 2:1-18
[196] *Judges* 13:2-5
[197] *Luke* 1:13-15
[198] *Exodus* 1:9-22
[199] *Jasher* 67:11-20
[200] See Act Three: The Themes—*A Hero for the Ages*
[201] *The Many Faces of Christ: The Thousand-Year Story of the Survival and Influence of the Lost Gospels*, Philip Jenkins; Basic Books, 2015, p. 83
[202] Ibid. pp. 86-87
[203] Ibid. p. 88
[204] *Matthew* 12:38-41; *Luke* 11:29-32
[205] *Matthew* 16:3-4
[206] *Hebrews* 11:1, 5, 17-19, 22, 24, 26, 35, 39
[207] *Second Corinthians* 5:17
[208] *First Corinthians* 15:54
[209] *John* 1:3
[210] *Genesis* 1:1
[211] *Acts* 3:15
[212] *Hebrews* 2:10; 5:9; 12:2
[213] *Romans* 10:17
[214] *Galatians* 3:5
[215] *First Enoch* 104:7-11

THE TRANSLATION - *A Matter of Style*

[216] *On the Film: The Passion of the Christ*, Wikipedia: The Free Encyclopedia, 2015
[217] *Edgar Johnson Goodspeed: Articulate Scholar*, James I. Cook; Scholars Press, 1981, p. 24
[218] *The Making of the English New Testament*, Edgar J. Goodspeed; The University of Chicago Press, 1925, p. 110
[219] Ibid. p. 110
[220] *What's the Big Deal?: Butch Cassidy and the Sundance Kid*, Eric D. Snider; Film.com, 2011
[221] *Edgar Johnson Goodspeed: Articulate Scholar*, James I. Cook; Scholars Press, 1981, p. 28
[222] Ibid. p. 28
[223] Ibid. p. 29
[224] *Hebrews* 11:24-26

THE INTERLUDE - *The Curtain Rises*

[225] See Act Three: The Players—*Enoch as: The Go-Between*
[226] *Romantic Quest and Modern Query: A History of the Modern Theater*, Tom F. Driver; Delacorte Press, 1970, pp. xi-xii
[227] Ibid. p. xiii
[228] Ibid. p. xiii
[229] See Act Three: The Players—*Adam as: The Defendant*
[230] Ibid.—*Abraham as: The Stranger*
[231] Ibid.—*Pilate as: The Public Defender*

THE SEGUE - *The New Paradigm Shift*

[232] *Paradigm Change in Theology: A Symposium for the Future*, Hans Küng, David Tracy (Editors); The Crossroad Publishing Company, 1989, p. 21
[233] Ibid. p. 25
[234] *Surviving the Swastika: Scientific Research in Nazi Germany*, Kristie Macrakis; Oxford University Press, Inc., 1993, p. 97
[235] *Scientific Autobiography and Other Papers*, Max Planck; Philosophical Library, 1949, pp. 33-34
[236] *Paradigm Change in Theology: A Symposium for the Future*, Hans Küng, David Tracy (Editors); The Crossroad Publishing Company, 1989, p. 20
[237] *Scientific Autobiography and Other Papers*, Max Planck; Philosophical Library, 1949, p. 184
[238] Ibid. p. 186

THE PLAYERS - *Enoch as: The Go-Between*

[239] *Genesis* 5:24
[240] *Hebrews* 11:5
[241] *Matthew* 22:30; *Luke* 20:35-36
[242] *First Enoch* 15:6-7
[243] *John* 14:1
[244] *First Enoch* 41:1
[245] *Secrets of Enoch* 61:1
[246] *Second Corinthians* 5:1
[247] *Mark* 13:26-27
[248] *First Enoch* 61:10-11
[249] *Matthew* 17:5; *Mark* 9:7; *Luke* 9:35
[250] *Luke* 9:35
[251] *Isaiah* 42:1
[252] *First Enoch* 45:3-4
[253] Ibid. 45:4
[254] Ibid. 61:10
[255] *Matthew* 13:11; *Mark* 4:11; *Luke* 8:10

THE PLAYERS - *Adam as: The Defendant*

[256] *Genesis* 3:5
[257] Ibid. 3:12
[258] *Numbers* 22:28-30
[259] *First Adam and Eve* 17:6-8
[260] *Genesis* 3:14
[261] Ibid. 3:15
[262] *First Adam and Eve* 27:1-12
[263] *Dreyfus: His Life and Letters*, Alfred Dreyfus; Yale University Press, 1937, p. 175

[264] *Genesis* 2:16-17
[265] *Epitome*, Apollodorus, c. 200 B.C., E.3.2-3
[266] *Banana: The Fate of the Fruit That Changed the World*, Dan Koeppel; Hudson Street Press, 2008, p. 1
[267] *Paradise Lost*, John Milton, 1667, Book Nine, verses 549-588
[268] *First Enoch* 31:2-5
[269] *Ephesians* 5:18
[270] *John* 15:5
[271] *Matthew* 26:27-29
[272] *Genesis* 3:12
[273] *Romans* 5:12
[274] Ibid. 5:12

THE PLAYERS - Abraham as: The Stranger

[275] *Genesis* 12:1-4
[276] *Romans* 4:11-25
[277] *Jasher* 9:4-6
[278] *Gods, Graves, and Scholars: The Story of Archeology*, C.W. Ceram; Random House, Inc., 1949, p. 344
[279] *Familiar Mysteries: The Truth in Myth*, Shirley Park Lowry; Oxford University Press, 1982, pp. 95-96
[280] Ibid. pp. 103-04
[281] *Matthew* 16:21-23; *Mark* 8:31-33
[282] *John* 12:23-34
[283] *Exodus* 2:1-10
[284] *Jasher* 8:2-4
[285] Ibid. 8:15-16
[286] Ibid. 8:33-34
[287] Ibid. 8:35-36
[288] Ibid. 9:5-6

THE PLAYERS - Pilate as: The Public Defender

[289] *Matthew* 27:24
[290] *John* 18:35
[291] See Act Three: The Players—*Adam as: The Defendant* (paragraph one)
[292] *John* 18:38
[293] *On the Embassy to Gaius: The First Part on the Treatise on Virtues*, Philo, 238.301 & 303
[294] Ibid. 238.302
[295] *First Apology*, Justin Martyr, Chapter 35
[296] Ibid. Chapter 48
[297] *John* 19:10
[298] *The Hero with a Thousand Faces*, Joseph Campbell; New World Library, 2008, p. 64
[299] *John* 10:18
[300] Ibid. 19:11
[301] Ibid. 19:12-14

THE THEMES - A Prophecy of Days

[302] *Time*, David Gilmour, Nick Mason, Roger Waters, Richard Wright; Pink Floyd Music Publishers Ltd., 1972
[303] *Ecclesiastes* 3:1-2, 8
[304] *Isaiah* 49:8
[305] *Daniel* 7:25
[306] Ibid. 8:19; 11:29, 33
[307] *John* 7:6
[308] *First Corinthians* 4:5
[309] *Romans* 5:6
[310] *First Adam and Eve* 3:1-2
[311] Ibid. 3:3-5
[312] Ibid. 3:6
[313] *Hosea* 1:4-8
[314] *Isaiah* 20:1-6
[315] *Ezekiel* 5:1-17
[316] *Hosea* 1:10
[317] *First Adam and Eve* 3:1-6, 16
[318] *Hosea* 1:10
[319] Ibid. 5:14-15
[320] Ibid. 6:1-3
[321] *Deuteronomy* 28: 15, 25, 37
[322] *Second Peter* 3:8; *Psalm* 90:4; *Jubilees* 4:30
[323] *Second Kings* 17:5-6
[324] *Israel-Britain*, Adam Rutherford (Author and Publisher), 1934, p. 161
[325] *Ezekiel* 37:1-14
[326] *Israel-Britain*, Adam Rutherford (Author and Publisher), 1934, pp. 181-82

THE THEMES - A Man of Substance

[327] *First Adam and Eve* 50:7
[328] *Exodus* 12:13
[329] *Matthew* 26:18-19
[330] *Luke* 7:18-20
[331] Ibid. 7:22
[332] *Luke* 4:16-18; *Isaiah* 4:18-19

THE THEMES - A Hero for the Ages

[333] *Psalm* 42:7
[334] Ibid. 42:3
[335] Ibid. 42:7
[336] *Matthew* 3:11
[337] *The Hollywood Reporter Book of Box Office Hits*, Susan Sackett; Billboard Books, 1990, p. 21
[338] *An Empire of Their Own: How the Jews Invented Hollywood*, Neal Gabler; Anchor Books, 1988, p. 173
[339] Ibid. p. 173
[340] *List of Highest-Grossing Franchises and Film Series*, Wikipedia: The Free Encyclopedia, June 2015
[341] *The Writer's Journey: Mythic Structure for Storytellers and Screenwriters*, Christopher Vogler; Michael Wiese Productions, 1992, pp. 181-82

THE SUBPLOTS - A Capstone to Time

[342] *Nicodemus* 22:10-13
[343] *Isaiah* 28:15-17
[344] Ibid. 19:19-20
[345] *Strong's Exhaustive Concordance of The Bible: Dictionary of Hebrew Words*, James Strong; MacDonald Publishing Company, 1890, p. 10
[346] Ibid. pp. 85-86
[347] *Genesis* 5:23-24

[348] *Pyramidology: Book I*, Adam Rutherford; The Institute of Pyramidology, 1957, p. 83
[349] *The Great Pyramid Decoded*, Peter Lemesurier; Element Books Ltd., 1977, pp. 375-76
[350] *The Great Pyramid of Egypt: Miracle in Stone*, Joseph A. Seiss; Porter and Coates, 1877, pp. 115-16
[351] *Job* 38:1-7
[352] *The Great Pyramid of Egypt: Miracle in Stone*, Joseph A. Seiss; Porter and Coates, 1877, pp. 61-62
[353] Ibid. p. 110
[354] Ibid. pp. 109-10
[355] *Job* 38:3-4
[356] Ibid. 38:6-7
[357] *Genesis* 6:4
[358] *Complete Books of Enoch*, Ann Nyland; Smith and Sterling Publishers, 2010, p. 20
[359] *Second Samuel* 24:15-16
[360] *Second Kings* 18:13, 17, 25; 19:1, 15-20, 32-35
[361] *Matthew* 28:2-3
[362] *Genesis* 6:4-7
[363] Ibid. 6:5
[364] *First Enoch* 7:1-7, 10-15; 8:2, 9
[365] *First Samuel* 17:4
[366] *Genesis* 6:15
[367] *The Merck Manual: Home Edition*, David N. Finegold, 2013, Genes and Chromosomes
[368] *Genesis* 3:6-8
[369] *The Legends of the Jews, Volume 1: From the Creation to Jacob*, Louis Ginzberg; The Jewish Publication Society of America, 1913, p. 76
[370] Ibid. p. 59
[371] Ibid. p. 76
[372] *Jubilees* 4:15
[373] *Genesis* 4:25
[374] Ibid. 5:29
[375] *Second Timothy* 3:7
[376] *John* 8:22
[377] *First Adam and Eve* 26:2-6
[378] Ibid. 26:9-10
[379] *Second Adam and Eve* 12:2, 5-6, 13
[380] *Numbers* 14:27-32
[381] *Jasher* 7:24-25
[382] *Second Adam and Eve* 18:13-14; 19:1; 22:1-2
[383] *The Egyptian Book of the Dead*, E.A. Wallis Budge; The British Museum, 1895, p. cxviii
[384] *The Great Pyramid of Egypt: Miracle in Stone*, Joseph A. Seiss; Porter and Coates, 1877, pp. 27-28
[385] Ibid. p. 28
[386] *Pyramidology: Book I*, Adam Rutherford; The Institute of Pyramidology, 1957, p. 150n
[387] *The Great Pyramid of Egypt: Miracle in Stone*, Joseph A. Seiss; Porter and Coates, 1877, p. 28
[388] Ibid. p. 28
[389] *Exodus* 25:10
[390] *Nicodemus* 22:10-14
[391] *Genesis* 15:9
[392] Ibid. 17:5
[393] *Number in Scripture: Its Supernatural Design and Spiritual Significance*, E.W. Bullinger; Eyre and Spottiswoode Ltd., 1921, Part II: Spiritual Significance, Five
[394] *Pyramidology: Book I*, Adam Rutherford; The Institute of Pyramidology, 1957, pp. 150-51n
[395] *Romans* 4:11, 16-17
[396] *Exodus* 13:18
[397] *Joshua* 1:14
[398] *Number in Scripture: Its Supernatural Design and Spiritual Significance*, E.W. Bullinger; Eyre and Spottiswoode Ltd., 1921, Part II: Spiritual Significance, Five
[399] *Genesis* 1:1-2
[400] *Treatise on Bible Chronology*, Adam Rutherford; The Institute of Pyramidology, 1957, p. 197; *Pyramidology: Book III*, Adam Rutherford; The Institute of Pyramidology, 1957, pp. 698-99
[401] *Acts* 18:28
[402] *Against Apion*, Flavius Josephus, c. 97, Book 1:1
[403] *Treatise on Bible Chronology*, Adam Rutherford; The Institute of Pyramidology, 1957, pp. 194-95; *Pyramidology: Book III*, Adam Rutherford; The Institute of Pyramidology, 1957, pp. 695-97
[404] *Studies in Biblical and Patristic Criticism, Volume 1*, William Sanday, S.R. Driver, John Wordsworth; Oxford University Press, 1885, p. 90
[405] *Commentary on Daniel*, Hippolytus of Rome, c. 205, Fragment 2:4-5
[406] *Nicodemus* 22:12-13
[407] Ibid. 22:11
[408] *Second Esdras* 14:21, 22, 24-27, 44-48
[409] *Nicodemus* 22:2-3
[410] *The Extant Fragments of the Five Books of the Chronology of Julius Africanus: On the Mythical Chronology of the Egyptians and Chaldeans*, Julius Africanus, c. 222, Fragment 1
[411] *Encyclopedia Perthensis: Or, Universal Dictionary of the Arts, Sciences, and Literature, Volume 9*, John Brown; Anchor Close, 1816, p. 91
[412] *A Dissertation on Sacred Chronology*, Nathan Rouse; Longman, Brown, Green, and Longmans, 1856, pp. 51-52
[413] Ibid. p. 22
[414] *The Patriarchal Age: The History and Religion of Mankind from the Creation to the Death of Isaac*, George Smith; Carlton and Phillips, 1854, p. 40
[415] *The Cave of Treasures: The Book of the Succession of the Generations*, Ephrem the Syrian, c. 350, Fol. 43b, col. 1
[416] *The Book of the Cave of Treasures: A History of the Patriarchs and the Kings, their Successors, from the Creation to the Crucifixion of Christ*, E.A. Wallis Budge; The London Religious Tract Society, 1927, pp. 7, 10
[417] Ibid. pp. 13-14
[418] *Genesis* 3:15
[419] *Jubilees* 4:15

[420] *The Luminous Eye: The Spiritual World Vision of Saint Ephrem the Syrian*, Sebastian Brock; Cisterian Publications, 1984, p. 55
[421] *Faith*, Ephrem the Syrian, c. 360, 4:9
[422] *The Luminous Eye: The Spiritual World Vision of Saint Ephrem the Syrian*, Sebastian Brock; Cisterian Publications, 1984, p. 56
[423] *Matthew* 21:42
[424] *Acts* 4:11
[425] *Psalm* 118:23
[426] *First Peter* 2:4-6
[427] *Ephesians* 2:19-22
[428] *The Great Pyramid of Egypt: Miracle in Stone*, Joseph A. Seiss; Porter and Coates, 1877, pp. 125-28
[429] *Isaiah* 19:19-20
[430] *The Great Pyramid Decoded*, Peter Lemesurier; Element Books Limited, 1977, p. 380
[431] *Phi: 1.618, The Golden Number: Golden Ratio Overview,* Gary Meisner; PhiPoint Solutions, 2014
[432] Ibid.
[433] Ibid.
[434] *First Corinthians* 13:12
[435] *Dramatic Prophecies of the Great Pyramid*, Rodolfo Benavides; Editores Mexicano Unidos, 1970, p. 123
[436] *Daniel: The Key to Prophetic Revelation*, John F. Walvoord; The Moody Bible Institute of Chicago, 1971, Chapter Nine: The Prophecy of the Seventy Weeks
[437] *Daniel* 9:24
[438] Ibid. 9:25-26
[439] *Mark* 4:11-12
[440] *Galatians* 4:4
[441] *Second Corinthians* 1:20
[442] *Matthew* 27:54; *Mark* 15:39
[443] *John* 19:31-34
[444] *Exodus* 12:46; *Numbers* 9:12; *Psalm* 34:20
[445] *Zechariah* 12:10
[446] *Matthew* 12:39-40; *Luke* 11:29-30
[447] *The Spear of Destiny*, Trevor Ravenscroft; Samuel Weiser, Inc., 1973, p. xii
[448] Ibid. pp. 14-17
[449] *Secrets of the Holy Lance: The Spear of Destiny in History and Legend*, Jerry E. Smith and George Piccard; Adventures Unlimited Press, 2005, p. 201
[450] *The Spear of Destiny*, Trevor Ravenscroft; Samuel Weiser, Inc., 1973, p. 5
[451] Ibid. pp. 26-27
[452] Ibid. p. 7
[453] Ibid. pp. 8-9
[454] Ibid. pp. 16, 18
[455] Ibid. p. 17
[456] Ibid. p. 17
[457] *Jasher* 7:30, 32-33
[458] *Genesis* 10:9
[459] *Jasher* 7:45-47
[460] *Last Days of the Third Reich, Part Three*, Walther Johann von Löpp (Compiler), Levi Bookin (Editor); The Propagander
[461] *World War II in Europe: The Death of Hitler*; The History Place
[462] *Exodus* 12:46; *Numbers* 9:12; *Psalm* 34:20
[463] *Zechariah* 12:10
[464] *Voltaire in His Letters*, Voltaire; G.P. Putnam's Sons, 1919, p. 232
[465] *On Liberty*, John Stuart Mill; Tickner and Fields, 1863, p. 40
[466] *First Corinthians* 15:14
[467] *The Blood and the Shroud: New Evidence that the World's Most Sacred Relic is Real*, Ian Wilson; Simon and Schuster, Inc., 1998, p. 19

THE SUBPLOTS - The End

[468] *First Enoch* 104:8-11; 105:1
[469] *New Science*, Giambattista Vico, 1725, Book 1, Establishment of Principles: XIII, 144
[470] *New World Encyclopedia*, Paragon House Publishers, 2015
[471] *Leonardo's Notebooks: Writing and Art of the Great Master*, Leonardo da Vinci; Black Dog and Leventhal Publishers, Inc., 2005, p. 404
[472] *The Legends of the Jews, From the Creation to Exodus: Notes for Volumes 1 and 2*, Louis Ginzberg; The Jewish Publication Society of America, 1925, p. 51
[473] *The Myth of the Phoenix: According to Classical and Early Christian Traditions*, Roelof van den Broek; Brill Archive, 1972, pp. 119, 121-25

THE CREDITS - Selected Biographies

[474] *James Bruce*, Edward Ullendorff, p. 133
[475] *Dictionary of National Biography*, Joseph Hirst Lipton, 1885-1900, Volume 58
[476] Ibid., Gordon Goodwin, 1885-1900, Volume 32
[477] *The Jewish Encyclopedia: Samson-Talmid Hakam*, Isidore Singer, Cyrus Adler (Editors), Funk and Wagnalls, 1860, p. 24
[478] *Dictionary of National Biography*, Cecil Bendall, 1901 Supplement
[479] Ibid., William Prideaux Courtney, 1885-1900, Volume 53
[480] *The Ancient Near East*, Cyrus H. Gordon; W.W. Norton and Company, Inc., 1965, p. 99

Cast of Characters

About the Author

SINCE 1976, W. KENT Smith has been an avid student of all things *Bible*, beginning at the age of sixteen when he read every book on the subject in his father's private collection. By age nineteen, having digested the works of William Barclay, Werner Keller, and C.S. Lewis, Kent embarked upon a lifelong quest that became the foundation for all that followed—a biblical timeline that systematically chronicled the history of God's dealings with mankind. As a result of this endeavor, he came to the realization that the traditional view of biblical history was fraught with contradictions and inconsistencies, and therefore required a radically original approach to reconcile these discrepancies.

2015 – Seeing the Light at the End of the Tunnel in completing the decades-long odyssey that is "Tales of Forever"

Then, in the mid-1980s, Kent was introduced to a body of ancient wisdom literature, which provided him with the missing pieces of a puzzle that is nothing less than the epic tale of God's control over history. This wisdom literature—extra-biblical literature, to be more precise—is known in modern parlance as pseudepigraphical literature, otherwise known as apocryphal literature. As it turned out, this fresh literary infusion not only opened up a brand-new chapter of biblical history for Kent, but it also provided him with a unique framework for every book he will ever write.

Kent is fifty-nine years old and presently lives in West Covina, California, an eastern suburb of Los Angeles. He can be contacted at wkent@loststorieschannel.com, or lodestarcinema@msn.com.

Made in the USA
Monee, IL
24 January 2020

20803674R10319